EXPLORATIONS IN PERSONALITY

EXPLORATIONS IN PERSONALITY

A CLINICAL AND EXPERIMENTAL STUDY OF FIFTY MEN OF COLLEGE AGE

By the Workers at the

HARVARD PSYCHOLOGICAL CLINIC

HENRY A. MURRAY, M.D., PH.D.
Assistant Professor in Psychology

WILLIAM G. BARRETT, M.D.
WALTER C. LANGER, PH.D.
CHRISTIANA D. MORGAN
ERIK HOMBURGER
H. SCUDDER MEKEEL, PH.D.
ROBERT W. WHITE, PH.D.

KENNETH DIVEN, PH.D.
JEROME D. FRANK, PH.D.
ELEANOR C. JONES
DONALD W. MACKINNON, PH.D.
SAUL ROSENZWEIG, PH.D.
R. NEVITT SANFORD, PH.D.
DAVID R. WHEELER, PH.D.

SAMUEL J. BECK, PH.D.
JAMES A. CHRISTENSON
ELIZABETH A. COBB
EDWARD INGLIS
KARL R. KUNZE
MERRILL MOORE, M.D.
M. RICKERS-OVSIANKINA, PH.D.
RUTH T. PETERSON
RICHARD N. SEARS, PH.D.
BENJAMIN J. SHEVACH, PH.D.
CARL E. SMITH, PH.D.
E. H. TROWBRIDGE
ESTHER M. WHITMAN
RICHARD E. WOLF

NEW YORK
SCIENCE EDITIONS, INC.
1962

Printed in the United States of America

This Book is Gratefully Dedicated

by its authors

to

MORTON PRINCE

who had the vision, raised the endowment and

was the first director of the Harvard Clinic,

to

SIGMUND FREUD

whose genius contributed the most fruitful

working hypotheses,

to

LAWRENCE J. HENDERSON

whose expositions of scientific procedure

established a methodological standard,

to

ALFRED N. WHITEHEAD

whose philosophy of organism supplied the

necessary underlying generalities,

and to

CARL G. JUNG

whose writings were a hive of great

suggestiveness.

ACKNOWLEDGEMENTS

THE AUTHORS WISH TO EXPRESS THEIR INDEBTEDNESS TO

THE ROCKEFELLER FOUNDATION

FOR THE GENEROUS ANNUAL GRANTS WHICH

MADE THESE RESEARCHES POSSIBLE

THE AUTHORS ARE EQUALLY GRATEFUL FOR LESS TANGIBLE GIFTS :

THE SERENITY, LOYALTY AND SUPERIOR COMPETENCE OF

MARJORIE C. INGALLS

WHO ORGANIZED AND SUPERINTENDED THE SCHEDULE OF

EXPERIMENTS AND TYPED THE COUNTLESS REPORTS AND THE

WHOLE OF THIS MANUSCRIPT

PREFACE

This is a book of many authors. But in writing it our purpose was to make an integrated whole, not a mere collection of articles on special topics. The planned procedure for achieving unity was this : to have all experimenters study the same series of individuals with the same concepts actively in mind, and then in assembly — a meeting being devoted to each case — to report their findings and collaborate in accomplishing a common purpose : the formulation of the personality of every subject. The degree of unity attained is for others, not us, to judge. Diversity is certainly conspicuous in spots ; so difficult is it, particularly in psychology, for a group of men to reach and hold a common outlook. Indeed, what is now so hard for us to realize is that the job was done at all, that for three years the many authors of this book were able to work, think and talk together with enjoyment and some measure of productiveness.

Four years ago every investigator at the Harvard Psychological Clinic was a pioneer with his own chosen area of wilderness to map. Each area was an aspect of human personality — a virgin forest of peculiar problems. Here he lost and sometimes found himself. Though there were plenty of opportunities for communication, his obligations to other experimenters were minimal and he was free to follow the wilful drifts of his own elusive thought. He enjoyed, in other words, relative autonomy in a Jeffersonian democracy of researchers — an atmosphere that is breath to the nostrils of every seeker after hidden truth.

All we workers were bound by a common compulsion : to inquire into the nature of man ; and by a common faith : that experiment would prove fruitful. We devoted ourselves, therefore, to the observation of human beings responding to a variety of controlled conditions, conditions which resembled as nearly as possible those of everyday life. Our emphasis was upon emotional and behavioural reactions, what previous experiences determined them, to what degree and in what manner. This preoccupation set our studies somewhat outside the university tradition. For it has been the custom in academic psychology to concentrate upon the perceptive and cognitive functions of the human mind or, more recently, upon the behaviour of animals.

The usual procedure at the Clinic was to compare the responses of a group of subjects in two contrasting situations ; each experiment having been devised to validate or contradict a prediction that if conditions were modified in a particular way the responses would also be modified in a particular way. The results which we obtained by following this well attested plan were, in general, of this nature : a majority — perhaps seventy per cent of the subjects — manifested the predicted change, but a minority reacted otherwise. One result, for instance, was this : after trying to complete a number of tasks, the majority remembered their successes better than their failures. Another was this : that the majority remembered best the tasks on which they had cheated. Yet another was this : that the majority persisted longer in an attempt to perform a mental operation after they had been humiliated in their initial attempt than they did after they had been commended. Now a statistical result of this kind may often be reservedly accepted as partial proof of the operation of a separable factor, but such a result conceals, as Lewin has pointed out, the other important forces, not selected for observation, which contributed to the common (exhibited-by-the-majority) response. In lay words, the subjects who gave the majority response may have done so for different reasons. Furthermore, a statistical answer leaves unexplained the uncommon (exhibited-by-the-minority) response. One can only ignore it as an unhappy exception to the rule. Averages obliterate the 'individual characters of individual organisms' (Whitehead), and so fail to reveal the complex interaction of forces which determines each concrete event.

Thus we were driven to the conclusion that the indecisiveness of our results was the inevitable outcome of a deficient method. The correct formulation of an experimental finding must, we came to feel, include more personality factors — or 'variables' as they are called — than the one which the given procedure had been devised to set in motion. Additional factors intuitively apperceived by an experimenter were of some aid in interpreting the results, but they were insufficient and there was no adequate proof of their operation.

We should, perhaps, have anticipated this conclusion since we were accustomed to conceive of personality as a temporal integrate of mutually dependent processes (variables) developing in time, and from this conception it follows that a large number of determining variables as well as their relations must be recognized, and approximately measured, if one is to give an adequate interpretation — analysis and synthesis — of a single human event. Since it is impossible to distinguish all these variables simultaneously, they must be discovered one at a time on separate occasions.

This conclusion led to our first important decision, which was : that all experimenters should use one and the same group of subjects. Each worker continued as before with his own problem, but under the new plan he had the findings of other observers to aid him in the interpretation of his results.

It then occurred to us that interpretation might be still further facilitated if we knew more about the past experiences and the aptitudes of the subjects. Our second decision followed : to add a number of interviews, free association hours and psychological tests to the schedule of experiments. The purpose of the entire procedure was to place at the disposal of each experimenter a wealth of information about his subjects and thus to assist him in interpreting his results and arriving at generally valid psychological laws. This was our initial intent, and since it will not be referred to again, I take this opportunity to express the opinion that the reason why the results of so many researches in personality have been misleading or trivial is that experimenters have failed to obtain enough pertinent information about their subjects. Lacking these facts accurate generalizations are impossible.

As I have said, our primary aim was to discover some of the principles that governed human behaviour, but as soon as we began to assemble and attempt to organize the biographical data we discovered that we were involved in a deeper and more fundamental problem : the problem of how to conceive of an individual life history. What should we agree to mean by the term 'personality'? What are the fundamental variables in terms of which a personality may be comprehensively and adequately described? Before we could compare and organize the results of different experiments it was necessary to construct a conceptual scheme which every experimenter would understand, agree to use and find efficient. This we tried to do. But, as might have been anticipated, we fell short of the goal. Even at the end, after many revisions, we could not think of our scheme as more than a rude array of concepts to classify our findings.

In our explorations each session—'session' being the general term which we shall use to denote a planned meeting between an experimenter (E) and a subject (S), whether it be a conference, a routine test or an experiment—was designed to reveal a certain segment of the personality; that is, to incite and thus bring into relief particular processes, or variables. Though it is supposed that personality is at all times an integral whole—that the constituent processes are functionally inseparable—it is clear that not all situations provoke the same variable to the same extent, and, consequently, it can be said that a specific situation serves to isolate, or dissect, a specific part of the personality. This part can rarely be understood by itself, but it can be studied as a clue to the general structure of the personality. These considerations have led us to the conclusion that if after assembling the results of many sessions the structure of the whole can be formulated, then each session may be reinterpreted—interpreted in such a way that it conforms to all the other sessions.

Now, to carry out this procedure—to conduct a long series of sessions and to organize the findings from all of them into an intelligible portrait of a subject—called for the co-operation of the entire staff. Each experimenter had to relinquish some of his dearly prized freedom. He had to use the terminology of a constantly revised scheme of thought, to arrange the time of his experiments to fit in with others and to participate in lengthy conferences. It seemed that to obtain the desired comprehensive formulations this amount of collaboration was necessary, yet there was the question of whether for each experimenter the goal was worth the partial sacrifice of intellectual independence. We did not wish to succumb to the great American compulsion to cooperate if it was not clearly necessary. The prospect of what might be achieved, however, appealed to us and so we made our plans and worked together, with many changes in our company, for three years.

It is true that we never completely succeeded in merging our separate ideologies. How could such a thing come to pass in a group composed of poets, physicists, sociologists, anthropologists, criminologists, physicians; of democrats, fascists, communists, anarchists; of Jews, Protestants, Agnostics, Atheists; of pluralists, monists, solipsists; of behaviourists, configurationists, dynamicists, psycho-analysts; of Freudians, Jungians, Rankians, Adlerians, Lewinians, and Allportians? To the fact that we never found a language suitable to all, that some of the experimenters entertained reservations to the last, the reader can ascribe some of the annoyance or pleasure he may experience when here and there throughout the book he encounters varieties of terminology or theory.

During the two and a half years of research fifty-one male subjects of college age were interviewed and tested. The first group, intensively studied over a two-weeks period, was composed of young men drawn from the ranks of the unemployed. All the rest of our subjects were college men. The second group composed of eleven students was studied over a period of three weeks, the third group of thirteen over a period of two months, and the fourth group of fifteen, in a more leisurely fashion, over a period of six months. No subject had any knowledge of the theories and practices of psychology. The college students were so chosen by the Harvard Employment Office that the Arts and the Sciences, high scholarship and low scholarship were equally represented. They were paid for their services at the current wage.

It has seemed to us that more progress could be made by conscientious clinical researches and by seeking experimental evidence for the validity of certain general intuitions about human nature than by devising tests to measure with precision things that have no influence on the course of life. Psychology should not lose sight of human nature as it operates in everyday existence.

We have speculated freely, with an understanding, let us hope, of what we were about. If a psychologist of personality had to limit his discourse to theories that were securely proved he would have nothing to recount. In his realm there are no certainties.

In our explorations we attempted to get below the social derm of personalities. Indeed, we became so bent upon the search for covert springs of fantasy and action that we slighted necessarily some of the more obvious and common phases of behaviour. This has resulted in a certain distortion which may seem great to those whose vivid experiences are limited to what is outwardly perceived and public, to what is rational and consciously intended.

Henry A. Murray

Cambridge, Massachusetts

CONTENTS

EXPLORATIONS IN PERSONALITY

EXPLORATIONS IN PERSONALITY

Chapter I
INTRODUCTION

H. A. MURRAY

MAN is to-day's great problem. What can we know about him and how can it be said in words that have clear meaning ? What propels him ? With what environmental objects and institutions does he interact and how ? What occurrences in his body are most influentially involved ? What mutually dependent processes participate in his differentiation and development ? What courses of events determine his pleasures and displeasures ? And, finally, by what means can he be intentionally transformed ? These are antique questions, to be sure, which in all ages have invited interest, but to-day they more insistently demand solution and more men are set for the endeavour. There is greater zest and greater promise of fulfilment.

The point of view adopted in this book is that personalities constitute the subject matter of psychology, the life history of a single man being a unit with which this discipline has to deal. It is not possible to study all human beings or all experiences of one human being. The best that can be done is to select representative or specially significant events for analysis and interpretation. Some psychologists may prefer to limit themselves to the study of one kind of episode. For instance, they may study the responses of a great number of individuals to a specific situation. They may attempt to discover what changes in the situation bring about important changes in response. But, since every response is partially determined by the after-effects of previous experiences, the psychologist will never fully understand an episode if he abstracts it from ontogeny, the developmental history of the individual. Even philogeny, or racial history, may have to be considered. The prevailing custom in psychology is to study one function or one aspect of an episode at a time — perception, emotion, intellection or behaviour — and this is as it must be. The circumscription of attention is dictated by the need for detailed information. But the psychologist who does this should recognize that he is observing merely a part of an operating totality, and that this totality, in turn, is but a small temporal segment of a personality. Psychology must construct a scheme of concepts for portraying the entire course of individual development, and thus provide a framework into which any single episode — natural or experimental — may be fitted.

The branch of psychology which principally concerns itself with the study of human lives and the factors that influence their course, which investigates individual differences and types of personality, may be termed 'personology' instead of 'the psychology of personality,' a clumsy and tautological expression.[1]

Personology, then, is the science of men, taken as gross units, and by definition it encompasses 'psycho-analysis' (Freud), 'analytical psychology' (Jung), 'individual psychology' (Adler) and other terms which stand for methods of inquiry or doctrines rather than realms of knowledge.

In its intentions our endeavour was excessively ambitious. For we purposed nothing less than (1) to construct methodically a *theory* of personality ; (2) to devise *techniques* for getting at some of the more important attributes of personality ; and (3) by a study of the lives of many individuals to discover basic *facts* of personality. Our guiding thought was that personality is a temporal whole and to understand a part of it one must have a sense, though vague, of the totality. It was for this that we attempted comprehensiveness, despite the danger that in trying to grasp everything we might be left with nothing worth the having.

We judged the time had come when systematic, full length

1. Some have objected that personology, as here defined, is what all men, except professional psychologists, call psychology. Since it has to do with life-histories of individuals (the largest unit), it must be the most inclusive, other types of psychology being specialties or branches of it. This view, however, is not generally accepted.

studies of individuals could be made to bring results. And more than this, indeed, it seemed a necessary thing to do. For if the constituent processes of personality are mutually dependent, then one must know a lot to comprehend a little, and to know a lot that may be used for understanding, good methods must be systematically employed. In our attempt to envisage and portray the general course of a person's life, we selected for analysis certain happenings along the way and, using these as points, made free drawings of the connecting paths. We judged that the spaces without definition would attract attention and it would become more evident than it has been in what quarters detailed research might yield important facts. For without some notion of the whole there can be no assurance that the processes selected for intensive study are significant constituents.

Actually, the scheme of concepts we employed was not exhaustive ; one reason being the inability of the mind to hold so many novel generalities in readiness. The amount of space and time and the number of examiners available put a limit to the number of experimental subjects and the number of techniques that could be used. Thus, in the end, our practices and theories were not as comprehensive as we thought they could and should be.

Since in the execution of our plan we went from theory down to fact, then back to theory and down to fact again, the book may be regarded either as a scheme of elementary formulations conceived of to explain the ways of different individuals, or as an assemblage of biographic data organized according to a certain frame of reference.

The Present State of Personology

It might be thought that a number of psychologists from the same or different universities, assembling in any suitably equipped clinic, could, after apportioning their work, become engaged without delay in a collaborative study of any group of normal individuals. This could occur in clinical medicine but not by any good fortune in psychology. For in psychology there are few generally valued tests, no traits that are always measured, no common guiding concepts. Some psychologists make precise records of their subjects' overt movements, others inquire into sentiments and theories. Some use physiological techniques, others present batteries of questionnaires. Some record dreams and listen for hours to free associations, others note attitudes in social situations. These different methods yield data which, if not incommensurate, are, at least, difficult to organize into one construction. There is no agreement as to what traits or variables are significant. A psychologist who embarks upon a study of normal personality feels free to look for anything he pleases. He may test for intelligence, or note signs of introversion-extraversion, he may focus on inferiority and compensation, or use the cycloid-schizoid frame of reference, or look for the character traits of pre-genital fixation, or measure his subjects for ascendance and submission; but he will not feel bound to any particular order of examinations, since there is no plan that custom has accredited. It must be acknowledged that personology is still in diapers enjoying random movements. The literature is full of accurate observations of particular events, statistical compilations, and brilliant flashes of intuition. But taken as a whole, personology is a patchwork quilt of incompatible designs. In this domain men speak with voices of authority saying different things in different tongues, and the expectant student is left to wonder whether one or none are in the right.

A little order is brought out of this confusion — though somewhat arbitrarily — by dividing psychologists into two large classes holding opposite conceptual positions. One group may be called *peripheralists*, the other *centralists*. The peripheralists have an objectivistic inclination, that is, they are attracted to clearly observable things and qualities — simple deliverances of sense organs — and they usually wish to confine the data of personology to these. They stand upon the acknowledged fact that, as compared to other functions, the perceptions — particularly the visual perceptions — of different individuals are relatively similar, and hence agreement on this basis is attainable. Agreement, it is pointed out, is common among trained observers when interpretations are excluded, and since without agreement there is no science, they believe that if they stick to measurable facts they are more likely to make unquestionable contributions. Thus, for them the data are: environmental objects and physically responding organisms: bodily movements, verbal successions, physiological changes. That they confine themselves to such events distinguishes them from members of the other class, but what characterizes them particularly is their insistence upon limiting their concepts to symbols which stand directly for the facts observed. In this respect they are *positivists*. Now, since we are reasonably certain that all phenomena within the domain of personology are determined by excitations in the brain, the things which are objectively discernible—the outer environment, bodily changes, muscular movements and so forth—are peripheral to the personality proper and hence those who traffic only with the former may be called *peripheralists*. If the peripheralists ever do indulge in speculations about what goes on within the brain, they usually fall back upon the conceptual scheme which has been found efficient in dealing with simpler partial functions. They resort to *mechanistic* or physiological explanations. Men of this stamp who study people usually come out with a list of common action patterns or expressive movements, though occasionally they go further and include social traits and interests. Such a man is apt, at least implicitly, to agree with Watson that 'personality is the sum total of the habitual responses.' This is one variety of the doctrine of elementarism. To repeat, the man we are distinguishing is a *peripheralist* because he defines personality in terms of action *qua* action rather than in terms of some central process which the action manifests, and he is an *elementarist* because he regards personality as the sum total or product of interacting elements rather than a unity which may, for convenience, be analysed into parts. Furthermore, the implicit supposition of this class of scientists is that an external stimulus, or the perception of it, is the origination of everything psychological. For them, the organism is at the start an inert, passive, though receptive, aggregate, which only acts in response to outer stimulation. From the point of view of consciousness, as

Locke would have it, mind is at first a sensorium innocent of imprints which, as time goes on, receives sensations from external objects and combines them variously, according to objective contiguities and similarities, to form ideas and ideologies. Those who hold this view are called *sensationists*.

In contrast to these varieties of scientists are a heterogeneous group, the *centralists*. The latter are especially attracted to subjective facts of emotional or purposive significance : feelings, desires, intentions. They are *centralists* because they are primarily concerned with the governing processes in the brain. And to these they think they are led directly by listening to the form and content of other people's speech. Their terminology is subjectively derived. For instance, to portray a personality they do not hesitate to use such terms as wishes, emotions and ideas. Though most of them make efforts to observe behaviour accurately, interpretation usually merges with perception, and overt actions are immediately referred to psychic impulses. Since the latter are intangible, personologists must imagine them. Hence, men of this complexion are *conceptualists* rather than positivists ; and further, in so far as they believe that personality is a complex unity, of which each function is merely a partially distinguished integral, they are *totalists*, naturally inclined to doctrines of immanence and emergence. Craving to know the inner nature of other persons as they know their own, they have often felt their wish was realized, not by making conscious inferences from items of observation but by an unanalysable act of empathic intuition. For this, perceptions, naturally, are necessary, but the observer is only dimly aware of the specific sensa which were configurated to suggest the underlying feeling or intention of the subject's momentary self. So hold the *intuitionists*. Finally, as opposed to the *sensationists* are the *dynamicists* who ascribe action to inner forces — drives, urges, needs, or instincts — some of which, inherited or suddenly emerging, may be held accountable for the occurrence of motility without external stimulation. These inner energies of which the personality may be wholly unaware seem to influence perception, apperception and intellection. The more or less mechanical laws of the sensationists are only true, it is believed, when a passive, disinterested attitude is adopted by the subject. But under most conditions, attention and conceptualization are directed by wants and feelings.

These two general classes of psychologists are heterogeneous. It is only certain underlying similarities which prompt us to put in one class peripheralists, objectivists, positivists, mechanists, elementarists, and sensationists; and to put in another centralists, subjectivists, conceptualists, totalists, and dynamicists. It is clear that a psychologist may belong in certain respects to one class and in others to another. For instance, some psychologists are eclectic, others vaguely hold a middle ground, still others attempt with more or less success to encompass both positions. Then there are those whose natural temper is emotionally subjective but who come to adopt, for their own equilibration, the extreme behaviouristic point of view. These are the holy zealots, the modern puritans of science. Mixtures and contrasts of this sort are not uncommon, but in the main the two classes are distinguishable (*vide* Extraception — Intraception, p. 211).

The peripheralists are mostly academic men addicted to the methodology of science. Being chiefly interested in what is measurable, they are forced to limit themselves to relatively unimportant fragments of the personality or to the testing of specific skills. The aim is to get figures that may be worked statistically.[1]

Among the centralists one finds psychologists of the 'hormic' school, psycho-analysts, physicians and social philosophers. These have no stomach for experiments conducted in an artificial laboratory atmosphere. They feel no compulsion to count and measure. Their concern is man enmeshed in his environment;

1. This may be regarded, perhaps, as one of many manifestations of a general disposition which is widespread in America, namely, to regard the peripheral personality — conduct rather than inner feeling and intention — as of prime importance. Thus, we have the fabrication of a 'pleasing personality,' mail courses in comportment, courtesy as good business, the best pressed clothes, the best barber shops, Listerine and deodorants, the contact man, friendliness without friendship, the prestige of movie stars and Big Business, quantity as an index of worth, a compulsion for fact-getting, the statistical analysis of everything, questionnaires and behaviourism.

his ambitions, frustrations, apprehensions, rages, joys and miseries.

In summary, it may be said that the peripheralists are apt to emphasize the physical patterns of overt behaviour, the combination of simple reflexes to form complex configurations, the influence of the tangible environment, sensations and their compounds, intellections, social attitudes, traits, and vocational pursuits. The centralists, on the other hand, stress the directions or ends of behaviour, underlying instinctual forces, inherited dispositions, maturation and inner transformations, distortions of perception by wish and fantasy, emotion, irrational or semi-conscious mental processes, repressed sentiments and the objects of erotic interest.

The divergencies thus briefly catalogued are rarely constant. And they are hardly more apparent than the divergencies within each group, particularly among the centralists. That the centralists should radically disagree in their interpretations is the result of their subjectivistic bias, the opportunities for projection being limitless. For man — the object of concern — is like an ever-varying cloud and psychologists are like people seeing faces in it. One psychologist perceives along the upper margin the contours of a nose and lip, and then miraculously other portions of the cloud become so oriented in respect to these that the outline of a forward-looking superman appears. Another psychologist is attracted to a lower segment, sees an ear, a nose, a chin, and simultaneously the cloud takes on the aspect of a backward-looking Epimethean. Thus, for each perceiver every sector of the cloud has a different function, name and value — fixed by his initial bias of perception. To be the founder of a school indeed, it is only necessary to see a face along another margin. Not much imagination is required to configurate the whole in terms of it. Such prejudiced conceptions, of course, are not unfruitful. To prove the correctness of their vision — to prove their sanity, one might say — scientists are led to undertake laborious researches. The analysts, for instance, have made wondrous discoveries by pursuing one instinct, observing its numerous guises and vagaries. Hunting other trails with like genius and persistence all the ways of personality may eventually be explored. Though this has proved to be a successful method of advance, the men who follow it are not well balanced intellectually. They are not well balanced because their thoughts are loaded, the favoured variable being turned up at every throw. Pursuing a single objective and disregarding numberless concatenations, they abstract too arbitrarily from the fullness of experience and upon one entity lay the full burden of causation.

What Course to Follow?

Now, in view of these divergent trends, what is the proper path to take? Is it possible that some order will emerge if a variety of methods are employed in the exploration of a group of subjects, the best of contemporary theories being judged in respect to their general success in interpreting the findings? In our minds the answer to this question was affirmative. Viewed in this way our work was an experiment in reconciliation. It was our thought, at least, that if we took account of what appeared to be the most important factors, and succeeded in measuring them approximately, the conceptual distortions which now exist might be rectified to some extent. It might even be possible, by slight modifications here and there, to construct a scheme which would fit together most of the prevailing theories. For a common theory and a common language is for psychology an urgent requisite.

Since science-making is a kind of working for agreement, the psychologic forces which give rise to controversy have been matters of concern to us. For instance, we paid some attention to the factors which determine the creation or adoption of a theory, as well as to those that make adherence lasting. Even among ourselves there were marked differences of outlook which were never satisfactorily combined, though attempts were made by some of us to expose by self-analysis any underlying twists that might be narrowing our perspective. We thought by taking steps to solve the problem of divergence our work might be, at least, the staking out of ground for an orderly development. This we take to be the scientific way — the only way, if the testimony of the last three centuries of practical and theoretical achievement has validity — of progressing towards agreement about 'truth.' One should begin at the beginning, and the beginning is proper method and accurate observation. We attempted first of all to make records of events as they occurred. These were the *facts*, facts not to be confused with the *theory* that seemed to fit them. In proceeding thus we were supported by the notion that the ability to observe — though no doubt a minor virtue — may, like the tortoise, in the long run win; and that a slow-witted man with a good method can often succeed where a clever man with a poor one fails. However, to choose this path is one thing, to follow it is another.

Difficulties that Confront the Investigator of Personality

The facts which should be observed in order to obtain a comprehensive view of a particular individual may be classified as follows:

A. OBJECTIVE FACTS

- i. The changing conditions of the physical and social environment that are perceptible to the subject.
- ii. The changing physiological conditions in the subject's body.[1]
- iii. The trends and action patterns (motor and verbal) of the subject. These may be initiations or responses.
- iv. The apparent gratifications (successes) and frustrations (failures) of the subject.

B. SUBJECTIVE FACTS

Reports given by the subject of his perceptions, interpretations, feelings, emotions, intellections, fantasies, intentions and conations.

What difficulties do these phenomena present to those who wish to make a study of them? In answer I shall limit myself to an enumeration of the factors which interfere with accurate and

1. Since the Harvard Clinic is not equipped for physiological studies, the latter could not be included in the present research.

sufficient observation under clinical conditions. In reviewing these factors brief mention will be made of the measures to surmount them that were tried out at the Harvard Clinic.

1. *Limitations of time, of the variety of conditions and of the number of experimenters.* To know a subject well one must see him many times, and observe or hear about his behaviour in many varied situations, when exposed to different treatment by different types of people. In professional studies limits are fixed by the amount of space, the number of experienced examiners and the funds available. In our case, we made a virtue of necessity by deciding that our purpose was to see how much could be discovered in a short time with relatively few sessions and few experimenters, many of whom were inexperienced.
2. *Peculiar effect of the laboratory situation.* Conditions in a laboratory or in a clinic are, at best, unnatural and artificial, and the subject is constantly reminded that he is being watched and judged. This usually makes him self-conscious and ill at ease, puts him on guard or prompts him to assume a favoured role. Though such attitudes are in themselves significant, they may not be indicative of how a man behaves in his accustomed haunts, which is what one most wants to know about. This difficulty was partly overcome by having subjects come to the Clinic off and on for a long period — time enough for the disappearance of whatever shyness, hostility or suspiciousness was due merely to the strangeness of the situation. Home-like surroundings and the friendliness of examiners helped to put a subject at his ease. The fact that we respected our subjects and became fond of them may have been the reason why in the main they were so natural, friendly, co-operative and confiding. This was important since to discover how a man is apt to act and feel in the ordinary situations of his life, one must rely upon his answers to tactful questions and what he writes about himself.
3. *Effect of the experimenter and the difficulty of estimating it.* Since in almost every session an experimenter is present, the latter, being of the same order of magnitude, is an intrinsic

member of the total situation. It is not that a solitary subject if secretly observed would reveal more of himself, because what one wants revealed is his behaviour with one or several human beings. Hence, there should usually be another person present. But the point is that the appearance, attitude and underlying needs of the other person are variables in the episode under observation and, since in most sessions the other person is none other than the experimenter, the latter must make concurrent judgments of himself in these respects, and this is not so easy. The difficulty was diminished to some extent by having experimenters trained in self-awareness, and, as we did in two sessions, by having a concealed observer judging the attitude and actions of both subject and experimenter.

4. *Limitations of perceptual ability.* Since reality is a process and the organism, as well as its environment, is changing every moment, only a small fraction of what occurs may be attended to, apprehended and retained in memory. This is because one's perceptual functions are, by nature, deficient in respect to speed and span. The limitation here may sometimes be partially surmounted by increasing the number of examiners or using various mechanical devices : a moving picture camera, speech-recording or movement-recording instruments, appliances to measure physiological changes and the like.

5. *Limitations of apperceptual ability.* Here we refer to deficiencies in the ability to *interpret* behaviour. *Interpreting* directional or purposive activity is so difficult that some psychologists, in the hope of obtaining uniformity, have confined themselves to the observation of simple movements. There is more agreement when this is done, but the records thus obtained are psychologically unimportant and cry out for understanding. But it is much more difficult to interpret records of this sort than it is to interpret behaviour at the moment of its occurrence. Thus, as we shall maintain in the chapter on the diagnosis of personality, apperception must accompany the original perception. To be sure, this introduces the greatest possibility of error, for the experimenter is required to go 'beyond' the facts, facts

which, at best, are fragmentary. For instance, he must often — since a fair proportion of acts are not successfully completed — base his diagnosis on the apparent trend (or intention) of the subject's conduct.

The difficulties of diagnosis are diminished to some extent by collecting in advance many common, concrete examples of the overt expression of the tendencies to be studied. But that such guides if taken 'literally' may lead to error must be apparent. To illustrate, take the act of 'kissing a person.' This would undoubtedly be classified as an expression of love or tenderness, and yet we have only to think of Judas Iscariot to recognize that a kiss may mean something else entirely.

6. *Unreliability of subjective reports*. There are many reasons why subjects' memories and introspections are usually incomplete or unreliable. Children perceive inaccurately, are very little conscious of their inner states and retain fallacious recollections of occurrences. Many adults are hardly better. Their impressions of past events are hazy and have undergone distortion. Many important things have been unconsciously repressed. Insight is lacking. Consequently, even when a subject wants to give a clear portrait of his early life or contemporary feelings he is unable to do so. Over and above this are his needs for privacy, for the concealment of inferiority, his desire for prestige. Thus, he may consciously inhibit some of his sentiments, rationalize or be a hypocrite about others, or only emphasize what a temporary whim dictates. Finally, one is occasionally confronted by out and out malingering. So as not to be too frequently deceived as to the reliability of what a subject says, the experimenter must hold in mind, if possible, every limitation and distortion which interferes with accuracy and be always skeptical, though tolerantly so. With most of our subjects there was ground for confidence and perhaps because we trusted their intentions they were disposed to truthfulness.

7. *Variability of the subject's personality*. In studying a subject over a four-month period it is assumed, as an approximation, that his personality remains *potentially* the same. The some-

times marked inconsistencies that occur are put down to the subject's characteristic range of variability, itself an attribute of personality. In many cases, however, the subject's reactions are not inconsistent; they are determined by factors of which the experimenter is unaware. There is little opportunity, for instance, to discover what daily shocks, victories, joys and sorrows occur in a subject's life. Sometimes he will volunteer such information and sometimes tactful questioning will draw it out of him, but usually an experimenter is ignorant of the immediately preceding happenings. Thus, many subjects come to a session with an emotional 'set,' occasioned by an accidental — and to the experimenter unknown — series of circumstances which gives him an uncustomary and evanescent manner and impulsion. This is a difficulty which was partially surmounted by seeing the subjects often over a relatively long period of time, the effect of unusual fortune being thereby minimized. One must consider the possibility, however, that during a four-month term a subject's potential personality may undergo a transformation; to some extent because of his attendance at the clinic. If such occurs, the experimenter is apt to discount it, believing merely that he is 'getting to know' the subject better.

8. *Limitation in the number and variety of subjects.* This becomes a confining factor if an experimenter expects to generalize his conclusions. It is always hazardous to apply what is discovered under certain conditions at a certain time with certain subjects to other conditions, times and subjects. Due to the preliminary nature of our studies we have not ventured to do this.

As to the variety of subjects examined at the Clinic, all of them, except for our first group of fourteen, were college students, some graduates and some undergraduates. They received remuneration at current prices (forty cents an hour). None of them was financially well-off. None had studied psychology. Since when they applied at the Employment Office none of them knew the nature of the work that would be offered them and since only one applicant refused the offer, there is no ground for believing that our subjects were selected on the basis of a morbid inclination to exhibit themselves. Different sections of the country were represented, different races and different religions. The staff of the Clinic had the impression that they were dealing with an exceedingly heterogeneous group of men, who resembled each other in only one respect: their willingness to assist the experimenters, even to the extent of revealing their mortifications, failures and ineptitudes.

9. *Inadequate conceptual scheme.* The experimenter is to a large extent bound by the categories defined and agreed upon before he commences to observe. He is 'set,' as it were, to perceive one or more of the phenomena which have been listed and nothing else. Thus, if the scheme is limited — as, at present, all schemes must be in personology — the original observations will be limited and much that is important will pass unnoticed. Ideally, the experimenter's mind should be stocked with variables which are well-defined, sufficient and appropriate to every circumstance. But since there is a limit to the number which a man may hold in readiness, a usable list of factors will always be deficient in completeness.

Ideally considered, an abstract biography, or *psychograph* according to our use of this term, would resemble a musical score and those who knew the signs might, by reading from left to right, follow the entire sequence of events. The analysis and reconstruction of each temporal segment would be represented by appropriate symbols among which would be found those which portrayed the environmental forces, the subject's inner set, his initiation or response, and the immediate outcome of the interaction. Reading the psychograph one could apperceive the relations between events and the development of the evolving personality. Such a reconstruction might be taken as the high and distant goal towards which our hesitating steps should be directed.

And now before I close this account of the difficulties that confront the personologist, I should mention one final limitation of any conceptual formulation of a man's experience. It must necessarily do violence to human feelings. It will never satisfy all the needs of anyone and it will surely insult the needs of some. This will be so because it is the substitution of heartless, denotative, referential symbols for the moving immediacy of living. By employing such a scheme a person's vital moments, once warm and passionately felt, become transformed into a cruelly commonplace formula, which dispossesses them of unique value. The subject himself is stripped and assimilated to a typological category. Much is thereby lost. The discomfort that people feel in the presence of a psychologist is in part the apprehension that they will be catalogued and filed away in his museum of specimens. The artist's representation of an experience, on the other hand, is a re-invocation of the original feeling or of a similar feeling, equally immediate, exciting and intense. The artist re-creates the 'feel' of it, the scientist substitutes the 'thought' of it. Passing over the point that many artists are likewise guilty of abstracting (as Norman Douglas's open letter to D. H. Lawrence illustrates), it should be pointed out in rejoinder that the non-sensuous scientific statement — though it may annul aesthetic feeling — does, by portraying relations, make the event intelligible to the understanding, and this is just the result that some men find so thrilling. The emotion has a different texture than that engendered by the artist, but it is for this that the scientist is willing to pay his price, the partial loss of immediate human feeling.

The Need for Hypothetical Formulations

A little reflection upon the general properties of human nature and the special liabilities of error in observing them — reviewed above and minimized if anything — should chasten what pretensions to authoritative truth we might be tempted to indulge. What must be known is so complex and our instrument for knowing so uncertain. Is it not a vast presumption to believe that this fragmentary consciousness of ours can perceive what is overt and then imagine what lies behind it; behind behaviour, as well as behind the mental processes that seek to comprehend behaviour, the various and subtly interweaving forces which make up personality? Is not doubt, suspended judgment, skepticism or utter silence the only dignified and knowledgeable attitude to take? Perhaps, but it is not likely to be taken, for, as history shows, the more complex a problem is and the fewer facts there are, the more inclined man is to voice opinions with conviction. But is conviction necessary or advisable?

The condition of affairs in personology can be illustrated by a diagram. The reader may look at this design and ask himself what kind of human face it represents:

figure 1

The figure portrays the items — three recorded facts, we may imagine — of a certain person's life. We should like to state the relationship between them in order to 'get a picture' of the personality. Shall we say (a) 'We do not know'; or shall we say (b) 'This is the explanation'; or shall we say (c) 'We suggest this hypothesis'?

Figure 2 presents two possible explanations. The dark lines stand for the facts, the light lines represent the imagined factors which, if present, would relate the parts into a more or less intelligible pattern. Interpretations x and y are obviously different, as different, let us say, as the conceptions offered by Ludwig and Freud, respectively, to explain the course of Kaiser Wilhelm's eventful life. Ludwig's biography,[1] one may recall, explains the grandiose ideas of the German ruler as overcompensations for organ inferiority: a withered arm acquired at birth. Freud, however, thinks that the important factor was a withdrawal of mother love 'on account of his disability. When the child grew

1. Ludwig, Emil. *Wilhelm Hohenzollern*, New York, 1927.

up into a man of great power, he proved beyond all doubt by his behavior that he had never forgiven his mother.'[1]

The response of a cautious scientist to *figure* 1 might be (a) 'I do not know'; whereas the response of an untrained person is commonly an *assertion* of some kind, (b) '*This* is the explanation' (x or y in *figure* 2). A child is also inclined to give such a response, not so much because he has not learned to reason, but

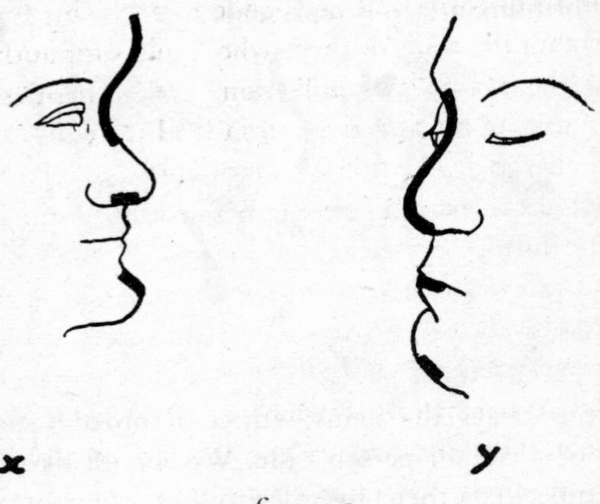

figure 2

because he has not learned to curb articulation of his thought. Piaget, in demonstrating the absence of self-criticism in the prelogical reasonings of youth, neglected to point out that children lack the necessary facts for arriving at satisfactory explanations. What a child studied by the staff of the Rousseau Institute *does not* say and the trained scientist faced by a situation of similar complexity *does* say is this : 'I do not know.' The child, much to the satisfaction of the experimentalist, gives voice to his intuitions ; whereas the academic thinker, perhaps heedful of his reputation, seldom does. To comprehend an occurrence — that is, to make a verbal picture of the interrelations of its parts — one requires a vast amount of data. Without them, everything is problematical. The child is usually willing to communicate his imaginative flights — often with a certain facetious whimsicality —, whereas

1. Freud, S. *New Introductory Lectures on Psycho-Analysis*, New York, 1933.

the scientist is not. What distinguishes the child from the scientist, however, is not so much his irrationality — because, as we have said, he has not enough data to be rational — but his readiness, his naïve, trusting, careless readiness, to guess in public and expose his ignorance to others. We know that the response of a trained imagination is often (c) 'I suggest this hypothesis' (x or y in *figure* 2). It is advanced as a tentative proposal, a man-made theory subject to correction or abandonment. This form of statement may chill the souls of those who hanker for authority, leave indifferent those who seek salvation, make enemies of restless minds clamouring for assertive action, and yet none other is justified when the goal of truth is paramount. No mind reviewing it's past errors can be but humble before the sphinx-like face of nature. The history of science is a record of many momentous defeats and a few tentative victories. Fortunate it is that most of the errors are eventually interred and truth lives after.

Now, at every stage in the growth of a science there is, it seems, an appropriate balance between broad speculation and detailed measurement. For instance, in the infancy of a very complex science — and surely psychology is young and complicated — a few mastering generalizations can be more effective in advancing knowledge than a mass of carefully compiled data. For in the wake of intuition comes investigation directed at crucial problems rather than mere unenlightened fact-collecting. Here we may point to the undeniable enrichment of our understanding and the impetus to further studies which has come from psychoanalytic theory. In its present stage personology seems to call for men who can view things in the broad ; that is, who can apperceive occurrences in terms of the interplay of general forces. A man who has been trained in the exact sciences will find himself somewhat at a loss, if not at a disadvantage. He will find it difficult to fall in with the loose flow of psychologic thought. He will find nothing that is hard and sharp. And so if he continues to hold rigidly to the scientific ideal, to cling to the hope that the results of his researches will approach in accuracy and elegance the formulations of the exact disciplines, he is doomed to failure.

He will end his days in the congregation of futile men, of whom the greater number, contractedly withdrawn from critical issues, measure trifles with sanctimonious precision. Perhaps the best course for such a man is to quit psychology for a simpler, more evolved and satisfying science — physiology, let us say. Nowadays, to be happy and productive in psychology, it is better not to be too critical. For the profession of psychology is much like living, which has been defined by Samuel Butler as 'the art of drawing sufficient conclusions from insufficient premises.' Sufficient premises are not to be found, and he who, lacking them, will not draw tentative conclusions can not advance. The self-analysis of thought may end by crushing what it feeds upon, imaginative spontaneity. As Jung says of himself : 'I have never refused the bitter-sweet drink of philosophical criticism, but have taken it with caution, a little at a time. All too little, my opponents will say ; almost too much my feeling tells me. All too easily does self-criticism poison one's naïveté, that priceless possession, or rather gift, which no creative man can be without.'[1]

It is just as well that man has always had at least a germ of faith in his omnipotence and omnicognizance. For without it the first assertions and assumptions would never have been made and, lacking these, the sciences would not have flowered. Though science preaches the need for caution, logical analysis and undisputed facts, it is much indebted to those who at the start made bold assumptions.

Our conclusion is that for the present the destiny of personology is best served by giving scope to speculation, perhaps not so much as psycho-analysts allow themselves, but plenty. Hence, in the present volume we have checked self-criticism, ignored various details, winked a little at statistics, and from first to last have never hesitated to offer interpretative hypotheses. Had we made a ritual of rigorous analysis nothing would have filtered through to write about. Speech is healthier than silence, even though one knows that what one says is vague and inconclusive.

It should be clearly understood, however, that every interpre-

1. Jung,C.G. *Modern Man in Search of a Soul*, New York:1934, p.135.

tative statement or conclusion in this volume is an hypothesis or theory which is ready to abdicate in the face of any facts which definitely contradict it. No theory has been set up as 'president for life.' We have, however, generally avoided qualifying phrases, the prefacing of statements with 'it seems' or 'it appears,' because in a long book this practice makes for monotony and is annoying to many readers.

The Order of Procedures at the Harvard Psychological Clinic

Personology, if it is ever developed, will rest upon an organized collection of facts pertaining relevantly to the long course of complex events from human conception to human death. They will be contained for the most part in case histories based on observations of behaviour in natural and experimental situations, together with the subject's memories and introspections. The questions : what are facts ? how are they discovered ? and how proved to others ? will always be fundamental to the science. But the discipline will not advance until it is possible to transform the raw data of experience into adequate abstractions. Now, as every experimenter knows, the latter must be constructed *before* the facts are sought. Naturally, the facts will compel a reformulation of the concepts, but if we approach personality without a tentative theory, we shall neglect much that is relevant and include much that is not. Therefore, in the order of events at the Clinic, the conceptual scheme came first.

A. CONCEPTUAL SCHEME

The business of every science is the construction of a conceptual scheme, and since a conceptual scheme is, by definition, a condensed abstract representation — a short word-picture, a reduced map, a symbolic formulation — of the actuality of immediate experience, its success depends upon the selection of a proper mode of analysis. Everything that is essential but nothing that is unessential to the structure of an event should be included. Naturally, opinions will differ as to which variables should be measured and which omitted. For the sake of thought, communication and action, an enormous amount of detail must be put aside as irrelevant, and, consequently, there is always the danger that something crucial has been disregarded. We must remember that our map is not the event itself. It is merely a much reduced and, at best, a very approximate mental reproduction of it. If possible, the scheme should be comprehensive, coherent, necessary and convenient.

The data out of which our original concepts emerged were: our own experiences, and the lives of others: patients treated at the Clinic, acquaintances, and characters in history and fiction. We were largely guided in the construction of our generalizations by the theories of Freud and McDougall, as well as those of Jung, Rank, Adler, Lewin and others. The problem, of course, was one of discriminative abstraction, that is, it was necessary to analyse out of a subject-object interaction those factors in the subject and in the object which influenced the course of events. As will be shown in the next chapter, we came down to a theory of directional forces within the subject, forces which seek out or respond to various objects or total situations in the environment. These are commonly termed *instincts*, or *part-instincts* by the Freudians, and were so termed by McDougall in his earlier writings. The latter now calls them *propensities*. Though the Freudians mention only two instincts explicitly, sex and aggression, in their explanations of behavioural phenomena, they refer to numerous other forces which, some think, might just as well be called instinctive: passivity, anxiety and avoidance, masochism, exhibitionism, voyeurism, and so forth. Though the naming and defining of these tendencies actually constitute a primitive classification, the Freudians do not speak of it as such. They are averse — sometimes with good reason — to defining terms or to building up their constructs systematically. In the beginning of a science this is perhaps the best course to pursue, but now, it seems to us, the time has come for a more orderly approach. In this we have followed McDougall who, in his classification of propensities, included most of the drives which the Freudians have enumerated.

Now, besides the variables defined as driving forces, we distinguished others, which may be variously described as dimensions, functions, vectors, modes, or traits of personality. Here we leaned heavily on Jung, Stern, G. W. Allport and a host of psychologists who have tried their hand at characterological description.

Then, since we were concerned with the genesis and history of tendencies and sentiments, we had to distinguish various modes of development ; processes of maturation, learning and socialization. In doing this we were guided by the principles of conditioning, association and organization worked out by Pavlov and the gestalt psychologists, and by such psycho-analytic concepts as fixation, substitution, compensation, sublimation and regression.

In summary, then, it may be said that our variables of personality consisted of a miscellany of general attributes, driving forces, relations between these forces and developmental modes. Each variable was defined to the satisfaction of all experimenters and a large number of concrete examples of its activity assembled to serve as guides for diagnosis. It was assumed that the degree of intensity of each variable could be marked on a 'zero to five' scale. With our first group of subjects we had but ten variables ; with our last we had over forty. In defining them and building up our theory of the total personality, we attempted to proceed systematically according to certain principles.[1] A systematic, objective, and perhaps tediously thorough approach seemed advisable, because the *ex cathedra* method commonly adopted would have accentuated, if anything, the differences and confusions which now prevail among personologists.

B. METHODOLOGICAL PLAN

A series of sessions — interviews, tests and experimental procedures — was devised to bring into prominence various aspects of personality, particularly those covered by the personality vari-

1. In working out our method of approach we were greatly influenced by Professor L.J.Henderson of Harvard who insisted upon a serious study of Pareto (Pareto,V., *The Mind and Society*, New York,1935).

ables. We employed whatever appropriate mechanical aids could be devised : speech-recording apparatus, galvanometer for measuring changes in skin resistance, tremor-recording apparatus, instrument for measuring sensorimotor learning, moving picture camera, and so forth ; but we did not believe that the use of instruments was, in itself, a mark of scientific worth.

Some psychologists have an almost religious attachment to physical apparatus taken over from the fundamental disciplines : physics, chemistry and physiology. Working with such contrivances they have the 'feel' of being purely scientific, and thus dignified. Sometimes this is nothing but a groundless fantasy, since what has made these methods scientific is the fact that applied to other objects they have yielded answers to important questions. It is dubious whether many crucial problems in psychology can be solved by instruments. Certainly if physical appliances do not give results which lead to conceptual understanding, it is not scientific to employ them. For the all-important characteristic of a good scientific method is its efficacy in revealing general truths.

We tried to design methods appropriate to the variables which we wished to measure ; in case of doubt, choosing those that crudely revealed significant things rather than those that precisely revealed insignificant things. Nothing can be more important than an understandnig of man's nature, and if the techniques of other sciences do not bring us to it, then so much the worse for them.

Our procedures are precisely described in Chapter VI. At this point it is enough to list the few general principles that our experience invited us to adopt.

1. Each subject should be exposed to *many varied* situations. This is basic. It rests upon the attested supposition that a person has almost as many 'sides' as there are different situations to which he is exposed.

2. Each subject should be observed and independently diagnosed by many different types of men and women. This follows

from the preceding principle : first, because one man has not the time to carry out all the necessary examinations, and second, because to vary conditions sufficiently one must vary the experimenter. There are also other reasons, the chief of which is the desirability of having many estimates and judgments of each subject. In no other way can an experimenter check his own interpretations. In our work we relied not only upon *many* judgments, but also upon the *weighted* judgments of the more experienced members of the staff.

3. Experience has taught us not only the necessity for varied sessions and a multiplicity of investigators, but also the necessity for experience in diagnosis. The experimenters, therefore, should be wisely selected and properly trained. The psychologist is and will always be the final judge of all questions pertaining to personality. No fine instrument can replace him. Therefore, as far as he is able, he must himself become an instrument of precision. Now, since in any group of experimenters there will always be some who have greater aptitude or who are more experienced than others, it is advisable to establish a diagnostic hierarchy. By weighting the opinions of the more competent, one gets the full benefit of *superior* judgments as well as of *many* judgments. The problem of diagnosis—of how the experimenter can get beyond his own sentiments and approximate what is ideally the true judgment—is, of course, one of the central problems of psychological procedure. It is a topic which we shall take up later in a special section. At present, we shall merely call attention to the principle of weighted judgments as a contribution to methodology.

4. The experimental sessions should be as life-like as possible. This is important because the purpose of personological studies is to discover how a man reacts under the stress of common conditions. To know how he responds to a unique, unnatural laboratory situation is of minor interest.

5. The subject's mind should be diverted from the true purpose of an experiment. This is usually accomplished by announcing a plausible but fictitious objective. If a subject recognizes the

experimenter's aim, his responses will be modified by other motives : for instance, by the desire to conceal the very thing which the experimenter wishes to observe.

6. One or more experiments should be observed by a second, concealed experimenter. In this way the reports of experimenters may be checked from time to time.

7. After some of the sessions, subjects should be asked to give a verbal or written report of their view of the experience : their impressions of the experimenter, their inner, unexpressed feelings, and so forth.

8. Each experimenter should attempt a hypothetical interpretation of the behaviour of each subject. The tentative character of such inferences should be recognized.

C. SESSIONS

A group of about thirteen subjects were engaged to come to the Clinic three or four hours a week over a period of several months. [The first group of subjects was asked to come much more frequently than this and the entire period of examination lasted less than two weeks.] The subjects were examined individually. With the last group of subjects about two dozen procedures were used, each procedure consisting of one or two sessions of one hour's duration. The entire program of sessions amounted to about thirty-five hours. Each subject underwent all the sessions and in the same sequence. Twenty-four experimenters took part in these examinations ; each of whom recorded his observations, his markings on each variable and his hypothetical interpretations of every subject. These conclusions, independently arrived at, were later brought together for comparison with the judgments of all the other experimenters.

Use was also made of a number of specially devised, comprehensive questionnaires, or reaction-studies, from which were obtained marks for every subject on every variable, based, in this instance, on his own reports of his usual behaviour in everyday life. In addition, each subject was asked to write a short autobiography.

D. DIAGNOSTIC MEETINGS

Five of the more experienced experimenters were selected to constitute a Diagnostic Council. This Council conducted a conference with each subject, the conference being the first in the sequence of sessions to which the subject was exposed. Thus, at the very outset, the members of the Council received an impression of the subject and were able to assign tentative marks on each variable. Subsequently, the Council held meetings to hear and discuss reports presented by other experimenters and, on the basis of these, revised, when necessary, their original markings and interpretations.

E. FINAL MEETING

At the end of all the examinations, a meeting, usually lasting five or six hours, was held on each subject. At this meeting each experimenter read a report of his session with the subject. A specially appointed 'biographer' conducted the meeting. He opened with a short summary of the findings, made comments on each report and concluded with a psychograph, or reconstruction of the subject's personality from birth. After the psychograph was read, there was general discussion and, at the end, the markings of the subject on each variable were discussed and finally established by majority vote.

F. STATISTICAL ANALYSIS

Many of the tests were susceptible of quantitative treatment, and so rank orders of the subjects could be obtained and intercorrelated. Rank orders on each of the personality variables, based on ratings by the staff as well as on the results of questionnaires, were likewise intercorrelated. Finally, the test results and the personality variables were intercorrelated. In this way there was an opportunity of discovering what variables were commonly or rarely found together and what variables were potent in determining the outcome of each test. Furthermore, correlations of variables gave a ground for dropping some and compounding others. In the mathematical treatment of results, we relied chiefly upon Allport and Vernon whose treatise, *The Measurement of Expressive Movements*, is a model of its kind.

The statistical analysis of the variables finally retained demonstrated that certain of them intercorrelated repeatedly to a significant degree. Most of these clusters seemed to correspond to our observations of people in everyday life. Hence, we concluded that they might be regarded as syndromes of functionally related factors which, for economy, could be used instead of the separate variables to portray a character. Our results showed, furthermore, that a variable may be an item in several different syndromes, and that its nature is modified by the character of the ensemble of associated variables in which it is found.[1]

G. THEORETICAL DISCUSSIONS

The experience of the experimenters in classifying the subjects' behaviour and of the biographers in reconstructing comprehensible life histories provided a basis for estimating the validity of the conceptual scheme originally devised. The question was asked: did this or that subject display any characteristic not adequately covered by one or more of the variables? If so, what is the psychological significance of this characteristic; on what underlying processes does it depend; and how should these processes be defined? In discussing such questions the adequacies and inadequacies of the scheme became more apparent. A verification of the scheme was found in its general success. Invariably, there were revisions and redefinitions of the variables and of the dynamic principles determining their operation. Thus, with a new theoretical outline and a new program of sessions, the staff of the Clinic was ready to engage another group of subjects, to carry out again the entire sequence of events.

This order of procedures repeated several times may be termed 'the method of successive approximations.' The theory which is evolved is the product of an assemblage of minds on the field of

1. The chapter on the intercorrelation of variables and syndromes had to be omitted from this volume.

action. It bears marks of its empirical derivation, but it has the advantage of being agreed upon by many different judges before being presented as a workable conception.

Our Methods Compared to those of Psycho-analysis and Academic Personology

The techniques employed in the present exploration resemble in some respects those developed by psycho-analysis and in others those devised by personologists in universities. But, because of our emphasis upon inhibited or unconscious tendencies as well as our persistent attempt to trace things back to infantile experiences, our work was more closely allied to the concerns of analysts.

We differ from psycho-analysis in respect to the length and depth of our explorations. Most psycho-analyses take about two hundred hours, and some take much longer, up to three or four years. With us, however, a subject participates in but thirty-five one-hour sessions, of which only about five are devoted to the recovery of past experiences. Thus in the same period of time we examine about six times as many subjects, but the analyst obtains about six times as much data from each, and because of his close and prolonged personal relationship with the patient he has revealed to him more of the 'depths' of personality. Here, however, it may be said that the length of the analyses is dictated by therapeutic considerations; that as far as understanding is concerned they are usually carried beyond the point of diminishing returns. Nevertheless, it must be admitted that the psycho-analytic technique is superior to ours in respect to the amount of evidence obtained.

The advantages of our procedure, however, are not negligible:

1. The collaboration of many experimenters who contribute their observations and take part in the final reconstruction of each subject's personality does not permit a one-sided viewpoint. A subject displays different facets of his personality to different experimenters, and despite what most analysts say to the contrary, it is for them to disprove what much evidence seems to show, namely, that the personality of the analyst determines

to an appreciable extent the attitude that the patient assumes, the course of his free associations, and thus the final diagnosis which is made. Here, we may include the advantage of exposing a person to a large number of very different situations.

2. In our theoretical scheme, as well as in our methodological approach, we paid more attention to the manifest personality than psycho-analysts are prone to do. Moreover, we had a better opportunity of judging overt social conduct and demonstrable abilities. Thus, the total personality — including the relation between the conscious and the unconscious, the manifest and the latent — could be seen with greater definition. A psycho-analytic case history seldom portrays the patient as an imaginable social animal. Even in describing normal people the psycho-analysts put emphasis upon the aberrant or neurotic features, because these are the things which the practice of their calling has trained them to observe. It is as if in giving an account of the United States a man wrote at length about accidents, epidemics, crime, prostitution, insurgent minorities, radical literary coteries and obscure religious sects and made no mention of established institutions : the President, Congress and the Supreme Court.

3. The fact that we studied a series of individuals — small though it was — gave us a basis for estimating individual differences, the normal range of each variable, what variables commonly occurred together, what variables were influential in determining the outcome of each test, and so forth. Such statistical results are certainly of some value in establishing common tendencies and syndromes and in arriving at general principles.

4. By our procedure there was opportunity to test certain hypotheses under experimental conditions ; and unless one is prepared to throw aside what cumulative experience has shown to be the most effective instrument for arriving at relative certainty, it must be conceded that this is a decided advantage. Most psycho-analysts, by temperament and training, are unsympathetic or opposed to experimental research.

With us the concepts were considered hypothetical and tentative, and every session was taken as an opportunity to correct or verify them. Thus, the entire organized procedure may be regarded as an experiment to test the ability of the constructed theory to classify and causally relate the facts.

Now that these differences have been pointed out, it should be said that, although we find something to criticize in psychoanalysis, we are not unmindful of the fact that from the start it has been our most constant guide and source of illumination. Without it these studies would never have been planned or finished.

From academic psychology — particularly, as said above, from the work of G. W. Allport — we learned much in respect to an orderly method of procedure and a proper statistical treatment of our findings. We included some of the procedures commonly employed in academic studies : intelligence tests and a variety of questionnaires ; but these contributed very little to our understanding. American personologists base their conclusions on a much larger number of subjects than we studied, and in this respect their findings are more representative than ours. What they usually study, however, are the physical attributes of movement, manifest traits and superficial attitudes, facts which subjects are entirely conscious of and quite willing to admit. Thus, their researches do not penetrate below the level of what is evident to the ordinary layman. To discover the traits of subjects, confidence is placed upon self-estimates or upon what a few untrained judges say about them. The original data, then, are of uncertain value, and no amount of factor analysis can make them more reliable. Furthermore, since these students of personality are apt to ignore the past history of their subjects, their final formulations are generally too static. To fully understand a trait one must know its genesis and history.

In short, then, we might say that our work is the natural child of the deep, significant, metaphorical, provocative and questionable speculations of psycho-analysis and the precise, systematic, statistical, trivial and artificial methods of academic personology. Our hope is that we have inherited more of the virtues than the vices of our parents.

The Future Prospect

As we approached the end of our exploring, innumerable ideas came bubbling up to plague us, ideas of further searches, experiments and tests which should be done in order to settle some tantalizing problem or get a clearer view of certain personalities. If we had been in touch with a medical clinic or a physiological laboratory, where, let us say, examinations could have been made of the cardiac, gastro-intestinal or endocrine systems of our subjects; or if we had had with us a sociologist to make detailed studies of the families and communities from which the subjects came, then, surely, many things which now are dubious would be less so. Numerous experiments of different kinds occurred to us as profitable ventures, and it was galling to realize that none of them was possible. We were definitely limited by lack of time, space, number of trained experimenters and apparatus. We came to view our work as a mere point of departure and the Clinic as an *anlage* of some future institute where more exhaustive studies could be made. Such an institute might eventually bring about a unification of the various schools of psychology and thus lead to a state of affairs such as now prevails in medicine, where all are working within a common scheme.

Reasons could be readily advanced for such studies besides the essential ones that knowledge is *per se* a final good and that man is of all objects the most inviting. There are many who believe that an understanding of human nature is the great requirement of this age; that modern man is 'up against it,' confused, dissatisfied, despairing and ready to regress; that what he needs is the power to change and redirect himself and others; and that the possession of this special power can only be won through knowledge. If it is true, as some reasonable men affirm, that culture—the best of man's high heritage—is in jeopardy, and that to save and further it man, its creator and conserver, must be changed — regenerated or developed differently from birth — then the immediate requisite is a science of human nature.

To study human nature patiently, to arrive at understanding, to gain some mastery ; there would be little hope in the enterprise if it were not for the history of science, the steady, unassertive, conquering pace of disinterested observation, experiment and reflection. Three centuries ago did the fancy of the most imaginative men foresee the miracles of thought and technics that would mark the way of science ? Absorbing this tradition, man may now explore his soul and observe the conduct of his fellows, dispassionate to the limit, yet ever animated by the faith that gaining mastery through knowledge he may eventually surmount himself.

Chapter II

PROPOSALS FOR A THEORY OF PERSONALITY

H. A. MURRAY

It is now necessary to set forth the conceptual scheme which guided our explorations. It is not a rigid system that was instituted in the beginning and maintained throughout. It has been repeatedly modified to accord with observed facts, and is still evolving. Hence, we can do no more than take a snapshot of it in mid-career, and offer this as a tentative make-shift for orienting thought and directing practical action. The reader will observe that the scheme is the outcome of a prejudice in favour of the dynamical, organismal viewpoint. It is, if he chooses to so regard it, a rationalized elaboration of the perception that a human being is a motile, discriminating, valuating, assimilating, adapting, integrating, differentiating and reproducing temporal unity within a changing environmental matrix.

Since psychology deals only with motion — processes occurring in time — none of its proper formulations can be static. They all must be dynamic in the larger meaning of this term. Within recent years, however, ' dynamic ' has come to be used in a special sense : to designate a psychology which accepts as prevailingly fundamental the goal-directed (adaptive) character of behaviour and attempts to discover and formulate the internal as well as the external factors which determine it. In so far as this psychology emphasizes facts which for a long time have been and still are generally overlooked by academic investigators, it represents a protest against current scientific preoccupations. And since the occurrences which the specialized professor has omitted in his scheme of things are the very ones which the laity believe to be 'most truly psychological,' the dynamicist must first perform the tedious and uninviting task of reiterating common sense. Thus he comes on the stage in the guise of a protesting and perhaps somewhat sentimental amateur.

The history of dynamic organismal psychology is a long one if one takes into account all speculations that refer to impelling forces, passions, appetites or instincts. But only lately have attempts been made to bring such conceptions systematically within the domain of science. We discover tentative signs in the functionalism of Dewey and Angell with its emphasis upon the organization of means with reference to a comprehensive end, in Ach's 'determining tendency,' and in James's notion of instinct, but not until we come to McDougall[1] do we find a conscientious attempt to develop the dynamic hypothesis. Since then, some of the animal psychologists, notably Tolman,[2] and Stone,[3] have worked with an objectively defined 'drive' which is strictly in accord with dynamical principles, and Lewin,[4] representing the gestalt school of psychology, has made 'need' basic to his system of personality. But the theory of drive or need has not been systematically developed by the latter investigators, their interest in external determinants of behaviour being predominant.

Outside the universities, the medical psychologists — and here we may, without serious omissions, start with Freud[5] — have for five decades been constructing a quintessentially dynamic theory. For this theory the academic psychologists, with the exception of McDougall, found themselves entirely unprepared. The psychoanalysts not only presented facts which had never entered the academic man's field of observation or thought, but they used a novel nomenclature to designate certain obscure forces which they thought it necessary to conceptualize in order to account for their findings. McDougall and the analysts have been kept apart by numerous differences, but in respect to their fundamental dynamical assumptions they belong together.

1. McDougall,W. *Introduction to Social Psychology*, London,1908 ; *Outline of Psychology*, New York,1923.
2. Tolman,E.C. *Purposive Behaviour in Animals and Men*, New York,1932.
3. Stone,C.P. *Sexual Drive*. Chapter XVIII, in *Sex and Internal Secretions*, ed. by Edgar Allen, Baltimore,1932.
4. Lewin,K. *A Dynamic Theory of Personality*, New York,1935.
5. Freud,S. *Collected Papers* (4 vols.), International Psycho-analytical Library, London,1924–25 ; *A General Introduction to Psycho-analysis*, New York,1920 ; *New Introductory Lectures on Psycho-analysis*, New York,1933.

The theory to be outlined here is an attempt at a dynamic scheme. It has been guided partly by the analysts (Freud, Jung,[1] Adler [2]), partly by McDougall and by Lewin, and partly by our subjects — whose actions so frequently corrected our preconceptions. As I have said, the theory is vague and incomplete. At many points it does scant justice to the precisely stated conceptions of other psychologists, even those with whom we find ourselves in substantial agreement. Compared to analytical speculations — some of Jung's intuitions, for example — it is limited and superficial. The truth is that we have taken from our predecessors only what could be used with profit in the present study.

This book is not a theoretical treatise and there is not the space for a thorough presentation of our concepts. It is only possible to state the principal assumptions and enumerate in the briefest manner the steps that led us to adopt the theory which served us as a plan of action. And in order to get over the ground of fundamentals with as little circumlocution as possible, it has seemed best to crystallize the broad facts of observation, as they have appeared to us, into a set of general postulates or propositions. It will be seen that some of these are mere commonplaces, others are cloudy, hardly verifiable generalities, still others are highly problematical and call for refutation or further study. The reader should not be deceived by the dogmatic form of statement. Each proposition is provisional. It is asserted flatly so that it may more readily be checked or contradicted.

A. PRIMARY PROPOSITIONS

1. The objects of study are individual organisms, not aggregates of organisms.
2. The organism is from the beginning a whole, from which the parts are derived by self-differentiation. The whole and its parts are mutually related ; the whole being as essential to an

1. Jung, C.G. *Psychology of the Unconscious*, London, 1919 ; *Psychological Types*, London, 1924.
2. Adler, A. *The Neurotic Constitution*, New York, 1921 ; *The Practice and Theory of Individual Psychology*, New York, 1924.

understanding of the parts as the parts are to an understanding of the whole. (This is a statement of the *organismal* theory.[1]) Theoretically it should be possible to formulate for any moment the 'wholeness' of an organism; or, in other words, to state in what respect it is acting as a unit.

3. The organism is characterized from the beginning by rhythms of activity and rest, which are largely determined by internal factors. The organism is not an inert body that merely responds to external stimulation. Hence the psychologist must study and find a way of representing the changing 'states' of the organism.
4. The organism consists of an infinitely complex series of temporally related activities extending from birth to death. Because of the meaningful connection of sequences the life cycle of a single individual should be taken as a unit, the *long unit* for psychology. It is feasible to study the organism during one episode of its existence, but it should be recognized that this is but an arbitrarily selected part of the whole. The history of the organism *is* the organism. This proposition calls for biographical studies.
5. Since, at every moment, an organism is within an environment which largely determines its behaviour, and since the environment changes—sometimes with radical abruptness—the conduct of an individual cannot be formulated without a characterization of each confronting situation, physical and social. It is important to define the environment since two organisms may behave differently only because they are, by chance, encountering different conditions. It is considered that two organisms are dissimilar if they give the same response but only to different situations as well as if they give different responses to the same situation. Also, different inner states of the same organism can be inferred when responses to similar external

1. Here the wording has been taken from E.S.Russell (*Form and Function*, London, 1916; *The Interpretation of Development and Heredity*, Oxford, 1930) who has stated most admirably the organismal viewpoint elaborated by W.E.Ritter (*The Unity of the Organism*, Boston, 1919) and others.

conditions are different. Finally, the assimilations and integrations that occur in an organism are determined to a large extent by the nature of its closely previous, as well as by its more distantly previous, environments. In other words, what an organism knows or believes is, in some measure, a product of formerly encountered situations. Thus, much of what is now *inside* the organism was once *outside*. For these reasons, the organism and its milieu must be considered together, a single creature-environment interaction being a convenient short unit for psychology. A *long unit* — an individual life — can be most clearly formulated as a succession of related *short units*, or *episodes*.

6. The stimulus situation (S.S.) is that part of the total environment to which the creature attends and reacts. It can rarely be described significantly as an aggregate of discrete sense impressions. The organism usually responds to patterned meaningful wholes, as the gestalt school of psychology has emphasized.

> The effect on a man of a series of unorganized verbal sounds or of language that he does not understand is very different from the effect of words organized into meaningful sentences that he does understand (or thinks he understands). It is the meaning of the words which has potency, rather than the physical sounds *per se*. This is proved by the fact that the same effect can be produced by quite different sounds : by another tongue that is understood by the subject.

In crudely formulating an episode it is dynamically pertinent and convenient to classify the S.S. according to the kind of effect — facilitating or obstructing — it is exerting or could exert upon the organism. Such a tendency or 'potency' in the environment may be called a *press* (*vide* p. 115). For example, a press may be nourishing, or coercing, or injuring, or chilling, or befriending, or restraining, or amusing or belittling to the organism. It can be said that a press is a temporal gestalt of stimuli which usually appears in the guise of a *threat of harm* or *promise of benefit* to the organism. It seems that organisms quite naturally 'classify' the objects of their world in this way: 'this hurts,' 'that is sweet,' 'this comforts,' 'that lacks support.'

7. The reactions of the organism to its environment usually exhibit a *unitary trend*. This is the necessary concomitant of behavioural co-ordination, since co-ordination implies organization of activity in a *certain direction*, that is, towards the achievement of an effect, one or more. Without organization there can be no unified trends, and without unified trends there can be no effects, and without effects there can be no enduring organism. Divided it perishes, united it survives. The existence of organisms depends upon the fact that the vast majority of trends are 'adaptive': they serve to restore an equilibrium that has been disturbed, or to avoid an injury, or to attain objects which are of benefit to development. Thus, much of overt behaviour is, like the activity of the internal organs, survivalistically purposeful.

8. A specimen of adaptive behaviour can be analysed into the bodily movements as such and the effect achieved by these movements. We have found it convenient to use a special term, *actone*, to describe a pattern of bodily movements *per se*, abstracted from its effect. To produce an effect which furthers the well-being of the organism a consecutive series of sub-effects must usually be achieved, each sub-effect being due to the operation of a relatively simple actone. Thus, simple actones and their sub-effects are connected in such a way that a certain trend is promoted. It is the trend which exhibits the unity of the organism. The unity is not an instantaneous fact for it may only be discovered by observing the progress of action over a period of time. The trend is achieved by the bodily processes, but it cannot be distinguished by studying the bodily processes in isolation.

This proposition belongs to the organismal theory of reality. It is in disagreement with the common practice of studying a fraction of the organism's response and neglecting the trend of which it is a part. One who limits himself to the observation of the bodily movements, as such, resembles the sufferer from semantic aphasia.

> In semantic aphasia, the full significance of words and phrases is lost. Separately, each word or each detail of a drawing can be understood, but the general significance escapes ; an act is executed upon command, though the purpose of it is not understood. Reading and writing are possible as well as numeration, the correct use of numbers ; but the appreciation of arithmetical processes is defective. . . A general conception cannot be formulated, but details can be enumerated. (Henri Piéron) [1]

9. A behavioural trend may be attributed to a hypothetical force (a drive, need or propensity) within the organism. The proper way of conceptualizing this force is a matter of debate. It seems that it is a force which (if uninhibited) promotes activity which (if competent) brings about a situation that is opposite (as regards its relevant properties) to the one that aroused it. Frequently, an innumerable number of sub-needs (producing sub-effects) are temporally organized so as to promote the course of a major need. [The concept of need or drive will be more fully developed later.]
10. Though the organism frequently seeks for a certain press — in which case the press is, for a time, expectantly imaged — more frequently the press meets the organism and incites a drive. Thus, the simplest formula for a period of complex behaviour is a particular press-need combination. Such a combination may be called a *thema*.[2] A *thema* may be defined as the dynamical structure of a simple *episode*, a single creature-environment interaction. In other words, the endurance of a certain kind of *press* in conjunction with a certain kind of *need* defines the duration of a single *episode*, the latter being a convenient molar unit for psychology to handle. Simple episodes (each with a simple thema) may relatedly succeed each other to constitute a *complex episode* (with its

1. Quoted from Korzybski, Alfred. *Science and Sanity*. Lancaster, Penn.1933,p.19.
2. I am indebted to Mrs. Eleanor C.Jones for this term.

complex thema). The biography of a man may be portrayed abstractly as an historic route of themas (*cf.* a musical score). Since there are a limited number of important drives and a limited number of important press, there are a greater (but still limited) number of important themas. Just as chemists now find it scientifically profitable to describe a hundred thousand or more organic compounds, psychologists some day may be inclined to observe and formulate the more important behavioural compounds.

11. Each drive reaction to a press has a fortune that may be measured in degrees of realization ('gratification'). Whether an episode terminates in gratification or frustration (success or failure) is often decisive in determining the direction of an organism's development. Success and failure are also of major importance in establishing the 'status' of an organism in its community.
12. In the organism the passage of time is marked by rhythms of assimilation, differentiation and integration. The environment changes. Success and failure produce their effects. There is learning and there is maturation. Thus new and previously precluded combinations come into being, and with the perishing of each moment the organism is left a different creature, never to repeat itself exactly. No moment nor epoch is typical of the whole. Life is an irreversible sequence of non-identical events. Some of these changes, however, occur in a predictable lawful manner. There are orderly rhythms and progressions which are functions of the seasons, of age, of sex, of established cultural practices, and so forth. There is the 'eternal return' ('spiral evolution'). These phenomena make biography imperative.
13. Though the psychologist is unable to find identities among the episodes of an organism's life, he can perceive uniformities. For an individual displays a tendency to react in a similar way to similar situations, and increasingly so with age. Thus there is sameness (consistency) as well as change (variability), and because of it an organism may be roughly de-

picted by listing the most recurrent themas, or, with more abstraction, by listing the most recurrent drives or traits.

14. Repetitions and consistencies are due in part to the fact that impressions of situations leave enduring 'traces' (a concept for an hypothetical process) in the organism, which may be reactivated by the appearance of situations that resemble them ; and because of the connections of these evoked traces with particular reaction systems, the organism is apt to respond to new situations as it did to former ones (redintegration). Some of the past is always alive in the present. For this reason the study of infancy is particularly important. The experiences of early life not only constitute in themselves a significant temporal segment of the creature's history, but they may exercise a marked effect upon the course of development. In some measure they 'explain' succeeding events. ['The child is father to the man.']

15. The progressive differentiations and integrations that occur with age and experience are, for the most part, refinements in stimulus discrimination and press discrimination and improvements in actonal effectiveness. Specific signs become connected with specific modes of conduct, and certain aptitudes (abilities) are developed. This is important because the fortune of drives, and thus the status of the individual, is dependent in large measure upon the learning of differentiated skills.

    In early life the sequences of movement are mostly unrelated. Trends are not persistent and disco-ordination is the rule. Opposing drives and attitudes succeed each other without apparent friction. With age, however, conflict comes and after conflict resolution, synthesis and creative integration. ('Life is creation.' Claude Bernard) Action patterns are co-ordinated, enduring purposes arise and values are made to harmonize. Thus, the history of dilemmas and how, if ever, they were solved are matters of importance for psychology.

16. Since in the higher forms of life the impressions from the external world and from the body that are responsible for

conditioning and memory are received, integrated and conserved in the brain, and since all complex adaptive behaviour is evidently co-ordinated by excitations in the brain, the unity of the organism's development and behaviour can be explained only by referring to organizations occurring in this region. It is brain processes, rather than those in the rest of the body, which are of special interest to the psychologist. At present, they cannot be directly and objectively recorded but they must be inferred in order to account for what happens. A need or drive is just one of these hypothetical processes. Since, by definition, it is a process which follows a stimulus and precedes the actonal response, it must be located in the brain.

17. It may prove convenient to refer to the mutually dependent processes that constitute dominant configurations in the brain as *regnant* processes ; and, further, to designate the totality of such processes occurring during a single moment (a unitary temporal segment of brain processes) as a *regnancy*.[1] According to this conception regnancies correspond to the processes of highest metabolic rate in the gradient which Child [2] has described in lower organisms. It may be considered that regnancies are functionally at the summit of a hierarchy of subregnancies in the body. Thus, to a certain extent the regnant need dominates the organism.

> The activities of the nerve-cells and muscle-cells are necessary conditions of the whole action, but they are not in any full sense its cause. They enable the action to be carried out, and they limit at the same time the possibilities of the action. . . Putting the matter in another way, a knowledge of the nature of muscular and nervous action would not enable us fully to interpret behaviour.[3]
>
> We distinguished in general the *modes of action* of higher and lower unities — from the mode of action of the organism as a whole down to the modes of action of those parts of the cell which, like the chromosomes, show a certain measure of independence and

1. The term ' regnancy ' was suggested to me by Mrs. Eleanor C.Jones.
2. Child,C.M. *Senescence and Rejuvenescence*, Chicago,1915.
3. Russell,E.S. *The Interpretation of Development and Heredity*, Oxford:1930, p.186.

> individuality. We came to the conclusion that the modes of action of the subordinate unities condition, both in a positive and a negative sense, the modes of action of the higher unities. Being integrated into the activity of the whole they render possible the vital manifestation of these activities by imposing on them a particular form.[1]

Occurrences in the external world or in the body that have no effect upon regnancies do not fall within the proper domain of psychology.

18. Regnant processes are, without doubt, mutually dependent. A change in one function changes all the others and these, in turn, modify the first. Hence, events must be interpreted in terms of the many interacting forces and their relations, not ascribed to single causes. And since the parts of a person cannot be dissected physically from each other, and since they act together, ideally they should all be estimated simultaneously. This, unfortunately, is not at present possible. Much of what has been discovered by other methods at other times has to be inferred.
19. According to one version of the double aspect theory—seemingly the most fruitful working hypothesis for a psychologist—the constituents of regnancies in man are capable of achieving consciousness (self-consciousness) though not all of them at once. The amount of introspective self-consciousness is a function of age, emotional state, attitude, type of personality, and so forth. Since through speech a person may learn to describe and communicate his impression of mental occurrences (the subjective aspect of regnant events) he can, if he wishes, impart considerable information about the processes which the psychologist attempts to conceptualize.
20. During a single moment only some of the regnant processes have the attribute of consciousness. Hence, to explain fully a conscious event as well as a behavioural event the psychologist must take account of more variables than were present

1. Russell, E.S. *The Interpretation of Development and Heredity,* Oxford: 1930, p.280.

in consciousness at the time. Consequently, *looking at the matter from the viewpoint of introspective awareness,* it is necessary to postulate unconscious regnant processes. An unconscious process is something that must be conceptualized as regnant even though the S[1] is unable to report its occurrence.

21. It seems that it is more convenient at present in formulating regnant processes to use a terminology derived from subjective experience. None of the available physico-chemical concepts are adequate. It should be understood, however, that every psychological term refers to some hypothetical, though hardly imaginable, physical variable, or to some combination of such variables. Perhaps some day the physiologists will discover the physical nature of regnant processes and the proper way to conceptualize them ; but this achievement is not something to be expected in the near future since an adequate formulation must include all major subjective experiences : expectations, intentions, creative thought and so forth. Tolman,[2] however, has already shown that many of the necessary variables can be operationally defined in terms of overt behavioural indices.

It is not only more convenient and fruitful at present to use subjective terminology (perception, apperception, imagination, emotion, affection, intellection, conation), but even if in the future it becomes expedient for science to use another consonant terminology it will not be possible to dispense with terms that have subjective significance ; for these constitute data of primary importance to most human beings. The need to describe and explain varieties of inner experience decided the original, and, I predict, will establish the final orientation of psychology.

22. One may suppose that regnancies vary in respect to the number, relevance and organization of the processes involved, and that, as Janet supposes, a certain amount of integrative

1. Throughout this book 'S' will be used to stand for 'subject' (the organism of our concern) and 'E' will signify 'experimenter' (physician or observer).
2. Tolman, E.C. *Purposive Behaviour in Animals and Men*, New York, 1932.

energy or force is required to unify the different parts. Regnancies become disjunctive in fatigue, reverie and sleep, as well as during conflict, violent emotion and insanity. The chief indices of differentiated conjunctive regnancies are these: alertness, nicety of perceptual and apperceptual discrimination, long endurance of a trend of complex action, increasingly effective changes of actone, rapidity of learning, coherence, relevance and concentration of thought, absence of conflict, introspective awareness and self-criticism.

23. Because of the position of regnancies at the summit of the hierarchy of controlling centres in the body, and because of certain institutions established in the brain which influence the regnancies, the latter (constituting as they do the personality) must be distinguished from the rest of the body. The rest of the body is as much outside the personality as the environment is outside personality. Thus, we may study the effects of illness, drugs, endocrine activity and other somatic changes upon the personality in the same fashion as we study the changes produced by hot climate, strict discipline or warfare. In this sense, regnant processes stand between an inner and an outer world.

24. There is continuous interaction between regnancies and other processes in the body. For the chemical constitution of the blood and lymph, as well as a great variety of centripetal nervous impulses originating in the viscera, have a marked effect on personality. Indeed, they may change it almost completely. The personality, in turn, can affect the body by exciting or inhibiting skeletal muscles, or through the power of evoked traces (images) can excite the autonomic nervous system and thereby modify the physiology of organs (*cf.* autonomic neuroses). The personality can also vary the diet it gives the body, it can train it to stand long periods of intense exercise, drive it to a point of utter exhaustion, indulge it with ease and allow it to accumulate pounds of fat, poison it with drugs, bring it in contact with virulent bacteria, inhibit many of its cravings, mortify it or destroy it by suicide.

The relations between a personality and its body are matters of importance to a dynamicist.

25. *Time-binding*. Man is a 'time-binding'[1] organism; which is a way of saying that, by conserving some of the past and anticipating some of the future, a human being can, to a significant degree, make his behaviour accord with events that have happened as well as those that are to come. Man is not a mere creature of the moment, at the beck and call of any stimulus or drive. What he does is related not only to the settled past but also to shadowy preconceptions of what lies ahead. Years in advance he makes preparations to observe an eclipse of the sun from a distant island in the South Pacific and, lo, when the moment comes he is there to record the event. With the same confidence another man prepares to meet his god. Man lives in an inner world of expected press (pessimistic or optimistic), and the psychologist must take cognizance of them if he wishes to understand his conduct or his moods, his buoyancies, disappointments, resignations. Time-binding makes for continuity of purpose.

Here we may stop in order to consider in some detail three crucial theories: the theory of unconscious processes, the theory of needs, and the theory of press.

B. UNCONSCIOUS REGNANT PROCESSES [2]

We have adopted the version of the double-aspect hypothesis which states that every conscious process is the subjective aspect of some regnant brain process, but that not every regnant process has a conscious correlate.[3] It appears, indeed, that to explain any conscious event, as well as to explain any behavioural event, one must take account of more variables than those which are at the moment present in consciousness. 'Regarded as events,' Köhler

1. Korzybski, Alfred. *Manhood of Humanity*. New York, 1921.
2. Much of what is contained in the following exposition is quoted (by permission of the editor, Dr. Carl Murchison) from an article by the author which appeared in *The Journal of General Psychology*, 1936, *15*, 241–268.
3. The theory is impartial on the question of whether every process has a 'psychic' correlate or pole (according to some metaphysical definition of 'psychic').

points out, 'the facts and sequences of our direct experience do not, taken by themselves, represent complete wholes. They are merely parts of larger functional contexts.'[1] The following examples, some of which are taken from Köhler, support this opinion.

1. The perception of the 'Dipper' is an immediate experience in which the form is given as-a-whole. The stars are not organized into this common shape by a conscious process. The form comes to us 'ready-made.' Presumably there have been previous impressions of actual dippers which have left traces in the brain, and in the present act of perception some interaction between the memory image of a dipper and the impression from the heavens occurred. But this memory image is not in consciousness.
2. In the recognition of a person whom we have met once and not seen for a long time we are frequently conscious of the interaction between the memory image and the present impression. But later, after frequent encounters, immediate recognition occurs. On such occasions, though the memory image is not in consciousness, to explain the recognition we must suppose that it is still functioning.
3. When of an evening I am conversing with a friend, I am reacting from moment to moment on the basis of a great many realizations and suppositions which are not in consciousness. For instance, that the floor stretches out behind me — I should be anxious if there were a yawning chasm behind my chair —, that I will be free to leave at a certain hour, and so forth. Such assumptions, though not conscious, are providing a time-space frame for conscious events and hence are determining their course.
4. One may pass a man in the street and immediately think : 'he appears anxious, as if he were about to face some ordeal.' The conscious perception of the man's face as a physical schema, however, may have been so indefinite that one is

1. Köhler, W. 'The new psychology and physics.' *Yale Review*, 1930, *19*, 560–576.

utterly unable to describe the features which contributed to the apperception of his inner state.

5. When one is learning to drive an automobile, one is, at first, aware of every accessory intention and subsequent motor movement, but later, when proficiency has been attained, the details of the activity are seldom in consciousness. We must suppose, nevertheless, that ordered activations are occurring at the motor pole of successive regnancies.
6. Absent-minded acts which involve movements of the body as a whole are performed without awareness of intentions similar to those which usually precede such actions.
7. When, let us say, a man is building a house he is usually conscious from moment to moment of his intention to realize a particular subsidiary effect. Though the idea of the major effect — the image of the completely constructed building — is not in consciousness, it must be active, since each conscious conation and movement is so clearly subservient to it.
8. Unconscious influence is clearly manifested by the operation of a mental 'set' or 'determining tendency' (ex: fixed intellectual viewpoint).

> The firm determination to submit to experiment is not enough; there are still dangerous hypotheses; first, and above all, those which are tacit and unconscious. Since we make them without knowing it, we are powerless to abandon them. (H. Poincaré)[1]

These examples point to the fact that the extent of regnancies is greater than the extent of consciousness. It is as if consciousness were illumined regions of regnancies; as if a spotlight of varying dimensions moved about the brain, revealing first one and then another sector of successive, functionally-related mental events. The examples demonstrate, furthermore, that, since a conscious experience depends upon interrelated, extra-conscious variables, it can be understood only when it is viewed as part of the larger whole. Thus, to explain a conscious event, as well as

1. Quoted from Korzybski, A. *Science and Sanity*, Lancaster, Penn. 1933, p. 1.

to explain a behavioural event, all the major variables of a regnancy must be known. According to this conception, then, the goal of the introspectionists and the goal of the behaviourists become the same: to determine the constitution of significant regnancies. To agree about this matter, however, the introspectionists must accept the theory of unconscious regnant processes, and the behaviourists must attempt — as physicists, chemists, and biologists have attempted — to conceptualize the phenomena which underlie appearances.

In the examples cited above none of the variables operating unconsciously were considered to be enduringly inaccessible to consciousness. The very next moment the S might have become aware of one or more of them. There are other unconscious processes, however, — processes with which psycho-analysis is preoccupied — which seem to be *debarred* from consciousness. They are inhibited or repressed, according to theory, because they are unacceptable to the conscious self (Ego). Also there may be a vast number of potential tendencies — some of them, as Jung has suggested, vestiges of earlier racial life — which seldom, or never, find their way into consciousness because they lack the requisite verbal symbols. Some of these tendencies are exhibited distortedly in insanity. Thus, on the 'deepest level' we must consider traces of the racial past and the early infantile past which lack adequate verbal associations (the 'unverbalized,' as Watson would say). Then, on a 'higher level,' we have the inhibited, once verbalized tendencies, many of which are infantile. Finally, we have processes that 'pass,' as it were, in and out of consciousness; as well as those that have become mechanized (habits and automatisms) which can, but rarely do, enter consciousness.

If it is agreed that subjective terminology should be used to stand for regnant processes, and if it is agreed that all conscious processes are regnant but not all regnant processes are conscious, then, just at this point a much debated question presents itself: if at one moment a variable — let us say the trace of a perception of food (unconditioned stimulus) — is conscious (as an image of food) and therefore regnant, and at another moment it is unconscious though still regnant — because it causes salivation — what term shall we apply to it at the second of these two moments ? There are some men who have argued that the word 'image' as well as every other consciously derived variable applies to an element in consciousness, and that to use the term for something that is unconscious is to commit a logical fallacy. To designate an unconscious process these thinkers favour the use of a term which refers to a physical entity in the brain. I find it impossible to agree with this conclusion because we do not require two terms to designate the same process, and it is particularly confusing if one of the terms is of introspective and the other of extrospective origin. Having chosen the vocabulary of conscious processes we should adhere to it, and not be embarrassed if this practice leads to what sounds like verbal nonsense ('unconscious conscious processes'). Figures of speech are sometimes useful and in this case are no more metaphorical or absurd than are terms derived from physics when applied to conscious processes.

Since any concepts which can be developed to describe unconscious regnant processes must necessarily be hypothetical (convenient fictions), it is scientifically permissible to imagine such processes as having the properties of conscious processes if, by so doing, we provide the most reasonable interpretation of the observed facts. That the theory of unconscious psychic processes has great resolving power becomes apparent when one applies it to the heretofore mysterious phenomena of psychopathology.

It is possible to define regnant processes, as Tolman and MacCurdy have shown, on the basis of objective data alone. Thus, such symbols as 'perception,' 'image,' 'conation' may be used to refer to hypothetical physical processes — the nature of which may or may not be known — and, if there is sufficient objective evidence, they may be used whether or not the processes for which they stand are accompanied by consciousness. MacCurdy[1] uses the term 'image,' or 'imaginal process,' in this way. His definition is as follows :

1. MacCurdy, J.T. *Common Principles in Psychology and Physiology*, London: 1928, p. 14.

An imaginal process, from the standpoint of an objective observer, is some kind of a reproduction of a specific bit of past sensory experience, which is inferred to exist from the presence of a reaction for which the specific experience would be the appropriate stimulus — this reaction not being completely accounted for by any demonstrable environmental event.

C. THE CONCEPT OF NEED OR DRIVE [1]

A NEED is a hypothetical process the occurrence of which is imagined in order to account for certain objective and subjective facts. To arrive at this concept it seems better to begin with objective behavioural facts, for by so doing we align ourselves with scientists in other fields, and, what is more, shall be on firmer ground for it is easier to agree about objective facts than about subjective facts.

In starting with a consideration of behaviour we suppose that we are focussing upon one of the most significant aspects of the organism, and hence of the personality. For upon behaviour and its results depends everything which is generally regarded as important : physical well-being and survival, development and achievement, happiness and the perpetuation of the species. We are not interested in overt behaviour to the exclusion of other aspects : inner conflicts, feelings, emotions, sentiments, fantasies and beliefs. But, in accord with many psychologists, we believe that it is best to start with behaviour. And, since here it is my aim to describe behaviour rather than the external factors which determine it, I shall, for the present, have little to say about the nature of the environment.

We must begin by limiting ourselves to a definite temporal unit — a temporal unit which holds together psychologically and is marked off by a more or less clear-cut beginning and ending. For such a behavioural event the following formula is as simple and convenient as any :

$$B.S. \rightarrow A \rightarrow E.S.$$

1. Here, by permission of the editor, Dr. Carl Murchison, I shall quote freely from an article of mine appearing in *The Journal of Psychology*, 1936, *3*, 27–42.

where B.S. stands for the conditions that exist at the initiation of activity; E.S. for the conditions that exist at the cessation of activity; and A for the action patterns, motor or verbal, of the organism. The difference between B.S. and E.S. (what might be called the B–E form of the behavioural event) describes the *effect* which has been produced by the action patterns.

No matter how a behavioural event is analysed, whether it is taken as a whole (molar description), or whether it is analysed into parts (molecular description), the action patterns (bodily movements of the organism) and the B–E form (effect produced) can be distinguished. One may always ask, 'What is done?' (i.e., 'What effect is produced?') and 'How is it done?' (i.e., 'What means are used?'). These two objectively apparent aspects of a behavioural event, though always intimately connected, can and should be clearly differentiated. For instance:

	B.S. →	A →	E.S.
(1)	Food placed before a child with an empty stomach	Crying, followed by swallowing of food that is offered by mother	Food in the stomach
(2)	Food placed before a child with an empty stomach	Eating with a knife and fork	Food in the stomach

It should be noted that the B–E forms in the two events are similar, but the action patterns are different.

Though the introduction of new terms is sometimes confusing and should be avoided if possible, I require, at this point, a single term which will refer only to bodily movements as such (the mechanisms, means, ways, modes) and not at all to the effects of such movements. The word 'action' cannot be used because it is commonly employed to describe both the movements and the effect of the movements. Hoping, then, for the reader's tolerance, I shall introduce the term *actone* to stand for any action pattern *qua* action pattern. And, since action patterns are mostly of two sorts, I shall divide *actones* into: motones (muscular-motor action patterns) and verbones (verbal action patterns).

A motone is a temporal series of more or less organized muscular contractions and a verbone is a temporal series of more or less organized words or written symbols. The verbone is constituted by the actual words used. The intended or actual effect of a verbone is something quite different.

Now, since the first systematic step in the construction of any science is that of classification, we, as students of behaviour, must find proper criteria for distinguishing one form of conduct from another. The problem arises, shall we classify in terms of actones or in terms of effects? We may, of course, and shall eventually, classify according to both criteria, but the question is, which method is the more profitable for scientific purposes? We can predict that the two classifications will not correspond. According to one method we shall find in each category a number of similar actones, and according to the other method we shall find in each category a number of similar effects. Since it is obvious that similar actones—putting food in the mouth and putting poison in the mouth—may have different effects, and different actones—putting poison in the mouth and pulling the trigger of a revolver—may have similar effects, *the aspects of conduct that are described when we classify in terms of actones are different from those described when we classify in terms of effects.*

Practical experience has led me to believe that of the two the classification in terms of effects organizes for our understanding something that is more fundamental than what is organized by the classification in terms of actones. Without minimizing the great significance of the latter, I should like briefly to enumerate the reasons for this opinion.

1. Physical survival depends upon the attainment of certain effects; not upon what actones are employed.

If oxygen, water and nutriment are not assimilated or if injurious substances are not avoided, the organism will die.

2. Certain effects are universally attained by living organisms, but the actones that attain them vary greatly from one species to another.

Some organisms kill their prey with teeth and claws, others by injecting venom.

3. During the life history of a single individual certain effects are regularly attained, but the actones change.

The embryo assimilates food through the umbilical vessels, the infant sucks it from the tendered breast of the mother, the child eats with a spoon what is put before him, and the adult has to work, or steal, to get money to buy food.

4. According to the Law of Effect, which is widely accepted in one or another of its modifications, the actones which become habitual are for the most part those which, in the past, have led most directly to 'satisfying' end situations. Hence, effects determine what actones become established.

5. When confronted by a novel situation, an organism commonly persists in its 'efforts' to bring about a certain result, but with each frustration it is apt to change its mode of attack. Here, the trend is the constant feature and the mechanism is inconstant.

6. There are some effects which can only be attained by entirely novel actones.

As a rule, laughter in others is only evoked by a *new* joke.

7. That actones are of secondary importance is shown by the fact that many biologically necessary effects may be brought about by the activity of another person.

The essential wants of a sick or paralysed child may be supplied by its mother.

We may see, I think, from this brief list of observations that certain effects are more fundamental to life and occur more regularly than any observed action patterns. This agrees with Skinner's conclusions. The latter found in his experiments with rats that if one takes a particular effect—the depression of a lever — as the criterion for the rate of responding, one gets quantitatively lawful results; whereas if one takes a particular actone — for instance, the movement of the rat's right paw (on the lever) — one gets irregular and inconsistent results. In other words, the rat may use one of a number of different movements to depress the lever. The movements, Skinner concludes, are 'all equally elicitable by the stimulation arising from the lever, they are *quantitatively mutually replaceable*. The uniformity of the change in rate excludes any supposition that we are dealing with a group of separate reflexes, and forces the conclusion that "pressing the lever" behaves experimentally as a unitary thing.'[1]

In passing, it may be said that the 'depression of the lever' is what we should call a subsidiary effect (sub-effect), since, according to the conditions of the experiment, it is an effect which must occur before the major effect — 'getting food into the stomach' — is accomplished.

At this point a new concept should be introduced, for there are many acts which, because of some accident or because of the organism's lack of innate or acquired ability, never reach an end situation, that is, the total effect (B–E form) is never realized. In such cases, the direction of the movements is usually evident enough, or their preliminary results sufficient, to allow an experienced observer to predict with a reasonable degree of accuracy what total effect is being promoted. Such a succession of minor, subsidiary effects (sub-effects) may be called a *trend*. Thus, a *trend* describes the direction of movements *away from* the B.S. — movements which, if unembarrassed, would reach a certain kind of E.S. By the use of this concept we may include for classification actions which, though incomplete, manifest a tendency to achieve a certain end.

'Trend' should be a satisfactory term for psychologists who admit the directional character of behaviour but do not wish to employ a concept that points to something 'behind' the tangible facts.

1. Skinner, B.F. The generic nature of the concepts of stimulus and response. *J. Gen. Psychol.*, 1935, *12*, 40–65.

Now, let us assume that the actual business of classifying in terms of B–E forms has been accomplished. In this classification each category (B–E form) is merely a phenomenal concept, since it is no more than a general description of a trend exhibited by organisms. In other words, it is merely a collective term for a certain class of occurrences. If we were radical positivists, or if we were primarily concerned with environmental changes, we might stop here. But we are not, and so we ask ourselves : what process or force within the organism brings about the observed effects ? We say force because, according to physical theory, all manifest effects of any kind are due to energy overcoming resistance, i.e., force. For the physicist force has now become a measurement of motion, a mere symbol in an equation ; but for generations the notion of force as a propelling activity was indispensable to the physicist and, in my opinion, it will be indispensable (i.e., a convenient fiction) to the psychologist for a long time to come. If the psychologist could deal directly with the brain and measure a drive process (such as I am now conceptualizing), then, perhaps, its force might be defined in terms of pointer readings ; but, unlike the physicist, the psychologist must infer intensities in the brain on the basis of productions that have no meaningful physical dimensions. For example, one psychological index of the degree of a person's passion is the word that he uses to express it. Take 'like,' 'love,' 'adore.' Such a gradation is not representable in physical units.

Here we have to do with nervous energy or force, of which we know little, and, therefore, when we use this term in psychology we are referring to something which is analogous to, but not the same as, physical force. We need such a term for it is impossible to construct a dynamical theory without it. We are able to measure differences in the intensity and duration of directed activity. To what may such differences be referred if not to differences in the force of an organic drive ? Furthermore, as Lewin has pointed out, the notions of organization and equilibrium necessitate a concept of force. It is always a matter of balance, economy or least action of energy. A number of other considerations favourable to this hypothesis will be advanced later. Are there any adequate reasons for hesitating to do what physical scientists have consistently done before us : conceptualize processes 'behind' appearances ?

Now, to explain the observed phenomena — the realization of a certain effect — what attributes must be possessed by an organic force ? Let us see. It must be something : (a) that is engendered by a certain kind of B.S. ; (b) that tends to induce activity, activity which, at first, may be restless and random, but, later, becomes effectively organized ; and (c) that tends to persist until a situation (E.S.) is reached which contrasts with the B.S. in certain specific respects. The E.S. *stills* the force which the B.S. *incites*. Thus, the force tends, by producing a certain trend, to bring about its own resolution.

On the basis of this characterization we have constructed a hypothetical entity which has been termed a *need* (or *drive*). Each need has (a) a typical directional or qualitative aspect, (B–E) form, which differentiates it from other needs, as well as (b) an energic or quantitative aspect, which may be estimated in a variety of ways . Thus, the first and best criterion for distinguishing a certain need is the production by the subject of a certain effect, or, if not this, the occurrence of a certain trend.

Between what we can directly observe — the stimulus and the resulting action — a need is an invisible link, which may be imagined to have the properties that an understanding of the observed phenomena demand. 'Need' is, therefore, a hypothetical concept.

Strictly speaking, a need is the immediate outcome of certain internal and external occurrences. It comes into being, endures for a moment and perishes. It is not a static entity. It is a resultant of forces. One need succeeds another. Though each is unique, observation teaches that there are similarities among them, and on the basis of this, needs may be grouped together into classes ; each class being, as it were, a single major need. Thus, we may speak of similar needs as being different exhibitions of *one need*, just as when we recognize a friend we do not hesitate to call him by name though he is different from the person with whom we conversed yesterday. Between the different appearances of a certain kind of need there may be nothing to suggest it, but everyday experience and experiment show that if the proper conditions are provided the need (i.e., another manifestation of the same kind of need) will be activated. Thus, we may loosely use the term 'need' to refer to an organic potentiality or readiness to respond in a certain way under given conditions. In this sense a need is a latent attribute of an organism. More strictly, it is a noun which stands for the fact that a certain trend is apt to recur. We have not found that any confusion arises when we use 'need' at one time to refer to a temporary happening and at another to refer to a more or less consistent trait of personality.

With successive activations each need tends to become more fixedly associated with the actones which have successfully led to end situations ; or, in other words, stereotypes of response commonly become established (mechanization of behaviour). When this occurs 'habit pattern' may to some extent replace 'need' as an explanatory concept (*cf.* Woodworth[1]).

The seven points which were listed to demonstrate the importance of trends and effects are equally favourable to the concept of need, since a need is, by definition, the force within the organism which determines a certain trend or major effect. There are sixteen additional arguments in favour of needs which may now be set down.

8. An enduring directional tendency (disequilibrium) within the organism accounts for the *persistence* of a trend (furthered by a great variety of actones) towards a certain general effect. In some cases no single action pattern endures or recurs ; but something else (some intra-organic factor such as anoxemia or dehydration) must endure or recur because the trend endures or recurs. Difficult to interpret without a concept of directional tension are the following : the *resumption* of unpleasant work after interruption and the *increase* of striving in the face of opposition.

9. Complex action is characterized by the occurrence of mus-

1. Woodworth, R.S. *Dynamic Psychology*, New York, 1918.

cular contractions in widely separate parts of the organism — contractions which manifest synchronous and consecutive co-ordination. Such organizations of movement must be partially determined by a directional process — which is just what a need, by definition, is. Furthermore, the directional process must occur in some central area of communication — in this instance, nervous communication. Thus, the need process must be placed in the brain, for this is the only area to and from which all nerves lead. It is even conceivable that some day there may be instruments for measuring need tension directly.

10. The concept of a directional force within the organism is something to which one may refer differences in the intensity and duration of goal-directed behaviour. The strength of the action cannot be ascribed to the actones *per se*, since these may, and commonly do, vary from moment to moment. Not infrequently, for instance, it seems that the intensity of directional activity is maximal at the very time when one actone is being replaced by another (ex : violent trial and error movements).

11. An investigator may often interrupt the action pattern of his subject by bringing about the appropriate effect (the 'goal' of the subject) himself. This may be termed a *gratuity*, or gratuitous end situation. According to the need theory this should relieve the need tension and, as it usually does, stop the action. But if the actone itself were the dynamic factor, the presentation of the E.S. would not interrupt it. The actone would continue to its completion.

12. That a need is an important determinant of certain kinds of behaviour is shown by the fact that when it is neither active nor in a state of readiness responses to specific stimuli do not occur.

(a) Animals recently fed do not commonly respond to food. (b) Female guinea pigs exhibit the copulatory reflex only during oestrous.

13. When a particular need is active, common objects in the environment may evoke uncommon responses — responses however which promote the progress of the active need. Thus, the usual s-r (stimulus-response) connection may not be exhibited.

When a boy, who is quarrelling with a playmate, sees an apple, he may not respond, as he usually does, by eating it, but, instead, may throw it at his antagonist.

It seems highly probable that many of the s-r connections which are considered stable by experimenters are stable only under the conditions of their experiments, that is, when the same need — usually hunger — is active in the organism.

14. When a need becomes active a characteristic trend of behaviour will usually ensue even in the absence of the customary stimuli.

An animal will *explore* for food, and a man will *search* for a sex object.

15. Positivists are usually disinclined to accept the concept of drive, because they cannot, as it were, get their hands on it. It seems like a vague, airy conception — perhaps a disguised emissary of theology and metaphysics. That some day definite *sources* of the drives may be discovered is suggested by certain recent findings, and these constitute another argument in favour of the concept.

(a) The recent researches of Riddle [1] indicate that prolactin, a pituitary hormone, is responsible for the nurturing, or parental activity of rats. (b) The findings of Young [2] show that two secretions, the luteinizing hormone from the pituitary and progesterol from the ovary, bring on oestrous in guinea pigs.

A hormone may be the generator of a drive, but it cannot be the drive itself. A chemical substance, is one thing, the excitation which it sets up in the brain is another.

Up to this point the evidence in support of the concept of internal driving forces has been derived from extrospection. I have presented only external public and objective facts. I shall now, without shame, turn to the testimony offered by internal, private or subjective facts, including a few additional objective facts for full measure.

1. Riddle,O., Lahr,E.L., & Bates,R.W. 'Maternal behavior induced in rats by prolactin.' *Proc. Soc. Exper. Biol.*, New York,1935,*32*, 730–734.
2. Young,W.C. Paper presented at the Harvard Psychological Colloquium, April 22, 1936, 'The hormonal production of sexual receptivity in the guinea pig.'

16. Introspection has given us a good deal of information about the subjective entities that are necessary for the formulation of mental, and, hence, we must suppose, of cerebral events. If the double aspect theory is correct, every subjective entity must have a physical correlate. Consequently, we should expect to find a cortical or sub-cortical process co-existing with the experience of desiring (volition, conation, etc.). 'Wishing for something' or 'the desire to do something' may be as actual and definite as the fact that one 'sees a tree out there.' Since a need, as defined, closely resembles in all its relations the inner feeling of tension which seems to impel us to strive for a certain goal, we may tentatively suppose that a need is an electro-chemical process of some sort which is inwardly felt as the force of desire.

The subjective experience of desiring, intending, or planning usually precedes the experience of striving. It is, therefore, pre-motor, just as a need, by definition, is pre-motor.

Since a need is commonly aroused by certain afferent processes, and since it may justly be considered the physical correlate of the force of desire, and since, finally, as we shall see, it directly affects perception and thought, we may tentatively suppose that it is located in the brain, 'between' the sensory and motor areas. It is, let us say, a directional tension (one might almost say a facilitation) which is the resultant of certain electrical or chemical processes originating in other, more or less specific parts of the body. This, of course, is highly speculative.

If we assume, then, that desire and drive are two aspects of the same thing, we may use introspection to reveal to us some of the possible internal relations of drives. For instance, it is reasonable to suppose, as objective researches and introspection suggest, that every need is associated with traces (or images) representing movements, agencies, pathways, and goal objects, which, taken together, constitute a dynamic whole, *need integrate*. This need integrate may exhibit itself as a fantasy which depicts a possible and perhaps expected course of events. It seems reasonable to think of a drive as a force in the brain exciting a flow of images — images which refer, for the most part, to objects once perceived in conjunction with the activity of that drive.

With this in mind, we may consider a number of other facts, mostly subjective, which seem to call for such a concept of directional tensions in the brain region.

17. Among the commonest subjective experiences is that of conflict between desires, and that of having one desire inhibit another. If psychology limits itself to concepts which refer only to external movements, there will be no way of formulating important psychological events of this sort.

18. Although many psychologists may describe events without explicit mention of affection (pleasure or unpleasure) they are unable to get along without this variable when they have to deal practically with themselves or with others. This is not the time to discuss psychological hedonism, but at least, I may say, what most people, I think, would agree to, namely, that pleasure is closely associated with a successful trend : the moving towards and final achievement of a major effect. It is less closely associated with activity *qua* activity — movements, let us say, which achieve nothing. Furthermore, introspection seems to reveal that a need does not cease (is not 'satisfied') until pleasure is experienced. In fact, it often happens that we do not properly distinguish a need until an object that brings pleasure informs us of what it was we wanted. The point that I am making here is this : that because of its close connection with happiness and distress, a need is more 'important' than an action pattern.

19. Experience seems to show that a certain desire may sometimes give rise to a dream or fantasy and at other times promote overt activity. Without the concept of an underlying drive one could not adequately represent the obvious relationship between fantasy and behaviour.

There is a good deal of evidence to support the view that under certain conditions fantasy may partially relieve the tension of a need ; that is, it may be the equivalent of overt action.

20. Introspection and experiment demonstrate that a need or an emotion may determine the direction of attention and markedly influence the perception and apperception (interpre-

tation) of external occurrences. To influence sensory and cognitive processes a need must be some force in the brain region.

(a) Sanford [1] has shown that hunger will influence a child's completion of unfinished pictures. (b) Murray [2] has shown that fear will change a child's interpretation of photographs.

21. Everyday experience informs us that sentiments and theories are to a varying extent determined by desires. A man likes and tries to prove (by rationalizations) the value of what he wants. He also 'projects' his own needs into his psychological theories.

Every impulse is a tyrant and as such attempts to philosophize. (Nietzsche)

Metaphysics is the finding of bad reasons for what we believe on instinct. (F. H. Bradley)

22. Introspection and clinical observation reveal that different desires (or trends) may be related in a variety of ways : one form of behaviour may satisfy two or more desires, a desire may inhibit another, one trend may serve finally to promote another, a trend may be succeeded by its opposite, etc. Such relationships cannot be formulated without a concept of different directional processes interacting in one region of the body, the brain.

23. Without a concept of motivating forces most of the phenomena of abnormal psychology would be wholly unintelligible. This applies to compulsion, conflict, repression, conversion, displacement, sublimation, delusion and so forth. And without such a concept a therapist would be literally tongue-tied. He could communicate neither with his patients nor with his colleagues.

When we consider that no therapist or, indeed, anyone who has to deal in a practical way with human beings, can get along without some notion of motivational force (instinct, purpose, aim, intention, need, drive, impulse, urge, attitude, inclination, wish, desire, or what not), the suspicion naturally arises that those who entertain a prejudice against such a concept do so on metaphysical or 'religious' grounds.

1. Sanford, R.N. 'The effects of abstinence from food upon imaginal processes : A preliminary experiment.' *J. Psychol.*, 1936, 2, 129–136.
2. Murray, H.A. 'The effect of fear upon estimates of the maliciousness of other personalities.' *J. Soc. Psychol.*, 1933, 4, 310–339.

Need as a Dynamic Concept

In so far as a need is defined as a disequilibrium which stresses toward equilibrium, it falls into the category of finalistic concepts, of which the Second Law of Thermodynamics is typical. The latter has been stated as follows : 'In all processes with which we are acquainted, every known form of energy at a high potential always tends to run down to energy at the lowest potential circumstances will allow.' According to this principle, affairs tend to take a certain course. The need theory calls attention to a similar phenomenon observable in human behaviour. A trend is like a tropism, a movement away from or towards some source of stimulation, or, again, it is similar to the attraction and repulsion of chemical substances.

Suppose that two hydrogen atoms are some distance apart with the total energy necessary to make a molecule. If they begin to move towards one another under some attractive influence which they exert we display no surprise. But they are moving towards a final end, which is an end, even though they are of course unconscious of it ; and provided that nothing interferes they will reach one another, form a molecule, and the process will be consummated. The atoms move under an irresistible law of attraction towards a final condition which is unavoidable unless outside influences prevent it. The system of the two atoms develops necessarily towards a consummation, and the process has in this sense a teleological quality, though this need not mean that any god or man had consciously planned the end for these particular hydrogen atoms.

Thus all heat processes tend towards an approximate uniformity of temperature, and chemical reactions also move towards a final condition.[1]

It seems peculiar that psychologists should make such obstinate attempts to evade the directional or *finalistic* aspect of living processes, in the name of science, when most sciences have recorded and conceptualized such tendencies. Physiologists, for example, have always been guided by the notion of function. They have always asked themselves, 'What is the function of this process ?' and by 'function' they have meant 'survivalistic

1. Whyte, L.L. *Archimedes, or The Future of Physics*, New York, 1928.

value.' Take homeostasis, for example.[1] The concept expresses the fact that the various activities of the body are organized in such a way as to maintain and, if it is disturbed, restore a steady state in the body. Homeostasis calls attention to the *direction* of co-ordinated physiological action.

A need is clearly an emergence from the immediate past, or, as Schopenhauer would have it, 'a push from the rear,' rather than a 'pull from the future.' The environment may, of course, be effective in arousing this 'push,' and to consciousness the field that lies before its vision or the imagery which seems to anticipate such a field commonly appears in the guise of a pull, positive incentive, or attraction. We should say that the notion of an attracting or repelling object (press) is a necessary complement to the need concept ; also that some reference to a possible future is an intrinsic determinant of the moment. But the future does not exist. There is merely the present situation with a field extending before the subject either as meaningful, patterned percepts or meaningful, patterned images. The laying out of images 'ahead of time' expresses that aspect of human experience which is designated by the words 'anticipation,' 'expectation,' 'hope.' However, the imaginal representation of the goal (conscious purpose) does not always occur. To put it metaphorically, a need may have no inkling of *what* it needs. It may be a blind impulse, but an impulse which does not as a rule completely subside until a situation of a certain kind has been arrived at. It is because of this that we speak of drive as a finalistic rather than a mechanistic concept. Those who use finalism in some other sense should not apply it to the need theory as here developed. This, of course, does not supersede the mechanistic account of things. For we must also take cognizance of the stimulus-response sequences, the linked actones and agencies by means of which the closing situation is achieved and the tension lowered.

I hesitate to use the term 'mechanism' for, as Whitehead has said, 'nobody knows what mechanism is.' However, in modern psychology, 'mechanism' and 'dynamism' have been used as

1. Cannon, W.B. *The Wisdom of the Body*, New York, 1932.

convenient labels for two contrasting points of view and I think it will not be confusing if I limit them to this application. The words are not important to us. It is the two seemingly opposite mental sets that are important. At one pole stands the psychologist who attempts to show that a human being behaves like a very complicated man-made machine, and at the other stands the psychologist who believes that human behaviour is determined by conscious purpose. My own position is that in some events it is mechanism and in others it is dynamism that prevails (providing that the dynamic factor is given a strictly present organic status [ex: an existing process in the brain]). In most behavioural events both principles seem to be operating (in different proportions). I am presenting the facts that favour dynamism, because at present—in America particularly—mechanism as a general proposition requires no further demonstration. It enjoys a large prestige. It is almost synonymous with 'righteousness' and 'purity.' It attracts all the young scientific climbers. Its facts are rather obvious. They are relatively clear and tangible. They have already been well presented. Everybody agrees—up to a point. But dynamism, despite McDougall's able advocacy,[1] is still 'out of court.' It is 'unscientific,' 'mystical,' 'vague.'

A machine gives an invariable response which may be predicted by a study of the physical relations of its parts. With this in mind mechanistic psychologists have looked for actones which invariably followed specific stimuli (automatic reflexes). They have succeeded in finding a number of them (ex: the knee jerk) and in showing that they can be adequately explained by reference to the passage of impulses over a certain circuit of nerve fibres. Thus, mechanistic principles apply to some actions. However, it does not seem that they apply to others. There is adaptive behaviour, for example; and even mechanistic psychologists use the term 'adaptation,' despite the fact that it stands for an activity which has characteristics opposite to those of a reflex. Adaptive

1. McDougall,W. *Psychologies of 1925*, Worcester, Mass.,1927; *Psychologies of 1925*, Worcester, Mass.,1930; with Watson,J.B. *The Battle of Behaviourism*, New York,1929.

behaviour is marked by a *change* of actones. What consistency there is in adaptive behaviour is found in the *trend* that follows a certain kind of stimulation and this, as we have suggested, must be attributed to some drive process in the brain. The introduction of this hypothetical factor disturbs the mechanists because they cannot find a corresponding 'something' in the nervous system. But suppose it were a chemical substance (hormone) that is extrinsic to the nervous system? It is interesting to note that mechanistic psychologists attempt to explain everything solely in terms of the cerebro-neuro-muscular (somatic) system. (Hence they draw most of their analogies from physics.) They rarely mention the fluid conditions in the brain. Dynamicists, on the other hand, may go so far as to regard the exterofective nervous system as a mere instrument of the body (torso), an instrument that is used to organize the locomotions and manipulations which are necessary to bring about the effects that facilitate (rather than obstruct) the processes of life in the vital organs. The dynamicists get more instruction from chemistry than they do from nineteenth-century physics. At this point I might suggest that the controversy could be described as one between 'limb' psychology (focussing on reflexes, motor co-ordination and behavioural intelligence) and 'torso' psychology (focussing on digestion, respiration, endocrines, erogenous zones and reproduction).

The first distinguishing characteristic of dynamism, then, is this: an emphasis upon the lawful connection between a certain kind of stimulus (press) and a certain kind of trend (effect), rather than the connection between a stimulus and an actone. In order to make the record that he desires the mechanist must observe the *bodily movements* and the dynamist must observe the *situation which is changed* by the bodily movements. For example, the pupillary reflex might be described as a 'movement of the iris' (mechanism) or as a 'shutting out of light' (dynamism). The same effect might have been accomplished by shielding the eyes with the hand. Dynamism's second distinguishing characteristic is the conceptualization of (qualitatively and quantitatively different) pre-motor excitations or *forces*, which are evoked by appropriate stimuli (press) and remain active until the situation is modified. The point is that *they are not discharged by a bodily response as such*. Thirdly, dynamism emphasizes the relation of such forces to the well-being of the organism. It can be observed that a trend moves almost invariably towards supplying a lack, relieving a distension, or getting rid of an irritant. Thus, the final effect upon which everything depends is an occurrence *inside* the organism which can be described as the *rectification of a disturbed vital function*. For this reason it seems necessary to put the dynamic variable beneath the skin. Finally, dynamism is distinguished by its gross or *molar* descriptions of behaviour, some of which merely record the difference between the beginning and the end situation. A dynamicist might say, for example, 'The man built a house,' without feeling that it was necessary to record the numberless bodily movements, tools, materials, and pathways that were employed in the construction. This point of view can be compared to that of thermodynamics.

> The characteristic feature of thermodynamics is that it permits us to deal with energy changes involved in a physical change of state, or in a chemical reaction, without in any way requiring information regarding the molecular mechanisms of the process under investigation.[1]

The dynamicist, of course, admits that there are innate reflexive patterns. But it is easier for him to see how these developed philogenetically (as they do ontogenetically) from trial and error adaptive movements and became fixed, than it is to see how fixed reflexes can, by mere combination, produce creatively effective action.

Dynamicists can point to the fact that most reflexes are now adaptive or were once adaptive. Thus, even what appears now as mechanism was dynamism once. Reflexes that have no adaptive value are either mere reactivities to proximate blows (ex : the tendon reflexes) or vestigial remnants of past adaptations. Indi-

1. Lewis,W.C.McC. *A System of Physical Chemistry*, London,1920, p.1.

vidual life is conditioned by a multitude of previous life cycles. Perhaps the elimination of a species in the evolutionary struggle is favoured by over-mechanization ('trained incapacity').

If the evidence advanced here is valid, the conclusion should be that mechanism and dynamism represent two complementary aspects of organic life. Certainly there is no dynamism without mechanism. Furthermore, there are, it seems, gradations between actions which are predominantly dynamic and those that are predominantly mechanical. As an example of mechanical activity we may mention, besides simple reflexes: more complex chain reflexes, automatisms and tics of various sorts, obsessional fixations to certain objects, stubborn and invariable habits, inflexible stereotypes of gesture and expression. We note that these forms of activity are more common during fatigue, periods of absent-mindedness and old age. We speak of a personality becoming mechanized or of a mind becoming 'ossified,' and we mean by this expression the disappearance of novelty, the decrease of adaptability and the loss of creativity. On the other hand, there are forms of behaviour which are far from being mechanical: the appearance of unique adaptations, intuition and insight into new relations, witty repartee, spontaneity and flexibility in manner and expression, and all types of truly creative thought. The poet may be taken as a prototype. To be successful he must write a new poem; that is, he must do something that has never been done before. All poets have the same elements to work with, namely, the words of the language, but a poet of merit puts these words together in a way that excites wonder and pleasure.

To psychologists who bristle when 'purpose' is mentioned, I am tempted to quote Whitehead: 'Scientists animated by the purpose of proving that they are purposeless constitute an interesting subject for study.'[1]

From this exposition it should be clear that the term 'need' or 'drive' does not denote an observable fact—the direction of activity, for example. For this we have the terms 'behavioural trend' or 'behavioural effect.' Nor does 'drive' refer to any

1. Quoted from Sullivan, J.V.N. *Limitations of Science*, New York, 1933.

attribute of general activity as such. It refers to a hypothetical process within the brain of an organism which, perseverating for a time, 'points' activity and co-ordinates it. If opposed by another need process, however, it may not manifest itself overtly.

Again, it should be clear that the term 'need' or 'drive' does not stand for any physiological occurrences (visceral tension or endocrine secretion) which may lead up to or evoke the directive processes in the brain. The former may be termed 'sources' or 'provokers' of needs, but they are not themselves need processes.

The word 'need' (and to a less extent the word 'drive') seems to disturb some psychologists more than the concept itself, for it smacks of anthropomorphism. The dynamicists are accused of the 'sin of animism' (projecting life into inanimate objects) despite the fact that the objects of psychological concern are not inanimate. The only sin of this sort that is possible is the 'sin of inanimism' (projecting a machine into life), and of this the mechanists are certainly guilty. However, we might have avoided a great deal of misunderstanding if we had used the letter 'n' (as we shall frequently do) to represent the vectorial magnitude in the brain.

An activity in the brain has been conceptualized because it is the regnant processes in this region which we, as psychologists, must ultimately attempt to formulate. If we do not, we shall never bring together into one conceptual scheme the facts of behaviour, the facts of brain physiology and pathology and the facts of consciousness. It does not seem possible to place the factor which determines the directional effectiveness or intensity of behaviour either in the afferent or in the efferent systems. It must be post-afferent and pre-efferent. The fact that we cannot conjure up an image of what such a cephalic field force might resemble is no reason for hesitating to use the concept as a working hypothesis.

If we were concerned with the individual merely as a unit in a field of social forces, then perhaps he might be treated as physicists treat a body: his behaviour might be represented by an arrow (*cf.* Lewin[1]). But we are equally interested in field forces within

1. Lewin, K. *A Dynamic Theory of Personality*, New York, 1935.

the brain: conflicts between rival tendencies, the inhibition of emotion, 'overcoming temptation,' dissociation, and so forth. The individual is not always a unified being. This makes it necessary to conceptualize regnant (mental) forces.

We did not start the present discussion with an assertion. We merely pointed out that an hypothesis of a driving force helps to order some of the facts. According to this view a need is not a reified entity extrinsic to the system. It stands for the momentary direction of regnant processes in the brain region. It is always in a state of mutual dependence with other cephalic forces. It may change from one split second to the next. To say that an organism has a certain drive when that drive is not at the moment active is to make a very abstract, though convenient, statement. It means that a certain trend has commonly occurred in the past and, if conditions are suitable, it will probably recur in the future.

'Instinct,' the noun, is a word to be avoided, because it has been so extensively used in two different senses: to signify innate actones and to signify innate needs.

> It is true that if we consider the structure of the action pattern only, disregarding for the time being its origin, we cannot easily distinguish instinct from habit, for both are in their pure form, automatic stimulus-response processes.[1]

> It is not the details of the response that are fixed by the innate factor we have called instinct, but rather the general nature of the end towards which the response shall move; the details are fixed by the limitations of the creature's intelligence and the structure of its sensory-motor mechanism.[2]

Another reason for discarding the term 'instinct' is that it limits one to needs which can be proved innate. The problem of whether this or that need is innate is difficult of solution. Most of the primary viscerogenic needs, such as hunger and thirst, seem to be innate in the usual sense of the term. Presumably they are provoked by internal conditions regardless of the environment. Other needs, called by us 'psychogenic needs,' though found to

1. Bernard, L.L. *Instincts*. New York, 1924.
2. Garnett, A.C. *The Mind in Action*. New York, 1931.

operate without obvious dependence upon the viscerogenic needs, were perhaps once subsidiary to the latter. Furthermore, though their manifestations have been observed in all peoples, they are influenced to a great extent by cultural forms, particularly when the latter are represented by the parents.

Needs from a Subjective Standpoint

Using the deliverances of introspection for all they are worth, experience seems to show that the earliest intimation of a succeeding action is a kind of inner tension, viscerogenic or psychogenic. This inner state may be taken as the subjective aspect of what we have termed 'need.' There may be no awareness of what is needed. It may be simply the experience of a vague 'lack' or 'pressure' giving rise to unrest, uneasiness, dissatisfaction. If images of the need object or needed activity appear in consciousness, one commonly speaks of 'desire' or 'wish,' an experience which may occur without motor involvement. We may imagine that an increase of need activity leads to an intention (the decision to perform a certain act) and finally to a conation, or the experience of striving, which, we may assume, corresponds to the excitation of actones.

Desire, intention, conation may be conveniently grouped together. It is even possible that they belong on a single continuum. They appear, in any case, to be irreducible facts of inner experience that call for an objective correlate. Though we are using 'need' and 'drive' synonymously, 'need' seems to be the better word for the initiating apperception of an obstruction (lack, harm) leading to desire, whereas 'drive' designates more appropriately the ensuing activity (conation).

Some desires and intentions are subjectively felt to be in conflict with the chief aim of the self or with the 'selected personality' (Ego Ideal): what the S wants to be or to become. Such impulses appear as 'temptations,' 'seductive suggestions' or 'irresistible compulsions.' According to a scheme that shall be presented later, all drives that subjectively seem to come from 'without' the self, that are unacceptable or opposed to the 'best intentions' of the personality, have been termed 'Id' needs (idn). Id needs may or may not be resisted (inhibited or repressed). Then there are needs, evoked by sudden, close stimuli, that are impulsively and emotionally objectified without a preceding conscious intention. These may be termed emotional needs (emn). Many 'emotional' needs are also Id needs, opposed to the selected personality. Then there are some needs that are not represented in consciousness by an explicit desire, the trend and action pattern being objectified 'automatically.' The first phase in an emotional need is also automatic (*cf.* startle response [1]), but the behaviour that we are now distinguishing 1, is not emotional ; 2, is usually acceptable to the personality ; and 3, conforms to previous patterns of behaviour. It is comparable to a pattern of adapted chained reflexes. The theory is that it has been 'stamped in' by repetition. It has become a habit ; or, in other words, the actonal factor is now more conspicuous than the drive factor (mechanization of behaviour). This we shall term an 'actonal' need (an). A need may also be objectified (as unwittingly as an actonal need) in conformity with a perceived trend exhibited by another person (imitation) ; or in response to demands or persuasions (compliance). Finally, one should mention the needs that are engendered by a dissociated part of the regnancy, as one finds in hysteria (fugues and conversion symptoms).

Needs, Viscerogenic and Psychogenic

Up to this point only two criteria for distinguishing needs have been stressed : the kind of trend (effect) observed objectively and the kind of effect which the subject says that he intends or desires. Though these provide an insufficient basis for a satisfactory classification, we shall, nevertheless, now offer a list of the needs that we have found it profitable to distinguish, in order to assist the reader in following the further elaboration of the theory.

Needs may be conveniently divided into : 1, primary (viscerogenic) needs, and 2, secondary (psychogenic) needs. The former

1. Hunt, W.A. and Landis, C. 'Studies in the startled pattern ; I, II & III.' *J. Psychol.*, 1936, 2, 201–219.

are engendered and stilled by characteristic periodic bodily events, whereas the latter have no subjectively localizable bodily origins; hence the term 'psychogenic.' They are occasioned by regnant tensions, with or without emotion, that are closely dependent upon certain éxternal conditions or upon images depicting these conditions. Thus, speaking loosely, we may say that from a subjective standpoint the viscerogenic needs have to do with physical satisfactions and the psychogenic needs with mental or emotional satisfactions.

The viscerogenic needs are: 1, n Air, 2, n Water, 3, n Food, 4, n Sex, 5, n Lactation, 6, n Urination, 7, n Defecation, 8, n Harmavoidance, 9, n Noxavoidance, 10, n Heatavoidance, 11, n Coldavoidance, and 12, n Sentience. We also recognize a need for Passivity, which includes relaxation, rest and sleep, but this may be neglected for the present.[1]

It is hard to decide whether one should concoct new words as names for the needs or attempt to get along with old and ill-used terms. In the present endeavour sometimes one and sometimes the other of these two possibilities was adopted but without conviction. It was found that no system of nomenclature could be consistently maintained: appropriate words were not forthcoming.

The words used for most of the viscerogenic needs indicate in each case what effect is brought about by the need action. The n Noxavoidance refers to the tendency to avoid or rid oneself of noxious stimuli: to look or draw away from repulsive objects, to cough, spit or vomit up irritating or nauseating substances. The needs for Heatavoidance and Coldavoidance together refer to the tendency to maintain an equable temperature: to avoid extremes of heat and cold, to clothe the body or seek shelter when necessary. The n Harmavoidance refers to the tendency to avoid physical pain: to withdraw, flee or conceal oneself from injuring agents. It includes 'startle' and 'fear' reactions generally, to loud noises, loss of support, strangers. The n Sentience refers to the

1. It is heartening to discover, as P.T.Young's recent book (*Motivation of Behavior*, New York, 1936) makes evident, that psychologists are reaching agreement in regard to the most convenient classification of viscerogenic drives.

inclination for sensuous gratification, particularly from objects in contact with the body : taste sensations and tactile sensations (ex : thumb-sucking). The need moves in a direction opposite to that of the n Noxavoidance and the n Harmavoidance. But it may be associated with any one of the other needs : local sensations are an important part of sexual activity and they may accompany urination and defecation ; moderate changes in temperature are sensuously agreeable and food may give rise to delicious olfactory and gustatory impressions.

The effect of the need action in each case can be represented by the B–E form.

B.S.	E.S.
Lack of food	Repletion
Genital tumescence	Detumescence
Fluid in the bladder	Evacuation
Pain	Absence of pain

A few remarks at this point may not be amiss :

1. Some of the needs here distinguished represent gross groupings of a number of more specific needs. The n Food, for instance, could be divided into separate needs for different kinds of food. Here they are combined for convenience because they all involve 'feeding behaviour' and the objects are all nourishing.

   i. Certain animals go to salt licks — as certain tribes used to travel to salt mines — for the sole purpose of adding this necessary ingredient to their diet. ii. Diabetics have an appetite for sugar ; sufferers from deficiency diseases 'need' this or that vitamin, and so forth.

2. It will be noticed that the B.S. for most of the viscerogenic needs are afferent impulses from some region of the body.
3. The viscerogenic needs are of unequal importance as variables of personality. The personological significance of a need seems to depend upon whether there are marked differences between individuals in the frequency, intensity and duration of its

activity, and upon whether the strength of any psychogenic needs are functions of such differences. A need, furthermore, does not usually become a dominant element of personality if there is no obstruction to its satisfaction. If its activity and gratification can be 'taken for granted,' it may be neglected. The n Air, for example, is perhaps the most essential of all the needs from a biological standpoint, since if the organism does not attain this need's E.S. in three or four minutes, it dies. And yet the n Air is rarely of any personological importance. Air is free and most human beings get enough of it. There is little competition for air. The n Sex, on the other hand, ordinarily depends upon the co-operation of another person, is commonly interfered with by rivals, is highly unstable, and is hemmed in by all kinds of social restrictions. This is enough to account for its importance.

The viscerogenic needs enumerated above may be grouped in a number of ways. One convenient grouping (which calls for the division of the n Air into inspiration and expiration) is the following.

A. *Lacks* (leading to intakes)		1. n Inspiration (oxygen)	POSITIVE
		2. n Water	
		3. n Food	
		4. n Sentience	
B. *Distensions* (leading to outputs)	Secretion (life-sources)	5. n Sex	
		6. n Lactation	
	Excretion (waste)	7. n Expiration (carbon dioxide)	NEGATIVE
		8. n Urination	
		9. n Defecation	
C. *Harms* (leading to retractions)		10. n Noxavoidance	
		11. n Heatavoidance	
		12. n Coldavoidance	
		13. n Harmavoidance	

The first six needs may be called 'positive' or 'adient' needs because they force the organism in a positive way towards other objects : air, water, food, sensuous patterns, a sex object, a suckling. The last seven needs, on the other hand, may be called 'negative' or 'abient' needs because they force the organism to separate itself from objects : to eliminate waste matter or to avoid unpleasant or injuring agents. The positive needs are chiefly characterized subjectively by a desire to reach the E.S., whereas the negative needs are chiefly characterized by a desire to get away from the B.S. The division of needs into lacks with intakes, distensions with outputs, and harms with retractions may also be found useful.

The secondary or psychogenic needs, which are presumably dependent upon and derived from the primary needs, may be briefly listed. They stand for common reaction systems and wishes. It is not supposed that they are fundamental, biological drives, though some may be innate. The first five pertain chiefly to actions associated with inanimate objects.[1]

n Acquisition (Acquisitive attitude). To gain possessions and property. To grasp, snatch or steal things. To bargain or gamble. To work for money or goods.
n Conservance (Conserving attitude). To collect, repair, clean and preserve things. To protect against damage.
n Order (Orderly attitude). To arrange, organize, put away objects. To be tidy and clean. To be scrupulously precise.
n Retention (Retentive attitude). To retain possession of things. To refuse to give or lend. To hoard. To be frugal, economical and miserly.
n Construction (Constructive attitude). To organize and build.

Actions which express what is commonly called ambition, will-to-power, desire for accomplishment and prestige have been classified as follows :

n Superiority (Ambitious attitude). This has been broken up into two needs : the n Achievement (will to power over things, people and ideas) and the n Recognition (efforts to gain approval and high social status).
n Achievement (Achievant attitude). To overcome obstacles, to exer-

1. To some extent the same tendencies are exhibited towards people (acquiring friends, maintaining loyalties, possessiveness, organizing groups).

cise power, to strive to do something difficult as well and as quickly as possible. (This is an elementary Ego need which alone may prompt any action or be fused with any other need.)

n Recognition (Self-forwarding attitude). To excite praise and commendation. To demand respect. To boast and exhibit one's accomplishments. To seek distinction, social prestige, honours or high office.

We have questioned whether the next need should be distinguished from the Recognition drive. In the present study the two have been combined.

n Exhibition (Exhibitionistic attitude). To attract attention to one's person. To excite, amuse, stir, shock, thrill others. Self-dramatization.

Complementary to Achievement and Recognition are the desires and actions which involve the defence of status or the avoidance of humiliation :

n Inviolacy (Inviolate attitude). This includes desires and attempts to prevent a depreciation of self-respect, to preserve one's 'good name,' to be immune from criticism, to maintain psychological 'distance.' It is based on pride and personal sensitiveness. It takes in the n Seclusion (isolation, reticence, self-concealment) which in our study was considered to be the opposite of n Exhibition and, for this reason, was not separately considered. The n Inviolacy has been broken up into three needs : n Infavoidance (the fear of and retraction from possible sources of humiliation), n Defendance (the verbal defence of errors and misdemeanours), and n Counteraction (the attempt to redeem failures, to prove one's worth after frustration, to revenge an insult). Counteraction is not truly a separate need. It is n Achievement or n Aggression acting in the service of n Inviolacy.

n Infavoidance (Infavoidant attitude). To avoid failure, shame, humiliation, ridicule. To refrain from attempting to do something that is beyond one's powers. To conceal a disfigurement.

n Defendance (Defensive attitude). To defend oneself against blame or belittlement. To justify one's actions. To offer extenuations, explanations and excuses. To resist 'probing.'

n Counteraction (Counteractive attitude). Proudly to overcome defeat by restriving and retaliating. To select the hardest tasks. To defend one's honour in action.

The next five needs have to do with human power exerted, resisted or yielded to. It is a question of whether an individual, to a relatively large extent, initiates independently his own behaviour and avoids influence, whether he copies and obeys, or whether he commands, leads and acts as an exemplar for others.

n Dominance (Dominative attitude). To influence or control others. To persuade, prohibit, dictate. To lead and direct. To restrain. To organize the behaviour of a group.
n Deference (Deferent attitude). To admire and willingly follow a superior allied O. To co-operate with a leader. To serve gladly.
n Similance (Suggestible attitude). To empathize. To imitate or emulate. To identify oneself with others. To agree and believe.
n Autonomy (Autonomous attitude). To resist influence or coercion. To defy an authority or seek freedom in a new place. To strive for independence.
n Contrarience (Contrarient attitude). To act differently from others. To be unique. To take the opposite side. To hold unconventional views.

The next two needs constitute the familiar sado-masochistic dichotomy. Aggression seems to be either 1, the heightening of the will-to-power (Achievement, Dominance) when faced by stubborn opposition, 2, a common reaction (fused with n Autonomy) towards an O that opposes any need, or 3, the customary response to an assault or insult. In the latter case (revenge) it is Counteraction acting in the service of n Inviolacy. One questions whether n Abasement should be considered a drive in its own right. Except for the phenomenon of masochism, Abasement seems always to be an attitude serving some other end : the avoidance of further pain or anticipated punishment, or the desire for passivity, or the desire to show extreme deference.

n Aggression (Aggressive attitude). To assault or injure an O. To murder. To belittle, harm, blame, accuse or maliciously ridicule a person. To punish severely. Sadism.
n Abasement (Abasive attitude). To surrender. To comply and accept punishment. To apologize, confess, atone. Self-depreciation. Masochism.

The next need has been given a separate status because it involves a subjectively distinguishable form of behaviour, namely *inhibition*. Objectively, it is characterized by the absence of socially unacceptable conduct. The effect desired by the subject is the avoidance of parental or public disapprobation or punishment. The need rests on the supposition that there are in everybody primitive, asocial impulses, which must be restrained if the individual is to remain an accepted member of his culture.

n Blamavoidance (Blamavoidance attitude). To avoid blame, ostracism or punishment by inhibiting asocial or unconventional impulses. To be well-behaved and obey the law.

The next four needs have to do with affection between people ; seeking it, exchanging it, giving it, or withholding it.

n Affiliation (Affiliative attitude). To form friendships and associations. To greet, join, and live with others. To co-operate and converse sociably with others. To love. To join groups.
n Rejection (Rejective attitude). To snub, ignore or exclude an O. To remain aloof and indifferent. To be discriminating.
n Nurturance (Nurturant attitude). To nourish, aid or protect a helpless O. To express sympathy. To 'mother' a child.
n Succorance (Succorant attitude). To seek aid, protection or sympathy. To cry for help. To plead for mercy. To adhere to an affectionate, nurturant parent. To be dependent.

To these may be added with some hesitation :

n Play (Playful attitude). To relax, amuse oneself, seek diversion and entertainment. To 'have fun,' to play games. To laugh, joke and be merry. To avoid serious tension.

Finally, there are two complementary needs which occur with great frequency in social life, the need to ask and the need to tell.

n Cognizance (Inquiring attitude). To explore (moving and touching). To ask questions. To satisfy curiosity. To look, listen, inspect. To read and seek knowledge.
n Exposition (Expositive attitude). To point and demonstrate. To relate facts. To give information, explain, interpret, lecture.

On the basis of whether they lead a subject to *approach* or *separate* himself from an object, these derived needs may be divided into those which are *positive* and those which are *negative*, respectively. Positive needs may again be divided into *adient* needs : those which cause a subject to approach a *liked* object, in order to join, amuse, assist, heal, follow or co-operate with it ; and *contrient* needs : those which cause a subject to approach a *disliked* object in order to dominate aggressively, abuse, injure, or destroy it. Negative needs, following Holt,[1] are *abient* needs.

This classification of needs is not very different from lists constructed by McDougall, Garnett, and a number of other writers. At first glance it is quite different from the scheme most commonly used in psycho-analysis. According to the latter there are two fundamental urges, or two classes of drives : ego instincts and sex instincts. Among the ego instincts is the hunger drive and the need for aggression. Hunger is rarely mentioned, but within recent years aggression has become one of the chief variables in the analyst's conceptual scheme. Aggression, the concomitant of hate, is considered to be the force which is operating when an individual attacks, injures and murders others. It may also be turned inward, in which case the subject may abuse, mutilate or even kill himself. Contrasting with aggression and other unnamed ego instincts are the sex instincts — the force underlying them all being termed 'libido.' Under sex has been subsumed :

1. The sex instinct proper, as biologists have described it, that is, the force which leads to the development of sexual characteristics and to intercourse between the sexes (n Sex).

2. All tendencies which seek and promote sensuous gratification (n Sentience), particularly the enjoyment of tactile sensations originating in certain sensitive regions of the body (the erogenous zones). Thus, analysts speak of oral, anal, urethral and genital erotism.

3. All desires and actions which are attended by genital excite-

1. Holt, E.B. *Animal Drive and the Learning Process*, New York, 1931.

ment or by that characteristic emotional state — the palpitating, ecstatic-like feeling — which is the usual accompaniment of sexual activity. Here one speaks of the erotization of a need (fusions with n Sex).

4. All manifestations of love and humane feeling: the emotions of a lover, feelings of friendship, social inclinations (n Affiliation) and maternal tenderness (n Nurturance). Here the sex instinct takes the place of the biologist's herd instinct. It binds people together and leads to peace and concord.

5. Self-love, or Narcism, is also considered to be a manifestation of the sex instinct, but here it is the sex instinct turned inward upon the subject (Narcism, or Egophilia).

Periodicity of Needs.

Many of the viscerogenic needs are characterized by rather regular rhythms of activity and rest, rhythms which seem to be determined by an orderly succession of physiological events: inspiration and expiration, ingestion and excretion, waking and sleeping. Within certain limits, these rhythms may be modified by the will of the subject or by regimentation imposed from without.

Among psychogenic needs we also find some evidence of periodicity, particularly in the alternations of contrasting needs: sociability and solitude, talking and listening, leading and following, helping and being helped, giving and getting, work and play. Though in most cases, the frequency of such activities may be readily changed, under stable conditions a need may acquire a rhythmic habit which will determine its objectification irrespective of the immediately presenting environment. The organism will search periodically for an appropriate object.

The fact of periodicity speaks for the dynamic importance of intraorganic successions. It also speaks for a theory of dynamic forces rather than theories which attempt to explain behaviour on the basis of chained reflexes.

For convenience, a single need cycle may be divided into: 1, a *refractory* period, during which no incentive will arouse it; 2, an *inducible* or *ready* period, during which the need is inactive but susceptible to excitation by appropriate stimuli ; and 3, an *active* period, during which the need is determining the behaviour of the total organism.

A need which is aroused in a subject and not completely objectified may *perseverate* for some time afterwards. During this period the subject will meet situations that present themselves with a *need set.* That is to say, the need in question will be in a state of high *inducibility* or high *readiness*, with a low *threshold of stimulation.* For example, if it is anger (n Aggression) that has been aroused, the subject will be apt to vent his emotion upon the first object that crosses his path, the object, in such a case, being called a *substitute* object (Freud).

Interrelation of Needs

In everyday life a subject may, within a short space of time, exhibit many needs in succession, each of them evoked by some newly arising circumstance. In such events there is no reason for conceptualizing an integration of needs within the personality. Likewise, when a subject makes a decision to follow some particular course of action, he usually has the prospect of satisfying a number of needs in succession. More frequently, however, one finds evidence of a definite, and sometimes enduring relation between needs.

Fusion of Needs. When a single action pattern satisfies two or more needs at the same time we may speak of a fusion (F) of needs. Confluences of this kind are extremely common.

Ex : F n AcqExh : An exhibitionistic subject gets paid to sing a solo in public.

Subsidiation of Needs. When one or more needs are activated in the service of another need, we may speak of the former as being *subsidiary* (S) [1] and the latter as being *determinant.* The determinant need regulates the action from the beginning, but may not itself become overt until the terminal phase of the total event.

1. The letter 'S' standing between two needs signifies that the former is subsidiary to the latter. In other contexts 'S' means 'subject.'

A politician removes a spot from his suit (n Noxavoidance) because he does not wish to make a bad impression (n Infavoidance), and thus diminish his chances of winning the approval and friendship of Mr. X (n Affiliation) from whom he hopes to obtain some slanderous facts (n Cognizance) relating to the private life of his political rival, Mr. Y, information which he plans to publish (n Exposition) in order to damage the reputation of Mr. Y (n Aggression) and thus assure his own election to office (n Achievement) : (n Nox S n Inf S n Aff S n Cog S n Exp S n Agg S n Ach).

The subsidiation of one major need to another is similar to the subsidiation of sub-needs to a major need. For, as we have pointed out, many consecutively organized accessory actions are usually necessary before an end situation is attained.

To cure a patient suffering from an acute abdominal condition many separate, though integrated, acts are required. The operating room must be prepared for the patient ; instruments, sponges, sheets, and gowns must be sterilized ; the operator and his assistants must wash up and disinfect their hands ; the anaesthetic must be properly administered ; each step in the operation must be effectively performed ; and from then on during the entire course of the convalescence proper measures must be taken to bring about the patient's recovery. Each procedure is an act accessory to the need for Nurturance and, perhaps, also to other needs (Achievement, Acquisition).

Since each sub-need has an end situation (sub-effect) of its own, any need-determined action may be regarded as composed of a progressing series of transitional closures (sub-effects). During activity a subject will usually be attentive to the single procedure which confronts him. He will have a specific intention (sub-need) in mind, the major need to which the given intention is integrated being 'out of mind.' During an operation the surgeon is not imagining the final goal of all his endeavours, the patient leaving the hospital well and happy. His mind is preoccupied with the problem of the moment, clamping that spurting artery, making a clean incision through the fascia, separating the muscles and getting good retraction. Each step properly performed is a minor accomplishment (n Ach).

We see, then, that in most cases a succession of accessory effects must be realized before the major or final effect can be achieved. Thus, the evocation of any need will secondarily excite a series of sub-needs, each of which may be designated, if it is expedient to do so, by referring to the specific minor effect (task) which it aims to achieve. Though each subsidiary effect is but a part of a larger temporal whole, at any moment the attention of the subject is directed towards the accomplishment of just that effect.

Contrafactions. Needs are commonly related to their opposites in a temporal configuration. A phase of Dominance is succeeded by a phase of Deference. A wave of Aggression is followed by a wave of Nurturance or of Abasement. Abstinence follows indulgence ; passivity, activity, etc. The second trend is called a contrafaction, since it opposes or serves to balance the effects of the first. It may, for instance, be the exaggerated expression of a need following a prolonged period of inhibition. Under this heading should be listed counteractions, defence mechanisms, atonements, reformations. The two opposing needs combined may be termed an ambitendency (A). The life patterns of some subjects allow for such contrafactions.

1. A man acts like a Napoleon at home, but in his business is obedient and servile (n Dominance — A — n Abasement). 2. A man is very stubborn and resistant with his wife but is worshipfully compliant to his mistress (n Autonomy — A — n Deference).

Conflicts. Needs may come into conflict (C) with each other within the personality, giving rise when prolonged to harassing spiritual dilemmas. Much of the misery and most of the neurotic illness in the world may be attributed to such inner conflicts.

1. A woman hesitates to satisfy her passion because of the disapproval of her family (n Sex — C — n Blamavoidance). 2. A man hesitates to satisfy his desire to fly an aeroplane because of fear (n Achievement — C — n Harmavoidance).

To explain the occurrence of contrafactions and conflicts it seems that one must refer to directional forces which oppose or balance each other. It is as if there were a tendency for psychic equilibration which operates in such a way that an exaggerated objectification of one need must be eventually balanced by an exaggerated objectification of its opposite (*cf.* the balance of sympathetic and parasympathetic tendencies). If these two consecutive phases of behaviour are merely regarded as expressions of two superficial traits, or attitudes, there is no answer to the question, why did the second phase follow the first? Only when one supposes that each attitude is the resultant of a central force that is usually balanced by an opposing force does the matter become intelligible. This is an argument for the need theory.

Needs, Emotions and Affections

All experimenters know that emotion is a topic about which there is no agreement at the present day. To us it seems preferable not to attempt to discuss it in the short space that is at our disposal, but to come directly to our present tentative conclusion without marshalling evidence.

Without pretending to settle anything we may state that for us 'emotion' is a *hypothetical concept* that stands for an excitatory process in the brain — most probably in the interbrain (thalamic region) — that may manifest itself subjectively or objectively or both. Thus an emotion may occur without the subject's being aware of it (unconscious emotion). Usually it is felt, the subjective manifestation being that quality of an experience which is generally designated by the word 'emotional' ('excited'). The objective manifestation is a compound of autonomic disturbances ('autonome'), affective actones, and the intensification or disorganization of effective behaviour (motor and verbal). Sometimes the faintest moistening of an eye or the quiver of the voice is enough for a diagnosis. At other times the experimenter requires more evidence: the occurrence of a sufficient press, signs of vegetative upset, characteristic tremors, gestures and exclamations, confusion of thought, disorganization of actones and a subjective report of having been 'much upset.'

It is possible that the separable emotions are differentiations from an elementary general excitement (Stratton[1]) or startle (Hunt and Landis[2]). They grade into one another and are sometimes difficult to distinguish objectively or subjectively. Usually, however, they are definite enough to be named. In practice, for instance, temper tantrum, phobia, guilt feelings, contempt and depression are useful categories, not often confused.

Our own observations agree with common opinion (and McDougall's[3] theory) that certain emotions are linked with certain tendencies to action (disgust with retraction, rage with combat etc.). We do not find, however, that all emotions have drives or all drives have emotions, but the more important emotions (ex: 1, fear, anger, disgust, pity, shame, lust and 2, elation, dejection) are associated either 1, with a certain drive, or 2, with the fortune—facilitation (success) or obstruction (failure)—of a drive. The association of particular emotions and drives supplies us with another index for differentiating some of the needs.

We are using 'affection' to refer to hedonic feelings: pleasure, happiness, 'eupathy,'[4] contentment and elation (positive affection), and unpleasure, unhappiness, 'dyspathy,'[4] discontent and dejection (negative affection). Here we shall deal with this age-old problem as we did with the problem of emotion, giving only the briefest outline of our working hypothesis.

Affection is considered to be a hypothetical concept which stands for some process in the brain—probably in the interbrain—that manifests itself subjectively as feelings of pleasure or unpleasure (which vary in intensity), and objectively (with much less clearness) as a compound of affective actones (a certain bearing, demeanour, intonation of speech, tempo of movement, etc.). Our most direct information about feelings must come from introspection, but it should not be supposed that an affection

1. Stratton, G.M. 'Excitement as an undifferentiated emotion,' in *Feelings and Emotion*, The Wittenberg Symposium, Worcester, 1928.
2. Hunt, W.A. and Landis, C. 'Studies of the startle pattern: I, II & III.' *J. Psychol.*, 1936, 2, 201–219.
3. McDougall, W. *Outline of Psychology*, New York, 1923.
4. 'Eupathy' is a convenient term for psychical well-being, joy, contentment; and 'dyspathy' for its opposite: mental distress.

(as defined above) is always or even usually conscious. Now, if we construct an hedonic scale leading from extreme unpleasantness through the point of indifference to extreme pleasantness, and say that every occurrence which tends to move affection up the scale (i.e., to make the subject feel *less unpleasure*, or *more pleasure*) is *hedonically positive*, and everything that tends to make it move down the scale is *hedonically negative*, then the results of observation and introspection may be stated as follows: there are three sorts of pleasure, or three distinguishable kinds of events that are hedonically positive: 1. *Activity pleasure,* accompanying the rise of 'energy' (zest) and its discharge ('overflow') in uninhibited movement or thought. This corresponds to Aristotle's and Hamilton's definition of happiness[1] and to Bühler's 'function' pleasure.[2] It is marked by free, playful, actonal movement: the catharsis of inner tension. The instant an obstruction is met or fatigue sets in the level of affection falls. 2. *Achievement pleasure*, accompanying the conquest of oppositions to the will. This is Nietzsche's correlate of happiness. It is different from activity pleasure in as much as here the subject welcomes obstacles (physical or mental), selects the hardest tasks—things that demand great exertion and courage—, in order to experience the elation of mastering them. If the body and its cravings are regarded as oppositions to the will, the overcoming of inertia, fatigue, fear, appetite or lust brings pleasure. The greater the demands on the subject, the greater the experienced pleasure if he is able to meet them. The performance of an easy or habitual task brings no satisfaction, and failure in accomplishment markedly lowers the level of affection. Repeated failures lead to disquieting inferiority feelings.[3] 3. *Effect pleasure*, accompanying the satisfaction of need tension. Every need arises out of a disequilibrium (lack, distension, harm or threat) which considered by itself is

1. Hamilton, William. *Lectures on Metaphysics*, 1859–60.
2. Bühler, K. 'Displeasure and pleasure in relation to activity,' in *Feelings and Emotions*, The Wittenberg Symposium, Worcester, 1928.
3. Achievement pleasure is like activity pleasure in as much as it accompanies activity, but it is still more like effect pleasure because it depends on the *results* of activity. It might be called 'Ego effect pleasure.'

unpleasurable. This does not seem to be a fact to many other psychologists but it is a fact to us. We should say that *dissatisfaction* is the common attribute of every need *qua* need. The dissatisfaction, however, is commonly obscured by 1, the initiation of behaviour bringing activity pleasure or, in some cases, achievement pleasure; but much more commonly by 2, anticipatory images of successful terminal activity which tend to raise the affective level. The greatest pleasure seems to be associated with a relatively rapid lowering of need tension (Freud,[1] Bousfield[2]). The ratio : degree of realization/degree of expectation, is also an important factor. Thus, roughly speaking, since the beginning situation is unpleasurable and the end situation is pleasurable, and since the need action leads the S from the former to the latter, it may be said that the *activity of drives tends to be hedonically positive.* Opposition interferes with progress, postpones satisfaction and not infrequently diminishes expectations of close end pleasure. Failure to attain the goal often leads to two kinds of dissatisfaction : that arising from the frustrated, perseverating need and that arising from the failure of the Achievement drive ('I was not able to do it'). For example, a man who is jilted by a woman may lose self-esteem as well as the desired object.

Most people do a great many things everyday that they do not enjoy doing. 'I don't do this for pleasure,' a man will affirm, thinking that he has refuted the principle of hedonism. But in such cases, I believe, introspection will reveal that the man is determined (consciously or unconsciously) by thoughts of something unpleasant (pain, criticism, blame, self-depreciation) that might occur if he does not do what he is doing. He goes to the dentist to avoid future pain or disfigurement, he answers his mail in order not to lose social status, and so forth. If it is not the thought of expected unpleasantness that prompts him, it is the thought of expected pleasure, possibly in the very distant future. Visions of heaven after death, for example, have often encouraged men to endure great suffering on earth.

1. Freud, S. *Beyond the Pleasure Principle*, London, 1922.
2. Bousfield, W.R. *Pleasure and Pain*, New York, 1926.

These considerations commit us to one variety of the now almost abandoned theory of psychological hedonism. We think it is important to re-affirm that :

1. Affection (i.e., the hypothetical physiological counterpart [correlate] of *felt* affection) may be conceived of as a delicate index of diffuse well-being (health of mind and body) or its reverse. It is made negative by any obstruction to a vital process that arouses a need. Every obstruction, to be sure, is due to some *specific* factor (lack of oxygen, lack of companions, etc.) which evokes a *specific* type of behaviour, but the point is that all obstructions giving rise to needs are *hedonically negative*. This is their common attribute. Furthermore, all adaptive behaviour tends to rectify this state, to facilitate the obstructed process and thereby raise the affective level. Hence, it seems proper to say that need action obeys the pleasure principle (Freud)

2. Instead of saying that all behaviour is a search for pleasure, it seems better to say that all behaviour is the riddance (or avoidance) of painful tension, encouraged perhaps by pleasure-evoking images of expected goals. The emphasis upon 'escape from pain' was given by Plato, Kant, and Schopenhauer.

3. Previous and present levels of expectation and aspiration must never be neglected in attempting to account for a given affective state (*cf.* William James[1]).

4. It is important to distinguish the three separable kinds of hedonically positive occurrences : i, mere uninhibited activity ; ii, overcoming difficult obstacles ; and iii, moving to end situations (relieving wants). These different sorts of pleasure-seeking or pain-riddances are often in conflict with one another. Freud, by neglecting i and ii, gives a one-sided theory which fails to account for the pleasure of exercise and contemplation and fails to provide an hedonic basis for the structuration of the Ego (the development of will power, etc.).

If the above propositions are approximately correct the experimenter is furnished with another index for distinguishing needs. The exhibition of satisfaction at the attainment or at the gratuitous

1. James, W. *Psychology* : Briefer course. New York, 1892, Chap. XII.

arrival of a certain end situation suggests a need for just such a situation. And of like diagnostic value is the exhibition of dissatisfaction when a certain trend is frustrated.

As the concept of need or drive was developing it was noticed that we were applying it to two somewhat different kinds of phenomena : 1, *wishes for a certain end situation*, together with evidences of satisfaction when it occurred (regardless of the kind of behaviour exhibited by the S) ; and 2, *behaviour* which tended directly to bring about a certain situational transformation. A subject, illustrating the first phenomenon, might crave a specific result but exhibit a trend commonly associated with quite a different need. For example, a girl who wanted revengefully to hurt her parents (n Aggression) exposed herself in a thin nightgown to wintry weather with the hope of catching pneumonia (n Abasement) — in which attempt, by the way, she was successful. She did it with the anticipation of her parents' subsequent repentance and grief. Numerous other illustrations of this sort of behaviour come to mind. I remember, for instance, a friend of mine saying : 'If you want to destroy a man, flatter him to death.' One thinks also of the tendency of some women to spurn (n Rej) the very man they wish to attract (F n AffSex). The contrasting phenomenon is exhibited by a subject who 'blows off steam' by openly expressing his aggression (catharsis), but does not particularly enjoy the fruits of his conduct (that is, the injury suffered by the object). There is a distinction between these two forms of expression which we did not at first perceive clearly : the emphasis on the former case being upon the desired end situation and in the latter upon the behaviour that is exhibited.

The instinct theory of McDougall emphasizes the impulsive, emotional type of behaviour, illustrated by our second case, but does not seem to take account of the more indirect or deliberate type of conduct. McDougall, with the laudable intention of showing the connections between functions, puts into one category a certain emotion, a certain actone and a certain trend (or effect). Thus, one instinct might be called 'fear,' or 'flight' or 'security' ; another 'anger,' 'assault' or 'object-injury.' To be sure, these different aspects of need action are found together very commonly in animals and not infrequently as reactions to sudden stimuli in adults (emotional needs). But, according to our experience, a theory of motivation must be carried beyond the primitive, impulsive (thalamic) level of action. It must be made to include cool, carefully planned conduct : conduct that does not display characteristic emotional actones. Here we believe, with Garnett,[1] that it is better to have the fundamental concept stand for the more inclusive thing : the obstructing organic disturbance (beginning situation) which of course implies its opposite, the facilitating organic satisfaction (end situation) ; and allow everything to vary, as it does, between the beginning and the end situations.

Our own reflections have led us to formulate the two above-described phenomena as follows : the need that is overtly expressed is put down as a subsidiation of the need that is finally satisfied (determinant need). For example, the formula ' n Aba S n Agg ' indicates that the subject allowed himself to be harmed in order to harm someone else (masochistic aggression). If the determinant need is entirely concealed (not expressed directly) it is said to be latent (ln Agg), and if it is unconscious, as well, this fact is also represented by a symbol : uln Agg. Simple overt aggression, on the other hand, as illustrated by our second case, is put down as it occurs (n Agg), or more precisely, if it is an emotional outburst, it is symbolized thus : emn Agg.

Emotional needs (emn) — needs accompanied by agitation of thought and body — are most apt to set off actones which are reminiscent of animal, savage or infantile behaviour. The action is regressive and instinctual in so far as the more lately acquired actones do not function. An explanation of this phenomenon might be that the occasion has aroused thalamic centres, generating energy that tends to discharge by the shortest routes — the shortest routes being the innate, instinctual or primitive action patterns. Supposedly, the cortex, or some of it, is short-circuited. The action occurs without conscious effort (will). The body moves automatically, just as the leg kicks up when the patellar

1. Garnett, A.C. *The Mind in Action*, New York, 1932.

tendon is struck. In the latter case the blow seems to 'do the work,' though we know that 'nervous energy' comes from the excited neurones in the spinal cord. In emotional action it is the *sudden, close, pressive* situation that seems to 'do the work' by releasing energy in the motor centres of the interbrain which, in turn, leads to action that is effortless. Indeed, it is the attempt to *inhibit* such behaviour rather than to promote it that is felt to be effortful.

It appears that if an emotional need is abruptly restrained — the energy not being discharged — residual tension will perseverate and lead, perhaps, to a variety of after-effects. These after-effects do not seem to occur if a deliberate, unemotional, consciously-intended action is inhibited. A driving emotion — one that is linked with a directional tendency — may be regarded as a heated deed momentarily deprived of embodiment. Release of emotion, therefore, has a cathartic effect (activity pleasure) : a subjective value, which may, however, be out of harmony with the results of the executed act. Symbolic behaviour — let us say, the killing of an animal in a religious festival — can give vent without dire consequences to savage fantasies locked within the organism. It seems that emotional needs are desires for *action* of a certain kind more than desires for specific end situations. In the distant racial past, it may be supposed, the end situation of successfully executed emotional action was completely satisfying. Under these conditions an individual could remain unified. But as soon as the time arrived that successful emotional action led to distressing results — remorse and guilt feelings —, persisting inner conflict came into being : conflict, let us say, between the forebrain and the interbrain.

Needs, Actones, Vectors

The word 'actone' has been used to stand for a simple bodily movement, such as pouting, lowering the eyes, smiling, coughing, extending the hand (simple motone) ; a compound of movements, such as rising from a recumbent position, walking, manipulating, kneeling and bowing (complex motone) ; a single word or phrase, such as 'Yes,' 'Hurry up,' 'I like you,' 'Go to Hell' (simple verbone); and a compound of words, such as occurs in a long conversation or speech (complex verbone). Now, these are all objective occurrences and they may be recorded and measured in terms of frequency, speed (tempo), strength (emphasis), duration, conjunctivity (organization) and a host of other defining dimensions. Many of these actones are commonly considered to be outward signs of a particular emotional state, whereas others are regarded as manifestations of temperament or temper. The term 'expressive movements,' which indicates that these events reveal something that is 'inside' and are not to be taken merely as patterns, is currently used to include all such phenomena.

Though, in the present study, we have neglected the problem of temperament—having been unable to arrive at any satisfactory scheme for distinguishing its varieties—we have observed the presence or absence of numerous variables which are commonly used as indices of it. These observations may eventually lead to something, but at the moment we have nothing to contribute to the subject. Later, when the matter of general traits is considered, the variables that seem pertinent will be defined.

Putting aside, then, the importance of the general dimensions of actones we turn to the question of their relations to needs. It may first be noted that *affective* actones—despite the negative findings of laboratory experimentalists (Landis,[1] Sherman[2])—are employed in everyday life with considerable accuracy as indices of emotional states, and, further, that the commonest of these emotions, as McDougall has pointed out, are associated either 1, with a particular drive or 2, with the fortune of a drive. In the first case the affective actonal pattern may be taken as an index of the occurrence of the associated drive (ex: anger is a sign of Aggression) and subsumed under the latter concept; whereas when an actone portrays gratification or frustration we are in-

1. Landis,C. Emotion: II. 'The expressions of emotion,' in *A Handbook of General Experimental Psychology*. Worcester, Mass.1934.
2. Sherman,M. and Sherman,I.C. *The Process of Human Behavior*, New York,1929.

formed of the fact that 'something' (which can be nothing else than a need) is being facilitated or obstructed, and the nature of the total situation tells us what need it is.

Furthermore, almost every *effective* actone is commonly associated in a given culture with a certain effect (aim), physical or social (usually the actone and its effect are bound together as two aspects of one act) ; and there are no effects which do not further the fortune of some need. That is to say, every effect may function as a sub-effect to some major effect (goal of a need). Consequently, even though the actone is incompetent (has no effect), by observing it one can guess the need. Indeed, there are many actones which are, as it were, 'logical mechanisms' for a particular need. For example : crying (n Succorance), peering or cocking the ears (n Cognizance), striking out with the fist or kicking (n Aggression), smiling or waving (n Affiliation), turning the head away (n Rejection), reclining (n Passivity). Most of these are socially effective, because they are accepted cultural norms, but the point is that they are customarily associated with a particular need and, knowing the culture, one can usually guess correctly the need that is operating. It is because of the common association in animals of certain actones (or sub-effects) with certain needs that McDougall, in developing his formulation of instincts, was able, without much misunderstanding, to stress action patterns (flight, combat, caring for offspring) rather than goals.

Psycho-analysis has quite conclusively shown, in certain cases, that many simple actones (ex : hysterical conversion symptoms) 'mean' something ; that is, they are dissociated parts of a larger context and derive their significance from that context, at the core of which there is always some unconscious need or fusion of needs.

These considerations lead us to the conclusion that in most cases actones may be taken as indices of a need, conscious or unconscious ; a conclusion which is not in harmony with the point of view that enjoys the widest acceptance in the United States. In this country it is generally considered that the elementary units of behaviour are action patterns (actones) rather than directional tendencies. It is affirmed that the responses which are most constant and characteristic (that get 'fixed' in the personality irrespective of the forces that may have engendered them) are reflexive actones (demeanours, gestures, manners, attitudes, specific forms of movement and speech) which have become divorced from and hence may be considered apart from the needs which — if there are such entities — they once may have satisfied. According to this view the dynamic factor is in the neuro-motor system itself (just as the force of a simple tendon reflex is derived from energy liberated in anterior horn cells) and not in some pre-motor, possibly endocrine chemical factor (need). In judging this point of view it should be noted first that almost invariably a trend (or effect) is surreptitiously introduced into every action pattern that is distinguished (ex : 'feeding behaviour' includes the fact that food is taken into the mouth). If no effect were achieved the action pattern could not be adaptive (adaptation itself being a general effect). But if we disregard this flaw in the case for mechanism (*vide* the trend vs. actone discussion, pp. 56–58) we must admit that there is much truth in this conception. It stresses what may be called the 'mechanization of behaviour' (actonal needs), and the fact that the actones thus established by repetition may in a constant environment become as determining as the needs. As the condition progresses the personality becomes more constant, rigid and less adaptable to new conditions (to the delight of personologists who seek consistency). As an illustration of this, a form of behaviour described by Mapother may be cited :

> In 1918 I was billeted in a kitchen with a brick-tiled floor. I had a kitten which had been separated from its mother as soon as its eyes were open. There was snow outside, and the kitten could not go out. In fullness of time it developed a practice of scrabbling at the brick floor with its front paws, turning round and defaecating and scrabbling again in a typically feline and perfectly futile attempt to cover up its faeces.[1]

One can hardly deny that mechanization occurs as well as its counterpart, socialization (the inculcation of culture patterns) ;

1. Mapother, E. 'Tough or tender.' *Proc. R. Soc. Med.*, 1934, 27, 1687–1712.

otherwise chloroform at forty would not have been recommended. Nevertheless, mechanized behaviour exhibits trends — they were once adaptive even though they are no longer — and these trends are classifiable according to the scheme that is employed for needs. That is to say, similar trends may and should be put together, regardless of whether some are novel patterns arising out of consciously present needs and others are automatisms. The difference between these two kinds of behaviour is attributable in our scheme to a difference in the strength of another variable (Sameness, or rigidity). Furthermore, even though a need, from the point of view of consciousness, has been 'worked out' of behaviour, it must nevertheless be in the 'background.' The mechanisms, if they are adaptive, must automatically facilitate 'something,' and they must do it before that 'something' becomes so obstructed that it creates tension in the regnancy (consciousness). It is perhaps only when frustration occurs (when the mechanisms fail) that the inner obstruction, exhibited as a need, comes to consciousness. For instance, we do not become conscious of needing and seeking air (respiration is automatic) until partial asphyxia occurs. My own opinion is this : mechanization (actonal consistence with one's self) and socialization (actonal consistency with cultural norms) are widespread, important phenomena but only under rare or abnormal conditions do we find behaviour patterns that exist for long without satisfying underlying needs. And, even if it were shown that such patterns do occur, most of them achieve effects (which would satisfy certain needs if they were present) ; consequently, actonal actions can be classified, as the needs are classified, according to their effects.

Since an actone can be compared to a piece of apparatus (the muscularly controlled limbs being instruments for facilitating the life of the vital organs), the present point may be illustrated by taking the case of a research man in science who has learned certain technical methods. Which is more correct, to say that the man is prompted by intellectual curiosity (n Cog) to investigate and solve certain problems, or to say that the scientific procedure which he has learned determines his behaviour ? It seems obvious to us that both factors are effective to varying degrees depending on personality and circumstance. Since an individual cannot become equally proficient in all techniques (actones), his conduct is limited (determined) by the abilities and readinesses that he is able to develop. One might say that the needs that are objectified and the goals that are selected are the ones which can be most easily realized by the actones at a man's disposal. An extreme case would be a technician of a single apparatus who spent his days making countless measurements of everything that came to hand, thus allowing the instrument to determine the problems. Looking at the matter from the opposite point of view, it seems that the learning of a scientific technique must be prompted and sustained, by a desire to investigate (to probe into things, gain knowledge, solve problems) as well as by other needs. If there was no need of this, or some other, sort to be satisfied by the acquired actones, the individual would tend to change his vocation, to develop abilities which would satisfy a more positive requirement of his nature. Or, if the man possessed veritable intellectual interest the chances are that he would become absorbed in certain problems, and in his attempt to solve them he would learn or invent new procedures. He would not be limited by stereotyped methods. The emphasis on technique seems to be more appropriate for certain personalities and the emphasis on needs and goals for others. Also, a psychologist who views men superficially—'extraceptively' (*vide* p. 211), 'peripherally' (*vide* p. 6)—will be impressed by repetitions of technique (actones), whereas the psychologist who apperceives them deeply—intraceptively (*vide* p. 211) centrally (*vide* p. 6)—will be impressed by the aim which sustains the technique or endures throughout many changes of technique.

There is, in addition to the actonal viewpoint, another conception which remains to be considered. It is the one which affirms that all people have the same needs in the same measure and, consequently, they cannot be differentiated on this basis ; what distinguishes them are the modes (other than actones) which they employ to satisfy their needs. No doubt there is much truth in this proposition, how much we are not prepared to judge. That we have given it a place in our scheme the reader will discover when, in the succeeding chapter, the various forms of need expression are listed. Some of the modes are covered by the concept of subsidiation. To illustrate : a man may establish a friendly relation (n Affiliation) by flattery (n Deference), by imparting interesting information (n Exposition), by asking questions that the O enjoys answering (n Cognizance), by agreeing with the O (n Similance), by expressing sympathy (n Nurturance), by tactfully exhibiting his own talents (n Recognition), and so forth.

But besides these and others to be discussed later, there are modes which are distinguishable according to the type or general direction of spatial movement. For example, adience and abience (*vide* p. 79) describe movements towards and away from external objects. Following Lewin,[1] these may be termed *vectors* (v). The Adience vector furthers the positive needs (Food, Sex, Sentience, Achievement, Recognition, Affiliation, Deference, Nurturance, Dominance, Exhibition, Succorance), whereas the Abience vector favours the negative needs (Harmavoidance, Noxavoidance, Blamavoidance, Infavoidance). Contrience (Aggression) may be included with Adience, and a new vector 'Encasement' (surrounding the self with a defensive and forbidding 'wall') may be classed with Abience. This gives us a dichotomy that roughly corresponds to extraversion-introversion. This way of viewing behaviour has been applied by Alexander [2] and Homburger [3] to the activities centring about the erogenous zones. For example, the mouth may be used to passively take in, aggressively bite into or disgustedly spit out objects ; and the anus may function to retain or expel, and so forth. This conception can be usefully extended, as Homburger has shown, to characterize the play of children, particularly in their trafficking with objects. For in-

1. Lewin,K. *A Dynamic Theory of Personality*, New York,1935.
2. Alexander,F. 'The influence of psychologic factors upon gastro-intestinal disturbances,' *Psychoanal. Quart.*,1934,*3*, 501–588.
3. Homburger,E. Configurations in play, *Psychoanal. Quart.*,1937,*6*, 139–214.

stance, among children there are those who greedily grab and snatch, those who collect and patiently construct, those who secretively hoard and retain, and those who reject and violently throw down. Finally, there are movements of penetration into objects as well as those of entering and breaking out of enclosures. Though it is clear that certain vectors favour certain needs, we find in most cases that a single vector may serve several needs and a single need may be realized through one of several vectors. According to this broadened viewpoint a vector describes an objective trend (of a general sort) that may facilitate one or more needs. Thus the question arises, which is the better criterion for distinguishing individuals? We cannot give an answer at the present time because we arrived at vector analysis—following Mr. Homburger's exposition of it—as we were approaching the termination of our studies and there was not time to test it systematically. The following list of vectors are tentatively proposed:

1. Adience vector, approaching desirable objects. This favours all the affiliative needs.

2. Ingression vector, seeking and entering an enclosed space or haven (claustrum) and staying there (n Passivity, n Seclusion, n Harmavoidance, n Rejection). This movement which suggests a 'return to the womb' is probably highly correlated with the Abience, Encasement and Adherence vectors.

3. Adherence vector, reaching for and clinging to a supporting object (n Affiliation, n Harmavoidance). This is the characteristic movement of infantile dependence, the mother being the preferred object (n Succorance). It may be fused with the Ingression vector (entering and refusing to leave a sanctum).

4. Contrience vector, attacking external objects, the objects being usually disliked (n Aggression). This may be fused with Injection, or even Ejection (damaging objects by throwing them about or soiling them).

5. Abience vector, retracting or fleeing from disliked, scorned or feared objects (n Harmavoidance, n Infavoidance, n Rejection). This may be associated with Ingression or Adherence (n Seclusion, n Succorance).

6. Encasement vector, remaining fixed and holding one's ground

against intruders by erecting a wall, holding up a shield or making aggressively defensive movements. This is represented on the verbal level by reticence, taciturnity, 'psychological distance' (n Inviolacy, n Passivity, n Seclusion, n Defendance, n Infavoidance, n Blamavoidance). Logically, this should be correlated with the Ingression and Retention vectors.

7. Egression vector, leaving or breaking out of an enclosed place (claustrum). This suggests the re-enaction of birth as well as the angry liberating movements displayed when a child is restrained (n Autonomy). This vector is commonly fused with Locomotion.

8. Locomotion vector, moving rapidly through space, running from one spot to another, leaving places (n Autonomy). This is a very general attribute of behaviour. It is probably correlated with Adience, Egression and Injection. It includes what is commonly termed exploratory activity.

9. Manipulation vector, moving objects about or using them as tools or instruments with which to do things (n Dominance over things).

10. Construction vector, combining and configurating objects, building things (n Construction).

11. Reception vector, sucking or passively taking things into the body (particularly into the mouth), which often suggests dependence upon others for nourishment, affection, comfort, support, possessions, energy, knowledge, encouragement (n Succorance). It should perhaps also include the passive enjoyment of sensuous impressions (sights and sounds). It is commonly fused with Adherence.

12. Acquisition vector, grabbing or aggressively acquiring objects (perhaps to put in the mouth and bite). This goes with Adience, Contrience, Locomotion, Reception.

13. Ejection vector, expelling (pushing out) something (particularly excretions) from the body. This is also exhibited when a child throws things down, smashes objects on the floor, creates disorder, smears and soils. It is not certain whether the following should be included : spitting up, blowing out, vomiting, making loud noises, exploding, dynamiting, tearing apart, logorrhoea, slanderous gossip.

14. Retention vector, retaining something (particularly excrement) in the body. Constipation is the physiological prototype of this, but there is also mutism and secrecy, possessiveness and miserliness and the unwillingness to give time, energy or affection to others. This is often fused with Encasement.

15. Injection vector, sticking an object into something. This trend characterizes the phallic phase of sexual development. Children like to put their fingers into things, to bore, to force sticks into holes, to throw knives, shoot arrows and so forth.

One advantage of vector analysis is the fact that it is based on readily discernible spatial changes, and for this reason there is apt to be good agreement among those who make the initial observations. However, since the vectors are of negligible importance until they are interpreted, the 'personal equation' is not diminished.

To conclude the topic of mode, we may say that under this term we list not only all the varieties of action by which a need may be realized, but also the materials, implements, vehicles, machines (agency objects or technics) which the limbs manipulate in order to achieve the desired goal.

Since, as we have said, there is a close relation between certain needs and certain actones (the former being dependent for their satisfaction upon the latter), and since the effective operation of actones requires ability (innate and acquired talent), it is highly probable that early abilities determine in large measure what needs develop and become dominant. Since actones and effects must be mutually dependent, invention may be the mother of necessity as often as its daughter. We did not make full use of this conception in the present study, though the attempt was made to discover the more prominent abilities and disabilities of each subject (*vide* p. 441). Interests should perhaps also be mentioned at this point, since many of them involve a particular set of motones (ex: swimming, tennis, mountain climbing, fishing) or a particular class of verbones (ex: political speaking, logic, poetry) which call for special abilities. Interests, abilities and actones are closely interrelated (*vide* p. 228).

Cathected Objects, Interests

An object (O[1]) that evokes a need is said to 'have cathexis' (c) or to 'be cathected' (by the subject or by the need). This is

1. O = object, an entity (thing, person, institution) which evokes reactions in the subject (S).

one of Freud's many valuable concepts.[1] If the object evokes a positive adient need (indicating that the S likes the O) it is said to have a positive cathexis (value) ; if it evokes a positive contrient or a negative abient need (indicating that the S dislikes the O) it is said to have a negative cathexis. Such cathexes may be temporary or enduring. Sometimes one object is endowed with both positive and negative cathexis (ambivalence). Cathexes may be further classified according to the need which the O evokes in the S. Common cathexes, for example, are the following : garbage (c Noxavoidance), lightning (c Harmavoidance), doctor (c Succorance), sobbing child (c Nurturance), hero (c Deference), autocrat (c Autonomy). A need that is concentrated upon one object or upon objects of a well-defined class may be called a 'focal' need ; one that is moved by a wide variety of objects may be called 'diffuse' (free-floating). The word 'object' is used to indicate a single object or a class of objects : sensuous patterns (ex : music, the landscapes of Van Gogh), inanimate objects (ex : tools, a Ford runabout), animals (ex : cats, Fritz), persons (ex : Slavs, George Smith), institutions (ex : colleges, the G.A.R.) and ideologies (ex : utopias, the theory of natural selection, communism). Different *interests* centre about different cathected objects.

A personality is largely revealed in the objects that it cathects (values or rejects), especially if the intensity, endurance and rigidity of each cathection is noted, and if observation is extended to the cathected groups with which the individual is *affiliated* (has 'belongingness'). In this fashion a reasonably adequate portrait of the social personality may be composed. Institutions and cultures can also be profitably analysed from the standpoint of their cathected objects, what they value and what they depreciate.

It would be possible to collect facts in favour of the proposition that the kind of objects that an individual cathects is of more significance than the relative strength of his needs. Everyone is

1. Lewin and Tolman use the term *valence* to describe approximately the same facts.

friendly (n Affiliation) to somebody and discriminates (n Rejection) against certain others. What should interest us particularly is the nature of the objects accepted and the nature of the objects rejected. With this opinion we agree readily—up to a point. As we see it, the need factor and the object factor are complementary. Indeed, one can often guess what needs are dominant in an individual by knowing the objects of his positive and negative sentiments. Disliking the boss suggests Autonomy, preferring an inferior suggests Dominance, a fondness for unfortunates suggests Nurturance, a hatred of snobs suggests Inviolacy, and so forth. In our experience, the positive or negative cathection of a particular person can often be reasonably well 'explained' on the basis of a fusion of needs, since the object (the other person), being himself a compound of several needs, is able to satisfy more than one in the subject. However, this falls short of the mark, for there are a great number of enduring cathexes which are due to circumstance rather than to the relative strength of needs. Objects can be cathected (by primary displacement), because, let us say, of their association with birthplace, nationality, parents, an unusual traumatic experience, a glamorous relationship or some other fortuitous event. Then there is secondary displacement with all the mythological imagery of the unconscious to choose from. But we are not concerned here with explanations of conditioning ; we are faced with the fact of different sentiments in different individuals, and with their striking importance in determining attraction or repulsion, respect or disrespect, friendship or enmity. The problem is to generalize for scientific purposes the nature of the cathected objects ; for it does not seem that we can deal with concrete entities in their full particularity. It can have no scientific meaning to say that an S likes Bill Snooks, or enjoys the works of Fred Fudge, or has joined the Gamma club, or belongs to the Eleventh Hour Adventists, though to the gentlemen involved with the S in these associations it may be a matter of concern. Our own opinion is that it is important to know that there is *some* object cathected, but the object, as such, can have no scientific status until it is analysed and formulated as a compound of psychologically relevant attributes. The theory of press, we venture to hope, is a step in this direction.

In our work we chiefly distinguished among objects as persons : those that were superior (older, of higher status, stronger, more competent, dominant or more intelligent) and those that were inferior (younger, of lower status, weaker, ineffective, submissive, stupid). A need that was directed towards a superior O was termed supravertive, and one directed towards an inferior object, infravertive. Thus :

n suprAffiliation, the seeking of friendships with people of higher status.
n infrAggression, bullying younger objects.
n supraRejection, disrespect for adults.

Furthermore, we distinguished ideologies (programs of action, rationalized sentiments, party platforms, mores, philosophies, religious beliefs) from all other objects ; having observed that a need might manifest itself towards a principle, an idea, a theory, as well as towards the personalities who supported it. Thus

n ideo Dominance, to argue in favour of one's theory.
n ideo Nurturance, to see value in another person's theory and to assist in elaborating it

Besides the great variety of objects in the external world that are candidates for positive cathection, there is the self or Ego— firstly and perhaps lastly beloved. An unusual attention to one's body, feelings and thoughts and a narrow devotion to one's interests, disregarding the well-being of others, is termed Narcism (egophilia or Ego-cathection). Needs which bring effects that chiefly benefit the subject are called ' egocentric ' (or ' egophilic '). Most actions are egocentric. But there are needs which are also exhibited in behalf of a group or institution (ex : one's country). These are called ' sociocentric ' (or ' sociophilic '). Sometimes men have to be urged to serve the State, in which case circumstances may compel them to manifest Dominance, Aggression, Exhibition and so forth.

Needs that are turned in upon the subject are said to be intravertive. For example :

n intrAggression, self-blame, remorse, self-injury, suicide.
n intraNurturance, self-pity, nursing a wound.
n intraDeference, self-admiration.
n intraDominance, self-control, will power.

Among significant questions pertaining to cathection are the following :

1. The ratio of positive/negative cathexes. Does a subject like more objects than he dislikes ?

2. The intensity, endurance and inflexibility of the cathexes.

3. The distance in space and time of the cathected objects. Does, for example, a subject admire his father or is it a mythological figure that appeals to him ?

4. To what extent does a subject support his cathexes by reasoned arguments (rationalizations) ?

5. Are the cathexes imitations for the most part or have they been independently arrived at ?

6. Are they conservative or radical ?

7. Does the S identify himself with his cathected objects and experience their fortunes as if they were his own ?

The concept of cathection may be employed for still another purpose : to represent the characteristic value or potency of the subject in the eyes of other men. One can ask, what are the kinds and intensities of cathexes he possesses for his acquaintances, or, if the S is a public character, for the members of his native culture ? Is he annoying (c Aggression) ? Does he command respect (c Deference) ? Does he attract friends (c Affiliation) ? Does he evoke sympathy (c Nurturance) ? Do people generally ignore him (c Rejection) ?

Need Integrates

Everyday observation instructs us that with development each need tends to attach to itself (to be commonly evoked by) certain objects or certain classes of objects, other objects or classes being disregarded. And, likewise, each cathected object attaches to *itself* an aggregate or fusion of needs. Also, certain characteristic modes (actones, sub-trends, agency objects and pathways) become quite regularly utilized in connection with these needs and objects. Such consistencies of connection lead to the conception of relatively stable organizations in the brain, a notion which is substantiated by introspection. One might say that traces (images) of cathected objects in familiar settings become integrated in the mind with the needs and emotions which they customarily excite, as well as with images of preferred modes. A hypothetical compound of this sort may be called a *need integrate*, or *complex*. The integrate may enter consciousness as a fantasy or plan of action, or, under appropriate circumstances, it may be objectified, in which case it can be operationally defined as a reaction pattern that is evoked by certain conditions.

When a need is aroused it has a tendency to seek or to avoid, as the case may be, the external objects that resemble the images with which it is integrated. Failing in this, it projects the images into the most accessible objects, causing the subject to believe that the latter are what is desired or feared. The thing 'out there' looks like or is interpreted to be the cathected image of the need integrate. This theory accounts for the content of dreams, hallucinations, illusions and delusions. It also makes intelligible the selectivity in attention and response which individuals exhibit when confronted by a heterogeneous environment. In some people selectivity is so marked that the environment, as objectively 'laid out,' seems of little importance. The subject makes what he will out of it. 'If a man has character he has his typical experience which always recurs' (Nietzsche). Thus, 'need integrate' or 'complex' is a concept that will 'explain' relatively specific recurrent phenomena. It is an internal constellation which establishes a channel through which a need is realized. Compared to it the concept of need is highly abstract. Complexes differ chiefly in respect to the needs, the modes (actones, sub-needs, technics) and the stimulus-objects or goal-objects which compose them. Cultures, as well as individuals, may be portrayed as organizations of such complexes.

Manifest and Latent Needs

Need integrates commonly become objectified and exhibit themselves in overt action, when they are aroused. One can observe repeatedly in some people the same directional tendency carried along by the same mode towards the same object. Integrates of this sort tend to become loosely organized into a characteristic temporal sequence : a daily schedule which gives shape to a person's life. Some need integrates, however, do not become objectified in real action when evoked. They take one of a number of other forms, all of which we have termed *latent*. 'Covert' or 'imaginal' would have been a happier word, since in these cases the complexes are not strictly speaking latent. They are active fantasies which are merely not manifested objectively, or, if so manifested, follow an 'irreal' (Lewin's term[1]) course. Let us list briefly the chief courses or levels of need expression.

1. *An objectified (overt or manifest) need*. This includes all action that is 'real' (seriously and responsibly directed towards actual objects), whether or not it is preceded by a conscious intention or wish.

2. *A semi-objectified need*. Here we class overt activity that is playfully and imaginatively (irresponsibly) directed towards real objects, or that is seriously directed towards imagined objects.

2a. Play, particularly the play of children, but also many of the things that adults do 'for fun,' let us say, when they are intoxicated.

2b. Dramatics : expressing a need integrate by playing the preferred role in a theatrical production.

2c. Ritual, religious or semi-religious practices that are expressive of some relatedness to imagined higher powers.

2d. Artistic expression : singing a song, playing a musical composition or reciting a poem that gives expression to a complex.

2e. Artistic creation : composing a work of art (painting sculpture, music, literature) that portrays a complex, in whole or in part.

1. Lewin, K. *Principles of Topological Psychology*, New York, 1936.

3. *A subjectified need*. This covers all need activity that finds no overt expression. The following are significant :

3a. Desires, temptations, plans, fantasies, and dreams. Information as to these important processes must be obtained directly from the subject.

3b. Vicarious living. Here, the subject occupies himself with the objectification by *another object* of tendencies similar to his own inhibited impulses. He empathically participates in the action. The following are sources of stimulation :

- i. contemporary events, actual happenings in the present world which the subject observes (ex : an execution, a marriage or a funeral), or hears about from his acquaintances or reads about in the newspaper ;
- ii. fiction, fairy tales, stories, plays and movies that the subject especially enjoys ; or
- iii. art objects which represent some element in a need integrate. The art object may stand for an object of desire or of fear, or it may be something with which the individual can identify himself.

When, in an adult, a need with its integrate is not actually objectified one usually supposes that it is inhibited. Since such inhibitions are matters of importance in understanding a personality we have found it necessary to distinguish between needs that are overt (manifest) and those that are not. In our study the latter (semi-objectified and subjectified forms of activity) were classed together as 'latent' needs (ln).

In judging an individual it is important to observe which needs are periodically satisfied and which are repeatedly frustrated. Here we have to take account of specific abilities. Frustration may lead to inhibition of a need, to atrophy from hopelessness or to exaggerated re-striving. It is necessary to note the occurrence of gratuitous end situations (unnaturally facile climaxes), common in the lives of the over-privileged. With the latter, needs may be so easily satisfied that they rarely enter consciousness. Hence these people may appear as if they had none. Here, the conclusion must be that it is hard to judge the strength of needs without knowing which of them are being regularly stilled during times when the subject is not being observed.

The word 'attitude,' so widely used in social psychology, seems to describe a state intermediate between subjectification and objectification. It is an 'obvious readiness' to act in a certain way. If the attitude is barely obvious it might be considered inhibited, covert, latent. If it is very obvious it might be judged to be overt and manifest. Anyhow, it seems that 'attitude,' in so far as it refers to behaviour, can be subsumed under the need concept, because the latter is the more inclusive. Need is defined to cover everything from the most incipient inclination toward assuming a certain attitude to the most complete expression of such a tendency. Attitude is limited to the mid-region between latency and full realization. It would be hardly appropriate to say that an erotic fantasy was an attitude or that committing murder was an attitude. Attitudes make up the derm of a personality. Most of the social attitudes can be classified as the needs have been classified (affiliative, nurturant, dominative, rejective, etc.). This also applies to attitudes about ideologies (political platforms, religions, philosophies). Verbal activity in connection with such programs and beliefs we have termed ideological needs. For example:

n ideo Aggression, to demolish a theory.
n ideo Affiliation, to be friendly to an idea.
n ideo Rejection, to scorn or vote against a proposition.

The positive adient needs are expressed by different types of positive attitude (favourable to an object); whereas the contrient and abient needs are expressed by different types of negative attitude (unfavourable to an object).

Conscious and Unconscious Needs

It is important to distinguish the needs which are relatively *conscious* from those which are relatively *unconscious* (un).[1] By consciousness we mean introspective or, more accurately, immediately-retrospective awareness. Whatever a subject can report upon

1. Conventional abbreviations are as follows: Cs = conscious; Ucs = unconscious. We have used 'un' to stand for 'unconscious need.'

is considered conscious ; everything else which, by inference, was operating in the regnancy is considered unconscious. According to this convenient pragmatic criterion, consciousness depends upon verbalization. Thus, conscious facts (for the experimenter) are limited to those which the subject is able to recall. Consequently, in all organisms below man every regnant variable, being unverbalizable, is treated as if it were unconscious.

A conscious as well as an unconscious need (un) may be either subjectified or objectified. For example, many conscious desires are never put into action and many unconscious needs are exhibited in actions which can be interpreted by others. The manifestations of unconscious needs are usually rationalized or 'explained away' by the subject. They are attributed to another need or to some other factor : habit, convention, imitation, bad influence, etc. As a general rule, unconscious needs are in opposition to the social personality. Together they constitute what has been called the *alter ego*, a partly dissociated self, composed of tendencies that are not 'let out' in everyday life. It is this subterranean part of an individual that may, by a sudden eruption, produce an unpredicted transformation : contrafaction, conversion, regression or creative progression. A dual personality (ex : Dr. Jekyll and Mr. Hyde) is a limiting case. What is unconscious is much more difficult to modify than what is conscious. Hence, one of the steps in the development of personality is that of becoming conscious of what is unconscious.

Unconscious needs commonly express themselves in dreams, in visions, in emotional outbursts and unpremeditated acts, in slips of the tongue and pen, in absent-minded gestures, in laughter, in numberless disguised forms fused with acceptable (conscious) needs, in compulsions, in rationalized sentiments, in projections (illusions, delusions and beliefs), and in all symptoms (hysterical conversion symptoms particularly). In the present study we became less interested as time went on in conscious overt behaviour — it was obvious and the subject knew about it — and increasingly absorbed in the exploration of unconscious complexes.

At this point, a special difficulty arises in connection with the subject who is disturbed or depressed but does not know what is wrong or what he needs. He is like a sick man ignorant of medicine. For example, there is no instinct that leads a patient with scurvy to drink orange juice. He must be told what he needs. If left to himself he might seek (that is, act as if he 'really' needed) a great variety of things. Similarly it appears that many people do not know what it is they 'really' want, what they 'really' need for their own well-being. They recognize it only when they find it, after much fumbling about or after being shown by someone else. Parents, nurses, educators, psycho-therapists, priests and moral philosophers make it their business to tell the young, the depraved and the sick what they need. Perhaps they are wrong most of the time, but when it can be shown that such a prediction is right, that a certain heretofore unexhibited trend of action brings contentment in place of inner disturbance, then there is reason to suppose that a need has been satisfied, a need that was previously active, though entirely unconscious. If, however, there has been no antecedent discontent we must consider the possibility of a new integration of needs, or even of the generation of a new need. It is often fruitful to consider an individual from the point of view of what needs are currently satisfied and what needs (common in others) are not ; and then to consider which ones of the satisfied and which ones of the unsatisfied are really important to his well-being.

D. CONCEPTS OF PRESS AND THEMA. DEFINITION OF NEED

It has been maintained that personology conceptualizes the reactions of individuals on a molar (gross) level. Though it is not limited to the construction of such formulations, this is its distinctive task. The concepts of need, trend and effect, for example, are molar concepts. They describe the general course of behaviour. They might even be used (in the case of an individual whose entire life has been ordered by a controlling purpose) to summarize a biography. But this mode of abstraction results in a one-sided portrait that leaves us in the dark as to many dynamic factors about which we quite naturally require information. The representation of the personality as a hierarchical system of general traits or need complexes leaves out the *nature of the environment*, a serious omission. We must know to what circumstances an individual has been exposed.

To some extent an application of the notion of cathection will fill the gap, because an enumeration of the positively and negatively cathected objects tells us what entities in the environment had drawing or repelling power. However, the enumeration of concrete cathected objects has meaning only for those who have had experience with them and can, by an intuitive leap, imagine why they repelled or appealed to the subject in question. To say that John Quirk had a focal Affiliation drive is equivalent to the statement that 'he maintained a life-long friendship with George Smythe,' since we have no information about the attributes of George Smythe. Concrete objects and events constitute the data of science, but they cannot be incorporated in a discipline until they can be described as patterns of general attributes. We must build a conceptual home for our perceptions.

What seems to be necessary here is a method of analysis which will lead to satisfactory dynamical formulations of external environments. To us it seems that few psychologists have correctly envisaged this problem. Those who study behavioural reactions record, usually quite scrupulously, the particular stimuli which evoke each response, and when the reaction system is defined it is described as a kind of activity that is evoked by a certain class of stimuli. But upon examination it becomes apparent that the class of stimuli has but one uniformity : the power to evoke the reaction in question. Thus, reactions of class A are responses to stimuli of class X ; and stimuli of class X are those that arouse reactions of class A. In other words, the abstract description of the effective (behavioural) environment, as usually given, is mere tautology. An obvious way to avoid tautology is to become concrete and mention the specific objects or situations which in each instance provoked the behaviour. But it is just here that we do not want to rest, because to arrive at the generalizations that science demands we must find similarities (uniformities) among events and to find similarities it is necessary to abstract from the concrete. The question is, how shall we classify situations *in their own right* (i.e., irrespective of the *response* that they evoke in the organism) ? As psychologists, of course, we must limit ourselves to the parts of the environment with which human beings make contact and to the aspects which 'make a difference.' The usual classification — as represented by common speech and the dictionary — assigns a name to objects which have similar physical properties, but this mode of symbolization, though it classifies objects in their own right, is of no use to us because it is dynamically (personologically) irrelevant. If we attempted it we should discover that objects which have quite similar physical dimensions (ex : two men that resemble each other) may affect the organism entirely differently and give rise to different reactions, and that objects which are perceptually very different (ex : a stroke of lightning and a wild animal) may affect the organism similarly and bring about similar reactions. As Koffka [1] has emphasized, the physical environment and the behavioural (or psychological) environment are two different things.

Failing to make progress by using any of the above described methods, we finally hit upon the notion of representing an object or situation according to its effect (or potential effect) upon the subject, just as we had become accustomed to represent the subject in terms of his effect (or intended effect) upon an object. By 'effect' here we *do not mean the response that is aroused in the subject* (a mode of classification that has been abandoned) ; we mean what is done to the subject before he responds (ex : belittlement by an insult) or what might be done to him if he did not respond (ex : a physical injury from a falling stone), or what might be done to him if he did respond by coming into contact with the object (ex : nourishment from food). Thus, one may ask : does the object physically harm the subject, nourish him, excite him, quiet him, exalt him, depreciate him, restrain,

1. Koffka, K. *Principles of Gestalt Psychology*, New York, 1935.

guide, aid or inform him ? Such questions are the outcome of a dominating conception of the organism as a 'going concern' (a system of vital processes), the behaviour of which is mostly directed by occurrences that facilitate or obstruct these processes. On the personological level we must deal for the most part with social factors which facilitate or obstruct the psychological well-being of the individual, but they can be viewed in the same way as a physiologist views the culture medium of an organism. Does it contain poisons ? Is there sufficient oxygen ? Does it allow for the elimination of waste products ?

Our conclusion is that it is not only possible but advisable to classify an environment in terms of the kinds of benefits (facilitations, satisfactions) and the kinds of harms (obstructions, injuries, dissatisfactions) which it provides. When this is done it may be observed that in the vast majority of cases the organism tends to avoid the harms and seek the benefits. The troublesome exceptions to this general rule can be put aside for the present. What we want to represent is the kind of effect that a given object does (or can) have upon the subject. If it is a 'bad' effect the subject tends to prevent its occurrence by avoiding it or defending himself against it. If it is a 'good' effect the S will usually approach the object and attempt to get the most out of it. A single object, of course, may be capable of numerous effects, both harms and benefits.

It may readily be seen that when the objects of the environment are human or animal, they can be symbolized as the subject is symbolized in terms of this or that drive. The natural environment, as we shall see, may be treated in much the same fashion. Thus, the external world appears in the guise of a dynamical process and the complete behavioural event as an interaction of forces.

We have selected the term *press* (plural *press*) to designate a directional tendency in an object or situation. Like a need, each press has a qualitative aspect — the kind of effect which it has or might have upon the subject (if the S comes in contact with it and does not react against it) — as well as a quantitative aspect, since its power for harming or benefitting varies widely. Everything that can supposedly harm or benefit the well-being of an organism may be considered *pressive*, everything else *inert*. The process in the subject which recognizes what is being done to him at the moment (that says 'this is good' or 'this is bad') may be conveniently termed *pressive perception*. The process is definitely egocentric, and gives rise almost invariably, to some sort of adaptive behaviour.

Most stimulus situations are not in themselves directly effective. As such, they are not harms or benefits to the organism. But they are potent evokers of behaviour because they appear as signs of something that is to come. Some people, for example, are more disturbed by omens of disaster than they are by actual misfortune; and others are more thrilled by thoughts of future events than by these events when they occur. Similarly, there is such a thing as fore-pleasure and fore-unpleasure. Indeed, the power of a stimulus situation does not usually depend upon *pressive perception*—'the object is doing this or that to me'—but rather upon *pressive apperception*—'the object may do this to me (if I remain passive) or I may use the object in this or that way (if I become active).' Such pressive apperceptions are largely determined, as investigations have shown, by the impressions and integrations which have occurred in the brain as the result of past experiences. Pressive apperception, indeed, may be defined as a process by which a present situation excites images (conscious or unconscious) that are representative of pressive situations of the past. Through them the past is made to live actively in the present. Thus every conditioned response depends upon pressive apperception, for it is this process which connects an existing, otherwise inert situation with the impression (trace) of a former pressive perception. What is important to note is that pressive apperception is usually unconscious. The creature merely reacts. If it happens to be a mature human being, he will often give reasons to himself or to others for his behaviour, but his explanations will seldom coincide with the unconscious determining integration.

Because the conception of press came to us rather late in the course of our explorations it was not suitably compounded with our other concepts. Nor has it yet been applied sufficiently to the interpretation of personality and social cultures. And there is not even space here for an account of what in the theory has already been found usable. Suffice it to say that one can profitably analyse an environment, a social group or an institution from the point of view of what press it applies or offers to the individuals that live within or belong to it. These would be its dynamically pertinent attributes. Furthermore, human beings, in general or in particular, can be studied from the standpoint of what beneficial press are available to them and what harmful press they customarily encounter. This is partly a matter of the potentialities of the environment and partly of the attributes of the subject. Some individuals, because they are ugly or disorderly or courteous or quiet, have a cathexis for certain kinds of press. That is to say, they arouse certain needs—Rejection, Aggression, Deference, Nurturance—in others.

Our present classification of press is not considered satisfactory, but a bare outline might be offered at this point :

Press may be classified in a rough way as *positive* or *negative*, and as *mobile* or *immobile*. Positive press are usually enjoyable and beneficial (ex : food, a friend) ; negative press are usually distasteful and harmful (ex : poison, insult). Mobile press are moving forces which may affect the subject harmfully or beneficially if he remains passive (ex : an animal or human being). Mobile press may be either *autonomous* or *docile*, autonomous when the activity is initiated in the O, docile when regulated by the S (ex : a compliant subordinate). Immobile press can have no effect unless the S approaches, manipulates or influences them in some way (ex : a glass of water). A *positive autonomous* (mobile) press would be exemplified by a sympathetic mother, an affectionate friend, a bestowing philanthropist, a benevolent leader. And the apperception of the S might be : 'he (or she) will be friendly, help me, praise me.' A *positive docile* (mobile) press would be exhibited by a river that is used to drive a mill, a domestic animal, a servant, a disciple. Here the apperception of the S might be : 'I can control it, he will obey me, he is respecting my wishes.' A *negative mobile* press would be exemplified by lightning, a storm at sea, a carnivorous beast, an angry parent, a gangster, the 'hand of the law,' a bore, a troublesome child. A negative mobile press is always autonomous, since a S does not use an object to bring displeasure to himself. A *positive immobile* press is manifested by inorganic objects which cannot or usually do not act on the subject unless he approaches or manipulates them. The following might be mentioned : nourishing food, water, shelter, toys, money, building stones, all manner of material possessions. The apperceptions of the S might be : 'It will taste good, it will warm me, I can play it, I can give it to someone.' A *negative immobile* press would be exemplified by quicksand, ice cold water, a precipice, a barrier, poison ivy, useless instruments, an ugly object and so forth. Here apperception will report : 'It is dangerous, it will hurt me if I touch it, it cannot be used.'

What we have been describing is the external world in the guise of a psychological environment : objects in changing settings characterizable as foods, poisons, sensuous patterns, supports, harbingers of danger, friends, guides, enemies, suppliants that are prospective of certain consequences if approached, manipulated, embraced, commanded, flattered, obeyed or otherwise responded to. The *press* of an object is what it can *do to the subject* or *for the subject*—the power that it has to affect the well-being of the subject in one way or another. The cathexis of an object, on the other hand, is what it can *make the subject do*.

In our work we concentrated upon press that were manifested by human objects (mobile, autonomous press) and we enlarged the notion to include lacks and losses of positive press (ex : a barren monotonous environment, lack of food objects, poverty, no friends, etc.). A few illustrations will suffice :

p Affiliation, a friendly, sociable companion
p Nurturance, a protective, sympathetic ally
p Aggression, a combative O, or one who censures, belittles or fleers
p Rival (Recognition), a competitor for honours
p Lack (Economic), the condition of poverty
p Dominance : Restraint, an imprisoning or prohibiting object.

The diagnosis of press is fraught with the same difficulty as the diagnosis of need. It is always an interpretation, but an important one. Every individual must make such guesses many times a day : 'Will this object please and benefit me, or will it displease and harm me ?' The knowledge of what is good and what is bad for man is a large part of wisdom. In identifying press we have found it convenient to distinguish between 1, the *alpha* press, which is the press that actually exists, as far as scientific inquiry can determine it ; and 2, the *beta* press, which is the subject's own interpretation of the phenomena that he perceives. An object may, in truth, be very well disposed towards the subject — press of Affiliation (*alpha* press) — but the subject may misinterpret the object's conduct and believe that the object is trying to depreciate him — press of Aggression : Belittlement (*beta* press). When there is wide divergence between the *alpha* and *beta* press we speak of delusion.

Pre-actions and Outcomes

Behaviour is inaugurated not only by newly arising internal wants and freshly presented press, but by preceding occurrences. Among the latter we have found it convenient to distinguish 'pre-actions' and 'outcomes.' Any action which determines the course of future behaviour, may be called a 'pre-action.' Some pre-actions are of the nature of promises and pledges. They call for some later fulfillment : a further 'living out' or a repetition of the word or deed. Others, however, are followed by actions of an opposite sort : borrowing by returning, lending by demanding payment, generosity by stinginess, depreciating by praising, fighting by peaceful overtures, rudeness by courtesy (contrafactions). If the status of the subject is lowered by his own pre-action (ex : humiliation), then the 'sequent-action' is very likely to be an attempt to re-instate himself (ex : self-vindication). Whereas, if another human being is diminished by the pre-action, there will be a tendency for the subject to bring about a restitution (ex : apology, gift, compliment). Influencing many of these acts is a vague sense of 'justice,' of a balance between what is due the subject and what is due the object. This is closely related to inferiority feelings and guilt feelings.

Besides pre-actions it is necessary to take account of outcomes (the fortunes of previous strivings). A man, for example, may react to *success* by inflation (self-confidence, boasting, demands for recognition) or by deflation (modesty of the victor). Similarly, *failure* may give rise to aggression and extrapunitiveness or to abasement and intrapunitiveness (*vide* Dr. Rosenzweig's paper, p. 585). It may also be followed by Defendance (verbal self-vindication), Succorance (appeals for help or generosity), Infavoidance (withdrawal), Play (attempts to make a joke of it), Recognition (telling about one's success in some other field) and so forth.

Concept of Thema

A thema is the dynamical structure of an event on a molar level. A simple thema is the combination of a particular press or pre-action or outcome (o) and a particular need. It deals with the general nature of the environment and the general nature of the subject's reaction. For example:

p Rejection → *n Rejection*: the S is rejected (snubbed) by the O and responds in kind.

o Failure → *n Achievement*: the S makes renewed, counteractive attempts to succeed after failure.

Thus, a thema exhibits the press of the stimulus to which a subject is exposed when he reacts the way he does. Since fantasies as well as actual events have themas, every need integrate is also a thematic tendency; the theory being that in such cases there is an inhibited need for a particular form of behaviour to be aroused by a press which the individual secretly (perhaps unconsciously) hopes to find embodied in some actual person. In our experience, the unconscious (*alter ego*) of a person may be formulated best as an assemblage or federation of thematic tendencies.

Definition of Need

Marshalling the facts and reflections reviewed in this section it is possible to enlarge upon our initial definition of a need.

A need is a construct (a convenient fiction or hypothetical

concept) which stands for a force (the physico-chemical nature of which is unknown) in the brain region, a force which organizes perception, apperception, intellection, conation and action in such a way as to transform in a certain direction an existing, unsatisfying situation. A need is sometimes provoked directly by internal processes of a certain kind (viscerogenic, endocrinogenic, thalamicogenic) arising in the course of vital sequences, but, more frequently (when in a state of readiness) by the occurrence of one of a few commonly effective press (or by anticipatory images of such press). Thus, it manifests itself by leading the organism to search for or to avoid encountering or, when encountered, to attend and respond to certain kinds of press. It may even engender illusory perceptions and delusory apperceptions (projections of its imaged press into unsuitable objects). Each need is characteristically accompanied by a particular feeling or emotion and tends to use certain modes (sub-needs and actones) to further its trend. It may be weak or intense, momentary or enduring. But usually it persists and gives rise to a certain course of overt behaviour (or fantasy), which (if the organism is competent and external opposition not insurmountable) changes the initiating circumstance in such a way as to bring about an end situation which stills (appeases or satisfies) the organism.

From this definition it appears that the indices by which an overt or manifest need can be distinguished are these:

1. A typical behavioural trend or effect (transformation of external-internal conditions).
2. A typical mode (actones or sub-effects).
3. The search for, avoidance or selection of, attention and response to one of a few types of press (cathected objects of a certain class).
4. The exhibition of a characteristic emotion or feeling.
5. The manifestation of satisfaction with the achievement of a certain effect (or with a gratuity), or the manifestation of dissatisfaction when there is failure to achieve a certain effect.

These objective indices have subjective correlates: a subject is usually aware of wanting and striving for a certain effect, he can report upon what attracted his attention and how he interpreted it. He can describe his inner states of feeling, emotion and affection. He can say whether he was really pleased or just pretending. Thus, if the above-mentioned five kinds of phenomena are observed, subjectively and objectively, there will be ten criteria upon which to base a diagnosis of manifest need.

Latent needs (like manifest needs) are parts of integrates composed of actones, sub-needs, feelings, and cathected images embodying press, but either 1, they are objectified in play or ritual or artistic compositions, the objects being make-believe or symbolic (semi-objectifications); or 2, they are portrayed in the behaviour or art productions of others, the S being merely an empathic observer (vicarious living); or 3, they are not objectified in any form, the E becoming aware of them only when the S speaks aloud his free-associations or reports upon his dreams and fantasies (*vide* p. 111). Special methods have been invented for evoking latent, imaginal needs and objectifying them in fictional forms. These will be discussed later (*vide* p. 529).

The strength of a single exhibition of a need is measured in terms of intensity and duration. The strength of a need as a consistently ready reaction system of personality is measured by noting the frequency of its occurrence under given conditions. In our scoring these three indices of 'strength' were lumped together; a high mark indicating that the need in question was exhibited with great frequency, or occasionally with great intensity or persistence. The criteria of intensity will be discussed in a later section (*vide* p. 251).

Since, according to our conception, a need manifests itself in a variety of ways, it is not possible to confine oneself to a single operational definition. It seems that the best objective basis is the behavioural attainment of an apparently satisfying effect, an effect which brings the activity to a halt (usually by facilitating a vital process). The best subjective criterion is the occurrence of a wish or resolution to do a certain thing (to bring about a certain effect). According to some psychologists subjective processes are outside the pale of operationism. Naturally, they do not come within the domain of physics, but that a physicist might include them if he took up the study of psychology is indicated by Bridgman's choice of a subjective process to illustrate operationism.

> As a matter of self-analysis I am never sure of a meaning until I have analysed what I do, so that for me meaning is to be found in a recognition of the activities involved. These activities may be diffused and nebulous and on the purely emotional level, as when I recognize that what I mean when I say that I dislike something is that I confront myself with the thing in actuality or in imagination and observe whether the emotion that it arouses is one with which I associate the name 'dislike.' The emotion awakened which I call 'dislike' permits of no further analysis from this point of view, but has to be accepted as an ultimate.[1]

As we have said, the objective and subjective criteria above mentioned are but two ways in which a need makes itself known; others are almost equally valid and useful. Thus, although it is necessary that an experimenter be able to give a clear and accurate account of the occurrences upon which he has based a diagnosis of need — he must always be able to distinguish fact from theory — he cannot, in the present state of psychology, base his diagnosis (or his definition) on a single operation. Here, he is in the same predicament as a physician who makes a diagnosis on the basis of numerous incommensurate signs or operations (subjective pain, temperature, blood count, urine examination, etc.) and next day, when faced by another subject, makes correctly the same diagnosis on the basis of a somewhat different collection of signs.

Furthermore, since during any occasion a need is but one of many interacting processes, all of which vary qualitatively and quantitatively from occasion to occasion, measurements of need strength must necessarily be crude and various. For instance, there seem to be about twenty equally valid indices of the intensity of a drive (*vide* p. 253). All of which leads us to the conclusion that a rigorous operational definition of need is inadvisable, and perhaps impossible at the present time.

Some psychologists have strenuously objected to the concept

1. Bridgman, P.W. *The Nature of Physical Theory*, 1936, pp. 8, 9.

of need, on the basis that it is either a simple tautology or a hazardous unscientific guess. A friend of mine writes : 'I observe a man enter a room and sit down on a couch. What do I add to an understanding of the event by stating that he had a "need to sit on that couch" ?' The answer to such a question is that the 'need to sit on that couch' is either a concrete example of a certain class of needs (ex : need for Passivity) or it is a sub-need which furthers the trend of one or more determinant needs : perhaps a need for Similance (other people are sitting down), a need for Cognizance (to discover whether the couch is comfortable or not), a need for Affiliation (to be near a cathected object who is sitting on the couch), etc. One cannot say which of a number of possible needs are operating without further facts. The experimenter must observe how the subject behaves when he sits down, must ask, 'Why did you sit down on that couch ?' and so forth. The attribution of a particular need is always an hypothesis, but one which can sometimes be substantiated by sufficient evidence (subjective and objective), and when so substantiated may lead to important generalizations about a personality. The mere fact that a particular S sat on a particular couch, however, is of no scientific interest. It is an outcast fact begging to be understood and to be accepted with others of its kind.

When it is stated that an individual has a strong need for Aggression, let us say, it means merely that signs of this need have recurred, with relative frequency, in the past. It is an abstract statement which requires amplification, for it does not tell us : 1, whether the manifestations of Aggression are emotional (accompanied by anger) and impulsive (emn Agg), or deliberate and calm, or habitually automatic and actonal (an Agg) ; or 2, what actones are habitually employed — motones (fists) or verbones (words of belittlement) — or what needs act in a subsidiary capacity ; or 3, whether the need is focal or diffuse, and, if focal, what are the negatively cathected objects (people, institutions, ideas) and what press do they exemplify (does the S attack prohibiting authorities [n suprAgg] or weaklings [n infrAgg] ?) ; or 4, whether the need is directed inwardly

(intrAgg) resulting in self-condemnation and guilt feelings ; or 5, whether the need integrate is objectified in overt behaviour or inhibited and latent (ln Agg), manifesting itself only in fantasy or in a preference for aggressive scenes and stories ; or 6, whether the subject is conscious of his wish to belittle others and of his enjoyment over their defeats ; or 7, whether the need is sustained by an aggressive Ego Ideal or exemplar ; or 8, whether the activity is in the service of another need (to redress an injury [n Agg S n Inv] or to attain power [n Agg S n Dom]) ; or finally, 9, whether the aggression serves the subject only or whether it furthers an important social cause (n socio Agg).

What factors determine the establishment of a need as a ready reaction system of personality ? This is an important problem to which only vague and uncertain answers can be given. In the first place, observation seems to show that the relative strength of needs at birth (or shortly after birth) is different in different children. Later, the strength of some needs may be attributed to intense or frequent gratifications (reinforcements), some of which rest on specific abilities. Indeed, some needs may emerge out of latency because of gratuities or the chance attainment of end situations through random movements. (The need for morphine, which can be more potent than hunger, is developed solely by repeated gratifications.) Some needs may become established because of their success in furthering other more elementary needs. The gratification or frustration of a need is, of course, largely up to the parents, since they are free to reward or punish any form of behaviour. Certain innate or acquired abilities will favour the objectification of some needs and not of others. There is much evidence to show that the sudden frustration of a need — particularly if preceded by a period of intense gratification — leads to residual tension. This seems to be particularly true for emotional 'thalamic' needs that are abruptly obstructed or inhibited. A 'thalamic charge,' let us say, perseverates in such a way as to control fantasy and, if the occasion offers, to explode into overt behaviour. Such inhibited 'thalamic' needs often become fused with the Sex drive. In this way they become 'erotized.' A need may also become established by repetition, due to the frequent occurrence of specific press. But if the stimulus becomes stale, habituation sets in and the need becomes less responsive. Emulation (n Similance S n Superiority) is a potent factor in accentuating certain needs — the S wanting to be like his exemplar —, and so is Deference: Compliance, and Affiliation. Here we have to do with cultural factors. Certain cultures and sub-cultures to which an individual is exposed may be characterized by a predominance of certain needs. Not infrequently Contrarience (the desire to be different from or the exact opposite of a disliked object) operates to enhance the strength of some need. There are still other factors, no doubt, that work to determine what needs become dominant. For instance, there is the occurrence of conflict and the inhibition of one need by another. However, in view of our ignorance of such determinants, we require observation and experiment rather than any further reflections of this sort.

E. MISCELLANEOUS CONCEPTS

Energy

AMONG the facts of subjective experience is the feeling or the quality of feeling to which the term 'energy' is very commonly applied. Not only can an individual introspect at any moment and give an estimate of the degree to which he feels 'energetic'; but his judgement will often be found to correspond with what an observer would say on the basis of external signs. Evidently we are dealing here with a continuum between two extreme states, subjectively and objectively discernible: *zest* and *apathy*. The various aspects of zest may be designated by such words as alertness, reactivity, vigilance, freshness, vitality, strength, 'fire,' 'pep,' verve, eagerness, ardour, intensity, enthusiasm, interest; whereas under apathy may be subsumed lassitude, lethargy, loginess, 'brain fag,' indolence, ennui, boredom, fatigue, exhaustion. The former state yields prompter, faster, stronger, more frequent and persistent reactions — reactions that are apt to be more correct, relevant, novel, adaptive, intelligent, imaginative or creative than those produced during the latter state. Zest is highly correlated with pleasure and activity (physical and mental), apathy with unpleasure and inactivity.

To the topic of energy (vital energy, psychic energy) much thought and many words have been devoted, but, as yet, no theory acceptable to the majority of psychologists has been proposed. Psychologists who deal with small segments of the personality have usually been able to dispense with the concept, but few practical psychologists agree that it is possible to do so, even a crude notion being better for them than none. The consequences of feeling fresh and energetic are so very different from the consequences of feeling stale and exhausted that to omit all observations bearing on this point is to leave a great gap in one's account of personality. We are certainly dealing with a magnitude which is correlated with the capacity to do work, but the variable is only roughly analogous to energy as the physicist conceives it.

In the development of the need theory the notion of energy or force was employed to account for differences in the intensity and endurance of directional behaviour. It seemed necessary to express the fact that some needs are 'stronger' than others. To use energy in this connection is to fall in line with the hormic theory of McDougall,[1] as I understand it. Here, however, we are talking about energy that is 'general' or associated with functions (actones), not the energic aspect of drives. That the two are different is demonstrated by the fact that a need may be intense — a man may be starving or extremely desirous to accomplish an intellectual task — and yet, if he is 'worn out by over-work' he will not move a muscle or a thought. The need is great, but there is no available 'energy' (we say) in the actones (muscular system or intellectual system) that must be employed to reach the goal. It seems that fairly strong needs may occur in the absence of actonal energy — in which case they remain latent — and actonal energy may exist without needs. But it does not follow from this that general (or actonal) energy and drive energy are unrelated.

1. McDougall, W. in *Psychologies of 1930*, Worcester, Mass., 1930.

For when a person is fresh, his drives commonly partake of the increased tone ; they seem stronger in themselves. Similarly, when a person is exhausted all his appetites are usually diminished. This fits in with an observation that has been made repeatedly : animal or human subjects that are rated high in one positive need are usually rated high in others. This applies even to needs that are antipolar. For example, the most assertive (n Dom) and aggressive (n Agg) child may also be the most affiliative (n Aff) and sympathetic (n Nur). Some of the animal psychologists have concluded that it is necessary to conceptualize a general drive factor, and at times this has seemed to us the best solution. The 'need for Activity' was what we called it, and in contrast to it we defined the 'need for Passivity.' At other times it has seemed best to 'explain' intensity of movement and speech by referring to Energy : general, widely-disposable energy ('blood-stream energy') or energy residing in the actones (muscular system, intellectual system) by means of which the drives fulfil themselves. According to the latter formulation it is actonal energy which, when combined with ability, allows for the quick and effective expression of all drives that employ the functions in question.

The concept of Energy 'overflowing,' as it were, into action — or, with equal justification, the concept of 'need for Activity' — may be utilized to account for random behaviour in children and adults. Random behaviour is displayed most clearly during the first weeks of life. At this time one can observe periods of almost incessant activity (flexions, extensions, rotations, squirmings), activity that is inco-ordinated and therefore ineffective — the eyes, head, arms and legs may all move at once in different directions. These movements are not dependent upon external stimulation, nor do they appear to 'seek' anything. Since the child does not even attend to his movements, it is not possible to say that during these periods he is trying to achieve mastery of his limbs. The most that can be said is that random behaviour is the expression of vitality, of actonal metabolism (katabolism after anabolism). It belongs to the givenness of life.

We might speak here of actonal energy, associated with physical movements and associated with thought (speech), which in the absence of drive tends to become kinetic, giving rise to restlessness, play, random actions, disjunctive fantasy, voluble speech. Indeed, there is evidence for supposing that this actonal energy may precede need tension, that a need may be generated and become established as a result of the discovery by random action of a satisfying end situation (*cf.* drug addiction).

These facts and reflections lead to the conclusion that every functional system (we can profitably confine ourselves to the muscular system : physical action, and the thought system : verbal action) assimilates and builds up a certain amount of energy, which tends (of its own accord), if nothing intervenes, to become kinetic. It does this, as it were, for its own 'satisfaction.' The exercise is a catharsis. It helps to oxidize ineffective accumulations. It facilitates life. (The reader will excuse me, I hope, if for the time being I speak of 'energy' as if it were a thing rather than a measurable attribute of an event.)

The concept of specific actonal energies is proposed to account for the fact that the fatigue of one function (intellection, let us say) diminishes but little the energy available for another function. Physical exercise may be vigorous after the mind has been worn out by exertion, and vice versa.

Besides the specific energies of each system we must also distinguish general ('bloodstream') energy which is closely related to the actonal energies. This general energy factor seems to be determined partly by the condition of the blood (oxygen, carbon dioxide, waste products, presence of thyroxin, adrenin and other hormones), partly by metabolic conditions in the separate systems (which contribute oxidation products to the blood) and partly by the fortunes of the drives (success or failure, or expectations of success or failure). General energy is also affected by the weather, diet, drugs, physical illness and so forth. Our conception of energy has some relation to Spearman's 'g,'[1] but it is a different variable in as much as it has been entirely abstracted from skill or ability.

1. Spearman, C. *The Abilities of Man*, New York, 1927.

In our studies we put the various actonal energies together with general energy under one heading, Energy, which, for greater clarity, was divided into two variables : Intensity and Endurance (*vide* p. 208). From what has been said it will be clear that the following indices of Energy are appropriate :

1. Subjective and objective signs of zest (as briefly defined above).
2. Subjective and objective signs of activity pleasure.
3. A relatively large total of vigorous activity per day (as compared to the amount of rest and sleep).
4. The prevalence of random motilities (physical movements and speech). Here we refer to excessive actones : a surplus of abundant, rich, extravagant or playful flourishes of gesture and language.
5. High intensity and duration of all positive drives, particularly Achievement, Play, Dominance, Aggression, Affiliation, Deference, and Nurturance.

As we progressed in our studies it became apparent that there were two factors, not one, to be distinguished : the general energy level and the disposition of a subject to discharge as contrasted with the disposition to conserve whatever energy is available. Closely correlated with this dichotomy are the opposing tendencies : 1, to play a stimulating or initiating role (n Dom) in social or sex relations, and 2, to remain passive or receptively compliant (n Def). It was here that the concepts 'need for Activity' and 'need for Passivity' became particularly useful. It seems that the need for Activity (overt motility) is usually associated with a high energy level and the need for Passivity with a low level, but there are numerous exceptions. In some people spontaneous activity is decidedly low, despite the fact that the energy level, as far as one can estimate it, is sufficient. The need for Passivity seems, on the one hand, to be related to the force of inertia and, on the other, to be in the service of the need for rest ; that is, the organism seeks to conserve its energies, to avoid exhaustion, and to be free of the necessity of decision. The tendency for Passivity is subjectively represented by the desire to relinquish the will, to relax, to drift, to daydream, to receive impressions. In the face of external forces it yields because this is easier (or more exciting). The tendency inclines a person towards a placid, vegetable existence, free from excitation or stimulation, or towards a life of waiting for external stimulation (let us say, for a lover). Freud describes Passivity as the tendency to reduce excitations to a minimum, to 'return to the womb,' or even to an inorganic state. We may suppose here that the stressful integration of the regnancy breaks down ; that 'it goes into solution.' The operation of this tendency, then, leads to a state of relaxed disjunctivity, to sleep, to unconsciousness. One commonly finds it after an intense or prolonged exertion of the will, particularly if the will has been exercised against a social group. When, in an utterly exhausted state, the will relaxes, a person may experience a most blissful feeling. (We have reports that such affections occur just before a drowning man loses consciousness.) The need for Passivity may also arise as the aftermath of inner conflict. It is, indeed, one of the best means of resolving tension. A person says : 'What difference does it make to me ? ' He relaxes mind and body and the disturbing turmoil passes over. His troubles fall away like water. The efforts of Orientals to reach the state of Nirvana may be taken as an extreme instance of this general tendency.

When fused with the Sex drive Passivity leads to the attitude which is classically feminine : deference and abasement in erotic interaction. Its presence in a man is a mark of bisexuality, which, in turn, is correlated with homosexuality. Heterosexual Activity in women and heterosexual Passivity in men, however, are very common present-day phenomena.

Though Passivity was not defined soon enough to be given a place in our conceptual scheme we found that we could not get along without it. Consequently, the reader will find references to this somewhat vague factor in the succeeding pages.

Divisions of the Personality

Freud and the psycho-analysts after him have distinguished three parts of the personality : the Id, the Ego and the Superego. As determinants of behaviour these functions may be characterized as follows: the Id is the aggregate of basic instinctual impulses; the Ego is the organized, discriminating, time-binding, reasoning, resolving, and more self-conscious part of the personality; and the Superego is the intra-psychical representative of the customs and ideals of the community in so far as they have been communicated by the parents.

This scheme has proved its usefulness in formulating and treating the neuroses, all of which are the result of moral conflict between elementary needs and social standards (that have become assimilated to form conscience). This almost universal dilemma can be well represented as an opposition of Superego and Id, the Ego standing between as puppet or final arbiter. Although the conception is a vague oversimplification, which leaves many facts unexplained, we have not been able to improve on it. In fact, we have found it as helpful in dealing with normal subjects as in dealing with abnormals.

The Id. This is the generic term under which all innate drives are subsumed, among which the viscerogenic needs should be especially emphasized. We are apt to use the term when we observe the excitation of emotional impulses associated with primitive actones (savage assault, panicky fear, flagrant exhibitionistic sexuality). At such times conscious control is in abeyance and the individual merely reacts. He feels that he is overcome by irresistible forces outside himself. Strong temptations and compulsions are also assigned to this category.

The Id, however, is not composed entirely of active passions. The need for Passivity (which may manifest itself as indolence and slovenliness) belongs to it. Hence it is often necessary to stir up the Id instead of checking it.

Furthermore, all impulses of the Id are not asocial or antisocial as most analysts affirm. There are, for example, certain gregarious and conforming tendencies (empathy, imitation, identification) which operate instinctively and unconsciously. Also, the highest as well as the lowest forms of love come from the Id.

Viewing the Id from the point of view of perception and intelligence, we find that its operations are carried on by associations of imagery, mostly unconscious, that do not conform closely to the course of natural events. To the Id we ascribe hallucinations, delusions, irrational beliefs as well as fantasies, intuitions, faith and creative conceptions. Thus almost everything, good and bad, has its primitive source in the Id.

The Superego System. Since the environment is a factor in every episode of personality, and since from a psychological point of view the social environment is more important than the physical, it is necessary to pay particular attention to the culture in which the individual is imbedded, the 'culture' being the accepted organization of society as put into practice and defended. For our purposes, the organization may be partially described in terms of the time-place-mode-object (tpmo) formulas which are allowed or insisted upon for the expression of individual needs. A child is allowed to play during the day but not at night (time). He may defecate in the toilet but not on the floor (place). He may push other children but not hit them with a mallet (mode). He may ask his father but not a stranger in the street for money (object). No need has to be inhibited permanently. If the individual is of the right age and chooses the permitted time, the permitted place, the permitted mode and the permitted object, he can objectify any one of his needs. However, the Id impulses of no child are readily modified to fit civilized patterns of this sort. They come insistently (cannot wait for the proper time or place), erupt in primitive forms (with instinctual actones) and are directed indiscriminately towards this or that object. To socialize a child the proper tpmo formulas are gradually imposed by a variety of methods : suggestion, persuasion, example, rewards, promises, punishments, threats, physical coercions and restraints. This is done first by parents, surrogates and nurses, and later by other elders : teachers, priests, policemen and magistrates. To the child, then, as well as to the adult, the culture is a compound of behavioural patterns that are imposed by stronger authorities. It is fear of the pain or of the belittlement these authorities can inflict or of the distress that the withdrawal of their love and protection will engender that is most influential in finally bringing about a sufficient acceptance of social forms. The tpmo pattern, as a loose organization of 'Do's' and 'Don'ts,' preached and perhaps practised by the parents, asserted to be the only 'Right,' sanctioned by religion and strengthened by the image of an ávenging deity, becomes, to a greater or less degree, internalized as a complex institution, known commonly as conscience. This may be termed the Superego system. A strong Superego is usually more exacting than current laws and conventions. It may be elevated far above worldly considerations by fusion with the Ego Ideal. It endures, with certain modifications, throughout life. It is, as it were, always there to influence the composition of regnancies. Its first function is to inhibit asocial tendencies, its second is to present cultural or religious aims as the 'highest good.' Its operations are largely unconscious.

The Ego System. Introspection yields much information in regard to the internal factors that influence behaviour. Everyone has experienced 'resolving to do something' or 'selecting a purpose.' Such an experience must modify the brain (i.e., must leave a latently perseverating disposition), because at some future date it will be found that behaviour is not the same as it would have been if the 'resolving' experience had not occurred. Decisions and intentions of this sort — 'accepting a goal,' 'planning a course of action,' 'choosing a vocation,' as well as promises, compacts and 'taking on responsibility' (all of them related to time-binding and the establishment of expectations and levels of aspiration) — seem to be attended by a relatively high degree of consciousness, and, what is more, by a feeling that the 'self' is making the decision, freely *willing* the direction of its future conduct. We should say that such conscious fixations of aim were organized to form the 'Ego system.'

Introspection also teaches us that when other non-instituted (unaccepted) needs and impulses (impulses that seem to disrupt, oppose or nullify the established Ego system) arise in consciousness, they are felt to come from 'outside' the self, or from a 'deeper layer' of the self, from the 'bodily' or 'animal part' of the self. All such unacceptable impulses have been subsumed under the term 'Id.' Need integrates of the Id are usually to be distinguished by their instinctual (animal-like), primitive (savage-like) or infantile (child-like) modes and cathexes. They are usually restive and insistent and impatient of the schedule of activity instituted by the Ego. It may be said, I think, that though the Ego derives its original strength from emotional needs and is repeatedly refreshed by them, it can operate for periods without their urgent activity (just as a man who has no appetite can force himself to eat). Every need is associated, of course, with numerous modes, some of which belong to the Ego system and some to the Id. Thus, the Aggression drive expressing itself in verbal criticism of the President or in physical assault upon a gangster might be part of an Ego system, whereas other more violent forms of expression might belong to the Id.

The concept of Ego emphasizes the determining significance of 1, conscious, freely-willed acts : making a resolution (with oneself) or a compact (with others) or dedicating oneself to a life-long vocation, all of which 'bind' the personality over long periods of time ; 2, the establishment of a cathected Ego Ideal (image of a figure one wants to become) ; and 3, the inhibition of drives that conflict with the above mentioned intentions, decisions and planned schedules of behaviour. One index of the degree of structuration (strength) of the Ego is the ability of an individual to 'live by' his resolutions and compacts.

The Ego system stands, as it were, between the Id and the Superego. It may gradually absorb all the forces of the Id, employing them for its own purpose. Likewise, it may assimilate the Superego until the will of the individual is in strict accord with the best principles of his society. Under such circumstances what the individual feels that he wants to do coincides with what he has to do (as prescribed by his culture). The Ego, however, may side with the Id against the Superego. It may, for example, inhibit or repress the Superego and 'decide' in favour of a criminal career. A strong Ego acts as mediator between Superego and Id ; but a weak Ego is no more than a 'battleground.'

Interests. If we observe a series of objective episodes (external press and overt trends) occurring in the life of an individual, we never fail to notice certain resemblances. The personality exhibits sameness. We say that the man possesses certain consistent traits. However, we can usually observe more than this. Viewing successive episodes over a sufficient span of time we can note developments. We can perceive that some episodes are the logical outgrowths of others and that together they form temporal systems bound together by the persistence (constant repetition) of one or more needs integrated with certain modes and directed towards certain cathected objects (things, people, institutions, ideologies). Every such system may be called an *interest* (complex need integrate).

The concept of interest focusses attention upon the cathected objects and modes of activity rather than upon the needs that are engaged. It takes the needs for granted. A man enters politics and almost overnight much of his behaviour becomes oriented in such a way as to further this interest. This is certainly a fact of significance and it can be stated without considering what combination of needs prompted his decision or what needs are satisfied by his political activity. He may be affiliative, dominative, aggressive, exhibitionistic or seclusive, but this is another matter.

The concept of interests is closely related to the concept of cultural patterns or organizations, since most interests are not only possessed in common with other people, but they have an accepted institutional or ideological form. These sometimes quite rigid communities of mode and purpose stand ready to canalize the random activity of each new generation. Their suggestive and dominative influence is so great and omnipresent that some psychologists have been tempted to think of personality as constituted by its different memberships. A person may be sufficiently described, it is claimed, in terms of the mores and aims of the different groups (sub-cultures) to which he belongs. This point of view can be accepted with several important qualifications. Institutions are congealed need patterns shared by many; they are supported by new members with similar integrates; and they are modified or abandoned by members whose needs change.

They do, however, determine specifically what actones and what objects will be cathected.

Institutions and needs are complementary forces. From the point of view of the drive theory, an institution is engendered and maintained because it tends to satisfy certain needs that are held in common by many people. Among numerous existing institutions the individual tends to select for membership those which give the best opportunity for the fulfilment of his particular set of tendencies. As the needs of the members change the institution changes, though here there is usually a certain lag. A whole-hearted member of an institution — one who transfers value from himself to the object — acts for the institution as he would act for himself. He attempts to further its aims in competition with other institutions, he is hurt when it is ridiculed, feels depressed when it declines, defends it, fights for it, belittles other groups, and so forth. Thus an institution will allow a sociocentric man of this stamp to express all his needs in behalf of a 'cause' (opposed to other 'causes') as well as in his own behalf.

The endurance and progressive development of interests make it necessary to conceptualize the gradual establishment of persisting organizations of control in the brain. Without a notion of such interest systems one cannot explain why many successive samples of an individual's behaviour — sometimes nearly all his behaviour for months or years (*cf.* Balzac's *Quest of the Absolute*) — can be meaningfully related to each other according to their function in furthering a dominant aim. A purposive system conserved in the brain is the conceptual cord upon which we string our beads, the observed episodes. All such organizations of interest may be assigned to the Ego System, though many of them have come to operate because of Superego influence.

The Habit System. Behaviour that has become automatic, that proceeds without much conscious intervention, that recurs repeatedly in the same form, may be conveniently ascribed to a *habit system*. This is formed by the structuralization (mechanization) of what has frequently recurred, whether determined by the Superego, the Ego or the Id. The habit system accounts for most rigidities, particularly those which the individual himself cannot abandon.

Thus, as we see it, regnancies are the resultants of external press, of freshly aroused emotional needs (Id), of conscious intentions (Ego), of accepted cultural standards (Superego) and of customary modes of behaviour (habit system) in varying proportions. The relative strength of these influences determines what tendencies will be objectified.

This brings us to the end of this long, yet all-too-brief, summary of the theory and concepts that guided our researches. Now it is necessary to give an account of the variables of personality which we attempted to distinguish and measure in our subjects.

Chapter III
VARIABLES OF PERSONALITY

H. A. MURRAY

AUTHORS whose works are read with enjoyment cover the bare framework of their thought with prose that moves like muscle, employing lively images and graceful turns of speech to bring its contours to the semblance of palpitating life. At no point does a bony surface unpleasantly protrude. But here it must be different. This section is the first chapter of an anatomy. There is room in this place only for the disarticulated bones of thought. Perhaps later they will be made to rise from the dead and support something more living than themselves — the red cells of the blood, we may recall, are born in cavities of bone — but now these elements must be examined in isolation.

Does not every elementary textbook of chemistry, botany, zoology, etymology, human anatomy and medicine begin with a tedious account of the different entities that constitute its subject-matter ? Is there any way to avoid memorizing a classification ? Is it not necessary that a surgeon, though ceaselessly engaged with life, hold fixed in mind the name and place of every bone, muscle, tendon, organ, artery, vein and nerve in the body ? And if pointing, describing, defining, naming and classifying is necessary in the more fundamental sciences, is it not reasonable to suppose that psychology must follow the same path ? I am convinced that the answer to this question is 'yes,' despite the current tendency among psychologists to legislate against the 'class' theory and fashion their science in the likeness of physics. We believe that a primary task for psychology is the proper analysis of behaviour into functions or phases, each of which, though necessarily concrete and unique in every actual occasion, may be subsumed under a construct, a construct that defines a uniformity (a class of such entities).

Without objects conceived as unique individuals, we can have *no Classes.* Without classes we can, as we have seen, define *no Relations,* without relations we can have *no Order. But to be reasonable is to conceive of order-systems, real or ideal. Therefore, we have an absolute logical need to conceive of individual objects as the elements of our ideal order systems.* This postulate is the condition of defining clearly any theoretical conception whatever. The further metaphysical aspects of the concept of an individual we may here ignore. *To conceive of individual objects is a necessary presupposition of all orderly activity.*[1]

In this chapter will be found an attempt to define and illustrate each of the variables of personality that were employed in the present study. Though the list is the outcome of two years' experience, we do not regard it as more than a rough, preliminary plan to guide perception and interpretation. If we had thought that personality could be well viewed as the working of one major tendency this chapter might have been made more interesting to the casual reader. For it is possible to become emotionally identified with a single urge if the author animates it to heroic proportions and gives the reader a dramatic account of its vicissitudes, conflicts, frustrations and successes. A volume on the 'will-to-power' may be as exciting as a biography of Napoleon. A chronicle of the sexual instinct is as intriguing as the memoirs of Casanova or St. Anthony. But if one has been driven to the view by observed facts that personality is the outcome of numerous forces — now one and now another being of major import then it is impossible to choose a hero. And what is more distressing is that it is necessary to include an account of many entities within a space that ordinarily would be assigned to one. If a volume could be devoted to each variable, something as interesting as fiction could be written, but when every concept must be torn out of its concrete living embodiments only minds disciplined to hard labour will be able or willing to follow the account.

In the preceding chapter it was made clear that our conceptual scheme was biased in favour of the dynamic or motivational as-

1. Josiah Royce, — quoted in Korzybski, Alfred, *Science and Sanity*, Lancaster, Pa., 1933, p. 131.

pects of personality. We have especially had 'our eyes out' for objective facts pertaining to trends or effects of motor and verbal action, and we have attempted to correlate the observed directions of behaviour with subjective reports of intention (wish, desire, impulsion, aim, purpose). From these and other sorts of facts we have attempted to infer the operation of one of a class of hypothetical directional brain tensions (drives or needs). Some psychologists may prefer to regard each variable as a mere label to denote a category into which a great number of behavioural patterns have been arbitrarily placed. Even to these, if we have been successful in putting together what belongs together, the classification may be of some use.

Forty-four variables in all were distinguished.[1] Twenty of these were manifest needs, eight were latent needs, four referred to certain inner states, and twelve were general traits. An alphabetical list of these variables (with their abbreviations) will help the reader to understand the more comprehensive descriptions that follow.

Alphabetical list of manifest needs

1. n Aba = n Abasement (Abasive attitude).
2. n Ach = n Achievement (Achievant attitude).
3. n Aff = n Affiliation (Affiliative attitude).
4. n Agg = n Aggression (Aggressive attitude).
5. n Auto = n Autonomy (Autonomous attitude).
6. n Cnt = n Counteraction (Counteractive attitude).
7. n Def = n Deference (Deferent attitude).
8. n Dfd = n Defendance (Defendant attitude).
9. n Dom = n Dominance (Dominative attitude).
10. n Exh = n Exhibition (Exhibitionistic attitude).
11. n Harm = n Harmavoidance (Fearful attitude).
12. n Inf = n Infavoidance (Infavoidant attitude).

    n Inv = n Inviolacy (Inviolate attitude). This need is considered to be a composite of Infavoidance, Defendance and Counteraction.

1. From this point on all the variables that have been used in the present study will be capitalized in order to distinguish them from other psychological terms.

13. n Nur = n Nurturance (Nurturant attitude).
14. n Ord = n Order (Orderly attitude).
15. n Play = n Play (Playful attitude).
16. n Rej = n Rejection (Rejective attitude).
    n Sec = n Seclusion (Seclusive attitude). This need has been taken as the opposite of Exhibition, not as a separate variable.
17. n Sen = n Sentience (Sentient attitude).
18. n Sex = n Sex (Erotic attitude).
19. n Suc = n Succorance (Succorant attitude).
    n Sup = n Superiority (Ambitious attitude). This need is considered to be a composite of Achievement and Recognition (see below).
20. n Und = n Understanding (Intellectual attitude).

The following needs are occasionally referred to but were not systematically used in the present study :

n Acq = n Acquisition (Acquisitive attitude).
n Blam = n Blamavoidance (Blamavoidant attitude).
n Cog = n Cognizance (Inquiring attitude).
n Cons = n Construction (Constructive attitude).
n Exp = n Exposition (Informing attitude).
n Rec = n Recognition (Self-forwarding attitude). This was included under Exhibition.
n Ret = n Retention (Retentive attitude).

The twenty needs listed above were rated in terms of the frequency and intensity of their overt behavioural manifestations. In the first two years of experimentation considerable disagreement in respect to such ratings arose because some of the experimenters found in the subjects evidence of need tensions which were not objectified. It was thought that a rating should reflect the subjectified as well as the objectified tensions. According to theory it is *inhibition* which blocks the objectification of need tension. Hence, given a certain amount of tension the degree to which a need is objectified is a function of the strength of the inhibiting barrier. Consequently, to determine the total strength of a need one should consider the amount of internally inhibited tension as well as the amount of externally exhibited activity.

The former has been called, for convenience, a latent need and the latter a manifest need.

In conformation with clinical impressions, our findings indicated that inhibited needs produce marked subjective effects and indirectly influence overt behaviour. It seemed important, therefore, to take account of them. Experience justified the selection of eight needs as being those most commonly inhibited. It seemed that the amount of inhibited tension of each of these needs could be very approximately estimated by the use of specially devised techniques.

Alphabetical list of latent needs

1. ln Aba = repressed Abasement (Passivity and Masochism). The desire to suffer pain, to succomb sexually.
2. ln Agg = repressed Aggression (Hate and Sadism). The desire to injure and inflict pain.
3. ln Cog = repressed Cognizance (Voyeurism). The desire to see and inspect. To probe into private matters.
4. ln Dom = repressed Dominance (Omnipotence). The desire for complete power. To magically control Os.
5. ln Exh = repressed Exhibitionism (Exhibitionism). The desire to show off and expose one's body in public.
6. ln Sex = repressed Sex. The desire for heterosexual relations.
7. ln Homo-sex = repressed Homosexuality. This is really not a separate need. It is the Sex drive focussed on an O of the subject's sex.
8. ln Suc = repressed Succorance (Anxiety of Helplessness). The desire for security, support, protection, sympathy, love.

Besides these eight latent needs there were four other internal factors which we attempted to distinguish and estimate :

Alphabetical list of miscellaneous internal factors

1. EI = Ego Ideal : the operation of images portraying the subject (or an accepted exemplar) achieving noteworthy successes. High levels of aspiration. This is a manifestation of a latent or unrealized Achievement drive.
2. N = Narcism : self-love in any of its various forms.
   Se = Superego : 'Conscience' : inhibiting and punishing images rep-

resentative of parental, social and religious authority. The operation of this factor may be 'quiet' (unconscious inhibition without conflict) or it may be 'disturbing' (conflict). Thus, we have two distinguishable conditions :

3. SeI = Superego Integration : a condition in which the dictates of 'conscience' have been so far accepted by the Ego that the subject *wills* the obligatory (the socially demanded action).
4. SeC = Superego Conflict : a condition of conflict in which asocial impulses are 'at war with conscience.' There may be some asocial conduct or there may be merely asocial desires (conscious or unconscious). These are opposed by domineering and prohibiting forces. The effects of the latter are as follows : 'pangs of conscience,' guilt feelings, remorse, diffuse anxiety, obsessions of doom and disaster, self-corrective compulsions, depressions, neurotic symptoms and so forth. (The n Blamavoidance seems to be sufficiently covered by these two variables.)

In addition to these thirty-two variables twelve other traits were selected for measurement.

Alphabetical list of general traits or attributes

1. Anx = Anxiety : startledness, apprehension, timidity, worry.
2. Cr = Creativity : manifest ability to produce and develop original ideas ; to devise new methods, construct hypotheses, offer novel explanations, compose works of artistic merit.
3. Conj/Disj = Conjunctivity/Disjunctivity ratio.

   Conj = Conjunctivity : co-ordination of action and thought ; organization of behavioural trends and purposes. This describes the *ability* to make a coherent pattern of one's life. Unsuccessful efforts that the subject makes in this direction are not included in the rating.

   Disj = Disjunctivity : disco-ordination of action and thought ; disordered and conflicting behaviour.
4. Emo = Emotionality : the amount of emotion, affection and autonomic excitement that the subject manifests : zest, elation, anger, fear, dejection, shame, etc. The opposite of Emotionality is Placidity.
5. End = Endurance : the protensity of a behavioural trend. This includes 'power of endurance,' persistence and conative persevera-

tion. Opposite to these are transience, impersistence and imperseveration.

6. Exo/Endo = Exocathection/Endocathection ratio.

   Exo = Exocathection : the positive cathection of practical action and co-operative undertakings. A preoccupation with outer events : economic, political, or social occurrences. A strong inclination to participate in the contemporary world of affairs.

   Endo = Endocathection : the cathection of thought or emotion for its own sake. A preoccupation with inner activities : feelings, fantasies, generalizations, theoretical reflections, artistic conceptions, religious ideas. Withdrawal from practical life.

7. Intra/Extra = Intraception/Extraception ratio.

   Intra = Intraception : the dominance of feelings, fantasies, speculations, aspirations. An imaginative, subjective human outlook. Romantic action.

   Extra = Extraception : the disposition to adhere to the obviously substantial facts. A practical, 'down-to-earth,' skeptical attitude. Enjoyment of clearly observable results. An interest in tangible or mechanical results.

8. Imp/Del = Impulsion/Deliberation ratio.

   Imp = Impulsion : the tendency to act quickly without reflection. Short reaction time, intuitive or emotional decisions. The inability to inhibit an impulse.

   Del = Deliberation : inhibition and reflection before action. Slow reaction time, spastic contraction, compulsive thinking.

9. Int = Intensity : strength of effort ; quick and forceful movements ; emphasis and zest during activity ; ardently expressed opinions ; power of expression.

10. Proj/Obj = Projectivity/Objectivity ratio.

    Proj = Projectivity : the disposition to project unconsciously one's own sentiments, emotions and needs into others. To maintain wish-engendered or anxiety-evoked beliefs. Mild forms of the delusions of self-reference, persecution, omnipotence, etc.

    Obj = Objectivity : the disposition to judge oneself and others in a detached and disinterested manner ; psychological realism.

11. Rad St/Con St = Radical sentiments/Conservative sentiments ratio.

    Rad St = Radical sentiments : the origination, promulgation or defence of sentiments, theories or ideologies that are novel, questionable or opposed to tradition.

Con St = Conservative sentiments : the maintenance of well-accredited conventional views, and a rejection of new ideas. A dislike of innovations.

12. Sa/Ch = Sameness/Change ratio.

Sa = Sameness : adherence to certain places, people and modes of conduct. Fixation and limitation. Enduring sentiments and loyalties ; persistence of purpose ; consistency of conduct ; rigidity of habits.

Ch = Change : a tendency to move and wander, to have no fixed habituation, to seek new friends, to adopt new fashions, to change one's interests and vocation. Instability.

A brief review of the forms of need activity (described in the previous section) may be helpful.

a. *Motones*. i. *Exterofactive system*. Needs may be satisfied by overt physical acts : eating, pushing, embracing, holding, etc.

Erogenous Zones.

Oral : Oral-Succorance (sucking), Oral-Aggression (biting), Oral-Rejection (spitting), etc.

Anal : Anal-Retention (constipation), Anal-Aggression (soiling), etc.

Genital : Genital-Abasement (Masochism), Genital-Aggression (Sadism), etc.

ii. *Enterofactive system*. Needs may be manifested by observable autonomic changes and expressive movements : fear, anger, shame, love, etc.

b. *Verbones*. Needs may be satisfied by speech : calling, persuading, praising, boasting, condemning, inquiring, etc.

c. *Ideological*. Needs may be directed towards ideas rather than people. n ideo Dom (forcing opinions on others), n ideo Rej (ignoring the ideas of others), n ideo Aff (harmonizing opinions), etc.

d. *Intravertive*. The needs, as given, are considered to be directed outward, toward or away from objects (extravertive needs). But they may also be directed inward, toward the body or toward parts of the personality. Here we have to do with *intravertive* needs. Thus, extrAggression would be expressed by criticizing or injuring others, whereas intrAggression would be expressed by criticizing or injuring the self (Ego-depreciation or suicide).

e. *Latent (Subjectified and Semi-objectified).* Inhibited desires, fantasies, dreams, play, artistic creations and religious ritual.
f. *Focal.* A need may be manifested only towards one or a very few kinds of objects. If focality is not specified a need is assumed to be *diffuse.*
g. *Egocentric or Sociocentric.* A need may be purely personal (narcistic) or it may be engendered by social pressure : n socioAgg (fighting in an army), n socioDom (commanding to gratify a group), etc.
h. *Infravertive and Supravertive.* A need may be directed towards a superior O or an inferior O ; infrAffiliation (to make friends with inferiors), supraAggression (to attack an authority), n infraDeference (to praise children), etc.

In marking a subject on a given variable a, b, c, g and h are lumped together ; whereas d, e and f are taken up separately.

Most of the needs to be described are social reaction systems which lead a subject (1) to raise his status ; (2) to conserve and defend the status he has attained ; (3) to form affiliations and to co-operate with allied objects (or institutions), as well as to praise, direct and defend them ; or (4) to reject, resist, renounce or attack disliked hostile objects. An individual may be predominantly eager and ambitious, retiring and defensive, sociable and helpful, or critical and aggressive. But equally important is the nature of the cathected objects, values, or interests in respect to which he is ambitious, retractive, affiliative or hostile. A man may desire prestige but since he cannot excel in everything, he must select certain lines of endeavour and neglect others. What he chooses will constitute his system of values, and this will determine in large measure whom he likes, whom he praises, whom he excludes and whom he attacks. He will feel inferior about some things — his poverty, his game of golf, his flat nose, his lack of taste, his accent — but he will not hide and conceal himself when the social situation calls for other virtues : humour, physical agility, scientific knowledge. These considerations make it necessary to construct a rough classification which will order according to some intelligible scheme the main fields of interest and ability.

This catalogue will be presented at the end of the present chapter, after the behavioural trends which orient themselves in respect to these instincts have been outlined.

After describing the various manifestations of each variable we shall list the statements covering that variable which were used in our behavioural questionnaire, and, in the case of some needs, append a list of aphorisms (used in a sentiments questionnaire) which might appeal to a subject who ranked high on the variable in question.

For the general reader the first paragraph devoted to each variable will suffice as description.

n Dominance	n Autonomy	n Aggression
n Deference		n Abasement

This group of five needs may be taken together. The Dominance drive is manifested by a desire to control the sentiments and behaviour of others. Those who are willing to follow and co-operate with an admired superior object are swayed by the Deference drive. Usually a man is deferent to those above him and dominative to those below him. The n Autonomy controls those who wish neither to lead nor be led, those who want to go their own way, uninfluenced and uncoerced by others. It appears as defiance or as an escape from restraint (for example, when a man moves to a more tolerant environment). The Aggression drive is accompanied by anger and operates to supplement Dominance when the latter is insufficient. It is aroused by opposition, annoyances, attacks and insults. Thus, it is opposed to Deference but may fuse with Dominance or Autonomy. When Aggression is fused with Sex the ensuing behaviour is called Sadism : erotic-like pleasure in inflicting pain. Directly opposite to Aggression is Abasement. This is probably a sub-need, subsidiary to n Harmavoidance, n Blamavoidance, or n Infavoidance. However, in the form of Masochism — erotic pleasure in suffering pain — the Abasement drive, fused with n Sex, seems to have its own peculiar end situation. In a sense, n Dominance, n Autonomy and n Aggression are also subsidiary, since they are almost always called forth when there is 'something else to be done.' A leader orders (n Dom) a subordinate to build something (n Cons) ; a child wants freedom (n Auto) to play (n Play) ; Aggression is aroused because some other need (n Sex) is thwarted, and so forth. Likewise, the average subject is deferent only when the action suggested by the leader conforms to his own system of needs.

n Dominance (n Dom)

Desires and Effects : To control one's human environment. To influence or direct the behaviour of Os by suggestion, seduction, persuasion, or command. To dissuade, restrain, or prohibit. To induce an O to act in a way which accords with one's sentiments and needs. To get Os to co-operate. To convince an O of the 'rightness' of one's opinion.

Feelings and Emotions : Confidence.

Trait-names and Attitudes : Dominative, forceful, masterful, assertive, decisive, authoritative, executive, disciplinary.

Press : infraDom : Inferior Os ; p Deference : Compliance ; p Abasement.

supraDom : Superior Os ; p Dominance ; p Rival.

Gratuities : Children, servants, disciples, followers.

Actions : General : To influence, sway, lead, prevail upon, persuade, direct, regulate, organize, guide, govern, supervise. To master, control, rule, over-ride, dictate terms. To judge, make laws, set standards, lay down principles of conduct, give a decision, settle an argument. To prohibit, restrain, oppose, dissuade, punish, confine, imprison. To magnetize, gain a hearing, be listened to, be imitated, be followed, set the fashion. To be an exemplar.

Motones : To beckon, point, push, pull, carry, confine.

Verbones : Commands : 'Come here' — 'Stop that' — 'Hurry up' — 'Get out,' etc.

Mesmeric influence : To hypnotize.

ideo Dominance : To establish political, aesthetic, scientific, moral, or religious principles. To have one's ideas prevail. To influence the 'climate of opinion.' To argue for one cause against another.

socio Dominance : To govern a social institution.

Fusions : The commonest fusion is with n Agg (Autocratic power).

Coercion : To force an O (by threats) to do something.

Restraint : To put up barriers. To limit motion. To forbid certain acts. To enforce the law.

Also with : n Ach (to achieve things as leader of a group), n Exh (to be dramatically forceful in public), n Aff (to be a genial, humane leader), n Sex (to take an assertive erotic attitude), n Nur (to guide and correct a child), n Sec (the silent man of power behind the throne).

Needs which may be subsidiary to the n Dom : n Agg (to punish in order to control), n Exh (to dominate Os by fascination), n Suc (to control Os by exciting pity), n Aff (to be friendly to voters), n Sex (to control through sexual attraction — *femme fatale*).

Needs to which n Dom may be subsidiary : n Ach (to persuade a group to get something done), n Auto (to argue for freedom), n Aff (to bring about harmony within a group), n Acq (to put over a business deal).

Conflicts with : n Aba, n Inf, n Suc, n Auto, n Aff, n Nur, n Play, n Def.

intraDom : Will power. To develop self-control. To restrain instinctual drives. To be master of oneself.

Subjns and Semi-objns : Magic and sorcery. To control the gods.

Pathology : Delusions of omnipotence.

Social forms : The government of a country : King, President, Congress, Parliament, Legislature, Courts of Law. With n Agg : Army, Navy, militia, police.

Statements in Questionnaire [1]

1. I enjoy organizing or directing the activities of a group — team, club, or committee.
2. I argue with zest for my point of view against others.
3. I find it rather easy to lead a group of boys and maintain discipline.
4. I usually influence others more than they influence me.
5. I am usually the one to make the necessary decisions when I am with another person.
6. I feel that I can dominate a social situation.
7. I enjoy the sense of power that comes when I am able to control the actions of others.

1. In the questionnaire given to the Ss the statements for this variable (as well as those for other variables) are not presented consecutively (as above). Each statement is separated from its fellow by nine statements illustrative of other, different variables (*vide* p.436).

8. I assert myself with energy when the occasion demands it.
9. I feel that I should like to be a leader and sway others to my opinion.
10. I feel that I am driven by an underlying desire for power.

n Deference (n Def)

Desires and Effects : To admire and support a superior O. To praise, honour, or eulogize. To yield eagerly to the influence of an allied O. To emulate an exemplar. To conform to custom.

Feelings and Emotions : Respect, admiration, wonder, reverence.

Trait-names and Attitudes : (a) *Deferent*, respectful, admiring, laudatory, worshipful ; (b) *compliant*, obliging, co-operative ; (c) suggestible.

Press : Superior O ; p Dominance, p Exhibition. The O has greater directional force or more attracting power (' mana ') than the S.

Gratuities : A parent or allied leader with an admirable character.

Actions : General : To move towards, fix gaze upon, salute, bow down to an admired O. To believe in conformity with the wishes of a superior O. To accept the leadership of a more experienced O.

Acclaimance : To watch, listen attentively to, praise, applaud or honour a superior O. To eulogize, celebrate or acclaim an O. To elevate, vote for or give a title to an O. To elect an O to high office. To idolize a leader. To choose a superior ally. Hero worship. To raise a statue. To express gratitude or give thanks.

Compliance : To do willingly what a superior O suggests or dictates. To co-operate eagerly. To perform little services. To work happily in a subordinate position. To follow advice.

Fusion with n Similance S n Superiority : To emulate a great man. To become superior by resembling a superior O.

ideo Deference : To admire the ideology of an exemplar. To become a disciple. To accept the ideas of others. Credulity and suggestibility.

Hypnotic Suggestibility : A variety of suggestibility.

Focal n Def : Admiration for one or a few great men. The Ego Ideal figures are constructed from such exemplars.

Fusions with : n Suc (to follow a sympathetic guide), n Cog (to learn by accepting the opinions of a superior O), n Aba (to humbly serve a domineering person), n Sex (to feel erotic pleasure in yielding), n Nur (to praise in order to console), Sa (to remain loyal to the same Os), Ch (to change allegiances), Con St (to follow conservative leaders), Rad St (to follow radical leaders), n Sup (to emulate a great man).

n Dom and n Def : An S who is loyal to superiors, dominant to inferiors.

Needs to which n Def may be subsidiary : n Rec (to obey orders in order to be promoted), n Blam (to flatter in order to avoid opposition and censure), n Dom (to flatter in order to be chosen leader), n Acq (to serve for pay, to act as an S in an experiment), n Inf (to obey and thus avoid responsibility for failure), n Aff (to praise in order to make a friend).

Conflicts : Any need (supported by the n Auto) which impels an S along another course : n Dom, n Ach, n Rec, n Rej, n Agg, n Exh.

Measurement : Subjects are marked according to the amount of diffuse Deference. Intense focal Deference is treated as a separate factor.

intraDef : Willing submission to conscience. Consecration to an ideal.

Subjns and Semi-objns : Religion : worship of deities, ceremonials of deference, hymns of praise, offerings of gratitude, serving God and obeying his laws. The poet's submission to his 'Muse.'

Social Forms : All members of a State or institution are expected to be deferent : to obey the leaders, to praise and defend the 'faith.'

Statements in Questionnaire

1. I am capable of putting myself in the background and working with zest for a man I admire.
2. I see the good points rather than the bad points of the men who are above me.
3. I accept suggestions rather than insist on working things out in my own way.
4. I am considered compliant and obliging by my friends.
5. I often seek the advice of older men and follow it.
6. I give praise rather freely when the occasion offers.
7. I often find myself imitating or agreeing with somebody I consider superior.
8. I usually follow instructions and do what is expected of me.
9. In matters of conduct I conform to custom.
10. I express my enthusiasm and respect for the people I admire.

Sentiments of Deference[1]

1. No gift is more precious than good advice.
2. The fairest lives are those which regularly accommodate themselves to the human model.
3. The first duty of every citizen is to regard himself as made for his country.
4. Let a man keep the law, any law, and his way will be strewn with satisfaction.
5. The victory always remains with those who admire rather than with those who deride.
6. It is not so necessary to find heroes as to see the hero in every man.
7. It does not take great men to do things, it takes consecrated men.
8. Only by compromise and the closest co-operation may we abolish the evils that confront us.
9. Love is a willing sacrifice.
10. Before you begin get good counsel; then, having decided, act promptly.
11. Laws deliver man from anxiety; they choose a side for one, and give one a master.
12. We acquire the highest form of freedom when our wishes conform to the will of society.
13. Honour thy father and thy mother.
14. Without the authority conferred on government the human race cannot survive.
15. Our chief want in life is somebody who will make us do what we can.

n Autonomy (n Auto)

Desires and Effects: To get free, shake off restraint, break out of confinement. To resist coercion and restriction. To avoid or quit activities prescribed by domineering authorities. To be independent and free to act according to impulse. To be unattached, unconditioned, irresponsible. To defy conventions.

Feelings and Emotions: (a) Feeling of restraint. Anger. (b) Independence and irresponsibility.

1. As in the behavioural questionnaire, the sentiments of each variable (in the sentiments questionnaire) were interspersed with the sentiments of other variables.

Trait-names and Attitudes : (a) *Autonomous,* independent, free, wilful, unrestrained, irresponsible ; (b) rebellious, insurgent, radical, defiant ; (c) *negativistic,* stubborn, resistant.

Press : Negative : p Physical restraint (Barriers, Confinement).
p Dominance and p Aggression : Coercion, Prohibition, Restraint.
Positive : p Open Spaces. p Tolerance.

Gratuities : Indulgent parents. A progressive school. A 'free' country.

Actions : General : To do as one pleases regardless of rules or conventions. To refuse to be tied down by family obligations or by a definite routine of work. To avoid organized athletics or regular employment. To look on marriage as a form of 'bondage.' To love adventure and change, or seclusion (where one is free to do and think as he likes).

Motones : To break loose from physical constraint. To escape from prison. To run away.

Verbones : To speak one's mind. To defy authority. To demand 'free speech.' To swear and blaspheme. 'To hell with you !'

Freedom : To escape from the confines of four walls. To play truant. To avoid the dominance of authority and convention by running away, resigning, leaving the country. To wander. To seek independence in isolation (open spaces, wilderness), or in tolerant, uninhibited communities (the Latin Quarter, Tahiti). To quit civilization. To travel alone and unencumbered.

Resistance : To refuse to comply with the directions or commands of another O. To argue against authority. To be 'as obstinate and stubborn as a mule.' To disobey one's parents. Negativism. Defiance.

ideo Auto : To advance original or revolutionary theories.

Fusions : The commonest fusion is with n Agg (the revolutionist). Also with : n Ach (to achieve things without guidance), n Rej (to shut out objectionable Os who interfere with concentration), n Play (irresponsible amusement), n Cog (to be a pioneer, an explorer, an experimenter), n Exh (to attract attention by being eccentric), n Dom (to lead a new movement), n Inf (to escape from failure and coercion).

Needs which may be subsidiary to n Auto : n Dom (to argue for freedom), n Aff (to join an association to fight for liberty), n Suc (to plead for freedom).

Needs to which n Auto may be subsidiary : Any needs which are blocked, for instance : n Play (to miss school in order to play), n Ach (to be independent in order to achieve a purpose), n Cnt (to refuse to obey out of pride), n Inf (to refuse to comply in order to avoid a potentially humiliating situation), n Sex (to enjoy free love).

Conflicts with : n Aff (ties of all kinds), n Blam, n Ach, n Def, n Suc, n Nur.

intraAuto : Free-will. To liberate the Ego from the restraints of conscience and reason. To be irresponsible. Laughter.

Subjns and Semi-objns : Playful mirth. Drunken orgies. Celebrations, festivals, and reunions. Black Mass and Saturnalia.

Social forms : Radicals and Progressives. Creators. Criminals and law breakers.

Statements in Questionnaire

1. I am unable to do my best work when I am in a subservient position.
2. I become stubborn and resistant when others attempt to coerce me.
3. I often act contrary to custom or to the wishes of my parents.
4. I argue against people who attempt to assert their authority over me.
5. I try to avoid situations where I am expected to conform to conventional standards.
6. I go my own way regardless of the opinions of others.
7. I am disinclined to adopt a course of action dictated by others.
8. I disregard the rules and regulations that hamper my freedom.
9. I demand independence and liberty above everything.
10. I am apt to criticize whoever happens to be in authority.

Sentiments of Autonomy

1. He shall be the greatest who can be the most solitary, the most concealed, the most divergent.
2. A man can learn as well by striking out blindly on his own as he can by following the advice of others.
3. The greatest fortunes are for those who leave the common turnpike and blaze a new trail for themselves.
4. The superior individual has no respect for government.
5. Society everywhere is in conspiracy against the manhood of every one of its members.
6. As men's prayers are a disease of the will, so are their creeds a disease of the intellect.
7. Whoso would be a man, must be a nonconformist.
8. There is a time in every man's education when he arrives at the conviction that imitation is suicide.

9. The state is made for the individual ; the individual is not made for the state.
10. A member of an institution is no more nor less than a slave.
11. Adherence to convention produces the worst kind of citizen.
12. A man must make his own decisions, uninfluenced by public opinion.
13. A member of a group is merely an unnecessary duplicate. It is the man who stands alone who excites our admiration.
14. The individualist is the man who is most likely to discover the best road to a new future.
15. To accept a benefit is to sell one's freedom.

n Aggression (n Agg)

Desires and Effects : Physical : To overcome opposition forcefully. To fight. To revenge an injury. To attack, injure or kill an O. To oppose forcefully or punish an O.

Verbal : To belittle, censure, curse or ridicule maliciously an O. To depreciate and slander. (The end that is sought is the expulsion or the painful humiliation of the O.)

Feelings and Emotions : Irritation, anger, rage (temper tantrum) ; also revenge and jealousy. Hatred.

Trait-names and Attitudes : (a) *Aggressive*, combative, belligerent, pugnacious, quarrelsome, argumentative ; (b) irritable, malicious, resentful, revengeful ; (c) destructive, cruel, vindictive, ruthless ; (d) critical, accusatory, abusive ; (e) domineering, severe, despotic.

Press : p Aggression : Assault, Belittlement, Censure, Ridicule, Punishment ; p Dominance : Coercion, Opposition, Prohibition, Restraint ; p Superiority : Any object who is too self-assured, boastful, vain, pompous ; p Rival ; p Rejection ; p Repellent O.

suprAggression : Aggression against superior Os : parents, authorities, leaders, the State (*cf.* parricide).

infrAggression : Aggression against inferior Os : children and defenceless animals. Bullying.

Common agency objects : Stones, sticks, knives, guns, poison.

Actions : General : To move and speak in an assertive, forceful, threatening manner. To jostle and push Os out of one's way. To curse or blame those who impede one's progress. To adopt a terrifying attitude and take the best by force. To experience 'fits of rage,' to scream, kick and scratch.

Physical aggression : Assault : To strike, to 'pick a fight.'

Murder : To kill an O.

Destruction : To break things. To dismember.

Zonal aggression : Oral Agg : Biting ; Anal Agg : Soiling.

Verbal aggression : *Belittlement* : To criticize, depreciate, slander.

Censure : To reprimand, blame or scold.

Ridicule : To make fun of an O. Malicious satire.

ideo Aggression : To attack a system of thought or of sentiments.

socio Aggression : To fight for one's country. To punish criminals and traitors. To kill enemies.

Fusions with : n Dom (aggressive leadership), n Sex (sadism), n Auto (to use force to escape confinement), n Exh (prize fighting), n Dfd (to fight in self-defence), n Acq (to fight for possessions, to rob a man).

Needs to which n Agg may be subsidiary : n Sex, n Rec, n Dom, n Cnt (to defend honour), n Auto (to kill a tyrant).

Conflicts with : n Harm, n Blam, n Inf, n Aba, n Aff, n Def, n Nur.

intrAgg : Self-criticism (inferiority feelings). Self-censure (guilt feelings). Self-mutilation (castration). Suicide.

Subjns and Semi-objns : Murder stories. Public executions. Religious blood-lettings (Mithraic ceremonial).

Social forms : *Fn Dom* : Autocratic despot. Army, navy and police. *Fn Auto* : Revolutionary movements. Law breakers.

Statements in Questionnaire

1. When a friend of mine annoys me, I tell him what I think of him.
2. I am apt to enjoy getting a person's goat.
3. I like physical competition — such as football, boxing or wrestling — the rougher the better.
4. I protest sometimes, when a person steps in front of me in a waiting line.
5. I treat a domineering person as rudely as he treats me.
6. I try to get my own way regardless of others.
7. I argue or bluff my way past a guard or doorman if necessary.
8. Sometimes I use threats of force to accomplish my purpose.
9. I get into a fighting mood when the occasion seems to demand it.
10. I often blame other people when things go wrong.
11. I get angry and express my annoyance when I am treated with disrespect.
12. I am considered aggressive by some of my acquaintances.

13. When a good fight is on, I am one of the first to pitch in.
14. I am apt to express my irritation rather than restrain it.
15. I often let myself go when I am angry.
16. I often disregard the personal feelings of other people.
17. I enjoy a good hot argument.
18. Occasionally when a youngster gets fresh with me, I threaten to punish him.
19. I can become quite dictatorial when I am dealing with a subordinate.
20. I rebuke my friends when I disapprove of their behaviour.

Sentiments of Aggression

1. When swords are drawn, let no idea of love, not even the face of a father, move you.
2. Destroyers of tyranny have contributed most to humanity.
3. A person seldom falls sick without the bystanders being animated with a faint hope that he will die.
4. Men are just what they seem to be, and that is the worst that can be said of them.
5. A bold attack is half the battle.
6. To keep a secret enemy — that is a luxury which even the highest men enjoy.
7. Interiorly most people enjoy the inferiority of their best friends.
8. Anger is one of the sinews of the soul ; he that lacks it has a maimed mind.
9. Anger in its time and place may assume a kind of grace.
10. Every normal man must be tempted, at times, to spit on his hands, hoist the black flag, and begin slitting throats.
11. Love force, and care little how you exhibit it.
12. Revenge is a luscious fruit which you must learn to cultivate.
13. It does not matter much what the man hates as long as he hates something.
14. Marriage is a field of battle.
15. We are much nearer loving those who hate us, than those who love us more than we like.

n Abasement (n Aba)

Desires and Effects : To submit passively to external force. To accept injury, blame, criticism, punishment. To surrender. To become resigned to fate. To admit inferiority, error, wrong-doing or defeat. To confess and atone. To blame, belittle or mutilate the self. To seek and enjoy pain, punishment, illness and misfortune.

The n Aba is perhaps always a sub-need, but because of its general importance it is given a separate status.

Feelings and Emotions : Resignation or aboulia. Shame, guilt, remorse or contrition. Inferiority or humility. Helplessness or despair.

Trait-names and Attitudes : (a) *Abasive,* submissive, acquiescent, pliant, meek, humble, servile ; (b) impotent, passive, patient, resigned ; (c) contrite, penitent, prostrate ; (d) timorous, weak, cowardly.

Press : p Aggression and p Dominance.

Actions : General : To adopt a passive, meek, humble, or servile attitude. To stand aside, take a back seat, let others push by and have the best. To submit to coercion and domination without rebellion or complaint. To allow oneself to be 'talked down.' To accept censure without rebuttal. To allow oneself to be bullied, dispossessed of objects. To receive physical injuries without retaliation.

Surrender : to 'give in,' to acknowledge defeat.

Renunciation : To give up material Os, or narcistic aims. To resign in favour of another O.

Penitence : Self-blame, self-accusation.

Atonement : To do something to balance a wrong. To expiate or atone for a sin by humiliating oneself. To wear sack-cloth and ashes. Under this may be classed many self-mutilations, self-inflicted illnesses and suicides.

Fusions with : n Suc (to pray meekly), n Exh (to make an exhibition of martyrdom), n Def (to be very humbly compliant, to suffer in order to show devotion and reverence), n Cnt (to suffer pain stoically, to 'will the obligatory'), n Sex (masochism).

Needs which may be subsidiary to the n Aba : n Auto (to disobey so as to be punished), n Agg (to pick a fight in order to be licked).

Needs to which the n Aba may be subsidiary : n Harm (to surrender in order to avoid more pain), n Aff (to confess in order to retain friendship), n Blam (to apologize in order to avoid censure ; to atone for a crime), n Rec (to 'fish for compliments'), n Inf (to stand back or surrender in order to avoid further failure), n Agg (to be injured by an O in order to have the right to retaliate).

Conflicts with : n Cnt, n Dfd, n Ach, n Agg, n Dom, n Auto, n Inf, n Rec, n Ret.

intrAba : To offer no resistance to instinctual or Superego tendencies. To be overwhelmed by Ucs forces. To repress nothing. Psychic deflation.

Pathology : Masochism (to enjoy pain and suffering).

Subjns and Semi-objns : Religious acts : Confession of sins, atonements and self-mutilations.

Social forms : Slaves.

Statements in Questionnaire

1. I am seldom able to hold up my end in a fight.
2. When something goes wrong I am more apt to blame myself than to blame the other fellow.
3. There are times when I act like a coward.
4. I am more apt to give in than to continue a fight.
5. My friends think I am too humble.
6. I feel nervous and anxious in the presence of superiors.
7. I am rather submissive and apologetic when I have done wrong.
8. I am shy and inhibited in my relations with women.
9. I am sometimes depressed by feelings of my own unworthiness.
10. I feel that I must suffer before I can achieve my purpose.

Sentiments of Abasement

1. A man who knows that he is a fool is not a great fool.
2. The moral man does not desire anything outside of his position.
3. When Heaven is about to confer a great office on any man, it first disciplines his mind with suffering.
4. Do little things as though they were great things and you will live to do great things as though they were little things.
5. There is nothing which the body suffers which the soul may not profit by.
6. There is no man living who would willingly be deprived of his right to suffer pain for that is his right to be a man.
7. Charity should begin with your enemies.
8. Meekness is better than vengeance.
9. Render good for bad ; blessings for curses.
10. Perhaps the only true dignity of man is his capacity to despise himself.
11. 'Tis vain to quarrel with our destiny.
12. The first step to self-knowledge is self-distrust.

13. All fortune is to be conquered by bearing it.
14. The life of no man is free from struggle and suffering.
15. If you wish to mount the ladder you must begin at the lowest rung.

n Achievement Ego Ideal

The n Achievement may accompany any other need. It is the desire or tendency to do things as rapidly and/or as well as possible. Thus, there is a great variety of acts — from blowing smoke rings to discovering a new planet — which may gratify the Achievement drive. The Ego Ideal is merely the aggregate of the imagined goals of the n Achievement (In Ach). It is, let us say, a conception of the ideally successful self. It may take any one of many different shapes — from the perpetrator of the 'perfect crime' to the prophet of a new religion.

n Achievement (n Ach)

Desires and Effects : To accomplish something difficult. To master, manipulate or organize physical objects, human beings, or ideas. To do this as rapidly, and as independently as possible. To overcome obstacles and attain a high standard. To excel one's self. To rival and surpass others. To increase self-regard by the successful exercise of talent.

Kinds of Achievement : The n Ach is focalized according to kind of Interest (*vide*). For instance : n Ach (Phys), the desire for athletic success ; n Ach (Caste), the desire for social prestige ; n Ach (Intell), the desire for intellectual distinction.

Feelings and Emotions : Zest, ambition. (These may come as counteractions to inferiority feelings.)

Press : p Task ; p Rival.

Trait-names and Attitudes : Achievant, ambitious, competitive, aspiring.

Actions : To make intense, prolonged and repeated efforts to accomplish something difficult. To work with singleness of purpose towards a high and distant goal. To have the determination to win. To try to do everything well. To be stimulated to excel by the presence of others, to enjoy competition. To exert will power ; to overcome boredom and fatigue (intraDom).

Fusions and Subsidiations : The n Ach fuses readily and naturally with every other need. Indeed, it is considered by some that the n Achievement — often called the 'will-to-power' — is the dominant psychogenic need. Perhaps in most cases it is subsidiary to an inhibited need for Recognition.

Conflicts with: n Aba, n Inf, n Blam, n Play, n Aff, n Exh.

Subjns and Semi-objns: Great deeds in fantasy and play. Writing 'achievement' stories.

Social forms: Every recognized profession or occupation may be regarded as a channel for the n Achievement.

Statements in Questionnaire

1. I am driven to ever greater efforts by an unslaked ambition.
2. I feel that nothing else which life can offer is a substitute for great achievement.
3. I feel that my future peace and self-respect depend upon my accomplishing some notable piece of work.
4. I set difficult goals for myself which I attempt to reach.
5. I work with energy at the job that lies before me instead of dreaming about the future.
6. When my own interests are at stake, I become entirely concentrated upon my job and forget my obligations to others.
7. I enjoy relaxation wholeheartedly only when it follows the successful completion of a substantial piece of work.
8. I feel the spirit of competition in most of my activities.
9. I work like a slave at everything I undertake until I am satisfied with the result.
10. I enjoy work as much as play.

Sentiments of Achievement

1. Fame! Glory! They are life-giving breath and living blood. No man lives unless he is famous. (n Rec)
2. Ambition is a gallant madness.
3. Power is the morality of men who stand out from the rest and it is also mine. (n Dom)
4. When a man is no longer anxious to do better than well, he is done for.
5. I like best that which flies beyond my reach.
6. Ambition is the parent of many virtues.
7. Only ambition will bring a man's mind into full activity.
8. My aspirations are my nearest friends.

9. Man is complete and upstanding only when he would be more than man.
10. Better to reign in hell than serve in heaven (n Dom).
11. To be superior a man must stand alone (n Auto).
12. No bird soars too high if he soars with his own wings (n Auto).
13. It is not to die we fear, but to die poorly : to fall forgotten, in a multitude (n Rec).
14. God, give me hills to climb, and strength for climbing.
15. Freedom cannot exist alone. Power must accompany it.

Ego Ideal (E I)

The Ego Ideal is composed of all the fantasies which portray the subject, or a hero, accomplishing great deeds or achieving recognition. These are the desiderata of the need for Achievement. Taken together at any stage of a subject's life, they represent his highest hope, the dramatization of himself as a man of destiny. This instituted fantasy—always partially unconscious—goads the individual to ever greater efforts. Failure to actualize it depresses him.

The E I is in truth a subjectification of the Achievement, but because of its importance it is given the status of a separate variable.

Kinds of Ego Ideal. The Ego Ideal is focalized according to the kind of Interest (*vide*).

Relation to other variables. The Ego Ideal is the best indication of an unfulfilled Achievement drive (ln Ach). It is usually accompanied by action, but it may lead to paralysis of action — when the Ego Ideal is so high that it is futile to strive for it. If the Ego Ideal is very high and the individual believes that he has approached it, or if he finally identifies himself with it, it is an indication that Narcism is dominant (delusions of omnipotence and grandeur). The Ego Ideal usually consists of a composite of internalized exemplars. Thus, its formation is preceded by the need for Deference, admiration of another object being accompanied by a tendency to emulate it. If the n Achievement is extremely high, however, the S will usually admire very few people. In such an individual the needs for Rejection and Autonomy will be high and the need for Deference will be low. Here, Deference may be intense but it will be focal.

Measurement. The height of the E I; the vividness, perseveration and frequency of E I imagery; the determining effect of this variable upon other variables.

Statements in Questionnaire

1. I dream a good deal about my future successes.
2. I feel that most of my acquaintances have a rather low standard of achievement.
3. I feel that some far goal deserves my effort more than any daily duty.
4. I admire immensely and attempt to emulate in one way or another certain great men of the past.
5. I am guided in most of my decisions by an over-riding ambition.
6. I am repeatedly swayed to action by exultant hopes of possible success.
7. I spend a good deal of time planning my career.
8. I energize myself by dramatizing my life as an ascending struggle against opposition.
9. No immediate compensation could console me for the failure of my highest hopes.
10. No one can demand from me as much as I demand from myself.

n Sex — n Exhibition
n Sentience — n Play

This group of needs is loosely related. They are directed towards the enjoyment of 'sensations': erotic excitement, sensuous pleasure, dramatics, humour, fantasy and play.

n Sex (n Sex)

Desires and Effects: To form and further an erotic relationship. To have sexual intercourse.

Feelings: Erotic excitement, lust, love.

Trait-names and Attitudes: Erotic, sensual, seductive.

Press: p Sexual O.

infra or supra Sex: The selection of a younger or an older O.

Homo or Heterosexual: The selection of the same or the opposite sex.

Actions: General: To make advances, to 'pick-up' a man or woman, to seduce a sexually appealing O. To enjoy the company of the opposite sex, to be fond of mixed parties, to like dancing.

To be in love. To desire only the chosen object : to work and play together, excluding others ; to exchange sentiments and ideas.

Motones. To hold hands, embrace, kiss, copulate.

Verbones. To flirt, praise, express sympathy, make love.

Fusions with : n Aff (Erotic love), n Agg (Sadism), n Aba (Masochism), n Exh (Exhibitionism), n Cog (Voyeurism), n Suc (Anaclitic love), n Nur (Nurturant love), n Def (Idolatry), Dom and Agg = Active role. Def and Aba = Passive role.

Needs which may be subsidiary to the n Sex : n Aff (to win the affection of an object). n Exh (to fascinate an O), n Ach (to demonstrate talent).

Needs to which the n Sex may be subsidiary : n Acq (prostitution), n Aff (to maintain an enduring love), n Dom (to gain control over an O), n Cnt (to avoid being called innocent and inexperienced), n Nur (to have a child).

Conflicts with : n Ach, n Blam, n Inf, n Rej.

intraSex : Auto-erotism and masturbation.

Subjns and Semi-objns : Erotic fantasies and dreams. Romantic poetry, love stories, etc.

Social Institutions : Marriage. Organized prostitution.

Statements in Questionnaire

1. I spend a great deal of time thinking about sexual matters.
2. I fall in love rather easily.
3. I feel that my sexual instinct is as strong as my ambition.
4. I have more pleasure with a woman than with a man.
5. I sometimes lose myself in extravagant sexual fantasies.
6. I have difficulty controlling my sexual impulses.
7. I am attracted by every good-looking woman I see.
8. I regard every attractive woman with searching curiosity, looking her over from head to foot, measuring, discriminating, estimating possibilities.
9. I prefer women who have a strong sexual appeal.
10. I have had a good deal of actual sex experience.

n Sentience (n Sen)

Desires and Effects : To seek and enjoy sensuous impressions.

Feelings and Emotions : Sensuous or aesthetic feelings.

Trait-names and Attitudes : Sentient, sensuous, sensitive, aesthetic.

Press : p Sensuous O.

Zones of Sentience : 1. *Perceptive :*

(a) Tactile (n tSen). To stroke and be stroked. To touch fabrics. Fusion with n Sex : Stimulation of erogenous zones : oral, mammary, urethral, anal, and genital. Thermal sentience (warm water, rays of sun).

(b) Olfactory (n oSen). Pleasurable odours, scents, perfumes.

(c) Gustatory (n gSen). Delicious food, sauces, desserts, wines.

(d) Auditory (n aSen). Natural sounds, human voice, poetry and music.

(e) Visual (n vSen). Pleasurable sights : colour, light, form, movement, a beautiful face, clothes, decoration, landscapes, architecture, painting and sculpture. Vivid imagery.

(2) *Kinetic :* Kinaesthetic (n kSen). Pleasurable muscular movements ; dancing, skating, gymnastics, diving, etc.

Actions : To seek and find delight in the enjoyment of any of the above sense impressions. To have delicate, sensitive perceptions.

To perceive and comment upon the sensuous quality of objects. To remark upon the atmosphere, the temperature, colours in the room, pictures, various sounds and odours. To remember and in the description of events include sensuous details.

To use expressive language. To use exact and novel metaphors.

To display a genuine delight in one or more of the Arts.

Fusions with : n Sex (diffuse libidinous satisfactions), n Aff (to be with a beautiful person), n Exh (to give an artistic performance in public), n Def (to yield to the enticing power of a beautiful O).

Needs which may be subsidiary to n Sen : n Suc (to cry for the mother's body), n Auto (to break away from puritanical conventions).

Needs to which n Sen may be subsidiary : n Sex (sensations to excite erotic feeling).

Conflicts with : n Ach, n Blam, n Rej, n Dom.

intraSen : To delight in the beauty of one's own body. To enjoy sensuous imagery.

Social forms : Restaurants, perfumery shops, theatres, concert halls, museums, parks, picture galleries.

Statements in Questionnaire

1. I notice and am responsive to slight changes in the colour of the sky, in the temperature and quality of the atmosphere.

2. I enjoy myself observing in great detail the facial expressions, gestures and mannerisms of the people I see.
3. I enjoy the sensuous quality of my own imagery.
4. I repeat to myself certain thrilling phrases I have heard or read.
5. I observe and am affected by the decorations and colour tones in a room.
6. I amble about in the country or lie in the grass — attending only to the odours of the earth, the drift of clouds, the rustling of leaves, the song of birds.
7. I think that the arts are more important to me than the sciences.
8. I can be as intensely excited by a novel or a poem as I am by anything else.
9. I wish that I could own objects purely for the aesthetic pleasure they give me — etchings, pottery, ironwork, carved figures, paintings.
10. I attach great value to certain words purely because of their sound.
11. I feel that a certain perversity adds a flavour to pleasure.
12. I find that a smell or fragrance will evoke very vivid memories in me.
13. I find that apathy or depression can be transmuted by an object, a sound or a scene of beauty, into sheer delight.
14. I enjoy the rhythm as much as the meaning of good prose.
15. I search for sensations which shall be at once new and delightful.
16. I love good food and good wine, and have become quite a connoisseur in such matters.
17. I prefer good music to the disturbing presence of most people.
18. I have found that any overpowering feeling — even sorrow — pleases me privately.
19. I get pleasure from anything which has a long legendary past, a special pleasure coming from the associated richness.
20. I find myself 'feeling into' objects and people, and within myself experiencing their essence.

n Exhibition (n Exh)

Desires and Effects : To make an impression. To be seen and heard. To excite, amaze, fascinate, entertain, shock, intrigue, amuse or entice Os.

Feelings and Emotions : Vanity. Exuberance and self-confidence.

Press : p Audience. A cathected O to be attracted.

Trait-names and Attitudes : Exhibitionistic, histrionic, dramatic, spectacular, conspicuous.

Actions : Motones : Self-display. To make the self conspicuous by wearing unusual or colourful clothing. To seek the limelight, pose for effect, enjoy it when all eyes are upon the self. To wear little clothing or go naked. To join a Nudist colony.

Verbones : To talk a good deal : tall stories, anecdotes and jokes. To hold the floor, monopolize the conversation. To attract attention by mannerisms, expressive gestures, emphatic or extravagant speech. To enjoy an audience.

To attempt to entertain others. To speak, or perform in public. To act, take part in dramatics, play music, dance, show-off. To play the clown.

Oral-Exhibition : to sing, or speak with poetic feeling.

To talk a lot about the self, to exaggerate one's part in an adventure, to dramatize the self, to pose as a unique, mysterious, incalculable person, a person with hypnotic power.

Indirect form : to represent the self in art forms ; to write self-revealing novels or autobiographies.

Fusions with : n Ach (to work at something in public), n Sen (to display beauty or perform on a musical instrument in public), n Aff (to interest others and be the life of the party), n Play (to amuse others by playing the fool), n Dom (to persuade others with dramatic force, to be a 'spell-binder'), n Sex (to display genitals), n Suc (to make a pitiful, tragic spectacle of the self, to excite sympathy by exhibiting one's wounds).

Needs which may be subsidiary to the n Exh : n Ach (to work on a performance which is to be done in public).

Needs to which n Exh may be subsidiary : n Sex (to seduce an O), n Aff (to win affection by fascinating or amusing Os), n Dom (to dominate by fascination and enticement), n Acq (to earn a living by acting on the stage, by selling goods in public — auctioneer).

Conflicts with : n Inf (fear of failure), n Blam (fear of blame — 'vanity is unbecoming'). The antipole of the n Exh is the n Seclusion (the desire for privacy and concealment).

Measurement : n Exhibition = n Exh minus n Sec.

intraExh : Self-dramatization.

Social forms : Public performances : theatres, vaudevilles, circuses, hippodromes, amusement parks. Magicians and monologists. With n Sentience : Concerts and operas.

Statements in Questionnaire

1. Sometimes when I am in a crowd, I say humorous things which I expect strangers will overhear.
2. I often dramatize a story which I am telling and demonstrate exactly how everything happened.
3. I talk rather freely about myself, even to casual friends.
4. When I am in a group, I try to increase the enjoyment of others by telling amusing stories.
5. I prefer to be looked at than not.
6. I like to have people watch me do the things which I do well.
7. I am apt to show off in some way if I get a chance.
8. I often take the lead in livening up a dull evening.
9. I do a thing sometimes just to watch the effect it will have upon other people.
10. I amuse others by playing the clown when the occasion warrants it.
11. I boast a bit about my achievements from time to time.
12. I feel pleasantly exhilarated when all eyes are upon me.
13. I do quite a bit of talking when I am in mixed company.
14. I act on the principle that a man will never get ahead if he does not blow his own horn from time to time.
15. I am rather successful at entertaining others.
16. I enjoy holding the floor or performing before a group — playing the piano, showing tricks, acting in charades, etc.
17. I am pleased if I am called upon for a story or a speech.
18. I often exaggerate my part in an event in order to make myself appear in a more interesting light.
19. I feel dissatisfied if I remain unnoticed.
20. I love to talk and it's hard for me to keep quiet.

n Play

General Description. Some people devote their free time to various forms of amusement : sports, dancing, drinking parties, cards and other indoor games. A playful attitude may also characterize their working hours. They like to laugh and make a joke of everything. We attribute this to the operation of the n Play : the tendency to act for 'fun,' without further purpose.

This variable manifests itself best in children's play : enjoyable, stressless, 'make-believe' activity. It is random, whimsical, fantasy-driven behaviour, which releases internal tension, but achieves no exterior effects. Subjectively, it is experienced as 'activity pleasure.' It ceases the moment a serious obstacle is encountered, the moment it is necessary to become 'serious,' to adapt to a stubborn fact. Thus play, like fantasy, is *undirected* ; it is not propelled and pointed towards a definite goal by a will process. There is an inseparable gradation between a playful attitude and an achievant attitude. They become fused when a child becomes intent upon accomplishing a chosen 'unreal' task, or later when the Achievement drive takes the form of sport. In our studies, Mirth — playing jokes and the enjoyment of humour — was subsumed under the n Play. It is questionable whether Play and Achievement should be included within the definition of need, but in the present study it was found convenient to do so. Play is sometimes an 'escape from reality,' an enjoyable relaxation of stress. Good-natured humour, even though slightly aggressive, is classed as Play.

Trait-names and Attitudes : (a) *Playful*, gay, jolly, merry, blithe, jovial ; (b) easy-going, light-hearted, sportive.

Statements in Questionnaire

1. I feel that if I were free from the necessity of making a living I should devote a good deal of time to the pursuit of unmixed pleasure.
2. When I am working, I spend a good deal of time planning or anticipating future pleasures.
3. I believe that I have the disposition of a 'man of pleasure' rather than a 'man of great ambition.'
4. I spend a fair proportion of my time amusing myself — parties, dances, shows, card-games or drinking bouts.
5. I prefer the company of amusing, fun-loving people.
6. I treat sex as an amusing game rather than a serious undertaking.
7. I cultivate an easy-going, humorous attitude toward life.
8. I seek, at the cost of some distant goal, whatever makes me feel most cheerful here and now.
9. I act on the principle that a wise man is known by his ability to play.
10. I seek amusement as an antidote for worry.

n Affiliation — n Rejection, Narcism

The n Affiliation describes a positive tropism for people, the n Rejection a negative tropism. Occasionally, one finds one or the other extreme : a person who likes almost everyone or a misanthrope. But usually both needs operate, the need that is aroused being determined by the object encountered or the class to which the object belongs (profession, political party, nationality, religious sect, etc.). Narcism is Affiliation turned inwards.

n Affiliation (n Aff)

Desires and Effects : To draw near and enjoyably co-operate or reciprocate with an allied O : an O who resembles the S or who likes the S. To please and win affection of a cathected O. To adhere and remain loyal to a friend.

Feelings and Emotions : Trust, good-will, affection and love. Sympathetic empathy.

Trait-names and Attitudes : Affiliative, friendly, sociable, genial, affectionate, trusting, good-natured.

Kinds of Affiliation : Interests (*vide*) may determine the O preferred.

Press : Positive : p Allied object : p Affiliation.
Negative : p Friendless Environment.

infra or suprAffiliation : Friendships with inferior or superior Os.

Actions : General : To meet and make the acquaintance of Os. To form, maintain or accept synergies with Os. To show good-will and love. To do things which please an O. To avoid wounding, to allay opposition.

Motones : To draw near and stay with. To wave, shake hands, go arm in arm, place hand on the shoulder, embrace.

Zonal : Oral : Kissing.

Verbones : To greet, say hello and goodbye, question in a friendly way. To give information, tell stories, exchange sentiments. To express trust, admiration, affection. To confide in an O.

Contiguance : To approach, touch, accompany, and live near allied Os. To be gregarious.

Similance : To feel and act like an allied O. To imitate and agree with, to be ' as one with.'

Co-operation : To achieve things with an O.

Reciprocation : To communicate or play with an O. To converse, telephone, write letters. To share benefits, possessions, knowledge or confidences with an O. To enjoy erotic relations with a beloved O (Fn Sex Aff).

ideo Aff : To be receptive to ideas. To harmonize one's sentiments with those of others. To resolve differences.

Types of Affiliative Synergies : The aim of the n Affiliation is to form a synergy : a mutually enjoyed, enduring, harmoniously co-operating and reciprocating relation with another person. The S must like and be liked by the O before a synergy is possible. A synergy should result in the reinforcement of emotions and needs. Hence, some degree of similarity seems to be essential. The following varieties may be recognized : Fn Suc Aff (friendship with a sympathetic protecting O), Fn Def Aff (friendship with an admired exemplar), Fn Nur Aff (friendship with a younger dependent O), Fn Dom Aff (friendship with a compliant O), Fn Exp Aff (friendship for a pupil), Fn Cog Aff (friendship for a teacher). The following are also of interest : Complementary Aff (friendship based on contrast), Supplementary Aff (friendship based on similarity). *Diffuse Aff*. Many friends of different types. *Focal Aff*. One or a few friends. *Sa & Aff*. Long enduring synergies. *Ch & Aff*. To drop friends and acquire new ones. To be fickle and changeable.

Fusions : Since most things may be done in co-operation with another, almost every need may fuse with the n Aff. For instance : n Ach (to collaborate in accomplishing anything), n Agg (to fight together against a common enemy), n Nur (to co-operate in caring for a child). Likewise, *reciprocation* involving any two antipolar needs may occur : n Cog and n Exp (to ask or answer questions), n Nur and n Suc (to give or receive sympathy).

Needs which may be subsidiary to the n Aff : All needs, as suggested above. Also : n Auto (to break out of prison to join a beloved O), n Aba (to apologize, to admit mistakes), n Blam (to avoid doing anything that would annoy an O), n Acq (to make money in order to entertain friends), etc.

Needs to which the n Aff may be subsidiary : All needs, as suggested above. n Dom (to make friends in order to be elected to high office).

Conflicts with : N, n Ach, n Rej, n Dom, n Agg, n Auto, n Inf, n Cnt.

Measurement : *The chief criteria are* : 1. friendly feeling ; 2. desire to associate, play and converse ; 3. efforts to resolve differences, co-operate and maintain harmony ; 4. readiness to trust and confide ; 5. the number, intensity and duration of friendships.

intrAff : To be on good terms with one's self. To regard one's own weaknesses with humorous tolerance. To resolve conflicts. Narcism.

Subjns and Semi-objns : An imaginary companion.

Social forms : Clubs and social organizations. (with n Sex) Marriage.

Statements in Questionnaire

1. I am in my element when I am with a group of people who enjoy life.
2. I become very attached to my friends.
3. I give myself utterly to the happiness of someone I love.
4. I feel 'out of sorts' if I have to be by myself for any length of time.
5. I like to hang around with a group of congenial people and talk about anything that comes up.
6. I make as many friends as possible and am on the lookout for more.
7. I accept social invitations rather than stay at home alone.
8. If possible, I have my friends with me wherever I go.
9. I am desperately unhappy if I am separated from the person I love.
10. I make a point of keeping in close touch with the doings and interests of my friends.
11. I become bound by strong loyalties to friends and institutions ; it may be a college, a club, a vocational group or a political party.
12. I make friends rather quickly and feel at ease in a few minutes.
13. I go out of my way just to be with my friends.
14. I make special efforts to promote good feeling when I am with other people.
15. I enjoy co-operating with others more than working by myself.
16. I feel that friendship is more important than anything else.
17. I enjoy myself immensely at parties or other social gatherings.
18. I like to play around with people who don't take life too seriously.
19. I am very free in expressing cordiality and goodwill to others.
20. I have a good word for most people.

Sentiments of Affiliation

1. A man's friends are his magnetisms.
2. The feeling of friendship is like that of being comfortably filled with roast beef.
3. Humanity is not a vain word. Our life is composed of love, and not to love is not to live.

4. The humblest of friendships is a treasure more precious than all the triumphs of genius.
5. One of the greatest experiences in life is to give some of one's innermost soul into the safekeeping of a friend.
6. One cannot be in love with life if he does not love humanity in general.
7. Go often to the house of thy friend, for weeds choke up the unused path.
8. He has achieved success who has lived well, laughed often and loved much.
9. Goodwill subdues its opposite, as water fire.
10. The ornament of a house is the friends that frequent it.
11. It is more important to cultivate the heart than the head.
12. We arrive at wisdom through our intimacies with people.
13. A man's wealth is measured by his friendships.
14. Wherever you go plant companionship as thick as trees.
15. There is no satisfaction in any good without a companion.

n Rejection (n Rej)

Desires and Effects : To separate oneself from a negatively cathected O. To exclude, abandon, expel, or remain indifferent to an inferior O. To snub or jilt an O.

Feelings and Emotions : Disgust, scorn, boredom, indifference.

Trait-names and Attitudes : (a) *Rejective,* exclusive, forbidding, scornful, aloof, haughty, snobbish ; (b) insulated, detached, indifferent ; (c) discriminating, critical, selective.

Kinds of Rejection : Interest (*vide*) may focalize the need.

Press : infraRej p Inferior O. p Repellent O.

supraRej : To reject a disliked superior O, to out-snub a snob.

Actions : General : Vulnerability to annoying, coarse, rude, vulgar, stupid, boring, childish, mean, cheeky, presumptuous, unattractive Os. To be sensitive, easily repelled, hard to please. To adopt a disdainful, forbidding, superior attitude. To remain aloof and indifferent. To be a severe critic. To be unwilling to suffer fools. To demand a high standard of ability, intelligence, wit or imagination. To be very discriminating and critical in the choice of friends and exemplars. To reject a suitor. To break with a friend. To withhold love (N).

Motones : To debar unpleasant Os. To close and lock the door. To avoid meeting stupid people. To cross the street, refuse invitations.

Zonal : Genital : Frigidity and impotence.

Verbones : Silence. 'I shall never speak to you again.' To eliminate or exclude : 'Shut up' — 'Get out of here' — 'Leave the room' — 'I'm through with you.'

Zonal : Oral : Mutism. To be close-mouthed.

Exclusion : To keep out unwelcome intruding Os. To remain secluded and unapproachable. To be psychically insulated. To refrain from intimacies and confidences. To blackball. To refuse to admit, invite, shake hands with, or marry an inferior.

Expulsion : To expel, disinherit, excommunicate.

Abandonment : To desert a child. To drop a friend.

Withdrawal : To leave home. To resign from a group : club, institution, or business. To avoid people. To seek solitude.

Contrarience : To be different from inferior Os. Not to do as the Philistines do. To be distinguished by contrast.

Belittlement : To criticize other Os scornfully (Fn Agg).

Censure : To blame other Os scornfully (Fn Agg).

Fusions with : n Sec (to withdraw so as to enjoy privacy), n Auto (keeping interference at arm's length), n Inf (excluding people who might ridicule), n Agg (to punish an O by exclusion, exile, excommunication, boycotting ; to slander an O as a moral pariah).

Needs to which n Rej may be subsidiary : n Cnt (to reject an O who might reject the S), n Ach (to exclude Os who divert S from the pursuit of his goal), n Aff (to exclude uncongenial Os for the sake of harmony).

Conflicts with : n Aff, n Suc, n Exh, n Nur, n Blam, n Def, n Aba.

intraRej : Criticism, inhibition and repression of what the S considers to be weak, childish, disgusting, or unseemly in himself. Scorn of one's own past.

Social forms : Immigration laws. Institutions, clubs, or places to which only the élite, the cultured or the otherwise distinguished are admitted.

Statements in Questionnaire

1. I am intolerant of people who bore me.
2. I maintain a dignified reserve when I meet strangers.
3. I am very discriminating in my choice of friends.
4. I get annoyed when some fool takes up my time.
5. I am offended by the tastes of many people I meet.

6. I often seclude myself, so that every Tom, Dick and Harry cannot bother me.
7. I usually ignore rather than attack an opponent.
8. I feel superior to certain forms of competition.
9. I find it easy to 'drop' or 'break with' a friend.
10. I avoid very close intimacies with other people.
11. I often cross the street to avoid meeting someone I know.
12. I am indifferent to the petty interests of most of the people I meet.
13. Sometimes I think that the vast majority of people are either fools or knaves.
14. I am a bit scornful of people whose ideas are inferior to my own.
15. I usually keep myself somewhat aloof and inaccessible.
16. I am repelled by people with bad manners.
17. I often snub or 'high-hat' a person I dislike.
18. I often express my resentment against a person by having nothing more to do with him.
19. I will do anything rather than suffer the company of tiresome and uninteresting people.
20. I prefer the company of older, talented or generally superior people.

Sentiments of Rejection

1. Solitude is one of the highest enjoyments of which our nature is capable.
2. Life is a well of delight, but where the rabble drink, there all fountains are poisoned.
3. Fish and visitors smell after three days.
4. The world is full of people who are not worth speaking to.
5. Every blackguard is pitiably sociable, but true nobility is detected in the man who finds no pleasure in the companionship of others.
6. The more I know of men the more I admire dogs.
7. The friendships of the world are oft confederacies in vice.
8. The man who walks in solitude is the one who in the long run achieves the greatest success.
9. Playing around with a crowd of people spoils the character.
10. As a rule, a man is sociable in just the degree to which he is stupid and lazy.
11. Few men are raised in our estimate by being too closely examined.
12. Familiarity breds contempt.
13. Society is a hospital of incurables.

14. Clubs are for the bores and the bored.
15. Love is the business of the idle.

Narcism (N)

Narcism (or Egophilia) is technical for self-love. The term designates the object upon which positive cathexes are localized, namely the *self*. It is often accompanied by obliviousness or disrespect of others.

Direct manifestations. (1) Self-absorption, self-admiration, self-pity, autoerotism ; (2) Superiority feelings and delusions of grandeur ; (3) Self-display and extravagant demands for attention, praise, honour, aid, compassion or gratitude ; and (4) Susceptibility to neglect or belittlement, hypersensitiveness, excessive shyness and delusions of persecution.

Indirect manifestations. (1) Ruthless self-seeking, demands for benefits, attempts to dominate and demonstrate power, delusions of omnipotence ; (2) Object depreciation : indifference, belittlement, exploitation, suspicion or hatred or others, misanthrope ; and (3) Egocentricity and projectivity : the perception and apperception of the world from an entirely personal or subjective standpoint.

These are extreme manifestations of the following : intraDeference, intrAffiliation, intraNurturance, intraSex, n Superiority, n Exhibition, n Succorance, n Inviolacy, n Aggression, n Dominance, n Autonomy and n Rejection.

Antipole of Egophilia is Altrophilia (or object-love). The equator of egophilia and altrophilia is Sociophilia.

Sociophilia. (1) Respect for the commune and forgetfulness of private interests ; (2) Suitable self-confidence, readiness to co-operate, to fulfill any function ; (3) Fair demands, good-natured resiliency ; (4) Justice, thoughtfulness of others ; (5) An objective, social attitude.

Another antipole of Egophilia is *Ego depreciation* : (1) Self-criticism, inferiority feelings and delusions of unworthiness ; (2) Seclusiveness, modesty and humility ; (3) Acceptance of criticism and censure, readiness to confess and atone ; (4) Self-abnegation and abasement ; (5) Deference, acknowledgement and praise of others, self-sacrifice and devotion. This tendency may alternate with Narcism.

Statements in Questionnaire

1. I often think about how I look and what impression I am making upon others.

2. I can become entirely absorbed in thinking about my personal affairs, my health, my cares or my relations to others.
3. My feelings are easily hurt by ridicule or by the slighting remarks of others.
4. When I enter a room I often become self-conscious and feel that the eyes of others are upon me.
5. I dislike sharing the credit of an achievement with others.
6. I love to talk about my innermost feelings to a sympathetic friend.
7. I dislike being with a group unless I know that I am appreciated by at least one of those present.
8. I talk a good deal about myself, my experiences, my feelings and my ideas.
9. I feel that I am temperamentally different from most people.
10. I often interpret the remarks of others in a personal way.
11. I enjoy it immensely when I am left alone with my own thoughts.
12. I feel that my own judgements uncorrupted by other men's experience are most valid.
13. I feel that I should like to write or create something which would express my inner vision of the true values of life.
14. I spend a good deal of time trying to decide how I feel about things and why I feel as I do.
15. I easily become wrapped up in my own interests and forget the existence of others.
16. I feel that I have enough on my hands without worrying about other people's troubles.
17. I feel that other people have not counted much in my life.
18. I am secretly 'put out' when other people come to me with their troubles, asking me for my time and sympathy.
19. I pay a good deal of attention to my appearance : clothes, hats, shoes, neckties.
20. I have great faith in my own ideas and my own initiative.

n Succorance n Nurturance

The n Succorance is the tendency to cry, plead, or ask for nourishment, love, protection or aid ; whereas the n Nurturance is the tendency to satisfy such needs in a succorant O. Thus, the two needs are complements. The Succorance drive seeks a nurturant O and the Nurturant drive seeks a succorant O. The most obvious example is the child-mother relationship. The Succorant need is always a sub-need, in as much as it is evoked in the service of some other drive : n Food, n Water, n Harmavoidance, n Affiliation, and so forth.

n Succorance (n Suc)

Desires and Effects : To have one's needs gratified by the sympathetic aid of an allied O. To be nursed, supported, sustained, surrounded, protected, loved, advised, guided, indulged, forgiven, consoled. To remain close to a devoted protector. To have always a supporter.

Feelings and Emotions : Anxiety of helplessness ; feelings of insecurity, forsakenness, despair.

Trait-names and Attitudes : (a) *Succorant*, dependent, helpless ; (b) forlorn, grieving, tragic ; (c) suppliant, petitioning, begging, pleading.

Press : Negative : p Insupport : Physical (Danger of falling or drowning), Parental (Family Discord, Inferior Father), Economic (Poverty), Social (Insolidarity). p Loss : Death of Parents. p Rejection : Unconcern, Abandonment, Expulsion.

Positive : p Nurturance : Sympathy and Aid.

Gratuities : p Support : Enclosed place (claustrum), Parental (Family Concord), Economic (Family Affluence), Social (Solidarity). p Nurturance and p Affiliation.

Actions : General : To attract or seek out nurturant Os. To capitalize mishaps. To be particularly drawn to nurturant Os — sympathetic Os who are in a position to give advice, aid or support. To crave affection and tenderness. To 'blossom' when treated with kindness. To accept favours unhesitatingly. To enjoy being fussed over. To avoid being alone. To adhere closely to a haven.

Motones : To weep, adopt a pathetic or tragic attitude, hold out arms, extend the hand (beggar's cup). To exhibit wounds. A tantrum of despair.

Zonal : Oral Succorance : To suck nourishment from the breast.

Verbones : To cry for help : 'Murder ! Fire ! Police !' S.O.S. To tell of misfortunes, hardships, accidents and failures. To exaggerate an injury, an illness, a mental symptom. To complain of being miserable, depressed, sad, worried, tired. To appeal to an O's good-nature, mercy or forbearance. To seek advice. To go frequently to doctors.

ideo Suc : To seek aid in arriving at a philosophy of life.
socio Suc : To plead for a cause.

Fusions with : n Harm (to move away from danger towards a protector — a child clinging to its mother), n Aff (anaclitic love — a relationship with a stronger, wiser, nurturant O), n Exh (to make an exhibition of one's wounds), n Aba (to humbly, abasively plead for aid), n Dom (to rely entirely upon servants).

Needs which may be subsidiary to the n Suc : n Aba (to suffer or become sick in order to excite pity and receive undivided love).

Needs to which the n Suc may be subsidiary : Any need, but more particularly : n Food and n Water (crying for nourishment), n Harm (calling for help in a dangerous situation), n Acq (to beg for money, to plead for a toy), n Aff (appeals for friendly sympathy), n Sex (to excite erotic compassion), n Auto (a child crying to get his own way, a petition for freedom), n Dom (to control an O through pity, the despotism of the invalid), n Blam (to ask for clemency), n Nur (to plead in behalf of another O).

Conflicts with : n Cnt, n Ach, n Nur, n Rej, n Dom, n Dfd.

intraSuc : To look within for consoling thoughts. To 'wait upon the spirit.'

Subjns and Semi-objns : Supplications and prayers to deities.

Social forms : Children, orphans and widows. Beggars. Unemployed. The blind, the sick.

Statements in Questionnaire

1. I feel anxious and uncertain when I am suddenly faced by a critical situation.
2. I usually tell my friends about my difficulties and misfortunes.
3. I prefer to have some friend with me when I receive bad news.
4. I think of myself sometimes as neglected or unloved.
5. I find that tears come to my eyes rather easily.
6. I enjoy the comforting realization that I know one or two older people whose wisdom and sympathy I can rely upon.
7. I feel lonely and homesick when I am in a strange place.
8. I like sympathy when I am sick or depressed.
9. I experience a vague feeling of insecurity when I must act on my own responsibility.
10. I am rather easily discouraged when things go wrong.
11. I 'feel out' the opinions of others before making a decision.

12. I like it when people ask me about my health or state of mind.
13. I am rather dependent upon the presence and judgement of my friends.
14. I think that most people are rather self-centred and heartless.
15. I am drawn to women who are sympathetic and understanding.
16. I feel that my lot in life has been a hard one.
17. I am apt to rely upon the judgement of some member of my family.
18. I feel lost and helpless when I am left by someone I love.
19. I am apt to complain about my sufferings and hardships.
20. I want sympathy, affection and understanding more than anything else.

n Nurturance (n Nur)

Desires and Effects : To give sympathy and gratify the needs of a helpless O : an infant or any O that is weak, disabled, tired, inexperienced, infirm, defeated, humiliated, lonely, dejected, sick, mentally confused. To assist an O in danger. To feed, help, support, console, protect, comfort, nurse, heal.

Feelings and Emotions : Pity, compassion, tenderness.

Trait-names and Attitudes : (a) *Nurturant*, sympathetic, compassionate, gentle, maternal ; (b) protective, supporting, paternal, benevolent, humanitarian ; (c) indulgent, merciful, charitable, lenient, forbearing, forgiving, tolerant.

Press : Positive : p Succorance.

supraNur : Caring for a superior O — nursing a sick parent.

Gratuities : Children, dependents.

Agency Objects : Medicines. Also food, candy, money, toys, valuable Os.

Actions : General : To be particularly attracted to the young, the unfortunate, the sorrowing. To enjoy the company of children and animals. To be liberal with time, energy and money when compassion is aroused. To be moved by the distress of others. To feel more affectionate when an O exhibits a weakness. To be moved by tears.

To inhibit narcistic needs in the presence of an inferior O. To refrain from bothering or annoying an O. To be lenient and indulgent. To give freedom. To condone. To become indignant when children are maltreated.

Motones : To do things to gratify the needs of an inferior O. Thus any need may be subsidiary to the n Nur. To embrace, support, defend, heal. To give refuge.

Zonal : Mammary Nur : To give the breast to an infant.

Verbones : To encourage, pity, console, sympathize with an unhappy O. To express condolence. To assuage, calm, appease, pacify, encourage with praise.

Bestowal : To give material Os. To give money to the poor, toys to children, food to wayfarers.

ideo Nur : To encourage creative work. To help a pupil in the construction of a philosophy. To be generous with one's ideas. To be tolerant of the theories of others.

Fusions with : n Aff (a tender affection for a sick friend), n Sex (erotic feeling for an unfortunate person), n Dom (to guide a person for his own good), n Play (to play with children), n Def (to care for a sick parent), n Aba : Atonement (self-sacrifice as an expiation), n Agg (to perform a surgical operation), n Dfd (to defend an abused friend).

Needs which may be subsidiary to the n Nur : n Agg (to fight an O who has been molesting a child), n Sex (to marry solely for children), n Aba (to allow a child to win).

Needs to which the n Nur may be subsidiary : n Aff (protecting an O so as not to lose it), n Dom (doing kindnesses to win votes), n Blam (assisting an O so as not to be considered selfish).

Conflicts : N, n Rej, n Agg, n Harm, n Inf, n Suc, n Ach.

intraNur : Self-pity. Sulk. Pre-occupation with an injury to one's own body — favouring a lame leg.

Subjns and Semi-objns : Worshipping the Christ child. Caring for pets, feeding pigeons and squirrels, watering plants. Playing with dolls.

Social forms : Churches, Charities and Social Service Agencies. Hospitals, asylums, orphanages, almshouses. Societies for the Prevention of Cruelty.

Statements in Questionnaire

1. I take pains not to hurt the feelings of subordinates.
2. I will take a good deal of trouble to help a younger man — to get him a job, to intercede for him or in some other way to further his interests.
3. I go out of my way to comfort people when they are in misery.
4. I enjoy the company of younger people.
5. I give my time and energy to those who ask for it.
6. People are apt to tell me their innermost secrets and troubles.

7. I am easily moved by the misfortunes of other people.
8. I am drawn to people who are sick, unfortunate or unhappy.
9. I am especially considerate of people who are less fortunate than I.
10. I feel great sympathy for an ill-used or defeated 'under-dog,' and I am apt to do what I can for him.
11. I feel the needs and interest of others almost as if they were my own.
12. I often go out of my way to feed, pet or otherwise care for an animal.
13. I enjoy putting my own affairs aside to do someone a favour.
14. I am considered, by some of my friends, as too good-natured, too easily taken in.
15. I praise or otherwise encourage people who are depressed.
16. I sympathize with people more often than I blame them.
17. I am quite gentle and protective in my relations with women.
18. I enjoy playing with children.
19. I feel the failures of my friends as if they were my own.
20. I am always ready to give or lend things to others.

Sentiments of Nurturance

1. Unselfishness and sympathy are more desirable than high ideals and ambitions.
2. Weaklings deserve respect and consideration. The world should not merely belong to the strong.
3. Sweet mercy is nobility's true badge.
4. Altruism is the rock of life.
5. What we win through authority we lose ; what we win through devotion we keep.
6. Pity is the touch of God in human hearts.
7. If you would fall into any extreme, let it be on the side of gentleness.
8. It is not enough to do a generous thing, you must do it generously.
9. Man shall be as the shadow of a great rock in a weary land.
10. We are all born for love. It is the principle of existence and its only end.
11. Pity is the last consecration of love, is, perhaps, love itself.
12. To lay down your life for a friend. This is the summit of a good life.
13. Love is more just than justice.

14. Better do a kindness near home than go far to burn incense.
15. Love is wiser than ambition.

n Blamavoidance Superego

A man living in a society must inhibit, if he wishes to avoid the possibility of punishment, whatever impulses arise which do not conform to the patterns (tpmo formulas) of his culture. The n Blamavoidance is the mechanism which operates to save the individual from the moral censure and retribution of society. The S does not objectify an asocial wish because he fears external punishment (pain, penalty, confinement, rejection). When it is an inner punishment (guilt feelings and remorse) that the S fears, we attribute the inhibition to an additional factor, the Superego.

n Blamavoidance (n Blam)

This variable was not used in the present study, but it is outlined here as an introduction to the two variables that were employed : Superego Integration and Superego Conflict.

Desires and Effects : To avoid blame or rejection (loss of affection). To inhibit narcistic, asocial impulses and to perform altrophilic or sociophilic acts in order not to be rebuked by other Os (parents, teachers, friends). To be inoffensive.

The original form of the need is that of escape, i.e., to flee from punishing Os after a misdeed has been committed. Later, images of punishment become associated with asocial forms of behaviour, and then n Blam becomes an inhibiting force.

Feelings and Emotions : Anxiety and apprehension. Guilt feelings and remorse.

Trait-names and Attitudes : (a) *Blamavoidant*, inhibited, over-anxious, fearful ; (b) scrupulous, unobjectionable, conscientious, conventional, dutiful ; (c) propitiatory, apologetic, remorseful.

Press : p Aggression : Punishment, Censure. p Dominance. p Rejection.

Actions : General : To be concerned about public opinion, what 'the neighbours will say.' To be careful to do nothing that will annoy, antagonize or alienate the affections of others. To be afraid of provoking opposition or hostility. To wonder whether people are disapproving.

Inhibition : To inhibit and repress asocial impulses : narcistic Acq, Agg, Auto, Dom, Exh, Sex. Not to cheat or lie if there is any likelihood of getting caught. To be respectable, polite, courteous, decorous, proper, ethical.

If the n Blam is strong and the asocial impulses are weak the S will always act in a socially-responsible manner. But if an asocial tendency does become objectified (a misdeed or crime is committed) the n Blam will operate in one of several ways :

Fusion with n Aba : apology, contrition, confession, atonement.
with n Sec : concealment, obliteration of clues.
with n Harm : flight, escape from disapprobation.

ideo Blam : To inhibit the expression of unconventional ideas.

Fusions with : n Def (to be obedient in order to avoid blame), n Aff (to please and not to displease), n Nur (to avoid offending an O), n Inf (to avoid the humiliation of censure), n Sec (to be silent and thus to avoid saying anything which might offend).

Needs which may be subsidiary to the n Blam : n Aba (to be humble in order to avoid censure), n Def (excessive politeness in order to avoid punishment), n Dfd (giving excuses in order to avoid blame).

Needs to which n Blam may be subsidiary : n Ach (to avoid offence, to be diplomatic, in order not to provoke opposition), n Auto (to obey the law in order to avoid interference or imprisonment).

Conflicts with : n Auto, n Acq, n Agg, n Exh, n Dom, n Sex.

Measurement : A low n Blam is more easily inferred than a high. It is indicated by selfish, inconsiderate, irritating, asocial, immoral behaviour.

intraBlam : Repression of guilty memories and thoughts.

Subjns and Semi-objns : (*cf.* Superego Conflict) Fantasies of punishment, eternal torture, Hades, Purgatory, an avenging deity.

Statements in Questionnaire

1. I feel upset if I hear that people are criticizing or blaming me.
2. I refrain from expressing unconventional opinions to people who may disapprove of them.
3. I apologize profusely when I am blamed for something.
4. I keep out of trouble at all costs.
5. Before I do something I am apt to consider whether my friends will blame me for it.
6. I never do anything that will provoke opposition if I can help it.

7. I do a great many things just to avoid criticism.
8. I feel mortified if I am told that I have acted selfishly.
9. In coming to a decision I always take other people's interests into account.
10. I take pains not to incur the disapproval of others.

Traces of punishments or threats of punishment or threats of rejection (*cf.* 'Your parents won't love you') become aggregated in a child's mind and fused with the general inhibiting system. This compound of images (of the unhappy consequences that might follow certain forms of behaviour) acts as an internal resistance. This barrier has been named 'Superego' by Freudian analysts. It appears to be a product of the n Blamavoidance, but it is so important that it has been given the status of a separate variable.

Superego (Se)

The Superego may be defined as the aggregate of all the internalized or imaginatively constructed figures of moral authority, functioning as conscious or unconscious images to inhibit or otherwise modify asocial behaviour. This instituted composite of parental and cultural influences corresponds roughly to the system of rewards and punishments administered during childhood.

But the Se is more than the images of punishment which may be anxiously anticipated if certain prohibitions are broken, for when fully developed it is positively cathected by the Ego and accepted as a scheme of ethical principles which must be obeyed (Fn Def Blam). Hence, if narcistic, asocial or 'evil' impulses do become objectified, the subject will submit to self-punishment; that is, there will be guilt feelings and remorse, self-imposed resolutions and prohibitions, confessions and atonements. Thus, the Superego is synonymous with 'conscience.' It may be discerned from this that the Superego process is a subjectified (or semi-objectified) form of the need for Blamavoidance. Instead of the external dominative object, we find a figure of fantasy: the Lord, the God, the Father, the omnipotent, the omnipresent, eternal Judge.

Positive Superego. As a positive force the Superego presents to the individual certain ideals of social or saintly conduct, the conception of a life consecrated to mankind or God. This usually involves objectified, semi-objectified or subjectified forms of the n Deference (obedience) and the n Nurturance (charity).

Negative Superego. The Superego is much more important as a negative or prohibiting force ; its primary function being to inhibit asocial tendencies : narcistic n Acq, n Agg, n Auto, n Sex, etc. If successful in this (intraDominance), it is 'silent,' that is, it only manifests itself negatively by the non-appearance of asocial actions (Superego Integration). If it is only partially successful as an inhibitor, signs of internal conflict may appear : the symptoms of a 'bad conscience' (Superego Conflict). These are :

1. Guilt feelings and remorse. Self-accusations.
2. Morbid anxiety, apprehension, free-floating fear.
3. Nightmares of being pursued, mutilated, devoured, punished.
4. Depressions and suicidal thoughts.
5. Obsessional doubts, perplexities and hesitations.
6. Self-corrective compulsions : repeating, counting, ordering, cleansing, praying. Compulsive thinking.
7. Pre-occupation with moral and religious ideas.

These processes are the result of intrAggression. The needs involved are chiefly the following : n Harm, n Aba, n Suc, and, of course, n Blam.

Statements in Questionnaire : Superego Integration (SeI)

1. I have developed a good deal of self-control.
2. I avoid gay and irresponsible pleasure-seekers.
3. I seldom do anything for which anyone could reproach me.
4. I am scrupulous about telling the truth.
5. I prohibit myself the enjoyment of certain unprofitable pleasures.
6. I control my sexual impulses by instituting prohibitions and restrictions.
7. I carry a strict conscience about with me wherever I go.
8. I have a strong sense of responsibility about my duties.
9. I think that I have a more rigorous standard of right and wrong than most people.
10. I am seldom tempted to do anything wrong.

Statements in Questionnaire : Superego Conflict (SeC)

1. I often ask myself : 'Have I done right ?'
2. I am apt to lower my eyes when someone looks me square in the face.
3. I am sometimes depressed by feelings of my own unworthiness.

4. I feel sometimes that people disapprove of me.
5. I am concerned about moral problems and dilemmas.
6. I have had a few severe nightmares.
7. I feel remorse when I think of some of the things I have done.
8. I am apt to be peculiarly bothered by certain problems which keep recurring to my mind.
9. Sometimes I feel — after I have done something — that I have not done it correctly, and that I must repeat it to satisfy myself.
10. Sometimes I have a vague feeling of anxiety as if I had done wrong and would be found out.

Sentiments of Superego

1. The moral man watches diligently over his secret thoughts.
2. To starve is a small matter ; to lose one's virtue is a great one.
3. I find that there is no worthy purpose but the idea of doing some good in the world.
4. Be not lenient to your own faults ; keep your pardon for others.
5. He that loses his conscience has nothing left that is worth keeping.
6. He conquers who conquers himself.
7. The higher type of man makes a sense of duty the groundwork of his character.
8. The real fault is to have faults and not try to amend them.
9. There is no medicine for a tortured mind.
10. The evil that men do lives after them.
11. It is better to be faithful than famous.
12. Every evil deed brings with it its own angel of vengeance.
13. Not to attain happiness, but to be worthy of it, is the purpose of our existence.
14. Virtue is merely a struggle wherein we overcome our weaknesses.
15. He who says what he pleases, must hear what does not please him.

n Infavoidance — n Defendance
n Counteraction

In this group are to be found the behaviour patterns which resist the descent of a person's status. Under n Infavoidance have been classed desires to avoid situations which might lead to a lowering of self-regard ; under the term n Defendance are grouped the attempts to defend the self verbally against depreciating and belittling judgements, and under n Counteraction we have classified the efforts that are made to regain a valuation of the self by positive action. These were once considered to be different aspects of one need — n Inviolacy : the tendency to maintain status, to remain or become uncriticizable by self or by others.

n Infavoidance (n Inf)

Desires and Effects : To avoid humiliation. To quit embarrassing situations or to avoid conditions which may lead to belittlement : the scorn, derision or indifference of others. To refrain from action because of the fear of failure.

Feelings and Emotions : Inferiority feelings. Before and during an event : nervousness, anxiety, embarrassment. After the event : shame, mortification.

Expressions of Emotionality : Hesitation, speechlessness, confusion, flurry, trembling, blushing, stammering, sweating.

Trait-names and Attitudes : Infavoidant, sensitive, shy, nervous, embarrassed, self-conscious, shrinking.

Narcisensitivity : Susceptibility to adverse opinion. The disposition to be easily 'hurt.'

Kinds of Inferiority : These conform to the classification of interests (*vide*).

Press : p Aggression : Belittlement, Ridicule. p Rejection.

Actions : General : To avoid doing or to stop doing something which one does not do well. To avoid repeating a failure. To be hesitant to make friendly advances. To fear rejection. To be afraid to propose marriage. To avoid tests of strength and athletic skill. To avoid doing things in public. To avoid strangers or critical audiences. To avoid the company of superior contemptuous Os. To associate with inferiors.

Promotion of Ailment : To get sick in order to avoid a difficult situation or test. To escape participation by staying in bed.

Concealment : To hide parts of the body or of the mind. To cover blemishes. To conceal a mutilation or disfigurement : lame foot, withered arm, deafness, freckles, etc. To conceal ignorance. To avoid certain topics of conversation. To conceal humiliating facts.

Withdrawal : In the midst of a humiliating moment to retreat, retire or take flight. To slink out with 'tail between legs.' To resign, change one's job, leave the country.

Fusions with : n Dfd (to offer anticipatory extenuations and justifications), n Sec (to remain silent and unexposed), n Exh (to demonstrate an excellence in order to draw attention from a blemish ; to be conspicuous in order not to be a nonentity), n Aba (to admit inferiority — 'I'm no good at this' — in order to ward off criticism), n Rej (to scornfully exclude Os who have made S feel inferior), n Ach (substitute achievement), n Blam (to avoid moral inferiority and censure).

Needs which may be subsidiary to the n Inf : n Suc (to appeal to another O for assistance), n Rej (infraRejection : to avoid association with inferior Os, so as not to be identified with them), n Def (to let others make decisions in order not to have to take the blame for failure).

Needs to which the n Inf may be subsidiary : n Ach (failures and humiliations detract from S's accomplishments).

Conflicts with : n Ach, n Dom, n Agg, n Acq, n Sex, n Aff, n Exh.

intraInf : To repress and forget humiliations and failures.

Statements in Questionnaire

1. I worry a lot about my ability to succeed.
2. After I have made a poor showing before others, I usually recall the occasion with distress for a long time afterwards.
3. I often avoid open competition because I fear that I may appear in a bad light.
4. I get rattled when I have to speak before a group.
5. I usually lack self-confidence when I have to compete against others.
6. I feel that my self-esteem has been shaken when I fail at something.
7. I keep in the background when I am with a group of confident and boisterous people.
8. I feel nervous if I have to meet a lot of people.
9. I am easily hurt by the snobbishness or exclusiveness of others.
10. I am awkward in asserting myself.
11. Before presenting some work which I have done, I often apologize or explain why it has not been done better.
12. I hesitate to put my abilities to the test, because I dread the humiliation of failure.
13. When I meet a stranger, I often think he is a better man than I am.
14. I often shrink from a situation because of my sensitiveness to criticism and ridicule.

15. I have fits of depression and think of myself as a failure.
16. I am cautious about undertaking anything which may lead to humiliating consequences.
17. I am nervous and apprehensive before taking an important examination or test.
18. I feel embarrassed and uncomfortable in the presence of people who are socially gifted.
19. I think that I have made more than the usual number of blunders for a person of my age.
20. I think that some of my acquaintances look down upon me.

n Defendance (n Dfd)

Desires and Effects : To defend the self against assault, criticism and blame. To conceal or justify a misdeed, failure or humiliation. To vindicate the Ego.

Feelings and Emotions : Guilt feelings, inferiority feelings. Anxiety. Indignation.

Trait-names and Attitudes : Defendant, self-defensive, self-vindicative.

Press : p Aggression : Assault, Punishment, Belittlement, Ridicule, Censure.

Actions : Motones : The S defends himself physically.

Verbones : The S defends himself verbally. He is 'on his guard'; bristles when criticized; has a 'chip on the shoulder'; interprets harmless remarks as slurs. He suppresses his ineptitudes. He resists inquiries into his private affairs. He will not admit guilt under fire. He is ready with excuses. He 'argues back.'

ideo Dfd : The S defends his sentiments and theories.

Vindication : To explain, justify, offer extenuations for, or rationalize inferiority, guilt or failure.

Suppression : To suppress, conceal or fail to mention something which is considered discreditable. To maintain a wall of reserve.

Disavowal : To deny or refuse to admit guilt, inferiority, weakness. To rationalize it away as unimportant. To lie.

Fusions with : n Agg (to fight back, to justify the self by criticizing the accuser), n Suc (to rationalize misdeeds and beg for mercy), n Sec (to remain defensively apart), n Nur (to defend a friend), n Rej (to ignore accusers).

Needs to which the n Dfd may be subsidiary : n Inv (to maintain self-respect), n Harm (to ward off injury), n Blam (to escape censure by justifying one's actions).

Conflicts with: n Aba, n Def, n Aff.

intraDfd: The S condones his own actions. He regains self-respect by thinking of extenuations. Self-justification.

Social forms: Lawyers and Legal Aid Bureaus who defend the accused.

Statements in Questionnaire

1. I can always think of something to say in my own defence.
2. I am put on my guard by anybody who seems to want to know about my personal affairs.
3. I am apt to get into arguments with people who criticize my way of living.
4. I keep my private feelings concealed behind a wall of reserve.
5. If I believe some man is going to snub me I snub him first.
6. I am usually unwilling to admit that I am in the wrong.
7. I can usually find plenty of reasons to explain my failures.
8. I am on the defensive when my abilities are being tested.
9. I usually manage to justify my conduct, to myself and others.
10. I stick to my own opinions when I am opposed.

n Counteraction (n Cnt)

Desires and Effects: To master or make up for a failure by restriving. To obliterate an humiliation by resumed action. To overcome weaknesses, to repress fear. To efface a dishonour by action. To search for obstacles and difficulties to overcome. To maintain self-respect and pride on a high level.

It was not apparent at the time the experiments were being done that the n Counteraction should be regarded as the n Achievement acting as a subsidiation to the n Inviolacy: when an S accomplishes something in order to wipe out or compensate for a failure, disability, etc. The concept is nevertheless useful in so far as it characterizes a particular sort of behaviour: efforts directed towards the hardest goals, unwillingness to receive aid, attempts to efface injuries and belittlements.

Feelings and Emotions: Shame after a failure or an exhibition of cowardice. Determination to overcome. Pride. Zest for restriving.

Trait-names and Attitudes: Counteractive, resolute, determined, indomitable, dauntless, dogged, adventurous.

Kinds of Counteraction : (*vide* Interests).

Press : p Obstacle. A frustration or previous failure.

Actions : The actions are the same as those of the n Ach, with this addition : they are done for pride's sake or for honour's sake. To re-enact after a trauma the same event until anxiety is mastered or, after a failure, to try to accomplish that very thing. The activity that is required depends upon the kind of humiliation that has occurred. The n Cnt is usually focal. For instance : Restriving for Achievement (Econ) : To attempt to make up a financial loss. Traumatic Restriving (Accident) : to make efforts to deal successfully with a formerly traumatic situation.

Independence : To accomplish things unaided. To repress Anxiety, n Harm, n Suc, n Aba, n Inf. Stoical behaviour.

Fusions with : n Ach (to seek adventure and opposition, to enjoy the most difficult tasks), n Agg (to revenge an insult by a superior O), n Auto (to do forbidden things just to prove they can be done), n Dfd (to 'take a dare,' to defend himself against the accusation of cowardice), n Sex (to engage in sexual intercourse so as not to be scorned as inexperienced).

Needs which may be subsidiary to the n Cnt : To do this or that because if the S did not do it he would feel ashamed. n Auto (to refuse to comply for pride's sake), n Agg (to fight so as not to be called a coward).

Conflicts with : n Harm, n Inf, n Suc, n Aba, n Def, n Aff, n Blam.

Subjns and Semi-objns : In dreams, fantasies and play the child overcomes traumas and becomes a hero (counteractive Ego Ideal).

Statements in Questionnaire

1. I often do something just to prove that I can do it.
2. I can usually inhibit an emotion which I do not wish to feel.
3. I enjoy dangerous undertakings.
4. I try to work things out for myself when I am in trouble.
5. I usually refuse to admit defeat.
6. When I get bad news, I hide what I feel and behave as if I didn't care.
7. I go out to meet trouble rather than try to escape it.
8. I return to a task which has stumped me, determined to conquer it.
9. To me a difficulty is just a spur to greater effort.

10. Sometimes I feel that I must do everything myself, that I can accept nothing from others.
11. I am apt to turn away from those who try to sympathize with me.
12. I dislike it when I am asked about my health or about my frame of mind.
13. I would rather go without something than ask a favour.
14. I usually refuse to admit that I am tired or disappointed when I am.
15. I am determined to conquer all my fears and weaknesses.
16. I usually say 'No' when others offer to assist me.
17. I will go to any length rather than be called a quitter.
18. I often refuse to take suggestions from others out of pride.
19. I seldom admit that I feel embarrassed or inferior.
20. I prefer difficult tasks to easy ones.

n Harmavoidance — Anxiety

The primitive reaction of withdrawal from a painful stimulus and the tendency to fear and avoid such stimuli at a distance have been grouped with other acquired fears (fears of bodily injury, disfigurement, illness and death) under the heading Harmavoidance drive. n Infavoidance and n Blamavoidance are supposedly derived from (originally conditioned to) the n Harmavoidance.

n Harmavoidance (n Harm)

Desires and Effects: To avoid pain, physical injury, illness and death. To escape from a dangerous situation. To take precautionary measures.

Feelings and Emotions: Fear, anxiety, apprehension. Fright, terror.

Expressions of Emotionality: Trembling, sweating, pallor, stammering, verbal disjunctivity.

Trait-names and Attitudes: (a) *Apprehensive*, fearful, anxious, timid, frightened, panic-stricken, pusillanimous; (b) cautious, hesitant, wary, prudent, careful, vigilant.

Press: Negative: p Danger: Physical danger, Infection; p Insupport.
Positive: p Refuge; p Nurturance.

Kinds of Fear: (a) Natural dangers: Lightning, earthquakes, volcanoes, storms at sea, floods, tornadoes, fire.
(b) Animals: wild animals, bulls, watch dogs, snakes, rats, etc.

(c) Accidents: railroad, automobile, airplane. Also falling from heights, riding horseback, drowning.

(d) Brutality: rough games, boxing, fighting, gangsters, burglars, enemies.

(e) Physical punishment: spanking, flogging, torture, mutilation.

(f) Infections: general or specific: gonorrhoea, syphilis, fevers.

Agency Objects: Lifeboat, lifebelt, fire extinguisher, fire escape, parachute, weapons of defence, drugs, antitoxin, disinfectants, etc.

Actions: General: To avoid danger. To be cautious and hesitant about undertaking something. To hang back; shun, evade, or shrink from a perilous situation.

Flight: To recoil, retreat, draw back, withdraw or flee from danger.

Concealment: To hide from an enemy. To stand still and make no noise so as to be unobserved. Immobilization reaction (sham-death).

Prevention: This form becomes fused with intraHarm (fear of internal disease). To avoid infection. To avoid contact with contaminated Os. To take measures to prevent illness: to wear rubbers or a heavy coat, to abstain from alcohol and certain foods, to be inoculated. To take drugs — alkalis, etc.

ideo Harm: The fear and avoidance of disturbing ideas and doctrines. To inhibit the expression of beliefs because of the fear that they will be disproved, that one will be left without strong supporting convictions.

Fusions with: n Dfd (to defend the self against assault), n Inf (to avoid both injury and humiliation), n Blam (to inhibit asocial tendencies in order to escape physical punishment), n Sec (to seclude one's self and avoid harm).

Needs which may be subsidiary to the n Harm: n Suc (S.O.S., to go to a doctor for assistance), n Acq (to acquire a protective weapon), n Cons (to build an ambush), n Aba (to surrender in order to avoid further injury), n Def (to follow a guide in order to avoid danger), n Aff (to take a friend along in case of danger), n Agg (to have an enemy put to death).

Needs to which the n Harm may be subsidiary: n Ach (to keep well in order to accomplish something), n Nur (to keep well in order to be able to nurse a child), n Exh (to keep well for appearances' sake).

Conflicts with: n Ach, n Cnt, n Rej, n Dom, n Agg, n Def, n Aff, n Nur.

intraHarm: (a) Fear and avoidance of illness and death. Hypochondria. Bodily phobias: fear of heart disease, cancer, stomach trouble, etc.

Avoidance of exertion. Cautious dieting. Excessive rest and sleep. This may occur with Prevention (extraHarm). It is also closely associated with Superego Anxiety (*cf.* n Blam). (b) Fear and inhibition of overpowering asocial impulses. Fear of mental confusion and chaos. Fear of insanity.

Subjns and Semi-objns : Nightmares. Delusory fears. Belief in Hell and the Devil.

Pathology : Ucs Fears : Autonomic neuroses : tachycardia, hyperthyroidism, asthma, gastric ulcer, colitis, etc. Free-floating anxiety. Fear of closed or open spaces. Specific phobias. (*cf.* n Blam : Superego Conflict.)

Statements in Questionnaire

1. I avoid passing through certain districts at night on account of a vague fear of assault.
2. I think that I would be timid and fearful if I were challenged to a fight.
3. I fear certain things, such as lightning, high places, rough water, horseback riding, aeroplaning, etc.
4. I am conscious of a vague fear of death.
5. I am afraid of physical pain.
6. Sometimes I experience a vague dread that I may be attacked by someone.
7. Sometimes I fear that I may be injured in an accident.
8. I am afraid of certain animals : snakes, bulls, watchdogs, etc.
9. I am somewhat afraid of the dark.
10. I am apt to be apprehensive when I am alone in an empty house at night.

Anxiety (Anx)

Experience and reflection led us to divide apprehensive avoidance reactions into three classes : Harmavoidance, Infavoidance, Blamavoidance. These distinctions are based chiefly on the press that are feared and avoided : an object that can cause physical pain, an object that can scorn and belittle, an object that can morally blame and punish, respectively. The feelings and emotions are similar in the three classes and the reactions are often alike : riddance, avoidance or inhibition. Whether we were wise in making the above divisions is questionable. Being uncertain, we decided to add another variable, Anxiety, which would stand for apprehension and worry of every sort. This factor includes all emotional reactions associated with the three avoidances (n Harm, n Inf and n Blam), as well as those related to other possible sources of dissatisfaction (worry about collegiate standing, money matters, love and so forth). The objective signs of Anxiety have already been described.

n Order
Conjunctivity/Disjunctivity
Sameness/Change
Impulsion/Deliberation
Emotionality/Placidity

The variables in this group are all related to the degree of organization, stability or rigidity of a personality. The n Order describes behavioural trends that are directed towards the organization of a subject's immediate environment : cleanliness and care of his body and its vestments ; arrangement of his possessions, putting everything in its proper place ; orderliness of bureau drawers, desk, books, furnishings ; upkeep of his garden, lawn, car ; neatness and scrupulous precision in his work. Conjunctivity describes co-ordination of movement, speech, and purposes, the 'shape' of a person's day and the orderly progression of his life. Sameness stands for fixation and repetition : consistency, dependability and rigidity of character. Deliberation describes the tendency to reflect before acting, to consider all sides of a question, to plan out a course of behaviour. Placidity stands for a calm, passive, phlegmatic or well-controlled emotional system. Co-variation of these factors is common, but not by any means universal.

n Order (n Ord)

The n Order seems to be related to the n Construction (*cf.* creation of forms), a need which is not included in this study ; to Sameness (*cf.* repetition compulsions) ; to a high Superego and to the n Blamavoidance (*cf.* scrupulousness and precision to avoid censure). In a sublimated form it may be related to the n Sentience (enjoyment of balance and significant design), particularly if there is a preference for classical art forms ; though artists themselves, in respect to their personal appearance and belongings, are proverbially unkempt and disorderly. It is as if their need for Order was expressed in their creative work, and that everything else, including themselves, was left in disorder.

Desires and Effects : To put things in order. To achieve cleanliness, arrangement, organization, balance, neatness, tidiness and precision.

Feelings and Emotions : Disgust at disorder.

Actions : General : To be neat and clean in one's personal appearance. To sit and move about in an orderly, restrained manner. To arrange work, dust off the table, put things in their place. To have a special place for everything. To straighten things. To write neatly in a straight line, erase, keep papers clean, copy a page if it is untidy. To keep accounts. To be exact and precise in speech, in the routine of the day and in transactions with others. To be scrupulous. To aim for perfection in details. To keep a room in order ; to sweep, dust, polish ; to hang pictures straight ; to arrange the furniture ; to pick-up. To keep a country place in order, mow the lawn, cut the hedge, rake the path, throw away rubbish.

Fusions with : n Ach, n Sen, n Blam, n Inf, n Aba, n Exh.

Conjunctivity (Conj)

This is scored as the ratio of Conjunctivity to Disjunctivity (Conj/Disj). Some persons function in a coherent, co-ordinated and integrated fashion ; others are confused, unco-ordinated, and disorganized. We have used the term Conjunctivity to describe the former and Disjunctivity to describe the latter.

It is convenient to distinguish :

First-degree Conjunctivity : co-ordination and organization in performing a single unit of work.

Second-degree Conjunctivity : organization and integration of interests as exemplified by a subject's behaviour during a phase or epoch of his life : harmony among purposes, freedom from conflict, well-ordered plan of life.

In the laboratory only first-degree conjunctivity can be observed. It may be recognized as an attribute of motones, verbones or trends of behaviour.

1. Motor Conjunctivity: muscular co-ordination, integration of skilled movements, manual dexterity and athletic skill. Manual dexterity may be measured by special tests.

2. Verbal Conjunctivity: verbal clarity, coherence of ideas, rationality of thought. Lucid well-structured sentences.

3. Conative Conjunctivity: co-ordination of purposeful trends, organized behaviour, economy of movements that reflect regnant processes: intentions and decisions.

Statements in Questionnaire

Conjunctivity

1. I know what I want to say without having to fumble about for the right word.
2. I stick to a plan of action which I have decided upon.
3. I am on time for my appointments.
4. I am systematic and methodical in my daily life.
5. I usually get through my work efficiently without wasting time.
6. I organize my daily activities so that there is little confusion.
7. When I have to undertake something difficult, I make out a scheme of procedure.
8. I can maintain the thread of a conversation without making unnecessary digressions.
9. I say what I have to say in a few simple words so that I am easily understood.
10. I have arranged my life so that it runs smoothly and without conflict.

Disjunctivity

1. I have so many ideas that my conversation lacks clarity and continuity.
2. I find it difficult to exclude irrelevant ideas and pin myself down to one line of thought.
3. I go about my work in a somewhat inefficient and unco-ordinated manner, making many useless moves.
4. I often go from one thing to another in my daily life without much plan or organization of thought or action.
5. I lack simplicity, consecutiveness and logical sequence when I try to explain something to someone.

6. I often interrupt the trend of a person's thought by interposing inconsequential ideas or by describing a personal anecdote.
7. I find it difficult to lead an orderly life because my impulses are so conflicting.
8. I am somewhat fitful and contradictory in some of the opinions I advance.
9. My desires are often at war with one another.
10. There are times when my life lacks clear purpose, order or design.

Sameness (Sa)

Here the score is based on the ratio of Sameness to Change (Sa/Ch). Sameness is measured in terms of (1) degree of fixation, (2) frequency of repetition and (3) degree of rigidity.

Sameness. (1) Fixation. To measure the degree of fixation the S must be observed (or a history must be obtained) over a span of months and years. The characteristic finding is that the same object, or the same class of objects, is cathected from year to year. These are some of the signs : to adhere to one place (the same room, house, neighbourhood, city) ; to select a few chosen pathways and haunts (the same streets, restaurants, shops) ; to like and associate with the same people (members of the family, school and college friends) ; to maintain the same tastes, sentiments and beliefs (political party, preferred authors, creed) ; to wear the same clothes, smoke the same brand of cigarettes, like the same dishes, enjoy the same music, etc.

(2) Repetition. This applies to regularity of routine, moods, modes of behaviour and purposes. Characteristic attributes : to rise at the same time, exhibit a consistent attitude, follow a prescribed order of behaviour, use stereotyped gestures and modes of speech ; to be a 'creature of habit' : dependable and consistent.

(3) Rigidity. This stands for a lack of plasticity, a dislike of novelty, an inability to change cathexes or modes when conditions require it.

Change. (1) Lack of Fixation. To have no fixed habitat, to enjoy moving from place to place, to wander and travel. To have few permanent attachments. To seek novelty, experiment, adventure. To be fickle in love. To enjoy new sights, new books, new people, new ideas.

(2) Lack of Repetition. To be irregular in rising, eating, working, playing and resting. To exhibit mood swings, unpredictable responses, sudden inconsistencies of purpose.

(3) Plasticity. The ability to move, change loyalties or adopt new modes of behaviour when necessary.

Sameness represents the conserving force in nature. It binds and holds things together. It is the power of association. It brings about the structuration of function. Memory is based upon it. It leads to repetition which is a necessary part of the learning process. Repetition is also used as a disciplinary measure. The child is taught to repeat correctly whatever he has done incorrectly. Thus such actions become associated with Superego activity, repetition being the commonest of the self-corrective compulsions.

Sameness men are set in a mould ; *Change* men are as unstable as the weather. The reactions of the former are predictable, their interests constant, their attachments fixed. The latter, on the other hand, are flexible. They change their methods, their habits and their preferences. They are more adaptable, more easily influenced, readier to shift their allegiances from one object to another. They are opportunists who are usually, but not always, impersistent. If they do persist in an endeavour to reach a goal, they are quite ready to change their tactics, their loyalties and their principles to attain it. Sameness seems to increase with age.

Statements in Questionnaire

Sameness

1. I can become devotedly attached to certain places, certain objects and certain people.
2. I am somewhat disturbed when my daily habits are disrupted by unforeseen events.
3. I respect custom and consequently am somewhat resistant to untested innovations.
4. I find that many of my tastes and sentiments have remained relatively constant.
5. I am guided in my conduct by certain principles which I have accepted.
6. I find that a well-ordered mode of life with regular hours and an established routine is congenial to my temperament.
7. I am consistent and dependable in my dealings with others.
8. I am a creature of habit ; I can even endure monotony without fretting.
9. I prefer to associate with my old friends, even though by so doing I miss the opportunity of meeting more interesting people.

10. I am usually consistent in my behaviour : go about my work in the same way, frequent the same preferred places ; follow the same routes, etc.

Change

1. I crave variety and contrast ; enjoy anything for a change.
2. I frequently start new projects without waiting to finish what I have been doing.
3. I find that novel prospects — new places, new people, new ideas — appeal to me immensely.
4. I have often experienced rather marked 'swings of mood' from elation to depression.
5. I could cut my moorings — quit my home, my parents and my friends — without suffering great regrets.
6. At times I act and express myself quite differently than I do ordinarily.
7. I find it difficult to keep to any routine.
8. I find that my likes and dislikes change quite frequently.
9. I am quick to discard the old and accept the new : new fashions, new methods, new ideas.
10. I am rather fickle in my affections.

Impulsion (Imp)

This is scored as the ratio of Impulsion to Deliberation (Imp/ Del).

Impulsion is the tendency to respond (with a motone or verbone) quickly and without reflection. It is a rather coarse variable which includes : (1) short reaction time to social press, (2) quick intuitive behaviour, (3) emotional drivenness, (4) lack of forethought, (5) readiness to begin work without a carefully constructed plan. The S is usually somewhat restless, quick to move, quick to make up his mind, quick to voice his opinion. He often says the first thing that comes into his head ; and does not always consider the future consequences of his conduct.

Statements in Questionnaire

1. I often act on the spur of the moment without stopping to think.
2. I waste no time in asking for what I want.
3. I often act impulsively just to blow off steam.

4. I have a ready word for most occasions.
5. I act as the spirit moves me, obeying whatever impulse is strongest.
6. When I have to act, I am usually quick to make up my mind.
7. Sometimes I start talking without knowing exactly what I am going to say.
8. I am easily carried away by an emotional impulse.
9. I am apt to say anything — though I may regret it later — rather than keep still.
10. I am rather spontaneous in speech and action.

Deliberation is easier to observe than Impulsion. It is marked by : (1) long reaction time to social press, (2) inhibition of initial impulses, (3) hesitation, caution and reflection before action, (4) a long period of planning and organizing before beginning a piece of work. The S may have obsessional doubts : a 'load' of considerations which he must 'lift' before beginning. He usually experiences difficulty in an emergency.

Statements in Questionnaire

1. When suddenly confronted by a crisis I often become inhibited and do nothing.
2. I repress my emotions more often than I express them.
3. I think much and speak little.
4. I am slow to decide upon a course of action.
5. I consider a matter from every standpoint before I form an opinion.
6. I am slow to fall in love.
7. I usually make a plan before I start to do something.
8. I dislike making hurried decisions.
9. I do most things slowly and deliberately.
10. I am poor at repartee, quick retorts, snap-judgements.

Emotionality (Emo)

This variable is estimated in terms of the frequency, intensity and duration of manifest emotion (emotional expression) and of reported 'felt' emotion. The following are signs : To be frequently excited ; to show emotion (anxiety, fear, embarrassment, anger, elation, affection, grief) on slight provocation ; to speak with passion ; to exhibit marked fluctuations of mood ; to exhibit autonomic changes : trembling, sweating, blushing, palpitation of the heart, stuttering, inco-ordination of movement.

Statements in Questionnaire

1. My feelings and emotions are easily aroused.
2. I give full vent to my sentiments when I am stirred.
3. I have unaccountable swings of mood, elations and depressions.
4. I am considered somewhat excitable by my friends.
5. I am rather sensitive, impressionable and easily stirred.
6. I have intense likes and dislikes.
7. I display 'temper' when the occasion warrants it.
8. I can get quite 'heated-up' over some matter which interests me.
9. I find it difficult to control my emotions.
10. I am influenced in my decisions by how I happen to be feeling at the time.

The opposite of Emotionality is termed Placidity.

Statements in Questionnaire

1. I am calm and placid most of the time.
2. I usually express myself dispassionately, with caution and restraint.
3. I take part in things without much display of enthusiasm.
4. I am moderate in my tastes and sentiments.
5. It takes a good deal to make me angry.
6. I am considered rather phlegmatic by my friends.
7. I find that my life moves along at an even tenor without many ups and downs.
8. I do things in a leisurely sort of way without worry or irritation.
9. My emotional life is marked by moderation and balance.
10. I am rarely very excited or thrilled.

Creativity (Cr)

Creativity was introduced to describe responses that were neither repetitious, consistent, stereotyped, rigid, banal (Sameness) nor random, merely novel, sensational, irresponsible, inconsistent, fickle, odd (Change). The variable was applied to insightful adaptations to new conditions (ingenuity, intuition, quick learning). This might be called 'behavioural' Creativity.

The term was most especially employed, however, to cover originality and imagination in the handling of words and ideas (artistic and scientific thought). As many of our procedures called for imaging, plot construction and story-telling the artistic type of imagination was given more opportunity to display itself than was the conceptual. Thus our marks on this variable were in most cases based on judgements of the quality of literary fancy and creativeness.

Intensity Endurance

These variables may be regarded as two measures of liberated vital energy (a concept which was discussed at some length in the preceding chapter, *vide* p. 129). We shall not review the evidence already presented, but shall content ourselves with a brief list of the manifestations of energy :

1. Subjective and objective signs of zest : alertness, vitality, vigour, enthusiasm, effort.

2. Subjective and objective signs of activity pleasure (enjoyment of action 'for its own sake' : physical exercise, conversation, thought).

3. Long periods of activity (n Play or n Achievement), few or short periods of rest ; the ability to get along without sleep.

4. A large amount of random motility (physical or verbal) : restlessness, excessive motion, talkativeness, abundance of extravagant language, etc.

5. Speed, strength and long duration of all behavioural reactions. At this point one can hardly differentiate between general energy and drival energy.

Energy also leads to vigorous emotional responses (particularly of lust and anger). It has been found convenient to divide this factor into two variables, Intensity and Endurance.

Intensity (Int)

Some persons impress themselves more forcefully than others upon the objects of their environment. They are more 'energetic.' Various aspects of this factor may be represented by the following common words : power, strength, force, gusto, zest, eagerness, enthusiasm, emphasis, vividness, loudness, demonstrativeness. All these may be regarded as evidences of tension, effective or affective, liberated in a moment of time. The tension may express itself by an unusual number or a marked strength of physical or verbal acts. The demonstration may not endure. It may be followed by a period of temporary exhaustion. The opposite of Intensity is Apathy.

An apathetic S may :

move about in a slow and lethargic manner ; sink into a chair, loll, slouch, lie back with feet outstretched, yawn, sigh, appear to be fatigued ; look with ennui and without enthusiasm at people and things ; appear unconcerned, disinterested, supercilious, bored ;

relax his muscles ; wear a placid, unresponsive countenance ; respond slowly and without emotion ; work lazily without manifesting effort or concern ;

express himself but little and then without ardour ; speak quietly in a low voice or in a monotone without inflection or emphasis, as if his words were not important and he did not care whether he were heard or not ; use flat, banal expressions ; show little emotion, except possibly shyness, timidity, apprehension or nervousness.

Statements in Questionnaire

1. I am intense about the things which interest me.
2. I go at things with considerable zest and gusto.
3. I feel fresh, vigorous and ready for anything, most of the time.
4. I express myself with emphasis when I am interested in a topic.
5. I work hard when I work, and play hard when I play.
6. I am energetic in the development and expression of my ideas.
7. I work like a fiend at a problem that interests me.
8. I spend myself freely, since I have plenty of energy.
9. Sometimes I tackle a job as if my life depended on it.
10. I can expend a great deal of effort in a short time.

Endurance (End)

This variable was selected to stand for the persistence of effort (vigorous activity). Intensity expresses how hard a man works ; Endurance how long he works. The latter is an easier concept to deal with, because it is simply a matter of determining the duration of directed action. When it is mental activity that is being measured, however, there may be some difficulty (unless it is accompanied by verbal expression) to rule out undirected fantasy.

In the clinic it is hardly possible to measure Endurance. The sessions are too short and other factors, such as the amount of interest that is aroused by a given task, are too obtrusive.

The S with low Endurance may:

show signs of fatigue even when dealing with interesting material; fall off in his performance as time goes on; complain of weariness; explain that he has not had enough sleep; find it difficult to concentrate for any length of time, etc.

The rating on this variable is based mostly on the subject's autobiographical reports.

Statements in Questionnaire

1. I can work at an arduous task for a long time without getting tired of it.
2. I can stand very long periods of exertion.
3. I am a horse for work. I am seldom exhausted.
4. I finish most everything I commence.
5. I can enjoy a long spell of continuous activity.
6. I stick at a job even though it seems I am not getting results.
7. I enjoy long discussions. They rarely weary me.
8. I am able to keep working, day in and day out, without getting bored or tired.
9. I can get along with less than the average amount of rest and sleep.
10. I usually persist in the pursuit of a purpose. My motto is: 'Never say die.'

Extraception/Intraception Projectivity/Objectivity
Exocathection/Endocathection

With this group of variables the attempt was made to segregate some of the factors which were included by Jung under the terms extraversion and introversion (*vide* the discussion of Jung's concepts, p. 232). We were concerned first with what is commonly called subjectivity and objectivity, a dichotomy which we found great difficulty in formulating. The former (called by us Intraception) seemed to be an attitude that is engendered by strong personal feelings, fantasies, sentiments, and wishful speculations ; whereas the latter attitude (Extraception) seems to depend on the determining influence of sense data (physical and social factors) and the disposition to come into accord with them. The subjective attitude leads to self-expression and the emotional valuation of events. The objective attitude leads to the dispassionate recognition of fact, as well as to conformity in social behaviour (reasonableness). These tendencies are only opposites in the sense that one arises out of internal conditions and the other is provoked by external requirements. As with all other contrasting variables they are both exhibited in some measure by everyone. It is only for convenience that one speaks of intraceptors and extraceptors.

Endocathection describes a turning inward (reverie or reflection) and a cathexis of the products of mental activity. This is different from Intraception, for a man may turn outward to engage in practical affairs (Exocathection) with his head full of romantic aspirations and ideals (Intraception) ; or he may turn inward (Endocathection) to speculate about the physical properties of Nature (Extraception). Projectivity describes the tendency to misinterpret (because of the influence of desire, emotion, and sentiment) natural and social occurrences, the motivations of others and one's own inner experiences.

Extraception (Extra)

This is scored as the ratio of Extraception to Intraception. Extraception is a term that describes the tendency to be determined by concrete, clearly observable, physical conditions (tangible, objective facts). The sense of touch seems to control the personality, material substance, in one form or another, being the most undeniable (*cf.* Dr. Johnson kicking the stone) and valued fact. The subject is drawn to solid things. He needs them to support his locomotions (*cf.* 'He keeps his feet on the ground'), to employ as tools, to sustain his sense of reality. He likes to explore his surroundings, observe the workings of Nature, and produce tangible results. His thinking is dominated by the disposition t bring ideas into accord with observed facts or by the need t further some practical aim. Thus a person of this type (extra ceptor) has an inclination to invent implements, construct ma chinery or engage in experimental research. In human dealing extraception leads to an emphasis upon overt behaviour and ob servable traits, the tendency to accept social standards, and readiness to co-operate impersonally in group activity.

Intraception, on the other hand, is the disposition to be deter mined by diffuse personal feelings and inclinations (intangibl subjective facts). For such a man the desire for happiness seem basic. Thinking is dominated at first by fantasies : wishful crea tions or imaginative reconstructions of external happenings. Late the intraceptor may attempt to describe his emotional impression of actual events or to conceptualize the facts of his inner life The behaviour of the intraceptor is very apt to be the outcome o mere energy, of a mood, a fantasy (ex : play of children), cherished scheme, romantic desires or utopian speculations. Th intraceptor is controlled by a valuating (aesthetic or moral) atti tude which impels him to make judgements (that may be of de ciding importance) as to the human good of this or that, bu which interferes with his disinterested observation of objectiv occurrences. In his relations to other people the intraceptor is in clined to make immediate inferences as to their affections an motivations ; he becomes personal and subjective and finds it diffi cult to co-operate with those whose sympathies he does not share

The extraceptor is commonly characterized by several of th following adjectives : objective, factual, accurate, impersonal, prac tical, denotative in speech, empirical, utilitarian, impartial, coo and phlegmatic, reasonable in action, insensitive, sociocentric conforming, tough-minded, inductive, systematic in observations scientific, psychologically superficial, materialistic, mechanistic pluralistic.

The following adjectives are commonly used to describe the intraceptor : subjective, imaginative (fanciful), somewhat in- accurate, personal in his dealings, impractical, connotative in speech, metaphysical, partial in his opinions, warm and passionate, 'unreasonable' in action, sensitive, egocentric, individualistic, tender-minded, deductive, intuitive in his observations, artistic or religious, psychologically penetrating, idealistic, dynamistic, monistic or dualistic.

It is very difficult to describe these two tendencies since they manifest themselves in so many ways; the differences among extraceptors or among intraceptors (due to other factors) being as great as the differences between extraceptors and intraceptors.

Extraceptive perception and apperception are marked by the exclusion of everything except bare sense data (objective facts): tangible objects and their physical relations and the outward behaviour of other people. It is usually orderly, systematic and conventional.

Intraceptive perception and apperception on the other hand are characterized by the intrusion of affections and images evoked by the facts: sentiments, imaginal elaborations, symbolic meanings, interpretations of the feelings and motives of other people. It is selective; emphasizing and elaborating upon one or more details to the exclusion of others.

The intraceptive mode of apperception seems to be basic to an intuitive understanding of other people. It may be largely unconscious and inarticulate; and it is certainly liable to err grossly, but there is no other way of immediately apprehending the primary tendencies which explain the multiplicity of superficially dissimilar phenomena. The organism, as a whole, is controlled by regnant processes in the brain, and for these we have only terms which represent their subjective aspect. Thus, to understand human beings in a dynamical situation we must know what motivating forces are in operation at the moment, and since these are concealed and cannot be perceived, they must be inferred. The fundamental process involved in making this inference is 'participation' (empathy, emotional apperception). This primitive process is natural to children, and well developed in artists and women. It is enhanced by passivity and obstructed by a highly conscious, critical, and rationalistic attitude. The intraceptive person who becomes conscious and critical of his own psychology may learn to correct for the projections which commonly occur, and by constant practice his interpretations of others may become reasonably reliable. The extraceptive person, on the other hand, by not using the process of 'participation,' permits it to remain in an undeveloped state. Thus he may be confused by complex emotional situations, and he will be deficient in his interpretations of the more irrational phases of human experience : dreams, fantasies, the play and perversities of children, the erotic impulses of adolescents, the religious practices of savages, the poetical and metaphysical utterances of adults, the vagaries of neurotic and psychotic patients.

If an extraceptive person becomes personally implicated in a tense emotional situation, or if he is asked in a test to interpret the underlying motives of some other individual, he will often project more than the intraceptive person. This is to say, there will be a greater degree of personal reference in his interpretations than in the explanations given by an intraceptor of equal age and development. The reason for this is that participation is an undifferentiated process in the extraceptor. It has never been exposed to the discipline of self-criticism.

The extraceptive attitude usually involves conscious attention to external affairs and a separation of the ego from the unconscious. Though such people are usually alert, with a clear focus of consciousness, the area of consciousness is relatively small ; since they are not continuously influenced by nor aware of the intraceptor's marginal, semi-conscious flow of imagery and feeling. Looking at the matter from this standpoint, the extraceptive person seems to be extraordinarily simple, uncomplicated and unconscious. What is not plain and outspoken is for him non-existent. For this reason the person with extraceptive apperceptions will find that dealing with physical phenomena, as in strict science, is an enterprise especially congenial to his temperament.

Extraceptive thinking is predominantly inductive. It leads to the explanation of natural events in terms of the mechanical interaction of physical bodies, and of human events in terms of bodily appetites, economic pressures and social custom. It starts from bare facts or practical operations, analyses them, constructs classifications and finally arrives at generalizations (useful fictions) which describe the data in a summary form. It is anti-sentimental, disinterested and skeptical. It is congenial to operationism and positivism (*vide* the discussion of peripheralists and centralists, p. 6).

Intraceptive thinking is apt to be deductive, its deepest sources being vague diffuse feelings (acceptances and rejections). It leads quite naturally to the development of social, aesthetic, philosophical or religious theories. Such theories are usually influenced by wishes, by optimistic or pessimistic sentiments or by experienced values. As a rule the intraceptive thinker strives for internal coherence, logical form, and aesthetic balance. But the fruits of his cerebration may also take the form of metaphorically phrased mystical ideas or sharp aphoristic illuminations. Despite its habitual subjective bias, intraceptive thinking has made numberless contributions to science (ex : Periodic Law in Chemistry). For the emergence of a seemingly plausible generalization often acts as a stimulus which impels the thinker to seek illustrative exemplifications in the external world. There is a tendency among intraceptors to explain physical occurrences as resultants of energic processes and to interpret human action in terms of motivating forces (ex : the world will, *élan vital*, libido, demi-urge, instinct).

Extraceptive action is aimed at the achievement of tangible results : manufacture of objects, money, power, status, office, prestige. It is practical and usually effective, since much attention is paid to technique and method. It strives for quantity, speed and economy. Its ends have survivalistic or comfort-giving value. This is best manifested by applied science and business. The extraceptor is inclined to regard human beings as objects to be manipulated. He is sensible and hard-boiled.

Intraceptive action is the outcome of personal feelings, 'hunches,' valuations, enthusiasms. It expresses the personality, gives vent to a point of view or objectifies desire. The action is often a catharsis or self-dramatization, which is not always adapted to the imagined goal, though it may have considerable inner value. This is best manifested by the play of children, dancing, courtship and artistic creations. It is an intraceptor that is usually the initiator of a new movement, but extraceptors are required to make it function effectively.

Extraceptive feeling is apt to conform to the pattern of the culture. It leads to social adaptation and co-operation. It induces the subject to join and become an effective member of groups and institutions, particularly those of good standing. Such a person is usually restrained and matter of fact. He enjoys plain dealings with plain people, and avoids situations that may become too personal, for he is uncomfortably disturbed by irrational processes in others as well as in himself. Engaged in social action he can submerge his personality and endure co-operation and routine without revolt. He may express a good deal of fellow-feeling but his appreciation of art and his understanding of psychological subtleties are usually meagre. Most of his tastes and sentiments are echoes of authoritative judgments. He chooses what is generally considered good, in contrast to the intraceptor who accepts only what is good for him.

Intraceptive feeling is personal and individualistic ; and often opposed to current opinion. It commonly takes the form of aesthetic or moral tastes and sentiments. It may lead the subject to prefer solitude or the company of a few congenial friends ; or possibly to choose writing as a medium of self-expression. Though sensitive, the intraceptor is often impelled to make vehement public declarations of his views. He may be expansive, or given to daydreaming and self-analysis. In any case he cannot abide a cold, indifferent human climate. He blossoms when he feels that he is warmly appreciated. Being more aware of his feelings than the extraceptor, he is quick to realize what is humanly wrong in existing social conditions. Thus, he is apt to sympathize with the individual rather than with the group (authorities). His temperament is that of an artist and at some point one can always find tenderness, wonder and reverence.

It should be pointed out that there may be an ambitendency involving Intraception and Extraception. An individual may veer from one extreme to another. Particularly is it likely that an essentially intraceptive person will come to hold an extraceptive doctrine. He may be forced to adopt this attitude as a balance to an extreme emotionality in everyday life, or he may come to it because of the respectability it now enjoys. Thus, a man's expressed theories cannot be used as infallible indices of the Extraceptive/Intraceptive ratio. We suspect, for instance, that many who violently attack Intraception are attempting unconsciously to rid themselves of this very tendency. The diagnosis can often be made by watching such a person's behaviour in concrete situations.

The influence of Intraception and Extraception upon widely different functions, and the lack of clarity in our own minds in respect to the exact nature of these variables, led us to employ eighty statements (a ' shotgun ' questionnaire) as a preliminary exploration of the range of the two factors.

Statements in Questionnaire

Intraception :

1. I enjoy psychological novels more than other kinds of literature.
2. I believe that I have an instinctive understanding of the underlying motives of other people.

3. I enjoy an intimate conversation with one person more than a general conversation with several.
4. I feel that I know a good deal about my own motives and feelings.
5. When I hear a person speak, I think more about his personality than I do about what he is saying.
6. I am apt to become rather deeply and emotionally involved with one person or another.
7. I like to review in my mind the impressions which other people have made upon me.
8. I think that I have a fair understanding of women.
9. I often think I can feel my way into the innermost being of another person.
10. I feel things deeply and personally, and am sensitive to the deeper feelings of others.
11. My fantasies are an important part of my life.
12. In the conduct of my life I bother very little about practical details.
13. I often imagine myself accomplishing great deeds.
14. I feel that ideals are powerful motivating forces in myself and in others.
15. I like to dramatize events in which I am participating.
16. I am influenced in the conduct of my life by a vision of my destiny.
17. I often do things merely for my private emotional satisfaction, no matter whether anything is accomplished or not.
18. I feel that a person's life should be the full expression of his innermost self.
19. I often hope for a situation which will allow me to act out one of my fantasies.
20. I am apt to make up stories by myself about the private thoughts and experiences of the people whom I meet.
21. I have moods of expansive elation when I feel like embracing the whole world.
22. My hopes and expectations are very exuberant when I embark upon a new enterprise.
23. I accept the verdict of my own feelings as the surest guide to what is right.
24. I have, at times, been utterly dejected by disillusionment.
25. My best thoughts often come at times of emotional stress.
26. I feel that the heart is as good a guide as the head.
27. I like to associate with people who take life emotionally.

28. Without zest and excitement life seems pale and shallow.
29. My head is full of ideas clamouring for expression.
30. I believe that the world may be well lost for love.
31. I usually see things as a whole ; am apt to disregard minor details.
32. I live in my imagination as much as I do in the external world.
33. I believe in the value and importance of inner revelation.
34. I generalize freely ; am apt to make rather sweeping and exaggerated statements.
35. I rely as much on intuition or faith as I do on the results of past experience.
36. I give my imagination free sway when I am thinking or talking.
37. I am thrilled by ideas which are large and all-embracing.
38. I am apt to see an underlying symbolic meaning in the stories that I read.
39. Some of my friends think that my ideas are impractical if not a bit wild.
40. Sometimes I think of natural objects as possessing human qualities.

Extraception :

1. I am more interested in a person's behaviour than in his inner life.
2. In the moulding of character I think that external conditions are more important than inner tendencies.
3. I dislike morbid psychological novels.
4. I spend very little time worrying about problems of love and sex.
5. I like to work with mechanical appliances : machinery, electrical apparatus and so forth.
6. I enjoy scientific articles more than fiction or poetry.
7. I am apt to judge people in terms of their tangible accomplishments.
8. Mathematics has been one of my best subjects.
9. I am rather detached and impersonal in my dealings with other people.
10. I am often at a loss to explain the behaviour of people who are emotionally unstable.
11. I am practical and efficient when there is something to be done.
12. I am interested in the business and financial problems of the day.
13. I am interested in all kinds of new mechanical devices.
14. I am much more apt to think of an object's utility than of its symbolic value.

15. I stick to the unadorned facts when I tell about something that happened.
16. I spend very little time thinking about distant goals and ultimate ideals.
17. I work for tangible and clearly-defined results.
18. I find it rather easy to work out an effective, sober plan of action.
19. I accept the world as it is and do not try to imagine how it might be.
20. I always attempt to substantiate the facts of a case before giving a judgement.
21. My anticipations remain within the realm of what is probable, i.e., they are based on past experience.
22. I am temperamentally opposed to the 'romantic' point of view.
23. I have few, if any, emotional problems.
24. I find it easy to think things out calmly without the interference of sentiment.
25. I like to keep myself free from emotional entanglements.
26. I act on the principle that a man's first duty is to adjust himself to his environment.
27. I am rather moderate and judicious in my judgements of other people.
28. I am quite conventional in my behaviour.
29. My relations with other people are simple and uncomplicated.
30. I keep my feet on the ground, i.e., I adopt a common-sense and matter-of-fact attitude towards life.
31. I should say that my ideas were sound and sensible, rather than unusual or imaginative.
32. When I tackle a subject I read what others have written about it before I begin.
33. I am specially interested in ideas that are thoroughly practical.
34. I believe that the economic interpretation of history is as valid as any.
35. I adopt a somewhat skeptical or agnostic point of view towards most theories.
36. It is easier for me to deal with concrete facts in one special field than with general ideas about man or nature.
37. I am rather 'tough-minded' or 'hard-boiled' in my interpretations and judgements.

38. I am inclined towards a mechanistic (or materialistic) conception of nature.
39. I believe that science offers as good a guide as there is to the future.
40. When I think out a problem I keep very close to the facts.

Projectivity (Proj)

This is scored as the ratio of Projectivity to Objectivity. Projectivity describes egocentricity in perception, apperception and conception. The S 'projects' into others his own wishes, fears, interests, and pet theories. He may be animistic towards the inanimate or inanimistic (projecting a 'machine') towards the animate. Common signs are these : The S misinterprets events, gives fantastic explanations, seriously ascribes various motives to others on insufficient evidence (people seem to be looking at him, praising him, blaming him, scorning him, plotting to injure him, etc.). He quarrels with people because of some trivial misunderstanding. His thinking is guided by sentiment, he sees his theories exemplified by the course of events, is dominated by prejudice, and influenced by 'halo' tendencies. He holds beliefs that conform to hopes or worries, is unable to see another person's point of view, misinterprets his own behaviour, refuses to admit the operation of bias. In extreme cases hallucinations and unmistakable delusions occur.

Piaget [1] uses the term egocentricity to describe certain phenomena characteristic of the child. They are also characteristic of Projectivity as we define it. The child does not differentiate clearly between the images in his mind and the objects in the external world. His dreams are considered at first to be events which have occurred in the environment about him. His vivid fantasies are associated with a conviction of actuality and his make-believe is as real as stubborn facts. In his adventures the obvious happenings become so inseparably merged with his elaborate imaginations that in his subsequent accounts of things he cannot distinguish what was outside from what was inside. His parents are apt to

1. Piaget, J. *The Language and Thought of the Child*, New York, 1926 ; *Judgment and Reasoning in the Child*, New York, 1928.

think that he is telling lies for his own amusement or their deception. The child is animistic and is inclined to favour allegorical and anthropomorphic explanations of the natural events : there is a man in the moon, the sun is a benevolent father, the clouds are malicious devils, the wind is the breath of God. He plays games in which the action is more affective than effective ; that is, it expresses tensions and emotions without achieving tangible results. Many of such activities are similar to the practices and rituals of primitive people. The child identifies himself with objects of some remoteness, with animals and with the heroes of story books. When a toad is run over by an automobile he feels the pain as if it were in his own body. He has convictions in regard to the feelings and motives which sway members of his circle. His own emotions are uniquely important to him. They are hyperbolically expressed and ardently dramatized. His thoughts are often fantastic, being mere associations of emotionally determined images. His conceptions of the world are frequently vague and extravagant. The trend of his fantasies leads him to suppose that natural occurrences bear some reference to his welfare, that his parents are continuously thinking about him, that the stars are watching him, that the flight of a bird conveys a special message to him of good or evil.

Objectivity describes the absence of Projectivity. The S is impartial, detached, disinterested, tolerant, understanding. Common signs are these : The S is aware of and responds to the conditions that actually exist. He observes the plain facts, clearly differentiates between what is subjective (within his self) and what is objective (outside his self), is conscious of his inner feelings and inclinations and regards them with an impartial eye. He observes behaviour accurately and makes reliable inferences as to the probable inner states of other people. He has true insight, and is able to interpret the motives of his acquaintances reasonably well.

Since the S is by definition unconscious of his own projections (at the time they occur), it is hardly possible to get evidences of Projectivity by direct questions. Consequently, this variable was not covered in the questionnaire.

Exocathection (Exo)

This is scored as the ratio of Exocathection to Endocathection. The variable has to do with the relative importance to the subject of : (1) practical, concrete, physical or social action, and (2) fantasy, reflection, imagination or abstract thought. This dichotomy is often confused with Extraception and Intraception.

Exocathection. The S is most interested in practical activity and the affairs of everyday life, domestic, economic, political and social. His chief interests are earning a livelihood, competing with others, and participating in contemporary events. He wants to be actively in the 'thick' of things, adapting to reality.

1. *Exo + Extra :* To adapt to the world as it stands ; to be interested in tangible results ; to be very practical ; to amass a fortune. To secure a permanent position ; to become a member of clubs and institutions. To be without illusions ; to conserve established values. To work effectively with mechanical appliances.
2. *Exo + Intra :* To live imaginatively ; to dramatize the self ; to express one's sentiments and beliefs in action. To initiate and further progressive social movements. To speak against abuses ; to propose reforms. To concoct new schemes : business ventures, political innovations ; to be guided by a vision of the future. To seek adventure ; to become involved in amorous affairs.

Endocathection. The S is most interested in 'things of the mind' : cultural and intellectual pursuits. He gives the highest value to general ideas, symbols and artistic productions. He enjoys serious discussions or creative activity rather than immediately practical action. He seeks solitude for uninterrupted speculation and reverie.

1. *Endo + Extra :* To be interested in ideas and theories about substantial events (ex : physical sciences). To reflect and write about external occurrences and systems : history, economics, government, education. To collect data and think inductively.

2. *Endo + Intra:* To devote oneself to artistic or religious representations. To dream, brood and introspect; to become absorbed in the attempt to solve inner conflicts and spiritual dilemmas. To seek the deepest psychological truths. To think deductively or idealistically; to develop a metaphysical system.

Statements in Questionnaire

Exocathection:

1. I can deal with an actual situation better than I can cope with general ideas and theories.
2. I have a rather good head for business.
3. I like being in the thick of action.
4. I am interested in everything that is going on in the world: business, politics, social affairs, etc.
5. I am extremely interested in the activities of other people.
6. I like to do things with my hands: manual labor, manipulation or construction.
7. I am a practical person, interested in tangible achievement.
8. I like to have people about me most of the time.
9. I would rather take an active part in contemporary events than read and think about them.
10. Money and social prestige are matters of importance to me.

Endocathection:

1. I am inclined to withdraw from the world of restless action.
2. I would rather *know* than *do*.
3. I spend a lot of time philosophizing with myself.
4. I think more about my private feelings or theories than I do about the practical demands of everyday existence.
5. I dislike everything that has to do with money — buying, selling, and bargaining.
6. I would rather write a fine book than be an important public figure.
7. I like above all to discuss general questions — scientific or philosophical — with my friends.
8. I would rather grow inwardly and achieve balance and fullness of experience than win success in practical affairs.

9. I am more interested in aesthetic or moral values than I am in contemporary events.
10. I am apt to brood for a long time over a single idea.

Two variables were added at the last moment : n Understanding and Radical Sentiments.

n Understanding (n Und)

We were never able to decide as to whether differentiated *thinking* (cognition) should be considered a drive or a function. Cognition is usually involved as a process in adaptive behaviour. In James's words, thinking is 'delayed action.' But there are forms of thought which do not lead the thinker to action ; they inhibit action or lead away from action. There is thought which has as its final aim the representation in symbols of the order of nature. To understand (conceptualize) relations is sufficient. It is a final value. Perhaps this activity represents an endopsychic form of the need for Construction, since it is a structurally coherent system (of ideas, to be sure, rather than materials) which the metaphysician, as well as the scientific rationalist, attempts to create. An edifice of logically inter-articulated concepts is the end situation which satisfies and quiets the tension. If the scheme can be shown by observation and experiment (n Cognizance) to fit the facts that are turned up by nature then the thinker (the extraceptive thinker at least) has his final reward. This sort of intellectual activity requires disinterested detachment rather than vigorous action, and even when the construction that a philosopher imposes on nature is merely an intricate rationalization of his own behavioural sentiments, it does not usually lead the creator himself to adopt a new course of action, though it may, of course, affect others in this way. For these reasons, we have chosen to regard intellection as a need, the trend of which is to analyse experience, to abstract, to discriminate among concepts, to define relations, to synthesize ideas, and to arrive at generalizations that are comprehensive and verifiable. The need may be regarded as primarily endopsychic, though it may result eventually in spoken or written aphorisms, propositions, hypotheses, theories, systems of thought. The extraceptor tends to become an operationist (physical scientist), the intraceptor an interpreter of subjective experience. Naturally there is a high correlation between n Understanding and Endocathection. The latter, however, is more inclusive, since it embraces reverie, inner brooding, mystical experience and artistic imaginings. The artist, like the scientist and the philosopher, orders and reconstructs his impressions, but his aim is to embody his experience in a concrete form that has perceptual and emotional, rather than conceptual, value. This activity was not subsumed by us under the n Understanding. It was our practice to classify it as Creativity and n Sentience, although the advisability of so doing is questionable.

Under the n Understanding we have classed: the tendency to ask or to answer general questions; interest in theory; the inclination to analyse events and generalize; discussion and argument; emphasis on logic and reason; self-correction and criticism; the habit of stating opinion precisely; insistent attempts to make thought correspond to fact; disinterested speculation; deep interest in abstract formulations: science, mathematics, philosophy.

Statements in Questionnaire

1. I enjoy reflection and speculation as much as anything.
2. I am more excited by general ideas than by concrete facts.
3. I am rather logical and coherent in my thinking.
4. I search for the most general interpretation of every actual occurrence.
5. I spend hours formulating my ideas as clearly as possible, so that I can be understood by others.
6. I enjoy reading books which deal with general ideas — books on science, aesthetics, philosophy, etc.
7. I have often brooded for a long time in an attempt to solve some fundamental problem.
8. When I wish to arrive at the truth, I make a conscious attempt to eliminate sentiment and prejudice.
9. I enjoy debating with my friends about the relative value of various ideas or theories.

10. I am interested in facts and events only in so far as they manifest the operation of general laws.
11. I feel that I should like to dedicate my life to the search for truth.
12. I lay great emphasis upon words or concepts which exactly express my thought.
13. I feel that the attempt to arrive at a deep understanding of life is more important than practical activity.
14. I feel that I should like to devote my life to teaching and scholarship.
15. I am more practiced in dealing with general ideas than in making decisions.
16. I think that *reason* is the best guide in solving the problems of life.
17. I find that I can usually defeat others in an argument.
18. I am critical of current ideas and theories.
19. I feel that I have a number of ideas which some day I should like to put into a book.
20. I feel that I have the general disposition of a philosopher.

Radical Sentiments (Rad Sts)

This was scored as the ratio of radical to conservative sentiments (Rad Sts/Con Sts). The variable stands for the proportion of expressed sentiments, tastes and opinions that are (1) novel, original, unique ; or (2) contrary to those held by the majority of respected citizens. The radical subject usually exhibits the n ideo Aggression against long-established customs, conventional views, prevalent mores. Sometimes such radicalism is diffuse. The S favours modern art, the rejection of sex taboos, socialism, the freedom of the press, the elimination of religion, nudism, progressive schools, the humane treatment of criminals, etc. Radicalism is usually opposed to authority, to any force that restrains liberty. It favours the weak, the dissatisfied, the oppressed minority. Thus, radicalism is often an indication of suprAggression (inhibited) and infraNurturance. It may be an expression of the stern father and rebel son thema.

Special tests and questionnaires are used for measuring the strength of this variable. Much is also revealed in interviews. It should be understood that it does not apply to radical behaviour. Among our subjects the most radical sentiments were expressed by succorant, abasive and infavoidant subjects.

Miscellaneous Variables

The conceptual scheme used with our final group of subjects included a few additional variables, some of which seemed to direct attention to important aspects of personality. Here, however, our data is not sufficient to warrant definition and exposition. A list will be enough : n Acquisition, n Retention, Expansive/Contractive, Social Solidarity (security of belongingness in one or more stable groups), Superiority/Inferiority feelings, Optimism/Pessimism, n Cognizance (taking the form of diffuse curiosity), Neuroticism.

The list of separable factors employed during the last two years of experimentation may be conveniently arranged on a sheet for scoring :

PERSONALITY MARKING CARD

Manifest Variables : Marking Scale : 0 to 5
(2, Just Below and 3, Just Above Av.)

n Aba		n Cnt		n Rej		n Play		n Exh		Se I	
n Suc		n Dfd		n Def		n Ach		Exo/Endo		n Ord	
Anx		n Auto		n Aff		Ego Ideal		Intra/Extra		Sa/Ch	
n Harm		Rad St		n Nur		Narcism		Proj/Obj		Conj/Disj	
n Inf		n Dom		n Sex		Int		n Und		Imp/Del	
Se C		n Agg		n Sen		End		Cr		Emo	

Latent Variables : Marking Scale : 0 to 3

n Suc (Helplessness)		n Agg (Sadism)		n Exh (Self-display)		n Sex	
n Dom (Omnipotence)		n Aba (Masochism)		n Cog (Voyeurism)		n Homo-Sex	

Values, Interests and Abilities

Cathected Attributes and Conditions

People commonly admire themselves or others because of certain endowments, gratuities, acquired abilities or achievements. What they specifically admire determines to a large extent their system of values. It is a matter of sentiments : the kinds of interest and the kinds of ability that are valued. The best of these, being represented in a subject's Ego Ideal, control the direction of the n Infavoidance and the n Counteraction, or may form the basis for inferiority feelings and the need for Defendance. The values that are realized by others may canalize the n Deference in a subject and provoke n Similance as well as the n Affiliation. The values that are not realized by others may focalize the n Rejection (ex : a scorn for those who do not measure up to a particular standard). Thus, from one point of view, the important thing is not whether a subject has a need for Achievement or for Affiliation or for Rejection, but rather *what* it is he wishes to achieve, affiliate himself with, or reject.

Our classification of the most commonly cathected attributes may be convenient, but it has no scientific significance. The following list is by no means exhaustive :

Gratuities (Endowments of inheritance or fate) :

Race Superiority. To belong to a great race.

National Superiority. To be the citizen of a great nation.

Caste Superiority. To belong to the upper class ; to come from an aristocratic family.

Consanguineous Superiority. To be descended from or related to a great man. To have a distinguished father.

Economic Superiority. To be born of rich parents ; to inherit a fortune.

Gratuities or Achievements :

Physique Superiority. To be comely, beautiful, lithe. To have a powerful or well-proportioned body.

Possessions Superiority. To own more Os or more valuable Os than others.

Superiority by Contiguance. To come from a superior county, state, or city. To live near superior people. To be near a superior O. To have visited the homes of the great.

Superiority by Similance. To resemble a superior O in one way or another : physique, habits, tastes, theories. To do as the great have done.

Affiliation Superiority. To know many Os. To be on familiar terms with superior Os.

Contrarience Superiority. To be unique. To be different and thus exceptional.

Experience Superiority. To have had many experiences. To have travelled, participated in many events, known many people, perceived and suffered. To have known 'life.'

Innate Superiority. To be sensitive to the most rewarding experiences. To discriminate values with assurance. To have a deeper understanding of life. To have a superior 'soul.'

Abilities or Achievements :

Physical Ability, n Ach (Phys). Athletics. The ability to play games which demand bodily skill or prowess : football, baseball, rowing, hockey, tennis, golf. Physical agility or endurance : swimming, riding, skiing, mountain-climbing, exploration.

Mechanical Ability, n Ach (Mech). The ability to understand and manipulate mechanical appliances and instruments ; to repair and construct apparatus : electrical and mechanical. Technical skill in the applied sciences.

Economic Ability, n Ach (Econ). The ability to make money, to understand economic problems and make the most of financial opportunities. A 'good head for business' ; to buy and sell at profit. To bargain and speculate successfully. (n Ach fused with n Acq.)

Dominative Ability, n Ach (Dom). The ability to influence, lead and govern others in an effective way. To act promptly and decisively, and to inspire or persuade others to do likewise. To take responsibility in emergencies. To maintain discipline. To construct plans and systematize co-operative endeavours. (n Ach fused with n Dom.)

Social Ability, n Ach (Soc). The ability to make friends easily, to 'get on' with people, to be liked and trusted. A gift for enduring friendships. Also the ability to express oneself in the presence of others ; to amuse and entertain ; to be popular. (n Ach fused with n Aff.)

Erotic Ability, n Ach (Sex). The ability to please, attract and excite the opposite sex. To court successfully ; to love and be loved. (n Ach fused with n Sex.)

Intellectual Ability, n Ach (Intell). The ability to comprehend, remember and 'handle' general ideas ; to extract the intellectual content of a book and discourse about it intelligently. The capacity for learning and scholarship. (n Ach fused with n Und.)

Scientific Ability, n Ach (Sc). The ability to comprehend and deal with scientific ideas ; to understand natural phenomena : physical and chemical processes ; to think in terms of abstract theories, scientific concepts and mathematical laws. (n Ach fused with n Und.)

Aesthetic Ability, n Ach (Aesth). Artistic appreciation and judgement. The ability to feel with delight the sensuous qualities of objects ; to be sensitively attentive to impressions : sights, sounds, tastes and odours ; to discriminate values in art, literature or music, to appreciate the beautiful. (n Ach fused with n Sen.)

Art-Creative Ability, n Ach (Art-Cr). The ability to create in the realm of art ; to give adequate expression to feeling and imagination ; to write poetry, short stories or musical compositions ; to model or paint. (n Ach, n Sen and Creativity.)

Theory-Creative Ability, n Ach (Th-Cr). The ability to construct explanatory concepts in science ; to make up plausible theories in philosophy or in the humanities ; to build a rational system of coherent principles ; to devise good hypotheses. (n Ach, n Und and Creativity.)

No one who has had the patience to read through this section can be expected to come away from it now with a clear head. Just as after a momentary uncovering of a heterogeneous array of objects on a table one finds oneself unable to give a complete account of what has been perceived. Neither names nor meanings have become rooted. A mere list of concepts is like a series of nonsense syllables. No item calls forth and becomes a member of a society of relevant associations ; nor is there time to discover or manufacture relations between the separate items. It is because of the impossibility of holding more than a few things in mind at once that one often welcomes an author who directs attention to a single factor. One can agree or disagree, both of which are emotionally satisfying. But if too much is mentioned one is left unattached and uninterested.

However, if life *is* complex, if an event *is* the concrescence of numberless mutually dependent factors, and if an adequate formulation of it *must* take account of many of them, what then ? The answer would appear to be that a student has to set himself to the task of memorizing the elementary anatomy of a science before he can think about the subject at all. The concepts must be so actively alive in him that they pop into consciousness without deliberation, time and time again. In the present case perhaps the best method of orientation is that of selecting and holding constant a certain press (or varying it systematically) and observing differences of response (in different individuals or in the same individual at different times). For example, in an emergency (p Danger) does an S become emotional (Emo), act impulsively (Imp), exhibit disco-ordination (Disj), or is he calm, deliberate and conjunctive ? Is his behaviour predictable (Sa) or fickle (Ch) ? Does he retract from the situation (n Harm or n Inf), does he ask for help (n Suc), does he surrender (n Aba) or does he face it manfully (n Cnt, n Ach) ? Or again, if the press is that of criticism (p Aggression : Belittlement), what is the commonest response : blaming the other fellow (n Agg), defending the self (n Dfd), humbly accepting the blame (n Aba), pleading for gentleness (n Suc), taking it all as a friendly joke (n Aff, n Play) ? After failure (o Frustration) does an individual return to the same task with greater determination to succeed (n Cnt, n Ach), or, avoiding that task, does he strive for another goal (n Inf, n Ach) or does he become discouraged and give up the fight (n Aba) ? Does he attempt to prevent loss of prestige by offering justifications and excuses (n Dfd), or disarm criticism with flattery (n Def) or by getting a laugh (n Exh, n Play), or does he withdraw and seek isolation (n Inf, n Sec) ? Or again, when a subject is introduced to a sociable group (p Affiliation, Group) does he reciprocate on equal terms (n Aff), or, being impressed by the importance of the company, does he become over-courteous and suggestible (n Def), or does he show off (n Exh) and attempt to dominate the situation (n Dom) ? If someone proposes a course of action (p Dominance) does the S become stubborn (n Autonomy) and go off in a huff (n Rej), or does he readily comply (n Def) and co-operate in a friendly manner (n Aff) ? In every case we are dealing with a thema (the combination of a certain press and a certain need), which, in our minds, is a suitable method of analysing an event dynamically. The behavioural reaction alone is an abstraction hanging in the air if its connection with a press or a preceding event is not exhibited. And besides the press, one should know also the nature of the activity, object or topic that is involved in the situation. What kind of interest is expressed by the object whom the S rejects or flatters ? What kind of ability does the task require ? What kind of value does the S fail to achieve ? Finally, there is the outcome for the subject, success or failure. With this information the chief gross factors of a behavioural occurrence may be portrayed on a molar level.

Before closing this chapter on variables I feel that I should say a few words about the two pairs of attitudinal traits which have been most widely accepted by personologists. I refer to extraversion-introversion and ascendance-submission.

Extraversion and Introversion

To Jung belongs the credit of being the first to call attention decisively to two opposing tendencies in personality, named by him *extraversion* and *introversion*. He affirmed that both attitudes occurred in every individual, but as a rule one or the other clearly predominated (in frequency and intensity). Hence in most cases one could legitimately speak of either an extraverted type or an introverted type. Within a few years after the publication of Jung's long and thickly documented book (*Psychological Types*, 1923) all the world was using his terms and personologists, in America particularly, were busily engaged devising paper and pencil tests to measure the strength of each tendency in different individuals.

To his own preferred pair of opposites Jung assimilated numerous previously suggested dichotomies (Apollononian and Dionysian, Promethean and Epimethean, shallow consciousness and contracted consciousness, emphatic and abstractive, tender-minded and tough-minded, classic and romantic, and so forth). He approached the problem from different standpoints, arriving always at his own conception, which he illustrated by countless examples drawn from many realms of knowledge. Sensitively he penetrated to the deeper springs of human action, drawing many subtle distinctions. Among others he came to the conclusion that it was necessary to distinguish four functional modes—*thinking*, *feeling*, *sensation* and *intuition*—each of which was usually modified by an extraverted or introverted attitude. Considered *in toto* Jung's descriptions of type differences are more insightful, richer in anecdote and reference and more suggestive theoretically than anything that is to be found in the literature of personology. It is, therefore, particularly unfortunate that he did not systematically set down in one place a condensed list of what he considered to be the crucial indices of extraversion and introversion, respectively. This would have clarified his position and saved the confusion that has arisen as a result of the selections and projections of personologists of diverse temperaments. American psychologists, for example, with their emphatic preference for clear-cut behavioural differences, have seen fit to neglect much of what Jung considered important and to use only what fitted their own somewhat limited point of view. The result has been a miserable vulgarization of the original concept—an operation which has become only too common in this country. Would that we had been able to escape this error ourselves. The American personologists cannot be blamed entirely ; for amid the abundant illuminations in Jung's book one runs foul of many vague metaphors, confusions and contradictions. Perhaps some one will attempt an exhaustive systematization of what he has written. Here I must content myself with the briefest outline.

The fertility of Jung's thought is exhibited by the number and variety of contrasting tendencies that he has set forth to illustrate different aspects of what he considers to be the basic pair of opposites : extraversion and introversion. One can find scattered through his writings[1] innumerable significant distinctions, only a few of which can be listed here :

a. *Degree and manner of social participation and expression.* The extravert is heartily gregarious, he makes friends easily, feels at home even among strangers and rarely loses touch with the spirit of a gathering ; the introvert, on the other hand, prefers solitude or the company of a single trusted friend ; in a group he feels himself 'on the outside looking in,' but would rather remain unnoticed than be called upon to express himself before all the others. The extravert is uninhibited in his social actions, he takes the initiative and may, according to his nature, be cordially affectionate, dominant, exhibitionistic or aggressive ; the introvert, being more sensitive and self-conscious, is held back or rattled in his responses by fear, shyness or feelings of inferiority. The extravert is demonstrative, open and accessible ; the introvert is reticent, taciturn, shut-in and impenetrable, as if enveloped by a defensive shell. The extravert is more trusting of the average man's goodwill as well as more assured of his own ability to cope with hostility if it should arise ; the introvert, however, is apt to be suspicious of others and distrustful of his own readiness to do the right thing in an emergency. In a fight the extravert takes the offence, the introvert the defence. The extravert expresses his emotions smoothly and fully (though perhaps crudely) on suitable occasions ; whereas the introvert, uncertain of consequences, restrains the expression of his feelings but cannot end them, for they perseverate *malgré lui*, perhaps to explode at some later, less appropriate moment. All these inhibitions, defensive barriers, and avoidances (n Harm, n Inf and n Blam) of the introvert, it seems to me, may be put down to hypersensitiveness (narcisensitivity).

b. *Cathection.* The extravert gives determining value to the

1. Jung,C.G. *Psychological Types*, New York,1923 ; *Two Essays on Analytical Psychology*, New York,1928 ; *Contributions to Analytical Psychology*, New York, 1928 ; *Modern Man in Search of a Soul*, New York,1933.

outer world (social relations, possessions, power, prestige, public opinion) ; the introvert cathects the inner world (his feelings, fantasies, personal judgements, reflections, theories). The extravert is excited by and adapts his behaviour to contemporary events, in which he wants to play an active role, whereas the self-absorbed introvert remains relatively indifferent, being habitually under the spell of a moody drift of reverie, an inner dilemma, an absorbing idea, or a great scheme for future achievement. The extravert does not brood or introspect, he escapes from himself by ceaseless activity and thus he is almost bound to be superficial about psychological matters ; in contrast to this is the introvert's tendency to dream, mull over his experiences and analyse his motives. The extravert will talk to almost anyone about what he has seen and done but he has little to say about his subjective life, because even when he is aware of it — which is relatively seldom — it does not particularly interest him ; the introvert, however, though defensively secretive and aloof with strangers, may reveal some of his precious inner life to a sympathetic friend. The extravert talks to please, to inform or to influence people, whereas the introvert is more concerned about finding the exact words to express his thought. The extravert is stimulated to think and say his best things by the presence of others ; the introvert prefers to debate a problem with himself, to read and put his ideas into writing. The differences in this class are covered by the concepts Exocathection and Endocathection.

c. *Degree of social conformity*. The extravert's course of action is determined by his desire for social approval ; being no better than his day, he is gratified by any sort of praise or public acclaim. The introvert, on the other hand, is more apt to do something solely because it pleases him ; he rejects easily won applause and is only satisfied when he comes up to his own exacting standard. The extravert works for immediate rewards ; the introvert for a far-off goal (posterity, an ideal). The extravert is vain, the introvert proud. The extravert keeps his eye on what others are doing and he conforms to and is moulded by the groups of which he is a member ; but the introvert rarely feels himself a *bona fide* participant ; he may acquiesce and 'go through the paces' in a perfunctory manner, but inwardly he remains separate and unique. The extravert takes the prevailing moral order for granted, he may or may not succeed in living up to it but he rarely doubts that what the 'best people' say is 'Right' ; the introvert, on the other hand, is more apt to reject accepted dogmas and come to his own conclusions ; he may not be actively defiant but he is often radical in his sentiments and stubbornly resistant in his behaviour. The extravert is ready for opportunities as they arise, is quite suggestible to invitations and falls into line when the occasion dictates ; the introvert, on the other hand, dislikes suggestions, wants to follow his own routine without interruption and becomes negativistic when coerced. The extravert is more adventuresome in action but does not hesitate to ask favours or call on his friends for aid whenever it might benefit him ; the introvert, though perhaps secretly more dependent, generally refuses assistance, preferring to 'go it alone,' to make his own decisions and be solely responsible for his achievements. The introverted symptoms falling into this group are sufficiently described by n Inviolacy, with n Rejection : Contrarience, n Defendance : Concealment and n Autonomy : Resistance as subsidiations.

d. *Degree of activity and free energy.* The extravert is active and kinetic, the introvert passive and potential. The extravert, responsive, impulsive and impatient, acts confidently without reflection ; whereas the introvert is a slow, deliberate and cautious fore-thinker. These differences may be subsumed under high *vs* low Intensity (Energy, n Activity) and Impulsion *vs* Deliberation).

e. *Degree of contracting perseveration.* The extravert is characterized by a large and varied intake and output (expansive or porous reciprocity), he seeks, takes, bestows and wastes much ; the introvert, on the other hand, is contractive and conservative, he assimilates only what has meaning for him, preserves it and gives out little. The extravert gambles recklessly for large returns, the introvert holds steadfastly to what he has. The extravert seeks change, excitement and fresh adventure ; the introvert is satisfied to remain in one place (immobilization) surrounded by familiar objects, and pursue his chosen occupation. The extravert is quick to absorb the latest ideas and put them into practice ; the introvert, distrustful of novelty, is inclined to adhere to his own fundamental beliefs. The extravert likes to get things done quickly and hurry on to something new, neglectful of details, since he finds it easy to abandon a task if it bores him ; the introvert, on the other hand, perseverates (long secondary function), hates to be hurried, distracted or forced to change the trend of his thought, can endure monotony and is often bothered by the persistence of obsessional ideas. The extravert is apt to be carefree, and perhaps irresponsible and disorderly ; whereas the introvert is more often scrupulously neat, precise and, in his chosen work, a perfectionist. The extravert is diffuse, variously involved in a multiplicity of relations ; the introvert is focal with a narrow range of deeper and more concentrated interests and friends.

The distinctions in this group are quite important for psychology, but we are uncertain as to how they can best be formulated. One might speak of *expansive motility* vs *contractive immotility*, using the first term to include Change, quick intake (Reception vector), quick output (Ejection vector), talkativeness, movement and travel (Locomotion vector), and leaving places (Egression vector). In contrast to this, *contractive immotility* might include Sameness, staying in a closed place (Ingression vector), adhering to a supporting object (Adherence vector), perseveration, collecting and hoarding objects (Retention vector), and developing an impenetrable psychological 'wall' (Encasement vector). It will be observed that *contractive immotility* is distinguished by the same symptoms as Freud's anal-erotic character [1] (secondary reactive anal erotism or anal antherotism in our terminology, *vide* p. 379).

f. *Perceptive and cognitive attitude*. The extravert perceives, understands and values the world as it affects his senses, par-

1. Freud,S. *Collected Papers*, Vol.II, London,1924, No.iv. 'Character and anal erotism,' (1908) p.45, and No.xv. 'On the transformation of instincts with special reference to anal erotism,' (1916) p.164.

ticularly the sense of touch, hard substance being for him the ultimate fact ; the introvert, on the other hand, being chiefly influenced by psychic processes, perceives motility and behind motility the working of energies and directive forces. The extravert emphasizes observable facts and inductions arising from them ; the introvert assimilates the facts to his own system of fantasies and deductive speculations. The extravert is insensitive, objective, practical, impersonal and experimental ; the introvert is sensitive, subjective, theoretical, personal and philosophical. The extravert is materialistic and tough-minded in the sense that he values most what is obvious and irrefutable (money, position, prestige) ; the introvert is idealistic and tender-minded in so far as he takes the testimony of his own feelings and sentiments as the criterion of what is true, good and beautiful. The extravert is at his best when dealing with inorganic matter ; the introvert when dealing with human emotions. The distinctions in this class were first separated from the other manifestations of extraversion and introversion by Hinkle[1] who called her pair of opposites *objective* and *subjective*. We have followed her example, but for several reasons have termed our variables Extraception and Intraception (*vide* p. 211).

Ten years' work and reflection have led me to the conclusion suggested by the preceding summary, namely, that Jung has subsumed under the term 'extraversion' and under the term 'introversion' a number of variables which are not always correlated, and he has not stated clearly which of these he considers most typical of the underlying disposition. To illustrate, we might suppose that the following tendencies have been mentioned as symptoms of extraversion : A1, B1, C1, D1, E1, F1, G1, H1 ; and the following contrasting tendencies as symptoms of introversion : A2, B2, C2, D2, E2, F2, G2, H2. Systematic observation indicates that a small proportion of individuals may be found who exhibit most of the extravert symptoms and a small proportion who exhibit most of the introvert symptoms but the vast majority of

1. Hinkle, B.M. *The Re-Creating of the Individual*, New York, 1923.

people are mixtures of extravert and introvert qualities. Hence, if a person with A1, B2, D2 and H1 is encountered, one is uncertain as to what diagnosis should be made. If it were agreed that A and H were fundamental indices there would be no confusion, but no such agreement exists. In short, as others[1] have concluded, it seems that extraversion and introversion are not unitary variables.

Putting aside Extraception and Intraception (objectivity and subjectivity) which seem to describe attitudes that are clearly different from the other factors, we come down to a very crude division between the outward and more social and the inward and less social. The extravert seems to be the simple, healthy, uninhibited, readily adapting herd animal, whereas the introvert is somewhat held back within himself. My own opinion is that Jung has been misled by the supposition that there must be one reason why the introvert is held back. It is true that he has mentioned many reasons — in fact, I can think of no possibility that he has omitted —, but he has consistently attempted to subsume them all under one heading. We have been led to differ at this point by the fact that not all of the variables into which we analysed introversion were found to correlate. For this reason, they cannot legitimately be put into one category. However, several syndromes of intercorrelating variables do emerge from the data and these can be used as a basis for distinguishing the more important varieties of introvert.

I. *Passive introvert.* Low Intensity (Passivity) and low Impulsion (Deliberation) are consistently correlated (.24 to .62). Since sleep represents the extreme of introversion as well as the extreme of Passivity, and since both are related to low metabolism, there is reason to suppose that due to difference in glandular balance, the rate of energy release (as exhibited by physical, verbal or mental motility) differs among individuals. Those with a high degree of kinetic energy would tend quite naturally to be more

1. Guilford, J.P. and R.B. Personality factors S, E and M, and their measurement, *J. Psychol.*, 1936, 2, 109–127.

alert, to respond with greater speed and emphasis, to have stronger positive drives, and on this account to become assertive, dominant and aggressive (extraversion).

II. *Sensitive, avoidant introvert.* All the avoidant needs (Harmavoidance, Infavoidance, Blamavoidance) have repeatedly been found to intercorrelate (.37 to .85). These tendencies are linked with timidity, narcisensitivity and inferiority feelings. Intraception and Narcism are also common in this type of subject. Since there is reason to suppose that some children are innately more susceptible than others to pain, frustration and belittlement (or made so by early illnesses and traumas), narcisensitivity is probably at the core of this syndrome. Such children are generally fearful ; they retreat, whimper or sulk with slight provocation ; and their mothers discover that they must be treated with unusual gentleness. Due to narcisensitivity unpleasant occurrences seem to be remembered with more poignancy than pleasant ones and this leads to a generalized tendency to inhibit the outgoing positive needs. The possibility of innate differences in the ratio of inhibitory/excitatory nervous processes, unrelated to sensitivity, fear or anxiety, cannot be dismissed ; but until shown to occur it is only necessary to conceive of inhibitory predominance arising from fear of insupport, danger, rejection, ridicule, punishment and so forth. This would be sufficient to explain the characteristic caution, hesitation, avoidance of new situations, clinging to trusted objects, retraction, shyness and confusion of the introvert. A fair proportion of individuals combine syndromes I and II, but if large groups are taken the correlation between the two is rarely significant (.03 to .24).

III. *Reserved, inviolate introvert.* We have not been able to find an adequate formulation for this type : a 'wall' of diffident reserve that conceals and protects a proud and sensitive soul (Encasement vector). There is no timidity or inferiority apparent — these have been repressed —, but instead there is a resistant barrier or bristling defence. Such a person keeps his distance, is 'hard to get to know,' appears self-sufficient, indifferent, somewhat haughty, or depreciative of others, hides his emotions, refuses aid and cannot be victimized by praise or affection. We have to do here with Inviolacy and Seclusion and the negative aspects of Rejection (firm exclusion), Autonomy (negativistic resistance) and Defendance (self-concealment). The last three needs intercorrelate consistently (.38 to .62), but the syndrome as a whole correlates negatively with syndromes I and II.

IV. *Abstracted, imaginative introvert.* It seems that some children are more absorbed than others by their fantasies and reflections. Such Endocathection may be intensified by social frustrations and subsequent avoidances or by long periods of solitude, but imaginative and intellectual power should also be taken into account. For the mere fact of having 'brains' will often incline a boy towards reading, reflection and creative thought, all of which require solitude, inwardness and some diminution of social activity. With this in mind, it is entirely understandable that Jung originally connected introversion with thinking and extraversion with feeling. Anyhow, there seems to be no basis for denying that intellectual activity, particularly if it is creative, generally leads to introverted modes of living. Endocathection correlates highly with n Understanding (.70) and both of these variables correlate with syndrome II (.26 to .56).

V. *Contracted, perseverating introvert.* The variables Sameness, Order and Retention (*vide* p. 80) usually intercorrelate positively (.00 to .50). To these may be added 'cognitive perseveration,' a variable which we once employed but later dropped. These define a fairly clear type, marked by : limitation of the field of activity ; focalized and enduring attachments ; persistent cogitations and obsessive broodings ; attentiveness to order, neatness, cleanliness and precise detail ; secretiveness ; resistance to change, to interruptions or to demands for haste. The syndrome correlates variably with syndrome I (—.09 to .73) and variably with syndrome III (—.14 to .48).

In summary, we venture the opinion that, excluding Extraception and Intraception, five factors : passivity, avoidant inhibition, protective diffidence (the two latter being due to narcisensitivity), endocathection, and contractive perseveration, may be held accountable for various aspects of what has been called introversion. We should suggest that if extraversion and introversion are used as variables they should be treated separately, not considered to form a single continuum. For there are some individuals who are both more extraverted and more introverted than others. Like manic-depressive subjects, they swing from active, social participation to periods of solitary, passive reverie.

Ascendance and Submission

Though our results indicated that the Allports' A–S Reaction Study [1] was the most reliable of the dozen-odd paper and pencil questionnaires which were used at one time or another in our explorations, we did not adopt the traits 'ascendance' and 'submission,' because, as defined by the test, each of them is analysable into three or more of our own variables. Ascendance, for example, breaks up into Dominance (leading and guiding groups), Aggression (expressing irritation when annoyed or frustrated); Exhibition (showing off in public); and Submission may be analysed into Infavoidance, Blamavoidance, Seclusion and Abasement. It might be possible, I think, to unify each of these two groups of diverse behavioural trends if one could find the two proper, contrasting *underlying* factors. I suggest that self-confidence (superiority feelings) and self-distrust (inferiority feelings) would serve to unite in a psychologically intelligible manner all the reactions under ascendance and submission respectively. The fact that several of the responses that are used as indices of ascendance are examples of adolescent bumptiousness or crusty ill-humour rather than veritable 'ascendance,' leads one to suspect that among those who get high scores on this test there would be many individuals whose self-assurance was a not-too-convincing mask for repressed inferiority feelings, as well as those whose confidence was built on a basic sense of security and solid achievement.

1. Allport, G.W. and F.H. 'The A–S Reaction Study,' described in the *J. Abn. & Soc. Psychol.*, 1928, *23*, 118–136.

Chapter IV
JUDGEMENTS OF PERSONALITY

R. WOLF AND H. A. MURRAY

THE relations between variables (hierarchical order, fusions, subsidiations, contrafactions, conflicts, inhibition of one need by another, as well as what Allport and Vernon [1] have termed the 'congruence' of traits) are as important as the variables themselves. But one can hardly describe relationships without a preliminary identification of the variables that are related. Hence, leaving aside the possibility that by one act of intuition a subject may be apperceived as a unified whole, that without any intervening process of analysis he may be immediately 'recognized'—as one recognizes a square—leaving this unproved supposition aside, it may be said that in its first stages the diagnosis of personality consists of crudely quantitative estimates of the attributes which successively attract attention.

a. The Diagnosis of Needs

Some of the variables that constitute our conceptual scheme are general traits, not difficult to distinguish. Attributes such as reactivity, speed of movement, impulsiveness, emphasis, discoordination, emotionality, endurance, expansiveness, are on the very face of behaviour. They are its manifest dimensions, and it is likely that someday psychologists will have an appropriate battery of tests for each of them. But the diagnosis of social acts (some of which are automatic or unconscious) and the diagnosis of latent inhibited tendencies present difficulties that seem insurmountable. Besides the characteristics common to all activity which make observation and recording unreliable—the speed of its progression, its complexity, the fact that it is not repeated, etc.—there are the special characteristics of adaptive behaviour to confuse and trouble the experimenter. Generally speaking, it is pos-

1. Allport, G.W. and Vernon, P. *Studies in Expressive Movement*, New York, 1933.

sible to observe action patterns with a sufficient degree of accuracy. A subject makes certain movements which a camera can register, or he says certain things which a stenographer can record. The facts stare the judges in the face and the probability of their agreeing among themselves is relatively high. Agreement about actones, however, is but a little step towards an understanding of personality, for actones *qua actones* are usually of minor importance. According to our theory, at least, what the personologist has to discover is the need, desire, intention or direction of striving *within* the subject. In short, all but the most superficial studies of personality are concerned with motivation. As Allport put it: 'The only really significant congruences in personality must be sought in the sphere of conation. It is the striving of a man which binds together the traits, and which shows how essentially harmonious they are in their determination of his behaviour.'[1]

The question is, how is motivation to be diagnosed by observation? Assuming for the moment that every act is preceded by a conscious wish or intention, can we objectively infer the intention by listening to a subject's words and watching his movements? It follows from what has been said about trends and effects that if a subject is thoroughly capable and unopposed he should succeed in achieving an effect that corresponds to his intention. Observing the effect one could infer the intention. Unfortunately, affairs do not usually progress in this clear-cut fashion. There are many complicating factors that disturb a simple intention-effect relation. In the first place, an intention is not usually realized in social life, due to opposition, interruption, internal conflict or the subject's inability. And even when the effect is realized it may be even harder to detect than the intention of the subject, since very often the effect of a successful social act is a change of state *within* another human being: the arousal of interest, mirth, pleasure, irritation, friendliness, sympathy. Thus again we are confronted by the problem of something that is 'inner.' Furthermore, it is no

1. Allport, G.W. 'The study of personality by the intuitive method.' *J. Abn. & Soc. Psychol.*, 1929, 24, 14–27.

the effect actually achieved that we primarily want to know about (it might have been a mistake, a chance result). We want to know the need, the intended effect.

If sometimes no effect is produced and at other times the effect is inappreciable or equivocal, it might be concluded that the E should focus on the actones of the S and from them guess the effect intended, but this too is difficult. Great differences of intention may be expressed by the slightest modifications of tone and gesture. An operational definition of a need in terms of actones is out of the question. The actones change from culture to culture, from week to week. There are fashions in speech, new words are invented and meanings are modified. The culture may even determine specific gestures for the expression of emotion and feeling.

We have been speaking as if needs were conscious intentions, in which case we might solve our problem by getting the subject to state his desire. We might ask : what are you trying to do ? Here, however, we are confronted by more problems ; for the S is often unconscious of his motives or, if conscious, is unwilling to reveal them. The S may have a host of secondary conflicting motives. He may want to show himself in the best light, to be consistent, to exhibit independence, to be different, to give the normal response, to mislead or please the E, to amuse himself, and so forth. Then there are the fusions and subsidiations to complicate matters. An action that is commonly employed in the service of one need may be used in the service of an opposed need. For example : (1) damning with faint praise, (2) telling a negativistic child to do the opposite of what you want it to do, (3) separation to increase another's love, (4) making a boy pay a debt (to you) in order that he may preserve his self-respect.

One could write a volume on the difficulties of judging motives which might be bewildering enough to drive a rational man out of personology, or, if not this, to persuade him that only the simplest reflexes can be brought into the realm of science. It seems to me, however, that matters are not so hopeless as they appear on the surface. Man has powers beyond mere perception and rational inferences. He has feelings and emotions which can be trusted to aid him in understanding others. Although little is known about the processes involved, it is clear that in everyday life there is more understanding than misunderstanding. If this were not so, human relations would be chaotic and unreliable.

Up to the present, no one has succeeded, so far as I know, in giving an adequate account of the intuitive process when applied to the understanding of human behaviour. We have reason to believe that it involves a rather special ability which is not equally distributed in the population. The ability seems to depend on factors that are innate and factors that are acquired through personal experience and constant exercise. Novelists and dramatists are proverbially 'uncanny' in their ability to see behind the face of things, whereas most physical scientists are below the average. Is it that the kinds of bits into which events are broken by the scientist's objective eye do not reproduce, when recombined, the original whole? Is it that the artist's perceptions follow more closely the true trend of action? The temperament and training of a scientist lead him to rely on analytical perception and rational induction and to repress emotion and feeling; and I suspect that it is just this repression, when it becomes automatic, that so diminishes his ability to apperceive psychological events. If this is correct, the psychologist would make more progress if, instead of adopting the technical attitude found efficient in the physical sciences, he adopted the one which now gives the best results and attempted to perfect and discipline it. My own opinion is that psychology should begin as the physical sciences did originally — and as psycho-analysis has done recently — with the methods used in everyday life.

> In every science we can use only the senses we actually possess, although we can increase their exactness and eliminate to some extent their defects. Psycho-analysis in contrast to earlier psychological methods has simply refined and systematized the everyday methods used to understand other persons' mental situations.[1]

1. Alexander, F. *Lectures to the Harvey Society*. 1930–31.

It seems that personological diagnosis is an apperceptive process which does not proceed consciously by logical steps. Adams[1] is perhaps correct in saying that it is an inference based on the assumption that a person who moves and speaks in a certain way must be experiencing subjectively what we experience when we behave in that way. It is certainly true that it is hard to understand behaviour that does not resemble anything we have ever done ourselves or felt like doing. But the assumption and inference which Adams refers to must be unconscious, since in most cases the interpretation is given to us directly. Moreover, it seems to be accompanied by a sensitive feeling process which, like a resonator, is set off by the gestures and words of the subject. The name for this process is 'empathy,' an involuntary occurrence whereby an observer experiences the feelings or emotions which in his personality are associated 1, with the situation in which the subject is placed or 2, with the forms of behaviour that the subject exhibits. It does not seem possible to account for correct interpretation on the basis of sensory experience alone, as Köhler[2] does, since two people may give the same report of a perceived event (the objective signs) and yet differ markedly in their interpretations of it.

The complement of empathy is projection. We feel something (by empathy) and we imagine that the other person feels the same (projection). This seems to be the initial phase of all intuitive understanding. After repeated experiences we may cease to feel recognizable emotions, but we still have a resonating mental process that is like an emotion recollected in tranquillity. And, with training and experience, we cease to project with conviction. Every projection is merely an emotional hypothesis which we permit to occur, but which we immediately expose to the criticism of objective facts and whatever rational considerations are pertinent. The two phases together might be called 'critical empathy.' Consciously 'putting oneself in the place of another' or allowing the flow of one's thought and feeling to follow his words (identi-

1. Adams,D.K. 'The inference of mind.' *Psychol. Review*,1928,*35*, 235–252.
2. Köhler,W. *Gestalt Psychology*, New York,1929, Chap.7.

fication) furthers the empathic process. The results are most reliable, of course, when the experimenter is observing an event that falls within his personal experience.

Then, there is another emotional process (which so far as I know has not been described) that aids understanding. It is not the resonating supplement, but the complement (reciprocal) of the subject's inner processes. The E sets himself opposite to, rather than flowing with, the subject's movements and words, and, becoming as open and sensitive as possible, feels how the subject's attitude is affecting him (the E). In this way he apprehends the press (as it 'hits' him). If he feels excluded he imagines Rejection in the S ; if he feels that he is being swayed to do something he imagines Dominance ; if he feels anxious or irritated he infers Aggression, and so forth. Finally, there is the cathexis (rather than the press) of the subject. An E can ask himself : what drive is the S evoking in me ? Anger and aggression in the E suggest the same in the S ; compassion and tenderness suggest Succorance, and so forth. For this I cannot think of a less awkward term than 'recipathy' (reciprocal feeling rather than resonating feeling). Recipathy seems to be the mode most commonly adopted with strangers, whereas empathy is more appropriate for familiar, allied objects. Perhaps recipathy is the preferred method of the introvert (to whom all men are strangers) and empathy the habitual mode of the extravert (as Jung suggests).

It must be obvious that such participating feelings (empathy and recipathy) promote projection and hence distortion. However, the distortion is not as great as that which occurs when the emotional processes in the E are unconscious and denied. And herein lies the fallacy of the mechanized (over-scientificated) psychologist who believes that he can keep his feelings out of it. If he has unresponsive feelings, then well and good. He cannot make a sensitive interpretation and he usually knows that he cannot and does not attempt it. If, on the other hand, he has a medley of emotions which he denies or believes have been excluded, then, ten to one, they will operate unconsciously to prejudice all his observations. Better to make allies than enemies of one's emo tions. To rid oneself of troublesome projections one must become aware of them, make allowances for them in judging and by constant practice check their sovereignty. To become aware of them, introspection and self-analysis are necessary ; and a psychoanalysis by a trained practitioner may help.

What we are advocating here is more time and thought devoted to training psychologists in sensitivity and accuracy, and less time, if need be, to the perfecting of mechanical instruments. We hold no brief for uncontrolled, free-floating intuition. But we do maintain that critical emotional participation (empathy and recipathy) may be cultivated to advantage and, when corrected by all other means at our disposal, is the best instrument that we possess for exploring the ' depths ' of personality.

It is easy to see why so many psychologists have been repelled by approaches that rely on apperception. There is no science without agreement, and to date the results of experiments clearly show that interpretations of psychologists do not agree. Everyone has read of how, a century ago, the ' personal equation ' dilemma arose in the field of astronomy. At present, it is the cause of obsessional neuroses among psychologists. No one, so far as I know, has tested the ability of specialists to judge wishes, desires, intentions or drives in human subjects, but there have been experiments in judging more ' outward ' and hence less equivocal attributes, namely traits ; and the results have been thoroughly disheartening. (Arlitt,[1] Rugg,[2] Hollingworth,[3] and others.)

With the conviction that a science of personology can never be reared on ground so unstable as that provided by the concept of trait, a number of psychologists have attempted to discover what units of behaviour judges could agree about. D. S. Thomas,[4] for

1. Arlitt,A.H. ' Variability among a group of judges.' *Psychol. Bull.*,1926,*23*, 617–619.
2. Rugg,H. ' Is the rating of human character practicable ? ' *J. Educ. Psychol.*, 1921,*12*, 425–438, 485–501; 1922,*13*, 81–93.
3. Hollingworth,H.L. *Vocational Psychology and Character Analysis*, New York : 1929.
4. Thomas,D.S. *Some New Techniques for Studying Social Behavior, Child Development Monograph No.1*, Teachers College, Columbia University, New York,1929.

example, set herself the task of devising procedures for observing the social behaviour of children which would be as free as possible from the 'personal equation.' It became clear that judges could not agree about complex behaviour. And though there was more agreement when simpler categories ('hit,' 'point,' 'push,' 'embrace,' 'pull') were selected to guide perception and recording, even here reliability was disappointingly low. It was only later when other still less questionable, though more general, behavioural units (contacts with other individuals, contacts with materials, no contact with either individuals or materials) were set up that the observational records of different judges were found to agree. The results were of 'apparently great precision.'[1] This was an achievement in technique which may lead eventually to important findings.

We have been attempting to approach the same goal — agreement about behavioural units — from exactly the opposite direction. Instead of trying to find something (no matter what) about which we could agree, we have tried to find ways for coming to an agreement about something important. In other words, we have been more ashamed of triviality than of disagreement.

The lack of success in reaching agreement is partly due to the neglect of frequent discussion as well as to the vagueness and confusion of even the best terminology. The problem is essentially the same as that which confronts the medical diagnostician. The latter observes the physical signs and with the help of a detailed subjective report of symptoms infers the nature of the underlying condition. This inference is his diagnosis. Agreement is usually reached by repeated conferences and re-examinations. We have attempted to do the same. The facts are recorded and interpretations are discussed. But even when agreement has been reached we are not inclined to regard the diagnosis as anything but a more or less probable conclusion.

We might have made a better scientific showing if we had

1. Thomas, D.S., Loomis, A.M., Arrington, R.E. *Observational Studies of Social Behavior*, Vol.I, *Social Behavior Patterns*, Institute of Human Relations, Yale University, 1933.

termed our drives 'behaviour mechanisms,' and, stressing the objective trends and effects, offered neat operational definitions of each. This cannot be done and anyone who attempts to perpetrate such a hoax is willing to do anything for prestige ; or he has been woefully misled by a current fad. Motivation is the crux of the business and motivation always refers to something within the organism. But we must now turn to another aspect of diagnosis : quantitative estimations.

b. Estimations of the Strength of Needs

To participate in social life is to make, implicitly or explicitly, countless judgements of the character of one's fellow-men. And what should now be pointed out is that most of these judgements are of the nature of rough measurements of the *strength* of this or that trait. When it is said that a certain person is cautious, it means that he is cautious more *frequently* or more *intensely* than most people. It is not considered unintelligent to ask, 'How cautious is he ? ' Thus people think quantitatively about many of the attributes of personality. Gross errors, misinterpretations and exaggerations constantly occur, but, on the whole, experience seems to show that even the rough calculations of untrained people are worth something. They determine to a large extent what attitudes are adopted towards objects, and as a general rule these attitudes are suitable.

The question is, 'Can these estimates be made more accurate, more reliable, more scientific ? ' Can experimenters agree among themselves in respect to such estimates ? The attempt to measure the strength of the variables of personality is an endeavour which in the minds of some is premature and doomed to failure. A variable exhibits itself in so many different and incommensurate forms and, in each of its appearances, is so differently combined with other variables — some of which are entirely unknown — that only a very naïve and uncritical person can suppose that reliable measurements are possible. It is a matter of degree, of course. Truly reliable measurements are not possible. But, if, as experience shows, the unreliable measurements of everyday life are sufficient for adaptation, it is reasonable to suppose that by a critical study of the commonly employed indications of quantity one might learn to make judgements that are consciously controlled and hence more reliable.

The basic proposition is that there is no *elementary* variable which is not possessed and manifested, at least occasionally to a slight extent, by everyone. In the case of needs, our indefiniteness as to what is being measured must be admitted. A psychologist cannot, as a chemist can, physically break up a behavioural compound and measure each of its constituents separately. Even if we should assume that a defined variable represents a separable process, it must be evident that the intensity or frequency with which it is displayed will depend largely upon the strength of other operating variables, some of which facilitate and some of which oppose it.

Thus what one measures is always the resultant of numerous concatenating influences. Psychology is a long way from its ideal : the formulation of events as the interaction of forces of different strength. The vision of such a possibility, however, encourages us to continue our studies despite the barrenness and artificiality of the initial results.

In judging the strength of needs it is necessary to keep constant if possible, or make allowances for, the factors which affect the phenomenon measured. Of these the most important are : level of diffuse energy, general intelligence, special abilities, degree of inhibition, knowledge of the presenting situation.

Estimations of Manifest Needs

Since there is reason to believe that every drive is manifest to some extent and latent to some extent, it is not strictly correct to speak of a 'manifest drive' and a 'latent drive.' Such expressions, however, are more convenient than their equivalents : 'the amount of drive manifested' and 'the amount of drive that is not manifested.' A drive is manifested when it is embodied (objectified) in overt behaviour (physical or verbal) that seriously engages itself with real objects. It is latent (unmanifested, subjectified, inhibited, covert or imaginal) when it does not lead to serious overt behaviour, but takes the form of desire, resolutions for the future, fantasy, dreaming, play, artistic creation, watching or reading about the exhibition of the need in others. For the present, we shall confine ourselves to the measurement of what is manifest.

Overt needs, as we have pointed out, exhibit themselves in several different ways, of which the most direct are (1) an effect or trend (series of sub-effects) and (2) a simple or complex actone. The principal indirect manifestations are these: (3) cathection of (attention to) objects, (4) an initiating emotion, and (5) affection: pleasure with the attainment and unpleasure with the unattainment of an end situation. These three indirect manifestations may occur without overt action, and when they do they may be used as indices of a latent, rather than a manifest, need.

Needs may be distinguished *qualitatively* in terms of the kind of trend, the kind of actone, the kind of object cathected, the kind of emotion and the kind of end situation which arouses affect. Since a trend (effect) cannot be achieved without actones, these two aspects of need activity must be considered together. Consequently, there are four types of reaction and the question before us is this: what criteria of quantity are applicable to each type?

The generally accepted criteria are four: frequency, duration, intensity and readiness. Since each of these may be used in connection with any one of the four aspects of need activity, we are provided at the outset with sixteen measures of need strength. A strong drive, for example, would be indicated by any of the following occurrences:

1. A frequently recurrent behavioural trend or emotion;
2. Intent staring at an object for a long time;
3. Vehement and emphatic speech;
4. A readily aroused quick response;
5. Dejection that persists for days after frustration.

The measurement of frequency and duration is a relatively simple matter. For the former one has only to count, and for the latter one needs only a watch that keeps time. The estimation of intensity, however, is another matter. How does intensity manifest itself ? Our own experience and reflection have led us to accept the following measures of the intensity of overt behaviour :

i. Tempo of action, rapidity of movement or speech.

ii. Speed of learning, the time it takes the S to learn the method of reaching the goal.

iii. Actonal potency, the effectiveness of the actone utilized in objectifying the need. Physical acts, for example, are usually more effective than verbal acts, and some physical acts are more extreme or immoderate than others.

Ex : A graded series for the n Aggression might be : criticism given with a smile, a laugh at the O's expense, a mild insult, a severe accusation, a violent push, a blow in the face, murder.

iv. Amount of terminal activity, size or number of objects with which the S deals.

Ex : A hungry man will eat a huge meal.

v. Strength of action : weight, stress or emphasis of movement or words.

vi. Number and magnitude of the obstacles that are overcome to reach the end situation.

vii. Number and strength of the negative needs that are inhibited.

Ex : An ambitious man will endure pain and privation to attain his end.

viii. Number and strength of the positive needs that are sacrificed : what pleasures an S will forego.

These eight measures can only be used in connection with actones and effects. Together with those mentioned above this gives us twenty-three indices of need strength.

As measures of readiness the following have been utilized :

i. Speed of response, length of latent period.

ii. Strength of press, or 'stimulus-value' of the object. Here we have to do with different thresholds of response. Other factors being equal, the stronger the need the lower the threshold.

Ex : Some men get excited at the slightest provocation.

iii. Inappropriateness of the cathected object. If no fitting objects are available a man may be aroused by an unsuitable object, one that is commonly connected with another need.

Ex : A hungry man will eat shoe-leather.

iv. Level of aspiration. The need for Achievement is strong when a S selects a difficult goal or unavailable object towards which to direct his efforts.

The first three of these measures are applicable to overt behaviour, attention to objects, emotion and affection. Hence we have twelve instead of four indices of readiness, which, combined with level of aspiration (applicable to behaviour alone), gives us a total of thirty-two criteria of need strength.

All of these more or less valid measures are objectively discernible, but they should be taken in conjunction with subjective reports. When dealing with honest and insightful subjects the latter can be trusted to give reliable clues as to the strength of a need. A subject can and usually is willing to tell what O's attracted his attention and why, whether he responded more quickly, worked faster or harder than usual ; he can measure the intensity of his desire and can tell to what degree he was absorbed ; he can estimate the difficulty for him of the obstacles encountered, the amount of unpleasure endured and pleasure sacrificed ; he knows most about his level of aspiration and can often describe in detail the qualitative and quantitative aspects of his emotional experience ; he can report the amount of pleasure or unpleasure associated with the terminal situation ; and, finally, he can tell the E how frequently in everyday life he behaves as he did when observed. Thus, subjective reports are invaluable in checking and refining objective results.

Some of the indices that have been enumerated are hardly distinguishable from each other. For example, it may be hard to distinguish : mildness of the stimulus from inappropriateness of the stimulus, these from speed of response, speed of response from tempo of action, tempo from strength of action, level of aspiration from amount of terminal activity, number of obstacles overcome from number of negative needs inhibited, duration from frequency, and so forth. Some of these indices apply to some conditions and not to others; some are appropriate as measures of some needs and not of others.

It is obvious that each index measures the resultant of a multiplicity of factors, of which the tension of the need is merely one, and also that each index is determined by a different set of factors. Therefore, there is little reason to suppose that more than a few of the indices will intercorrelate positively. For example, it is improbable that the S who responds the quickest will be the one who perseveres the longest, that the S who manifests the most emotion will be the one who overcomes the most obstacles, that the S who is most easily aroused will be the one who inhibits the most negative needs. Strictly speaking, each index measures a specific combination of factors, and in some instances the tension or the need may be of negligible importance relative to the other factors.

Our practice has been to take into account, if possible, as many indices as can be measured and on this basis arrive at some coarse rating for the 'lump' of them.

This is somewhat facilitated by estimating separately some of the general factors that modify each result: Intensity, Endurance, Impulsion, Emotionality and so forth.

Estimations of Latent Needs

We must now deal with needs which are not objectified in action. That is, we must examine the criteria for measuring the strength of tensions which are resisted by other tensions, the latter being due in most cases to the activity of negative needs. Since it is usually a matter of partial, rather than total, inhibition, an inhibited need may display itself for a moment before it is checked. The E may then have the opportunity to observe a quick glance of the eye, a tremor of the hand, a fleeting gesture, a blanching of the face, a slip of the tongue; which, if he is intuitive, will be sufficient to reveal an underlying impulse.

Completely inhibited needs have no true objectifications. They express themselves only as subjectifications (imaginal processes) and semi-objectifications (make-believe actions). The common varieties of subjectification are as follows : (1) plans, desires, fantasies, free associations, dreams ; (2) empathic feelings and imagery (identification) while reading literature, conversing, reciting or observing events, contemplating works of art ; (3) verbal or musical expressions of sentiment and emotion ; (4) projections : misperceptions and misapperceptions ; (5) rationalizations : the projection of wishes and fears into thinking, and (6) artistic creations. Examples of semi-objectifications are these : (1) play (of children) ; (2) dramatics ; (3) erotic fantasy enactions ; and (4) religious practices.

The chief differences between an imaginal need and an overt need is that the former enjoys in reading, or represents in fantasy, in speech or in play what the latter objectifies in serious action. Thus, instead of pushing through a difficult enterprise, an S will have visions of doing it or read books about others doing it ; or instead of injuring an enemy, he will express his dislike of him to others or enjoy playing an aggressive role in a play. It should be understood, of course, that a need may be partially objectified and partially inhibited, that only some forms of the need may be repressed. Also, what is imaginal to-day may be objectified to-morrow. The term 'imaginal need' is convenient for the expression 'the amount of need tension that exhibits itself in thought and make-believe action.'

To recognize the needs that are promoting the course of a given series of imaginal processes is difficult, since one is rarely certain of the meaning of the images to the subject. If, as often happens, an image is merely a substitute or symbol for an *unconscious* image, the subject cannot be of much assistance to the experimenter. Without many hours of free association interpretations will be necessarily very hypothetical.

Most of the criteria of quantity that have been discussed are applicable to the measurement of imaginal or inhibited needs, since imagined behaviour or make-believe behaviour is not essentially different from overt behaviour. For example, fantasies may vary in respect to their : (1) inducibility, (2) actonal potency, (3) level of aspiration, (4) amount of terminal satisfaction, (5) degree of concentrated absorption ; (6) number of external incentives rejected or positive needs inhibited, (7) endurance, (8) frequency, (9) accompanying emotion, (10) accompanying pleasure or unpleasure. These indices may also be applied to the measurement of trends excited in dreams ; or excited while reading, observing events or conversing ; or projected into perception, apperception or intellection ; or represented by the S in works of art. It must be obvious that trends exhibited in play or in religious ritual are susceptible to measurement in terms of similar criteria.

Space forbids the enumeration of every index that may be applied in measuring each form of imaginal expression. A compressed account must suffice.

Brief Summary of Certain Criteria of Quantity

1. *Frequency, intensity and duration of an imaginal thema.* The length of time that a fantasy or topic of conversation endures, the number of times it recurs, the potency of its content are measures of an underlying tension which determines the associations. These indices may also be applied to imagery (its vividness), word associations, projections and so forth. For example :

a. *Selection of topics of conversation and verbal associations.* The course of a person's conversation should be noticed : what topics (objects) are discussed or avoided and what associations are made. Or better, the psycho-analytic technique of free associations may be used. Finally, formal tests may be presented calling for single word associations or chained associations. The stimulus words may be more or less suggestive of certain complexes. Word completion tests should also be included here. It is necessary to estimate the number of times that words depicting a certain class of objects occur, the intensity with which they are mentioned, the duration of the discussion.

b. *Sentimentive intensity.* Expressed sentiments, favourable or unfavourable, are indications of the amount of cathexis with which objects of a certain class are endowed. Thus if a sentiment can be properly interpreted, its intensity and the frequency with which it is expressed are measures of the associated imaginal need.

c. *Creative productions.* What objects a person constructs, draws, models or writes about may be used for interpretation. If a subject does not do one of these things of his own accord, he may be asked to do it as an exercise or test. He may, for example, be asked to write a story on a particular theme or to construct and present a play with puppets or dolls.

2. *Speed of response.* In word association tests a short reaction time suggests uninhibited imaginal need tension. A long reaction time, on the other hand, indicates obstruction, and thus an inhibited complex. This has been shown repeatedly in association tests.

3. *Inappropriateness of associations.* Here we have to do with far-fetched, bizarre or subjectively-determined associations. The theory is that when a fantasy or topic of interest is in a highly inducible state almost any word, image or picture will bring it to mind. To an outsider the association may seem highly irrational.

Ex : i. Jung's researches[1] in word association demonstrated the complex-revealing significance of unusual responses. ii. With some people, no matter how a conversation may commence, it is sure to be brought into the channels of their major interest. (Here we may recall Uncle Toby (*Tristram Shandy*) who was wounded while fighting in Flanders and could think of nothing else : ' " Sir," replied Dr. Stop, " it would astonish you to know what improvements we have made of late years in all branches of obstetrical knowledge, but particularly in that one single point of the safe and expeditious extraction of the foetus — which has received such lights, that, for my part (holding up his hands) I declare I wonder how the world has " — " I wish," quoth Uncle Toby, " you had seen what prodigious armies we had in Flanders." ')

4. *Multiplicity of forms.* The number of different equivalent modes by which a need expresses itself is usually taken as a sign of its strength. This is similar to the phenomenon of spread or irradiation in the cortex. Imaginal needs offer the most striking

1. Jung, C.G. *Studies in Word-Association*, London, 1918.

examples of this process, which exhibits itself as the repetition of the same thema in a variety of forms or the spread of associations about a central nuclear idea.

Ex : i. A subject (Veal) interprets a certain picture as the representation of a man descending into a mine to save some imprisoned miners by leading them out of a secret exit ; hearing a piece of music at another time he thinks of a man saving the occupants of an overturned coach ; later, he says that his favourite story is that of Jean Valjean in *Les Misérables* carrying the wounded Marius through the great sewer of Paris to its exit into the Seine. ii. A subject (Virt) says of one picture that it is a man who has just failed to save his sweetheart from drowning ; of another, that it is a woman who has been separated from her lover and is about to die ; of another, that it is a man who is prevented from rescuing his wife from a burning building.

5. *Projective distortion.* A strong need is apt to perceive and apperceive what it 'wants,' or, in the case of a negative need, what it 'fears' ; that is, an S under the influence of a drive has a tendency to 'project' into surrounding objects some of the imagery associated with the drive that is operating. The measure is the *amount* of distortion, that is, how much the O is changed.

Projection commonly occurs without overt action. It may be experimentally induced and the press of the projected imagery may be used as an index of imaginal or inhibited need tension. Here it is necessary to estimate the frequency with which objects of a certain class recur as well as their vividness and potency.

a. *Perceptive projections.* Illusions that occur under natural conditions may be noted. Or, the senses may be stimulated by various ambiguous presentations (ink-blots, pictures presented very rapidly with a tachistoscope, music, indefinite vocal sounds, complex odours, etc.) and the subject asked to name the objects, scenes or dramatic occurrences that are evoked (pseudo-projections). Picture completion tests are also of value.

b. *Apperceptive projections.* The interpretations which a person makes of the events of everyday life — particularly if he ascribes motives to other objects — may be noted. Formal tests may be devised with pictures or written material : apperceptions of motive, thematic apperceptions, story completions and so forth.

c. *Cognitive projections.* Here we refer to the amount of wishful thinking. The aphorisms, theories and philosophical principles which a person attends to or adopts may be recorded, with special regard to the amount of rationalization that occurs. At present, there are no formal procedures which bring this factor to the foreground, but it seems that proper techniques could easily be devised.

6. *Level of aspiration.* A high level exhibited in fantasy is an index of a high Ego Ideal (n Achievement in imaginal form).

Ex : 'I think I'm in hell, thought Eugene, and they say I stink because I have not had a bath. Me ! Me ! Bruce-Eugene, the Scourge of the Greasers, and the greatest fullback Yale ever had ! Marshal Gant, the saviour of his country ! Ace Gant, the hawk of the sky, the man who brought Richthofen down ! Senator Gant, Governor Gant, President Gant, the restorer and uniter of a broken nation, retiring quietly to private life in spite of the weeping protest of one hundred million people, until, like Arthur of Barbarossa, he shall hear again the drums of need and peril.

'Jesus-of-Nazareth Gant, mocked, reviled, spat upon, and imprisoned for the sins of others, but nobly silent, preferring death rather than cause pain to the woman he loves. Gant, the Unknown Soldier, the Martyred President, the slain God of Harvest, the Bringer of Good Crops. Duke Gant of Westmoreland, Viscount Pondicherry, twelfth Lord Runnymede, who hunts for true love, incognito, in Devon and ripe grain, and finds the calico white legs embedded in sweet hay. Yes, George-Gordon-Noel-Byron Gant, carrying the pageant of his bleeding heart through Europe, and Thomas-Chatterton Gant (that bright boy !), and François-Villon Gant, and Ahasuerus Gant, and Mithridates Gant, and Artaxerxes Gant, and Edward-the-Black-Prince Gant ; Stilicho Gant, and Jugurtha Gant, and Vercingetorix Gant, and Czar-Ivan-the-Terrible Gant. And Gant, the Olympian Bull ; and Heracles Gant ; and Gant, the Seductive Swan ; and Ashtaroth and Azarel Gant, Porteus Gant, Anubis and Osiris and Mumbo-Jumbo Gant.' [1]

Quantitative intensity is one of the best indications of the strength of an imaginal need. It is a matter of how extravagant, dramatic and emotionally charged the words, images or themas

1. Wolfe,Thomas. *Look Homeward, Angel*, pp.591–92, quoted by permission of the publishers, Charles Scribner's Sons, New York.

appear to be. At one extreme we have banal words and stories which indicate very little; at the other, we have unique plots, portentous words, nightmarish visions.

7. *Degree of absorption*. The importance of a fantasy or of a topic of conversation can be roughly estimated in terms of the degree of distractibility. Is the subject's attention easily diverted and, if diverted, how soon, if at all, will he return once more to his former line of thought?

8. *Degree of affection*. The amount of pleasure that accompanies a dream or a fantasy, the zest with which a topic of conversation is pursued, the thrill of excitement attending creative work are all indicative of underlying tension. Likewise, one commonly finds that certain images and ideas evoke a marked degree of revulsion. To discover what objects are associated with pleasure and unpleasure an S may be asked to rate a series of words according to the affect which they evoke.

c. An Experiment in Judging Personalities[1]

In our experiments the variables were marked on a 0 (zero) to 5 (five) scale. Each rating referred to a section of the normal frequency curve, as shown in the figure.

It will be noted that the divisions between scores are erected at even sigma units from the mean. Thus, for each variable the standard of comparison was the normal distribution of that variable in the entire college population (as roughly held in mind by each E). This was the first of many sources of error: the different conceptions of the normal distribution of each variable. If 10,000 instead of 28 college men had been examined we should have found the marks were distributed about as follows: 0 and 5 each, 2%; 1 and 4 each, 13.5%; 2 and 3 each, 34%.

This scale was admirably suited to our purposes. It was possible, for example, in order to facilitate certain calculations, to divide subjects into two groups: those in whom a variable was below

1. Much of what follows is quoted, by permission of the editor, from an article by the authors (Wolf,R. and Murray,H.A., 'An experiment in judging personalities.' *J. of Psychol.*, 1936,*3*, 345–365).

the mean (0, 1 and 2) and those in whom it was above (3, 4 or 5). For other purposes it was more convenient to make three groups : low (0 or 1), average (2 or 3) and high (4 or 5).

Each score (for a single subject on a single variable) was a composite of frequency, duration and intensity. What each examiner had to decide was whether the S displayed the given variable more frequently and intensely or less frequently and intensely than the average (mean) man of his age and status ; and to what extent. An S who displayed mild chronic irritability might

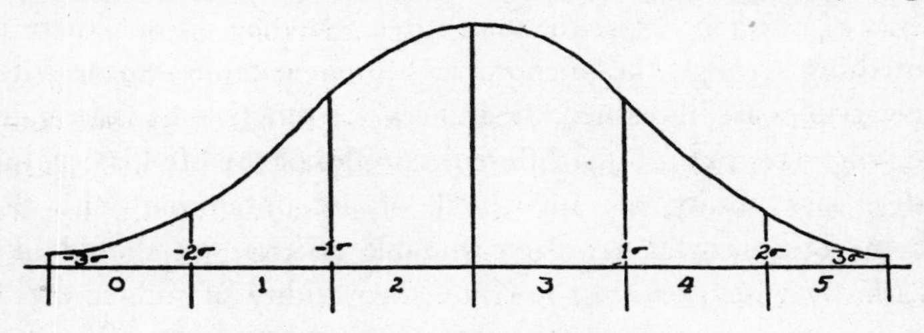

Meanings of Ratings (0 *to* 5)

get the same score on manifest Aggression as one who flew into a rage occasionally. A more refined method of marking might have taken account of such differences, but we relied on other variables, Emotionality, Impulsion, Change etc., to represent them.

In the beginning we put needs that had an opposite direction on a single continuum (Aggression — Abasement, Affiliation — Rejection, Autonomy — Deference etc.). This proved to be a mistake, and although we continued the practice with certain other variables (Impulsion — Deliberation, Conjunctivity — Disjunctivity, Intraception — Extraception etc.) we do not propose to do it in the future. This also applies to most rating scales and questionnaires (Extraversion — Introversion, Ascendance — Submission etc.), for it is not at all uncommon to find individuals who manifest opposite impulses to an extreme degree (*cf.* manic-depressive cases, sado-masochistic conflicts etc.). If in such a case one averages the marks (found at both ends of the continuum) the final score will put the individual near the mid-line, just where he never is. A rating should never obscure an ambitendency.

The Problem of the Reliability of Estimates

To list the subjective and objective indices of drive strength is one thing ; to use them efficiently in practice is another. We have repeatedly called attention to the difficulty of perceiving and retaining enough of what a subject does and says to provide a basis for rational interpretation. In an interview things happen very rapidly and there is much that perishes unrecorded. Judgements can certainly be made, but the question is, do the judgements of different experimenters agree ? If they do not, there is something wrong : the phenomena are too complex to measure, the variables are ill-defined, the indices of strength are inadequate, the judges are examining different samples of the life history, the judges lack ability, are untrained, or are unfamiliar with the scheme of concepts. Are there suitable criteria, we should like to ask, by which one can measure the validity of judgements ? Are there some attributes of personality about which judges can agree and others about which they cannot agree ? Should the latter be eliminated ? Are there marked differences in the ability to make diagnoses of personality ? Can an experimenter be trained to make more reliable judgements ? What influence has the personality of the E upon his judgements ?

These are fundamental questions which call for solution, because all personological studies involve judgements (interpretations) of observed facts, and if these judgements are unreliable everything that follows — speculation, statistical analysis, the construction of hypotheses and laws — will be still more unreliable.

Tentative answers to some of these questions are provided by the results obtained in the study of groups III and IV (28 subjects in all). And the best we can do now is to review them.

We shall confine ourselves to a study of the ability of judges to make reasonably reliable ratings on a zero to five scale. The less measurable, though more valuable, ability to see relations or to apperceive a personality as a whole will not be examined here.

The burden of diagnosis fell most heavily on the Diagnostic Council of five judges (A, B, C, D and E, respectively) who worked together for two years. Each S was first seen by this Council, sitting as a body, for a 45-minute session, termed 'the conference,' at which he was asked questions and given certain simple tasks to perform. After the conference each judge independently marked the S on each of the 40-odd variables. The average of the judges' marks on each variable was termed the 'conference mark.' During the course of the year the Council held meetings to hear the reports of subsequent sessions and independently to re-mark each S on the basis of the new evidence. Thus, there were several sets of independent ratings which were averaged and thoroughly discussed by the Council. These scores were supplemented by the ratings of other experimenters. The subjects also marked themselves, or, to be more exact, they filled out a comprehensive questionnaire of 600 items which was designed to cover the manifest variables. At the end of all the examinations a five-hour meeting was held on each S, at which all the reports and marks were read and discussed and a final mark for each variable was decided upon by majority vote.

Obviously, this procedure afforded many opportunities for influence among judges. A judge who was articulate and could clearly present the evidence for his opinion frequently persuaded other judges to change their markings. This, we believe, is as it should be. For, since the prime aim is to find the 'true' mark of each S, each E, before he finally makes up his mind, should be acquainted with the observations and interpretations of all the other judges, some of whom are more competent or have had better opportunities to observe than he. The marks agreed upon by all judges at the last meeting were called 'final marks.' We could not think of any method of reaching more reliable estimates and so in lieu of anything better these have been accepted as standard. As such they provide us with figures with which the earlier estimates of individual judges may be profitably compared.

The present study is principally concerned with the accuracy of the judgements that were independently made by the five members of the Council immediately after the initial conference. Assuming that the final mark is 'correct' one may ask : How accurate were the independent ratings and how accurate the pooled ratings of five experimenters after observing a new subject for forty-five minutes ? How well did they agree after observing the same event ? Were there marked differences in diagnostic ability among the judges ?

As to relevant facts about the judges, it may be said that they were males varying from 30 to 40 years of age, two of whom (B and E) were physicians, four of whom (B, C, D and E) had been psycho-analysed. One of them (D) had recently arrived from Europe. All of them worked and lunched together for two years. Thus, they became acquainted with each other's personality under natural and informal conditions.

Indices of Diagnostic Ability

How can the accuracy of judges' ratings be determined ? The usual method is to estimate the amount of agreement among judges on the principle that what people agree about is most apt to be true. In our studies, however, since we decided each final mark by majority vote after prolonged discussion, there were no figures for estimating the extent of ultimate agreement. To give others some assurance of the reliability of the final marks, we can only point to our entire procedure : the four months of examination, the number of tests and interviews, the number of experimenters, the specially selected and trained Diagnostic Council, the frequent markings and discussions. In our own minds, confidence was based upon (a) the number of unequivocal facts which supported each rating, (b) the psychological congruence of each mark with the marks on all other variables, and (c) the fact that each final mark was the decision of a majority. Since our primary aim was to discover the 'right' rating rather than to test the amount of agreement, discussion between judges constituted an important part of our procedure. We were well aware of the power of suggestion, persuasion and 'halo,' but we were convinced that marking by majority vote after discussion is more accurate than averaging marks that are independently assigned. What we usually found in each case was that one of the experimenters had observed some crucially important response or was able to give a more plausible explanation of the facts. If the other experimenters had rated the subjects before being told of such facts, on hearing them they would have said, 'Oh, if we had known *that* we would have marked the subject differently.' Thus, we followed the time-honoured practice of physicians when they assemble to establish a diagnosis.

Although we have no mathematical index of the reliability of the final marks, it has been possible to estimate the validity of the ratings of the Diagnostic Council after the initial 45-minute conference in terms of three indices.

(a). *Index a: agreement among judges in terms of σ.* On the assumption that the *average* of a number of judges' ratings is generally more valid than the rating of any one judge—that, lacking other measures, it is the most reliable measure obtainable—, a crude index of the competence of each judge is the standard deviation of his ratings from the average ratings for each subject on each variable. We could not use Shen's reliability coefficient of personal ratings[1] because this function is based upon a comparison of the ranks of subjects assigned by different judges and according to our procedure the subjects were not ranked by each judge; nor, since such a large proportion of subjects were assigned the same mark, could valid rank orders be obtained. It seemed worthwhile, however, to calculate the σ of each judge on all variables and the average σ of the five judges.

The standard deviations of the individual judges will be given later. Here, we shall merely record the average σ of the five judges. The results on the manifest and on the latent variables will be given separately.

In 1934–35, each judge independently marked the subject immediately after the conference, but in 1933–34 there was a short discussion after the conference before the subject was marked, which undoubtedly served to minimize gross differences between

1. Shen, E. 'The reliability coefficient of personal ratings.' *J. Educ. Psychol.*, 1925, *16*, 232–236.

the judges. Thus the techniques in the two years were not comparable and we are unable to determine how much, if any, improvement of diagnostic ability, as measured by better agreement, occurred between the first and second year. As might be expected, the average standard deviation on the manifest variables was lower in 1933–34 (σ .67, PE .03). In 1934–35 it was σ .80, PE .02. In 1933–34 estimations of latent variables were not made, but in the following year the average σ on these was .85, PE .02. Thus, the disagreement was hardly greater than it was on the manifest variables.

(b). *Index b : agreement with final ratings in terms of σ.* Since the final marks, we believe, are about as accurate as they could be, they may be used as standards with which to compare the conference marks, and thus another index of the validity of the latter may be obtained. As a valid measure of agreement we have used the standard deviation between the two sets of marks. When we examine this function as calculated for the two years, we are surprised to find that, despite the benefit to agreement which was afforded by the discussion after the conferences in 1933–34, the results obtained in the first year were less accurate than those obtained in the second. The average standard deviation in the first year was 1.13, PE .09, whereas in the second it was .89, PE .03. This result may be interpreted as indicating improvement in the diagnostic ability of the judges from the first to the second year. The average standard deviation between conference and final marks on the latent variables (1934–35) was .92, PE .06, which suggests that the diagnosis of latent variables is not appreciably more difficult than the diagnosis of manifest variables.

(c). *Index c : agreement with final ratings in terms of the correlation between rank orders of subjects.* Assuming again that the final ratings are correct, it is possible to estimate the accuracy of the conference marks by calculating for each variable the correlation between the rank order of subjects based on the conference marks and the rank order based on the final marks. The average of these correlations can be taken as an index of the reliability of the judges at the conference. The results are as follows: 1933–34, r = +.66; in 1934–35, r = +.63. Considering the advantages of discussion before marking enjoyed by the judges in the first year, this finding also points to an improvement in the diagnostic ability of the judges.

We have considered three indices of the diagnostic ability of the Council: (a) *Index a*, agreement among judges at the conference in terms of σ, (b) *Index b*, agreement between conference and final marks in terms of σ, and (c) *Index c*, agreement between conference and final marks in terms of the correlation between rank orders of subjects. Before considering the question of differences in diagnostic ability among judges we must report upon other matters.

Differences in the Measurability of Personality Variables

At the conference were some variables more accurately measured than others? To find a tentative answer to this question we may rank order the variables in terms of agreement as measured by the three indices above and compare the results. Here we shall consider only the manifest variables. The comparisons may be mathematically expressed by coefficients of correlation between each pair of rank orders. In Table 1 the results obtained the second year (1934–35) are placed *below* the results obtained the first year.

An examination of the table shows that in both years *Indices b* and *c* were positively correlated, whereas *Index a* (based on the agreement among judges) was correlated negatively once with *Index b* and twice with *Index c*. In other words, agreement about a rating at the Conference was, if anything, an index of the inaccuracy rather than the accuracy of the assigned mark. For example, in the first year the members of the Council agreed *best* in their markings on the variable Affiliation and yet these markings were *worst* in respect to their agreement with final ratings. Since, as we have said, the final ratings represent the best approximation to the 'truth' of which we were capable, we must conclude either (a) that the standard deviation is not a suitable index of agreement among judges, or/and (b) that agreement among judges after a 45-minute interview cannot be accepted as a measure of reliability. Before we take up this problem, however, we must conclude the present topic : differences in the measurability of variables. Since *Indices b* and *c* were highly correlated in both years, we may accept them as approximate measures of the facility with which the different personality

TABLE 1

RANK ORDER INTERCORRELATIONS (r's) OF THE MEASURABILITY OF VARIABLES AS DETERMINED BY THREE INDICES

	Index a	Index b	Index c
Index a		.01, PE .17 −.23, PE .13	−.26, PE .16 −.24, PE .08
Index b	.01, PE .17 −.23, PE .13		.73, PE .09 .65, PE .08
Index c	−.26, PE .16 −.24, PE .08	.73, PE .09 .65, PE .08	

variables may be diagnosed after a short formal interview. If, now, the two rank orders of variables (as determined by *Index b* and *Index c* respectively) are combined to form a composite rank order, one for 1933–34 and one for 1934–35, and these two composite rank orders are correlated, the result is $r = +.50$, PE .13. This positive correlation justifies our combining the two composite rank orders into a final composite rank, which represents, as nearly as we can estimate it, the ranking of variables in terms of their measurability or *apperceptibility*.

Inspection of this final rank order fails to reveal a single differentiating characteristic which holds for all of them. Examining the variables that stand near the bottom of the list, however, we notice (a) that for some (Sex, Creativity) the conference situation provided no adequate stimulus, and (b) that others (Succorance, Deference) were among the variables that aroused the most discussion during the months of experimentation, the ones that were most inadequately defined. Examining the variables near the top of the list we observe that here the opposite is true, and, furthermore, that among them are the variables most commonly associated with emotion (Anxiety, Emotionality, Impulsion, Aggression). More than this we cannot say at present.

The Use of ϵ as an Index of Agreement among Judges

The results just reported suggest that σ is not a good measure of validity. No doubt, we should have realized this in the beginning since it is clear that the standard deviation function fails to take account of the range and distribution of the marks. To illustrate : if in marking a diverse group of subjects in respect to a certain trait the judges tended to give conservative (average) ratings, the standard deviation would be low but the marks would not reflect the differences that existed between subjects.

These considerations [1] led us to employ the correlation ratio η (eta), the formula for which is :

$$\eta = \sqrt{1 - \frac{\overline{v}_a}{v}}$$

in which

$\overline{v}_a$ = the average variance of the scores about the means of their arrays, and

v = the variance of all scores about the mean of the whole table.

This formula, however, is not entirely satisfactory, since the ratio as it stands is not necessarily zero when no correlation is present. It merely tends towards zero. It is desirable to have a formula which will yield a score of 1 when there is perfect consistency and

1. We were instructed and guided in our statistical procedures by Dr. Dwight Chapman of the Harvard Psychological Laboratory, and we wish to take this opportunity to express our great indebtedness (Chapman,D.W. 'The statistics of the method of correct matchings.' *Amer. J. Psychol.*,1934,*46*, 287–298).

a score of 0 when there is no consistency. Such a formula may be obtained by applying Kelley's correction to the correlation ratio.[1] Kelley's formula for the corrected correlation ratio, ϵ (epsilon), is as follows :

$$\epsilon^2 = \frac{(N - 1)\,\eta^2 + 1 - k}{(N - k)}$$

in which ϵ = the corrected correlation ratio,
η = the uncorrected correlation ratio,
N = the population of the whole table,
and k = the number of arrays in the table.

The value of ϵ was calculated for the conference marks (1934–35) on each of the manifest variables. The average correlation ratio on all variables was .59. There was one 0 (zero) ratio, but all the others were positive between .37 and .84. In order to test the value of ϵ as a measure of validity the rank order of variables according to ϵ was correlated with the rank orders as determined by *Index b* and *Index c* respectively. The correlation with *Index b* (average standard deviation between conference and final marks) was r = +.02, PE .15, and the correlation with *Index c* (correlation of the rank orders of subjects as determined at the conference and at the final meeting respectively) was r = +.48, PE .10. These results are better than (—.22, —.24) those obtained when σ was used as an index of agreement between judges, a finding which substantiates our rational preference for ϵ. Nevertheless, the results with ϵ (+.02, +.48) are not encouraging enough to allow us to say that agreement at the conference is a good index of accuracy. For example, one variable (Radical Sentiments) stands second in the rank order of ϵ's (epsilons) but stands fifth from the bottom in our final composite rank order of measurability.

1. Kelley, T.L. 'An unbiased correlation measure.' *Proc. Nat. Acad. Sci.*, 1935, *21*, No. 9.

The Influence of Personality upon Judgements of other Personalities

In order to determine to what extent the marking of the subjects was affected by the personalities of the judges it was first necessary to obtain estimates of the latter. This was done by having each member of the Council mark himself and the other four Es on each of the personality variables. The *score* for each judge on each variable was obtained by averaging his self-rating with the average assigned by the other judges, his estimate of himself being considered as reliable as the combined estimates of his four friends.

By using the standard deviation of the self-ratings from these *scores* as an index, rank orders of self-insight on the manifest and latent variables respectively were obtained. Rank orders of ability to diagnose the other judges on the manifest and latent variables respectively were also obtained, using σ as an index. Before examining these rank orders, however, let us consider the question : do judges that rank high in a certain variable tend to assign high marks on that variable to others, and those that rank low tend to assign low marks ? Or do the judges that have high scores mark low, and those that have low scores mark high ? To put it more briefly, is there a prevailing tendency to mark by similarity or to mark by contrast ? It is generally supposed that most people project themselves into others and mark by similarity. Landis,[1] for example, has reported that tall people tend to overestimate height, that fat people tend to overestimate weight and that unstable people tend to overestimate instability. In discussing this question it will be convenient to use *score* to apply to a rating of a variable of a *judge's* personality determined by the method described above, and to use *mark* to apply to a rating of a variable of a *subject's* personality (assigned by a single judge). Thus the solution of the present problem calls for a comparison of scores and marks.

By averaging the marks assigned by each judge to the fifteen subjects on each variable it is possible to rank order the judges on

1. Landis,C. ' Questionnaires and the study of personality.' *J. Nerv. & Ment. Dis.*, 1936,*83*, 125–134.

each variable according to the average height of their *marks*. Each of these rank orders may then be compared in turn to the rank order of the judges' *scores* on the same variable. For example, see Table 2.

Examination of the two parts of Table 2 reveals a general tendency among the judges to mark by contrast on the need for Order. The highest marks are assigned by judges D and C who are themselves below average in orderliness, and the lowest ranks are assigned by judges A and E who are above average in orderliness.

TABLE 2

n ORDER

Average mark of 15 subjects as assigned by each Judge		Score of each Judge	
1. Judge D	3.15	1. Judge A	4.37
2. " C	2.57	2. " E	3.87
3. " B	2.33	3. " B	3.00
4. " A	2.20	4. " C	1.87
5. " E	2.13	5. " D	1.50

With no other variable, however, was there a clearly exhibited tendency to mark either by similarity or by contrast. To determine whether the judges exhibited a general tendency that operated to a slight extent throughout the series of judgements, the judges who stood first and second in the rank order of *scores* were classed as 'high' in that variable and those who stood fourth and fifth were classed as 'low.' The third (medium) position was neglected. The rank order of assigned *marks* was divided in the same way. The results have been tabulated in Table 3.

The findings indicate that the tendency to mark by contrast was, if anything, a little stronger than the tendency to mark by similarity.

Two other methods of dealing with the data were used, both of which indicated the same thing: that a very slight tendency to mark by contrast prevailed. On examining the marks given by the individual judges, however, it was discovered that only one of the judges (D) manifested this tendency (17 marks by contrast, and only 4 by similarity). In the other judges contrast and similarity were nearly equal in strength. Judge D was a European who felt that a few of the subjects were rather strange to him, unlike any of his acquaintances. Thus his marking might be accounted for by supposing that the personalities of some of the subjects were actually different, and were felt by him to be *very* different from his own.

TABLE 3

	Frequency	
	Manifest	Latent
Judges ranking *high* gave *high* marks	20	10
Judges ranking *low* gave *low* marks	23	12
Marking by similarity	43	22
Judges ranking *low* gave *high* marks	26	11
Judges ranking *high* gave *low* marks	28	10
Marking by contrast	54	21

Our calculations, then, furnished very little evidence of the occurrence of projection in any of the five judges when marking the fifteen subjects at the conference, a finding which testifies to their objectivity. Let us now consider another question.

Does a judge mark best those who are *like* himself or those who are *unlike* himself? The diagnostic success of each E in judging each other E was measured in terms of the standard deviation of his marks from the *scores* on each variable. Each *score*, it will be remembered, was obtained by averaging the judge's rating of himself with the average of the ratings assigned by the other four judges. A rank order of the accuracy with which each E marked each other E was made as follows:

1. B marking D .59
2. C " B .60
3. A " C .62
4. B " E .67 etc.

There were twenty such combinations. For comparison with this rank order every E was paired with every other E and a rank order of the ten pairs based on the degree of similarity of its members was constructed. Degree of similarity was estimated by calculating the standard deviation of the two sets of scores. These data may be examined in order to determine whether the most accurate marks are assigned by judges who most resemble the person judged. The results with the manifest variables may be summarized as follows:

A is *most* like C and judges C *best*.
A is *least* like E and judges E *worst*.
B is *most* like D and judges D *best*.
B is least like E but judges C worst.
C is most like D but judges B best (D second best).
C is *least* like A and judges A *worst*.
D is most like C but judges B best (C second best).
D is least like A but judges E worst (A second worst).
E is *most* like C and judges C *best*.
E is *least* like A and judges A *worst*.

Thus, 6 out of 10 cases support the proposition that a judge is most accurate when judging a person who most resembles himself, and least accurate when judging a person who is most different. In 3 of the remaining 4 cases the deviation from this rule is slight.

The results with the latent variables are as follows:

A is most like E but marks D best.
A is *least* like B and marks B *worst*.
B is most like E but marks C best (E second best).
B is least like D but marks A worst (D second worst).
C is *most* like E and marks E *best*.
C is least like D but marks A worst (D second worst).
D is *most* like A and marks A *best*.
D is least like B but marks E worst.
E is *most* like C and marks C *best*.
E is *least* like D and marks D *worst*.

Out of 10 cases, 5 give complete support and 3 partial support to the principle that judges mark best the subjects who most resemble them and mark worst those who least resemble them. In the 20 cases considered there was not a single instance of the opposite : that an E judged best the E whom he resembled least or judged worst the E whom he resembled most.

One explanation for this finding might be this : that a man tends to project his dominant variables into others and therefore he errs least when he judges someone who actually does resemble him. This notion, however, is not supported by our previous finding : that there was no predominant tendency on the part of these judges to mark by similarity. The best explanation seems to be the common one : that a man can only understand what he has already experienced. One might hazard the statement that without empathy a man cannot make an accurate diagnosis and he can best empathize with those whose responses resemble his own.

Differences in Diagnostic Ability among the Judges

As criteria of the diagnostic ability of individual judges we have *Index a* and *Index b*. *Index b* (agreement between conference marks and final marks) is a rather good criterion, if we use ' diagnostic ability ' to stand for the ability to give ratings on such variables as were used, but *Index a* (agreement with other judges at the conference), as we have seen, is a poor index. Nevertheless it may be of interest to examine our findings in order to see whether there were any consistent differences in deviation among the judges.

An examination of Table 4 reveals some consistent differences in rank. Judge B ranks 1st in 70% of the markings ; Judge D ranks 5th in 70% ; and Judge E is either 3rd or 4th in 80%. Judges C and A are less consistent. However, C ranks 1st four times and never 5th ; and A ranks 5th three times and never 1st. It has been pointed out that the standard deviation is an unreliable index, because, for one thing, it does not take account of the spread of a judge's ratings. But if we estimate the percentage of 2's and 3's assigned by each judge on the manifest variables we can get a rough idea of the spread of his marks. Assuming that the 28 subjects were a fair sample of the college population, the percentage of 2's and 3's (from -1σ to $+1\sigma$ on the normal frequency curve) should amount to about 68%. The findings are as follows: C, 62%; A, 59%; B, 54%; E, 50%; D, 46%. This result indicates that there was no noticeable central tendency and that the average for the group would have been somewhat better if the judges had kept the

TABLE 4

DIAGNOSTIC ABILITY OF THE JUDGES IN TERMS OF σ

			Year	B		C		E		A		D		
				R.O.	σ	R.O.	σ	R.O.	σ	R.O.	σ	R.O.	σ	Av.
Ss.	a	Mnf.	'34	1.5	.57	1.5	.57	3	.62	4	.72	5	.86	.67
			'35	1	.72	3	.78	4	.81	2	.75	5	.96	.80
		Lt.	'35	4	.88	1	.79	2	.81	3	.82	5	.97	.85
	b	Mnf.	'34	1	.93	2	1.08	4	1.19	3	1.16	5	1.31	1.13
			'35	1	.74	4	.94	3	.91	2	.83	5	1.05	.89
		Lt.	'35	1	.62	3	.99	4	1.08	2	.76	5	1.15	.92
Js.	a	Mnf.	'35	2	.76	1	.69	3	.90	5	.97	4	.96	.86
		Lt.	'35	4	.92	1	.70	2	.71	3	.84	5	.95	.82
Self	a	Mnf.	'35	1	.33	3	.46	4	.52	5	.72	2	.38	.48
		Lt.	'35	1	.34	2	.44	3	.45	5	.59	4	.46	.45
		Average		1.7	.68	2.1	.74	3.2	.80	3.4	.82	4.5	.90	

Ss = marks on subjects; Js = marks on judges; Self = marks on self.
a = Index a (average standard deviation from the mean).
b = Index b (average standard deviation between conference and final marks).
Mnf. = manifest variables; Lt. = latent variables.

frequency curve in mind. This applies particularly to Judges E and D who might have stood higher in the validity rank orders if they had marked more conservatively.

If we take the average results obtained with *Index b*, our most reliable criterion, the rank order of the judges is as follows: B, .76; A, .92; C, 1.00; E, 1.06; D, 1.17. This order agrees with the final average rank order except that A is two places lower in the latter. This drop in A's rank is due mostly to the extent of his deviations in self-ratings, a finding which may perhaps be ascribed to the fact that he was the only one of the judges who had not been psychoanalysed.

Each member of the council was required in 1934–35 to predict the rank order of subjects on three tests to be administered subsequently (*cf.* Hypnotic Test, Level of Aspiration Test, Ethical Standards Test). The average of the three coefficients of correlation for each judge between the predicted and the actual rank orders are as follows: B, r = +.34; D, r = +.32, E, r = +.31; A, r = +.22; C, r = +.13. Except that D and C have changed positions, this rank order, based on objective results, is similar to the ability rank order as given above.

One experiment in matching was attempted, when Judge D read the responses given by 5 subjects in a certain test, all remarks of a specifically personal character being omitted. The other judges were asked to guess what subject had given each production. Judge B guessed 3 correctly (to be expected by chance 9 times in 100); Judge C guessed 2 (to be expected 25 times in 100); Judges A and E each guessed 1 (to be expected 63 times in 100). This is approximately the same rank order that was obtained above.

Our findings, then, point to the conclusion that there are somewhat consistent differences among judges in respect to their ability to diagnose traits and predict behaviour. Comparing the experimenters it seems that the following factors are sufficient to account for the differences:

Judge B (R.O. 1) was older and had had two years' experience working with the scheme of variables.

Judge A (R.O. 4) was the only judge who had not been psychoanalysed.

Judge D (R.O. 5) was a foreigner. He neglected the frequency curve and hazarded numerous extreme ratings.

The differences between judges might have been greater if they had not been specially selected because of their proved aptitude for this kind of work.

In 1934–35, to determine whether some of the other somewhat

less experienced experimenters had greater or less ability than the members of the Diagnostic Council, four experimenters, who had not had the benefit of observing the subjects at the conference but who had seen them for a longer time under other conditions, were asked to mark the subjects. The rank order of their average standard deviations from the final marks was as follows : H, 1.04 ; F, 1.13 ; G, 1.18 ; J, 1.20. The average standard deviation was 1.11, definitely higher than .89, the figure obtained that year for the Diagnostic Council. The top man of the inexperienced group was about equal to the bottom man of the Diagnostic Council. This finding indicates that diagnostic ability is a function of experience.

Measurement of Latent Needs

Since the conference conducted by the Diagnostic Council offered little opportunity for the expression of latent needs, the ratings that were made at that session were hardly more than 'hunches' based on quite equivocal cues. Subsequently, however, there were several sessions specially designed to evoke images, fantasies and dramatic themes. These were examined directly for evidences of repressed infantile complexes, until a method was developed for dealing with them in a more systematic fashion. The present experiments were concluded, however, before we completed a scheme which would yield reasonably representative indices of the strength of the different needs and press. Nevertheless in the present experiments, the fantasy productions of our subjects provided sufficient data for deliberate judgements of the prevalence and force of certain underlying tendencies ; and we ended by feeling that our estimates of inhibited and unconscious needs were hardly further from the mark than were our estimates of the manifest needs.

Conclusions

Nothing has been definitely proved by the findings reported in this section. The data are insufficient and the sources of error too many. But a few very tentative conclusions may be drawn :

(1). There were rather consistent differences among the members of the council in respect to the validity of their ratings as measured by different indices: agreement with other judges, agreement with final marks, predictions of behaviour, correct matching. It seems that these differences can be accounted for by assuming the advantage of (a) a thorough acquaintance with the exemplifications of each variable, (b) experience in rating such variables, (c) keeping the frequency curve in mind when rating, (d) having been psycho-analysed. Some facts suggest that the disadvantage of being different from the subjects in respect to nationality (and perhaps also in respect to sex, age, social status, system of values, etc.) is considerable.

(2). The value of experience, of having judges who have worked together for some time, of establishing a methodological convention, is indicated by our findings. Inexperienced judges, for example, did not do so well as the members of the council. Also the ratings of the council were better the second year than they were the first.

(3). Agreement with other judges at the conferences (expressed in terms of σ) is a reasonably good index of the diagnostic ability of a single judge. But degree of agreement among judges in regard to the proper rating of a trait is not a good index of the validity of that rating.

(4). Kelley's ϵ (epsilon) is a better index of the validity of judges' ratings than the average standard deviation.

(5). There was no evidence of a prevailing projective tendency (to mark by similarity) among the judges.

(6). In marking other judges a judge usually marked best the judge who resembled him and marked worst the judge who least resembled him.

(7). There were rather consistent differences among the variables in respect to their measurability. The most readily diagnosed variables were those which (a) involved emotion, (b) were most readily evoked by the conference situation or (c) were best defined and understood.

Chapter V

THE GENETICAL INVESTIGATION OF PERSONALITY : CHILDHOOD EVENTS

H. A. MURRAY

THE estimation of separable variables, somewhat along the lines described in the last chapter, has seemed to us a necessary preliminary to the formulation of a personality. The outcome of the final synthesis is a portrayal of the subject as a loose organization of complexes (integrates), each of which is a compound of needs and modes oriented towards a fusion of press that emanate from certain cathected objects (people, institutions, ideologies), the complexes being conditioned to one or more cathected fields of interest (for example : athletics, finance, politics, art, etc.). These complexes may be objectified as overt action, may take the form of attitudes and verbally expressed opinions (rationalized sentiments) or may remain entirely latent. They are to varying degrees egocentric and sociocentric.

Formulations of this sort are, at their best, abstract representations of the status quo. They describe how the individual has been conducting himself recently, what causes he has been advocating or rejecting, what conflicts have been engaging his attention ; and if one is willing to lean on the principle of repetition and consist ency, they offer a basis for predicting the individual's behaviour, i certain situations present themselves, in the near future. However in our opinion, personality cannot be completely set forth as an integration of complexes at a particular point in time. An apparent cross section of this sort is a conception based upon the observation of a short temporal segment of the life history, a segment that may be less important and less representative than other segments. We should like to know, for example, to what extent the observed segment is a progression or a regression from previous periods. The more points we can obtain on the life curve the better can we extrapolate beyond the present. To conceive of personality as an historic flow or emergence of events is to be directed to the study of past occurrences. Abstract biography *is* the personality, as far as it can be formulated.

The exploration of the past, however, is dictated not only by our interest in the entire sweep (rather than in a single movement) of the life curve, but by a felt necessity to 'explain' what we observe. Why a man is habitually afraid of women, why he consistently refuses to join any club or association, why he is an atheist, why he is passionately fond of duck-shooting and poker, why he is affectionate with animals, why he is always very careful about his belongings and is scrupulously precise about money matters, why he suffers from indigestion, these problems remain unresolved until the psychologist pushes his inspection further, and further means inward or backward in time. The question, 'Why?' leads to another, 'What?' or 'How?' the beginning of a regress that is halted only by a dearth of facts.

The 'Why?' that follows the naming of a reaction system evoked by a certain press necessarily leads the psychologist inward (into the subject's brain), because he is called upon to explain why *this* individual reacted in one way and *that* individual reacted in another. As the situation has not changed objectively (for the E), *this* subject must be different from *that*; different in respect to how he apperceives the situation or different in respect to how he reacts to a similar apperception. Now, a vast amount of observation and experiment goes to show that a great many differences of personality can be attributed to differences in past experience. The press to which an individual has been exposed, the nature of the specific objects which have embodied each press, the benign objects that have been associated (in space or time) with the pressive object, the usual or occasionally intense success or failure of this or that need or mode, the amount of indirect knowledge (correct and incorrect) that has been accumulated about various situations — all these factors are capable under proper circumstances of modifying the structure of the brain. A subject who has repeatedly reacted in a certain fashion is different from one who has not. He has a different habit system. A subject who knows about certain matters is different from one who does not, and so forth. The general theory is that the perception and apperception of objects and of configurations of objects leave 'traces' (a hypothetical concept), and the activation of needs and actones leaves 'readinesses' (a hypothetical concept), and perception-conation sequences leave 'connections' (a hypothetical concept). These 'traces,' 'connections' and 'readinesses' are rarely fixed. They undergo countless modifications as the result of internal and external forces. This is theory, but theory that seems necessary if one is to explain the facts of what generally has been called 'conditioning.' It is necessary because in the formulation of an event, as Lewin has affirmed repeatedly, only factors that are operating at the moment can rightfully be included. The past, as experiments have shown, will explain some aspects of the present, but since the past *as such* has perished, it must be operating not *as such*, but in the form of a conserved impression (trace, memory) that is now a part of the organism. If it were possible to examine directly all these traces, connections and readinesses in the brain, as well as all the contemporaneous physiological happenings, one could name every process that was functioning within the organism. Since this is not possible, one must hypothesize the internal factors and substantiate the hypothesis with facts from the subject's past life. Usually one makes several hypotheses, and allows the facts turned up by further explorations to determine which one is the most probable. When the E finds himself unable to make any hypothesis, he must rely upon the biographical data for suggestions.

It was for these reasons that we resolved to undertake a genetical investigation of personality, and once the decision was made, we turned inevitably to psycho-analysis for guidance. Of course, we availed ourselves of what information could be obtained from other sources, but since analysis offers, as far as we know, the only conceptual scheme that orders in an intelligible fashion most of the phenomena of infancy and childhood, we adopted this point of view as a working hypothesis. The underlying conception of psycho-analysis calls attention to the impressionability of young tissue, the durability of the impressions received, and the determining effect of these upon the whole course of development. If this is true—and there is sound evidence from biology to support it—the earliest experiences, though unremembered by the subject, may be lastingly important. The psychologist must go back to the foetus, certainly not with the expectation of explaining everything, but with the hope of exposing some of the determinants of many things.

Psycho-analysis was led to its notion of the importance of infantile events by comprehensive studies of the recollections of adult neurotics. Evidence was accumulated to show that present symptomatology could be partially explained by referring to the earliest remembered events. But even these memories proved insufficient, since they did not include, except in rare instances, anything that had occurred during the first two or three years of life, and many of the subject's fantasies and dreams could be made psychologically intelligible only by assuming the endurance of traces established at that time. Further studies made it plain that some of these traces could not, by any chance, represent actual occurrences. However, they could conceivably have been engendered by fantasies, pre-logical imaginings of events. Finally, it was noted, first by Jung,[1] that there was much similarity among the fantasies of different children, children that were exposed to diverse family conditions. Since the environment could not be held accountable for the fantasies, it seemed necessary to resort to a theory of innate patterns of imagery (archetypal fantasies). This philogenetic conception of the mind was made credible by the discovery that the fantasies of children (as well as the delusions of the insane) resembled nothing so much as the folk tales, sagas and religious myths of primitive people. A possible hypothesis, then, would be this : that a child's imagination is successively influenced by unconscious configurating tendencies that were established (roughly in the same temporal sequence) during the course of man's development throughout the ages. This is the

1. Jung,C.G. *The Psychology of the Unconscious*, New York,1931.

theory which was proposed by Samuel Butler. The fact that so many myths (collective fantasies of former times) are carried along by images that so clearly call to mind the objects of infantile preoccupation suggests that it is the imaginings of the savage child rather than of the savage adult that were primarily responsible.

It may be supposed, I believe, that every modern child dreams his maturating way through these archetypal patterns. The march of the endocrines must be influential, as well as external conditions and the fortunes of needs : traumata, parental behaviour, gratifications, frustrations, and so forth. Due to certain circumstances, as yet only vaguely recognized, some of these fantasies 'stick' instead of perishing with their fellows in the limbo of the unconscious. They stick in the infant's mind and become connected in irrational ways to the objects of his world. Without some inkling of these weird fantasies, a psychologist will necessarily be at a loss to explain many of the less usual reactions of childhood. To what extent psycho-analysis has properly distinguished the common complexes and fantasies of infancy is uncertain. It is conventional, and probably correct, to say that analysts have limited themselves to phenomena which have sexual significance. If this is the case, one might suppose that they had overlooked many important phenomena. This conclusion, however, would hardly do justice to the flexibility of the pan-sexual theory. The analysts, it now appears, have overlooked very little ; which is due to the fact that they find significance in everything, since according to their theory, any action or any part of the body, or the body as a whole, or any object may become erotized (associated with pleasurable, erotic-like sensations or feelings). Thus, they speak of muscular erotism, erotization of thought, the body as phallus, etc.

Though many psychologists find it impossible to understand or to agree with Freudian theory, there is no dispute about what should be set down as the important activities of infancy : sleeping ; breathing ; sucking, biting and ingesting nourishment through the mouth ; excretion of urine through the urethra and faeces through the anus ; spitting up and vomiting ; retracting from painful stimuli ; thumb-sucking and scratching ; crying for the mother ; cooing and clinging to the mother ; struggling against physical restraint ; raging in a tantrum when frustrated ; attempting to co-ordinate and master objects : creeping, walking and manipulating ; exploring : touching, peering, smelling ; showing-off before admirers, and so forth. Later, one finds other activities : acquisition, collection and retention of objects, dreams of power expressed in play, destructiveness, assaults upon weaker objects (pets and young siblings), fantasied assaults upon stronger objects (parents and older siblings), primitive masturbation, curiosity about birth (after the arrival of a younger sibling), sexual fantasies, and a host of avoidances and anxieties : fear of falling, of injury, of rejection, of deprivation, of mutilation, of punishment, and so forth. This list is by no means exhaustive. It is, I suppose, what most people have observed and would agree to call outstanding. Nor would there be much argument about the fact that the following were important objects in the infant's world : parts of his own body, physical supports, what he eats and excretes, his mother with certain parts of her body (nipple, breast) specially cathected, his father, other siblings ; and later, dangerous situations, injurious objects, possessions, pets and playmates. Under mother we may include nurses and other older women who play the maternal role, and under father we may include older paternal men. Finally, there are the almost universal experiences : birth, teething, weaning, learning to walk without support, training in toilet habits, rivalry of siblings, the special devotion of the parent of opposite sex, interference by the parent of the same sex, numerous alarms and accidents and fevers, leaving home and entering school ; and, throughout the entire course of development : barriers, prohibitions, coercions and threats of punishment.

Out of these objects and events the child, driven by its needs, weaves its allegories, its science of life. There are great gaps in its knowledge, but the child fills them according to its inveterate tendency with whatever images it has at its disposal. Since, according to the evidence at hand, these pre-logical myths considerably influence development, it is the function of the 'depth' psychologist to reveal them. To do this he must be acquainted with prelogical and pre-realistical processes: syncretism, juxtaposition, animism, symbolization,[1] as well as a large number of typical infantile conceptions.

This 'streamlined' discussion of analytic findings and speculations leads to the conclusion that the first necessity is an account of the common events and fantasies of childhood ordered according to a conceptual scheme that makes them psychologically intelligible. Such a plan should lead to an abstract representation of the course of events that has exhibited each personality. It should make possible a comparison of cases. Naturally, all such schematizations will distort the facts to some extent. But if the psychologist attempts to get along without a plan that has an adequate theoretical foundation his case histories will consist of 'literary' accounts of experiences which the reader himself must, if he can, fashion for scientific use. If no uniformities or diversities are strikingly displayed, no generalizations will be possible. Science must overlook a great deal of the rich texture of concrete experience in order to put into relief the underlying interactions of forces. The relief resembles an X-ray photograph of a living man. We perceive none of the familiar features which in everyday life attract or repel us, but we see the structure that supports these features. The violence that is done to nature by scientific abstractions is grossest during the first stages of a discipline, marked as they are by the employment of large, all-embracing generalizations. Later, the initial, necessarily over-simplified conceptions become refined by detailed analysis and many previously neglected items are thereby distinguished and given place.

The scheme that we used was based on the theory that was outlined in the previous section, the analysis of events into themas: needs, press (cathected objects) and outcomes. As far as we have been able to observe, the behaviour of children exhibits much the

1. Piaget, J. *The Language and Thought of the Child*, London, 1926; *Judgment and Reasoning of the Child*, London, 1928.

same themas as does the behaviour of adults, though the modes of action and the objects cathected are often strikingly different. In our records of the reactions of subjects to the Clinic situation, it was possible to neglect the provoking press, since these were relatively constant for all subjects. But in dealing with the biographical material this omission would be disastrous. Here the press are of major import. Indeed, it is quite possible to portray a life, as some biographers do, as the almost inevitable outcome of the impact of external press.

Since the culture and the more or less acculturated parents are, as it were, in operation before the child is born, it seems more reasonable to start with this side of the equation, and to consider later the different reactions (drives) that such conditions commonly evoke in children. It will be convenient, in order to avoid endless repetitions, to classify the press and the needs separately. This procedure temporarily dislocates the thema (which symbolizes the dynamic integrity of an event) but this can be reconstructed later by combining the given press and the given need.

In view of the multiplicity and complexity of children's fancies and the difficulty of understanding such pre-logical compositions (primitive regnant processes), it seems advisable to limit ourselves to the facts of behaviour, and for the present, to events that occurred within the span of normal memory (after three years of age). Each category of the scheme will be illustrated by one or two samples culled from the autobiographies of our subjects. They will be presented as they were offered, without analysis or interpretation.

Classification of Childhood Events

A. PRESS

It is as difficult to diagnose a press as it is to diagnose a need, but if the diagnosis cannot be made an event cannot be dynamically interpreted. Furthermore, the strength of the press should be approximately estimated. For it is impossible to judge the reactivity of the child without knowing the degree of danger, of deprivation, of punishment or of indulgence (as the case may be) to which he is exposed. A zero (0) to five (5) scale is convenient for these ratings.

It is possible to distinguish in most cases the trend of the environmental force (physical or social) quite apart from the reaction which it initiates in the child. However, even when this objective standpoint is adhered to, each class of press will be felt — particularly by one who empathizes with the child — as something that is desirable or undesirable. This is inevitable, because every situation that is not inert will have an effect (actually or potentially) on the subject's well-being ; it will be a 'promise' to satisfy or a 'threat' to frustrate a need. A press, by definition, is just such a beneficial or harmful process.

The illustrations of press, having been culled from the autobiographies, are examples of beta press (apperceptions of the S) rather than alpha press (judgements of disinterested trained observers). We can only guess in each case to what extent the subject is a reliable witness. The beta press, of course, is the determinant of behaviour, since if a child believes that a situation signifies a certain thing it will be this conception that will operate rather than what psychologists believe the situation signifies. This has encouraged analysts (few of whom get reports from parents or other more impartial witnesses of their patients' early years) to say that the actual (alpha) conditions do not matter. It is the child's version that is all important. From a therapeutic standpoint this view seems to be sufficiently correct, but it would be of scientific interest, nevertheless, to know to what extent fantasy and a fallacious memory have distorted the facts. In our studies we made no attempt, except in a few instances, to get reports from parents. Consequently, some of the recorded press may mirror unconscious (archetypal) imagery more closely than they do the objective environment.

The press of childhood have been classified as follows :

CHILDHOOD EVENTS

Press

1. p Family Insupport	
a. Cultural Discord b. Family Discord	
c. Capricious Discipline d. Parental Separation	
e. Absence of Parent: Father Mother	
f. Parental Illness: Father Mother	
g. Death of Parent: Father Mother	
h. Inferior Parent: Father Mother	
i. Dissimilar Parent: Father Mother	
j. Poverty k. Unsettled Home	
2. p Danger or Misfortune	
a. Physical Insupport, Height b. Water	
c. Aloneness, Darkness	
d. Inclement Weather, Lightning e. Fire	
f. Accident g. Animal	
3. p Lack or Loss	
a. of Nourishment b. of Possessions c. of Companionship d. of Variety	
4. p Retention, Withholding Objects	
5. p Rejection, Unconcern & Scorn	
6. p Rival, Competing Contemporary	
7. p Birth of Sibling	
8. p Aggression	
a. Maltreatment by Elder Male Elder Female	
b. Maltreatment by Contemporaries	
c. Quarrelsome Contemporaries	
9. Fp Aggression-Dominance, Punishment	
a. Striking, Physical Pain b. Restraint, Confinement	
10. p Dominance, Coercion & Prohibition	
a. Discipline b. Religious Training	
11. Fp Dominance-Nurturance	
a. Parental Ego Idealism, Mother Father Physical Econ, Vocation Caste Intellectual	
b. Possessive Parent, Mother Father	
c. Over-solicitous Parent Fears: Accident Illness Bad Influences	

CHILDHOOD EVENTS (*Continued*)

PRESS

12. p Nurturance, Indulgence		Intraorganic Press	
13. p Succorance, Demands for Tenderness		18. p Illness	
14. p Deference, Praise, Recognition		a. Prolonged, Frequent Illness b. Nervous c. Respiratory d. Cardiac	
15. p Affiliation, Friendships		e. Gastro-intestinal f. Infantile Paralysis g. Convulsions	
16. p Sex			
a. Exposure b. Seduction, Homosexual Heterosexual c. Parental Intercourse		19. p Operation	
		20. p Inferiority	
17. Deception or Betrayal		a. Physical b. Social c. Intellectual	

1. *p Family Insupport.* A basic necessity for physical existence is the continued presence of solid support (*terra firma*), something that is wide and stable on which to lie, stand or walk. Loss of support is a press that always arouses fear in an infant and an earthquake may cause insanities of fright in adults. For a human child a supporting family structure is equally important since the satisfaction of all the child's needs depends upon it. First it is the mother who gives the child physical support (embraces it, puts it in its cradle, tightly tucks in the enfolding sheets), who feeds and cleans the child at regular intervals. Later, father and siblings contribute to the pattern of the child's universe. Family Support (Family Insupport 0, 1, 2) is exemplified by a consistent, stable, regular, dependable routine of devoted parental behaviour. Under these conditions the child can count on a constant tpmo schedule which provides periodic assistance for the gratification of its basic needs. No learning is possible in a chaotic world. As Pavlov has shown in dogs, ambiguities of meaning lead to neurosis. To supply orderly tender devotion the parents must themselves be stable:

happily united and secure. And to this a relatively solid surrounding culture is conducive.

Since a lack or loss of support (p Insupport) is more arresting than its opposite, we have chosen to view the family situation from the former standpoint. And under Insupport we have included the chief occurrences which disrupt for the child the sameness, regularity, consistency, or dependability of family life. The family's disorganization can often be attributed to disturbing social influences : financial panics, political upheavals, confusion and war (social insupport), but usually the child experiences these only indirectly. The more immediate factors are : periods of separation from one or both parents (involving changes of discipline), illness of a parent (which incapacitates the nurturant object and engenders worry), death of one or both parents, discord and quarrels between the members of the family, separation or divorce of the parents, irregular and capricious discipline by one or both parents, lack of congeniality with father or mother and family poverty sufficient to arouse feelings of insecurity in the household. The descent of family status should also be listed here. Since all children are more or less helpless such deprivations of assistance, particularly if they come abruptly and unexpectedly, are liable to arouse the anxiety of Succorance (feelings of insupport). There may be an underlying apperception of p Danger with a ready n Harmavoidance, or a fear that the elementary positive needs will not be satisfied. In an adventurous child, however, one in whom p Support is sometimes apperceived as a barrier, the loss of an unnecessary and perhaps restricting object does not come as a frustration of the Succorance drive, but as a gratification of the need for Autonomy (free motility). Thus when traces of p Insupport appear in the memories of a subject we may suppose the following : 1, a need for Succorance with fixation (dependence) upon former nurturant objects (cathexis of the past), 2, a need for Harmavoidance with fears directed towards open spaces, distances, darkness and strangers ; and possibly, 3, a high tendency for Sameness (contraction of the field of locomotion) together with a low need for Autonomy against restraint.

We have found it convenient to distinguish p Rejection (a cold, unloving, neglectful parental attitude) from p Insupport, despite the fact that the two are often combined and that p Rejection by itself is apt to provoke feelings of insecurity. For a number of reasons, however, the two press should be considered separately. For example, one may find orderly stable households in which expressions of love are lacking as well as the opposite: loving, indulgent parents who provide their children with no constant pattern of behaviour and sentiment. The first press of Insupport is the expulsion from the womb, the second is weaning and the third comes when the child is expected to walk unaided. Later, he is pressed to wash, dress and feed himself without assistance, and subsequently it becomes necessary for him to go greater distances alone: to walk to school or do an errand in the village, to pass a house where a dog will terrifyingly bark at him, to risk an encounter with a gang of toughs, to meet strangers, to go at bedtime into a dark room peopled with ghosts, and so forth. Thus, 'growing-up' involves a graded series of removals of support, and if a firm resilient structuration of personality is to result these removals should not be too alarming or too abruptly imposed.

1a. *p Family Insupport: Cultural Discord.* This is the condition that exists when the parents practice and teach a culture that is different from that of the locality in which they live, or when there are differences between the parents in respect to the culture which they represent to the child.

Zill: (My father) spoke English with less than the usual accent but was not entirely Americanized. . . This has often made me inwardly ashamed of him in many not uncommon situations (Inferior Father).

Roas: The meeting of two racial traditions was undoubtedly surcharged with many influences. . . I was christened in the Greek Orthodox Church, but brought up in the Methodist Church. There was a strong Quaker influence in my mother's family, and in the Quaker school which I attended. My Greek parentage resulted in one inconvenience. . . When I came to be of an age when matrimony might be at least thought of, my social availability was discounted.

1b. *p Family Insupport : Family Discord.* Disagreements and quarrels between the parents confuse and shake the balance of a child. They make a gap between his feet. He may become emotionally involved, take one side or the other and have a constant feeling of insecurity.

Abel : During these periods my father was quite quarrelsome, accusing my mother of infidelities which were without foundation. He always carried a cloak of pseudo-jealousy, but yet was outspoken in his admiration of other women.

p Family Support : Family Concord. This is the state that prevails when the father and mother, as well as the children and near relatives, are consistently in harmony ; thus offering the child a solid structure of goodwill.

Bulge : My parents were happily married and I can recall not one instance of an argument or discord of any kind in our home. . . I felt secure and utterly at peace in my relations.

1c. *p Family Insupport : Capricious Discipline.* When a child is exposed to an incalculable and irrational discipline — severity alternating with indulgence — it is hard for him to develop a stable character. Conditions provided by very emotional parents are classed here.

Outer : Sometimes she (mother) was kind to me, the next moment raging.

1d. *p Family Insupport : Parental Separation.* Separation or divorce of the parents is not uncommon. It usually comes after a period of quarrelling. It is apt to divide the child within himself and engender a feeling of insecurity.

Cling : Mother left my father. He was moody and selfish ; she irritable and hot-tempered . . . the ties of family had been broken before years had strengthened them. It was only long afterward that I regretted the absence of full and happy home life. . . I met few people through family contacts because of the unsettled nature of my home.

1e. *p Family Insupport : Absence of Parent.* One or both parents may be away from home a great deal, or the child may be left with relatives or be sent away to school. If the parents are divorced the child may be deprived of the support of one parent, usually the father.

Akeside : Both my parents were always away from home a great deal of the time, and there was very little home life.

1f. *p Family Insupport : Parental Illness.* One or both of the parents may be chronically ill ; a neurosis or psychosis being especially disrupting.

Outer : My mother's mental state gave way and she was sent to an asylum with 'brain fever.'

Abel : My mother's naturally fine disposition has been made ragged by nervous disorders, real and not affected. She has a heart condition and low blood pressure as a result of overwork and worry.

Vulner : My mother had a nervous breakdown when I was a baby and has devoted much time to studying and mastering her nerves.

1g. *p Family Insupport : Death of Parent.* The death of a parent during a child's impressionable years may disjoint his life. The death of the mother is usually more disturbing than the death of the father.

Bulge : My father's death was a terrific blow to my mother from which she never recovered. At my mother's death our family was separated.

Quick : After the death of my father, of whom I was very fond, I had a great depression. It took me a long time to recover.

Also under this heading may be included dangers which threaten the life of a parent.

Virt : My mother stood the danger of being killed, or if caught, of being hanged or maltreated by the soldiers.

1h. *p Family Insupport: Inferior Parent.* The father or mother may be inferior in one or more respects (physical, economic, social, intellectual) and on this account, be unable to win the attachment and respect of the child. The father, for example, may be a drunkard or a bankrupt. Perhaps the most important item in this category is Caste Inferiority, involving both parents.

Zeeno : (My father) has been content to live happily and although his income has been practically nothing for the last three years, he lacks the initiative or vigour to attempt anything else. . . His utter indifference to any pleasures outside of his home, and his mental simplicity has been a great consternation to me.

Gay : My father proved to be a social misfit. He took more and more to alcohol and we were neglected. We were taught to regard him as an erring human who must be brought to give up his evil habits.

p Family Support : Superior Parent. The child's father or mother may be a superior person (in the world's eyes or in the child's). The father, for example, may have a powerful physique, a magnetic presence, the ability to make money, or a high degree of intelligence. He may, in addition, be an important public figure. Or the mother may be a superior person in one or more respects ; she may play a dominant role in the family.

Zeeno : My mother is so different. She is a strong, businesslike, proud, and independent type of individual. . . She comes from a noble stock in her country. . . She is physically fine and possesses much initiative. Her desires are only to get along with her family and help us make up for my father's financial failings. . . My mother is father also, for she directs the discipline, the education, the morals, the work and the general activity of the whole family.

Irkman : My father had the acumen, the training, and the perseverance to succeed. I always felt he was superior to all other men.

11. *p Family Insupport : Dissimilar Parent.* A child may feel that he has nothing in common with his parents (mother and/or father). He may realize that their interests, sentiments and aims are quite different from his own, that they do not understand him and cannot share his point of view. In other words he does not find his parents congenial.

Kindle : My *mother* found that she could not understand my interests. Languages and literature meant little to her. Nor could she appreciate my fascination for the theatre.

p Family Support : Similar Parent. Some subjects feel that one or both parents can share their interests, can understand them and sympathize with their enjoyments.

Krumb : Mother and I were much more understanding of each other. I resemble mother.

1j. *p Family Insupport : Poverty.* If the family is in straitened circumstances, the child will necessarily be deprived of many advantages that other children enjoy. Moreover, his parents may worry a great deal about money and he may become infected with their feeling of insecurity.

Akeson : My parents have been so concerned with financial difficulties that the atmosphere has been unpleasant.

1k. *p Family Insupport : Unsettled Home.* Frequent changes of environment do not allow the child to familiarize himself with any fixed conditions. Friendships are unstable and it may even be hard to form regular habits.

Outer : At two years of age I was taken East. . . At four we moved again. . . Previous to moving I spent six months in a Catholic convent. . . We moved again, to another part of the city.

2. *p Danger or Misfortune.* In this category are included physical dangers from natural causes ; not those arising out of the neglect or hostility of other people. Thus Physical Insupport is classed here, despite its similarity to Human Insupport. Also the threats of animals are included, though in many respects they resemble and may be confused in the child's mind with the intended aggression of human beings. If the event is merely a *threat* of harm we speak of p Danger, but if the individual or his property is injured it is designated as p Misfortune. The remembrance and mention of such press suggest a high n Harmavoidance.

2a. *p Danger or Misfortune : Physical Insupport : Height.* A child is exposed to a press of Insupport whenever (during the time that it is learning to walk) it ventures to toddle alone across an open space. Under this heading we may also include : unstable ground, an earthquake, an icy slope, a chasm or crevass to jump across, a narrow bridge or log across a stream, the edge of a precipice, all conditions that unbalance the body. A timid person is apt to avoid such situations and merely mention that he fears heights. Hence, this complex is usually recorded under n Harm-avoidance. Falls (from ladders, buildings, overturned vehicles), however, are not uncommonly mentioned.

Asper : When I was one and a half years old I slipped off a table on which I was lying into a clothes boiler filled with hot water.

2b. *p Danger or Misfortune : Physical Insupport : Water.* Situations in which there is danger of falling into water, shipwreck or drowning, are grouped under this heading.

Cling : The tides were very high. . . Bill and I swam a few hundred yards to a sandbar which the low tide exposed. . . Suddenly . . . we turned and saw that the flats were covered for half a mile with water. Bill began swimming first, then I began. I lost sight of him. Very soon I grew tired and cold. A strong eddy current was carrying us beyond the nearest point. A fear seized me (n Harm). I shouted for help (n Suc). For a vivid moment the fear of death caught at my throat.

2c. *p Danger or Misfortune : Aloneness, Darkness.* Here we group all situations that are strange, weird or desolate, in which a child finds himself disoriented or alone, away from the protecting presence of an allied object. A child may find himself among strangers or lost in a wood. Such events usually involve Human Insupport.

Asper : I can remember another isolated incident wherein I was lost.

2d. *p Danger or Misfortune : Inclement Weather.* Children may be exposed to storms on land, to lightning, to high winds or to cold. These are sometimes frightening.

Cling : I remember one windy day walking to school, that I was afraid of the wind as I started to cross (the street) and that I clung to a lamp post until someone came and took me by the hand (n Suc : Adherence S n Harm).

Vulner : When I was a year old a lightning bolt struck a church near us. The lights went out and the ladies screamed . . . all of which frightened me terribly.

2e. *p Danger or Misfortune : Fire.* Some children are exposed to the injuring or demolishing power of fire. More commonly, perhaps, they see or hear about a house on fire and weave this phenomenon into a fantasy of Insupport.

Cling : My earliest recollection is of an apartment. . . I remember the details very clearly, flames bursting from the third storey window.

Outer : At three years of age I remember rather distinctly a fire which drove us from the housė in the middle of the night.

2f. *p Danger or Misfortune : Accident.* Here we mostly have in mind collisions of vehicles (automobile accidents and train wrecks) as well as injuries resulting from accidental impact (other than falls) ; also the rapid approach of destructive objects.

Asper : I can remember the incident of an accident when I was about four, when I split open part of my temple perilously near the eye.

Beech : At the age of six I lost my right hand. I was playing with dynamite caps which I set off.

2g. *p Danger or Misfortune : Animal.* An animal that threateningly approaches, pursues, attacks or bites a child falls into this category.

Gay : A strange dog came into our yard and bit me.

3. *p Lack or Loss.* The events in this category border on those under p Family Insupport, as it is usually due to the parents' poverty or absence that the child does not receive enough nourishment or toys, or does not meet other children of its own age. For the same reason this press is related to the press of Rejection : the unloving parent. If the child really wants something that it does not get it commonly attributes it to a wilful deprivation on the part of one or both parents. Here we are apt to imagine that the original frustration was oral : being kept waiting for food, interference with thumb-sucking, weaning and so forth.

3a. *p Lack or Loss: Nourishment.* Because of poverty (p Family Insupport) or illness a child may receive insufficient food or drink. He may long remember his hunger or thirst. Also it has been supposed that if the mother's milk disagrees with the child or if it is insufficient or if the child is allowed to cry for a long time before it is fed or if weaning occurs abruptly the child may conserve a dim impression of the lack of food.

Outer: I was brought up on canned milk in infancy as it was too cold up there for cows.

Gay: Our family doctor was very cautious about my diet and probably underfed me.

3b. *p Lack or Loss: Possessions.* A child may be given very few toys to play with or its toys may be taken away. The parents may use dispossession as a form of punishment; or the child may lose a valued object. Perhaps for the S to apperceive his lack, it is necessary that another child in the neighbourhood have more or better toys than he. When such episodes are remembered and recounted we may suppose that the S has, or once had, a high n Acquisition or n Retention.

Kindle: One of the boys who lived nearby . . . had a train, bigger and finer than mine.

Kast: I remember losing my new straw hat.

3c. *p Lack or Loss: Companionship.* An only child or a child brought up in an isolated region (barren environment) may suffer from the lack of playmates, or if he has playmates, they may leave him. The death or departure of a friend may be felt as an irretrievable loss.

Vulner: I was much alone.

Kindle: We were very much attached to each other. . . He spent a summer in France. . . I was very lonesome.

The apperception of this lack is supposedly due to the n Affiliation, which may, however, be inhibited by the n Seclusion or the n Infavoidance.

3d. *p Lack or Loss : Variety*. Here we group conditions that provide little change, gaiety or stimulation. The child is subjected to a barren home environment. Its activities are restricted and life becomes monotonous. This situation borders on the lack of possessions and companionship. It is based, supposedly, upon a frustration of the need for Play and of the tendency for Change.

Roon : Outside entertainments occurred only rarely . . . the one thing about my early life that I can never forget is the lack of holiday joys, particularly Christmas. No great joys, very little gaiety, nor much of the holiday spirit.

4. *p Retention*. Here have been grouped instances of withholding, and dispossession by the parents, parents who give few gifts, small allowances, and deprive children of the objects of their desire. This category is very similar to p Lack or Loss. It is frequently merged with p Rejection and occasionally with Fp Aggression-Dominance (when punishment takes the form of Dispossession). Later it seemed to us that this class was covered by p Lack or Loss, combined, as the case might be, with p Rejection or Fp Aggression-Dominance. ' p Deprivation ' (including both p Retention and p Acquisition) would be a better term for this sub-class.

Roon : We were given but little money to spend as we chose.

When this press is emphasized we may suppose a n Acquisition and perhaps a n Construction or n Retention in the child. There may also be an underlying n Succorance. The original trauma may be oral frustration.

5. *p Rejection*. Here we subsume all instances of lack or loss of parental love : the mother or father who does not cherish the child but instead disregards, neglects, scorns, repulses or abandons it. The occurrence of p Rejection among the subject's memories naturally suggests n Succorance. The original trauma may have been birth (expulsion from the womb) or weaning (frustration of sucking). This is perhaps the most important of all press in the life of a child. In some degree it is universally experienced, for if the child is to become self-reliant the parents must

gradually curb the expressions of their solicitous concern. Other events, such as the birth of another child, also conspire to bring about, even in the most loving parents, a diminution of displayed devotion. This press is closely associated with p Family Insupport and p Aggression. It would be possible, though I believe inadvisable, to put p Rejection on a single continuum with p Nurturance. A special sub-heading p Social Rejection (unpopularity with one's contemporaries) may conveniently be added here.

Outer : My family took no interest in my schooling whatever.

I received no co-operation whatever from home.

Kindle : I did not get along very well with children.

I was never very popular. . . By some I was utterly ignored. They didn't know of my existence.

Akeson : My parents have not made any serious attempts to understand my problems.

Veal : My father's attitude toward us was one of indifference.

6. *p Rival*. Under this heading may be classed the provoking presence of another person, a parent or sibling, who frustrates the child's desire for affection, for acquisition or for recognition. Hence, if p Rival is stressed in the subject's memories one suspects either n Succorance or Fn Achievement-Recognition.

Gay : My younger brother was liked more than I by all the family.

Nipp : My brother is my mother's favourite.

7. *p Birth of Sibling*. The birth of a sibling when a child is between 1 and 6 years old usually modifies the latter's personality. It may arouse the child's curiosity, a desire to investigate and probe into things, aggression against the newcomer, or a feeling that the mother has been faithless. Strictly speaking this event is not in itself a press. It may, however, manifest one or more press : p Rival, p Enigma, p Rejection.

Bulge : I was rather despondent for a while after the birth of Mary when I saw I was being neglected for this new stranger in our home.

8. *p Aggression*. The various forms of aggression merge into one another. There is *physical* aggression, which involves the use

of fists and weapons, and *verbal* aggression, which confines itself to criticism, ridicule and blame. There is *originative* (unprovoked) and *retaliative* aggression; the retaliations that are socially allowable or advised are termed *punishments* (punitive aggression). Punishments are classed under Fp Agg Dom (aggressive dominance), the usual aim of such measures being to educate the child and prevent further misbehaviour. There may, indeed, be Nurturance mixed with punitive aggression. If, however, the parent becomes unduly angry and the punishment is unnecessarily severe (unjust and cruel) an additional entry is made under p Aggression.

8a. *p Aggression: Maltreatment by Elder.* Some children are harshly and unjustly treated by adults (father, mother, older sibling, relative or nurse). This includes severe whipping, prolonged confinement, and all forms of cruelty. Injustices also belong here.

Maltreatment by Elder Female (Mother)

Zill: . . . what I still consider an unjust punishment. . . This is the first start of my feelings on the injustices rendered by school teachers or any 'bosses.'

Outer: . . . I was beaten several times by irate nuns.

She was ready to tear us to pieces if we made any remark. . . She acquired the habit of striking us on the slightest provocation. . . She would come home and for no reason at all, beat me. . . I used to receive whippings . . . which sometimes made my skin break open and bleed.

Maltreatment by Elder Male (Father)

Earnst: My father was at times a brutal man and inclined, when drinking, to be vindictive toward me. . . My father would make fun of me, call me unpleasant names, say that I would probably not live the year out, that it would be better if I didn't.

8b. *p Aggression: Maltreatment by Contemporaries.* Physical and verbal aggression may be lumped together in this category. The commonest forms are bullying, picking a fight, hazing, ridiculing, belittling and teasing. The offenders are playmates or neighbourhood toughs.

Kindle : I was frightened by the threats of the boys of the private school to which I was sent. They were going to put me through the paces of initiation.

Frost : I was bullied or ignored until I reached high school.

Oriol : I suffered from the barbaric joys of young boys. I was ridiculed and made the butt of low humour. In a series of posters and cut-out pictures I was exposed as a helpless baby, etc.

8c. *p Aggression : Quarrelsome Contemporaries.* In the life of a child there is quite commonly one or more other children (siblings or friends) with whom he occasionally or habitually quarrels. As contemporaries we may include children who are from five years younger to five years older than the S. As it takes two to make a quarrel most of the entries in this division will also appear under the need for Aggression. Here are to be especially listed the events in which the other person provokes the quarrel. The purpose of this category is to record the occurrence of many squabbles and arguments with other children (especially siblings) during the years of growth.

Oak : We had squabbled and argued and even fought at times.

Abel : My brother and I are getting along better than formerly, though we still have the usual squabbles.

9. *Fp Aggression-Dominance.* This is a special category reserved for punishments and threats of punishment. Punishments may vary in frequency and intensity : from mild verbal rebukes (0) to frequent spankings (5). If no punishments are administered we may suppose that the child is peculiarly co-operative or the parents are unusually affiliative and understanding (domination through love). Some parents are slovenly in their discipline whereas others are afraid to punish (afraid of losing the love of the child). The commonest forms of punishment are censure (verbal reprimand), striking (cuffs and spanking), restraint (limitation of action), coercion (enforced action) and disposses-

sion (refusing to give what the child expects to get or taking away what it has [forfeit or fine]).

9a. *Fp Aggression-Dominance : Striking.* Occasional spankings or beatings seem to be the rule in early life. Threats of mutilation may also be included here.

Roon : My early, most vivid impressions of (father) deal almost wholly with reprimands of a very tangible sort.

Outer : (My mother) would come home . . . and beat me.

Umber : My father threatened to cut off my thumb.

9b. *Fp Aggression-Dominance : Restraint.* Confinements or limitations of action enforced by the parents are classified here.

Zill : I begin to remember . . . the first big punishment from the teacher, being locked in the storeroom till school closed.

Outer : . . . taught us to lie on our backs perfectly still for an hour, as a punishment.

Kast : Mother once tied me in a chair in the darkness.

10. *p Dominance.* This covers all barriers to free motion and all persuasions and coercions to action as well as other modes of strong influence. Aggression or Nurturance may accompany these. Here are classed the parents who impose a definite system of social conduct : responsibilities and prohibitions. The system is mostly made up of laws that limit Autonomy, but they may be enforced without punishment, by kindly instruction and example.

10a. *p Dominance : Discipline.* This press is measured in terms of : height of imposed ethical standard, definiteness and rigidity, consistency of application.

Roon : By rigid family training (my sister and I) learned at a very early age just what we could do and what we could not . . . we lacked the freedom that other children our age enjoyed.

Kindle : Dancing, smoking, card-playing, and above all, drinking, was absolutely prohibited.

Mauve : Together by force, example and teachings my parents have inculcated into me a moral code almost inhibitory in its strictness.

10b. *p Dominance : Religious Training.* Here we have to do with the parents' inculcation, by act or precept, of religious ideals.

Kindle : Both my father and mother were brought up under the strictest of Puritanical households. For many generations the family has been Baptist, of the so-called 'hard-shelled' variety. . . I received the moral and religious instruction which my elders themselves had. Church and Sunday School in the Baptist Church which my mother's ancestors had helped to found.

Outer : God was in every room in the house, the housekeeper said. If you fell and hurt your thumb, it was punishment by the hand of God for something you had done recently. I had fear of God instilled deeply into me.

Bulge : I was trained to lead a clean, wholesome, honest life, to fear and love God, and to realize that this life is only a place of preparation for the eternity to come.

11. *Fp Dominance-Nurturance.* This is the fusion that occurs in most parents : the attempt to guide the child benevolently along the path of adaptation. Sometimes a parent, perhaps as a counteraction to his (or her) own frustrations in life, attempts to impose his (or her) unrealized ideal. Sometimes a parent, starving perhaps for affection, attempts to cling to the child. Sometimes a parent is of a worrying sort and for his or her own peace limits the activity of the child.

11a. *Fp Dominance-Nurturance : Parental Ego Idealism.* Under this heading may be classed the attempts of a parent to influence a child by suggestion and persuasion towards a certain goal of high achievement. The influence may come through the mother or the father. Often it is the case of a parent who hopes that the child will attain heights that he or she (the parent) failed to attain. Thus a child may be impelled to accept a very high Ego Ideal. Common forms of achievement urged upon children are physical, economic, vocational, caste, intellectual, aesthetic.

Zora : My mother was brought up in a deep faith in aristocratic tradition, but joined to that, a certain romantic idealism which has largely worked with the other influence to mould her own life and the lives of her children (Caste, Religious).

Abel : My father always instilled into me a desire to go to Harvard (Intellectual).

Akeside : My father would have liked to see me take up law and follow in his footsteps (Vocational).

11b. *Fp Dominance-Nurturance : Possessive Parent.* Here are classed the parents who are tenacious of their child's affection and jealous of his playmates and, later, of those upon whom he bestows his love.

Outer : She would always look at me strangely, as if she resented my having grown up out from under her eyes.

Mauve : Mother preferred that I read to going out and getting dirty playing with other boys.

11c. *Fp Dominance-Nurturance : Over-solicitous Parent.* The anxiety of some parents about the well-being of their child leads them to limit his activity and thus perhaps impede the growth of his independence. The chief parental fears are those having to do with : physical injury, sickness and bad influences.

Zill : My mother was timid and nervous about me. And I think this had much to do with the subordinate position I had when I was with the 'gang.'

Kindle : My parents, mother in particular, were overanxious about me. They nagged me about doing this and not doing that, and about taking care of myself. All this made me very impatient. I wanted to be left alone to take care of myself.

12. *p Nurturance.* Here are classed examples of cherishing parental affection, leniency, sympathy, generous bestowals (gifts) and encouragement (acclaimance). The extreme of this is 'spoiling' a child. Lack of discipline is classed under p Dominance and assigned a low mark (0 or 1).

Asper : Through some miraculous method Mother has kept me onto an essentially better existence by giving me almost complete freedom in my every act. I can always speak my mind and be understood. When she does not comprehend my peculiar reactions to things, she maintains a sympathetic silence.

Bulge : It was my mother who caressed my bruises and made them all well. She comforted my fears and made me feel ashamed of them, and who saved me from many a spanking which I justly deserved.

Vale: I received more attention as a baby than was good for me. . . I was somewhat pampered. . . My parents were affectionate and indulgent.

Quick: My mother is never cross or irritable and always loving and affectionate. If she has any fault it is that she is too lenient, for I have always considered myself spoilt in this respect. She has always given me whatever I desired.

This press may be taken as the antipole of p Rejection and p Aggression. It may, however, be exhibited to an extreme extent as a contrafaction to these press.

13. *p Succorance*. Some mothers attempt to control their children by playing upon their tenderness and chivalry with tears, illnesses and recitals of their sacrifices. They make bids for recognition, gratitude, devotion.

Cling: Mother sometimes cried when she was tired or if we acted thoughtlessly. . . (The fights with my brother) made my mother very unhappy.

Outer: (My mother) used to insist on having me repeat over and over again that she was my sweetheart and that when I grew up I would buy her a Pierce Arrow and protect her in other ways.

14. *p Deference*. A child may be given a great deal of recognition and praise by his parents or he may enjoy the obedient respect of a younger sibling or of his contemporaries. He may be an acknowledged leader, be elected captain of a team, receive prizes and honours. A girl may likewise be commended by her elders, achieve distinction and be greatly admired (p Deference, Social).

Zeeno: In grammar school I was captain. . . I recollect that I was always the idol of other less strong boys in my class.

Kindle: My education and experiences, far broader than (my sister's), have made me feel superior to her. She mildly worships me.

Mauve: I was admired and envied when in school because of my lack of study troubles and also because of my enigmatic self.

15. *p Affiliation*. Companionships with congenial children — children who like and respect the subject — are grouped in this

category. Since it takes two to make a friendship, items of this class are also entered under n Affiliation. Here should be especially included examples of unsolicited friendly advances. These signify that the subject has a cathexis for Affiliation.

Zora : I find most people of a friendly disposition towards me.

Kast : I made rapid strides socially. I discovered people liked me. I became increasingly popular.

Roll : I travelled with a gang. . . I have never had any trouble making friends with both sexes.

Roon : I always had many playmates. . . I was quite popular.

16. *p Sex.* Here may be classed early introductions to sexual facts and erotic practices, such as exposure of the genitals by members of the opposite sex or some variety of physical contact. The perception of the sexual activity of others may also be included here.

16a. *p Sex : Exposure.* Here may be subsumed situations in which a parent or child of the opposite sex exposes his or her naked body. This may shock the child and arouse anxiety or it may take the form of p Enigma.

Zill : About the age of ten I first discovered about the female organs in some of the 'house' or hospital games we played with the girls. I think these discoveries came before I had any curiosity on the matter.

Cling : A little girl said she would undress if I would. We did. I looked, she looked. But, my curiosity satisfied, I was bored and thought her a pretty nasty little girl.

16b. *p Sex : Seduction : Homosexual.* This describes an active sexual advance made by a member of the same sex.

Cling : There was an older boy in the room next to ours. At night when the younger boys were going to bed he used to sit on their beds and slipping his hand underneath the covers play with them. He did this once to me.

Roll : A boy performed masturbation on me.

16c. *p Sex : Seduction : Heterosexual.* Here are grouped early introductions to sexual practice by members of the opposite sex.

Roll : When I was nine, a girl of about sixteen initiated us into the mysteries of sexual intercourse.

16d. *p Sex : Parental Intercourse.* Some children overhear or witness the sexual activities of their parents, but it seems that most of them forget the event. Its occurrence, however, may be suspected when it is known that the child slept in his parents' room.

No memories of this kind were recorded in the autobiographies of our subjects.

17. *p Deception or Betrayal.* Some elders deceive a child by concealing facts or telling lies ; or disappoint him by betraying his affection or not fulfilling promises that they make. As a result the child may become unduly skeptical or cynical, a disbeliever in the honesty and good intentions of others.

Intraorganic Press

It is convenient to include among the press the bodily and intellectual disabilities and ineptitudes against which the will of the individual must contend. Chief among these are illnesses, operations and the various kinds of inferiority.

18. *p Illness.* Frequent or prolonged illnesses may readily increase the n Succorance in a child, since to be cared for in bed (spoiled by adults) re-establishes to a varying degree the infantile state of dependence. Suffering makes some children fretful and whiney (Fn Suc Agg) and weakens them, so that they are less fit to compete physically with their fellows. This engenders timidity and inferiority feelings. Narcisensitivity is apt to be high in children that have been sick. Lying in bed, however, may promote mental activity : Endocathection, Intraception and Projectivity.

It is supposed that an illness with a specific pattern of visceral effects leaves traces in the brain, which will be integrated with whatever fantasies are occurring at the time, whether or not these fantasies have been engendered by the illness. It is further supposed that if later these fantasies recur, one or more of the once-concomitant symptoms may be exhibited. There is reason to suppose that fantasies are intermediate links between physiological processes and conscious attitudes.

18a. *p Illness : General, Prolonged or Frequent.*

Earnst : As a baby I was constantly ailing, having one childhood disease after another, starting with measles at the age of six weeks. During the first years of my life there were times when all hope of my living was given up.

18b. *p Illness : Nervous.* Morbid anxiety, a neurotic symptom, hysteria, a nervous breakdown, as well as an out-and-out psychotic episode, may be grouped in this category.

Chew : . . . nervous breakdown. . . At a dinner party one evening I fainted, and was excused. I returned later and fainted again.

Krumb : In my fifteenth year I suffered a so-called nervous breakdown.

18c. *p Illness : Respiratory.* Whooping cough, bronchitis, pneumonia, and asthma are common afflictions in this group.

Kindle : I nearly died from whooping cough. This left me with weak lungs, bronchial tubes and heart. . . I suffered from asthma.

Bulge : As a child I was very sickly, having a severe attack of bronchitis and convulsions from which I nearly died.

18d. *p Illness : Cardiac.* Congenital disease, valvular insufficiency from infection, intermittent tachycardia, and irregular nervous heart are among the most frequent occurrences in this class.

Kindle : I have a nervous heart.

Krumb : I lay about the house . . . with tachycardia for three years intermittently.

18e. *p Illness : Gastro-intestinal.* The gastro-intestinal tract is subject to a great variety of disturbances, many of which are dependent upon irregularities of autonomic action which, in turn, may be engendered by emotional fantasies. Spasms and dilatations may occur at any one of several points from the mouth to the anus. We are familiar, for instance, with pylorospasm and Hirschsprung's disease in children. For all ages the commonest symptoms are : loss of appetite, nausea, vomiting, colic, diarrhoea and constipation.

Abel : It was hard to wean me on account of my stomach which has always caused me trouble unless I control my diet somewhat.

Krumb : I lay about the house with indigestion. . . I have much stomach trouble.

18f. *p Illness : Infantile Paralysis.* This illness commonly provokes (as a reaction to the trauma) rather marked counteractive efforts : strivings to compensate for and rise above the disability.

Bulge : I also had infantile paralysis.

18g. *p Illness : Convulsions.* There are a variety of causes of convulsions in children — high temperature, for example, — some of which may be related to a parasympathetic insulinization of the blood. Convulsions naturally suggest temper tantrums, hysteria and epilepsy.

Bulge : As a child I was very sickly, having a severe attack of bronchitis and convulsions from which I nearly died.

19. *p Operation.* Here we have a press from the outside world, coming from the surgeon or dentist, together with the incision or removal of a part of body (usually diseased). Hence, this event stands between p Aggression (subsidiary to p Nurturance) and p Illness (an intraorganic press). Common operations in children are : circumcision, tonsillectomy and appendectomy. It seems that any one of these may be interpreted as a castration (mutilation and dispossession), a retaliation or punishment for some fantasied sexual act. The pulling of a tooth may also be included in this group.

Kindle : I remember one especially bad time I had over an ulcerated tooth. It had to be pulled and I was frightened to death.

20. *p Inferiority.* Anything in the individual that is below the average, that provokes unfavourable comment or gives him a feeling of impotency or ineptitude is included here. The principal forms are : physical, social, intellectual. Caste inferiority is classified under p Insupport : Inferior Parents.

20a. *p Inferiority : Physical.* Smallness of stature, lack of physical strength and agility, awkwardness, athletic ineptitude and the inability to defend oneself in a fight may be grouped together in this category. This may be the consequence of p Illness. When an S mentions his inferiorities he usually speaks of inferiority feelings and infavoidances.

Earnst : I was too young to get anywhere fighting for myself.

Vale : I was inclined to be delicate, and was always more or less aware that a very little would lay me open to the dread charge of 'sissy.'

20b. *p Inferiority : Social.* General unattractiveness, lack of social talent, and the inability to get on with others and establish enduring friendship constitute this category. The S has a cathexis for Rejection or for Aggression.

Cling : I found that with the boys in my class I made no fast friends. I did not understand them. I was childish and irritable.

Kindle : I did not get along very well with children.

20c. *p Inferiority : Intellectual.* Low general intelligence, dullness, poor scholarship, flunking examinations and failure to be promoted in school, may be classified under this heading.

Zeeno : In the seventh grade I failed to get promoted . . . am still a very mediocre pupil.

Zill : I applied to a smaller college. . . But I was refused. . . I repeated the senior year.

B. NEEDS

Under this heading have been classified the chief types of reaction to the press that have been listed above. The events recorded in the autobiographies exhibit press and needs simultaneously and to separate them, as we have done, produces artifacts. The procedure was adopted for the sake of clarity and convenience.

With the affiliative needs we have listed some of the concrete positively cathected objects, and with the rejective and aggressive needs we have listed the negatively cathected objects. The combination of fused needs and objects (images) constitutes the major part of a need integrate. Strictly speaking, an object should be classed under one or more press, but this cannot be done if the attributes and behaviour of the object are not described. The Oedipus complex in a boy is suggested by a strong positive cathection of the mother and a negative cathection of the father.

The needs have been classified as follows :

BEHAVIOUR

1. Positive Cathexis	
Supra: a. Mother b. Female	
c. Father d. Male	
e. Brother f. Sister	
Infra: g. Brother h. Sister	
i. Contemporary	
j. Animal k. Possessions	
2. n Affiliation	
a. Friendliness b. n Suc: Dependence c. n Def: Respect d. n Nur: Kindness	
3. n Deference	
a. n Blam: Compliance b. n Aff: Respect c. n Nur: Devotion d. Ego Ideal, Emulation e. Suggestibility	
4. n Nurturance	
a. Sympathy & Aid b. n Aff: Kindness c. n Def: Devotion	
5. n Succorance	
a. Crying b. n Aff: Dependence c. n Harm: Appealance	

6. n Harmavoidance	
a. Timidity b. n Suc: Appealance c. Nightmares	
d. Fears: i. Insup., Heights & Falling ii. Water iii. Darkness iv. Fire v. Isolation	
vi. Assault, Lightning vii. Assault, Animals viii. Assault, Human General Hostility Father Mother Contemporaries	
ix. Illness & Death x. Miscellaneous	
7. n Infavoidance	
a. Narcisensitivity b. Shyness, Embarrassment c. Avoidance of Competition	
d. Inferiority Feelings i. General ii. Physical iii. Social iv. Intellectual	
8. n Blamavoidance and Superego	

BEHAVIOUR (*Continued*)

a. Sensitivity to Blame b. n Def: Compliance c. n Aba: Shame & Self-depreciation	
d. Directive Superego e. Religious Inclination	
9. n Abasement	
a. n Blam: Blame-acceptance b. n Def: Subservience c. n Harm or n Inf: Surrender	
10. n Passivity	
a. Inactivity b. n Aba: Acceptance	
11. n Seclusion	
a. Isolation b. Reticence c. n Inf: Shyness	
12. n Inviolacy	
a. n Dfd: Vindication b. n Ach: Restriving	
c. n Agg: Retaliation d. n Auto: Resistance	
13. Negative Cathexis	
Supra: a. Mother b. Female	
c. Father d. Male	
e. Brother f. Sister	
g. Contemporaries	
Infra: h. Brother i. Sister	
14. n Aggression	
a. Temper	
b. Combativeness	
c. Sadism	
d. n Dom: Coercion e. n Auto: Rebellion f. n Suc: Plaintance	
g. Destruction	
15. n Autonomy	
a. Freedom b. Defiance	
c. Inv: Resistance d. n Ach: Independence	
16. n Dominance	
a. Leadership b. Inducement c. n Agg: Coercion	
17. n Rejection	
a. Hypercriticalness b. n Inf: Narcisensitivity c. n Sec: Inaccessibility	
18. n Noxavoidance	
a. Hypersensitivity, Gen. b. Food	
19. n Achievement	
a. General b. Physical c. Intellectual	
d. Caste e. Rivalry	
f. Ego Ideal	
g. n Inv: Restriving h. n Auto: Independence	
20. n Recognition	
a. Recitals of Superiority b. Cathection of Praise c. n Exh: Public Performance	

BEHAVIOUR (*Continued*)

21. n Exhibition		26. n Order	
a. n Rec: Public Performance b. n Sex: Exhibitionism		a. Cleanliness b. Orderliness c. Finickiness about Details	
22. n Sex		27. n Retention	
a. Masturbation b. Precocious heterosexuality c. Homosexuality d. Bisexuality		a. Collectance b. Conservance	
23. n Acquisition		28. n Activity	
a. Greediness b. Stealing c. Gambling		a. Physical b. Verbal	
24. n Cognizance		29. Intensity	
a. Curiosity, General b. Experimentation c. Intellectual		30. Emotionality	
d. Sexual, Birth e. Genitals		31. Persistence	
25. n Construction		32. Sameness	
a. Mechanical b. Aesthetic		a. Constance of Cathexis b. Behavioural Rigidity c. Mental Rigidity	
		33. Inhibition	
		34. Elation	
		35. Imaginality	
		36. Deceit	

1. *Positive Cathexes.* Children may become enduringly attached to certain objects : father, mother, sibling, animal, thing. They join such objects, play with them and relish their company, cling and adhere, conserve and protect them. They dislike the loss or dispossession of the object and are annoyed by the intrusion of a competitor.

1a. *Positive Cathexis : Supra : Mother.* Most subjects in our group praised their mother.

Cling : My mother . . . was very beautiful . . . kind, considerate and unselfish. She was the only important influence on me.

Mother's occasional visits were my only happy hours.

Asper: The most interesting, intimate, truly remarkable personality whom I have ever met is my mother.

Bulge: To me my mother is the world's most lovely and noble creature. It was she to whom I always instinctively turned in all my joys and sorrows and was always sure of finding sympathy, understanding and advice.

Veal: My mother, of course, is my favourite parent.

1b. *Positive Cathexis: Supra: Female.* Some children, receiving more nurturance from some other older woman than they do from their mother, become attached to the former. It may be a nurse, grandmother, aunt, teacher or family friend. The mother substitute is very apt to be one who encourages the child and guides it towards a new path of achievement.

Kindle: Mother's mother I remember as very kind, with a spacious and comfortable lap, a refuge from irate parents. She could get me forgiven for anything.

One more member of the family circle should be mentioned. This was the maid, or colored mammy, once a slave in Virginia. She was a great comfort to me, one of the most kind-hearted souls alive. I remember the feel and fragrance of her even now.

Roon: I gained the friendship of one of my teachers. . . She had a great influence on my thinking, a very valuable one.

Roll: God knows, I love my grandmother enough. She is a swell person, the best I've ever known.

1c. *Positive Cathexis: Supra: Father.* The father is commonly cathected as an exemplar by the boy and as a love object by the girl.

Given: My favourite parent in my early years was my father, probably because he never punished me.

Irkman: For my father I have a sort of veneration. I always felt he was superior to all other men I ever met.

Outer: I grew to regard my father . . . as a great hero.

1d. *Positive Cathexis: Supra: Male.* An important stage in the development of a boy comes when he finds an older boy or man whom he can accept as an exemplar. The latter functions as a substitute father, providing another focus for the development of an Ego Ideal or Superego. In young girls, an older man is not infrequently the first object of erotic fantasies.

Roll : At this time a friend of the family, whom I have always practically worshipped, came to visit us and took me for a walk which I will always remember. He warned me against women who were easy to get, and against seducing an innocent girl, and I have always remembered his words.

Asper : The most eventful meeting in my entire life. He was 21, the picture of the ideal scholar. . . For me he was the most intelligent being on earth, and it wonders me now how he could have tolerated me — for we were together most of the time.

1e. *Positive Cathexis : Supra : Brother.* An older brother may function as an exemplar or love object.

1f. *Positive Cathexis : Supra : Sister.* A cathected older sister may determine the pattern of a boy's later love life. For example, he may be habitually attracted by women with a somewhat dominant attitude.

Roon : (My sister and I) have always been very close to one another. . . As we grew older our attachment became considerably stronger . . . we are the greatest and fastest of friends.

Vulner : My sister's temperament seems to complement mine completely, so there is complete understanding between us at all times.

1g. *Positive Cathexis : Infra : Brother.* Love for a younger brother is usually a sign of Nurturance, but the Nurturance may, in turn, be a contrafaction of Aggression.

Cling : Until I was twelve I used to kiss my brother quite frequently.

Quick : I have a great affection for my younger brother.

1h. *Positive Cathexis : Infra : Sister.* Love for a younger sister is indicative of Nurturance fused perhaps with Dominance.

Quick : I have a great affection for my youngest sister.

1i. *Positive Cathexis : Contemporary.* Here we have to do with a focal friendship that endures long enough to modify the personality. Such a friendship may, as Freud affirmed, be based upon repressed homosexuality, but in our experience most of these synergies manifest affiliation with no suggestion of erotic (sensuous) excitement.

Kindle : I struck up a deep friendship with an orphan lad of artistic temperament. . . We were very much attached to each other, our interests were the same. . . He spent a summer in France. I was very lonesome. In our senior year we were inseparable in our work.

Zora : I have had many friends, but one in particular, my own age, with whom I have grown up, and we are like a pair of old shoes.

1j. *Positive Cathexis : Animal.* Children commonly enjoy playing with animal pets. Sometimes they become affiliated and identify themselves in fantasy with a particular kind of animal, empathizing with it and imitating it. They like to read stories about it, draw or model it, collect pictures or reproductions of it.

Roon : I had two dogs for whom I had the greatest attachment. Whenever I could manage it, I would put them in bed with me at night. . . I still have a very strong love for animals, dogs particularly.

Roll : My favourite stories were about animals. I could tell anyone more about animals than he ever knew.

1k. *Positive Cathexis : Possessions.* Some children become very much attached to their toys or other possessions. Interest may become concentrated upon a single object or a single type of object (fetishism). Often the inanimate object takes the place of an animal or human being. A little boy, for example, may treat a Teddy Bear as if it were another child, play with it throughout the day, order it about, and take it to bed with him, clutching it as he goes to sleep.

Frost : I became very attached to a set of blocks and for several years played with them every day.

Kast : A toy electric motor was the pride of my life. A wagon was a favoured possession and I took great care of it.

2. *n Affiliation.* Under this heading are classed all manifestations of friendliness and goodwill, of the desire to do things in

company with others. It is hard to estimate the strength of this need on the basis of an autobiography, so much depends on whether the subject has been popular (the subject's cathexis for Affiliation). The child who attracts others is in company more often than the child who repels, but the latter's overt strivings for Affiliation may be greater. Furthermore, it is natural for a person to like those who like him. Hence, a subject who is attractive to others, will usually reciprocate by demonstrations of affection and friendships will result. This evokable or merely responsive form of Affiliation deserves a lower score than the initiating or active form, even when the latter is unsuccessful.

2a. *n Affiliation : Friendliness.* Affiliation, like other needs, is scored according to its diffuseness (generality of trait). But since diffuseness can be demonstrated only by a multiplicity of specific instances it forms a continuum with focality, the differentiating factor being the number of cathected objects (friends). The intensity and endurance of the friendships, however, must also be considered in scoring. A focal friendship (classed under 11. Positive Cathexes, Contemporary) may be a sign of a limited need for Affiliation.

Outer : I have had no end of friends, in several dozen circles.

Kast : I have a large number of friends and my social activities are extensive.

Quick : I have belonged to many clubs and have a large amount of friends.

2b. *n Affiliation fused with n Succorance : Dependence (vide* n Suc). Here we would include instances of enduring love and friendship for stronger sympathizing or protecting objects, usually one or both parents.

Given : My attachment to my family was a very close one — being an only child.

Quick : I have formed the habit of confiding to my mother everything I do, including my sexual relations.

2c. *n Affiliation fused with n Deference : Respect (vide* n Def). Here may be classed attitudes of respect and deference towards one's friends as well as the tendency to choose dominant objects as companions.

Asper: My early friends were to me distinctly superior beings.

Oriol: I have generally sought the friendships of mature people.

2d. *n Affiliation fused with n Nurturance: Kindness* (*vide* n Nur). This is manifested by sympathetic, generous or helpful attitudes. It is commonly associated with the choice of younger, inferior or less privileged objects as friends.

Kindle: With my friends . . . I am sometimes very kind and generous.

3. *n Deference.* Respect for authority, the desire to please parents and elders, the readiness to co-operate and comply, as well as the enthusiastic cathection, acclaimance and emulation of a distinguished person are grouped in this class.

3a. *n Deference fused with n Blamavoidance: Compliance* (*vide* n Blam). Respect and obedience to an allied authority may be classified here, the emphasis being upon an eager and trusting discipleship.

Zora: I think my attitude was generally obedient and co-operative. I should not like to say timid, but it was not assertive.

Asper: I tried to act, and still do, as I considered my society thought proper. Especially did I attempt to imitate those mannerisms to which society gave definite approval.

Sims: I had no inclination to get into trouble, and I tried to please my teachers.

Mauve: My attitude in class has always been adaptive, never guileful or recalcitrant.

Vulner: My general attitude was co-operative, which became a fault as it was carried too far.

My deportment was disgustingly good throughout.

I was too interested in making a good impression on the teachers.

3b. *n Deference fused with n Affiliation: Respect* (*vide* n Aff). Friendships commonly develop out of subject's admiration for a superior allied object. Here the S attempts to please the O, hoping that an enduring friendship will ultimately be established.

Kindle : I have always been on the best of terms with my advisers, tutors, and course professors.

Asper : I roomed with a certain Bohemian chap, who had interned in a hospital, and who had, for me, most marvellous stories to relate, of his own early life, of his many trials, of disease and death, of adventure. We would remain up for all hours of the night, and I would absorb eagerly all he had to say — and ask for more.

Akeson : I wanted to become friendly with tutors and instructors but was not very successful.

3c. *n Deference fused with n Nurturance : Devotion* (*vide* n Def). This describes a particular willingness to comply to the requests of a parent or elder when the latter is unwell or unhappy and appeals to the subject's pity. Obedience is the presenting phenomenon, but it is based upon compassion.

Mauve : I treated my mother with compliance when I felt that it would hurt her to disobey.

3d. *n Deference fused with Ego Ideal : Emulation* (*vide* Ego Ideal, n Ach). Under this heading may be classed : admiration for a hero and the emulation of his sentiments and aims, and on this basis the development of a determining Ego Ideal.

Roon : The actors were my heroes and I thought their life the most exciting and glamorous imaginable. I imitated their speech and diction ; it was so different from my Western twang. I did achieve some success in this.

Kindle : My heroes have been contemporary. . . At an early period my father. The professor whose work I admire. Then a whole list of minor heroes would consist of the actors and actresses of plays, rarely of movies, and most of all certain musicians and virtuosos I have admired to such a high degree that I worshipped them for a short time. I particularly admire the sensitivity and kindness of some, of others their daring and dashing innovations, spirit of adventure in dangerous places, the master mind, the pioneer. Certainly, I should include all the successful detectives of literature.

Zora : One of these mythological figures has either become myself or I have become it, I don't know which. It is the story of the Spartan boy who has caught a young wolf, and puts it beneath his robe, and the wolf gnaws at him, and the boy makes no outcry, but continues until he can no more. That image of stoicism seems to be ineradicable in me.

Bulge : I was goaded on in my ambition to become a doctor by the desire to become one like Dr. S——, a friend to all, and a perfect gentleman.

Sims : I read Shelley and Byron and resolved like them to throw off the restriction and limitations of society.

Oriol : In many ways I resemble Emerson.

My favourite hero was Robinson Crusoe, lonely and self-sufficient.

I want to picture myself as a martyr or Byronic hero.

3e. *n Deference : Suggestibility.* This applies to manifestations of suggestibility (gullibility and imitation) provoked by mildly cathected objects (a stranger or casual acquaintance). Since this phenomenon occurs unconsciously, one does not expect to find reports of it in autobiographies. Its presence may sometimes be surmised from such statements as the following :

Veal : My older brother convinced me I should go to college. He convinced me to adopt a policy of letting the future take care of itself.

4. *n Nurturance,* a parental or helpful attitude towards inferiors.

4a. *n Nurturance : Sympathy and Aid.* Evidences of kindness and compassion and of the willingness to exert oneself in behalf of others are classed here. The cathected object may be an animal.

Bulge : My ambition was to be a doctor and my motives for this were very altruistic . . . to be of some definite use to humanity, to be instrumental in relieving the sufferings of others.

Irkman : On finding a stray cat I would manage to get some milk for it. I once built a dog house for one.

4b. *n Nurturance fused with n Affiliation : Kindness* (*vide* n Aff). Here the emphasis is upon a benevolent compassionate attitude which precedes and perhaps determines the choice of an object as friend. No definite examples of this were found.

4c. *n Nurturance fused with n Deference : Devotion* (*vide* n Def). Here may be grouped instances of devotion and sympathetic helpfulness towards an admired superior object (a tired, ailing or aged parent).

5. *n Succorance*. This describes the need for or dependence upon a nurturing object that must be always at hand or within call in case the S wants anything : food, protection, assistance, care, sympathy, undivided devotion.

5a. *n Succorance : Crying*. Crying is the most effective mode of calling the mother or arousing her sympathy. It may persist as an emotional reaction which serves a variety of needs.

Sims : I cried a great deal as a baby and no amount of attention would keep me quiet.

Virt : I made my mother anxious through my continued crying.

5b. *n Succorance fused with n Affiliation : Dependence* (*vide* n Aff). The manifestations of anaclitic love (childish dependence on an adult) are classed here. Affectionate adherence, seeking protection, cuddling and homesickness are among the common signs.

Kindle : (The coloured mammy) was a great comfort to me. . . I would climb onto her broad lap, for she was a large woman, and beg her to cuddle me, and tell stories.

Bulge : I missed my mother and always did, and do so yet. All my life I have longed to have her, to run to her when I was sad, to share my secrets with her.

Frost : During my early years I was closer to my mother and was with her nearly all the time.

Mauve : During my four years of college I have felt a strong attachment to home which causes me to consult my parents still on important matters.

5c. *n Succorance fused with n Harmavoidance : Appealance* (*vide* n Harm). One of the commonest reactions of a child in the face of danger is to call (Appealance), run or cling to (Adherence) an allied object : a parent or some safe haven.

Cling : I used to have nightmares . . . until I woke, cold with sweat, and called to mother (Appealance).

Sudden fears often gripped me, and I ran home as if pursued by real and tangible dangers, and not just imagined bogeys (Flight to Security).

Krumb : When a snowball hurt too much I ran home crying.

Whenever I went anywhere I always had to be with one of my family.

Vulner : When the storm was over I would go to father, getting into his bed if it was night.

6. *n Harmavoidance*. The 'shock' reaction to sudden stimuli, withdrawal from painful or fearsome impressions and all avoidances and flights from physical danger are put into this class. Evidences of general timidity and apprehension are put into one class (6a) and the more common specific fears (phobias) under separate headings into another (6d).

6a. *n Harmavoidance : Timidity*. When a child is described as being timid but no mention is made of a particularly feared object, or when there are a great variety of objects that are habitually avoided, the subject is given a positive mark on this variable.

Krumb : I hate to go about. I am afraid of dangers everywhere.

Cling : I was in a sense timid. . . What other children did without thinking often gave me pause.

6b. *n Harmavoidance fused with n Succorance : Appealance* (*vide* n Suc). To this category may be assigned occasions of pain and fright that cause the S to cry out for help.

Cling : I shouted for help. For a vivid moment the fear of death caught at my throat.

6c. *n Harmavoidance : Nightmares*. Frightening dreams are put in a separate category. When the imagined object of fear is named the nightmare is also classified as a specific fear (6d).

Kast : For years I had nightmares, shouting and screaming in my sleep.

6d. *n Harmavoidance : Fears*. Children are apt to develop specific fears for one or another object or situation. Fears of insupport are supposedly related to the anxiety of helplessness and thus, in some cases, to the birth trauma. Fears of assault may be related to guilt and the fear of parental punishment.

6d. i. *n Harmavoidance : Fears : Insupport, Heights and Falling*.

Cling : Small jumps, in which a fall might have been painful . . . made me hesitate and I was usually the last to try such minor feats of agility. I almost never balked, but I was often very much afraid.

6d. ii. *n Harmavoidance : Fears : Insupport, Water.*

Berry : I was afraid of drowning and did not learn to swim until I was sixteen.

6d. iii. *n Harmavoidance : Fears : Insupport, Darkness.*

Cling : I used to be afraid of dark or lonely places.
Roll : I have always had a terror of the night.

6d. iv. *n Harmavoidance : Fears : Insupport, Fire.*

Oak : The only early fear I can remember is that the house would burn down. At night in bed I was constantly smelling smoke.

6d. v. *n Harmavoidance : Fears : Insupport, Isolation.* Here we refer to situations in which the S finds himself *alone* in a solitary place or in a crowd of strangers. This usually signifies a high n Succorance with dependence upon the supporting presence of a parent.

Cling : I used to be afraid of dark or lonely places. . . I used to be more afraid, I think, of crowded city streets and unfamiliar faces.
Krumb : I remember once getting separated from Dad in the Subway and being dreadfully frightened.

6d. vi. *n Harmavoidance : Fears : Assault, Lightning.* Lightning may sometimes be taken as ' the wrath of God ' (Se and n Blam) or as parental retaliation.

Vulner : I developed a terrible fear of thunderstorms.

6d. vii. *n Harmavoidance : Fears : Assault, Animals.* The fear of small animals may be determined by the fear of having something enter the body, whereas the fear of large animals may develop out of a fear of parental vengeance. It is generally supposed that the fear of a biting animal may be a result of the projection of oral Aggression. Later it may be related to the fear of castration.

Cling : There were some pigs there I liked ; but I was a little afraid of them after they chased my brother out of the sty.

Roll : I was very much afraid of a large cow which was one of my toys. When it 'mooed' I wanted to hide.

I have always had a terror of animals, particularly wolves. I used to be frightened to death when my grandfather would tell me wolves were after me. I am still haunted by dreams I have wolves chasing me. . .

6d. viii. *n Harmavoidance : Fears : Assault, Human.* The fear of strangers, gangsters or bullies, as well as the fear of aggression of parents and contemporaries, may be classed under this heading. The fear of doctors and dentists and the pain which they inflict may also be included here.

General Hostility

Earnst : I remember the talk of big guns and I had frightened visions of Germans shooting at me.

I acquired the fear of other people menacing me with physical punishment which is something I have never overcome.

Irkman : I remember having a form of nightmare — seeing in my bedroom a dark shroud the form of which was indistinguishable. I remember having called out, 'Black thing !' when it appeared to me.

Umber : My nights were a series of nightmares and fears — nightmares in the form of dreams whose central positions were occupied by giant fiends and ruthless men.

Cling : Sudden terrors often gripped me, and I ran home as if pursued by real and tangible dangers, and not just imagined bogeys.

Father's Hostility

Zora : I used to run from it (beating), and cry when I got it.

Earnst : I had such an acute terror of the whip that I usually went into hysterics at the mere sight of one.

Mother's Hostility

Outer : I soon learned to keep out of her (my mother's) way when she took these strange fits of conduct.

When I stepped into the house it was fearfully and with my eyes and ears tuned to my mother's whereabouts.

Hostility of Contemporaries

Zill : I had become more quiet and timid. . . I clench my fists often now when I think how cowardly or foolish I must have appeared to other boys as I showed my inability in fighting even smaller boys than myself.

Kindle : (The boys) were going to put me through the paces of initiation. I balked at the idea and for two or three weeks kept everybody busy trying to get me to go to school. There were many scenes, of which I am still very much ashamed.

Physically, I was no match for them. I knew that if I got into a fight I would be beaten . . . my impression of my relation with my schoolmates is one of very great anxiety. . . I was afraid of them.

6d. ix. *n Harmavoidance : Fears : Illness and Death.* Death is often related to the Day of Judgement and this to parental punishment for evil thoughts and deeds.

Zora : I had nightmares about the ending of the world.

Krumb : I was greatly scared at the idea of dying.

I have a dread of wet feet.

I have much stomach trouble and tachycardia which frightens me terribly.

Quick : I got the conception that I was going to die that night. When I went to bed a cold sweat broke over my whole body and I feared that I was never going to reawaken.

A friend of mine contracted infantile paralysis. I often went to see him. One morning I arose and in attempting to walk I thought my left leg was numb, and I walked with a perceptible limp. Half crazed with fear I reached my mother's room, uttered a groan, and fell in a dead faint on the floor. When I awoke I was shivering with fear. Sweat actually drained off my weakened body.

6d. x. *n Harmavoidance : Fears : Miscellaneous.* The fear of loud noises may be related to the fear of assault.

Irkman : I refused to go to the movies because the fear of hearing revolver shots fired drove me to tears.

The fear of claustral restriction and suffocation may be related to the birth trauma.

Kast : I once dreamed of being locked in a room where I could not breathe and attempting to get out.

Many fears seem to be based on rational considerations.

Krumb : I try to play with my set of chemicals but Dad has so cautioned me of dangers that I'm too scared.

7. *n Infavoidance.* This term describes the fears and avoidances associated with self-consciousness, shyness, social embarrassment. The subject cannot 'take' belittlement and ridicule.

7a. *n Infavoidance : Narcisensitivity.* This describes the readiness to be hurt (shamed) by the scorn or jibes of others. It pre-supposes Narcism, as well as inferiority feelings which may be focal or diffuse.

Zill : My name caused me much embarrassment. . . It made me the butt of many ignorant remarks . . . which I did not seem able to disregard and it became such an obsession that I winced every time the name was mentioned in school.

Asper : This sensitiveness with regard to myself and my relation to any person or group of people is, at present, the essential fault of my conduct.

Earnst : I was extremely sensitive and cried easily at such things.

Sometimes I see a person laughing on the street, and I have the impression that the person is laughing at me. This impression comes back again and again.

Vulner : I was called a 'sissy,' which made me utterly dejected for days at a time.

7b. *n Infavoidance : Shyness, Embarrassment.* Shyness and embarrassment form a separate class.

Cling : I was rather shy among strangers and older people. I felt completely at ease only with my mother, my father, my brother, and a very few of my teachers and schoolmates.

7c. *n Infavoidance : Avoidance of Competition.* The unwillingness to perform in public, the fear of failure and the withdrawal from open competition are grouped under this heading.

Gay : I never engaged in sports.

7d. *Inferiority Feelings.* Under this heading may be grouped instances in which the S feels that he is inferior in many or in one particular respect.

7d. i. *General.*

Akeson : I have always had a feeling of being a misfit.

Frost : In my early schools I acquired an inferiority complex.

Veal : I have felt inferior to my older brother.

7d. ii. *Physical.*

Gay : Whether it was that I never engaged in sports that made me puny, or vice-versa, I have always had a distrust and scorn for my body.

Virt : I was small in stature and felt that girls were not attracted to me.

Earnst : I was too puny to get anywhere fighting for myself.

7d. iii. *Social.*

Akeson : I envy my sisters the ease they display in their social relations.

Earnst : I acquired a feeling of inadequacy. I got the feeling there is something wrong with me and could hardly look another person in the eyes.

Kast : I was ashamed of the lack of worldliness of my father and mother.

I felt great chagrin when I realized how ill at ease I was among such surroundings. Her father remarked on my lack of polish and social ease.

Asper : So sensitively inferior did I feel to them that I must have behaved idiotically.

7d. iv. *Intellectual.*

Asper : I was struck with the mass of things to be learned and my own microscopic inferiority.

Krumb : My spirit was broken because I knew the adverse opinion my teachers held of me.

8. *n Blamavoidance and Superego.* Under this general heading are classed : sensitivity to parental and social disapproval, fear of censure, ready obedience, guilt feelings, remorse, confession of misdemeanours, fear of divine vengeance, as well as moral will

and the determination to live one's life according to ethical or religious principles. When anxiety and guilt feelings prevail we speak of Superego Conflict and assume the occurrence of asocial fantasies or acts. When the S is able to control himself, however, and acts willingly according to the demands of his culture we refer to Superego Integration, the inference being that a 'social character' (a structured Ego) has been developed.

8a. *n Blamavoidance : Sensitivity to Blame.* This is barely distinguishable from Narcisensitivity. Here the S is not so upset by a fall in his achievement level as he is by the disapproval of his parents or contemporaries. The fear of God's wrath or the fear of social censure is at the core of this trait.

Roon : I always had a fear of incurring (my parents') displeasure.

Outer : I had fear of God instilled deeply into me.

Valet : I was always loath to make enemies.

8b. *n Blamavoidance fused with n Deference : Compliance* (*vide* n Def). To please and not to displease are two aspects of one behavioural tendency. Hence, Deference and Blamavoidance are complementary. However, when there is temptation to do something that is not allowed, or when authority is uncommonly exacting, or when the subject lacks confidence, Blamavoidance rather than Deference dominates the personality.

Roon : I knew what was right and what was wrong ; and I was expected to abide by that code invariably. I rarely transgressed.

Vulner : I have never conceived of deliberate disobedience since I was 6 years old.

Zora : Some people think I am a goody-goody.

8c. *n Blamavoidance fused with n Abasement : Shame and Self-depreciation.* This describes the self-punishing reaction of a person with a high Superego to his own evil thoughts, impulses or misdoings.

Veal : I have scolded myself for not having tried to help out the straitened family after high school.

Bulge : I was ashamed when I found that kissing aroused sexual desires in me — likewise when I had erotic dreams.

Kindle : I was thoroughly ashamed of myself, and wondered if I could be freed from the habit.

Roll : My own masturbation gave me a feeling of shame — often occasioned a firm resolve never to do it again.

My smoking was a secret sin to me.

8d. *n Blamavoidance : Directive Superego.* Under this heading have been classified : the inhibition of primitive impulses (Sex and Aggression), the rejection of sexuality, overcoming temptation, ethical control, moral will power, reform, and all behaviour that is initiated by conscience.

Cling : When I realized the habit I had been forming, I began to struggle against it. I had terrific conflicts of will and desire, but finally . . . I cured myself completely. I never spoke to anyone about this.

Roon : This sense of strictness continued for many years and then seemed to be suddenly severed. I could do as I chose, act as I saw fit. But with the definite moral strictness that had been a very large part of my early life imbedded quite deep in me, I acted just as though I would incur the most drastic censure for a wrong action.

Abel : I never allowed myself to think about anything concerning sex for I was brought up with the idea that anything concerning sex was unclean, both morally and spiritually.

Bulge : I have always successfully conquered my passions.

Earnst : I always thought the practice of masturbation was indecent and I never indulged in it.

Kast : She begged me to have intercourse with her. I refused, realizing the situation had probably been my fault. For some reason, I couldn't let myself go that far. I felt we would regret it. I was afraid of the consequences. After such times I had quite a feeling of revulsion.

8e. *n Blamavoidance : Religious Inclination.* Fervent religious faith or practices, a pre-occupation with the problem of good and evil, church work and the desire to enter the ministry, may be grouped together as evidences of an underlying inclination to lead an irreproachable life.

Zora : As a child I was extremely religious, and, of my own volition, I did not read newspapers on Sunday and read the Bible every day.

Quick : I experienced a stupendous dream in which I imagined myself confronted by God at the time of my death. Awakening, terrified and amazed, I determined that I should give myself over to being strictly orthodox. After 16 I became really fanatically orthodox. Only recently has this sudden frenzy been completely removed.

9. *n Abasement.* This is usually subsidiary to some other need : n Harm, n Inf or n Blam. It describes reactions of self-depreciation or surrender as well as those of self-punishment and atonement for evil actions.

9a. *n Abasement fused with n Blamavoidance : Blame-acceptance and Atonement* (*vide* n Blam). Here we include unusual examples of self-blame, feelings of remorse and acts that are designed to appease a condemning authority. Subjects who accept unjust punishment without resistance also may be classed here.

Vulner : I attributed the thunderstorms entirely to God, and made myself miserable trying to appease Him. Among the reforms instituted for this purpose was the dropping of the finger sucking habit.

Oak : I can readily understand the punishment I got. It is a wonder that there wasn't more.

Veal : I never put up any defence when my brother criticized me. I would brood inwardly.

9b. *n Abasement fused with n Deference : Subservience.* Humility, docility, meekness, and the acceptance of a subordinate position in a semi-allied group are grouped under this heading. The unresentful acceptance of p Dominance and p Rejection, denoting a lack of social pride, may also be included.

Zill : . . . the subordinate position I had when I was with the gang.

9c. *n Abasement fused with n Harmavoidance or n Infavoidance : Surrender.* Surrender in the face of frustration is classified here. We may include : sudden despairing relaxations after muscular exertion, dejected cessations of effort, easy acceptance of defeat. A marked lowering of the level of aspiration is also considered a symptom (fusion with n Infavoidance). Passivity may accompany the Abasement drive and the n Succorance may be fused with it. Both Abasement and Succorance may be subsidiary to the n Harmavoidance.

Zill : More than once I broke out with that awful temper I was acquiring (n Agg) only to suddenly lower my fists (n Aba) and burst into tears (n Suc) whimpering that I couldn't fight or some other 'sissy' word.

Cling : I tried once or twice to fight back, but homesickness and loneliness (n Suc) overcame my resistance.

Krumb : When a bully threw snowballs at me I just stood there taking them. Never once did I try to defend myself.

10. *n Passivity*. The cathexis of sleep, the desire to relax, loaf and ruminate, the disinclination to exert oneself physically or mentally, the acceptance of fate, the inclination to let others take the initiative, may be grouped together.

10a. *n Passivity : Inactivity*. Here we class quietude, laziness, apathy, dreaminess, lack of persistence and excessive need for relaxation and repose.

Frost : Between the ages of 6 and 11 I lived almost wholly in a kind of sheltered passivity with my family.

Gay : I wanted to be allowed to read or do nothing.

Vulner : I spent much time lying still.

10b. *n Passivity fused with n Abasement : Acceptance*. Children who readily accept the inevitable, who remain passive and undisturbed in the face of frustration, belong to this category. They prefer to let others take the initiative. They do not go out to 'meet' or 'make' Fate ; they are 'hit' by it.

Cling : My wont was to accept everything with equanimity.

Zora : Much of my religiousness is past, to be replaced largely by world weariness.

Gay : In groups I was shy and acquiescent.

11. *n Seclusion*. Some believe that Seclusion is always subsidiary to another need : n Harm, n Inf, n Blam, n Pass or n Rej. But even if this view is correct, no great harm can be done by including it among the variables as it is at least an important mode of need activity.

11a. *n Seclusion : Isolation.* This describes the tendency to live, play and work at some distance from the mass of people or protected from them by walls. Such a subject dislikes groups. He likes to be by himself or with a few chosen companions.

Kindle : I played little with the boys in the neighbourhood, but rather with my sister. Mostly, however, I was left to myself.

Akeson : I had a very retiring nature.

My retiring nature turned me towards study and books as my chief occupation and recreation.

Frost : Living in such a dream world was probably the cause for my playing a great deal by myself.

The tendency to analyse people carefully and coldly has made me feel withdrawn from normal life.

Gay : I had deep moods of depression and desired to be alone.

Oriol : I love solitude.

I do not conceal too much and yet my identity seems to remain secret and isolated.

11b. *Reticence.* Silence, lack of talkativeness under most conditions, secrecy and the refusal to expose one's thoughts and feelings are grouped into one class.

Kindle : My natural New England reticence.

Vale : Friendship has always implied for me a large basis of personal reserve.

11c. *n Seclusion fused with n Infavoidance.* Very frequently seclusiveness is determined by a need to avoid belittlement and ridicule. Sometimes the n Harmavoidance or the n Infavoidance is also involved.

Kindle : I was always ashamed to show myself.

Earnst : Life became intolerable to me and I began to avoid as much as possible the company of other children.

I lived a painful and secluded existence.

12. *n Inviolacy.* Pride and the desire to maintain a high level of self-respect as manifested by a subject's efforts to make up for failure, or to defend, vindicate or revenge himself are grouped

together in one category. These reactions rest upon Narcism and grade off into Infavoidance. Differing from the scheme of needs presented in Chapter III, the Infavoidance drive has been put in a separate category. Here the need for Counteraction is covered by three fusions : with n Ach, n Agg and n Auto.

12a. *n Inviolacy : n Defendance.* This describes the readiness to deny accusations, to justify one's conduct and to offer extenuations for failure. It is based upon a refusal to accept belittlement and blame. Under this heading may also be included the concealment of inferior emotional reactions (fusion with n Seclusion). Defendance may be an exaggerated counteraction (defence mechanism) for guilt feelings.

Outer : I always had an alibi if a spanking seemed imminent.

Quick : I have always been stubborn and refuse to admit that I am wrong even when I am convinced of it.

12b. *n Inviolacy fused with n Achievement : Restriving.* Efforts to achieve something after failure or humiliation, to prove what one can do are grouped here.

Earnst : I fought in my own cause one day and was so braced up by my success that I never allowed myself to be picked on thenceforth unless my tormenters were large.

Vulner : There was one boy whom I could lick, and this I did regularly to bolster my pride.

My main ideal was to show these boys that I was brave and strong.

12c. *n Inviolacy fused with n Aggression : Retaliation.* Though this is perhaps the commonest type of Aggression, conforming to the law of talion, no clear illustration of it was found in the autobiographies.

12d. *n Inviolacy fused with n Autonomy : Resistance.* Stubborn refusals to be dominated (and hence, belittled) by others are placed in this category.

Krumb : I was recalcitrant.

I made a name for myself in school as the child who would not co-operate.

13. *Negative Cathections.* Under this heading are listed the important objects that repeatedly anger or are consistently disliked by the child. Since hate is a matter of crucial importance if it is directed towards somebody with whom one must have daily relations, it is particularly important to know whether one or another member of the family is negatively cathected. When ambivalent sentiments are entertained a score is given for positive cathection as well as for negative cathection.

13a. *Negative Cathexis : Supra : Mother.*

Outer : I remember praying each night that my mother would die, that she would be run over by an automobile.

I grew to hate my mother more and more.

Cling : I sometimes cursed my mother.

13b. *Negative Cathexis : Supra : Female.* The hatred of an older woman may signify a displaced hatred for the mother.

Outer : . . . the morbid life at home with my cousin, whom I often planned to poison.

13c. *Negative Cathexis : Supra : Father.*

Nipp : We none of us miss our father.

Veal : I have occasionally felt resentment against my father. I feel an inward wrath of his violation of parental duties.

Oriol : There is an undercurrent of antagonism between my father and myself which is in some measure kept under complete control.

13d. *Negative Cathexis : Supra : Male.* Hatred of a superior, an older person, a dogmatist, a recognized authority, a state official or the deity, may signify the perseveration and displacement of early parricidal tendencies.

Cling : I used to curse God when I was unhappy.

13e. *Negative Cathexis : Supra : Brother.*

Vulner : My brother is spoiled and peevish. He irritates me constantly.

13f. *Negative Cathexis : Supra : Sister.*

Kindle : I treated my older sister badly.

13g. *Negative Cathexis : Contemporaries.*

Krumb : I got to hate most of the boys at school.

13h. *Negative Cathexis : Infra : Brother.*

Cling : My brother and I used to have terrible fights . . . we were both hot-tempered and very childish.

13i. *Negative Cathexis : Infra : Sister.*

Outer : I soon learned to despise my younger sister.

Quick : I remember having almost daily quarrels with a sister who is two years younger than I.

Zora : I have a younger sister with whom I used to fight rather violently.

14. *n Aggression.* This describes the emotion of rage combined with overt acts of aggression against a thwarting, a competing or a belittling object. It also includes teasing or torturing objects that cannot defend themselves, as well as the destruction of property. Finally, there are the verbal forms of aggression : accusation, belittlement and malicious ridicule.

14a. *n Aggression : Temper.* In this class are the emotions that are commonly accompanied, though not always, by aggressive behaviour : irritability, anger, rage.

Zill : More than once I broke out with that awful temper I was acquiring.

Kindle : Whenever I was not given my own way I went into a tantrum. This was frequent.

14b. *n Aggression : Combativeness.* Here we include most of the physical and verbal forms of aggression : assaults, pushing, curses, angry accusations, criticism, blaming, irritable retorts, malicious jokes, destruction of possessions and heated arguments.

Roon : My sister and I are the only children of the family. . . We are of different temperaments and quarrels were always breaking out.

Outer : We four children fought . . . like animals.

Oak : We all squabbled and argued and even fought at times.

Kindle : I had quarreled much with my grammar school friends, somewhat with my friend from high school. I often disagreed bitterly with the chemist. But our friendship has continued unimpaired in spite of my fits of bad temper.

14c. *n Aggression : Sadism.* This describes pleasure that is felt when an object is hurt or belittled. It leads to the maltreatment of others : unjustly dominating, bullying, hurting or torturing a younger child or animal. Teasing is a mild form. No subject admitted to a marked degree of Sadism.

Cling : I used to pick on and bully him.

Quick : I have always enjoyed ridiculing others and am especially adept at satire.

14d. *n Aggression fused with n Dominance : Coercion* (*vide* n Dom). Rude assertions, the rough treatment of others, the frank expression of disturbing opinions, pugnacity and domination by threats belong in this category. A liking for rough physical encounters (athletics) may also be included.

Outer : My general attitude was aggressive and assertive when no one was around to stop me.

Zeeno : I turned to wrestling. I am very strong, but small.

Quick : I have many enemies whom I have alienated by my habit of speaking frankly.

Roll : I threatened to beat him to ashes.

14e. *n Aggression fused with n Autonomy : Rebellion* (*vide* n Auto). Aggressive resistance and flagrant disobedience are classified under this heading. It describes the ungovernable, defiant child. Anger evoked by authority belongs here. The tendency to oppose the opinions of others, e.g., the love of argument, may also be included.

Zill : I have often rebelled like a cranky child.

Quick : I have always loved to argue.

14f. *n Aggression fused with n Succorance : Plaintance* (*vide* n Suc). Here may be classed the manifestations of despairing rage (tantrums) found so frequently in infancy, as well as the complaints of later years. Blaming others for injustice and malice or reporting their misdemeanours may also be included.

Cling : The thwarting of my own desires was responsible for sullen brooding, or violent tantrums.

Together we decided to go to the headmaster.

Vulner : Telling tales made me very unpopular and incidentally very miserable.

14g. *n Aggression* : *Destruction*. Here we group destructive play, breaking toys, smashing windows, cutting or pulling things apart, dismembering dolls, throwing stones, upsetting things, lighting fires, and other forms of disruptive behaviour.

Kindle : I liked mechanical toys, particularly did I like pulling them apart.

Abel : My toys never stayed whole when I was young, and I understand it used to test my parents' ingenuity to give me something I couldn't get apart.

Roll : I had a mad idea about burning the house down to collect the insurance.

15. *n Autonomy*. This describes acts of resistance and defiance. Prompted by the general need for Activity and the tendency for Change there is first of all (a) breaking through barriers to free motility. Then, in the service of other needs (particularly n Sex) there is (b) defiance of prohibitions. The n Passivity, as well as other needs, may provoke (c) resistances to coercion and persuasion. Finally, behind many of these negativistic refusals is the n Inviolacy and the desire to become independent and self-reliant (n Ach).

15a. *n Autonomy* : *Freedom*. Under this heading we group all evidences of liberty-loving motility : breaking out of confinement, escape from routine, truancy, wandering away alone, irresponsibility and the disinclination to follow an established pattern. This egressive form of behaviour is usually combined with Rejection which may, in turn, be based on Infavoidance (running away from failure). Also it may be fused with n Aggression : struggling to get free.

Outer : 4 years . . . even at that age I wanted to run away from the convent.

I took long trips by bicycle away from home.

I dreamed often of running away.

I managed to break away on a very slight provocation.

Asper : Fred and I decided to take our ship's papers and break away from it all.

Abel : All unjust punishments were followed on my part by sullen periods wherein I made wild plans of joining the army when I grew up.

Quick : My special pleasures have always been to be out in the open air, a profound love of liberty knowing no restraint. I have always had a desire to join a Nudist Colony for the sincere enjoyment I would get in being liberated from the shackles of clothes, economic conditions, and social conventions. My greatest resentment arises when some one suggests my wearing more clothes (such as a tie or rubbers) since it is a direct insult to this unbridled love of freedom.

15b. *n Autonomy : Defiance.* This covers active disobedience disregard for authority, entering forbidden regions and law-breaking. Childish pranks as well as more serious misdemeanours belong in this group.

Outer : I used to be supposed to play with the nice boys of the neighbourhood, but instead sneaked off to a back alley where . . . I fraternized with ragamuffins and illiterate men's sons.

Oak : I was always in trouble for forgetting to do something I wa supposed to do and for raising too much childish Cain in the hall (a school). I almost set a record for hours of detention in one year.

15c. *n Autonomy fused with the n Inviolacy : Resistance (vid* n Inv). Here we group refusal to obey (negativism), passiv non-co-operation, resistance to persuasion and coercion, as we as persistent stubborn disagreements. Most of these acts take th form of verbal arguments against p Dominance. This may b fused with Aggression.

Zill : I often clashed with my father on religious ceremonies I had t perform.

Roon : I have always had definite opinions about matters that con cerned me and if they did not coincide with those of my father, I woul argue the matter out and still hold the opinion. It is a form of stubbornness that will give in only to undisputed authority.

Frost : My tendency is to react against the conventions of my surroundings.

15d. ***n Autonomy fused with the n Achievement : Independence*** (*vide* n Ach). Children who want to do things *alone* without help, who refuse aid offered by adults, who have initiative, and like to be 'on their own,' free and independent, belong in this class.

Outer : I was quite independent, due to my years spent with alley boys. . . I had ideas of my own, and paid little attention to schemes put out by others.

I soon became more independent, always went with boys three or two years older than myself . . . and grew generally very self-reliant.

Frost : I am completely self-sufficient mentally.

16. ***n Dominance.*** Here we have various manifestations of the will to power over other people : ordering, insisting, persuading, suggesting, or seducing. The effect desired by the subject is to have others work for him, help him or stop annoying him.

16a. ***n Dominance : Leadership.*** Attempts to control others, to manage an undertaking, to be the leader of a group are included in this category.

Roon : I soon had an attic theatre of my own. I was very intent on the managing of the project and soon had the whole neighbourhood as participants in the affair. My attitude here was entirely aggressive and I insisted on managing everything.

Kindle : I wanted to boss.

I was very active . . . leading and organizing young people's groups. . . I also was a leader of the younger boys. . . I thought such morality should be taught to others. I enjoyed teaching.

My ambitions have always been to be a professor . . . direct others in research.

Bulge : I being the boy and my mother's favourite, thought that I could boss all the girls.

Vulner : I entered enthusiastically into student government. I became a member of the student council, officer in Home Room, Editor of School magazine, and President of the Club.

Kast : I was president of my class for three years.

16b. *n Dominance : Inducement.* Under this heading may be classed various subtle or indirect forms of dominance : dominance by suggestion, flattery, friendly overtures, bribes, fascination or seduction.

Outer : I learned to become a very good and persuasive talker at this time.

Mauve : I have pretty much my own way with my mother.

16c. *n Dominance fused with n Aggression : Coercion* (*vide* n Agg). Fighting for power or the tyrannous domination of others may be put into this category.

Abel : My brother and I have the usual squabbles over ties and shirts and personal liberties and priority rights around the house.

Oriol : My domineering tendencies sometimes break through.

17. *n Rejection.* This describes feelings of indifference, revulsion, annoyance, scorn or disgust towards other people, accompanied by acts of exclusion, avoidance, withdrawal, expulsion and neglect.

17a. *n Rejection : Hypercriticalness.* Under this heading may be grouped the dislike and belittlement of others, feelings of scorn and disgust as well as the associated avoidant behaviour. There may be superiority feelings. We should also include skepticism, suspicion and distrust.

Outer : It made me suspicious of every proposition anyone made me after that.

I always regarded heroes with suspicion ever since an older boy promised to give me his wooden gun when I was four and he twelve, and disappointed me. I later became envious of all public heroes, and skeptical of their true natures.

Actually, my experiences with women have taught me to mistrust them. . . I have found every girl I have known (and I have known and gone with and 'necked' over a hundred) inferior to myself. They would not satisfy me in the long run, intellectually.

Asper : I now recognize my former friends as distinctly gross, uncouth, in fact, downright filthy specimens. . . How I ever escaped from their vile acts I cannot say definitely.

Frost : The tendency to analyse people carefully and coldly has made me feel withdrawn from normal life.

Vale : I taught in a boys' school and heartily detested it. I like boys well enough so long as I don't have to live with them or teach them.

Quick : There are only three people with whom I have great friendships. The rest are inferior.

17b. *n Rejection fused with n Infavoidance : Narcisensitivity* (*vide* n Inf). The subjects who especially dislike and avoid people who wound their vanity belong in this category.

Zeeno : My friendships are limited to those I care for. . . Usually, if I dislike a person I feel that I do so with justice. I feel that the few that dislike me are not really good themselves, for I feel that I am good and that people of discernment see and appreciate this feature in me.

Asper : Rebellion came shortly after I made a fool of myself at an initiation by almost breaking down, and I decided that henceforth I would be 'sufficient unto myself.' On that principle my life, up to very recently, has been conducted. I have had no real friend since the chap who introduced me to the society. I have met merely interesting individuals.

17c. *n Rejection fused with n Seclusion : Inaccessibility* (*vide* n Sec). Subjects who, because they dislike or distrust humanity, separate themselves from others by encystment, diffidence, going to a distance or erecting 'walls' belong in this class. Dislike of close contact, indifference, and an aloof, perhaps supercilious, attitude may also be included.

Asper : I decided from then on that I was somehow different from the rest of humanity, vastly superior to boys my own age — much too singular a creature to be understood. . . All my former acquaintances, almost to the last, I had dropped.

Sims : When I was a baby I had a great opposition to any kind of caressing or fondling. I am still sensitive to physical contact and am instantly repelled by it.

Mauve : I feel that old adage 'intimacy breeds contempt' has more truth in it than many suppose. I keep just a bit above everyone else.

Oriol : I meet people on an impersonal plane.

18. *n Noxavoidance*. This describes the readiness to be repelled by unpleasant sense impressions, disagreeable sights, sounds, smells, and tastes. It includes the avoidance of discomfort.

18a. *n Noxavoidance : Hypersensitivity : General.*

Zora : A fellow suggested the method by which I was myself begot. This filled me with a disgust and shame that almost made me sick. I am no longer disgusted, but even now I am impressed by a certain nastiness in the scheme of procreation.

Asper : The sex act itself was, at first, extremely repulsive.

18b. *n Noxavoidance : Hypersensitivity : Food.* The tendencies to spit and vomit, to suffer from indigestion and to reject certain kinds of food are classed here.

Roll : I used to be finnicky about food. This lasted into my teens.

19. *n Achievement*. Some children are conspicuous for the intensity, frequency or duration of their efforts to accomplish something. First it is a matter of controlling their muscles, gaining the erect posture, walking and climbing. Then they reach out to manipulate objects. Later, they must learn to direct their thoughts.

19a. *n Achievement : General.*

Oriol : I had ambition to excel.

Sims : I got three jobs and earned all my own expenses.

19b. *n Achievement : Physical.*

Zeeno : In the lower grades I was quite strong and athletic. In grammar school I was captain and pitcher on the baseball team. I used to hit home runs.

Outer : I found at school that in one particular branch of athletics, running, I was much better than the average.

Asper : I recall winning the 40 yard dash. I was most nearly interested in the body. The mind had not found itself as yet.

Bulge : Due to my athletic prowess I was popular.

19c. *n Achievement : Intellectual.*

Cling : I was very precocious in school, leading my class. . . I worked very hard, very long hours.

Outer : I managed to get admitted to the school, which had difficult standards for one of my education. I had to do a year of Latin myself in a month in the summer time.

For two years I had spent all my extra time studying for a national Greek scholarship.

Frost : When I was ten I had the sensation of a 'wall falling down' —and proceeded very rapidly. I went through Purdue in three years with an A— or B+ average. I acquired a great taste for literature and got A's in all my courses.

19d. *n Achievement : Caste.*

Kast : I associated with people of higher social status and more luxurious surroundings. I realized my lack of social ease and concentrated on improving myself at every opportunity.

19e. *n Achievement : Rivalry.* When an S is especially stimulated by the presence of a rival, enjoys open competitions and does better under such conditions he is given a positive score on this variable.

Zora : I found pleasure in competition.

Asper : There has been in my life as far back as I can remember the somewhat morbid practice of self comparison. The spirit of competition has been continuously a method of approach to another personality.

Earnst : When I found I could do better than other children in some studies I immediately concentrated my attention on school.

19f. *n Achievement : Ego Ideal.* The setting of a high level achievement, the determination to excel, the generation of a glowing fantasy of success may be put here.

Abel : My one big desire is to get an M.A. . . Unless I achieve this goal I shall be extremely disappointed.

Akeson : I felt the urgent necessity of doing something with myself, of accomplishing something worthwhile, of making my personality mean something.

19g. *n Achievement fused with n Inviolacy : Restriving* (*vide* n Inv). Attempts to replace failure by success, to select as lines of endeavour the very activities that have been associated with humiliation or defeat are grouped together in this class.

Kast : He remarked on my lack of social ease and from then on I concentrated on these things — and now I have as much polish as anyone.

Sims : I decided to make a come-back. I wrote for the college paper and made the board, which helped me to restore confidence in myself.

19h. *n Achievement fused with n Autonomy : Independence* (*vide* n Auto). The desire for singlehanded accomplishments and the refusal to accept assistance belong here.

Earnst : I was able to finish college without receiving aid from anyone.

20. *n Recognition.* This describes the desire for social approval, honour, position and fame. The usual manner of satisfying this need is through the n Achievement, but if a subject's accomplishments are not made public the approbation which he may desire from others will not be forthcoming. The need for Recognition is usually repressed because its objectification is annoying to others, but in some people it manifests itself as boasting, performing before others, publicizing, talking about one's adventures, displaying evidences of accomplishment and assuming a superior attitude. It is like the n Succorance in that it seeks something from others.

20a. *n Recognition : Recitals of Superiority.* Boasting and other ways of bringing one's accomplishments to the attention of others are classed here. No subject admitted that he was a boaster but some subjects evidently enjoyed the opportunity of recounting their accomplishments in an autobiography.

20b. *n Recognition : Cathection of praise.* Under this heading may be placed behaviour that is promoted by the hope or expectation of praise, commendation, special favours or prestige. Pleasure when one is flattered, displeasure when one is not, and annoyance when others are rewarded are signs of this variable.

Cling : I was fearful often that my brother's reward might exceed mine.

Kindle : I wanted . . . to be the object of their interest and attention.

Outer : . . . merely for the fun I got out of it . . . the feeling that I was playing a part, an important part, in the great play of life.

. . . dressed in expensive clothes, and speaking very correct English, I fraternized with ragamuffins and illiterate men's sons.

I took peculiar joy in showing them how I could steal cleverly.

I felt an irrepressible instinct to exhibit my salesmanship. . . I enjoyed standing in the crowd, having them remark on how beautiful my long curls were.

Vulner : The applause for my address and when my honours and activities were read gave me a tremendous thrill.

20c. *n Recognition fused with n Exhibition : Public Performance* (*vide* n Exh). The public demonstration of one's talents and the enjoyment of manifesting one's powers before others are classed here.

Oriol : I loved to talk and craved distinction and did not repress my desires.

Outer : I learned to love the applause of people when I acted and grew quite vain.

Zeeno : I used to hit home runs and I was always the idol of other less strong boys in my class.

21. *n Exhibition*. This describes direct exposure of the body or of the person. The subject wants to be seen even though he may not be applauded.

21a. *n Exhibition fused with n Recognition : Public Performance* (*vide* n Rec). Children like to show off and attract the attention of others. This is their method of winning acclaimance.

Zill : I made the usual bright sayings . . . most (of the older children) seem to have enjoyed my presence and childish wits.

Cling : I sang solos in chapel.

I acted in two plays.

Outer : (I took) several juvenile parts.

Quick : Boisterous, and at times puerile, I liked to be the centre of attraction.

21b. *n Exhibition fused with n Sex : Exhibitionism* (*vide* n Sex). Here we group instances of extraverted body Narcism, Exhibition in the service of sexual excitement or seduction.

Outer : At six I noticed that I had definite control of my own sex organs, and was reprimanded for displaying my powers to my mother.

Abel : I used to like to imagine a day at a nudist colony.

22. *n Sex.* This category is confined to genital manifestations of sexuality.

22a. *n Sex : Masturbation.* Infantile masturbation is believed to be universal. It usually stops at about five years of age and is not remembered afterwards. It may be revived during the latency period, but more commonly it does not reappear until the onset of puberty.

Zill : At the age of 12 I learned, very prematurely, I think, about sex from a boy even younger than myself. . . I masturbated often, but never openly. This I kept up till the age of 14 when a mysterious fluid began to come forth. I felt something was wrong and I was told so by an older boy. I have never masturbated since.

Cling : I noticed occasionally in climbing (a rope in the gym) a very pleasing and curious sensation. I had no idea what this was. I experimented. Without knowing what I was doing, I began to practise masturbation. I did this publicly whenever it occurred to me — in such a way that it was not directly evident what I was doing.

Oak : When I was 12 someone told me about masturbation and I did it several times a week for almost six years.

Roll : I discovered masturbation when I was 7 and practised it frequently. I reached the age of puberty and got into a rut of masturbation as there was plenty of chance to continue this practice unobserved.

Akeson : Retiring in nature as I was, I did not learn to masturbate until I was 19, a habit I have since not been able to throw off.

22b. *n Sex : Precocious Heterosexuality.* Some children show signs of 'falling in love' at an early age.

Zeeno : I was madly in love with two sweet young twins who occupied an apartment in our home. My feelings have always been that it was a youthful, sweet and innocent, and very deep love for two fine creatures.

My remembrance of early youth is several 'mimic' intercourses with a young girl a little older than myself.

22c. *n Sex : Homosexuality.* An erotic interest in a member of the same sex is classified here.

Kraus : One experiment, the result of curiosity, in sexual intercourse with one of my own sex was a decided failure for both of us, and it was never repeated.

Asper : I joined the Boy Scouts and my acquaintance narrowed down to four or five boys. . . There is a definite feverish element in my memory.

Krumb : I had a couple of mutual masturbation affairs.

I had a consuming interest in homosexual affairs. . . I reverted to these after being shocked by the pregnancy and abortion of the girl.

22d. *n Sex : Bisexuality*. Physical or mental attributes that are characteristic of the opposite sex are put in this category.

Cling : My voice did not begin to change until the end of my second year and did not completely change until the beginning of my senior year.

23. *n Acquisition*. This describes the desire for material possessions and acts designed to satisfy this desire : snatching or asking parents to give the S what he wants. A predatory, calculating, economic attitude may attend this need.

23a. *n Acquisition : Greediness*. Some children are very acquisitive. Toys and other objects attract them ; they grab, snatch, quarrel over their possessions and are continually asking their parents for things. Some are envious of their friends' possessions. They enjoy getting the best of a bargain or trade. A vivid memory of gifts received in the past usually indicates a strong n Acquisition.

Outer : I recall exhibiting tendencies for sharp bargaining and trade. I exchanged a penny for an apple and then persuaded the nun to give me back my money.

I was quick to exploit them, and used to ask them if they would give me money.

I told my mother that if she bought me an expensive set of tools I would make some articles of furniture and sell them, and pay her back her money. I almost believed myself.

I enjoyed . . . seeing them take out money and give it to me.

Bulge : I recall that company always thrilled me because I was usually given money by my relatives.

Quick : I am selfish for I want everything.

23b. *n Acquisition : Stealing*. This is the same as the preceding variable, but here the greediness is strong enough to overcome prohibitions or inhibitions.

Outer : We used to go into drug stores and steal lollypops.

Vale : I was once caught hooking candy in a store.

Zeeno : I remember stealing my father's cigars.

23c. *n Acquisition : Gambling*. Betting and playing games for money manifest the willingness to take risks for wealth.

Nipp : The love of gambling grew in our blood as we watched our father run poker games in the house. Even now we children would rather gamble than do almost any other thing in life.

My second year in college I joined the gang gambling every day and evening.

Shooting craps five nights out of seven between 10 P.M. and 1 A.M.

24. *n Cognizance*. This describes the exploratory activity of the child, gaining knowledge by manipulation, quiescent observation, the inspection of genitals, queries of all kinds, social curiosity and, finally, the reading of books for knowledge.

24a. *n Cognizance : Curiosity : General*. Here we group the various acts that are associated with diffuse curiosity : exploration, inspection, peering, overhearing conversations, asking questions.

Asper : We would remain up for all hours of the night and I would absorb eagerly all he had to say — and ask for more.

24b. *Cognizance : Experimentation*. Curiosity as to the outcome of manipulative activity, as well as the eagerness to attempt novel forms of artistic expression in order to note their effect, may be classed here.

Kindle : I was busied with Chemistry sets. This fascination for experiment in science lasted many years, and may explain why most of my friends at college were chemists, biologists, and so on.

My ambition has always been to carry on research.

Krumb : I devoted my spare time to experiment in my radio lab.

24c. *n Cognizance : Intellectual.*

Zora : I had an enthusiastic, whole-souled desire to read about Greek mythology. I remember staying in the schoolroom afternoons after class to read certain mythologic books.

Mauve : I was always looking for something to learn.

Sims : I began to get the reputation for being an inveterate reader of everything that came into the house.

24d. *n Cognizance : Sexual : Birth*. Curiosity about procreation is common in children. It is not infrequently frustrated by the evasions or falsehoods of parents.

Sims : I asked my father how dogs mated and what started the process of life going.

Vale : I asked the usual questions about where babies come from and was told that God put them in mother's bed.

Oriol : I wondered how a baby could be born through such a small aperture. My curiosity was not appeased until last year.

24e. *n Cognizance : Sexual : Genitals*. Curiosity about the organs of reproduction, the penis or lack of penis of the opposite sex, is a normal attitude for children.

Zora : I remember when I was six or seven visiting a small boy's house and as we took a shower we both observed that we had genital organs. Also, at a later time, a girl about the same age and I engaged in an experiment of sorts.

Earnst : A friend made his sister take her clothes off. We played with her genitals.

Gay : I had an interest in girls' bodies and tried to persuade a cousin to undress for me.

Veal : I wanted to see others naked, especially those of the opposite sex. I had a girl of my own age pull down her bloomers so I could see exactly what the difference was.

25. *n Construction*. This describes everything from the simple associative tendency, combining two things, to an interest in mak-

ing elaborate designs or buildings. It is an organizing or configurational tendency which may have either a utilitarian or aesthetical aim. It has been found convenient to include creative writing.

25a. *n Construction : Mechanical.*

Kast : I never tired of inventing new types of vehicles. I was continually experimenting with my electric motor to obtain different speeds.

Krumb : My real interest was electricity.

I wanted time to work at my radio construction.

25b. *n Construction : Aesthetic.* Artistic creations have been classified here, though to speak of them as constructions may be misleading.

Sims : I wrote some short stories.

Krumb : I took an interest in poetry and wrote some.

Vulner : I drew in pen, pencil and charcoal.

26. *n Order.* Under this caption we include three somewhat different tendencies : the activity of washing and cleaning up, the activity of arranging and putting things in their proper place, and a finnicky interest in detail.

26a. *n Order : Cleanliness.* To war against dirt and bad odours is a habit which some children acquire and others do not.

Irkman : I have always done my utmost to appear cleanly dressed.

26b. *n Order : Orderliness.* Neatness and order in the arrangement of one's possessions belong in this class. No illustrations of this or the next category were given in the autobiographies.

26c. *n Order : Finickiness about details.* An interest in precise and exact measurement or statement, scrupulosity, a concern about small matters, a fervour for the 'letter of the law,' a memory for detailed concrete facts ; these tendencies are frequently found in the same person. They seem to spring from a common root.

27. *n Retention.* The desires to collect, to conserve and to hold on to objects are grouped together under this heading.

27a. *n Retention : Collectance.* The gathering together of objects to form a collection is an extension of the acquisitive drive and is closely related to the n Construction and the n Order. It stands between these and true retentiveness. Hoarding and saving money may be included here.

Kast : I collected all kinds of things. Lately I have been making a collection of little wooden images.

Kindle : I had a work bench with all sorts of useless junk.

Earnst : I had been saving money carefully. I planned on saving enough to start college.

Kast : I was able to buy all my clothes and had saved $550 when I was ready for college.

27b. *n Retention* : *Conservance.* Care of one's possessions, efforts to preserve them from decay or weathering, concealing them or putting them under lock and key so that they will not be damaged by others may be grouped together under this heading.

Kast : Father is noted for the excellent condition in which he keeps his possessions. I am proud of these things.

28. *n Activity.* This is a large general category which describes the rate of overt activity, physical and verbal. It usually includes alertness, initiative, responsiveness, and a fast tempo of existence. Its opposite is Passivity, which was given a separate place, but this is probably inadvisable.

28a. *n Activity* : *Physical.* Some children are much more active than others in locomotion and manipulation. This is usually accompanied by exploratory excursions and the n Autonomy : Freedom. Restlessness and the inability to remain quiet in one place are characteristic. Such individuals usually like variety (Ch). This may lead to an interest in athletics (*cf.* myomania — exercise as a cure-all) or to movement for pure kinaesthetic enjoyment (muscular erotism).

Kindle : I entered into a life of great activity, was constantly busy — played tennis, did much walking and other exercises.

Asper : I enjoy dancing to fox-trot music. It is essentially an athletic enjoyment with a definite element of sex excitement. That the pleasure is athletic I can definitely feel when I dance quite alone and the body loosens in the swinging rhythm. I enjoy thoroughly a jazz orchestra that is essentially rhythmic and I have gone frequently to Harlem to hear them. It has the power for me to make me beat with my whole body.

Kast: I played at top speed, did nothing but run around.

28b. *n Activity: Verbal.* Talkativeness and garrulousness are put into this class. It is mostly a matter of the rate and amount of speech. Some children jabber endlessly.

Oriol: I loved to talk.

Quick: I am extremely loquacious, having the ability of talking hours at a time without saying anything of value.

29. *Intensity.* This term has been used to describe an attribute which seems to be distinguishable from Activity, Persistence and Emotionality. It refers to what in everyday language is called power, force, zest, enthusiasm, conviction, emphasis. Mere Activity (many movements or words per unit of time) may be lacking in strength, so also may persistent efforts. Emotionality may be entirely ineffective (*cf.* anxiety and grief).

Zora: I like to work intensely and I seldom do anything except with enthusiasm.

30. *Emotionality.* Here are grouped instances of frequent, or long-enduring intense emotional excitement.

Kindle: With my friends I am very temperamental, sometimes very kind and generous, sometimes given to bitter and sarcastic words.

Zora: I have often thought of myself as emotional, yet my self-discipline seems to be adequate.

Quick: I became fanatically orthodox. Only lately have the effects of this frenzy disappeared.

My moods are ones of excess. Great joy followed by great sadness.

Vulner: When my mother or sister played the piano I could work myself to tears thinking of my grandmother who died, though I had no real affection for her.

31. *Persistence.* This describes the tendency to 'keep at' something until it is finished. It involves the setting of a somewhat distant goal, the determination to reach that goal, lack of distractibility, endurance, will power in the face of fatigue, the

ability to endure monotony and so forth. It may belong under n Achievement.

Zora: When I am physically tired, I yet continue doing whatever I am doing, deprived of even the indications of enthusiasm.

32. *Sameness:* This term describes fixity, rigidity, inflexibility, stability or consistency of personality. Since this may perhaps be an attribute of processes at one level of integration and not at another it is questionable whether it should be accepted as a general factor.

32a. *Sameness: Constancy of Cathexis.* This designates the tendency of some people to maintain their cathections over a long period of time. The cathections may be strong (Intensity) or weak, but they endure. As illustrations one may mention adherence to the homestead, mother-fixation, family loyalty, the bearing of a grudge, the boy who never forgets an injury, fetishism, tenaciousness about possessions, the faithful servant, a 'die-hard,' the man of inflexible sentiments, a golden wedding. What we observe is the inability to accept substitutes for cathected objects, a preference for the familiar and a resistance to novelty.

Kast: I had toy soldiers and machines which I never tired of playing with.

Frost: I became very much attached to a set of blocks and for several years played with them every day.

32b. *Sameness: Behavioural Rigidity.* This describes the tendency to do the same things in the same order day in and day out. Such a person likes to plan what he is going to do and is disturbed by conditions or demands that require a change of plan. He is upset by the unexpected. If possible, he adheres to a regular routine, for he can tolerate monotony. He is apt to develop rigid habits.

32c. *Sameness: Mental Rigidity.* This describes the tendency to adhere to old conceptions and resist new ideas. The subject uses the same words to express the same banal opinions. He wants to hear similar opinions from others. This factor is separated from Behavioural Rigidity because the two are not highly correlated.

For example, there are some highly flexible and imaginative minds inhabiting bodies that pursue an inflexible routine. Mental Rigidity, however, may be the result of immotility and circumscription (confining one's life to a narrow environment and to a small circle of friends).

Zora : My view of society has come to be a view of the rural districts of Pennsylvania, for it seems to me that the life to be found there is the only life that my mind really comprehends.

Change is the opposite of Sameness. It describes the 'weather vane' person. As illustrations of this the following will suffice :

Quick : I have a very fickle nature, not only in my infatuations but in all my tastes and fancies.

Stubb : I can do more things than most people. Since twelve years of age I have held positions as an operator of a die-cutting machine in an envelope factory, as a chauffeur, as a swimming instructor, camp counsellor, director of camp, typist, clerk in grocery store, salesman, bar tender, tutor, bellhop, office boy, bookkeeper, publicity agent for crooner, publicity agent for masseur and various other jobs.

Asper : My mind is essentially unacademic.

33. *Inhibition.* Delayed reactions are usually the result of 1, Passivity (low Activity) : sleepiness, apathy, dullness, lag ; 2, lack of ability : ignorance or inexperience ; or 3, Inhibition. The latter factor is manifested by tenseness, spasticity, or rigidity which may be steady (the subject is 'frozen to the spot,' 'mute') or alternating (the subject's movements or words are jerky and disorganized). Under unemotional circumstances Inhibition takes the form of simple hesitation or caution. The factor of Inhibition favours all the negative needs. It may be a basic constituent of introversion. Combined with intellection, it manifests itself as delayed action : reflection and deliberation. 'Deliberation' is the term that was used for this factor in Chapter III. No clear illustrations of Inhibition were found in the autobiographies but there were many examples of its opposite, Impulsion.

34. *Elation.* It was considered important to have one variable which stood for a continuum of mood differences running from Dejection (including sorrow, depression, pessimism) to Elation (including joy, enthusiasm, optimism). Cycloid personalities, of course, vacillate from one extreme to the other.

Bulge : I was extremely happy. I had no troubles and no problem seemed worth worrying about. My life was one sweet song for four glorious years.

In the autobiographies depressions were recorded with more frequency than elations.

Outer : Now, for a while, it seemed as though I would become morbid.

Occasionally I find, if I am not busy, that I fall into the deepest fits of morbid despair, in which fits I am inclined to ponder over the efficacy of suicide.

Akeson : For the most part my life has been a series of disappointments, failures, unhappiness, dissatisfactions and deep depressions.

Earnst : My earliest impressions of life were miserable.

Oriol : I am moody and melancholy.

Quick : Periods of great happiness are followed by similar periods of great dejection. The moods are ones of excess, great joy — great sadness.

35. *Imaginality.* Under this heading we subsume fantasy and imaginative play. The variable describes the dreamy or imaginative child that is preoccupied and largely determined by its inner world, the sensitive and suggestible child that is frightened by its own shadow, the child that loves fairy tales and myths and the child that likes to make-believe.

Cling : My heroes were not men of history. I preferred strange, mythical characters, legends, and fairy tales. Jason, Ulysses, Perseus, or the younger brother of innumerable fairy stories were the people I longed to have been.

Sudden fears often gripped me, and I ran home as if pursued by real and tangible dangers, and not just imagined bogeys.

Roon : During the winter, when I read a great deal . . . my imagination would be very strong. I read simple adventure tales that would immediately set me dreaming of far-off, fantastic places.

Zora: Those mythologic figures are still the one thing in my mind that seem alive, and untouched.

Asper: I can always look for an evening of really deep pleasure when I hear music. It is a process of complete loss of self into an imaginary reality.

Frost: I lived in a most amazing dream world. This became very real to me and from merely playing with sticks impersonating men, I began to live with them, and a few dreams that I had convinced me of their reality. I used to play digging for gold mines. When asked about this I would say that I was actually digging for gold. By this deceit I eventually even convinced myself. These years formed my mind more than any others. It stimulated my imagination which later has helped me a great deal.

Vale: I was strongly addicted to the sort of fantasy in which I was the all-conquering hero, of having wild and romantic adventures; in superlative terms I was a soldier, an eloquent lawyer, an adventurer — always a man of action.

36. *Deceit.* This is a stray category which includes actions that seem to be important enough to be considered. The variable describes the tendency of a child to tell falsehoods, deceive or be excessively secretive about its conduct.

Outer: I always had an alibi if a spanking seemed imminent.

I grew very crafty in avoiding such show-downs.

I also found that an innocent pose always worked for the best, and cultivated an outward appearance of the utmost innocence and purity.

With the most hypocritical feelings we fawned on her and told her how glad we were to see her.

Infantile Complexes

The behaviour patterns and cathected objects listed above were illustrated by events that occurred after the age of three. Anyone can cull similar examples from his own past. It seems that such memories depend mostly, if not entirely, upon the possession of language, that only what has been verbalized can be recollected in thought. Hence, events which occur before the acquisition of language (during the pre-verbal period) are not recallable, though they may be partially re-enacted ('remembered,' as it were, by the motor system) and verbalized during the re-enaction in terms that seem to reproduce in a vague way the original situation.

An abundance of data collected by psycho-analysts, which cannot, of course, be reviewed here, strongly suggests that events of the pre-verbal period are in many cases as determining as, if not more determining than, later events. This conclusion has been arrived at by comparing some of the productions of adults (dreams of normal men, fantasies of neurotics, delusions of psychotics, as well as many artistic productions, myths and religious practices) to the events that can be observed in the life of infants. Without any doubt there is a connection. And there is nothing very extraordinary about this. It would be more extraordinary, from what we know about conditioning, if the reverse were true ; if something so plastic as an infant could not be radically modified by its experiences. Unfortunately, the child cannot tell us in so many words how it apperceives the world, how it feels and what it dreams about. Hence we must arrive at the contents of its regnancies by carefully observing external behaviour and by extrapolating backwards from the verbalizations that occur at a later age. Let the reader keep in mind the highly speculative character of what is now to be discussed, but let him also remember that some of it is supported by a growing mass of circumstantial evidence : hundreds of case histories in the files of practising analysts, only small fragments of which are in print. What I shall have to say about the themas which analysts have brought to our attention will be brief, somewhat superficial and necessarily unconvincing to anyone who has not had a long experience with free associations. The short space that is open for this topic does not permit me to do justice to what the more advanced analysts have written on the subject. Nor shall I confine myself to what is considered good doctrine. The basic conceptions, of course, come from Freud, to whom all psychologists are indebted ; but in the ensuing pages they are given the shape that our own observations and judgements have dictated.

The analysts have especially stressed five highly enjoyable conditions or activities, each of which is terminated, frustrated or limited (at some point in development) by external forces : (1) the secure, passive and dependent existence within the womb (rudely interrupted by the painful experience of birth) ; (2) the sensuous enjoyment of sucking good nourishment from the mother's breast (or from a bottle) while lying safely and dependently in her arms (brought to a halt by weaning) ; (3) the free enjoyment of the pleasurable sensations accompanying defecation (restricted by toilet training) ; (4) the pleasant sense impressions accompanying urination (these are not as restricted as other zonal pleasures and are of less significance) ; and (5) the thrilling excitations that arise from genital friction (prohibited by threats of punishment). Since the analysts are inclined to emphasize the tactuo-sensory phases of sexual activity, the four last mentioned zonal activities are considered to be rudimentary expressions of the Sex drive ; their connections with the more fundamental digestive functions being generally disregarded. Thus, it is the convention to speak of oral, anal, urethral and genital erotism. Leaving aside the Freudians' somewhat narrow and bizarre use of the term 'erotism,' the facts show conclusively : 1, that many children do derive absorbing and exciting pleasure from activities associated with one or another of these zones ; 2, that they may become fixated in respect to such activities ; and 3, that these fixations have a marked influence on the evolution of the sexual drive ; giving rise to the so-called perversions which are either overtly expressed or (more commonly) inhibited or repressed. Even when repressed, these tendencies have the power to influence thought and behaviour. Although, as Freud has suggested, these phenomena may depend primarily on endocrine activity, external factors are also important. It seems, for instance, that zonal fixations do not occur — one might almost say that the zonal activities do not become enduringly erotized — if there is no imposed frustration. The evidence suggests, indeed, that frustration followed by inhibition and repression may lead to the erotization of any drive : Aggression (sadism), Acquisition (kleptomania), Dominance (megalomania), Exhibition (exhibitionism), Cognizance (voyeurism). No plausible theory has been offered to account for this.

An enduring integrate (derived from one of the above-mentioned enjoyed conditions) that determines (unconsciously) the course of later development may be called a complex. A complex is considered abnormal only when it is extreme. The complexes which are now to be considered are constellated about : 1, an enclosed space (or 'claustrum' as we shall call it), 2, the mouth (sucking, biting and food), 3, the anus (defecation and faeces), 4, the urethra (urination and urine) or 5, the genitals (masturbation and the fear of castration).

A. CLAUSTRAL COMPLEXES

Under this heading we shall group all complexes that might conceivably be derived from the pre-natal period or from the trauma of birth. The following may be distinguished : 1, a complex constellated about the wish to reinstate the conditions similar to those prevailing before birth ; 2, a complex that centres about the anxiety of insupport and helplessness ; and 3, a complex that is anxiously directed against suffocation and confinement (anti-claustral tendency).

A1. *Simple Claustral Complex.* This integrate seems to be organized by an unconscious desire to re-experience the state of being that existed before birth. We have to do here with a compound of needs and actones associated with a certain type of object. The symptoms are as follows :

a. *Cathection of claustra.* It is not necessary to affirm that the child wants in any literal sense to enter the mother, for if, as is supposed, the womb was for him an agreeable place it must have satisfied certain prevailing needs, and after birth there are other places which may just as well or better satisfy these needs when they recur. An emphasis upon the external conditions of foetal life, however, establishes the cathexis of womb-like enclosures as the core of the complex. In order not to mix interpretation with fact it seems advisable to use the term claustrum (plural : claustra) to designate such places, particularly if they are small, warm, dark, secluded, safe, private or concealing. As illustrations of such objects or dream images the following may be mentioned : a crib, under the sheets, under the bed, a barrel, a box, a safe, a closet, a room of one's own, a sound-proof den, a home off the beaten track, a monastery, a castle, a citadel, a cathedral, a hut, a cave, a hogan, a secret hiding place, a tunnel into a mountain, a mesa, a mine, a tomb, a boat with a cabin, a barge, a stage coach, a limousine. One might also include islands, enclosed valleys, and certain versions of paradise. It is supposed that a subject with this complex is attracted to, seeks, or if not found, builds such objects, and is inclined to enter them (v Ingression) and remain in them (v Adherence) for some time, secluded from others. Claustral symbols may appear quite frequently in his dreams and fantasies. The subject gets a fixation on his habitation or sanctuary and hates to leave it or to move to another house.

b. *Cathection of nurturant objects (mother).* Since the mother furnished the original claustrum and since her embracing arms, her skirts and her protecting peaceful presence may function as a claustrum we may expect anaclitic love with fixation on the mother or on a mother surrogate. Homesickness is common. This would be characteristic of an extraverted claustral child. An introverted child is more likely to find or build a secluded material haven and act inwardly as its own parent (n intraNur). In a social situation the introvert's 'wall' of reticence functions as a claustrum. Institutions may act as protecting claustra (particularly for the extravert) : school, college (alma mater), lodge, church (mother church), hospital, almshouse, asylum, etc. God may be fantasied as a claustrum (ex : 'Rock of ages, cleft for me, Let me hide myself in Thee').

c. *n Passivity, n Harmavoidance, n Seclusion and n Succorance.* An emphasis on the drive aspect leads to the formulation of a compound constituted by needs that were satisfied in the womb : n Passivity (sleep, unconsciousness and inactivity), n Harmavoidance (freedom from pain, from loss of support, from shock, from loud noises and other dangers), n Seclusion (privacy and freedom from intrusive human stimulation), n Succorance (the close presence of another human body to gratify these as well as other needs : Food and Water). The great dependence upon home or upon a refuge (a safe haven of rest) justifies the expression 'claustral Succorance,' or even 'umbilical Succorance' (*cf. The Silver Cord*) when a subject does not dare to venture more than a certain distance from his homestead. Here the Harmavoidance drive commonly uses Succorance (adherence to a supporting O, or calls for help) as a subsidiary. The n Passivity is satisfied in sleep, the actones being those of curling up (ex : foetal position).

c i. *Cathection of death.* Related to the subject's underlying desire to return to his former state of passivity is the inclination to surrender, to fall ill, to drown in the waters, to depart this life or to 'enter the tomb and be swallowed up by mother earth.' It may be thought that 'death's bright angel' will bring a happy release from the coils of this mortal life. A milder version of this is

c ii. *Cathection of Nirvana.* Here the subject desires to attain utter passivity (without death), serenity resulting from the relaxation of tension and conflict, to lose his individual identity (Ego consciousness) by merging with (dissolving in) the infinite (becoming one with the universe, the atmosphere, the sea, the 'great mother,' the Godhead). This may lead to a separation from others, drug addiction, mystical exercises, or Yoga practices.

d. *Cathection of the past.* The S is attached to his birthplace. If he moves away, in later years he is apt to think back on his childhood with feelings of nostalgia. He may yearn to return to the old homestead, or he may idealize his childhood or he may glorify some epoch that is past, some historic period before his birth. ('Once things were better on the earth'—*cf.* myth of the Golden Age, myth of the Garden of Eden.) As a sub-heading may be added :

d i. *Epimethean sentiments.* The desire for security and immobility and the cathection of the past usually lead an S with a claustral complex to adopt and adhere to conventional and well-accredited patterns of behaviour and thought : morals, political principles, religious beliefs, aesthetical standards. He resists change, new ideologies, revolutionary doctrines. Sameness, Conjunctivity and Deliberation are apt to be high.

Illustrations (from the autobiographies) of the simple claustral complex must be sought under the proper headings : cathection of mother, n Passivity, n Seclusion, n Harmavoidance, n Succorance. Here it is only necessary to cite memories which relate to the cathection of claustra :

Krumb : I am able to take my exams at home, sheltered from the unthinkable agony of sitting in a room full of people.

I am afraid to leave my room. All I want is the quiet of my room.

Vulner : I loved to build tunnels in snow or under chairs with rugs thrown over.

The simple claustral complex may or may not be associated with the insupport complex.

A2. *Insupport Complex.* This is constituted by a basic insecurity or anxiety of helplessness (n Succorance S n Harmavoidance). The fears are rather typical.

Fears of insupport. The loss of physical support is one of the elementary conditions of fear. There are various kinds of fears which may be subsumed under this heading, the commonest being :

i. *Fear of open spaces* (agoraphobia). The subject cannot leave his house, or depart from the support of a wall, or expose himself to inclement weather, or cross a space, or feel at home in open country without the accompanying presence of a reliable and sympathetic friend or parent. One thinks here of a child learning to walk — moving cautiously from one fixed structure to another, not daring to hazard steps across the floor. This includes 'distance' phobias.

ii. *Fear of falling* (narrow pathways, insecure ground, heights). The subject is cautious in walking on rough ground or in crossing streams on a log or in jumping from rock to rock, or in climbing trees, or in shinnying up a pole, or in climbing mountains. He avoids heights if possible. Fainting or dizziness are common symptoms.

iii. *Fear of drowning* (water). The child is afraid when he first takes his bath. Later, he is very cautious when he begins to play along the water's edge. Because of fear he is slow in learning to swim, and when at sea he is afraid of rough water, afraid of capsizing. The idea of a shipwreck troubles him.

iv. *Fear of earthquake.* The thought of ground crumbling under him is alarming.

v. *Fear of fire.* Imaginations or dreams of his house being consumed in flames or falling on his head terrify him at night.

vi. *Fear of family insupport.* The S may be worried by discord between his parents. He may fear separation, divorce or the death of a parent.

vii. *Fear of life.* The subject fears novel situations, strangers, change, adventure. He does not feel capable of the effort and courage necessary to make his independent way in the world.

A3. *Egression (Anti-Claustral) Complex.* Psycho-analysts are apt to assume that the womb is the pleasantest of all environments and that every creature has an underlying desire to return to it. Certainly, in a child, the needs for Passivity and Succorance are strong, but it may be supposed that with foetal growth the womb sometimes becomes a press of confinement, which provokes the needs for Activity and Autonomy. We know, for instance, that the foetus is quite active during the last months. Recent findings indicate that a progressive anoxemia (asphyxia) in the child is the stimulus which initiates labor pains, and this is the very stimulus which is most certain to evoke Autonomy, movements to escape from restraint (particularly if it limits respiration) or from the confines of an airless space. The process of birth subjects the infant to extreme cranial pressure and is followed by a short period of more extreme asphyxia. Thus the press of asphyxia and physical restraint are intimately associated. It will be remembered that Watson and others have found that holding the head of a baby in a fixed position invariably provokes angry struggles for release. These facts suggest that we must consider the possibility of a complex directly opposed to the claustral complex.

Speculation suggests that the manifestations to be described constitute an integrate that is related to the trauma of birth. It may represent a re-enaction of the birth trauma in order to master the anxiety associated with it, or a long term perseveration of the n Autonomy (fused with the need for Air) set up and for a time frustrated by conditions just before and during birth. The symptoms of this complex are as follows :

a. *Egression vector.* This designates the fact that the subject is perpetually *leaving* a place, particularly an enclosed, stuffy, constraining, prohibiting or monotonous place. According to the emphasis at the moment we find :

i. *Cathection of open spaces and fresh air.* Some people have strong sentiments about the necessity for fresh air, wide open windows, deep and unimpaired breathing. They do not like to be confined indoors, to be 'cooped up.' They like to range freely, to roam or ride across country, to travel. They are apt to prefer large expanses : the sea, the desert, distant views from high mountains.

ii. *Locomotion vector.* This describes a recurrent reaction to environments, namely, separation. The subject cannot stay for any length of time in one place. He must be continually on the move. As examples we may cite : truants, hoboes, voyagers, adventurers, gentlemen of fortune, explorers, sailors, beachcombers.

iii. *Cathection of change.* There are subjects who hanker after new impressions, cannot tolerate monotony, are painfully bored by conventional people and trite speech. 'Anything for a change' is their motto.

iv. *Negative cathection of claustra* (claustrophobia). Here the subject is afraid that if he gets into an enclosed place, a room, an elevator, a subway, a train, a theatre, he will be unable to get out. When he does find himself in such a situation a fearful anxiety may arise (n Harm) and with it the thought that he is unable to breathe (fusion with n Air). This terrifies him and he will make frantic efforts to escape. The panic that sometimes possesses an audience when a fire breaks out in a theatre may be cited as an instance of a widespread temporary claustrophobia among normal people. A fear of closed spaces is not infrequently found in conjunction with a fear of open spaces. This is evidence in favour of the supposition that the basis for both of them is the same : the birth trauma. The fear of being buried alive should be included here.

b. *n Autonomy*. Typical of this complex is the Autonomy drive exhibited as an intolerance of barriers and restraining prohibitions, coupled with the tendency to break out and take flight from such confinements. Subjects of this stamp must feel free, and so whenever compliance is demanded (p Dominance) they rebel. ('Give me liberty or give me death.') They are apt to think that the 'authorities' are interfering with their rights. Open defiance, however, is less characteristic than escape to some more tolerant environment. With this integrate may go the cathection of primitive people (ex : the 'noble savage') and the expression of Promethean sentiments (ex : 'orthodoxy must be shattered ; there must be freedom ; a new "inspiration" must be brought to man').

Various interesting combinations of the three claustral complexes may be found. Ambitendency (vacillation from one extreme to the other) is not uncommon. We have, for example :

Rebirth thema, which combines Ingression (entering the womb [introversion] in order to gather new energies) and Egression (emergence from darkness [extraversion] in order to create something, take up a new life, or bring a 'message').

Orphan thema. The S may think of himself as having been unwanted by his parents, unloved, disinherited (*cf.* expulsion from paradise), misunderstood, pushed before his prime into an unkindly world (*cf.* claustral complex). He may dramatize himself as a pariah, an unbefriended wanderer over the face of the earth, wistfully craving or seeking the love that was once withheld, looking for the 'happy isles,' the 'forgotten way.'

Unfortunately, there is no data pertaining to the problem of whether such conditions as threatened miscarriage, protracted labour, marked asphyxia at birth and Caesarian section have an influence on the development of claustral complexes. There is evidence, however, which goes to show that later the press of Family Insupport (Discord, Separation, Death), the press of Rejection, and the press Birth of Sibling may promote or engender one of these integrates.

B. ORAL COMPLEXES

That the mouth is a zone which may function as an integral part of an erotic complex is demonstrated by the conjunction of kissing and sexuality, but more certainly by the occurrence of overt oral erotism (fellatio) and covert, inhibited oral erotism (unequivocally manifested in fantasies and dreams). These and other facts led Freud to the notion of a primarily erotized mouth. According to this theory it is from sucking that the infant derives its greatest sensuous delight. This theory, if given an operational definition, becomes a fact which no one who patiently observes the oral activity of babies can readily deny.

Though the activity of sucking may have originally acquired significance through its association with the satisfaction of hunger (n Food), it must be given the status of a more or less independent drive (n oral Sentience). For example, a child, after satiation of its appetite, will not infrequently push away the bottle and start sucking its thumb, just as, in later life, after a hearty meal a man will take a sweet (n gustatory Sentience) or light a cigar (n oral Sentience). The conclusion is that sucking, during a certain period of life, at least, is an actone which brings its own peculiar satisfaction. A child will exhibit the signs of extreme annoyance if this activity is interfered with. It seems likely, furthermore, that these mouth sensations are not only in themselves more sexual-like than anything else the child experiences, but they engender (by the spread of excitations through the parasympathetic nervous system) sensations in the genital region (fusion with n Sex). This would help to explain the frequency with which genital excitement follows upon oral stimulation (satisfied or frustrated).

Sucking is accompanied by a relatively passive, succorant attitude. The baby lies back (usually in its mother's arms) and receives its nourishment from her breast or from a bottle. Furthermore, the child is more or less helpless during the entire sucking period. Because of this association, one commonly finds oral automatisms and a succorant dependent attitude occurring overtly or covertly in the same individual. When this persists as an enduring complex it may be supposed that either the zonal fixation (as most analysts assume) or the receptive tendency is the basic constellating factor.

Having discovered evidence for what might be called the erotization of sucking, the analysts are prone to group all complexes that are associated with the mouth — biting, chewing, spitting, vomiting, breathing, tasting, food preferences, and speech phenomena — under the heading of oral erotism. To what extent this terminology is justified is uncertain. At present, there are not enough accurate observations of infant behaviour to warrant positive statements. Here we have limited ourselves to three oral complexes: 1, the mouth associated with n Passivity and n Succorance (Reception vector); 2, the mouth associated with n Aggression (Contrience vector); and 3, the mouth associated with n Rejection (Ejection or Encasement vector).

B1. *Oral Succorance Complex.* This is chiefly characterized by the conjunction of oral activity (automatisms and the cathection of oral objects) and passive, succorant tendencies (dependence and the cathection of nurturant objects). It bears some resemblance to the claustral complex in so far as it is engendered by a dependent physical connection with the mother (mouth-nipple) which is broken later, more or less abruptly. Expulsion from the womb and weaning are both imposed separations (frustrations) which may leave their mark on the personality of the child. Events of the feeding period, as well as the conditions of weaning, should have a determining effect upon the complex. Some children, for example, are weaned suddenly and show marked frustration reactions. The degree of trauma at weaning would appear to be determined by 1, the child's capacity to enjoy oral stimulation and the amount of previous gratification; 2, the rigidity and focality of the fixation; 3, the suddenness of the change; 4, the child's general irritability and intolerance of frustration ; and 5, the inability of the mother to provide adequate substitutes. The symptoms of an oral succorance complex are as follows :

a. *Oral automatisms : sucking.* Here we should include constant lip movements, sucking (of finger, pencil, etc.), frequent hand-to-mouth actones, excessive kissing and so forth.

Quick : I sucked my thumb until I was five.

Vulner : A bad habit I had was sucking my index finger and at the same time twisting my hair so that I developed a little bald spot.

Roll : One of my habits was pulling at my hair, getting a hair out by the roots, whereupon I put it in my mouth and sucked it. I have been trying to break this habit for years. I've even tried wearing a hat when I study.

b. *Cathection of oral objects : nipple, breast.* Originally, it was the nipple and breast or the nipple and milk bottle that satisfied oral Sentience. Later other objects (thumb, 'pacifier,' penis, cigars) may be accepted as substitutes and be cathected.

c. *Compulsive n Food or n Water, with cathection of food objects and drink.* Eating between meals, frequent inclinations to nibble or have a sip of something, a pre-occupation with diet (ritualistic habits), a prodigious appetite (stuffing), dipsomania, as well as the cathection of food objects (especially milk, ice cream, soft food, candy, 'all-day-suckers') and drugs that are taken by mouth ; these all suggest an oral complex. Memories of food and eating were profuse in some of the autobiographies, not at all in others.

Vale : I used to dream about having all I wanted to eat of the things I liked.

Kast : I remember father bringing me home some ice cream when I was sick. From then on I looked on ice cream as a benefit to life. I eat tremendous amounts of it in the summer.

Earnst : I remember drinking water for days, a sip at a time, to ease the feverish burning of my throat.

d. *n Passivity and n Succorance.* The desire passively to receive (v Reception) : nourishment, sympathy, protection, support, praise, recognition, money, love, is characteristic of this complex. The S appears to be starving for affection. The Acquisition drive is often fused with these needs (ex : a 'gold digger' on the lookout for a 'sugar daddy'). It is exemplified by those who 'make use of' people, who 'sponge' by accepting hospitality and money (ex : begging). An inhibited oral Acquisition tendency (exhibited by the infant who grabs and puts into its mouth whatever objects it can reach') may express itself as a fantasy of searching, inbreaking or digging in the ground for something valuable (oil, gold, etc.). Kleptomania may spring from this complex, as well as exaggerated envy.

It has been shown by Alexander [1] that gastric symptoms (indigestion, peptic ulcer) may be caused by covert oral receptive tendencies.

e. *Projections of n oral Succorance*. The subject fantasies that *other people* are trying to 'use' *him* (to make a 'sucker' out of him), and that his energies are being drained (Vampire thema). People, he says, ask for too much. This projection occurs when the S inhibits his own desire to take from others.

f. *Cathection of nurturant objects (mother)*. A dependent fixation on the mother or on some other sympathetically devoted object is common.

g. *Fantasies of oral impregnation*. Theories of fertilization by the inspiration or ingestion of a seed (*cf.* immaculate conception) are probably engendered by this complex.

h. *n oral Sex (fellatio)*. The fusion of Passivity and Succorance furthers the development of a feminine sexual attitude in men (Reception vector), and when this is combined with orality a passive homosexual complex (overt or covert) may result.

i. *Cathection of words*. There is evidence to suppose that a special interest in speaking and in the emotional value of words — loquaciousness, a neologistic tendency, a love of oratory or poetry — is a sign of orality. It is as if the poet's verses were just so many poignant cries for love (the 'lost Elysium').

1. Alexander, F. 'The influence of psychologic factors upon gastro-intestinal disturbances.' *Psychoanal. Quart.*, 1934, *3*, 501–539.

j. *Totalistic apprehension.* The reception vector operating with perception and apperception may lead to sensuous perceptiveness, empathic apprehension of a total situation (getting the 'feel' of something as a whole), 'drinking in' knowledge and apperceiving its 'essence' (rather than grasping and memorizing a bit at a time).

Weaning or the frustration of oral Succorance leads to further symptoms:

k. *Projections of p Rejection and p Retention.* This includes the Orphan thema ('I have been miserably deprived of parental support'). It displays itself as the belief that people are heartless, selfish, mean and miserly, as well as by a generally pessimistic outlook ('Nothing ever comes'—'You never get what you want'—'You can't trust anyone').

l. *n intraNurturance.* The S who believes himself rejected is apt to turn his love (n Nur, n Def, n Sex) inward. Self-pity is the root of one variety of Narcism. As with thumb-sucking, it may lead to a type of introverted self-sufficiency associated with a rejective attitude towards the world ('You can't expect anything from other people').

m. *Inhibited n Aggression.* The subject blames the world for giving him a 'raw deal.' His envy of what other people receive (by inheritance or luck) makes him particularly resentful of prosperous (well-fed), successful people.

B2. *Oral Aggression Complex.* This is constituted by the conjunction of Aggression and oral activity (biting). It functions not infrequently as a contrafaction to an underlying, though perhaps latent, oral Succorance.

a. *Oral automatisms: biting.* This includes chewing objects, nail-biting and grinding the teeth at night. In a baby this begins as the teeth appear (from about the fifth month onwards). Sometimes a child will bite its mother's nipple, an event which may necessitate weaning. In this case p Rejection (deprivation of the breast) may be interpreted as a punishment for biting (Aggression), and this may bring about regression to a less adaptive, passive attitude. The child may bite its own thumb (n intrAgg) until it becomes clubbed. A lover will sometimes bite the woman's body during sexual intercourse.

Oriol: I have always bitten the hair on the back of my fingers when I concentrate.

Zill: I was getting thinner and underweight and extremely nervous, bit my nails profusely.

b. *Cathection of solid oral objects.* Solid foods (meat and bones) or other objects (pencils, pipes, etc.) may be cathected. One of our subjects would chew through the stem of his pipe in a few months.

c. *n Aggression.* During phylogeny oral Aggression was associated with the n Food (the killing of prey) and a positively cathected object (something good to eat). Carnivora more frequently bite what they like (food) than what they dislike (an animal that is not good to eat). And if this is so, one would expect oral Aggression to be combined with a positive cathection (appetite, lust, love, admiration) of the object. This, indeed, is what one does find in the totem feast (eating the worshipped animal), in the Holy Communion, in cannibalism (incorporating the virtues of the bravest foes) and in infantile oral Aggression (biting the nurturing breast). In children oral Aggression is usually found as one phase of an ambi-tendency (contrafactive to oral Succorance), the Aggression having been evoked by an interference with sucking. Since, during the nursing period, hating usually objectifies itself as biting, the latter may be taken as a sign of oral frustration (weaning). Verbal Aggression (censure, criticism, belittlement, 'biting' sarcasm, insult) seems to be the most common sublimation of biting. It often takes the form of ideo Aggression: a destructive analysis and criticism of the sentiments and theories of others. It may exhibit itself also as nagging and commanding (n Dom) younger objects. Covert Aggression is more indicative of an early oral Aggression than is overt Aggression.

d. *Ambi-cathection of superior objects.* Oral aggression being originally directed at the depriving mother and later (quite com-

monly) at the interfering father, an upward orientation (sup
Agg) is thereby established which pre-determines the S, in lat
life, to select superior objects (dominating women, men of autho
ity, God) to attack and criticize. Whether or not the objects ha
been previously revered, they are usually respected secretly, eve
while they are being depreciated.

e. *Projection of oral Aggression*. Some children are arrested an
disturbed by stories, fantasies and dreams in which the hero
chased, attacked and eaten by a carnivorous animal. This may
due in part to the re-animation of archetypal images and fea
but is explained more immediately as a projection of the child
own oral Aggression. The infant sees the environment in its ow
image, as a world of biting objects. This accounts for the prev
lence of fairy stories and sagas about creatures that bite childre
and men : tales about dragons and giants (*cf.* 'The bogey ma
will eat you'), Little Red Riding Hood (*cf.* 'Who's afraid
the big, bad wolf ?'), Cronos devouring his children, the Wer
wolf legends and so forth. As a special instance of the ge
eral doctrine of Lycanthropy, we may cite the ancient Armenia
superstition that certain sinful women are punished for a ter
of years by being changed at night into wolves that crave th
flesh of their own children. Such wolf-women can pass throug
any door or window, and it is impossible to resist them. Here th
oral Aggression is projected onto the mother, but more frequent
the aggressor is a male figure (which has more basis in fact).

f. *n Harmavoidance and the negative cathection of biting an
mals*. A child may project Aggression onto some suitable objec
e.g., a dog or horse, and develop a phobia. Nightmarish fears
being chased and gobbled up may recur, these being the usu
accompaniments of projected Aggression.

g. *Identification with carnivorous creatures*. This applies
children who like to imagine or play that they are devourin
animals, or who especially enjoy stories of wild beasts and ca
nibals.

h. *Stuttering*. Stuttering is an inco-ordination or conflict of or
actones which may have its roots in an infantile conflict betwee

sucking and biting. The motor disjunctivity also involves respiration.

Akeson: I have been affected with stammering, a condition which varies in intensity . . . but which has always been with me and something I have been afraid of.

B3. *Oral Rejection Complex.* There is considerable uncertainty as to the nature and significance of this complex. There are first of all acts which illustrate the Ejection vector: spitting up and vomiting. These are basically derived from disgust (nausea) and the Noxavoidance drive. Then there are acts, such as turning away and firmly closing the mouth, which apparently have the same aim (to avoid noxious substances), but are characterized by spasticities at the oral orifice (rather than by oral reception followed by regurgitation). The problem is, what belongs together? Are we dealing with one complex, or are there two (*a*, ready reception and ready ejection and *b*, exclusion and retention)? These may be the result of autonomic (sympathetic) stimulation along the upper digestive tract (oesophageal, cardiac or pyloric spasm). The Freudians are apt to regard all of these rejections as repudiations of some underlying wish: to drain others (oral Succorance), to devour cannibalistically (oral Aggression), or to take into the mouth an erotic object (n oral Sex).

a. *Negative cathection of certain foods.* This is generally described as 'finickiness about food.' The child refuses to eat or spits up certain foods. The mother's milk or the doctor's feeding formula may not agree with the infant, or later, certain foods may become repulsive due to secondary displacement. In the child's fantasy they may stand for something else (flesh, faeces, penis). In some cases vegetarianism may represent a contrafaction to infantile cannibalism.

Zill: My appetite was very poor and many foods were repulsive to me because of some association they made in my throat with things slimy. Once after I had seen a crushed frog I could not eat for days.

b. *Inhibition of n Food.* The S may limit his diet or refuse to eat entirely (ex : hunger strike). Here, we may include dietary asceticism (eating meagre, simple fare) as well as suicide by starvation. A death wish may exhibit itself as an inability to swallow (oesophageal spasm). This may represent the guilty repudiation of an infantile wish to incorporate something loathsome (faeces, penis), or it may be a manifestation of utter spite ('I am dying because you rejected me. You are to blame and I hope self-reproaches will torture you to the end of your days').

c. *n Harmavoidance : Fear of oral infection.* Some subjects have a fear of being infected by mouth. They are apt to believe that food is dirty or decayed, or that it contains bacteria or parasites. The fear of kissing may have a similar origin as well as the delusion that another person is maliciously putting poison in one's food.

d. *n Rejection.* When the mother's milk does not satisfy the child it turns away. This happens sometimes immediately after birth. It makes bottle feeding imperative. There are no facts which tell us what effect this initial rejection of the mother may have. The child must henceforth cathect the milk bottle or its own thumb, rather than the mother's breast. Theoretically, this should lead to a state of relative independence, or one in which material objects are accepted as substitutes for affectionate contact. The Rejection drive may also be evoked by subsequent weaning (interpreted as p Rejection). It may function as a contrafaction to oral Succorance ('My mother is no longer of use to me'). This should lead to independence or exclusiveness (introversion) or to diffidence and aloofness.

e. *n Seclusion : Reticence.* The Encasement vector operating at the mouth should lead to reticence, secrecy, refusal to tell things, retaining information. This may be a subsidiation of the Rejection drive ('I shall never speak to you again'), or it may be in the service of privacy and Endocathection ('Leave me and let me enjoy my own thoughts'), or it may be for Retention ('I have a valuable secret which I am going to keep to myself'). Mutism is a not uncommon symptom in hysteria as well as in schizophrenia (catatonia).

f. *n Autonomy : Resistance.* Children who do not wish to eat, to talk, or to demonstrate affection are, as a rule, incessantly urged to do so by their parents. In order to defend themselves these children must develop habits of resistance and negativism.

g. *Negative cathection of nurturant object (mother).* The rejection is usually focussed upon the depriving parent. During the feeding period this is usually the mother. This original fixation may later give rise to constant depreciations of women or to the habit of refusing aid or sympathy from anyone ('I can take care of myself').

C. ANAL COMPLEXES

The psycho-analysts have clearly demonstrated that the association in infancy of certain general attitudes with defecatory activities may be of considerable importance in the later development of the personality. To account for this the original (and still widely held) theory was that defecation is one of several components of the Sex drive and that some children, due to a hypersensitivity of anal mucous membrane, derive special sensuous pleasure from this activity. Because of the resulting zonal fixation, certain behavioural tendencies associated with the period of bowel training : retentiveness, orderliness, cleanliness, obstinacy, become established as outstanding traits of personality. The observation that some children spend a long time on the toilet and resist efforts to hurry them has been put down to the fact that, because large faeces give more friction and hence more pleasure, the anally fixated child gets into the habit of retaining, accumulating and slowly discharging his excrement. One of the unhappy sequelae of this practice is chronic constipation. With these facts and theories as a nucleus the Freudians have expanded the concept of anal erotism to include almost everything that is commonly associated with defecation and faeces : diarrhoea, soiling, constipation, playing with faeces, smearing, sensitivity to bad odours, exhibitionistic expulsions, inspection of the defecatory activities of others, pruritus ani, back-house humour, and so forth.

We can say that in the main our own findings are in accord with analytical observations, but that they have led us to a somewhat different formulation. It seems that it is possible to distinguish two anal complexes : one connected with the tendency to expel (Ejection vector), the other with the tendency to retain (Retention vector). The primitive, natural tendency is to excrete whenever stimulation from the anal zone arises. This must be the original form of anal erotism. When training begins the first thing that the child must learn is to retain his faeces until the proper time and place are reached. He must also learn to eject at the time that a parent dictates. Thus, the original tendency is met by barriers and prohibitions ('You must not let go'), and then by coercions ('Now, you must give or produce something'). The more active, motile, expansive, impulsive, extraverted child finds difficulty in meeting the first demand ; whereas the more passive, immotile, contracted, inhibited, introverted child finds difficulty in meeting the second. Thus there is the possibility of two complexes, the main characteristics of which conform to those of the two stages of anal erotism postulated by Abraham.[1] Abraham distinguished a primary stage marked by the sadistic getting rid and annihilation of objects, and a secondary stage in which objects became cathected, acquired and held. Whereas analysts believe that these two impulses have their source in the erotogenic anal zone, we should say that they were general vectors which, though most clearly exhibited in connection with defecation and when pathologically exaggerated always associated with anal fixation, are commonly manifested before the period of anal training and can develop independently of excretory functions. For example, the youngest infants commonly pass through a period of belching and spitting up nourishment before they come to the stage of surely retaining it. Similarly with toys : they start by throwing them out of the crib and only later does the disposition to hold and collect them become dominant. There can be no certainty

1. Abraham,K. *Selected Papers*, London,1927.

about such matters, however, until the facts of infant development have been systematically observed and assembled. In the meanwhile the data at our disposal can be subsumed under two headings : anal ejection and anal retention.

C1. *Anal Ejection Complex.* The unequivocal phenomena at the core of this complex are : defecatory pre-occupation, the cathection of faeces, incontinence, soiling, frequent evacuations and diarrhoea. Associated with these are the tendencies characteristic of the Ejection vector, as well as certain commonly related needs.

a. *Cathection of defecation and faeces.* A special preoccupation with excretory activity (enjoyment, over-emphasis, worry, rituals, medication and so forth), lewd thoughts and language, anal humour, an interest in excrement or in somewhat similar material (dirt, mud, plaster, clay, paint, decayed flesh) and coprophagia may be grouped under this heading.

Vulner : Occasionally my mind would dwell on lewd or filthy subjects.

b. *Anal inspection and exhibition.* Here may be included curiosity in the excretory activities of others, as well as the display of one's own powers.

Outer : First notice of sex was at age of four when I used to play with a girl a year older. We used to make our toilets in alleys.

c. *Anal theory of birth.* Many children believe that babies are born from the rectum, but the theory seems to be more common among anally fixated children.

d. *Ejection vector and n Aggression : disorder, smearing.* Under this heading may be included not only 1, the excretion and expulsion of waste products and gases from the body, but also 2, dropping things down, throwing things about, making loud noises, setting off explosions, firing guns, disrupting, dismembering, mutilating. Subjects of this type are generally untidy, dirty, disarranged and unorganized. The vector may be fused with n Aggression, which in this connection takes on a distinctly destructive or sadistic aspect. Due to its association with katabolism and excrement, anal Aggression is accompanied by no love or respect for the object (as is oral Aggression). It wishes only to break apart, smash, shatter, burn. It may lead to an interest in horror, dead bodies, etc. It may exhibit itself as vandalism or as the disfigurement of objects by smearing. Using 'dirty,' 'foul' language or slandering the reputations of others (ex : yellow journalism) may be included here.

Oak : I found an old can of paint and proceeded to smear our car all up and there were many other things like it.

e. *Locomotion vector and n Autonomy : Freedom, Expansion, Impulsion and Change.* Subjects with a strong Ejection vector cannot stay in the same place for very long. Just as they find it difficult to control their bowel movements, so also do they find it impossible to restrain their incessant craving for locomotion, change, new sensations. As a rule they are 'wasters,' spending money freely when they have it and conserving nothing. There is the possibility of fusion with the egression (anti-claustral) complex.

f. *Anal Sexuality.* Pederasty associated with active or passive homosexuality is the complete expression of anal erotism ; but there are also milder and less direct forms that occur in conjunction with heterosexuality.

C2. *Anal Retention Complex.* Though one finds at the basis of this complex the same cathection of defecation and faeces that characterizes anal ejection, the outstanding manifestations are opposed to the latter tendencies. For the most part they are inhibiting defence mechanisms furthered by parental discipline and Superego formation. Hence the character that is established on this basis may be appropriately termed 'anal antherotic' (rather than 'anal erotic'). The first three and the last of the following list of symptoms are common to both anal complexes :

a. *Cathection of defecation and faeces.* Positive cathection is usually repressed and overbalanced by an exaggerated negative cathection : reticence, prudishness and disgust associated with defecation.

b. *Anal inspection and exhibition.* There may be a history of coprophilic curiosity in childhood.

c. *Anal theory of birth.*

d. *Encasement vector.* The subject is 'closed up,' 'shut-in,' 'close-mouthed,' reticent, secretive, taciturn. He has a 'wall' that holds others at a 'distance.' He does not like to be watched. Retardation of speech in a child may be associated with this general 'contractiveness.'

e. *n Retention.* The subject accumulates, piles up, collects and hoards his possessions. He also takes special measures to conserve them (n Conservance, *vide* p. 80). He repairs, paints, cleans, covers, puts away and locks up his 'treasures.' He is not inclined to lend things or give presents.

f. *Projection of p Acquisition.* The subject has fantasies or dreams of being dispossessed or robbed. He fears that others will borrow from him promiscuously or that he will be cheated of his inheritance or swindled in a business deal. These tendencies may date from the trauma of being given an enema in infancy. (Fantasies of this type may be fused with fantasies of rape or of homosexual assault.)

g. *n Autonomy : Resistance.* The subject is resistant to suggestions. He likes to concentrate on the things that interest him and take his own time. He becomes obstinate and negativistic when accosted by sudden demands. The Rejection drive (exclusiveness) is often strong.

h. *n Order : Cleanliness and Precision.* The S is obsessively orderly and tidy with his belongings, and keeps his body and vestments clean and neat. He is quick to notice and be upset by spots, mussiness or disorder. He is apt to be precise and scrupulous in his work as well as in his dealings with others.

i. *n Harmavoidance : Fear of microbes and insects.* The S may associate dirt with bacteria, and this may lead to obsessive cleanliness, or hygienic obsessions : squeamishness about touching such things as door-knobs, railings, towels or toilet seats in public places, a habit of gargling or rinsing his throat every morning, a compulsion to wash or bathe frequently, and so forth. Fears and revulsions involving insects and rodents may also be included here.

j. *Cognitive perseveration.* The S is as tenacious of an idea or a trend of thought as he is of money. He cannot 'drop' a topic, a trait that often leads to arguments. Sometimes he is bothered by worrying ideas that 'keep running in his head.'

k. *Anal Sexuality.*

D. URETHRAL COMPLEX

Under this heading may be grouped : bed-wetting and incontinence, urethral ejection (soiling), exhibitionism and clear-cut examples of urinary erotization.

a. *Bed-wetting and incontinence.*

Kast : Bed-wetting lasted until I was at least 12.

b. *Urethral ejection : soiling.*

Cling : One night I went outside to urinate and did so through a hole in the wall onto someone's bed (urethral erotism).

c. *Urethral erotism.*

Frost : I have had fairly regular wet dreams — usually about urinating.

The Freudian analysts have observed the common association with urethral erotism of ambition and the cathection of fire. We have found no data indicating that the former relationship is common, but the latter was clearly demonstrated by two of our cases.

E. GENITAL (CASTRATION) COMPLEX

There are several important complexes associated with the genital organs, some of which are considered in connection with the Sex drive, but here we may confine ourselves to the castration complex, which, according to many Freudian analysts, is at the core of all pathological anxiety. We cannot believe that this is generally true. And we suggest that in those cases in which it is possible to trace all exhibitions of anxiety to this source it will be found that there was a circumcision in babyhood. To make the analyst's contention worth considering, it is necessary to greatly extend the meaning of 'castration,' to have it include the loss of any pleasure-giving organ or object (mother's body or nipple, subject's hand, tongue, etc.). But even if given this larger meaning 'castration' does not cover all the eventualities which infants commonly fear : falling, being hurt, or being devoured by a wild animal or whipped by a parent or locked in a closet or buried alive. To us it seems better to confine the term castration complex to its literal meaning : anxiety evoked by the fantasy that the penis might be cut off. This complex occurs often enough, but it does not seem possible that it is the root of all neurotic anxiety. It usually comes as a resultant of the fantasies associated with infantile masturbation.

Hypothetical Events of Childhood

The greater part of this chapter has been devoted to a classification of common environmental press and common individual trends. A great many different combinations of press and trend, each of which constitutes a thema, can be observed in everyday life ; and, for us, the logically next step would be to define and name the most important themas. But even if this could be done within the limits of a chapter, it seems better to postpone the endeavour until a larger experience has taught us what press and what needs are of greatest import.

Though in selecting illustrations of press and needs I limited myself to the subjects' autobiographies, the latter were not our only source of information about childhood. For there were three sessions specially devoted to reminiscences (evoked by free associations and questions), and in several other sessions subjects had occasion to refer to past history. Thus we reaped a fair harvest of biographical facts. In formulating development, however, we did not confine ourselves to the episodes which the subject was able to recall and willing to recount. Depth psychology had taught us that it is necessary to take account of certain early occurrences no longer available to consciousness. The early occurrences that must be included are those which left traces that influenced the course of development and are still operating unconsciously to modify behaviour. It was Freud whose sheer genius discovered that these long enduring (though much modified) traces could be reached through the study of dreams, fantasies and free associations. But the current psycho-analytic procedure which grew out of this discovery requires many hours, extending over months ; and since, for us, this was a prohibitive amount of time, it was necessary to develop methods which would reveal more quickly the dominant unconscious traces and trends.

Instead of waiting for the repressed thematic tendencies to break through a gradually-made-permeable barrier of inhibition, we essayed a technique that would draw out the covert tendencies without arousing resistance or repression. The technique consists of asking a subject to demonstrate the limits of his imaginative capacity by making up stories (fantasies) suggested to him by a presented stimulus : a picture, a literary theme, a fragment of music, an odour and so forth (*vide* p. 529). It was found that these so-called 'projection methods' yield a large output of imaginative activity which, we have reason to believe, is closely related to and representative of prevailing thematic tendencies, of which some are conscious and some unconscious. The findings of psycho-analysis indicate that from this kind of material one may, by interpretation, infer the operation of traces established in childhood. The traces are enduring impressions of actual events or of fantasies, or more commonly of actual events distorted by fantasies. One rarely knows to what degree a given trace corresponds to an original experience. Perhaps it does not matter ; for a fantasy may be as determining as a fact. The point here is that a large collection of projected fantasies, a fair number of expressed sentiments, some free associations and a few recounted dreams provided us with ample imaginal material for interpretation. Interpretation took account of the contemporary situation, though it was directed more particularly to the genetical roots of the subject's present attitude. Thus, we arrived at a number of hypothetical occurrences or fantasies, many of which were supposed to have occurred during the pre-verbal period of childhood. We also inferred other events that had taken place later, but, having been subjected to repression, were no longer available to consciousness.

The kind of imaginal material that I have been discussing is of some significance *per se*, since an individual spends a large proportion of his life dreaming and imagining, and he may value this activity as much as he values his overt social acts. But these half-conscious twilight processes are also important because of their relation to infantile events, repressed complexes, neurotic symptoms and creative thought. At the moment we are particularly concerned with them as clues to the past. Our practice in the beginning was to do as most analysts do : interpret the fantasies immediately by intuition. The results were certainly interesting, but the amount of disagreement among interpreters made us skeptical of the results. Furthermore, it seemed that here as elsewhere — in contrast to psycho-analytic custom — one should analyse, classify and name fantasies as they are literally recounted (Freud's 'manifest content') before one goes on to refer them by interpretation to other categories (Freud's 'latent content'), just as in medicine a conveniently sharp distinction is made between symptoms and diagnosis. This conviction compelled us to consider the problem of how to analyse and classify the imaginal products obtained from our subjects. Reflection and experience led us to adopt the same mode of treatment as was used when dealing with overt events. We tried to make out the thema : the press, the responding need and the outcome ; remembering that a pre-active need or a preceding outcome could function as an internal press (*vide* p. 122). It was found that the categories of needs and press briefly defined in this chapter, though reasonably convenient for the classification of objective occurrences, had to be somewhat expanded to include the actions and objects which the imagination could invent. Since the systematic study and measurement of imaginal tendencies must depend upon the scheme to which they are referred, it is unfortunate that limitations of space require that the presentation of this part of our theory be kept for another volume.

A scheme for manifest content, however, is only a first step, since it is not the naming but the interpretation of the content that leads to the hypothetical conditioning events, the supposition of which will make intelligible many otherwise mysterious phenomena. Thus the second step throws one head over heels into the perplexing problem of interpretation.

Validation of Interpretations[1]

If scientific truth is what 'goes' among the intellectual élite, an experimenter should be more satisfied with his interpretations if he succeeded in convincing a sufficient number of others, or, better still, if a sufficient number of others separately arrived at the same conclusions. As a step in this direction we adopted the principle of the multiplicity of judgements. This certainly handi- caps the more intuitive and accomplished psychologues, for in- terpretation is a matter of 'insight' ('insight' into others), and insight—depending as it does upon the frequent exercise and training of a special aptitude—is certainly not equally distributed among those who profess psychology. Much greater than the dif- ferences in acuity of vision, hearing and taste are the difference in acuity of psychological intuition. Thus, at the frontier ther will always be those who see further than others. This, however does not make science. Science is democratic. It insists that th lame, the halt and the blind shall arrive and perceive. Thus, th intuitive pioneer, or those who follow him, must fashion instru ments, mechanical and conceptual, that will allow everyone t observe and understand what has already been observed and unde stood. But this is not the only necessity. For since most intuition of most pioneers are partially incorrect, the scientist must, for h own illumination if for no other reason, attempt to distinguis define and name every impression which led him to his co clusion.

Applying these general considerations to the problem at han the genetical interpretation of fantasies, it seems that the ne methodical step in scientification should be a systematic study symbolism. Is it true, and in what sense is it true, that a violi let us say, can symbolize the mother ? And if it can, what else ca

1. Here, by permission of the editor, I shall quote from 'Techniques for a sy tematic investigation of fantasy.' *J. Psychol.*,1936,*3*, 115–143.

it symbolize ? What else does it commonly symbolize ? Can it symbolize anything ? Is the sky the limit ? It will be long before science constructs a net to catch these irrational fish, but let her now essay it. It is of no profit to leave these most elementary and significant psychic processes for undisciplined people to talk about as they will.

The procedure that we are now pursuing is the laborious one of distinguishing the items that have led to each interpretation ; that is, of cataloguing imagined objects and actions together with the 'meanings' that have been assigned to each. And this brings us back to our main problem, the validation of assigned meanings. I have just mentioned the principle of the multiplicity of judgements, which by implication affirms that agreement among experimenters is one reason for accepting an interpretation. It is not, however, a very good reason. One knows too much about mutual suggestion and flattery in limited esoteric circles. Let us see what other modes of verification exist.

The problem may be simplified by taking the case of a single experimenter who, after reviewing his own results, comes to the conclusion that a certain infantile thema, X, has been an important factor in the development of one of his subjects. What methods are available for testing this inference ?

If variable X is an enduring determinant it should operate repeatedly and influence responses to diverse presentations. Also, it should be found to interact or articulate with other distinguishable factors according to a generally accepted 'logic' of the emotions. To ascertain if this is the case an experimenter may employ one or more of the following procedures :

a. *Correlation with a multiplicity of other fantasy tests.* The consistency of X is determined by noting the number of times it recurs in other tests. If it does not recur it should, at least, be dynamically related to the themas that do occur.

b. *Correlation with biographical data.* Experience goes to show that variables which strongly manifest themselves in fantasy (1) have usually been engendered or promoted by one or more concrete occurrences, and (2) are apt to lead to or influence subsequent occurrences. For this reason, the experimenter should avail himself of as much information as possible concerning each subject's life. The validity of X may then be partially determined by discovering how and to what degree it may be articulated with the facts disclosed in the biography. For example, the fantasy thema may be a repetition of, an escape from or a counteraction to some childhood event.

The finding that X recurs in other tests and that it seems to connect with other discernible factors would provide good ground for confidence if one were less familiar with the ability of men to combine things in thought and believe that they were so combined in nature. To determine whether fantasies produced by the same S for different experimenters show veritable (rather than rationalized) uniformities and articulations, one may employ the matching techniques.[1]

c. *Matching results from different tests.* An experimenter may attempt to guess, on the basis of his own findings, which of a group of subjects gave each set of results obtained in some other test.

d. *Matching test results with biographical data.* Ten biographies and ten sets of fantasies (with no names attached) were given for matching. One experimenter matched five, and two experimenters matched all ten correctly. This indicates that fantasies are related to the events of life in a distinguishable manner; that some of the dependencies that are apperceived have actually existed: they are not mere clever rationalizations.

e. *Guessing the occurrence of certain childhood experiences.* Solely on the basis of the fantasy material an E may attempt to name some of the critical experiences that occurred during the subject's infancy; to guess, for example, what gratifying, frustrating or traumatic events took place, what sort of relationship was established with the mother, the father and the siblings, how the child reacted to what difficulties in social adaptation. This

1. Chapman, D.W. 'The statistics of the method of correct matchings.' *J. Abn. & Soc. Psychol.*, 1929, *24*, 14–27.
Vernon, P.E. *Psychol. Bull.*, 1936, *33*, 149–177.

exercise puts the greatest stress upon the psychological knowledge and intuition of an experimenter. Though it has not yet been methodically attempted at the Harvard Clinic, many of the workers have independently and informally recorded their 'hunches' and attempted to verify them. The story in which 'the violin as mother' occurred may be taken as an example.

Subject Abel. When Abel was presented with a picture of a little boy gazing at a violin lying before him on the table, he gave the following story :

'This youngster has heard the violin played. When the player put the violin on the table he went over to look at the hole to see where the music came from. He is puzzled by the absence of any music maker inside, puzzled that the instrument could make such sounds. He doesn't connect the bow with the instrument. Pretty soon he will start fooling around with it trying to make sounds himself. The result depends on who hears him playing. The owner will be provoked, and take the instrument away. If no one hears him the strings will be taken apart, but he won't demolish the instrument.'

Here, the hypothesis was made that at the birth of a younger child Abel became perplexed about childbirth, suspected that the baby came out of the mother and entertained fantasies of aggressive exploration. When this diagnosis was made the experimenter did not know that Abel had a younger brother.

At a subsequent interview, on being asked whether as a boy he was inclined to dismember his toys, Abel responded exactly as follows without any prompting : 'Yes, I was always breaking things, always breaking everything to find out why or how it worked. I had a locomotive, I remember, and I had a wonderful time taking it apart. I learned to take the pedals of the piano apart. I used to peer inside the piano and wonder about it. I was terribly destructive, not just to destroy but to understand. I broke some plates to find out what they were made of and my mother scolded me for this. I would say that this destructive, curious period began when I was five and ended when I was eight. I remember when it began because my younger brother was born when I was five. My brother was born in the house and my mother was very sick afterwards. I couldn't see the connection between her sickness and the baby. I was told that he had been found in the flour barrel, but of course I didn't believe it. But after that I was awfully curious. I used to plague my parents to death asking the how and why of everything. This still persists as one of my strongest characteristics. My teachers in school told me that I was frightfully curious about everything and very inquisitive. I always want to know how things work.'

It was considered that these memories occurring in this sequence without direct questioning, together with other facts discovered, were good evidence for the experimenter's hypothesis.

f. *Predictions of future behaviour.* The E may attempt to predict on the basis of his material how each of his subjects will react when faced by a certain experimentally controlled situation. At the Harvard Clinic this has been systematically attempted only once. From the stories that fifteen subjects produced when presented with a particular picture (Thematic Apperception Test) an experimenter (Dr. White[1]) attempted to predict the relative hypnotizability of each member of the group. He made a rank order which correlated highly ($r = +.72$) with the rank order for hypnotizability which was established later.

g. *Consultation with the subject.* After an experimenter has completed his hypothetical reconstruction of a personality he may attempt, directly or indirectly, in a final interview with the subject to obtain evidence that bears upon the critical diagnostic issues.

By the use of these and other methods experimenters may check their interpretations and gradually assemble verified facts which bear upon the processes that are of special concern to modern psychology.

Creative productions and fantasies provide excellent material for the study of psychological inferences and the effect upon such inferences of the personalities and mental sets of judges. One should not suppose that any universal system of symbolism, similar to that which Freud set forth in his writings on the interpretation of dreams, will ever be the outcome of such studies. The power of the human mind to associate the most diverse objects is

1. White, R.W. 'Prediction of hypnotic susceptibility from a knowledge of subjects' attitudes.' *J. Psychol.*, 1936, *3*, 265–277.

almost limitless and the subject's personal experiences rather than his innate tendencies determine the meaning. It can be predicted, however, that if the experimenter looks for the thematic relations of the objects (images), he will discover significant resemblances between the most diverse fantasies and dreams, and some general principles will emerge.

Developmental Processes

Reviewing successive events in a person's life one is bound to observe several different types of sequence. There will be a varying amount of *Repetition* : similar events in which the tpmo (time-place-mode-object pattern) is not significantly changed—the consistency of behaviour patterns indicating that the S is holding his own but not progressing. Very similar is *Continuation*, which means the persistence of one system of aims and interests, with slight variations in the mode of approach. This signifies that work is being done (and hence, in an external sense, there is progression), but the man's nature is not undergoing conspicuous modification. In our scheme both repetition and continuation have been subsumed under Sameness. *Variation* is exhibited by a series of clearly dissimilar responses to similar conditions. There is novelty (Change) and inconsistency without noticeable progression or regression.

Progression is marked by changes which represent a decided advancement, according to some emotionally reasonable scale of values. It usually involves adaptive learning (increase in proficiency), integration (harmonious co-ordination of trends), socialization (adjusting to the tpmo formula of the culture) and individuation (self-reliance and uniqueness). Opposite to *Progression* is *Regression* (Freud). This stands for a decline of effectiveness as measured against an accepted scale of values. It is exhibited most commonly by the appearance of a formerly used but now less adaptive reaction system. *Substitution* (Freud) is a very general term which describes the displacement of cathexis from one object to another object. It often occurs after the S has been frustrated in an attempt to gain the first object. Substitution is also applied to other kinds of change: change of mode, of interest and of aim. The change may be progressive or regressive.

Socialization is a type of progression, namely, one that advances along the scale of social adjustment and conformity. This may represent a regression to a man who is striving to rid himself of limiting philistine claims.

Sublimation (Freud) has been variously defined, but at least everyone has agreed that it should be applied to a form of substitution in which a primitive act or cathection is replaced by an act or cathection that is less crude and less objectionable. Analysts take it as a synonym of socialization, but since socialization can be applied to the case of a sadist who finds employment in a slaughter-house, and sublimation can be applied to the schizophrenic transformation of a perverted sexual tendency into an overwhelming religious revelation, it seems that many socializations are not sublimations and many sublimations are not socializations. We suggest that the term sublimation be used to stand for any transformation (of an integrate) that departs from crudely biological (physical) acts and objects. The change from physical to verbal Aggression (reprimand without violence), or from physical to verbal Sex (love and flirtation without intercourse) would be included, as well as the replacement of a primitive object such as faeces by an acceptable object such as clay, provided the latter was not worked into a replica of faeces. Sublimation is most clearly exhibited, however, when a coarsely physical tendency, such as urination, sex or exhibitionism, takes a subjectified course, and, being modified by associations, dictates the themes of glorified fantasies, artistic designs or mystical illuminations. Sublimation may be an escape and, in that sense, a regression; but in most cases — as an adolescent phenomenon for example — it represents a healthy erotization of the mind which is a step beyond the unimaginatively sensual. Later a change of tendency from ethereal romanticism to physical objectification would be regarded by most people as a progression.

Inhibition and *Repression* can be found in the record of an individual's life by noting the disappearance of one or more objectified integrates with the march of time. The complexes that become repressed are those that are unacceptable to the individual (n Harm, n Suc, n Aba) or blameworthy in the eyes of society (n Agg, n Exh, n Sex, n Rec). Inhibition is the invariable accompaniment of progression, sublimation and socialization. *Contrafaction* is the succession of one integrate (pre-action) by its opposite (sequent-action). The pre-action may be something that in some way sacrifices or diminishes the S, in which case the sequent-action is an *Equilibration* : a demand for payment after lending money, a request for aid after doing someone a favour, boasting after self-depreciation, talking after listening, an outburst of anger after patiently enduring abuse. Or the pre-action may be something that diminishes or sacrifices the object, in which case the contrafactive sequent-action is a *Restitution* : payment after stealing, praise after criticism, kindness after cruelty, friendliness after rejection. Or the pre-action may be a misdemeanour or major crime that displeases conscience or an external object, and then the restitutive tendency is an *Atonement*. The latter may take the form of self-abasement : humble confession, suffering, suicide. *Reformation* is a contrafactive, restitutive process involving inhibition of a previous form of behaviour. It is usually involved in socialization. *Counteraction* is an equilibrating continuation of striving that re-instates the S after failure, or an equilibrating contrafaction that re-instates the S by substituting a courageous, superior mode of action for a timorous, inferior one : traumatic re-striving. This is a progression in the service of the Inviolacy drive.

Differentiation is the development of specialized functional systems (abilities, reaction patterns) each of which is adapted to certain materials or a certain set of conditions. The indices are : refined and subtle discriminations, precise interpretations of complex situations, accurate generalizations and effective, economical or poignant responses. Differentiation makes it possible for one function to operate without interference from other functions : thinking to occur without the influence of sentiment, feeling without the interposition of an ideology, sensuous enjoyment unopposed by practical considerations and so forth. Differentiation would break up the personality into an assemblage of talents if it were not for *Integration*, which organizes the separate systems into a harmonious whole, and *Unification* which raises certain interests to the apex of a hierarchy of aims. In extreme cases all the differentiated functions become subsidiary to the goal of highest aspiration. This is all that can be said here on the important topic of modes of development.[1]

1. Limitation of space required the omission of a chapter devoted to this problem.

Chapter VI
PROCEDURES

This chapter will be devoted to the procedures that were used in studying the last two groups of subjects (Groups III and IV). They will be described in the order in which their results were discussed at the final 'biographical' meetings. This order is approximately the same as that which was maintained during the period of examination.

PRELIMINARY INTERVIEW

H. A. MURRAY

BEFORE beginning the series of sessions this experimenter had a ten-minute interview with each prospective subject. The latter was told that the staff of the Clinic wished to try out various tests with the hope of discovering relations between certain types of ability and certain types of temperament. After outlining the three- or four-months program of attendance the candidate was asked whether he could conveniently afford the time required for these tests (about 36 hours in all), and whether he was willing to co-operate to the fullest extent. He was assured that if the results were published his identity would be concealed. He was then told that the first thing required of him was to write a short autobiography — about fifteen pages in length.

It was decided in advance that the men who seemed reluctant to co-operate or who wrote dull, superficial, or seemingly dishonest autobiographies would not be accepted as subjects. This rule, however, was never invoked since no man who applied failed to meet our standards. Thus there was no selection of subjects.

SCHEDULE OF PROCEDURES

1. Conference. *H.A.Murray.*
2. Autobiography. *H.A.Murray.*
3. Family Relations and Childhood Memories. *H.S.Mekeel.*

4. Sexual Development. *W.G.Barrett.*
5. Present Dilemmas. *M.Moore.*
6. Conversations. *E.C.Jones.*
7. Predictions and Sentiments Test. *K.R.Kunze.*
8. Questionnaires. *H.A.Murray.*
9. Abilities Test. *R.T.Peterson* and *E.Inglis.*
10. Aesthetic Appreciation Test. *K.Diven.*
11. Hypnotic Test. *R.W.White.*
12. Level of Aspiration Test. *J.D.Frank* and *E.A.Cobb.*
13. Experimental Study of Repression. *S.Rosenzweig.*
    a. Memory for Failures Test. *E.H.Trowbridge.*
14. Violation of Prohibitions. *D.W.MacKinnon.*
    a. Ethical Standards Test. *J.A.Christenson, Jr.*
15. Observations and Post-experimental Interviews. *R.N.Sanford.*
16. Sensorimotor Learning Test. *W.C.Langer.*
17. Emotional Conditioning Test.
    Galvanic Skin Response. *C.E.Smith* and *K.Diven.*
    Tremor Response. *W.C.Langer.*
18. Thematic Apperception Test. *C.D.Morgan* and *H.A.Murray.*
19. Imaginal Productivity Test. *D.R.Wheeler.*
20. Musical Reverie Test. *K.R.Kunze.*
21. Dramatic Productions Test. *E.Homburger.*
22. Rorschach Test. *S.J.Beck.*
23. Miscellaneous Procedures. *Sears, Whitman et al.*
24. Reactions to Frustration. *S.Rosenzweig.*
25. Social Interaction. *M.Rickers-Ovsiankina.*

1. CONFERENCE

H. A. Murray

The Conference was the first of the series of sessions. Its purpose was to allow the five members of the Diagnostic Council to obtain simultaneously their initial impression of the subject : to see him in the flesh, to observe his expressive gestures, to watch his reactions when confronted by a group of inquisitors ; and also to obtain certain facts of his life, to discover some of his dominant sentiments and interests. It resembled the prelude to an opera in that it included parts of themes (tests) which were to be fully presented in subsequent sessions. Though it lasted but 40 minutes it contained a little of much ; thus providing a rather broad basis for intuitive judgments.

At the end of the Conference each member of the Council independently marked the subject on all of the variables. This made it possible to measure differences in interpretation and relate them to differences in the personalities of the judges (*vide* p. 273).

Procedure. The subject was ushered into the library of the Clinic and given a chair at a large table around which the five members of the Diagnostic Council were seated. A stenographer was at another table, out of the direct range of vision of the subject ; her pad being concealed behind a stack of reference books which she pretended to consult. It was her function to write down every word that the subject said.

The subject was questioned in a friendly manner by each examiner in turn according to the schedule which follows. (After some of the questions representative answers have been appended.[1])

A. *Interests and Abilities*. (This part of the Conference was conducted by Dr. Barrett.)

1. *Mr. X, what is your field of concentration ?*
2. *Do you like it ?*
3. *How did you happen to choose it ?*

1. This has been the form used in examining male college students.

Given : The fact is, my father is more or less what you call 'in business.' Children follow after their fathers (n Def : Similance of father).

4. *Were your parents in sympathy with your choice?*

Nipp : Anything I do is all right (low p Dominance and probably low Se).

5. *What vocation are you intending to follow?*
6. *What other serious interests have you?*

Nipp : Success in life. I would like to be well off. If in one vocation, all right, if another, all right. The practical outcome is what I want (Exo, Extra, n Acq and probably low Se and low E I).

7. *Can you think of any individuals you were acquainted with or read about who influenced you in the choice of your interests or intended vocation?*

A boy may identify with his father, or with a father surrogate, and imitate him in his choice of vocation (n Def : Similance). This may occur unconsciously, the subject believing that he has independently arrived at his decision. He may be too proud to admit that he has been influenced (n Dfd : Disavowal S n Inv, and n Auto). On the other hand, a young man may be thrilled by the genius of some remote figure and gladly accept him as an exemplar (n Sup, n Def : Similance, E I). Some boys seem to have a 'natural bent' and are determined by it regardless of the influence of adults (n Auto) ; others without much ambition follow the easiest way or yield to social pressure (the trend of the majority).

Frost : Teaching is what my father is doing (n Def : Similance of father), but it isn't for that reason (n Dfd S n Inv, n Auto).

Nipp : No, I don't think so. . . I had a good man I worked under, but he didn't have much influence (low n Def).

Bulge : Why, yes. Dante was one, Chaucer another. You mean inspiration? A professor of mine at college who was quite a man in the poetical field (n Def : Similance).

Asper : Robinson, the American poet. . . He came along at the right time for me. I felt that life in college had been wasted — against my nature. It hadn't been made for me. My spirit hadn't entered into the academic atmosphere (N, Intra, Endo, n Auto, n Rej). Then I read

Robinson (n Def : Similance) and it seemed to dawn on me — hard to understand — society and school had twisted me instead of letting me develop according to my ability (n Auto). Of that, Robinson says : 'Don't give a damn about what these various agencies tell you (n Auto). Merely know yourself first, and then develop yourself according to your interests' (N, Endo). I tried to see myself as I am and I was disgusted (n Aba : Self-depreciation), but I accepted my various weaknesses and have tried to build on what I have.

8. *What kinds of things do you do best?*
9. *Have you ability with mechanical or electrical apparatus?*
10. *Have you artistic or literary talent?*
11. *Are you logical, good at arguments? Do you like to speculate and discuss theories?*

Frost : Yes. That is my main critical intention in order to get more logic into things. (Frost was one of our most irrational subjects.)

Zora : No, theories don't mean much to me (low n Und). (Zora was intuitive, aesthetic, religious). . . If I see a reflection of a certain light I am satisfied at having seen it (n Sen). But anyone can talk theories to me and I just get tired. (Light had the significance of a revelation to Zora.)

12. *What have you done in your life that you are most proud of?*

Roll : Probably making myself very proficient in sports after I had been sheltered so long (n Ach [Physical], n Counteraction).

Zora : If I write a decent sentence I think *that* an important accomplishment. I have written several and they *hang together*. They are all part of the same thing. . . I don't think there is anything more serious for anybody's life. I look upon fine prose as fine poetry. The harmony of life and the sounding of its depth seems to me the fulfilment of some recognition of the quality of life (Endo, Intra, n Sen).

13. *What are your chief amusements?*
14. *Have you ever made a collection of anything — such as stamps?*

B. *Social Experiences and Attitudes.* (This part of the Conference was conducted by Dr. Rosenzweig and later by Dr. Mekeel. It was designed to bring into relief the characteristic social attitudes of the subject.)

1. *Mr. X, what school did you go to?*

2. *Did you like the school?*

If the answer is a decided 'yes,' it usually means: 'I was a success and liked by the other boys.'

3. *How did you get on with the other boys at school?*

On this point subjects are distinguished according to 1, whether they suffered p Rejection or p Affiliation; 2, whether they were sensitive or insensitive to ridicule and neglect; and 3, whether or not they freely admit past successes and humiliations.

Asper: I knew practically no one. I adopted the attitude that I had been crushed by people, that I should build up a protection around myself (N, n Rej, n Sec, n Dfd).

4. *Were there girls in your class? How did you get on with them?*

Oak: I paid very little attention to them (low n Sex).

Given: Bored. I didn't even look at them while I was there (low n Sex).

To this question laconic or evasive answers were the rule, but occasionally a subject would attempt a complete exposition.

Oriol: Well, to answer that question necessitates a good deal of expansion. I am quite willing to go into it (N, n Exh). In high school I went with two definite sets. In this high school one third of them came from the West side. They were either rich or pretended to be. I came from the East side, where there were two definite sections. One of them was Jewish, and I was not particularly anxious to become brothers with them (n Rej [Caste]). I would have liked to be in distinguished society (n Sup [Caste]). I was more or less definitely isolated because the school was divided in social events of consequence — clubs, school papers, dramatic club. The debating club was all Jews. That would have automatically eliminated me from all girls in the wealthy set. I didn't care to know Jewish girls any better. And at that time I was trying to be a poet (n Ach [Art-creative]). The teacher discovered it. I became poet laureate of the school. I was labelled 'baby,' 'sissy,' 'infant' (p Agg: Ridicule). I became generally run down. That didn't help my neurosis any. Consequently, I didn't attract the female element very strongly (p Rej [Sex]). My whole social career in high school was nil.

I stayed pretty much by myself for these two reasons (n Inf). Of course, I looked at them differently than other people do (Egocentricity). I was an only child so I didn't have that normal association with them. But I never had any strange ideas (n Dfd). I read enough to overcome them. One fellow I did associate with. He had the same temperament. We both talked things over and avoided any misfortunes of that kind.

5. *Did you have any crushes at school?*

6. *Among the other boys did you have one or two friends or many friends?*

Here it is a matter of whether the subject 'belonged' (p Affiliation), and whether he had many fleeting friendships (Ch), or a few enduring ones (Sa), or rejected the group in *toto* (n Rej).

Given: Quite a number, I don't believe in getting too deep with anyone (Ch, n Aff, n Rej).

7. *What was the general opinion about you at school?*

Bulge: I imagine the general opinion was that I was a good scout (N, superiority feelings, n Aff).

8. *Were you ever a leader, or, if not, did you want to be a leader?*

Kast: Yes, I was captain of the basketball team for two years, and president of my class for three years (n Ach [Physical], n Dom).

9. *How have you got on at college? Have you found it easy or hard to make friends?*

10. *What is the worst blunder that you ever made?*

Nipp: Gambling. My sophomore year I averaged seven hours a day gambling. I was with a group of fellows every afternoon and evening unless we had an exam. . . I made $150 and paid my room rent in advance, and then I would be broke for a month. I couldn't afford to pay (n Acq, n Play).

Asper: Blunder, I can't say. I have never done anything that I shouldn't have done at the time (N, n Dfd, low n Aba, low Se).

Bulge: I think it was to insult a professor (n Agg).

Akeson: I have made a lot of mistakes. People used to pick on me quite a bit when I was a child. When I used to play war, I used to always be the captive and they locked me up (n Aba).

11. *What are your chief faults from a social standpoint?*

Nipp: Always talking about myself (N).

Roll: Bashfulness. It's pretty hard for me to hold up my end of the conversation (n Sec, n Inf).

Given: Well, lack of financial backing. It cramps my style quite an extent (p Insupport [Economic], n Agg : Censure).

Bulge: I think my worst quality is that I am a very bad loser. I can't take it (N, n Inv).

Zora: I think fundamentally I don't particularly have any faith ; that makes you doubt things in the Church, for instance. I feel and recognize the necessity of doctrine, and I think it's awfully necessary, but if I want to be downright honest, I don't believe it (Endo, Se).

Quick: I am pretty frank with people ; tell them exactly what I think of them (n Agg). I walk up to people I don't even know. . . I often embarrass people I am with by running off on a tangent (Imp). I start laughing out loud, go after people I don't know and tell them something (n Exh). . . I can see people think I am crazy (Disj). I wouldn't consider it a fault (n Dfd).

12. *What are your chief assets from a social standpoint?*

Nipp: I am very broad-minded. I will look at anyone's side of an argument (Sociocentric).

Bulge: Possibly a very straight-forward manner. (Bulge was one of the most self-deceived of our subjects.)

13. *Do you like animals?*

C. *Radical-Conservative Sentiments.* (This part of the Conference was conducted by Dr. R. W. White.)

E : 'Mr. X, I am going to read you a series of ten statements. After each statement make up your mind immediately as to whether you agree or disagree. If you agree with the statement, say "Yes." If you disagree with it, say "No." Then signify the extent to which you agree or disagree. Do this by adding to your answer a number on a scale from 1 to 5 : "Yes 1" to express mild or qualified agreement, up to "Yes 5" for complete agreement : "No 1" for mild or qualified disagreement, up to "No 5" for complete disagreement. Do you understand ? Then, in addition, give immediately one reason to support your judgement. Here is an example : (Statement) The American navy should be increased. (Answer) No 4. (Reason) "It is too hard on the taxpayer." You see, your response to each statement will consist of a "Yes" or "No," a number expressing the degree of your "Yes" or "No," and, lastly, a reason. Give your response quickly : this is a speed test, and I am going to keep the time it takes you to give your ten opinions. Ready ? '

Statements

1. The Constitution of the United States should be preserved intact.
2. Sexual freedom has gone too far in this country.
3. In a family the authority should rest entirely with the father.
4. Communistic propaganda should be prohibited in America.
5. Harvard is easily the best college in this country.
6. Children should be taught to go to church regularly.
7. Parents should discipline their children more than they do.
8. Companionate marriage should be forbidden.
9. Criminals should receive harsher punishments.
10. Social distinctions in the colleges should be maintained.

These ten statements were selected to represent sentiments in favour of the *status quo*, nationalism, authority and conventional morals. The answer 'No' should be given more frequently by negativists (n Auto : Resistance) and by radicals who favour social change. High numbers (pro or con) were taken as an index of 'sentimentive intensity' (strength of opinions).

D. *Thematic Apperceptions.* (This part of the test was conducted by Mrs. Morgan and later by Mr. Homburger.)
E : 'Mr. X, I am going to show you a picture, and I should like to have you make up a story for which this picture might be used as an illustration. Tell me what events have led up to the present occurrence, what the characters in the picture are thinking and feeling, and what the outcome will be.'

The E hands the S picture A (*vide* p. 542) and, if the latter does not give a sufficient plot, he is encouraged by such questions as : 'How did he come to do this ?' 'What is he thinking about ?' 'How will it end ?' If the S pauses, the E asks : 'May I help you ?'

After the S is through with picture A, he is handed picture B (*vide* p. 543) and told to proceed as before. The S is allowed about 1½ minutes on each picture.[1]

The E then hands picture C to the S and says : ' This is a young married couple. Suppose that both of them are friends of yours.

Picture C

The husband has come under the influence of another man who has taught him to take morphine, and he has become an addict. If you came upon this scene in real life what would you do ? '

In the stories which the subject composes for pictures A and B he should reveal some of his imaginal or repressed needs. If he hesitates, finds the task difficult, confines himself to a description

1. For a description of what this test may reveal see Thematic Apperception Test, p.530.

of what he perceives or makes up a short, banal story, Extraception is indicated. Picture A usually furnishes some information pertaining to the status of the Aggression-Superego problem.

Kast : This brings a picture to me of someone who is at the point of just realizing the consequence of some violent action he has taken against some person. There has been a physical attack (n Agg : Assault). . . I think he seems to be a bit penitent about the action he has committed (Se). . . I think there is a bit of fear coming into his eyes, and the natural thing will be to flee from this scene (n Harm : Quittance).

The response to picture C gives one an idea of how the subject might act in such an emergency : he might console the woman or aid the man ; reprimand or prosecute the other man ; take complete charge ; be helplessly inactive or selfishly indifferent. There is also the question of whether he will be attracted by the problem of the man or of the woman.

Kast : In the first place you would do what you could to sympathize with the woman (n Nur for women). I would try to take care of her, I think, and see that she is taken away from this scene (n Dom).

Roll : I would take the woman out of the room . . . and let her cry and try to comfort her (n Nur for women).

Oriol : As for the woman . . . I would probably tell her to stop crying . . . not too much sympathy. I wouldn't stay there if she didn't stop (N, n Dom, low Nur, n Rej).

E. *Miscellaneous Questions.* (This part of the Conference was conducted by Dr. Murray.)

The E hands the S a blank card (the same size as the cards used in the Thematic Apperception Test) and then says :

1. *Fix your eyes on this blank card. I should like to have you try to see or imagine a picture there.* (Then after a pause :) *Describe what you see.*

After the S has described the picture he is asked, as in the Thematic Apperception Test, to make up a story for which the picture might be used as an illustration.

Roll : There is a man lying on the ground. There is a lot of snow. There are a pack of wolves around tearing him. He won't last long. (As a child this subject was afraid of being devoured ; later he became an authority in lycanthropy.)

2. *Mr. X, will you please take the pencil and paper before you and immediately write down the names of the great men or women you admire the most. They may be living or dead.*

The sheet of paper lies on the table next to an ash tray. On it are some cigarette ashes. Therefore, in picking up the paper the S must either spill the ashes or empty them tidily into the ash tray (low or high n Order).

3. *Now, I should like to have you give me a brief character sketch of Colonel Charles Lindbergh.*

4. *Now, I should like to have you give me a brief character sketch of Mrs. Franklin Roosevelt.*

5. *In the box before you are the parts of a jigsaw puzzle. Please take them out and see whether you can fit them together to form a perfect square. I will allow you two minutes. Ready ?*

The jigsaw puzzle was made by cutting a thin square board into eight pieces of irregular size and shape. Since it cannot be solved in the time allotted, the Es are given the opportunity to observe the S's reaction to failure.

After two minutes have expired, the E says :

6. *Time is up.* (Then after a short pause :) *Would you like to take another puzzle or would you like to continue trying to solve this one ?*

Roll : I would like to keep on doing this (n Cnt).

Sims : I would like to try another (n Inf).

After the S's answer, the E says : 'Well, I guess we'll let it go. You got further than any other subject.'

7. *During the first minute, while you were doing the puzzle, did you feel that you would succeed or fail ?*

8. *Were you rattled doing the puzzle before all of us ?*

9. *Within the last year or so, have you had any general ideas or theories which have interested or excited you ?*

Frost : Yes, I think the idea of the classical approach to art and literature as a kind of life philosophy (n Ach [Aesthetic], n Und, Se). I am determined that you should not accept anything at its face value (n Dom). You can replace it with something that will work just as well. I think you can make a rational philosophy that will replace it. (In this answer Frost outlined a conflict that had persisted since childhood : the attempt to overcome certain irrational infantile fantasies and impulses by an intellectual *tour de force.*)

10. *Eye Test.* (This consisted of an abbreviated Moore-Gilliland Test.[1])
The S was first given the following directions : 'I am going to give you a number and I want you to add 1 to the number and announce the result, then add 2 to the result and announce that result, then add 3 and so forth up to 9. For instance, if I say 45, you say 46, 48, 51, 55, 60 and so forth. Do you understand ? I shall time you, because I want to see how fast you can do it. Ready ? ' The E then announced a number as he pressed a stop watch. Another E, who had the proper numbers on a card before him, corrected the S if he made a mistake, in this manner : '65 and 5 is what ? ' The time the S took to complete the series was recorded and then he was directed as follows : 'I shall give you another number and I want you to perform the same kind of addition. But this time look me straight in the eye while you are doing it. I want to see if you can keep your eyes steady while you are adding.' The subject's time was recorded and then he was asked to do the test over again both ways : without staring and with staring. In this manner the time of four performances was recorded : 1 and 3 without staring ; 2 and 4 with staring. Averaging all four times gave the *average time* ; subtracting the average of 1 and 3 from the average of 2 and 4 gave the *increase of time with staring.* The third index of interference was the *number of eye movements* as recorded by all the Es. A high mark on this test seemed to indicate Anxiety, Superego Conflict or n Infavoidance, n Abasement or low n Aggression and low n Dominance.

11. *What things or situations are you most afraid of?*

1. Moore,H.T. and Gilliland,A.R. 'The measurement of aggressiveness.' *J. Applied Psychol.*,1921,5, 97–118.

Nipp : Mostly afraid of ridicule (n Inv).

Oak : I always think about things that might happen when I get in crowds . . . in a theatre. I just wonder what the best thing would be to do in case of fire. I just wonder . . . if I would lose my head (Oak had been severely injured by an explosion in his youth).

Roll : Well, I don't know as I am afraid of anything very tangible. . . All I am afraid of is the supernatural. . . It takes the form of a fear of vampires and that sort of thing. (When Roll was 9 months old his mother died. In his autobiography he wrote : I used to be frightened to death, but with a pleasurable fear, when my grandfather, in fun, would scratch the sheets with his toes and tell me wolves were after me.)

Bulge : Deep water, because I had a painful experience of almost being drowned.

Zora : I suppose I am most afraid of — not personal danger, but the mob rule of the country. I should dislike it. Just in case they might. (It was supposed that his own instinctual impulses were the 'mob.')

Akeson : I am afraid of myself. . . I am afraid I won't do things I really should do (Se Conflict).

Abel : Well, I used to be afraid of the dark. At times I have a vivid imagination in that respect, and I imagine all sorts of weird things (Proj). Until about fourteen, if it was a weird looking night, I would see monkeys dropping out of trees. (He once had a fantasy of gorillas chasing him.)

12. *What part of this session did you find most annoying ?*

Nipp : The part where I was asked a question and have to give my answer and my reason. I could feel the answer I could give, but I couldn't discover a reason (Imp, low n Und).

Oak : I should have known more about what to say about the pictures (low Intra, n Aba : Self-depreciation).

13. *Thank you very much. That is all.*

The average duration of the Conference was 45 minutes.

Modifications of Procedure. The original schedule for the Conference was very different from the one described above. Many items were added as successive groups were examined and many were eliminated. The following procedures, for instance, were tried and discarded : dropping papers near the S to see whether he would pick them up, asking the S to read a paragraph of pornographic literature, have the subject : draw a bust that stands on a pedestal in the library, write his own name five times as fast as possible, whistle one of his favourite tunes. The complete Moore-Gilliland Test was tried and eliminated.

The following rank orders based on definite measurements were obtained from the Conference sessions : degree of radicalism, sentimentive intensity, speed of response to questions ; and on the Eye Test : average time, increase of time with staring, and number of eye movements.

The reader will note that about half of the Conference is spent in asking the S about various aspects of his personality. If the S could and would answer these questions correctly the attendance of the experimenters would be unnecessary ; in fact, the entire procedure of investigation would be unnecessary. A comprehensive questionnaire would be all that was needed to furnish the facts that would be required for constructing a psychograph. It is well recognized, however, that most individuals cannot, for a variety of reasons, give a reliable account of their own natures and, furthermore, that much of what they do know about themselves they are unwilling to expose. It is the function of the E to judge to what extent each answer is true or false, whether it states a fact or merely a pious wish. For example, subject Oriol said : 'My way of conducting life seems quite efficient to me. This is my greatest achievement—living like a rational thinking man, as most people, I think, don't.' But from this the experimenters did not suppose that Oriol was an outstanding example of n Understanding or Conjunctivity. It seemed more likely that for some time he had been the puppet of conflicting impulses and that he had only recently become aware of the necessity for Ego structuration. He had probably exerted himself in this direction, but that his thinking was still disorganized and confused was shown by many of his responses.

Immediately after the Conference the Es, working independently, gave the subject a mark on each variable. The average of these marks formed the first column of the score card which was used at all subsequent meetings of the Diagnostic Council. The validity and consistency of these initial marks has been discussed in the chapter on the Judgement of Personality (*vide* p. 243).

Within a few days of the Conference this experimenter analysed, interpreted and summarized at his leisure the stenographic record of the session. He was allotted fifteen minutes to report his findings at the first meeting of the Diagnostic Council. For an example of such reports the reader may turn to the Case Study (*vide* p. 620).

Summary. As an initial procedure or prelude to the subsequent sessions the Conference was found invaluable. Since the subjects were unfamiliar with the Clinic and unacquainted with the staff, this somewhat formal first meeting aroused in some of them considerable nervous tension which caused them to say things which they would not have said under less exacting circumstances.

2. AUTOBIOGRAPHY

H. A. Murray

Purpose. The primary purpose of this procedure was to secure information about a subject's early life and development. This was consonant with our general aim : to represent each individual as a temporal series of events which would reveal causal relations between early experiences and later dispositions.

Procedure. If the subject convinced the examiner that he would enjoy entering into the experiments and would do his utmost to meet the requirements, the examiner told him that the first thing he would be expected to do was to write a short account of his life. 'I shall give you an outline of what is required,' the E said, 'and at the first opportunity I should like to have you sit down, read the directions and write for at least two hours. You will be paid on the basis of two hours' work. Do not attempt to put it into good literary style. I do not care about correct spelling, punctuation or neatness. Do not bother to copy it over.' He was informed that since more than the necessary number of men had applied, the selection of subjects would be made on the basis of the completeness of the autobiographies.

Form for Autobiography

Directions. Please glance over this outline to get a general idea of what is required, and then write your autobiography without consulting it. When you have finished writing, read over the outline carefully and add, as a supplement, whatever information you omitted in your original account.

Family History

(a) *Parents:* (1) Race, education, economic and social status, occupations, interests, opinions and general temperament, state of health.

(2) General home atmosphere (harmony or discord). What was the attitude of each of your parents towards you: (affectionate, oversolicitous, domineering, possessive, nagging, anxious, indifferent, etc.)?

Attachment to family (close or distant); favourite parent; fantasies about parents; disappointments and resentments. Which parent do you most resemble?

Discipline in home, punishments, reactions to punishment.

Moral and religious instruction.

Special enjoyments at home.

(b) *Sisters and brothers*

Order of birth; characteristics of each.

Attachments and resentments; conflicts.

Did you feel superior or inferior to sisters and brothers?

(c) *Larger family circle.* Grandparents and relatives.

(d) *Physical surroundings of youth.* City or country; nature of home.

Personal History

Date and Place of birth.

Nature of birth (natural or Caesarean; short or long labour).

Time of weaning.

First experience you can remember.

Recollections of each parent during your early years. Did you feel secure and at peace in your relationship to them?

(a) *Early development.* Was it precocious or retarded? When did walking and talking begin?

(1) Illnesses.

(2) Habits: thumbsucking, nailbiting, bedwetting, stammering, convulsions ; tantrums, fears, nightmares, sleep-walking, revulsions, finickiness about food.

(3) Play. Toys and animals ; other children.

(4) Fantasies of self ; favourite stories and heroes.

(5) General attitude. Was your general attitude adaptive (co-operative and obedient) ; aggressive (competitive and assertive) ; timid (sensitive and fearful) ; guileful (teasing and wily) ; refractory (negative and resistant) ?

(b) *School and college history*

Age at entrance ; age at graduation.

Scholastic record ; best and worst subjects.

Friendships (many or few, casual or deep) ; quarrels ; moodiness and solitariness.

Association with groups ; how were you regarded and why ?

Were you ignored, picked-on, ridiculed, bullied ?

Attitude with groups (shy, submissive, genial, confident, forward, boisterous, aggressive).

Ambitions and ideals.

Hero-worship. Were there any particular people (historical or contemporary) whom you attempted to imitate ? What qualities did you particularly admire ?

Interests and amusements.

Sex History

(a) Early knowledge. Curiosity about the body, especially about sex differences.

What theories did you hold about childbirth ?

When did you discover about the sex relations of your parents ? Were you shocked ?

Sexual instruction.

(b) Early practices : masturbation, relations with the same or the opposite sex. Did you play sex games with sister or brother ? Did you want to see others naked or display your own body ?

(c) Puberty experiences of a sexual nature. Have you ever been in love ? How often ? Did you quarrel ? What type of person was selected ?

(d) Erotic fantasies ; reveries of ideal mate. What kind of activity was imagined as specially pleasurable ?

(e) What emotions accompanied or followed sex experiences (anxiety, shame, remorse, revulsion, satisfaction)?

(f) What is your attitude toward marriage?

Major experiences

Positive (events accompanied by great elation: success and joy).

Negative (events accompanied by great depression and discomfort: frights, humiliations, failures, transgressions).

Aims and Aspirations. What are your chief aims for the immediate future? If you could (within reason) remodel the world to your heart's desire how would you have it and what role would you like to play in such a world?

Estimate of Self and World

State briefly what you believe to be:

(1) Your general estimate of and attitude toward the social world.

(2) The world's estimate of and attitude toward you.

(3) Your general estimate of yourself.

This experimenter glanced over each autobiography in order to gain a rough impression of its psychological value: the relevance and interest of the material, the apparent completeness and frankness of the revelations. An autobiography is useful at the beginning as an index of the willingness of a subject to participate whole-heartedly in the experiments which are to follow. Any subject whose autobiography does not meet requirements may be dropped from the group to be studied.

After the Conference session, the experimenter analysed each autobiography and later presented a summary of the findings at the first meeting of the Diagnostic Council. Fifteen minutes was allotted to the reading of each report. For an example the reader may turn to the Case Study.

Results. In examining the autobiographies it was assumed that the subject was writing about the events of his early life as he remembered them. Many memories, no doubt, were unconsciously repressed, many were consciously withheld and of those that were recorded many were distorted. Despite these obvious limitations, every autobiography revealed something of importance. Besides the concrete facts there was evidence of the subject's attitude towards the facts. The method of interpretation was the same as that used in the analysis of all other verbal material. Note was taken of the amount of space or emphasis given to each topic, the omission of items listed in the form, interest in objective as compared to subjective happenings, Narcism, Intensity and Emotionality. The coherence of the account was a good index of verbal Conjunctivity. Marks on the n Order could be based on the neatness of the handwriting, absence of spots, smudges and so forth.

Most of the subjects were surprisingly frank in writing about their experiences, even though it entailed the exposure of inferiority and moral weakness. In one subject self-revelation was experienced as a not unpleasurable catharsis : 'The environment which I have been brought up in is one of unintentional reserve and it is shocking to me as well as a relief to write about matters which have never been aired before.' In the Form for Autobiographies the order of persons to be discussed is this : father, mother, self. Most of the subjects followed this order, the amount of space devoted to each object and the intensity of the characterizing words serving as a rough index of the object's cathexis. A few subjects, most of whom were high in Narcism, started with themselves. 'In many ways I resemble Emerson ; the Calvinistic theology, the moralizing, the painful self-consciousness which are always discernible in the Concord sage are likewise directing and determining my life and thought.' And later this : 'When I first graced this earth in 1911, the event was recorded in Albany papers. Forceps were used to extricate me at that time after a long labour on the part of my mother. According to my mother also I was weaned for about five months.' Another narcistic subject — this time a confirmed pessimist — began in this way : 'I first saw the darkness of night on the evening of January 23, 1916 . . . I was christened Abraham Caesar, a name which later caused me much vexation.' Reading this one feels intuitively that a long tale of woe and failure is about to be unfolded. Only one subject followed Henry Adams in speaking of himself in the third person : 'The boy Gifford was of his father's build. He was inclined to be nervous like his mother, and showed many other of her characteristics. She was his early favourite, and he is said never to have left her side when very young.' One subject started but did not continue in a humorous vein: 'My parents were God-fearing, God-loving Catholics—devout and earnest in prayer and work. My mother, whom I resembled most of all the children, was from that class of society that at that time might well have been styled the lace-curtain Irish.'

Subjects spent from one to three pages characterizing their parents. The more sociocentric subjects wrote about their aunts, uncles and cousins. Several subjects were graphic in their accounts of quarrels and dissensions between parents or between parents and children. Others pictured idyllic homes: 'Home atmosphere most harmonious and agreeable. Perfect mutual understanding, consequently no clash of interests. A watchful and helpful attitude towards children, but neither over-solicitous nor indifferent.' One can be sure that this subject is high in Defendance and that his Ego has been consolidated with the family pattern.

A large proportion of subjects were able to remember something about their early habits: finickiness about food and bed-wetting, etc. Almost all of them mentioned thumb-sucking. One subject, for instance, recalled an incident which occurred when he was three. 'The first thing I remember is standing on a second-story back porch sucking my finger. A neighbour passed below and when my mother chided me for sucking my finger in front of her, I pulled a woolen hat I was wearing down over face and finger.' This incident was an early objectification of what became a common pattern: a quiet, diffident exterior masking a free flow of fantasy. 'I spent much time simply lying,' he wrote, 'letting my imagination work, placing myself as boy hero in the wildest situations, particularly as boy President of the U.S. Occasionally my mind would dwell on lewd or filthy subjects and this while I was five or six years old.' His finger-sucking persisted for some time accompanied by the habit of twisting his hair. The result was a little bald spot on his head. Here we think of oral erotism accompanied by intrAggression (destruction of his own body) which is in turn to be associated with masochism

(n Aba) and Superego Conflict. 'A little later,' he continues, 'I developed a terrible fear of thunderstorms and with this a sort of superstitious religiousness. I attributed the storms entirely to God and made myself miserable trying to appease Him. Among the reforms instituted for this purpose was the dropping of the finger-sucking habit.' Several other subjects gave vivid accounts of the effect of religious ideas. 'I was given the religious education of an ordinary Jewish youth, that is, I was sent to a Hebrew School at an early age, but had little interest in the proceedings. Suddenly, shortly after my confirmation, I experienced a stupendous dream, in which I imagined myself confronted with God at the time of my death. Awakening, terrified and amazed, I determined from then on that I should give myself over to being strictly orthodox. This impulse was lost after three or four months of a sort of half-hearted attempt to become strict. From then until I was 16 my religious duties were raised to no higher degree than those of my family. But strangely enough, without any apparent reason I again became orthodox, only this time I became a really fanatic one. This state of affairs lasted for about nine months, and the relapse into my old ways was much more gradual. Only recently, and I am now over twenty, has the last effect of this sudden frenzy been completely removed.'

High Defendance was suspected when an autobiography described no failures, humiliations or sorrows. Only one subject, Mauve, portrayed his family and himself as entirely uncriticizable. His parents, he wrote, were 'of nobility of Ireland before English persecution . . . of family that continued with proud and pure blood.' Of himself he said : 'I was admired, I know, while in school, and envied a great deal because of my lack of study troubles, and also because of my enigmatic self. . . I took careful precautions to keep myself a closed book rather than an open one. . . Often I had a chap ask me how was it that I went to comparatively few dances, yet could dance so well. . . Others asked me boldly to tell them something about myself, as they couldn't figure me out.' Other subjects, on the other hand, did not seem to mind putting themselves in a bad light : 'I am extremely loquacious,' wrote Quick, 'having the ability, or rather the capacity, for talking hours at a time without saying anything of value. I love to tease people and I even go so far as to irritate them. . . Boisterous and at times puerile, I like to be the centre of attraction, much more than my mediocre talents will allow. I am fickle to the nth degree. . . My ambition is to have as happy life as it is possible for me to make, no matter by what means or at whose expense, thus exhibiting my selfish character.' A fusion of masochism and exhibitionistic Succorance was suggested by vivid emotional accounts, such as Zill's, of suffering and humiliation : 'Then I had a great physical misfortune. My skin broke out terribly, practically ruining all my social chances and affecting my mind. I grew morbid, extremely self-conscious and introspective. I worried about everything excessively, nothing seemed to break for me. Every new bit of sex knowledge got me thinking about its application to myself. When I learned more of homosexuality and its causes, a fear arose in me ; and I often tested myself. . . I want to be cordial but am mostly ill received. I seem to make a mess of everything I try.'

In describing their sex lives, subjects varied greatly. Some had very little to say. 'In time I made acquaintance with most of the erotic practices,' wrote Valet, 'but eventually found them uninteresting and a poor substitute for broader relations.' Others were prompted, as was Mauve, to prove their invulnerability. 'I actually have at times felt strongly inclined towards a certain girl, and instead of letting emotions rule my actions, I held her up to the critical eye of my code of standards, which inevitably proved too high for her, and hence I put her from my mind. I am not kidding myself into thinking that mind is superior to emotion ; I know it is in my case.' One subject, Zeeno, took a very matter of fact, almost scientific, attitude about his sex life. 'Until recently I never mingled in intimate relation with the opposite sex. But constant social intercourse wrought a change in me, so that just about a year ago I decided that I might indulge in sexual congress, due to my conviction that virginity in men or ignorance of sex life is conducive to mental incompatibility. I decided to copulate but only with an individual who would not cause me any revulsion or show the part of a strumpet. I have never desired to indulge with a virgin. Having found a very suitable person, I took part in coitus on various occasions.' Finally, there were subjects who wrote emotionally and without embarrassment about erotic experiences. One said : 'At 16 I got my first "thrill" when for the first time I touched a female breast. The reaction immediately caused masturbation and the flow was rather free. . . It was only last December that I touched the vicinity of a woman's womb, although it was covered by some clothes. The internal and external reaction on my part was tremendous. I masturbated freely, became terrifically hot and for the first time in my life, I believe, I felt the urge to commit sexual intercourse.'

In giving estimates of the world the subjects revealed their sentiments, sometimes in no unmistakable terms. From most of the Jews we came to expect critical judgements of modern civilization and suggestions for its improvement. 'If I could remodel the world,' wrote Veal, 'I would have it so that every individual with a worthy ambition could be allowed to draw upon a fund which would take care of all financial considerations involved in the attainment of the ambition.' One of our Catholic subjects, who had recently had a falling out with his girl, had a very poor opinion of the present state of affairs : 'I believe the world is going socially and morally to destruction. Society is on the downgrade now, even as that of Rome was around the year 200 A.D. And I believe this society will experience in time the same result as did that of Rome. Today, the world teaches that there is no God, no religion, no set standard of right or wrong.'

Summary. It can easily be appreciated that these autobiographies furnished indispensable data for composing the psychographs. The material which they contained was so important, indeed, that in the future we should advise allotting three or four hours to this item and encouraging the subject to write a longer and more detailed account.

3. FAMILY RELATIONS AND CHILDHOOD MEMORIES

H. Scudder Mekeel

Purpose of the Session : The primary purpose of the two interviews constituting this session was to determine some, at least, of the influences at work in the early conditioning of the S and what role the impress of these influences played in the behaviour and attitudes of the S as he was seen at the Clinic.

Procedure : The S was met in the waiting room and taken upstairs to the E's office. Some banal remarks were passed by the E to break the tension of first acquaintance. After the S had entered the office and the door had been closed the E assumed a business-like but friendly manner. The S was asked to lie on a couch and the E sat in a chair behind and facing the head of the couch.

At the first interview the E said : 'I am going to give you a memory test. You shall have thirty-five minutes and your task is to see how many experiences occurring before the age of seven you can recall. Tell me briefly in each case the circumstances and your reaction to them and any later results of the experience. Give your approximate age at the time the incident occurred. You might start by giving your first or earliest memory.'

When hesitant, the S was encouraged by such remarks as, 'Yes ?', or 'Yes, go on.' If and when the S's memories before the age of seven failed, he was asked to proceed with those occurring before the age of twelve. If the S continued up to the time allotted, he was stopped. The E, who noted as nearly verbatim as possible what the S related,[1] read over to the S what had been said, not only to make certain that the E had understood correctly, but also to find out whether the memories were recalled as pleasant, indifferent, or unpleasant. The S was asked to state, after the reading of each memory, the feeling-tone accompanying it by the use of the three terms : pleasant, indifferent, unpleasant.

The following two questions were asked the S at the end of

1. A phonographic record of the interview was made as well. This was used as a basis for the session report on each subject.

the session : 1, What was your favourite fairy story ? 2, Did you have any special fantasies or dreams ?

Immediately after the first hour the S was given the following questionnaire to fill out in the library. At the top was this statement and directions :

Directions. This questionnaire is to fill out the background for the early memories you have just recalled. Answer in detail any of the questions that you think require explanation or elaboration in your case. Use blank sheets of paper for your answers which you may number without rewriting the questions — as, for example, Group II D — then your answer.

Group I — *Family Relations*

(1) How many brothers and sisters have you ; any half-brothers or sisters, or step-brothers or sisters ? Have your parents lost any children through death ? Give the number of years' difference in age between you and each of your brothers and sisters, and state whether it is that much older or younger than you.

(2) What relatives lived with your family when you were a child ; what relatives visited you frequently or for long visits ; what relatives occasionally ? If they were grandparents, mention whether they were your father's or mother's parents ; if aunts or uncles, mention whether they were your father's or mother's brothers and sisters ; if cousins, mention the relationship of their parents to yours. Also mention what changes took place with these relatives and how old you were when they happened — such changes as moving away, death or marriage.

(3) Give the number of years' difference in age between your parents and state whether your father is older or younger than your mother.

(4) Outline the sleeping arrangements of your family — when you were a child and now. Give the number of sleeping rooms used and who slept in which. If you shared a room at any time, mention all changes chronologically from your babyhood to present time. Did your parents always share a room, and if so, did they use twin beds or a double bed ; any changes ?

(5) Describe your feeling about, and attitude toward, each member of your family you have mentioned above. Also mention any changes in your attitude that have occurred since childhood.

Group II — *School Relations*

(1) Did you go with a gang or play-group or organize a 'club'?
  (a) If so, what were its, or their, purpose and activities?
  (b) How many members did it, or they, have?
  (c) Did you hold any position in it, or them?
  (d) How old were you when a member of each; how long were you an active member in each? Give reasons for leaving.

(2) What extracurricular activities were you interested in in high school — sports, journalism, dancing, fraternities, etc.?

(3) Have there been any particular people in your life whom you looked up to or worshipped as a hero? If so describe them.

(4) What did you do when you had nothing to do?

Group III — *Kinds and Distribution of Authority*

(1) Which person set standards for family and which was considered the first authority?

(2) Was there conflict or co-operation between: parents; siblings and parents; parents and other relatives; siblings; siblings and other relatives?

(3) Was authority imposed kindly or harshly?

(4) Forms of punishment? Which preferred and by whom?
  (a) How did you react to these disciplinary measures?
  (b) Whose disciplining was most effective and taken most seriously by you? Why?
  (c) Whose disciplining did you fear most? Why?
  (d) If you had brothers or sisters did you ever or often feel that you were disciplined more strictly or harshly than they?
  (e) Were you often threatened with disciplinary measures which were not carried out? By which parent?
  (f) By which parent did you prefer to be disciplined or punished? Why?
  (g) Immediately after being punished, about what did you usually think or daydream?
  (h) If you had either brothers or sisters did you feel that you were your mother's or your father's favourite child or least loved child?
  (i) Did either parent tend to indulge you more than the other? If so, which one?

(j) Did either parent tend to frustrate you more than the other? If so, which one?

(k) Are you known to have had temper tantrums when very young?

(5) What special things or activities were prohibited to you in childhood? How did you attain your freedom later?

(6) Did you love your mother, nursemaid or older brother or sister for early care?

(7) What special interests or activities have your parents?

Group IV — (1) After the interview upstairs did you think of your memories as pleasant or unpleasant on the whole?

(2) What memories have occurred to you since the interview upstairs?

Before the second interview on the week following, the E read over the answers to the questionnaire and the account of the first interview which had been typed from the phonographic record. He then outlined specific points which needed clarification or further elaboration. The S was questioned for about fifteen minutes, after which he was asked to recall what memories he could of events occurring during the last ten years, in the same way in which he had done for the early memories.

Results: A. *Behaviour of subjects during interview.* All were co-operative. Some were uncomfortable about their backs being toward the E. One apologized for his back even though he knew he was supposed to sit in that position. Three turned the chair facing the E toward the end of the interview. Three or four were at first on the defensive. Two were not certain that they could co-operate because pictures from the family albums or often-told family anecdotes re-enforced or replaced actual memories. All but one or two seemed to enjoy the interview.

B. *The subjects' productions.* (1) *First Interview.* The majority of Ss took up the entire thirty-five minutes. Only one or two were not ready to stop. Just one, who stopped at the end of twenty-seven minutes, was very noticeably 'contractive.' Eight had to be allowed to draw on memories from the age of seven to twelve, and the other five also mentioned a few occurring in the same period.

The age of the earliest memory recalled varied from one and a half to six years.

Although it was surprisingly difficult to elicit the feeling-tone of each specific memory from the Ss, the general impression of the E was that pleasantness and unpleasantness were fairly evenly divided in the majority of subjects. Only three gave evidence of a prevailingly happy childhood ; two Ss harped on unpleasantness.

Aside from the excellent opportunity the E had of marking each S on most of the personality variables during the interviews, the main value of this session was to be found in its additions to and clarification of the autobiography.

(2) *Second Interview.* The second interview consisted in asking orally about the family constellation of attitudes from the S's point of view. Significant relatives as well as immediate family connections were charted. Such questions as sleeping arrangements, school activities, and the kinds of punishment administered at home were discussed in detail.

4. SEXUAL DEVELOPMENT

W. G. Barrett

Procedure. Upon entering the room the subject was greeted with a brief 'Good morning.' He was not addressed by name, but was asked in a friendly manner to make himself comfortable on the couch when the procedure would be described to him. The E then took his seat (just beyond the head of the couch and out of the line of vision of a reclining S) and explained the nature of the experiment, i.e., described free association. With those Ss who were reluctant to lie down the E added a remark to the effect that it would facilitate their co-operation thus to recline and relax in a position where the E would not be directly in view and, perhaps, intrude upon their thoughts. No difficulties were experienced beyond this point.

In describing free association the E used Freud's illustration of the man in a moving railroad train reporting the passing terrain to a blind geologist in order to get his opinion regarding the country. It was also described in terms of a moving picture, the S's mind being described as a screen upon which were projected images or ideas which should be reported in detail for the purposes of this experiment. The S was assured it was not necessary to 'make sense,' that he should have no concern about rounding off any topic he might be reporting at the moment a new idea appeared, that it was important to break off and report this new idea immediately.

In the hope that some reassurance might facilitate the S's bringing forward those fantasies which in everyday life are rarely communicated, the E remarked that certain thoughts might come to mind which ordinarily would not be mentioned but which were clearly a very important part of mental life. The S was assured that these revelations would never in any way be connected with him personally and was also told that the E was a psychiatrist and quite used to hearing about things not ordinarily discussed. It is an interesting commentary on the conditions of the experiment that, whereas in psycho-analysis the first session frequently offers material of a most private nature, in this experiment there was hardly an instance where the S spoke of such things as sexual experiences or overt fantasies of aggression until specific inquiry was made.

At the beginning of the free association period the Ss were encouraged to continue talking by such remarks as 'Go on, please,' 'What are you thinking now ?', 'What comes into your mind next ?', but the periods of silence were allowed to become increasingly longer. During silences the S's behaviour was noted and interpreted. When the S lapsed into narrative, the trend was interrupted with some such remark as, 'Don't forget the rule of talking about each new idea as it comes into your mind : you don't need to stick to any subject, you know.'

After a half hour of free association certain specific questions were put to the Ss. These were made as brief as possible, the S being permitted to develop the material coming to mind according to whatever implications he inferred in the questions. It was indicated that these questions should be used as points of departure for further free associations rather than answered by a limiting statement.

The topics introduced by the E were: (1) Earliest recollections from childhood. (2) Relations with parents and siblings in childhood and in later years. (3) First consciousness of sex and early discoveries and experiences with other children or with adults. (4) Childhood theories of origin, birth, and impregnation. (5) Beginning of masturbation, teachings regarding it and emotional attitude towards it. (6) Development of present sex practices and their nature. (7) Attitude towards the same sex and homosexual experiences. (8) An opportunity to question the E.

5. PRESENT DILEMMAS

MERRILL MOORE

Purpose. The primary purpose of this session was to discover the contemporary personal problems and dilemmas of each subject.

Procedure. Upon entering, the S was asked to lie down on the couch. Aside from this he was given no directions and the E did not ask any routine questions. Instead, the E, maintaining a sympathetic and receptive attitude, tried to encourage the S to a full exposition of his views. By informal and indirect queries the E attempted to get the S to express himself on the larger problems that confronted men of his generation; and then, by imperceptible gradations, to turn his attention to his own dilemmas and difficulties. By following this technique it was thought that each subject would, as it were, become a 'patient,' that is, an individual involved in a conflict of aims. In no two sessions was the procedure exactly the same. In some it was necessary for the E at last to question the S more or less directly, while in others the S appeared only too happy to discuss personal matters.

Results. Little difficulty was experienced in getting most of the subjects to come to the point, though in some instances it required tactful encouragement to get them to give a detailed account of their own plight and the possible solutions that had occurred to them. None of the Ss showed insurmountable reserve, and most of them appeared to welcome the chance to talk to a person supposedly informed about such matters. Some expressed regret that they were not given an opportunity to talk to their professors in this way.

Summary. The session was found to have value in that each subject became a 'problem' upon which all facts obtained in other sessions could be brought to bear. The time devoted to this topic might profitably be made longer, or a second interview arranged, for it was often noticed that the S was just beginning to 'warm up' when the hour came to an end.

6. CONVERSATIONS

Eleanor C. Jones

The purpose of these impromptu conversations, lasting from a few minutes to two hours or more, was to accumulate those casual yet contingent words and acts which occurred after, before, or during the more stringent course of something else when the S temporarily escaped, so to speak, out of the contracted-for bounds, as he was waiting for or leaving, working on or recalling a specific test, and when it was possible to catch particularly those echoes or repercussions, to record those verbalisms and gestures which emerged as apparent incidentals or as an aftermath of the task itself — and, as occasion spontaneously offered, to digress or to plunge into a general discussion of feelings and ideas.

The procedure consisted mainly in having little procedure at all, in relinquishing the formalities of technique or the wiliness of doctrine, and in the creation — when necessary — of an atmosphere of mutual pliancy. Apart from a series of definite questions concerning his recollection of two other experiments, the S talked as much or as little as he wished, lounged, expanded, or retracted himself, indulged in personalities. On the sidewalk, the stairs, in various rooms — in short, wherever and whenever encountered — the behaviour, mood, appearance of the S were under a close, minute-by-minute observation. At first, merely present in the library where the S worked on questionnaires, the E took no ostensible notes, being apparently busied with work of her own, or briefly leaving the room, in the event of a watchful S, to make them elsewhere — since it was not sufficient to trust all these minutiae to memory. When, however, several weeks later, set questions with regard to other tests were asked, the replies were written down with the most exact and obvious attention before the eyes of the S (and, of course, much more than the purely verbal information he gave). It was also possible to gain his own spontaneous help by saying something like : 'Naturally, I am going to write down what you tell me, otherwise neither of us would be here — and if it doesn't put you off, I will note down whatever you say in just the words that you say it, so that you may be fully represented and not have saddled upon you some insufficient and garbled report.' The S rarely failed to be willing to repeat what he had just said, with no objection to the E recording a hasty phrase exactly as he uttered it, even to slips or quickly corrected mistakes. In the largesse of spirit which he felt in conferring these benefits upon the attentive E who reached for his every syllable, his reckless generosity momently increased — a debt acknowledged by the E, and not without a certain amount of guilt. Above all, any slightest tinge of the official, patronizing, or informative was avoided and, indeed, never felt — as the moment became for the E, as well as occasionally for the S, an experience rather than an experiment.

The results of this rather anomalous venture would seem to have been something of a combination of free association and a kind of secondary thematic apperception — as when the eye of an S, glued upon a large emphatic Audubon engraving of two carrion-crows brooding above the sunken eye of a dead deer, transferred an eloquence of horror — mingled with sentience and aesthetic criticism — to the heretofore guarded tongue of a self-convinced rationalist ; or as when a chaotic and sentimental exhibitionist said of a marble bust of the classically cool Molière, 'He was just a modern man like us, except for the haircut.' One perceived also, in a few instances, the tentative emergence of a deeper awareness as the S, though in all cases certified to be psychologically innocent, seemed for a moment to gather the subliminal import which bided its time beneath his rationalizations. One discovered further, that whereas with the majority of subjects the most valuable responses were 'accidental' or indirectly 'evoked,' one or two others — notably Zora — most fully rewarded an explicit question, if asked with enough critically exact yet emotionally tinged care to accord with his metaphysical and nurturing pride: 'If only they would ask me what they want to know, I would tell them' — and humorous as this utterance will seem to an epicure of the unconscious, there proved to be a good deal of truth in it — his carefully considered statements corroborating to a remarkable degree the findings in the 'unconscious' experiments. But with the less developed, less poetically intense, and — paradoxically enough — less private natures, the casual method proved the most fruitful.

In envisaging further conceivable developments of such an undertaking, one imagines that as much as possible of a heightened sense of leisure, comfort, and security would best enhance a retrospect of feelings or experience. As one observed that an expressive relaxation from the fatigue, frustration or success of other experiments seemed the most propitious for communication, one would like to re-emphasize that a pliable opportunity — time to rehearse old voyages and plan for novel or traumatic restrivings — is especially rewarding — that whereas the door of the psychiatrist, opened and noticeably shut at a predestined moment, is valuable as a pressure over many months of sessions which have an avowed and enlisted therapeutic aim, so on the contrary, in meetings such as have been described, being both irregular and apparently 'irresponsible,' a fixed limit would waste more time than it would save. It goes without saying, as in any similitude to all-life-in-little, that where the extra minutes or hours are impracticable, by just so much is lost the possibility of the single syllable or look which might for the first time resolve some age-long and classic dilemma. It is equally a truism to insist that by just so much as the E is willing or able to expend, by just so much will he be recompensed, or even have the all-important extra jot thrown in. And as one more testimony to the success of the thematic apperception process, it would seem that in the actual setting, many objects — such as evocative pictures, sculptures, colours — might be chosen, arranged, lessened or augmented with a suitably considered view to inviting comment on those several needs implied, manifested or, indeed, lacking in them. Changes of temperature, as well as modest food of various kinds, cigarettes, confections and so on, might well be within reach — this brief interlude would seem best favoured by its indulgent and unexacting satisfactions — a slight inebriation of physical and mental comforts, surrounded by unobtrusive incitements to spiritual labour.

One might further ideally conceive of such a situation as developing for its own secondary ambition a more or less accurate response to the urgencies of tangential difficulties of the S himself. For this reason it would seem propitious that the E should be a good deal older than the S, able to meet in some slight measure the manifold obligation which might very well ensue in the course of such an enquiry, and — in certain rare cases — to fulfill something of the role described by Rilke in his 'Letters to a Young Poet,' as he comes to feel that what he knows should be placed at the service of the younger man.

7. PREDICTIONS AND SENTIMENTS TEST

Karl Kunze

Purpose. The general purpose of the Predictions and Sentiments Test is to obtain some measure of the degree to which sentiments influence judgements of fact. More specifically it measures the degree of similarity between an individual's predictions of the course of events in numerous fields of activity, and his hopes in regard to these events. Furthermore it provides an index of the intensity of his convictions, the extent of his radicalness, and the relative strength of his interests.

Procedure. The subject is given a questionnaire consisting of seventy predictions as to the course of future events in various fields (economic, political, social, scientific, etc.). He is asked to express his opinion and rate his certainty, pro or con, on each statement. Four months later he is again presented with the seventy statements but this time they are re-worded to read as statements of preference rather than statements of fact. The closeness of the predictions and the sentiments is taken as a rough index of wishful thinking.

At the start of the test subjects are asked to jot down, on separate sheets of paper, any comments, qualifications or elaborations they wish to make in regard to the statements, and are encouraged to append original predictions or sentiments. The number of words written for each of the listed fields of activity is computed and expressed as a percentage of the whole. In this way one obtains an idea of the distribution of the subject's interests. Outstanding or typical sentiments are detected by inspection of the test itself and by an interpretation of the written reactions to the statements. Many indirect signs of sentimentive intensity are commonly encountered such as recurring viewpoints, emotionally tinged remarks, swearing, disparaging and imprecatory statements, exclamation marks, and so forth. Manifestations of a fixed attitude may also be taken as indices of sentiments and interests. An intensely religious person, for instance, may react to the statements about education, science, and sociology from a religious point of view rather than from an educational, scientific, and sociological viewpoint respectively.

An index of sentimentive intensity is obtained by averaging the figures in both tests representing degrees of conviction or degrees of feeling. The scale allows for three of such degrees. In the Predictions Test, the categories represent degrees of certainty that the stated condition will exist fifty years hence ; 1, 2 and 3 in the 'Yes' column indicating increasing degrees of conviction. In the Sentiments Test, the columns represent degrees of agreement or disagreement, 'Yes' 3 indicating nearly complete agreement, and 'No' 3 nearly complete disagreement.

Analysis of the results so far obtained reveals a correlation of +.93 between the sentimentive intensities of the two tests, which shows that, with few exceptions, the subjects were consistent as to the strength of their opinions. Exceptions to this rule, however, may be significant. Those whose intensity in the Predictions Test is relatively low, for instance, may in general be more uncertain about the future of society than about their own feelings.

The correspondence of the tests is an indication of wishful thinking and thus specifies the extent of the subject's Projectivity. To be probable, judgements about the future must be based upon a consideration of past and present trends and the possibility for further change. If an individual projects his own needs into external events, he will of necessity neglect or minimize objective criteria. More rarely the correspondence of the tests may show that the S is in entire accord with modern trends and favours the changes that are likely to occur.

A lack of correspondence of the tests usually means Objectivity, but it may mean pessimistic wishful thinking. The S, out of the n Abasement, may unconsciously wish to demonstrate that nothing which he desires ever comes to pass.

The correspondence of the tests was calculated by summating the difference between the responses of one test and those of the other for each question. As an example, if statement #1 of the Predictions Test was checked in the 'No' 3 column, and in the Sentiments Test, 'Yes' 2, a variation of four points would be recorded. These variations were totalled, and the result divided by the index of sentimentive intensity to correct for the fact that those who consistently gave extreme responses would, in consequence, show a greater variability between the tests.

An Intraception/Extraception index was obtained from the written responses to the statements, by noting whether the S's emphasis was upon external facts or upon feelings, hunches and speculations. If, for instance, in response to the prediction that as time goes on education will become more vocational and utilitarian, the subject mentioned new courses that were recently added to the curriculum of his college, he would receive a mark for Extraception. If, however, his response were : 'God forbid,' as was the case with one student, he would be marked for Intraception. Each written response was marked on a scale of 0 to 5, 5 denoting the highest degree of Intraception.

Statements pertaining to politics, government, and some aspects of sociology were chosen as indicating conservatism or radicalism, and from responses to these items, a Radical/Conservative index was calculated. The conservative viewpoint for each statement was established, and the gross amount by which a subject varied from this norm represented his radicalism. Singularly enough, no correlation was found between sentimentive intensity and radicalness.

8. QUESTIONNAIRES

H. A. Murray

In order to obtain with the least expenditure of time a general impression of the everyday behavioural characteristics of our subjects, we asked each man to fill out (in two or three sessions) a long questionnaire specially designed to cover all the variables (except Creativity and Projectivity) that were used in our study. The questionnaire was divided into three sections, each section consisting of 200 items. Some of the variables could be covered by 10 items, each of which described a typical mode of response, but most of them required 20, and two (Intraception and Extraception) required 40. As in all our work a zero (0) to five (5) scale was used (*vide* p. 263), the subject being asked to put a check, after reading each question, in one of the six available columns.

The questionnaire was tested and modified a number of times by giving it to successive groups (other than our regular subjects) before the final form was composed and adopted. The testing consisted of an attempt to measure the diagnostic value or relevance of the separate items. To do this the percentage frequency of 0, 1, 2, 3, 4 and 5 responses to each statement was computed. This showed to what extent the responses to an item followed the normal distribution curve. Percentage frequencies were then computed for the twenty per cent of subjects who ranked highest, and for the twenty per cent of subjects who ranked lowest on the variable in question. By comparing these two computations it was possible to determine the agreement of each statement with the variable as a whole, and on this basis to rank it in respect to its ability to distinguish subjects in the upper division from subjects in the lower division. This provided a criterion for eliminating the least effective questions.

The subjects filled out the questionnaires in the library of the Clinic, sometimes alone, sometimes in groups of three or four ; the usual procedure being to devote a separate period (one hour) to each of the three sections. As it rarely took a full hour to complete a section there was time left over for informal conversation with the experimenter (Mrs. Jones) who was in constant attendance. This provided an opportunity to observe the subjects' reactions to the personal interrogations contained in the test.

The first page of the questionnaire was as follows :

PSYCHOLOGICAL INSIGHT TEST

Directions

In this test you are asked to compare your behavioural and emotional reactions with those of most men of your own age — with the hypothetical average among college men.

Read each statement carefully and make up your mind whether it is *more* or *less* true for you than it is for the average. Then, *make a check* in the proper column according to the following system :

Below Average

Column — (minus) 3 = I do, or I feel, or I think this thing *very much less* often (or intensely) than the average.

Column — (minus) 2 = I do, or I feel, or I think this thing *less* often (or intensely) than the average.

Column — (minus) 1 = average, but on the low side.

Above Average

Column + (plus) 1 = average, but on the high side.

Column + (plus) 2 = I do, or I feel, or I think this thing *more* often (or intensely) than the average.

Column + (plus) 3 = I do, or I feel, or I think this thing *very much more* often (or intensely) than the average.

Since the statements pertaining to each variable have been included in Chapter III it is not necessary to list them here. The first page of the questionnaire will suffice as an illustration of how the items were spaced :

SERIES A

	Below Av.			Above Av.			
	−3	−2	−1	+1	+2	+3	
I am in my element when I am with a group of people who enjoy life.							1
I can become devotedly attached to certain places, certain objects and certain people.							2
When a friend of mine annoys me, I tell him what I think of him . . .							3
I am capable of putting myself in the background and working with zest for a man I admire							4
I often think about how I look and what impression I am making upon others.							5
I am intolerant of people who bore me.							6
I notice and am responsive to slight changes in the colour of the sky, in the temperature and quality of the atmosphere.							7
I take pains not to hurt the feelings of subordinates.							8
Sometimes when I am in a crowd, I say humorous things which I expect strangers will overhear. . .							9

SERIES A (*Continued*)

I worry a lot about my ability to succeed							10
I become very attached to my friends							11
I am somewhat disturbed when my daily habits are disrupted by unforeseen events							12
I am apt to enjoy getting a person's goat							13
I can see the good points rather than the bad points of the men who are above me							14
I can become entirely absorbed in thinking about my personal affairs — my health, my cares or my relations to others							15
I maintain a dignified reserve when I meet strangers							16
I enjoy observing in great detail the facial expressions, gestures and mannerisms of the people I see							17
I will take a good deal of trouble to help a younger man — to get him a job, to intercede for him or in some other way to further his interests							18
I often dramatize a story which I am telling and demonstrate exactly how everything happened							19
After I have made a poor showing before others, I usually recall the occasion with distress for a long time afterwards							20

On this sheet one may find statements applying to ten variables. These occur in the following order : n Affiliation (1 and 11), Sameness (2 and 12), n Aggression (3 and 13), n Deference (4 and 14), Narcism (5 and 15), n Rejection (6 and 16), n Sentience (7 and 17), n Nurturance (8 and 18), n Exhibition (9 and 19), n Infavoidance (10 and 20). From this it may be noticed that the statements pertaining to the same variable have numbers that end in the same digit. Since this scheme is maintained throughout each section (until the last and 200th statement), the marking of the questionnaire is greatly facilitated.

Though the subjects (for their own clarification) were given a scale running from — (minus) 3 to + (plus) 3, the experimenter who marked the questionnaire paid no attention to this, but used the 0 to 5 scale. It was a matter of thirty seconds to add the scores on the twenty items representing one variable and divide the sum by 20. In this way one obtained a figure between 0 and 5 which, if the S had a fair knowledge of himself and others, measured his rank on the given variable in the community at large. As might be expected, however, it was found that there was a general tendency for the subjects to give themselves relatively high marks on the more desirable traits and relatively low marks on the less desirable. For example, when the questionnaire was given to a large group, the average mark, instead of being 2.5 (as it should have been if each subject had correctly measured himself against all the others), was about 1.6 for a variable such as Harmavoidance, and about 3.1 for a variable such as Affiliation. Consequently, it was necessary to compute, from the results obtained with large groups, the usual distribution of scores on each variable, and then by figuring even sigma units from the mean (*vide* p. 263) find the range of marks that correspond to each index figure (0 to 5) used in our scoring system. Having once obtained these figures for each variable, it was possible to translate a subject's score into absolute units immediately. Thus, the subject's self-estimate could be directly compared to the Clinic's estimate.

In the course of our explorations we used many different types of questionnaire (reaction studies, inventories and so forth), and though with experience our enthusiasm for them dwindled almost to the vanishing point, at the end we still felt they were useful adjuncts to studies such as ours. The average correlation between self-ratings (questionnaire ratings) and Clinic ratings on twelve variables for Group I was .20, on twenty-two variables for Group II was .22, on twenty-five variables for Group III was .48, and on thirty-three variables for Group IV was .54. It seems likely that the improvement was due partly to progressively better questionnaires and partly to progressively better marking by the experimenters. But it does not seem probable to us that if our studies were continued, the subjects' questionnaire scores and the scores assigned by the experimenters on the basis of their behaviour in the Clinic would continue to approximate. For even if the experimenters became maximally accurate there would always be a definite limitation to the reliability of the questionnaires, the reasons for which are not hard to find :

1. A questionnaire must necessarily be limited to a few among the many possible modes or situations in which a variable exhibits itself. Hence there will certainly be subjects who will get a low score because, though they possess the variable, they manifest it in situations other than those defined in the questionnaire.

2. Subjects mark themselves on the basis of their everyday life ; but since behaviour cannot be estimated apart from its conditions, and since each subject is exposed to a different set of conditions, and since these conditions are not stated by them in scoring the questionnaire, the scores cannot be accepted as reliable measures of personality.

Ex : Answers to the question, 'Do you suffer from moods of depression ? ' can not be justly interpreted if the E does not know that the mother of one subject has recently died, that the father of another has gone into bankruptcy, that another has just been awarded a scholarship and so forth.

3. When the S marks himself, he usually does so, consciously or unconsciously, in relation to others. (In our questionnaire he was specifically asked to do this.) He measures his behaviour

against that of his brothers and sisters, friends and acquaintances. For example, when he has to decide whether it is 'seldom' or 'frequently' that he gets angry with a waiter, he is apt to ask himself, 'Do I get angry less often or more often than my acquaintances?' Thus every man uses a different standard of comparison.

Ex: If, let us say, an S has a brother who is conspicuously lacking in application and industry, the S may have been frequently singled out by his parents as an example of perseverance. This may lead the S to think of himself as unusually persevering though, compared to the world at large, he may not be distinguished for this trait.

4. Subjects differ markedly in insight. There are differences in respect to the depth of their knowledge and differences in respect to their ability to remember and judge their social acts. Some can see themselves as others see them; but most people are protected from this knowledge by all manner of repressions and internal projections. They may refuse to acknowledge, for example, that they frequently act aggressively or feel depressed or enjoy sexual fantasies because the memory of such episodes is blotted out.

5. Subjects may intentionally misrepresent themselves. They may be ashamed of what they consider their weaknesses, or they may want to ingratiate themselves with the experimenter. Or perhaps a subject has half-wilfully dramatized himself as a certain kind of person, and he wants others to believe in the reality of his masquerade. But whatever the motive, the fact is he does not tell the whole truth as he knows it.

These are but some of the factors — minimized, to be sure, in the best procedures (ex: A–S Reaction Study) — which explain why questionnaires are always unreliable. If, however, they are supplemented by intimate interviews and used in conjunction with other examinations, they may be helpful. Indeed, they may be utilized to expose precisely those factors which usually make them almost valueless: the uniqueness of a subject's situation and associates, his lack of insight, his half-conscious distortions of the truth.

The popular questionnaires that we employed (Bernreuter's

for dominance, extraversion and self-sufficiency, Guilford's for extraversion, Thurstone's for neuroticism, Woodworth's for neuroticism, and so forth) were abandoned after three trials, because whatever they indicated was not sufficiently defined for our purposes. The results of the A–S Reaction Study (G.W. and F.H. Allport) correlated consistently with Clinic ratings of the corresponding variables, but since the latter were covered by our own behavioural questionnaire the Allports' test was superfluous (*vide* p. 242). The only well known pencil and paper test that proved indispensable was the Study of Values (Vernon and Allport[1]). The results of this test aided us in discovering a subject's hierarchy of interests. Interest in economic, politic or social affairs was accepted as a sign of Exocathection; interest in theoretic, aesthetic or religious activity as a sign of Endocathection. The ratio of the former to the latter provided an index figure for Exocathection, which in most cases was found to conform with Clinic ratings on this variable.

We devised a number of written tests ourselves of which the most promising was a series of six exercises[2] designed to reveal latent aggression. All of these pencil and paper methods, however, were eventually discarded.

9. ABILITIES TEST

RUTH T. PETERSON and E. INGLIS

Purpose. The object of this session was to make a general survey of each S's abilities. Since limitations of time and technique made it impossible to test these objectively, conclusions were based partly upon the S's estimates of his own abilities and partly upon the E's estimates after the S had offered a number of concrete examples to corroborate his ratings.

1. Vernon,P.E. and Allport,G.W. 'A test for personal values.' *J. Abn. & Soc. Psychol.*,1931,*26*, 233–248.
2. One of the tests used for latent aggression was reported by Barry,H., 'A test for negativism and compliance.' *J. Abn. & Soc. Psychol.*,1931,*25*, 373–381. Three other tests were briefly described by me in the *J. Abn. & Soc. Psychol.*, 1934,*24*, 66–81.

Procedure. A questionnaire was devised which listed 15 'Special Abilities,' with specific examples to illustrate each item ; the instructions called for self-ratings on a scale of 0 to 5. The test blank was given to the Ss, along with several other questionnaires, to be filled out at leisure in the library. Later, each S was interviewed by the E and asked to give as many examples as he could to illustrate his proficiency or deficiency in each ability. He was also encouraged to talk about his ambitions and vocational interests as well as his use of free time. The E then attempted to ascertain what factors determined his choice of interests—the influence of innate endowment, early training, identification—and, if possible, which abilities were 'natural' and which acquired by persistent effort. A second hour's session on another day was found necessary to complete this interview, after which the E scored the S on each ability, relying principally on the concrete examples provided by him in support of his own ratings.

The technique was altered somewhat in testing Group IV. With the earlier group, the E was a woman considerably older than the Ss ; with this group the E was a man of about their own age. In addition, the interview was limited to a single hour. Between them these two changes reduced the freedom with which Ss discussed themselves and their abilities, so that the original procedure is to be preferred for future use. A third change was introduced by requiring the S at the beginning of the interview, before discussion and the production of examples, to rate himself again without reference to his previous estimates. This was intended to permit a direct comparison between his ratings when alone and when face to face with an interviewer ; the changes, however, were slight, and the two self-ratings correlated +.90.

The list of abilities, as named and defined on the test blank, is as follows :

1. Physical Ability : the ability to play games which depend upon bodily skill or prowess — football, baseball, rowing, hockey, tennis, golf. Physical agility or endurance — swimming, riding, skiing, mountain-climbing.
2. Mechanical Ability : the ability to manipulate mechanical appliances

and instruments ; to take apart, repair and construct apparatus — electrical and mechanical. Technical skill in the applied sciences.

3. Leading and Governing Ability : the ability to lead and direct others in an effective way. To act promptly and decisively, and to influence, persuade and inspire others to do likewise. To take responsibility in emergencies. To construct a plan and systematize co-operative endeavours.
4. Social Ability : the ability to make friends easily, to 'get on' with people, to be liked and trusted. The expression of good-feeling and tact. A gift for loyal and enduring friendships.
5. Economic Ability : the ability to make money, to understand economic problems and make the most of financial opportunities. A 'good head for business' ; to buy and sell at profit. To barter, make deals and gamble successfully.
6. Erotic Ability : the ability to please, excite and attract the opposite sex ; to flirt or court successfully ; to love and to be loved passionately.
7. Attracting and Entertaining Ability : the ability to express oneself in the presence of others ; to amuse, entertain or excite people ; to talk fluently, to tell a good story, to hold attention, to act or perform in public.
8. Observational Ability : the ability to perceive events correctly and remember them accurately ; to be objective and reliable in recording facts ; to recall definitely what one has seen and read ; to remember names and faces.
9. General Intellectual Ability : the ability to comprehend, remember and 'handle' general ideas ; to extract the intellectual content of a book and discourse about it intelligently. The capacity for learning and scholarship.
10. Scientific Understanding : the ability to comprehend and handle scientific ideas ; to understand natural phenomena — physical and chemical processes ; to think in terms of abstract theories, scientific concepts and mathematical laws.
11. Psychological Understanding : the ability to feel the feelings of other people, to understand them — their attitudes and motives ; to have correct intuitions and express accurate judgements about them ; to analyse them and explain their behaviour.
12. Artistic Contemplation and Judgement : the ability to feel with delight the sensuous qualities of objects ; to be sensitively attentive to

impressions — sights, sounds, tastes and odours ; to discriminate values in art, literature or music ; to appreciate the beautiful.

13. Art-Creative Ability : the ability to create artistically ; to give successful expression to feeling and imagination ; to write poetry, short stories or musical compositions ; to model or paint.
14. Theory-Creative Ability : the ability to construct explanatory concepts in science ; to make up plausible theories in philosophy or in the humanities ; to build a rational system of coherent principles ; to devise good hypotheses.
15. Moral and Spiritual Understanding : the ability to apperceive spiritual values ; to appreciate moral integrity and virtue ; to have visions of the ideal and be influenced by them in guiding one's life ; to have intuitions in regard to one's inner development.

Results. In general, the interviews yielded a satisfactory picture of the Ss' abilities, together with considerable information about their ambitions, anxieties, and current dilemmas. The technique, especially with Group III, proved highly advantageous in disclosing each S's attitude toward himself, his tendency to wishful thinking, and the nature and strength of his Ego Ideal. Zill, for example, while working alone in the library marked himself above average on Art-Creative Ability ; when asked to support this rating he confessed that he had absolutely no such ability, but was influenced by an overwhelming desire to create. In another instance, that of Given, the wish intruded itself in a somewhat different way. This S marked himself low on Mechanical Ability, but in the discussion, which showed him to be fairly skilled in manipulating certain kinds of machinery, it appeared that he wanted to think of himself as a subjective person and was thus rejecting his mechanical attainments. Several Ss at first marked themselves low because they compared themselves with men who excel in the different abilities, or thought of particular incidents in which they had failed. Thus one S, remembering a disastrous financial experience which had caused him humiliation, marked himself low on Economic Ability, but it came out in discussion that he had often bought and sold with profit. The opposite type of distortion, the selective recall of successes, was also encountered in several cases, though here the E, depending upon the S's willingness or ability to recollect his failures, found it less easy to estimate the amount of error.

The Ss themselves were often able to discriminate between what they regarded as 'innate' abilities and those developed by effort. Zeeno, for example, considered business to be his natural ability. At an early age he showed a tendency to take economic responsibility, earning money in various ways and presently managing a shop for the summer. Later this interest was stimulated by managing an apartment house, which gave him an agreeable opportunity to direct people. He thus gained a reputation for 'being a wizard at making a good bargain and at managing financial affairs successfully.' Similarly, Vulner reported an early facility with pencil, pen and charcoal, and declared, 'I could easily become an artist, for drawing is as easy for me as breathing.' On the other hand, Oriol frankly recognized the counteractive nature of his attempts to succeed in track. As a child he was physically inferior to his playmates, and could not run fast enough to escape them. His present running, he said, 'sort of vindicates me ; now I can get away from anyone.' Sometimes an S reported an interest without the ability necessary to satisfy it. Such was the case with Umber, who said in regard to acting, 'I'm crazy about it ; I know I'm not good but I keep trying, and the deuce of it is that I am always shifted to scenery. . . I am terribly nervous about public speaking and sudden attention.'

Correlations. Four rank orders were calculated for purposes of correlation.

1. *Average Rating on Abilities, S's Estimate.* This rank order was made for both Group III and Group IV, but owing to a slight change in the rating scale the correlations are given separately. High coefficients were found in both groups with the following variables :

	Group III.	*Group IV*
n Achievement	+.65	+.68
n Dominance	+.70	+.80
n Exhibition	+.69	+.54
Ego Ideal	+.65	+.51

The meaning of these relationships is not at once obvious. It is possible that the variables in question are truly associated with general ability, but it is also not unlikely that they are connected with a tendency to overestimate one's self. Thus the n Exhibition might be correlated with superior talents, but on the other hand it might merely make the S represent himself as possessing such talents; while an S who stands high on the n Dominance might err by thinking of himself wholly in comparison with those he is accustomed to dominate. A tentative solution of this difficulty is indicated by results obtained with the second and third rank orders.

2. *Average Rating on Abilities, E's Estimate.* The E's estimate of abilities, based on the instances proffered by Ss in support of their ratings, probably comes nearer than anything else to an objective evaluation. The following coefficients were found with the variables just discussed: n Achievement, +.44; n Dominance, +.48; n Exhibition, +.04; Ego Ideal, +.27. Group IV was not included in this rank order, and the results, derived from only thirteen Ss, must be regarded as highly tentative. They suggest, however, the very plausible hypothesis that the n Achievement and the n Dominance are to some extent truly associated with superior abilities, while the n Exhibition gets into the first rank order purely because it leads to overestimation.

3. *Tendency to Overestimation: S's Estimate minus E's.* The correlations obtained with this index are in accordance with the hypothesis just advanced: n Achievement, +.33; n Dominance, +.36; n Exhibition, +.58; Ego Ideal, +.40. Again the results are for Group III only.

4. *Ratio of Exopsychic to Endopsychic Abilities.* In forming this ratio the S's and E's estimates were averaged. The rank order for Group C was found to correlate, as would be expected, with Exocathection (+.52) and negatively with Intraception (—.55). The following correlations were obtained with measures of a similar nature made at different sessions: ratio of exopsychic to endopsychic values in the Vernon-Allport Study of Values, +.72; ratio of personal to impersonal sources of stories in the Thematic

Apperception Test, —.60 ; ratio of exopsychic to endopsychic interests as estimated by the Diagnostic Council at the Conference, +.47.

Summary. The test served its primary purpose, a general survey of abilities, in a satisfactory manner. It also yielded valuable information in regard to the S's interests and ambitions, his objectivity, and the nature of his Ego Ideal. The session afforded an excellent opportunity for rating on the personality variables : Ss were required to volunteer information, be cross-examined and perhaps criticized, justify or retract statements, and discuss a wide range of intimate personal matters, all of which tested their conjunctivity and self-possession with no little rigour.

Intended primarily as an inventory, the test was not expected to throw clear light upon the vexed question of relationship between ability and interest, or upon the relative weight of endowment, environment, and early training in the history of present abilities. By keeping these questions in mind, however, considerable relevant material was gathered, and the method would seem to lend itself to such an investigation, especially if more time and emphasis were put upon the childhood history of interests and abilities and their continuity with contemporary ones. Evidence was found in the correlations for a relationship between abilities and the needs for Achievement and Dominance. The nature of this relationship, the possible priority of abilities or of needs, sets a problem which only further investigation can elucidate.

10. AESTHETIC APPRECIATION TEST

KENNETH DIVEN

Purpose. There were two general purposes involved in this test :

1. To obtain a rank order of Ss for insight and skill in the criticism of aesthetic material, which reflects three (perhaps more) somewhat different kinds of personal resources : (a) judgements of aesthetic excellence based upon technical knowledge of the medium ; (b) personal appreciation of, or satisfaction with, the material in regard to its form and content ; (c) taste,

a less palpable compound of technical knowledge, personal satisfaction, and probably additional factors.

2. To uncover attitudes held by the Ss toward aspects of the material which would help in diagnosing, corroborating or illustrating dynamic trends in their mental economy.

Procedure. Each S was shown successively ten poems and ten small reproductions of paintings and was asked to judge them on the basis of 'aesthetic merit.' The instructions were given conversationally, with as much informality as was felt consonant with serious application to the task, emphasizing a 'set' away from stereotyped replies and toward a personal reaction to the material. The standard preliminary explanation informed the S that the E was interested in 'some of the psychological aspects of aesthetic criticism,' not the technical canons of the critic and professional aesthetician; that what he wanted to get at was the immediate judgement and first impression a poem or picture brings to mind — the immediate valuation and the reasons for the feeling thus expressed. Ss were cautioned not to be deterred by the thought that they might acquit themselves better with more time to think it over, being informed they might have this opportunity later.

After the detailed criticism of the ten poems and pictures, the S was required to arrange them in what he considered their order of merit. As a basis for the first impression and detailed criticism, only one reading of the poem, at the S's own speed, had been allowed; but when he came to rank the poems in definite order a re-reading was permitted and encouraged. It was hoped that this device would throw into relief certain discrepancies between what he 'said' about a poem or picture and how it was finally valuated in relation to the others.

The test material was selected with two requirements in mind: (a) that it be diverse in quality, representing good, mediocre and poor art; and (b) that the content reflect as vivid and disparate sentiments as possible. This is, of course, a large order to fill with only ten poems and ten pictures; and whatever skewness there was in the material was toward themas and objects which because of their vividness seemed best calculated to evoke unequivocal opinions and attitudes in the Ss.

The poems used were (in order of their presentation) : Shelley, 'Political Greatness'; Thomas Hardy, 'To Life'; Teasdale, 'Barter'; Byron, 'And Dost Thou Ask the Reason of My Sadness ?'; Swinburne, 'Love and Sleep'; John Donne, Number Five from 'Holy Sonnets'; Keats, 'Sonnet' (to Fanny Brawne) ; Untermeyer, 'Infidelity'; Stephen Spender, 'My Parents Quarrel in the Neighbour Room'; Swinburne, a vampire theme taken from 'Chastelard.'

The pictures used were (in order of their presentation) : Arnold Wiltz, 'American Landscape'; Manet, 'Breakfast on the Grass'; P. V. Müller, 'Sacrificial Rock'; Mantegna, 'The Dead Christ'; Vermeer, 'Guitar Player'; Redon, 'Cain Killing Abel'; Eastman Johnson, 'Two Men'; anonymous, 'Mill on Fire'; Geoffrey, 'The Visit'; Redon, 'Painting.'

Results. The test was used only with the fifteen Ss of Group IV. All the Ss complied with the requirements, yielding bases for rating upon every point outlined above ; thus the primary aims of the test were fulfilled. Often the discrepancies between what an S 'said' about a poem or picture and his enhancement or depreciation of it, as reflected by where he placed it in his rank order of merit, were quite revealing.

In addition, there were numerous collateral findings, such as the turning up of objects, symbols and themas which were significant in the personality. Contrary to the practice with other sessions, no attempt was made to interpret results of this sort independently ; instead, the protocols were compared with the findings of other procedures, and a search made for congruent data. A few verbatim fragments from the protocols will illustrate, however inadequately, the kind and diversity of data obtained.

Poem 5 — Swinburne's 'Love and Sleep' — includes the following lines :

> 'I saw my love lean over my sad bed,
> . . . with bare throat made to bite,

. . . her face was honey to my mouth,
. . . her body pasture to mine eyes.'

Bulge, a young Catholic who has idealized his dead parents and whose sexual 'temptations' are always accompanied by the image of his 'sainted mother,' gave this key-note to his criticism: 'The sensuality detracts from the aesthetic . . . so offensive with its language . . . arouses me emotionally . . . the words "delight," "flanks," and "supple thighs" should be left out so as not to be so sensual.' Frost, who has a history of sexual conflict and is now a pedantic candidate for the doctorate in literature, consecrated to aggressive cultivation of 'the intellectual and aesthetic values' in himself and society at large, giggled several times while reading the poem and said, 'My dislike is of the *kind* of poetry it is. . . I would not re-read it.' In his final rank order of merit the poem was in second place.

Poem 7 — Keats' 'Sonnet' (to Fanny Brawne) — is on the following theme:

'I cry your mercy — pity — love!
. . . give me all.
Withhold no atom's atom or I die.'

This poem evoked an almost complete misconstruction from Bulge; 'Very good . . . a real unselfish love. . . I don't find this sensuous . . . it is the deep love of a husband for a wife . . . typical of ideal wedded bliss, my ideal . . . the party speaking has given all and wants all in return . . . love is more of soul than sensuality . . . fine, spiritual, unselfish.' Veal had this to say: 'There is a question of sincerity, it seems more said for the effect upon *her*, thus gaining his own ends.'

Poem 9 — Spender's 'My Parents Quarrel in the Neighbour Room' — contains these lines:

'How can they sleep, who eat upon their fear
And watch their dreadful love fade . . .

I am your son, and from bad dreams arise.
My sight is fixed with horror, as I pass
Before the transitory glass
And watch the fungus cover up my eyes.'

Bulge said, 'It's really their own fault for keeping awake quarreling. If they would rise to a firmer, more spiritual plane this needn't happen. . . Too bad the parents aren't finer . . . not a good poem.' Frost, who had found grave technical errors and metrical impossibilities in Shelley,

Keats, Donne and the others, found this poem the most congenial of all, saying : '. . . I like this a great deal better than the others . . . best in every way . . . but the third stanza should be re-written.' Veal said : 'Don't like it ; the very first sentence leads you to expect elucidation, whereas the conversation is just a normal conversation . . . he hasn't brought out the fear or bad feeling between the parents . . . all exaggerated with no proof. . . He is just outside . . . the third unwanted person . . . that's the way it's done . . . anybody that is old enough to write a poem should know that.' Zora, a graduate student in literature with almost pathological interest in light and all visual experience, said : '. . . you just can't be contented to let " the fungus cover up " your eyes. You've got to see the beauty in the worm . . . after all, maggots do arrange themselves in patterns. . .'

Picture 2 — Manet's 'Breakfast on the Grass' — represents four figures in a grassy opening of deep forest. The men are fully dressed, the women nude ; one woman is posed in the immediate foreground with the men, the other at some distance in the background. Bulge said of this, 'The men don't seem in the least disturbed, do they ? . . . Maybe it is a very young girl . . . morally perverse of the painter . . . are these women's clothes in the corner ? . . . I wonder what that other girl is doing back there ? ' Frost, something of a Francophile, said, 'The woman in the foreground is the most perfect French woman imaginable . . . they are real people.' Veal said, 'Artists in the wood with the immortals. . . If it is not this, it is silly . . . the incongruous composure of the woman, while the men have a philosophical discussion. . .' Zora's complex was activated to this characteristic comment, 'There must be more radiance than you can see . . . the light must be arrestingly lovely in the original.'

Picture 1 — Wiltz's 'American Landscape' — is a stylized modern, showing petroleum tanks, railroad tracks, cars and semaphores on the bank of a murky, steel-trestled river ; almost lost in the background is a drab dwelling house. Zora said, 'Attractive light . . . but barren.' Frost, the young rationalist who wishes to emancipate society with intellectual and aesthetic release for the worker, and who gave a history of childhood terrors from the story of a train wreck in which the cars fell through a bridge into the river, said : '. . . looks extremely bad technically . . . the cars are going to topple into the river . . . the one effective thing is the way the little house is dwarfed by the industrial foreground. . .' He was the only S who made any comment about these two objects. Bulge said, 'A bad picture . . . it has no beauty . . . common and dull . . . not true to life . . . the bridge and towers, whatever they are, all seem very artificial and ugly.'

Picture 8 — 'Mill on Fire' by some unknown painter — is a gaudy chromo of a blazing mill in a deep wood. Veal put this picture first in his rank order, saying, 'Very good, there are so many details . . . at a moment's glance . . . excellent.' Frost, who in addition to his terrified preoccupation as a child with the story of the train disaster in the river bed, gave a history of having erotic dreams, at the present time, involving rivers and urination, said, 'Too obvious colour . . . the stream bed is fair. . . Ah ! how I would have loved this as a boy — right over my bed ! ' Again he was the only S to mention this minor detail of the composition.

Correlations. To obtain as much objectivity as possible in ranking Ss for 'critical ability' and 'good taste,' the poems and pictures were ranked for merit separately by a number of experts in the respective fields. Composite rank orders of merit were thus obtained for the ten poems and ten pictures which served as a standard. The rank orders of merit of the poems and pictures arranged by each S were then correlated with the standard rank orders, the resultant coefficients serving as an index of the Ss' 'critical ability' and establishing a uniform and objective basis for ranking them in this regard.

The rank orders of Ss for expertness in this test were compared with the other tests and the variables, and certain correlations were found. Since only fifteen Ss were tested, no great weight can be attached to the figures, but some of the relationships may be briefly indicated. Rank order for poems correlated +.52, and pictures +.64, with Aesthetic Value in the Vernon-Allport Study of Values Test ; with Economic Value the figures were —.43 and —.43. Positive correlations were found with three different measures of sentimentive intensity, calculated from the Predictions Test (+.55, +.33), the Sentiments Test (+.41, +.05), and the Sentiments Questionnaire (+.29, +.43). Ability with jig-saw puzzles, as measured in the Ethical Standards Test, was correlated negatively with expertness in aesthetic criticism (poems —.31, pictures —.52). Positive correlations were obtained with the n Rejection (+.71, +.45). Three further coefficients may be mentioned, Sentience (+.47, +.35), Exocathexis (—.57, —.62), and Intraception (+.43, +.37) ; but they may be partly spurious, since data from the Aesthetic Appreciation Test contributed to the final ratings on these latter variables.

A point of considerable interest was touched upon in the experiment, but unfortunately could not be followed through. An attempt was made by a second E to predict from the other data collected on the S the rank order he would make of the poems and pictures. For the three Ss with whom this was tried, the correlations between predicted rank orders and those actually made were : poems, +.85, +.86, +.61 ; pictures, +.82, +.82, +.84.

Summary. Although this session does not purport to be a general test for ability in aesthetic appreciation or criticism, it nevertheless permitted a rough ranking of Ss in this respect. It was particularly valuable in turning up symbols and themas having special importance for the S. The twofold purpose was thus satisfactorily achieved. More work could profitably be done in predicting systematically the order of merit in which Ss will place aesthetic material. It is felt also that if the simpler methods of this test were developed to include a wider range of material, spaced experimental sessions, and a more exhaustive search into the reasons for appreciations and depreciations, a good deal of light might be thrown upon dynamic aspects of the aesthetic experience.

11. HYPNOTIC TEST

R. W. White

Purpose. The test designed to measure susceptibility to hypnotic suggestion was given for a double purpose. In the first place, this characteristic may well be expected to stand in some kind of relationship to the personality as a whole, a relationship the investigation of which has hitherto been far from satisfactory. In the second place, the test brought the subject into a somewhat unusual situation, fraught with unknown possibilities. Favourable conditions were thus created for noting inviolacies and anxieties, and for sensing the subject's willingness to throw himself into an event which might involve, if he held the ordinary supposition about hypnosis, surrender of voluntary control to a comparative stranger.

Procedure. The hypnotist endeavoured to act the role of a friendly person who, though interested in hypnotism, did not regard it as in any way out of the ordinary. He laid great stress on the necessity of the subject's co-operating if good results were to be obtained, and hinted that the outcome rested as much with the subject as with the operator. The preliminary details, such as drawing the shades, he treated in an offhand manner, and for an eye-fixation object picked up a pencil or paper-cutter, as though the thing chosen made little difference. He was at pains to avoid any appearance of domination. In all hypnotic experiments the result is strongly coloured by the method : a more dramatic procedure might have led to a quite different outcome.

The experiment was conducted in three sessions. On the first day the subject was engaged in conversation for ten minutes or more before the nature of the test was announced point-blank. After suitable instructions and remarks, designed to allay anxiety and invite co-operation, he was asked to lie down on the couch. Relaxation, drowsiness, and sleep were then suggested in a voice which gradually became subdued and monotonous ; this was continued for about five minutes, accompanied by occasional light stroking of the arms. When the subject appeared thoroughly relaxed and his eyes were closed, the following suggestions, previously used at the Clinic for scoring depth of hypnosis,[1] were given :

(i) You cannot open your eyes ; (ii) you cannot raise your arm from the couch ; (and after straightening the subject's arm in a vertical position) (iii) you cannot bend your arm ; (and after interlocking the fingers of both hands) (iv) you cannot separate your fingers ; and finally,

1. Barry,H., MacKinnon,D.W., and Murray,H.A. 'Hypnotizability as a personality trait and its typological relations.' *Human Biology*,1931,III, pp.9–10.

(v) you cannot speak your name. Before waking the subject, amnesia was suggested.

0 = No suggestions carried out. No tendency at all for them to be carried out.

1 = No suggestions carried out, but clear evidence of a difficulty or hesitancy in surmounting them.

1.5 = One suggestion carried out.

2 = Two or three suggestions carried out.

2.5 = Four suggestions carried out.

3 = All suggestions carried out.

Amnesia

0 = No loss of memory and no difficulty in recall.

0.5 = Difficulty in recall, cloudiness, but final memory.

1 = Partial loss of memory.

2 = Complete or almost complete loss of memory.

As a measure of hypnotizability (Hypnotic Index), the ratings for suggestibility and amnesia were added together for each subject. Consequently, the hypnotic index might vary from 0 (no hypnotizability) to 5 (complete hypnotizability).

After the subject had been awakened, he was questioned in such a way as to test the degree of amnesia, and if not amnestic was urged to give a full introspective report. This subsequent discussion was extended as long as possible after the second day's test, which otherwise was simply a repetition of the original session.

The third day, a fortnight or so later than the two test trials, the subject went to a different room for an interview with a different experimenter (Mrs. Jones). The object of this session was to secure a fuller and more candid introspective report which in the absence of the hypnotist might include the subject's feelings toward him, a vital aspect of the hypnotic relationship. The true attitudes of a number who had appeared politely compliant, though unhypnotizable, came to light in this subsequent interview.

In order to learn something about the subject's notion of hypnotism before he knew or suspected that it would be tried on him, a picture representing an hypnotic session was placed in the Thematic Apperception experiment for Group IV. The resulting stories added appreciably to the gleanings of the subsequent interview. In many cases it was possible to foretell from the story the subject's behaviour in the hypnotic test. Nipp, for instance, saw in the picture a scientific experiment, and said, 'It won't be a success because the youth has too much will and can't be overcome by the hypnotic spell.' He himself was not overcome in either trial. Kast, on the other hand, described a therapeutic scene, and said of the patient, 'He has complete faith in the hypnotist and is entirely under his control. The man will accept what is shown to him by the hypnotist and will believe. It will help him.' Kast scored above the average in the hypnotic test. In the case of Bulge, the hypnotic performance repeated with literal fidelity the story which the picture evoked, though four months had elapsed between them. 'The man on the couch,' ran Bulge's story, 'didn't believe in hypnotism. A friend who has this power wanted to show him. The friend put him to sleep. The experience was unique. He was convinced of his friend's power. He decides to read up about it and learn all he can about it, realizing the wonders of this field. He enjoyed the experience so much that he was grateful to his friend.' In the hypnotic test, Bulge was put to sleep by the hypnotist, and found the experience unique and enjoyable. 'The experiment impressed me,' he told the second interviewer, 'it is the most happy memory of any of my experiments;' and he went on to describe the comfort, the restfulness, the 'deliciously lazy' feeling. Like the pictured subject, he was convinced of the hypnotist's power. 'I was just waiting to hear his voice — whatever he told me to do, I would have done it. I suppose if he had told me to jump in the river I would have done it.' In addition, he copied the eager curiosity of the imagined subject, questioned the hypnotist closely on the wonders of the field, and expressed his wish to read about it at the earliest opportunity.

The correspondence was, of course, not always so remarkable, yet in only one case were the actual performance and the one in the story completely divergent. On the strength of the Conference, Autobiography and Childhood memories, the Diagnostic Council predicted the hypnotic scores for Group IV, and secured a correlation of +.50 with the actual indices. The hypnotist, using in addition the responses to the picture when making his prediction, obtained a correlation of +.70.

Results. The hypnotic indices covered the whole range of possible scores ; unquestionable amnesia was found in ten cases out of twenty-eight. With one exception, the subjects were personally unfamiliar with hypnotism, though most of them had seen or heard of it. Their attitudes ranged from skeptical to curious and, in a few cases, positively eager. Some who were not hypnotized could scarcely conceal their pleasure at this outcome, but others apologized ; Vale, for example, took his first unsuccessful performance to heart, and returned a week later to achieve with great determination an hypnotic score of 3.0. In a number of cases anxiety was visibly uppermost ; there were signs, as well as reports, of nervous tension, accelerated heart-beat and unnatural breathing.

Three subjects, all strictly unhypnotizable, did not like the informal way the hypnotist performed his task. They would have preferred mystery and magic, an exotic atmosphere. It may be imagined that the theme of power has special significance, fascinates the subject, and is cheapened when an ordinary citizen aspires to a role proper for not less than turbaned Orientals.

Among the more hypnotizable, it was possible to distinguish two types of trance. Some gave the impression of alert obedience ; suggestions were made to them and removed with equal ease, the responses, including the final waking, being prompt, and the signs of drowsiness slight. Others were almost from the start inert and sluggish. When told to make any movement voluntarily, for instance, to clasp their hands, they were scarcely able to stir, and at the close obeyed the suggestion to wake with obvious difficulty ; one, indeed, could not be completely awakened for nearly half an hour. Using as a criterion alert as contrasted with drowsy execution of voluntary movements, it was easy to place nearly all the more hypnotizable subjects in one or the other category, five in the alert-obedient, and five in the drowsy or sluggish group. The average hypnotic index of the former was 3.9, of the latter, 3.5.

Correlations. For purposes of correlation, the subjects of Groups III and IV, twenty-eight in all, were united in a single rank order of hypnotizability. Hypnosis plainly requires on the part of the subject a willingness to sacrifice, at least for the time being, his autonomy, and a somewhat deferent attitude toward the hypnotist. It is therefore not surprising to find significant correlations with the n Deference (+.43) and the n Autonomy (—.44), the two needs directly activated in the hypnotic situation. Subsequent reports of subjects who resisted the hypnotist's suggestions show how the experiment is affected when these needs are working against rather than for it. Deference was clearly not aroused in Umber, who observed to the second interviewer, 'When he said I couldn't raise my arm, I said to myself, "Well, watch me"'; nor can much rapport be inferred from Valet's statement, 'I couldn't help thinking how much of an ass he must feel, droning along, saying those stupid things.' Mauve, on the other hand, saw his autonomy in danger of outrage. 'My arm was in an unnatural position,' he protested, 'it really *was* heavy, not because he said so.' Zeeno was put off by the experimenter's confident, though unreasonable, assertions—'Of course, every time he said I couldn't, it was a natural challenge'—and it was this, to his mind, which spoiled what would otherwise have been an excellent autonomous performance. 'I was trying to sleep,' he told the hypnotist, 'your talking woke me up again.'

These two directly activated needs, despite their importance, cannot be regarded as the sole determinants of hypnotizability. Since a low n Deference and a high n Autonomy manifest themselves in quite unmistakable objective signs, especially when the subsequent interview is employed, it is possible to drop from the rank order those subjects who may be termed resistant. In this way a new group of sixteen can be formed, relatively free from resistance, yet covering the whole range of hypnotic scores. The correlation between n Deference and hypnotic index thereupon falls to +.24; that for the n Autonomy becomes —.32, both figures being of doubtful reliability. On the contrary, the other related variables, to be discussed directly, all rise to higher coefficients with the smaller group. Thus, by reducing the factor of essential unwillingness to be hypnotized, the determinants of hypnotizability in those for whom the experiment was not repugnant are thrown into bolder relief.

These further determinants are represented by the following four correlations : n Succorance, +.42, rising to +.46 for the group of sixteen ; n Abasement, +.44, rising to +.60 ; Anxiety, +.35, rising to +.41 ; and, lastly, Superego Integration, —.43, changing to —.48. On the surface, these relationships are far from intelligible. Experimental hypnosis awakens no expectation of p Nurturance, calls for co-operation rather than a true Abasement, would seem to be destroyed rather than abetted by anxiety, and has nothing directly to do with the Superego. This justifies a search for underlying factors which might be common to the several variables. Succorance, Abasement, and Anxiety show a very high inter-correlation. They form a syndrome of which the unifying feature seems to be Passivity, which is a mode of both Succorance and Abasement. It is reasonable to suppose that the subjects who stand high in this syndrome are those whom Activity, with the dangers it invites, makes tense and anxious, while Passivity, offering an escape from this unpleasantness, has a positive attraction. The hypnotic state, in which responsibility for action is transferred to the experimenter, can hardly fail to be alluring. This interpretation is further substantiated by the fact that the five subjects of the drowsy or sluggish group, those who appeared maximally passive, had without exception extremely high ratings on all three variables.

The negative correlation obtained with Superego Integration permits of being interpreted along similar lines. It is not so much the thing accomplished by the activity, as the mere fact of activity itself which establishes the negative relation. This way of viewing it is borne out by other correlations, not in themselves statistically significant, with variables whose mode is activity, though the things accomplished thereby are quite diverse. The n Counteraction shows a correlation of —.20, which becomes —.35 with the resistance-free group of sixteen ; the n Order is —.15, changing to —.34 ; and Conjunctivity, the variable which expresses some of the results of intrapsychic integrative activity, is —.30, changing to —.36. These three variables, together with Superego Integration, in a sense stand for the reverse of Passivity ; they show fairly high intercorrelations, and as a group yield the coefficient —.57 when compared with the passive syndrome.

These discoveries suggest as a tentative conclusion that the attraction of Passivity is of central importance in determining the outcome of an hypnotic experiment with those subjects who are not fundamentally unwilling. A closer scrutiny of the more hypnotizable subjects shows, however, that this is a half-truth, and explains why the correlations are no higher. Those individuals who comprise the drowsy or sluggish group, as described above, are indeed maximal in the variables which indicate Passivity. With the alert-obedient group, equally hypnotizable, the situation is different. These subjects stand near the average on Passivity, but distinguish themselves by uniformly high ratings on the n Deference and low ones on the n Autonomy ; they are, moreover, bunched at the top in respect to the n Affiliation. It is evident that the hypnotic trance can be entered on the strength of two quite different motives. It can be achieved because the subject is so deferent, so eager to fall in with and please the hypnotist, in which case the trance is of the alert type, or it can be attained for itself as a state of welcome Passivity, in which case it is of the sluggish or drowsy type. There are, it would seem, two distinct kinds of people who can be hypnotized under such circumstances as ours. This clearly indicated distinction may turn out to be not without value for the theory of hypnosis.[1]

Summary. The hypnotic test proves serviceable in discerning the

1. *Cf.* White, R.W., 'Two types of hypnotic trance and their personality correlates.' *J. Psychol.*, 1937, *3*, 279–289.

strength of the n Deference and the n Autonomy. It sometimes brings out indications of the n Dominance and latent omnipotence fantasies ; at other times, the anxiety which it evokes is a valuable clue. Its most striking function is exercised in those cases where it illumines a fundamental Passivity in the subject's relation to his surrounding press.

12. LEVEL OF ASPIRATION TEST

JEROME D. FRANK

Purpose. The purpose of the present study was to undertake a preliminary investigation of individual differences in the behaviour of aspiration as a function of achievement.

To make the above statement meaningful it will be necessary briefly to discuss the work of F. Hoppe,[1] on which this study is based. Hoppe calls the concept which he is primarily investigating the *level of aspiration* ('Anspruchsniveau'), and defines it as 'a person's expectations, goals, or claims on his own future achievement' in a given task.[2] So essential to the concept is its relation to success and failure, that this may well be included as part of the definition : 'The experience of a performance as a success or failure does not depend alone on its objective goodness, but on whether the level of aspiration appears to be reached or not reached.'[3] That is, a given performance is accompanied by a feeling of failure if it falls below the level of aspiration and by a feeling of success if it reaches or exceeds the level of aspiration. Hoppe seizes upon this as his main criterion of the height of the level of aspiration. The height of the level of aspiration is given primarily by the level of performance at which a success or failure experience occurs. A success experience indicates that the level of aspiration was lower than (or precisely the same height as)

1. Hoppe,F., 'Erfolg und Misserfolg.' *Psych. Forsch.*,1930,14, 1–62. The work of Hoppe is somewhat foreshadowed in T.Dembo. 'Der Aerger als dynamisches Problem.' *Psych. Forsch.*,1931,15, 50–56. (This study was completed before Hoppe's, though published after it.)
2. Hoppe,F., *op. cit.*, 10.
3. Ibid., 11.

the level of performance. The occurrence of a failure experience indicates that the level of aspiration was higher than the level of performance.

Hoppe's chief experiment consisted in giving the Ss a wide variety of simple tasks in a free situation, and studying the behaviour of the level of aspiration by means of the criterion mentioned above, as well as a few supplementary ones. The outstanding result of this experiment was that the level of aspiration tends typically to rise after a level of performance which has exceeded it ('a success'), and to fall after a level of performance which has failed to reach it ('a failure'). Of the many secondary results, only those concerning individual differences need concern us here. These are confined chiefly to a listing of those types of behaviour of the level of aspiration which, Hoppe feels, best indicate individual differences. Thanks to the remarkable properties of the German language, Hoppe gets them all into one sentence:

> The individual differences are related to the relative height of the level of aspiration; to the strength of the tendency to raise the level of aspiration after successes or to lower it after failures; to the tendency to make big or little steps in one direction or the other; to the strength of the tendency to break off entirely after failure rather than to lower the level of aspiration gradually; finally to the degree of effort to console oneself or to conceal the unpleasant realities through other methods. . . It is thus a question of differences that may be termed those of *ambition*, of *caution*, of *courage*, of *self-confidence*, of *fear of inferiority*, but also of the *security of self-confidence*, of the *courage to face reality*.[1]

Unfortunately, except for discussing a few individual cases in detail, this is as far as he goes.

Hoppe advances a theory to account for his results which, as it is the basis for the speculations to be found in this article, must also be briefly reviewed. In order to explain the behaviour of the level of aspiration, he introduces a new concept — the *ego-level* ('Ichniveau').[2] This concept is not rigorously defined, the fol-

1. Hoppe, F., 'Erfolg und Misserfolg.' *Psych. Forsch.*, 1930, 14, 38.
2. After much hesitation it was decided to use the literal translation 'ego-level' in preference to 'self-esteem,' 'pride,' 'self-confidence' and other terms which more or less approximate Hoppe's meaning. These terms were abandoned

lowing sentence being the nearest approach to a definition: '(The ego-level represents) the wide-embracing goals of the individual . . . which extend far beyond the single task . . . (and) . . . are related to the self-confidence ("Selbstbewusstsein") of the S.'[1] From this it seems that the levels of aspiration in different tasks are in a sense parts of the ego-level, or are, at least, closely related to it. The fundamental property of the ego-level is that it tends to be held high at all costs. In so far as the single levels of aspiration are related to the ego-level, they too tend to be kept high. On hedonistic principles, Hoppe makes the further assumption that the individual desires to have as many successes (pleasant experiences) and as few failures (unpleasant experiences) as possible. Since successes are produced by levels of performance which exceed the level of aspiration, there is a tendency to keep the level of aspiration low. As this is incompatible with the tendency to hold the level of aspiration high, springing from its relation to the ego-level, a conflict necessarily results. The behaviour of the level of aspiration represents the resultant of this conflict arising from the desire to keep the ego-level high on the one hand, and the desire to have as many successes as possible on the other.

The present experiment springs directly from Hoppe's study, and is an attempt to continue the investigation of individual differences in the behaviour of the level of aspiration where he left off.

Procedure. The procedure used embodies the same general technique as Hoppe's but contains several refinements with a view to yielding results which are more objective and more easily quantified. In order to measure the level of aspiration, S was given a task involving repetitions of a simple standardized performance — the printing of words standardized as to difficulty with a hand printing set. The 'goodness' of each performance was given by the number of seconds required to complete it, — the fewer the number of seconds the better the performance. After each trial

---

because they all drag connotations from everyday speech after them which tend to produce confusion of thought.

1. Ibid., 32.

S was told how many seconds he had required to complete the printing, and was then asked to state the number of seconds in which he intended to complete the next trial. This statement of S concerning the 'goodness' of his own future performance was taken to represent his level of aspiration. In this way the level of aspiration and level of performance were measured in terms of the same units.

In the experiment E sat across the table from S and timed him ostentatiously with a stop-watch. At the start E briefly explained the nature of the task to S who was then allowed a preliminary trial. At the completion of the trial he was told how many seconds he had required, and was then asked to state the number of seconds he thought he would require on the next trial. This procedure was repeated twenty-five times, with a short pause after the tenth and twentieth repetitions. Throughout the experiment, S was required to state his level of aspiration before seeing the words to be printed. As soon as he had stated his level of aspiration, he was given the card with the words on it, and allowed to study it as long as he wished, before starting to print.

With the Ss of Group I a more complex procedure was used. There were two tasks — the printing one described above, and sections of the Kelley Manipulation of Spatial Relationships Speed Test.[1] The procedure in the printing task was identical with that described above. Only those changes in procedure were made for the Kelley task which were necessitated by its different properties. There were two experimental sessions a week apart, in each of which there were fifteen repetitions of both tasks. The behaviour of the level of aspiration was so similar in the two tasks and sessions as to allow the elimination of the Kelley test in the later Groups : II, III, IV.[2]

The question at once arises as to whether the level of aspiration as obtained in this way is the same as the level of aspiration as defined by Hoppe. Rather than engaging in needless discussion

1. Kelley, T.L. *Crossroads in the Mind of Man*, Stanford, Cal., 1928, 171f, 184f.

2. For the correlations between the different tasks and sessions, *cf.* Frank, J.D., 'Individual differences in the level of aspiration.' *Amer. J. Psychol.*, 1935, 47, 119–128.

on this point, the present writer prefers simply to re-define the level of aspiration as that statement of S concerning his own future performance which is attained by the above technique. He does this with a clear conscience in the conviction that the concept remains essentially the same as that used by Hoppe. For the purposes of this investigation, then, the level of aspiration is *the level of performance in a familiar task which an individual explicitly undertakes to reach.*

It should be pointed out that the technique above described is superior to that used by Hoppe in two important respects. In the first place, the determination of the height of the level of aspiration is strictly objective. It is given by S's explicit statement rather than by such nebulous things (from E's viewpoint) as success and failure experiences. In the second place, this technique allows a quantitative statement of the height of the level of aspiration in terms of the same units as that of the level of performance. This makes possible the quantitative comparison of the heights of the level of aspiration and of the level of performance at any time.

Results. The data obtained were evaluated in terms of two measures—the average difference between the level of aspiration and the level of performance, and the rigidity of the level of aspiration. These measures do not show a consistent correlation (—.17 in Group III and +.49 in Group IV) and as they seem to represent somewhat different aspects of the personality, revealed in the differences of the personality variables with which they correlate, it seems justifiable to include them both.

In the calculation of both measures the first five trials were omitted in order to assure that the results obtained are based on S's behaviour only after he is familiar with the task.

The average difference between the level of aspiration and level of performance was obtained by subtracting the average level of performance on trials 5 to 24 from the average level of aspiration on trials 6 to 25 (the level of aspiration on each trial being based on the preceding performance). Thus the more positive the difference obtained, the higher was the average level of aspiration with regard to the average level of performance. This measure gave correlations of greater than +.20 in both groups with the following personality variables (listed in order of the average height of the correlation in the two groups) : Narcism, Aggression, Emotionality, Intraception, Ego Ideal, Dominance, Creativity, Sentience, Projectivity, and Intensity.

It may be noted in passing that this measure allows a quantitative expression of certain forms of behaviour of the level of aspiration mentioned by Hoppe as revealing individual differences (*vide* p. 462). It is a direct measure of the relative height of the level of aspiration. In addition, it is related to the readiness with which the level of aspiration is shifted after success or after failure, and to the tendency to shift it more markedly in one direction than in the other. Thus, a preponderance of failures, and greater shifts of the level of aspiration up than down, will be revealed in an average level of aspiration higher than the average level of performance. Conversely, in so far as successes predominate, and the downward shifts of the level of aspiration are greater than the upward shifts, the average level of aspiration will be lower than the average level of performance.

As a measure of the rigidity of the level of aspiration, was taken simply the number of trials in which the level of aspiration remained at the same height as on the previous trial. Thus, the larger the score, the more rigid the level of aspiration. This measure yielded positive correlations of +.20 or better in both groups with the following variables (listed as before in order of the average height of the correlation) : Counteraction, Impulsion, and Endurance. It yielded negative correlations of —.20 or better in both groups with Succorance and Harmavoidance.

Discussion. The average difference between level of aspiration and level of performance and the rigidity of the level of aspiration will be considered separately, as different attributes of the personality seem to underlie them.

The average difference between level of aspiration and level of performance seems to depend primarily on the interplay of the following three factors : (1) the desire to make the level of aspiration approximate the level of performance as closely as possible ; (2) the desire to keep the level of aspiration high in relation to the level of performance ; and (3) the desire to avoid failure, that is, a level of performance below the level of aspiration.[1] The desire to make the level of aspiration approximate the level of performance tends to make the average difference approximate zero. The desire to keep the level of aspiration high, in so far as it operates, tends to make the average difference positive ; while the desire to avoid failure tends to drive the level of aspiration below the level of performance, yielding a negative average difference.

The first desire presumably is based primarily on the all-pervasive tendency to keep one's estimate concerning one's ability in close relation to its actual height, which is simply a manifestation of the desire to keep in touch with reality, normally present in everyone.

Hence, unless disturbing factors are operating, the average level of aspiration may be expected not to differ appreciably from the average level of performance. In these cases, S's level of aspiration does not represent, strictly speaking, his aspiration at all, but is simply an intellectual estimate of the goodness of his future performance on the basis of past performance. We may say that S's estimate of the goodness of his future performance represents his aspiration, to a greater or less degree, only when his self-regard — or, to use Hoppe's term, his *ego-level* — is involved in the goodness of his performance, in that he regards it in some way as a measure of his own worth. This involvement of the ego-level in the task is responsible for the occurrence of experiences of success and failure, and to it may be traced both the desire to avoid failure and the desire to keep the level of aspiration high. According to Hoppe, the desire to avoid failure arises primarily from the desire to enjoy the pleasure of success and to avoid the unpleasantness of failure. In the present writer's opinion, a more significant factor in these experiments is the fear

1. *Cf.* Frank, J.D. 'Some psychological determinants of the level of aspiration.' *Amer. J. Psychol.*, 1935, 47, 285–293.

of the ridicule and embarrassment to which one is exposed when he publicly over-estimates his own ability. Since such ridicule is clearly a threat to the height of the ego-level, according to this view, fear of failure may be traced indirectly to the desire to keep the ego-level high. As the fear of failure did not predominate in any of the Ss used in these experiments, it will be ignored in the further discussion.

The involvement of the ego-level in the task will cause the level of aspiration to differ positively from the level of performance only when (1) it is involved mainly in the desire to do well, and (2) S is sufficiently subjective to allow this wish to influence his estimates.

With one or two Ss in these experiments the ego-level was involved primarily in the desire to guess the next performance as closely as possible. For such Ss a failure was represented not by a performance below the level of aspiration, but by a performance deviating markedly from it in either direction. With these Ss, as might be expected, despite marked involvement of the ego-level, the average level of aspiration did not differ significantly from the average level of performance.[1]

In order for the level of aspiration to differ markedly from the level of performance, the ego-level must be expressed by the *wish* to do well, since without it there is no incentive to keep the level of aspiration high. The wish to do well is often not accompanied by a *will* to do well, i.e., S may be largely satisfied with fantasy that he will do well the next time without ever seriously trying to give it reality. The presence of a strong *will* to do well may actually decrease the difference between the level of aspiration and level of performance, since it not only tends to raise the level

1. A negligible average difference between the level of aspiration and the level of performance might also conceivably be produced by an equilibrium between the desire to keep the level of aspiration high, and the desire to avoid failure. Both these cases can easily be distinguished from those in which lack of difference between level of aspiration and level of performance is due to the absence of ego-level involvement, by the presence of other criteria. Of these, the most significant are the occurrence of real experiences of success and failure (both of which are absent when the ego-level is not involved), and the appearance of emotionality.

of performance, thus bringing it closer to the level of aspiration, but implies a more objective attitude.

Finally, in order for the ego-level to find expression in the level of aspiration, S must also show a lack of Objectivity, allowing his judgement to be coloured by his wishes or fears. If S succeeds in preserving an objective attitude, his level of aspiration will remain an objective estimate of the goodness of his future performance on the basis of his past performance, and hence will remain close to the level of performance despite the desire to do well. Closely related to the factor of Projectivity is the ease with which S is able to disregard his failures or blame them on some external cause. The greater the ease with which S can dismiss his failures, the more easily can he keep his level of aspiration high despite them.

In short, the main factors causing the average level of aspiration to deviate positively from the average level of performance are the wish to do well (often unaccompanied by the will to do well), a subjective attitude, and the ability to dismiss failures.

In the light of these considerations, it is not surprising that the average difference between level of aspiration and level of performance correlates most highly with those personality variables in which one or more of these factors plays a significant role. Since each personality variable involves factors in addition to those here singled out, correlations of unity are not to be expected.

Thus, the average difference between level of aspiration and level of performance correlates primarily with those variables in which subjectivity (Intraception, Projectivity) plays a significant role. These correlations are lowered by the fact that some subjective Ss may not want to do well, in which case they have no incentive to over-estimate, or they may be dominated by pessimistic rather than optimistic feelings which would cause them to set their level of aspiration too low rather than too high. Positive correlations in both groups were obtained with Narcism, characterized by exaggerated occupation with self ; Projectivity with its tendency to misinterpret the outer world in accordance with one's own wishes; Intraception, implying domination by inner feeling rather than outer fact; Creativity, indicating an active fantasy and inner life; and Emotionality, involving subjectively coloured reactions to environmental influences.

Similarly, the ability to minimize failure, by whatever means, is possessed by the narcistic individual who must ignore failure to protect his Narcism; the projective person, whose wishful thinking is relatively undisturbed by hard reality; the dominating individual whose confidence is unshaken by failure; and the aggressive individual who regularly tends to blame the outside world rather than himself.

The wish to do well is again characteristic of the narcistic individual for whom a good performance is an additional reason for loving himself but who is often sufficiently satisfied with the fantasy of such a performance. It tends to be coupled with the will to do well in the individual with a well-developed Ego Ideal, since doing well helps him to live up to it; and in the dominating personality, which usually possesses an admixture of ambition.

To summarize, of the variables which yield a correlation of greater than +.20 in both groups with the average difference between level of aspiration and level of performance, Narcism involves subjectivity, the ability to minimize failures, and the wish to do well; Aggression, the ability to reject failures; Emotionality, subjectivity; Intraception, subjectivity; Ego Ideal, the wish and will to do well; Dominance, ability to minimize failures and the wish and will to do well; Creativity, subjectivity; and Projectivity, subjectivity coupled with the ability to minimize failures. Only Intensity and Sentience do not appear to involve one or more of the factors presumably mainly responsible for a difference between average level of aspiration and average level of performance.

That the set of variables with which this measure correlates consists for the most part not of a mere chance aggregation but of a few definite patterns, is shown by the fact that over half of these variables, and only they, may appear in a single syndrome. Thus, one syndrome contains Narcism, Ego Ideal, Projectivity, Creativity, Dominance and Intensity.[1] Another syndrome contains Intraception, Projection, Ego Ideal, Narcism, Creativity, Intensity, Emotionality, and no others. Looked at the other way, of the variables linked in this test Narcism and Projectivity occur together in no less than 15 syndromes; Narcism, Projectivity and Creativity occur in 12; these three with Ego Ideal occur in 7; and the above four with Intraception occur in 4.

It is more difficult to discern the factors which make for extreme rigidity or extreme lability of the level of aspiration, and here it is probably best to take our clues directly from the correlations obtained. Of the personality variables, rigidity correlates positively with Counteraction, Endurance and Impulsion. Of these, the common factor in Counteraction and Endurance seems to be *tenacity of purpose*, the refusal to yield an inch in the face of failure. This is clearly present in Counteraction, in which the characteristic response to failure is to set one's goal even more firmly and try even harder, and that it is a factor in Endurance is self-evident. The reason for the positive correlation with Impulsion is not clear. Conversely, rigidity tends to correlate negatively with Succorance and Harmavoidance, that is, Ss characterized by these variables tend to have very labile levels of aspiration. Both these variables imply a lack of stamina and a willingness to appeal for help, being thus in sharp contrast to Counteraction. With both of these variables the negative correlations are very low, indicating their very indirect relation to lability of the level of aspiration.

That these variables, too, are not merely a random aggregate but represent definite patterns is shown by the fact that Succorance is accompanied by Harmavoidance in 2 of the 3 syndromes in which it occurs, and Endurance and Counteraction occur together in 5 syndromes.

1. This syndrome contains only one additional variable, Exhibition, which gives a correlation of +.70 with our measure in Group III but none in Group IV. The presence of a correlation is to be expected in that Exhibition may involve the wish to do well as a means of showing off; its great variability is probably due to the frequent coupling of Exhibition with inferiority feelings which would tend to depress the level of aspiration.

13. THE EXPERIMENTAL STUDY OF REPRESSION

SAUL ROSENZWEIG

'I did that,' says my memory. 'I could not have done that,' says my pride, and remains inexorable. Eventually — the memory yields.

Nietzsche : *Beyond Good and Evil.*

I. *Introduction*

'The doctrine of repression,' says Freud,[1] 'is the foundation-stone on which the whole structure of psycho-analysis rests. . .' And elsewhere[2] he adds, 'It is possible to take repression as a centre and to bring all the elements of psycho-analytic theory into relation with it.' It was therefore natural that, when in 1930 the opportunity offered to subject analytic theory to laboratory study, the concept of repression suggested itself as a point of departure. A further and decisive inducement was the fact that certain aspects of this concept, in particular those relating to memory, seemed readily amenable to experimental procedures.

Accordingly, from 1930 to 1932 the writer was occupied almost exclusively with a series of experiments designed as a program for studying repression experimentally. A small fraction of the data thus obtained has been analysed and the results published, but the much larger part still awaits the necessary leisure. In this brief preliminary report an attempt will be made to summarize the results of the published work and to give some indication of what, at this writing, seems to be concealed in the as yet unpublished and, in some cases, only partially analysed data. The reader is asked to bear in mind the tentative character of most of the statements made here and is urged to view them as a basis for the hypothesis embracing hypnotizability, repression and frustration advanced toward the close of this paper.

The theory of repression is outlined by Freud[3] in an article contained in the fourth volume of his *Collected Papers*. Another

1. Freud,S. 'On the history of the psycho-analytic movement.' *Collected Papers.* New York,1924, Vol.I, p.297.
2. Freud,S. *Autobiography.* New York,1935, p.56.
3. Freud,S. *Collected Papers.* New York,1924, Vol.IV, pp.84–97.

theoretical discussion, written with a view to experimental investigation, has recently been published by Sears.[1] In the present context suffice it to say that repression is regarded by analysts as a mechanism of ego-defence resorted to in the face of intolerable frustrations occasioned by conflict between some positive drive and the need to preserve self-respect. In the process some *impulse* is usually denied expression and associated *ideas* or *images* are forcibly forgotten. It would seem convenient for expository purposes, and perhaps for experimental ones, to distinguish these two aspects of the process by the terms 'response repression' and 'stimulus repression,' the implication being that in the simplest case, say, an insult from some important person, one could study either the fate of the anger and retaliation *responses* denied expression or the fate of the *stimulus* presentations, such as the name of the insulting person or other circumstances of the humiliating incident, forgotten. In reviewing the studies of stimulus repression it is helpful further to distinguish between the *conscious* fate of the ideas or images—their supposed inaccessibility to normal recall—and their *unconscious* fate—their supposed persistence in the mind despite the content of consciousness. The same distinction is logically possible for response repression, since one could discuss the conscious fate of impulses, particularly their accompanying sensations and images, or their unconscious fate, especially in behaviour, but the investigations of this topic are not numerous and do not require such a division. Complete proof of stimulus repression would thus require evidence of both conscious forgetting and unconscious remembering. The demonstration of a complete repression cycle would require the addition of proof that the conscious representative of the unexpressed impulse had been forgotten and that the repressed response had gained substitute expression in some form or other.[2] No doubt this analysis violates the Gestalt-like character of the repression

1. Sears, R.R. 'Functional abnormalities of memory with special reference to amnesia.' *Psychol. Bull.*, 1936, *33*, 229–274.

2. A distinction between defensive and substitutive mechanisms of reaction to frustration is thus suggested. The former group would embrace projection, displacement, isolation, etc., while the latter would include sublimation, compensa-

process, but it is at least useful for the exposition of the experimental work in question.

Only a little of the experimentation thus far represented in the literature bears upon *response repression.* One of the rare instances of such research is Brun's [1] on drive conflicts produced in ants. He has studied the substitutive activities resorted to after repression has become necessary as a result of conflict and thus offers evidence of sublimation and regression. Some of the research of Lewin [2] and his associates belongs by implication in this same setting. Such work, despite its importance, bears only indirectly upon the present program. More directly related are certain studies of *stimulus repression* in which the *unconscious fate* of the ideas or images repressed was of special concern. Malamud and Linder [3] and Malamud [4] have investigated dreams from this standpoint, finding that when subjects are for a brief period shown and then asked to describe from memory certain types of pictures, they omit or distort items which reappear as unconscious or repressed material in the dreams they have soon after the experimental session.[5]

Of greatest relevance in the present context is that group of studies devoted to the *conscious fate* of *stimulus repression.* This work, well reviewed by Meltzer,[6] is, however, worthless as a test of repression because, as has been elsewhere [7] pointed out, it fails

---

tion, etc. Repression would, in the light of the above exposition, belong to both groups.

1. Brun,R. 'Experimentelle Beiträge zur Dynamik und Ökonomie des Triebkonfliktes (Biologische Parellelen zur Freuds Trieblehre).' *Imago*,1926,*12*, 147–170.
2. Lewin,K. *A Dynamic Theory of Personality.* New York,1935.
3. Malamud,W., and Linder,F.E. 'Dreams and their relationship to recent impressions.' *Arch. Neurol. & Psychiat.*,1931,*25*, 1081–1099.
4. Malamud,W. 'Dream analysis.' *Arch. Neurol. & Psychiat.*,1934,*31*, 356–372.
5. *Cf.* in this connection the work of O. Poetzl and that of Allers and Teller cited by Malamud and Linder, *op. cit.*
6. Meltzer,H. 'The present status of experimental studies of the relationship of feeling to memory.' *Psychol. Rev.*,1930,*37*, 124–139.
7. Rosenzweig,S., and Mason,G. 'An experimental study of memory in relation to the theory of repression.' *Brit. J. Psychol.* (Gen. Sec.) 1934,24, 247–265 (*cf.* 247–248).

to satisfy the necessary conditions of such a test. Either these studies have been concerned with memory for an impersonal type of unpleasant experience—sensory experience, such as odours, which the psycho-analyst does not include in his theory of forgetting—or, investigating as they should the recall of dynamically frustrating experiences, they have dealt with such episodes as occur in the everyday life of the subjects instead of producing these experiences in the laboratory itself. The latter defect involves the erroneous assumption [1] that pleasant and unpleasant episodes occur equally often in daily life. Studies based upon uncontrolled everyday experiences are further limited by the fact that repression may already have done its work by the time the subject makes his first report—and would hence go undetected—even if evidence of it fails to appear on subsequent reports of the same events. Properly to test the theory of repression in its relation to the conscious fate of the stimulus, it is necessary to bring about under controlled conditions experiences of conative striving which come into conflict with the pride of self-respect of the subjects, e.g., experiences of failure. If it is shown that such experiences are forgotten more frequently than comparable experiences of a successful nature, evidence of stimulus repression has presumptively been obtained.

Of the studies on stimulus repression which are satisfactory from the standpoint of the foregoing criteria, two are noteworthy. Koch [2] worked on students' recall of good and bad examination grades and obtained evidence that would appear to support the Freudian theory. Zeigarnik,[3] investigating the recall of finished and unfinished tasks, found that the latter were much more frequently recalled than the former. Although the tasks were not in general presented as a test of personal merit, when certain

1. *Cf.* Wohlgemuth,A. *A Critical Examination of Psycho-analysis.* London,1923, pp.28–39.
2. Koch,H.L. 'The influence of some affective factors upon recall.' *J. Gen. Psychol.*, 1930,*4*, 171–190.
3. Zeigarnik,B. 'Untersuchungen zur Handlungs—und Affektpsychologie. Herausgegeben von K.Lewin. III. Das Bahalten Erledigter und Unerledigter Handlungen.' *Psychol. Forsch.*,1927,*9*, 1–85. *Cf.* esp. p.77.

of them which had, for one reason or another, been so taken were interrupted, evidence of repression incidentally appeared. It will be seen later that the main evidence of this experiment is perhaps more important for the theory of repression than the obviously relevant incidental results.

II. *The Experimental Program*

1. *Technique.* The general features of the technique employed in the present experimental program may now be described. Subjects were given a simulatory test of intelligence in order to produce emotional tension in them and create experiences of success and failure.[1] The test consisted of a series of jig-saw picture-puzzles each of which when completed revealed some common object, such as a ship, a house or a coat, pyrographed upon its face. The subject was permitted to study a miniature picture of each object before undertaking the corresponding task. Usually he was allowed to succeed in half of the tasks but was made to fail in the other half. He was then asked to name the puzzles which had been included in the test.

The formal advantages of such a technique are readily apparent. All the tasks being of the same general type, they were characterized by a sufficient degree of uniformity to permit comparisons in recall and other aspects of behaviour on the basis of a few controlled variables. Such variables were the nature of the picture represented, the jig-saw design, and the outcome of the attempt to solve the puzzles. Quantification of the results was facilitated by the fact that the puzzles could be cut into any desired number of pieces and so made roughly to vary in difficulty. Obviously, the design of the construction was also a determining factor here. Moreover, the subject's success or failure could be estimated not only on an absolute basis, according to his having or not having completed the puzzle by the time he was stopped, but even more finely according to the number of pieces he had

1. For an account of some of the difficulties, such as the opinion-error, that arise when such methods of experimentally inducing need-tension are employed, *cf.* this writer's, 'The experimental situation as a psychological problem.' *Psychol. Rev.*, 1933, *40*, 337–354.

been allowed to assemble up to that time. In view of what has already been said about the simulatory character of the intelligence tests involved in this technique, it is hardly necessary to point out that in practically every instance described in the following experiments the degree to which a subject succeeded or failed in finding the solution of a puzzle was not a function of his ability but of the experimenter's purpose. Since the subject did not in general have any advance knowledge about the norms of the test, he was at the mercy of its administrator who could, according to the requirements of the investigation, stop him at any point in the solution.

By other devices further experimental control was possible. One such device was the preparation of two sets of puzzles identical in every respect except the number of pieces into which the corresponding boards were cut. One could thus obtain two parallel series of puzzles, one relatively easy, the other relatively difficult. Similarly, one could experimentally evaluate the significance of the pictures portrayed by having puzzles with nonsense syllable facings, and one could go even further in this direction by exactly duplicating the jig-saw design of such a series of puzzles and a corresponding picture series.

The foregoing technique with its numerous manipulative possibilities is the more important in view of the difficulties which one might well expect to encounter in any attempt at quantitative research involving *units of behaviour*. Its general success and wide applicability as an experimental method may be judged from the fact that by it such varied topics as repression, projection, rationalization, the experience of duration, hedonic tone, and repetition choice were all fruitfully investigated.

That the present technique actually motivated the subjects and created markedly emotional states is clear from the results. Both the behavioural notes of the experimenter and the introspective reports of the subjects abound in expressions such as 'hands tremble,' 'perspires freely,' 'beams,' 'clearly embarrassed' and 'very excited.' This is, however, not surprising if one considers that most individuals, being insecure, are highly sensitive to examinations and are really aroused by them. Through years of patient labour in the administration of intelligence and other tests psychologists have, moreover, unwittingly educated the public to accept the present type of *laboratory* or artificial situation as a *natural* or life-like one. In the case of the technique under discussion all of the following motivational factors were thus potentially present : (1) the obstacle for mastery represented by each of the puzzles ; (2) the set time within which each task had to be completed ; (3) competition with other individuals whom the subjects knew or were told about ; (4) critical scrutiny by the experimenter during the performance. The subjects were thus contending, in the ideal case, with an environmental problem having an unequivocal solution, with elapsing time and with a group of recognized competitors. To make matters worse, the watchful eye of the experimenter was ever upon the contest, thus helping to generate 'examination anxiety.'

2. *Preliminary experiments.* A first group of experiments on some forty summer school and regular students at Harvard and Radcliffe was designed to induce complexes through the experience of failure. Subjects were, for instance, given word lists for hedonic ratings *before* and *after* taking the so-called intelligence test. In the word list, among the names of many neutral objects, were those of the objects represented in the test. The purpose of the re-rating technique was to see whether the names of objects on which failure or success had been experienced would, unconsciously to the subjects, be affected in the second evaluation as compared with the first. In a number of cases this result was clearly obtained. In addition, a general shift in the hedonic ratings of the entire list was also occasionally found. Memory for the puzzles was tested by asking the subjects to name the tasks they had attempted. Though the opposite tendency was also disclosed, it was found that many individuals recalled a greater percentage of their successes than of their failures. Thus one Radcliffe girl who was given twelve puzzles to solve, half issuing in success, half in failure, recalled all six of the successful puzzles but only three of the equally numerous failures. This objective result

gained further significance in the light of her highly agitated behaviour during the test and her explanation that the continuation of her studies depended upon her obtaining a scholarship which, in turn, depended upon her receiving a superior grade in the psychology course from which she had been recruited for this experiment. Throughout the test her mind dwelt upon the lecturer in this course : 'All I thought of during the experiment was that it was an intelligence test and that he (the lecturer) would see the results. I saw his name always before me.' Under these circumstances the fact that she forgot half of her failures while remembering all of her successes might well be provisionally construed as repression.

While such tentative results were of interest as suggestions, it soon became clear that to obtain definitive conclusions the problem of repression would have to be approached at a much simpler level and only gradually developed to the point of complexity represented by these early efforts. In keeping with this plan a preliminary study was made of the relationship between success and failure, on the one hand, and hedonic tone, on the other. While common sense takes it for granted that success is pleasant, failure unpleasant, scientific psychology requires a more detailed and critical knowledge of this association before adopting a technique in which success and failure are to be treated as equivalent to pleasant and unpleasant experiences, respectively. Accordingly, some eight experiments were carried out to study hedonic tone as a function of success and failure.[1]

3. *Experiments on stimulus repression: conscious fate.* A series of circumscribed experiments on repression were now undertaken. The first of these [2] was done on a group of forty crippled children, with the result that the subjects could be divided into three groups according as they recalled a greater percentage of the names of the successful than of the unsuccessful tasks, a lesser percentage of the former than of the latter, or an equal percentage of each. Thus

1. *Cf.* Rosenzweig,S. *The Dependence of Preferences upon Success and Failure.* Doctoral thesis, 1932, Harvard University Library.
2. Rosenzweig,S. and Mason,G., *op. cit.*

far the data were obviously no more than one might expect according to the laws of probability. However, in view of the fact that the conditions under which the subjects had been working were relatively well defined, it was possible to go beyond this purely statistical finding. A first step in this direction was the discovery that the group who recalled successes better than failures was differentiated from the group who recalled failures better than successes by a more advanced average mental age and a higher average teachers' rating for the trait of pride. Of similar import but of even greater apparent validity was a correlation between the results of the present experiment and those of a previous one involving preferences in the repetition of successful and unsuccessful activities. In this earlier experiment [1] on the same subjects it was found that the younger ones consistently chose to repeat puzzles in which they had once had success, whereas the older ones chose to repeat puzzles in which they had experienced failure. This difference in repetition choice was associated with a difference in teachers' ratings on the trait of pride, in which the younger children had a markedly lower average than the older ones. It seemed likely by way of interpretation that the older children, because prouder, were more sensitive to failure and hence strove for self-vindication, whereas the younger children, not being wounded by failure, ignored it. The relationship of these results to the Freudian *pleasure* and *reality principles* is too obvious to require discussion. Now, in the present experiment on memory it was found that those subjects who tended to recall failures had formerly preferred to repeat successes while those who tended to recall successes had preferred failures for repetition. The

1. Rosenzweig,S. 'Preferences in the repetition of successful and unsuccessful activities as a function of age and personality.' *J. Genet. Psychol.*,1933,*42*, 423–441. Further experimental studies of repetition choice have since been made on groups of normal adults, normal children, feeble-minded individuals and schizophrenic patients. The results have led to the formulation of a concept of frustration tolerance — a factor both quantitatively and qualitatively variable and apparently increasing in the normal course of the individual's early development. *Cf.* Rosenzweig,S. 'The preferential repetition of successful and unsuccessful activities.' *Psychol. Bull.*,1936,*33*, 797 (abstract). An extended treatment is in preparation.

implication seemed to be that stimulus repression failed to occur in individuals who were still functioning naïvely in accordance with the pleasure principle ; or, more parsimoniously stated, that unless failure was experienced as wounding to self-respect and requiring social vindication, there was no basis for stimulus repression and it hence did not occur. These results may thus be construed as indicating that repression is a mechanism of defence resorted to relatively late in the development of the child.

As important incidental results of the experiment it was found that (a) there was a distortion in recalling the outcome — success or failure — of the tasks attempted that ran parallel with the tendencies shown in recalling the names of the tasks ; (b) with increasing age there was an increase in self-critical answers to the question, 'Do you feel that you did the puzzles well ? ; (c) the experiences of relatively shorter duration were much more frequently recalled than those of longer duration, presumably because of the prevailing dynamic conditions.

A second experiment on stimulus repression [1] was designed to verify the results of this first one, only now an attempt was made to control the external experimental situation so as to reproduce, with two groups of thirty adults each, the conditions which had obtained with the children by virtue of the genetic differences in their personalities. To the individuals in one of the two groups the tasks were presented as an intelligence test and under these conditions there was a tendency for the finished puzzles to be recalled more often than the unfinished ones. To the subjects in the other group, the tasks were presented in an informal spirit, the object of the appointment allegedly being to help the experimenter gain certain knowledge about the puzzles — not about the subjects — so that this information would be available for guidance in an experiment being planned for the near future. To avoid suspicion all records were kept by an assistant seated apparently with his own unrelated work at a desk on the further side of the

1. Rosenzweig,S. 'The recall of finished and unfinished tasks as affected by the purpose with which they were performed.' *Psychol. Bull.*,1933,*30*, 698 (abstract).

informal study in which the session took place. Under these circumstances there was a tendency for the unfinished puzzles to be recalled more often than the finished ones. Repression thus occurred in general under the expected conditions but did not occur otherwise. It is to be observed, however, that even under the adequate external conditions repression was not exemplified in the behaviour of every subject. In fact, some of those who performed the puzzles informally gave more evidence of repression than did certain of those who did the tasks as a test. One is led to suspect in these instances an underlying personality trait strong enough to over-ride the intention of the stimulus situation.

Zeigarnik's general results that unfinished tasks informally undertaken are better remembered than finished ones are in essential agreement with the present results, but the latter also explain why she found evidences of repression only very incidentally.

In attempting to interpret the above experiment more fully the problem arises as to whether the test situation resulted in the forgetting of the failures because these conditions aroused the *pride* of the subjects and hence provided a basis for *repression* or because they *excited* the subjects and thus produced a form of *dissociation*. While it is impossible to settle this question on the strength of the present evidence, it is worth noting that Breuer and Freud[1] were confronted with the same problem in their early attempts to account for the losses of memory they regarded as fundamental to hysteria. They pointed out that such instances of amnesia may be attributed to traumas which were insufficiently abreacted — the abreaction failing to occur either because the traumus involved humiliating circumstances which the patient did not wish to remember or because these traumas were experienced in an hypnoidal, exciting or otherwise abnormal state of consciousness. In either case 'associative elaboration' in the normal conscious state would be precluded and amnesia would thus ensue.

4. *Control experiments related to the foregoing.* It would obvi-

1. Breuer, J. and Freud, S. *Studies in Hysteria.* New York, 1936, pp. 6–8.

ously be difficult to design an experiment involving experiences of success and failure which would arouse emotional tension entailing reactions of pride without at the same time producing excitement, or *vice versa*, but such would be necessary to differentiate between the two sets of determinants under discussion. On the whole, the evidence would tend to give the pride factors greater *prima facie* importance since they would usually entail excitement whereas excitement alone might well occur apart from pride reactions. Further experimentation is, however, much needed at this point.

The studies which were actually undertaken at the stage of the program being described were designed to test some of the experimental artifacts that made even the general results just outlined questionable. Among these investigations, which need not be detailed here, were the two following : (1) an attempt to study the effect of changing the criterion of success so that a coincidence with completion would not be involved ; to accomplish this end all the puzzles were carried to completion but in some cases before, in others after a previously announced time limit within which the puzzles would need to be finished in order to be scored as successes ; (2) an attempt to rule out as a factor in recallability the familiarity of the objects depicted in the puzzles ; to achieve this purpose puzzles with nonsense syllable facings were substituted for those with pictures.

In this same connection may be mentioned another experimental variation involving some twenty subjects who were asked to recall the puzzles not *immediately* after their performance but *at some later period*. This experiment was intended to show the significance of delay as a factor in stimulus repression, but the obtained data are insufficiently analysed to be further discussed on this occasion.

5. *Experiments on stimulus repression : unconscious fate*. The investigations discussed thus far were all concerned with the *conscious* fate of stimulus repression. In addition, a series of experiments dealing with the *unconscious* fate of such repression were performed though the results are as yet for the most part in a raw

state. One group of these studies, in which about twenty subjects participated, five in each of four different experimental situations, was intended to compare *recall* of the problems with *recognition* of their names among a long list of objects. The subjects were asked not only to pick out the objects represented in the puzzles they had attempted, but to indicate in terms of a scale the degree of vividness of their recognition. If these results should reveal a poorer recall of the failures but a more frequent and more vivid recognition of them as compared with successes — which is what a first glance at the data seems to indicate — some evidence would be available for an unconscious or dispositional persistence of the failure experiences despite their not appearing in the consciousness of the subjects on account of stimulus repression.[1]

A very tentative investigation, with only four subjects taking part in it, may be mentioned for its suggestive value in relation to further work on the unconscious fate of stimulus repression. In this experiment a word list was first presented for hedonic ratings; after this, certain puzzles, the names of which were represented in the word list, were attempted as a test by the subjects with varying degrees of success. The word list was then given for re-rating. This experiment thus far resembles one of the preliminary studies reported above. Its unique feature was the use of a psycho-galvanometer throughout the session to measure changes in unconscious tension. From a very rough and unreliable analysis of the data it appeared that in some instances failure on the puzzles was accompanied by changes in the gsr, and that presentation after the test of the stimulus words referring to these failures gave significant deviations as compared with the original reactions to these same words. These results, if valid, would tend to support those of the preceding experiments on recognition memory. Both sets of data indicate a dispositional persistence of certain failure

1. *Cf.* in this connection the interesting experiment of C.A.Lynch, 'The memory value of certain alleged emotionally toned words,' *J. Exp. Psychol.*,1932,*15*, 298–315, in which memory for pleasant and unpleasant stimuli was studied by a recognition technique.

experiences not subject to voluntary recall. From the preliminary results of these separate studies further work in which the recognition technique was *combined* with measurement of the gsr during the same experimental session would seem to offer considerable promise.

It is also worthy of note that the above findings are in keeping with the experiment already discussed in which unfinished tasks performed under informal conditions, rather than as a test, were better remembered than finished ones. Zeigarnik obtained substantially the same results. The significance of these findings may now be more adequately understood. If undischarged tension connected with a need makes for better recall under unemotional conditions, it appears reasonable to suppose that when such undischarged tensions are repressed through pride and similar motives these tensions and their associated ideas or images will still continue more strongly in the mind than will corresponding experiences representing closed and unrepressed needs. Under these new conditions, however, the unclosed need situations will lead only a dispositional or — to use the Freudian terminology — an unconscious existence. From these considerations it becomes clear, too, why the equivalence of *incompletion* with *failure* in the experiments raises certain difficulties in such studies as the present. One must then be ever careful not to confuse the *unclosed need represented by the unfinished task* (perseveration) with the *unclosed need represented by the inhibited response*, say, of anger in the face of frustration. In keeping with this interpretation, evidence of repression obtained from experiments in which the criteria of failure is incompletion is particularly striking because under such conditions the repressive tendency can become manifest in terms of forgotten failures only after overcoming the competing perseverative tendency which would, by itself, make for the recall of the unfinished tasks. The problem inherent in this distinction underlay the control experiment described above in which success was defined by a criterion other than completion.

From these reflections to the problem of response repression in general is obviously only a short step, but until it be taken, little more can be profitably said on the present topic.[1]

III. *The Triadic Hypothesis*

One of the factors which kept cropping up throughout the preceding studies has as yet been left unmentioned. In one sense it represents the contribution of individual differences which obtruded themselves despite the systematically imposed external conditions of the experiments. But in another sense it implies a larger frame of reference than the concept of repression alone — a frame within which these individual differences are absorbed by a new set of general principles.

The factor in question concerns the way in which individuals seemed, according to the impression of the experimenter, to vary in their *immediate reaction to frustration or failure*. These variations in reaction appeared to correlate with subsequent predominance in recall of successes or failures. Briefly, it seemed that individuals who at the time of experiencing failure were inclined to blame the external world (e.g., the puzzles, the experimenter) — a type of reaction later called 'extrapunitive' — *or* to blame themselves — later called 'intropunitive' — tended characteristically to recall their failures, in contradiction to the repression hypothesis ; only those who tended to gloss over their failures as if inevitable and tried to rationalize them away at the time of their occurrence — a type of reaction later called 'impunitive' — recalled their successes better than their failures, i.e., displayed stimulus repression. It was accordingly suggested in a former publication [2] that each of the types of reaction might have a special relation to memory. One could speculate that both the extrapunitive and the intropunitive reactions would entail remembering the occasion of frustration, in the former case, as if in anticipation of revenge, in the latter, as if in preparation for nursing

1. The work of Lewin and his associates on substitute activities is of special interest in this connection. *Cf. op. cit.*, Chap. VI.
2. Rosenzweig,S. 'Types of reaction to frustration : an heuristic classification.' *J. Abn. & Soc. Psychol.*,1934,29, 298–300. *Cf.* pp.299–300.

the wounds to one's pride and 'eating one's heart out.' It could be maintained that the aggressive impulses were being preserved to be expressed later, in the former case, against outer objects, in the latter, against the subject's own self. The impunitive type of reaction, on the other hand, might be expected to entail a conscious forgetting of the occasion of frustration, as if in order to reconcile one's self — and others — to the disagreeable situation. The impunitive reaction would thus be summed up in the expression 'Forgive and forget,' whereas the other two types would involve neither forgiving nor forgetting. Thus the hypothesis soon arose that specific types of inadequate or subjective reaction to frustration might be found to be correlated systematically with special mechanisms of defence, repression being only one of these.

It was of interest to find after this hypothesis had arisen from the experiments that Freud's accumulating clinical experience had led him to a similar position. In a comparatively recent publication[1] he suggests that the concept of defence which he used in his earlier theoretical papers and which was later replaced by repression be now readopted. 'I now think that it confers a distinct advantage to readopt the old concept of defence if in doing so it is laid down that this shall be the general designation for all the techniques of which the ego makes use in the conflicts which potentially lead to neurosis, while repression is the term reserved for one particular method of defence, one which because of the directions that our investigations took was the first with which we became acquainted. . . The importance of such a nomenclature is increased if one considers the possibility that a deeper insight might reveal a close affinity between particular forms of defence and certain specific disorders, as for example between repression and hysteria. Our expectation even extends to the possibility of another important interrelationship. It may easily be that the psychic apparatus utilizes other methods of defence prior to the clear-cut differentiation of ego and id, prior to the erecting of a superego, than it does after these stages of organization have been attained.'

1. Freud, S. *The Problem of Anxiety*. New York, 1936, pp. 143–146.

The similarity between this position of Freud and that just outlined is striking though one should not overlook the fact that whereas Freud is emphasizing the special relationship between certain defence mechanisms and certain types of illness, the present hypothesis stresses a special relationship between certain types of defence and certain descriptively independent types of reaction to frustration. From the standpoint of this distinction MacKinnon's[1] experimental work on the violation of prohibitions is more pertinent than Freud's clinical observations. MacKinnon found that non-violators and violators exhibit consistently different behaviour patterns, the former having a close resemblance to what has been here described as intropunitive, while the latter appear to be either extrapunitive or impunitive. Violators who remember their violations well may be tentatively regarded as extrapunitive, those who tend to forget their violations would appear to be impunitive. The intropunitive subjects would be too full of guilt to commit violations and hence would in the experiment have none either to remember or to forget.

Since the concept of types of reaction to frustration seemed simpler than repression and appeared to be more amenable to measurement in the presenting experimental situation, the problem of preparing a measuring instrument for such types of reaction assumed definite importance. A behavioural device accordingly constructed is described in a later section.[2] A more complete description of the classification of reaction types provisionally adopted may also be found there. It should be mentioned, too, that MacKinnon and the writer are now standardizing a paper and pencil test which promises to help considerably in at least the gross determination of these types.

A final suggestion that has arisen from the experiments on stimulus repression refers to hypnotizability. From the clinical evidence of French psycho-pathology as to the *dissociability* of

1. *Cf.* p.491 ; also MacKinnon,D.W. *The Violation of Prohibitions in the Solving of Problems.* Doctoral thesis, 1933, Harvard University Library.
2. *Cf.* p.585 ; also Rosenzweig,S. 'A test for types of reaction to frustration.' *Amer. J. Orthopsychiat.*,1935,5, 395–403.

hysterical patients and from that of Freudian psycho-analysis as to the special relationship between *repression* and hysteria, it seemed profitable to investigate the possible association of repression as a mechanism of defence and hypnotizability as a personality trait. The availability of a measure of repression in the memory techniques made such an investigation feasible but only a preliminary study with about fifteen subjects has thus far been made. A rough analysis of the results tends to substantiate the expectation upon which the experiment was based, for the hypnotizable subjects appear to have recalled their successes better than their failures more often than did the non-hypnotizable ones.

A certain amount of reciprocal corroboration was obtained from an experiment in which a group of stutterers, sent by a physician in Boston, was compared with a group of Harvard students selected because they were active either in dramatics or in debating. By and large, the stutterers appear to have recalled their failures more frequently than did the public speakers. In view of the obsessional characteristics generally attributed to stutterers and their reputed refractoriness to hypnosis, this result is in good agreement with the hypothesis that repression is a mechanism of defence pathognomonic of hysteria only.

There thus emerges a triadic hypothesis according to which hypnotizability as a personality trait is to be found in positive association with repression as a preferred mechanism of defence and with impunitiveness as a characteristic type of immediate reaction to frustration.[1] Non-hypnotizability would, by implication, be linked with other defence mechanisms, e.g., displacement and projection, and with other types of reaction to frustration, e.g., intropunitiveness and extrapunitiveness. Should these inter-relationships be conclusively proved by experimentation yet to be done, a notable integration of certain concepts of French psychopathology (hypnotizability and dissociation) and of Freudian psycho-analysis (repression and other defence mechanisms) would have been achieved through the use of tools (techniques

1. For illustration of these relationships, *cf.* Case History.

for studying repression and types of reaction to frustration) made available by experimental psychology.

13a. MEMORY FOR FAILURES TEST

E. H. Trowbridge

Purpose. In a person's memory his successes and failures find representation, but not necessarily to an equal degree. Recall of successes and of failures may be conceived as forming a ratio, the value of which differs from one person to another. In the Memory for Failures Test an attempt was made to rank Ss in terms of this ratio as measured in a single controlled situation. It was hoped to determine what variables of personality are consistently associated with the ratio, and whether such a rank order can be predicted from other kinds of information. The test was administered only to Group IV.

Procedure. The test material consisted of rather simple jig-saw puzzles made up of eight or ten pieces. Each puzzle was stamped with a design representing some common object. This design was drawn upon the puzzle box, and the S was permitted to inspect it for fifteen seconds before beginning work. The E represented that he was giving 'a motor aptitude test, part of an examination for general intelligence.' He explained that there was a standard time limit for each puzzle, varying according to its difficulty, and that he would stop the S when the time was up. This fiction permitted the E to bring about an equal number of successes and failures in the course of the hour.

At the end of the session the E required an immediate recall of 'as many *designs* as you can remember irrespective of the order in which they were presented.' Five weeks later a delayed recall was secured, using the same instruction.

Results. The percentage of failures immediately recalled was subtracted from the percentage of successes and the Ss were ranked according to the size and sign of the difference. The same calculation was made for delayed recall. The results of immediate recall and of delayed recall showed a wide distribution. The two rank orders correlated only +.24, which precluded their combination into a single score. There was a slight (though statistically negligible) tendency for successes to be remembered better than failures. The prediction of the Diagnostic Council correlated +.43 with immediate recall and —.08 with delayed.

14. VIOLATION OF PROHIBITIONS

DONALD W. MACKINNON

a. Experiments : Personality Differences between Violators and Non-Violators of Prohibitions

Purpose. In an attempt to submit the psycho-analytic theory of repression to experimental investigation by determining the effect of feelings of guilt upon memory, an experimental situation was devised which left subjects free to obey or to violate prohibitions imposed upon them by the experimenter. The procedure employed in the experiment proved not only adequate to the answering of the original question — does a subject repress memories with which feelings of guilt are associated ? — but also revealed striking differences in personality between the violators and non-violators of the prohibitions. Since the findings in respect to the theory of repression have been reported elsewhere [1] and are not relevant to the investigations of personality reported in this book, only those findings which bear upon personality differences are reported here.

Procedure. The experimental procedure was as follows : the subjects were asked to solve twenty problems, each of which was printed upon a separate sheet of paper. The solution in each case was to be written below the problem. On the table at which the subject sat were two booklets which contained the solutions of the problems. The pages of these booklets were so cut and numbered as to indicate clearly the page on which the solution of any problem was to be found. Each subject was given permission to look at certain solutions but prohibited to look at the others. Each sub-

1. MacKinnon, D.W. *The Violation of Prohibitions in the Solving of Problems.* Doctoral thesis, 1933, Harvard University Library.

ject was left alone in the experimental room but the experimenter was able to see and to record all of his behaviour during the experiment through a one-way screen.

Results. Of the 93 subjects, all of whom were college graduates,[1] 50 (54%) were non-violators of the prohibitions, looking, if at all, only at allowed solutions. The remaining 43 subjects (46%) were violators of the prohibitions, looking at one or more of the prohibited solutions.

An analysis of the behaviour of the subjects during the experiments reveals interesting differences between the violators and the non-violators. Apart from exclamations of delight at a solution subjects tended to speak only when unable to solve a problem. Their verbal reactions were of four types: (1) remarks which indicated that the subject was trying to solve a problem, e.g., rereading the problem, speaking of a solution as it was being written, etc.; (2) simple explosive expressions of emotional tension directed against no object, e.g., 'Oh,' 'Gosh,' 'Oh, what the hell,' etc.; (3) emotional expressions directed at the object creating the frustration, verbal attacks upon the problems, not to solve them but to denounce and blame them, e.g., 'You bastard,' 'You crazy bitch,' 'These are the God damnedest things I ever saw,' etc.; (4) emotional expressions directed to oneself, blaming the self for failure and frustration, e.g., 'Jesus Christ, I must be dumb,' 'God, I must be a nitwit,' etc.

Violators and non-violators were equally expressive, about 65% of both groups speaking during the experiments, but differences between them were revealed in the relative frequency of occurrence of the four types of verbal reaction. Whereas 31% of the violators who spoke at all vented their anger upon the problems by deprecating them, not a single non-violator reacted in this manner. The verbal reaction of blaming oneself occurred very rarely, being manifested by 10% of the non-violators but by none of the violators. The diffuse emotional reactions occurred somewhat more often among violators (86%) than among non-violators (70%),

1. 19 at the University of Berlin, 14 at Radcliffe College, and 60 at Harvard College.

while non-violators (57%) more often than violators (45%) made overt verbal attempts to solve problems.

An analysis of the subjects' behaviour other than that of speech reveals that when frustrated in the attempt to solve problems the violators (31%), more often than the non-violators (4%), exhibited a destructive, aggressive restlessness manifested in scuffling the feet, stamping on the floor, getting up from the table and stamping back and forth across the room, kicking the leg of the table, pounding the fist, etc.

Non-aggressive types of restlessness were, on the other hand, more often seen in non-violators than in violators. Such behaviour as fidgeting, crossing and uncrossing the legs, hunching the shoulders, twisting the head to one side, etc., was shown by 39% of the non-violators and by 26% of the violators.

More striking differences between the groups were revealed in the relative occurrence of oral, nasal, and hirsutal activities. Oral activity, e.g., placing finger or thumb to mouth, sucking the thumb, biting finger-nails, licking the back of the hand, placing excreta from the nose or hair to the lips or into the mouth, etc., occurred among 83% of the non-violators but among only 48% of the violators. Nasal activity, e.g., picking the nose, smelling some part of the body, etc., was manifested less frequently, by 28% of the non-violators and by only 14% of the violators. Hirsutal activity of running the fingers through the hair or twirling a few strands around a finger, etc., occurred even more rarely but again about twice as often among non-violators (11%) as among violators (5%).

The picture of the non-violators thus obtained is suggestive of Freud's anal-erotic character type with its 'reliability and conscientiousness in the performance of petty duties,'[1] along with so much behaviour which would be considered by the psychoanalysts as merely disguised or substitute coprophilic activity.

In the frustration situation of the experiment the violator reacts aggressively, the non-violator regressively. The non-violator re-

1. Freud, S. 'Character and anal erotism.' *Collected Papers.* London, 1924, Vol. II, 45.

gresses when he sucks his thumb or bites his finger-nails. The violator tends, on the other hand, to push ahead and seek gratification not at a lower earlier level but at the level of frustration.

The violator may be thought of as turning his aggression outward in violating the prohibition. It is accordingly interesting to speculate concerning the extent to which the oral, nasal and hirsutal activity may be a manifestation of masochism and as such the result of aggression directed toward the self. Biting a fingernail and throwing it away is a destruction of a part of one's body. Picking one's nose, pulling out one's hair, biting the hair on the back of one's hands, etc., could all be interpreted as forms of masochism. To just the extent that such an interpretation is correct, the non-violators may be considered, in general, more masochistic than the violators.

Regardless of the interpretation of the findings, the fact that the violators express their aggression and the non-violators inhibit theirs is clearly indicated in both the verbal and non-verbal behaviour of the subjects.

In connection with the investigation of the theory of repression it was necessary to determine the emotional reactions of the violators to their having looked at prohibited solutions. It was, however, important that subjects should not know that they had been observed. Consequently, before they could be questioned about their emotional reactions to violations it was necessary to ask them if they had looked at any prohibited solutions and, if so, how many.

This question, put to most subjects four weeks after the original experiment, elicited from non-violators a simple denial of violations, but from violators three types of replies : either a complete denial or a partial admission or a complete admission.

The subjects who admitted, either partially or completely, the prohibited solutions which they had seen were asked : 'How do you feel about having looked at the prohibited solutions ? ' Of the 22 violators so questioned, only 6 admitted having felt badly or having experienced any feelings of guilt or wrong-doing. The other 16 denied that they had been in the least troubled by their actions.

It was impossible to put this same question to the violators who denied having seen prohibited solutions. Consequently, a hypothetical question was put to them, namely : 'If you had looked at any prohibited solutions how would you have felt about having done so ?'

Of the 10 violators so questioned only 2 stated that they would probably have experienced a bad conscience had they violated the prohibition.

If we combine these two groups of violators on the assumption that those who answered the hypothetical question were, like those answering the direct question, reporting their actual reactions, we find that 75% of the violators described their reaction as one of calm indifference, while only 25% described their reaction as one of guilt.

The replies of the non-violators to this same hypothetical question were strikingly different in that of the 37 subjects questioned only 6 (16%) reported that they would have been emotionally untroubled, the other 31 (84%) stating definitely that they would have felt guilty, conscience-stricken, ashamed, etc., had they seen the prohibited solutions, and so emphatic were the replies of these subjects that the experimenter could hardly escape the conviction that the subjects were describing an emotion which they had often vividly experienced, and that the reported feelings were the anticipated ones which in part served to keep them from violating the prohibition.

The difference between the replies of the violators and those of the non-violators at once suggests the fact that the criminal, a violator of social prohibitions, is characteristically untroubled by any feelings of guilt for his overt acts of aggression, while the submissive and compliant individual, a non-violator of social prohibitions, is peculiarly inclined to feel guilty as a result of the mere contemplation of acts which he never carries out.

This paradoxical fact, that he who has most cause to feel guilty is usually free of a feeling of guilt, while he who has least cause is most troubled, has invited the attention of Freud who on this point has written :

. . . The more righteous a man is, the stricter and more suspicious will his conscience be, so that ultimately it is precisely those people who have carried holiness farthest who reproach themselves with the deepest sinfulness. . . A relatively strict and vigilant conscience is the very sign of a virtuous man, and though saints may proclaim themselves sinners, they are not so wrong, in view of the temptations of instinctual gratifications to which they are peculiarly liable — since as we know, temptations do but increase under constant privations, whereas they subside, at any rate temporarily, if they are sometimes gratified.[1]

In other words, Freud considers that 'conscience is the result of instinctual renunciation.'[2] While some psycho-analysts[3] have considered that the thwarting of any instinctual gratification results in an increase in the feeling of guilt, Freud believes that this is valid only for the aggressive instincts.[4] Assuming that the renunciation in question is always a renunciation of aggression, he writes further that,

The effect of instinctual renunciation on conscience then operates as follows : every impulse of aggression which we omit to gratify is taken over by the super-ego and goes to heighten its aggressiveness (against the ego).[5]

If this theoretical formulation — that he who fails to gratify his aggressive impulses becomes the object of them and experiences as a result a feeling of guilt — is correct, the non-violators should experience feelings of guilt in everyday life more frequently than the violators.

These considerations led the experimenter to ask the subjects in the later experiments, 'Do you, in everyday life, often feel guilty about things which you have done or have not done ?'

Of the 48 subjects interrogated 24 were non-violators and 24

1. Freud,S. *Civilization and Its Discontents.* New York,1930, 109.
2. Ibid., 114.
3. Notably Alexander, Reik, Jones, Isaacs, and Klein.
4. Ibid., 114.
5. Freud,S. *Civilization and Its Discontents.* New York,1930, 114.

violators. Eighteen (75%) of the non-violators reported that they often feel guilty, and 5 (21%) that they almost never do, while the 1 remaining subject (4%) insisted that he could not answer the question. Among the violators, however, only 7 subjects (29%) admitted often feeling guilty, while 14 (58%) reported almost never experiencing such feelings. Three (13%) were unable to give a simple affirmative or negative answer.

The replies, then, of 48 subjects confirmed the theoretical expectations to a striking degree in that admissions of frequent feelings of guilt were made by 75% of the non-violators but by only 29% of the violators.

According to the psycho-analytic theory of psycho-sexual development, the first love object of the male child, other than his own body, is the mother, and the development of this love may be considered the first step in the socialization of the infant. The second step is made when the child extends his world to include the father. This step, termed by psycho-analysts the mastery of the Oedipus complex, is considered by them to be of the utmost importance for the later social development of the individual. In this step they describe the child as inhibiting and sublimating his earlier hatred of the father through identifying with him and wishing to become like him. If the Oedipus complex is not mastered, or if it is mastered only partially, the child will be less socialized than one who succeeds in identifying with the father.

A consideration of this single fragment of the psycho-analytic theory suggested that the violators and non-violators might show a differential parent preference, the violators tending to prefer the mother and the non-violators the father.

To test this, the question, 'Of which parent are you fonder ?' was put to all but the first 19 subjects. Of those questioned, 34 were violators and 40 non-violators. In reporting the replies, however, data are given for only 27 violators and 38 non-violators. In the case of 7 subjects, at least one parent had died when the subjects were so young there was no recollection of the dead parent. Two subjects, both violators, took offence at the question and refused to answer it.

Of the 27 violators 20 (74%) reported a preference for the mother, 6 (22%) stated that they were equally fond of both parents, while only 1 violator (4%) indicated a preference for the father.

In striking contrast were the 38 non-violators of whom only 14 (36%) were fonder of the mother, 13 (35%) equally fond of both parents, while 11 (29%) stated a preference for the father.

In other words, only 26% of the violators, as against 64% of the non-violators, were at least as fond of their fathers as of their mothers.

While confirming the theoretical expectations these findings raised a host of questions, answers to which were sought by giving the subjects a questionnaire upon their early child-parent relations. Since the experiments were over and most of the subjects had graduated from college before the questionnaire was devised, answers were obtained from only 28 subjects (all males) of whom 15 were non-violators and 13 violators.

The subjects were asked to check in a list of common forms of punishment those which had been most usually employed by each parent. The forms of punishment fell naturally into two groups, the first group being composed of those measures by means of which a child is actively and physically punished or frustrated; the second, of those measures which seek to have a child feel that he has fallen short of some ideal or that he has hurt his parents and consequently is less loved by them because of what he has done. The measures of the first group, though not doing so completely, place emphasis upon physical punishment, while those of the second rely more upon psychological effects, e.g., thwarting the desire for social approval or the desire to be loved.

The replies of the subjects reveal the importance of the father as disciplinarian. Whereas the more physically aggressive forms of discipline were employed more often by fathers of violators and least often by fathers of non-violators, the methods directed to make the child feel that he had fallen short of an ideal or was not worthy of the parents' love were employed least often by the fathers of violators and most often by fathers of non-violators.

Little difference is revealed, however, between the mothers of the violators and those of the non-violators in the relative frequency with which they employed the measures of the one type as against those of the other.

TABLE 1

THE FORMS OF DISCIPLINE EMPLOYED BY THE PARENTS OF THE SUBJECT

Parents of Subjects	Per Cent of Reported Forms of Discipline Which Were	
	Physical	Psychological
Fathers of Violators	78	22
Mothers of Non-Violators	62	38
Mothers of Violators	58	42
Fathers of Non-Violators	48	52

The non-violators are differentiated from the violators by the greater frequency with which they reported that the father's disciplining was more effective than the mother's, feared more than the mother's, but at the same time considered the more just. They also more often considered the father the final authority in matters of discipline.

All these reports are consistent in indicating that as children the non-violators tended to grant their fathers a favoured, respected, and somewhat feared position. The violators, on the contrary, showed no such tendency.

The answers given by violators and non-violators to the question, 'By which parent did you prefer to be disciplined or punished ?,' are interesting in that they indicate that the subjects, in general, preferred the more physical forms of punishment to those forms which were intended to make them feel inferior, unworthy, or unloved. The reasons for this preference are indicated in the subjects' descriptions of the manner in which they reacted to the two types of disciplines.

Typical reactions to the more physical forms of punishment were :

I was angered.

I sulked.

They antagonized me. I spitefully plotted ways of secretly repeating what I had been punished for. Sometimes my hot anger was drowned in tears leaving a residue of cold dislike.

Quite different were the typical reactions to the more psychological forms of punishment :

As a rule they made me resolve not to do the wrong again but to improve myself. Often I was ashamed.

I felt honestly sorry.

By trying to be good and doing what I was expected to do.

When one considers that the typical reactions to the frustration and physical pain of the more primitive forms of discipline were, as reported by our subjects, those of anger, stubbornness, resentment, antagonism, annoyance, obstinacy, hatred, cold dislike, etc., one would not expect great regard for authority and social prohibitions to develop in those individuals who were most often disciplined in this manner. Since the violators were more often physically punished, especially by their fathers, their violations of the prohibitions imposed by a male experimenter are not surprising but rather the expected behaviour in the light of what is now known about their early discipline and their reactions to it.

On the other hand, knowing that the non-violators were as children disciplined to a large extent, particularly by their fathers, by being made to feel inferior, unworthy, and temporarily unloved, and knowing that such disciplinary measures usually caused them to feel ashamed, sorrowful, conscience-stricken, repentant, desirous of apologizing, anxious not to offend again, etc., their regard of the prohibition is now more readily understood.

The findings of the present investigation lend support to a theory of the consistency of personality. Most investigators who have done work closely related to the present study, notably Hartshorne and May in their studies in deceit,[1] have argued for specificity of behaviour as against generality of traits and thus

1. Hartshorne,H. and May,M.A. *Studies in Deceit.* New York,1926.

against the consistency of personality. Subjects in the present experiment were not given a series of tests to determine whether those who were violators in one situation would also be violators in another. With this aspect of consistency, called by Newcomb 'specific behaviour consistency,'[1] the investigation was not concerned but rather with the broader aspects of personality consistency for which Newcomb[2] has suggested the term 'trait consistency' and which Allport and Vernon have called the 'congruence of traits.'[3]

Had the various aspects of the subjects' behaviour here reported been considered separately they would have been rather meaningless, but considered in relation to each other they have taken on significant meaning. So considered, they have revealed the violators, in general, to possess one congruent pattern of traits, the non-violators, in general, to possess an opposed but equally congruent pattern. Through the medium of their personalities the violators, on the one hand, and the non-violators, on the other, expressed themselves consistently both in the experimental situation and in their subsequent reports upon their experiences. The technique of this experiment has thus demonstrated what other less adequate techniques in the field of personality investigation have often failed to reveal, namely, the consistency of personality.

14a. ETHICAL STANDARDS TEST

J. A. Christenson, Jr.

Purpose. Using numerous suggestions from MacKinnon's work on the violation of prohibitions, the Ethical Standards Test was devised to investigate the effect of success and failure upon cheating. In addition, it provided the Ss with opportunities to cheat in a competition, and thus allowed the E to score them in respect

1. Newcomb, T.M. *The Consistency of Certain Extrovert-Introvert Behavior Patterns in 51 Problem Boys*, New York : Teachers College, Columbia Univ. Contributions to Education, No. 382, 1929.
2. Ibid.
3. Allport, G.W. and Vernon, P.E. *Studies in Expressive Movement.* New York, 1933.

to honesty. The present report will be concerned largely with this second purpose. The test was administered only to the fifteen Ss of Group IV, a number which does not warrant inferences in regard to the effect of success and failure.

Procedure. The test was conducted individually in two experimental sessions. It was presented to the S as a 'test of constructive aptitude,' consisting of jig-saw puzzles to be solved if possible within allotted time limits. The factor of speed was emphasized, and the task was put on a competitive basis with double remuneration for the three Ss who made the highest scores.

The E presented a series of seven puzzles, timing the performance with a stop-watch and making records of success or failure. He gave no assistance, evaded questions, and offered no comments while the S was at work. In the first session he interrupted each S, thus causing him to 'fail,' on the second and fifth puzzles, but allowed him to complete all the others. In the second session, a fortnight later, he reversed this procedure, so that the S 'failed' with all the puzzles except the second and fifth.

When the series of seven puzzles was completed, the E announced that he was obliged to leave in order to start the test in another room. He asked the S to attempt the rest of the puzzles in the forty minutes which remained, record his solutions on appropriate cards and put these in an envelope to be left in the secretary's office when he finished. Since the E would not return, the S might write on the back of the cards any comments which he wished to make.

Before leaving the room, the E pointed out a wall clock arranged to sound a bell at three- and one-minute intervals alternately. The S was instructed to begin a puzzle when the first bell rang, cease working at the next bell, and take up the succeeding puzzle when the bell once more sounded, continuing thus until the end. In the one-minute interval which this system created between puzzles, he was to record his solution on the appropriate card. Having explained this, the E started the clock and, as the first bell rang, went into an adjoining room where he observed the S through a one-way screen.

The puzzles were uniform in size (144 sq. in.), consisted of six to eight pieces, had no diagram on them, and were painted to obscure the grain of the wood. Each one had at least one tie-in, furnishing an internal angle which might serve as a clue. When solved they formed squares, rectangles, and equilateral triangles. The S was provided with cards having these figures already outlined upon them, and indicated his solution by filling in the arrangement of pieces.

A diagrammed solution of each puzzle was pasted on the bottom of the box which held it. During the first session this arrangement was fully revealed to the S, especially in connection with the two puzzles he failed to solve. When the E subsequently left the room, the S found himself with the opportunity to cheat either by consulting the diagrams or by ignoring the instructions relative to the bell. No direct prohibitions were imposed by the E except upon two Ss who in the second session asked if, out of curiosity, they could look at the diagrams of puzzles they had failed to solve. As honesty ratings were made from the average of both sessions, this minor deviation can safely be ignored in the scoring.

Results. The fact that the Ss had become so well affiliated with the Clinic in their previous visits tended to defeat the purpose of this experiment. Only three of the fifteen availed themselves of the opportunity to consult or copy diagrams. It was possible to secure a gradation in respect to honesty only by taking into account certain rather trifling violations. Two Ss, for instance, glanced at the very first solution before starting, but never did so again. Six others more or less frequently ignored the instructions relative to the bell, and there were only two out of the group who did not at some time work beyond the signal or start ahead of it. The inclusion, however, of such material in a rank order for honesty is far from satisfactory, and for this reason, as well as the small number to whom the test was administered, no attempt will be made to interpret the correlations. The following measures were calculated from the data :

1. *Ability.* The ability of Ss for the puzzle-solving task was

obtained by averaging their performance over all four periods of the two sessions, making suitable allowances for such cheating as occurred.

2. *Composite honesty rating*. Actual cheating either by copying or consulting the diagrams gave the primary ranking for honesty, outright copying without an attempt at solution being regarded as the more serious offence. The two Ss who looked once at the solutions were termed 'equivocal violators' and placed just above the violators in the honesty rating. A secondary rank order was calculated from the number of violations of instruction relative to the bell. The two rank orders were not averaged, the secondary being used to secure a gradation when Ss were tied in the primary. The resulting measure, called the composite honesty rating, was found to correlate, as might be expected, with Superego Integration (+.55). The attempt of the Diagnostic Council to predict honesty yielded a correlation of only +.23.

15. OBSERVATIONS OF EXPERIMENTS AND POST–EXPERIMENTAL INTERVIEWS

R. N. Sanford

Purpose. The twofold purpose of the exploratory study here reported was, first, to observe some of the press and trends exhibited by the E and the Ss respectively during an experimental session and, second, to add to our knowledge of each S's personality by taking a time sample of his behaviour under rather definite conditions.

That an S's performance of an imposed task is often profoundly influenced by factors other than those under immediate study has been frequently noted by experimenters, and it is a guiding principle of our explorations that, in formulating experimental results, account should be taken of as many factors of the S's personality as possible, and of the total situation in which he responds. In an experimental situation an S, who has emotional needs, personality traits and abilities, is presented with various social stimuli, that is, the appearance and behaviour of the experimenter, and with a task which has various characteristics and which presents the possibility of either success or failure. As in ordinary intercourse between two people there takes place between the experimenter and the subject an interplay of attitudes. An attitude or activity of the one, let us say the S, leads to some response by the E, and this response, in turn, becomes a press for further behaviour on the part of the S. The relatedness of the E and the S could be conceived of as a sequence of such press-trend combinations, which varies with and influences the S's progress with his task.

It seemed to us that our conceptual scheme was well adapted for a scientific description of the experimental session as a whole, and that an investigation of such a session, carried out with our concepts in mind, might throw further light upon the relations among the variables in our scheme. Making the tentative assumption that every act of the S is a behaviour pattern of some need, and that all need activity is the result of some press, we asked ourselves what needs and press can be observed in an experimental situation. The next questions were : How are these factors related ? What are the different kinds of need activity evoked by a given press and with what frequencies are they associated with this press ? What different kinds of press may arouse a particular need and with what frequency do we find these relationships ? Could we not with the use of these concepts gain so complete an understanding of this situation in which many variables operate as to make possible the formulation of some general psychological laws ?

According to our view, then, the S's mode of executing the experimental task was a phenomenon to be understood in its relation to many operating variables. Though it was our desire to aid the E in arriving at a complete account of his S's behaviour, on the basis of which he might explain individual differences with respect to the particular hypothesis being tested, actually we were no more interested in the S's performance of the task than in any other of the variables in the situation. For us, the experimental session was an instance of both the face-to-face social situation and the task situation, which together recur so frequently in life.

Though our primary concern was with the above general questions, the discovery of individual differences occupied much of our attention. We adopted the view that a complete diagnosis of a personality includes not only an estimation of the recurrent tendencies of that personality but a knowledge of the circumstances under which these variables manifest themselves. Thus, we inquired with what frequency are the particular needs of the individual subject manifested, and with what press are they associated.

Procedure. The E observed interpretatively from a position of concealment the events of the second session of the Ethical Standards Test and Memory for Failures Test, and at the close of these sessions he interviewed the S concerning his behaviour and experiences during them. The sequence of press-need combinations and as many as possible of the exact words and specific movements of the S and the E_1 [1] were recorded by the E, who used appropriate record blanks, a code of his own design, and a stop-watch which ran continuously throughout the hour. The record blank was a 9 x 12 sheet of paper, ruled to form one-minute intervals each of which contained three rows in which observations could be recorded. For example, the notations :

cr	enc	
	exc	aba-suc

would indicate that the E criticized the S and the S offered some excuse, whereupon the E encouraged the S who then expressed hopelessness mixed with an appeal for further encouragement. These records were analysed later to determine what press and needs had been manifested and in what relations.[2]

1. The expression E_1 stands for the experimenter who conducted the experiment under observation, while the observer is designated E.

2. The E_1 in each of the experimental sessions likewise made observations of his own and the S's behaviour. However, since (because of preoccupation with his other experimental duties) the E_1 was not able to keep records in time with those of the E, it was decided that rather than combine their observations each of the experimenters would make use of his own material in independently rat-

In interviewing the Ss the E assumed the attitude of one ignorant of the Clinic experiment. He attempted to gain rapport with the S as quickly as possible and to establish a situation which in its lack of tension was in contrast to the one which the S had just been through. The S was urged to recount in the order of their occurrence the events of the experimental session and to express himself freely concerning his reactions to the Clinic experiments in general, his attitudes toward puzzles, his attitudes and expectations with regard to taking part in this particular experiment, his motives, his effort, his opinion of his performance, his reactions to success and failure, his attitudes toward the experimenter, his interpretations of the experimenter's attitudes toward him, and other aspects of his behaviour and experiences during the session.

The S's reports and behaviour during the interview offer rich material for interpretation. In so far as these reports were objective they could supplement the records of the E in arriving at a complete account of the objective events of the experimental session, and they could sometimes supply knowledge of the experiences and inner tensions associated with the behaviour recorded. But the S's conscious and unconscious falsifications, distortions and omissions promised to be even more revealing. The degree to which the motives of the S influenced his report, as well as the direction of this influence, was a factor of importance. The reports of the S would depend upon his dominant needs and traits, upon tensions established in or as a result of the experimental session, and upon the events of the interview itself, particularly those springing from his relatedness to the E. The E attempted to take account of all these variables. Preoccupied as he was with making notes of the S's reports, he was not able to keep a precise record of the press-need combinations, but on the basis of notes he nevertheless drew some conclusions concerning this aspect of the problem.

---

ing the Ss on the variables of personality. It is clear, however, that in future work of this sort the E_1 should keep the same kind of record as the E. Or, better still, the motion picture camera and the microphone should be used.

About three months elapsed between Interview 1 and Interview 2. Unlike Interview 1, Interview 2 took place in the room in which the S had been working alone on puzzles. The E, knowing the time at which the session would be terminated, entered the room just as the S was concluding his work on the last puzzle. It was thus natural that discussion should be directed immediately to the experiment just concluded. The E attempted to reinstate the friendly relations previously established with the S. The points treated in Interview 1 were again discussed and the S was questioned at greater length than previously concerning his experiences at the Clinic, his reactions to and attitudes toward the particular experiments, and other issues which he himself raised.

This interview was observed by the E_1, who, being already in a position behind the one-way screen,[1] recorded as fully as possible the conversations of the E and the S. This material was used in conjunction with the E's notes in making interpretations of the session.

16. SENSORIMOTOR LEARNING

Walter C. Langer

The purpose of this investigation was to test the ability of subjects to learn a simple sensorimotor task, to distinguish and measure the separable factors that determine the rate and mode of solving it, and finally to discover which personality variables are correlated with each of these factors.

The task selected for this purpose was one in which the subject was asked to learn to associate each one of ten visual stimuli with a particular telegraphic key mounted on a keyboard. A special apparatus was designed and constructed at the Clinic which forced the subject to learn this task by the trial and error method, the order of the slides being never the same.[2] A waxed paper

1. See the technique of the Ethical Standards Test.
2. For full description of apparatus see : Langer, W.C. 'An apparatus for studying sensori-motor learning, retention and reaction time.' *J. Gen. Psychol.*, 1935, *12*, 228–238.

record was taken (throughout the learning performance) of each slide presented, all responses made to the slide and the time consumed. From this record it was then possible to measure each subject's performance in terms of errors, total time and number of repetitions, as well as time of responding, and perseveration on the keys.

The subjects in Group II learned three such key-slide systems, always using the same set of slides. Some of these slides had meaningful designs such as the square, circle, triangle, etc., and some had 'nonsense' patterns. In each key-slide system a given slide would correspond to a key different from that used in any previous systems. The subjects in Group III learned four key-slide systems. The first learning was with a set of slides the patterns of which were all meaningful and common in the life of every adult individual. The second, third and fourth learning performances were with a single set of 'nonsense' or meaningless slides. Group IV learned three key-slide systems. The slides used in all three systems were the 'nonsense' slides used with Group III. All three groups of subjects subsequently relearned all of the key-slide systems originally learned, and a comparison of the relearning performances with the original learning performance offered a measure of retention by the 'savings method.'

The experimental technique in all of the learning and relearning sessions was identical. The subject was taken into a small darkened room in which the keyboard rested on a table of typewriter height. The remainder of the apparatus was set up in an adjacent room, the slides being exposed to the subject through an aperture in the wall. When seated at the table with the keyboard the subject was given the following instructions:

Place your fingers on the keys so that the little finger of the left hand is on the key at the extreme left; the little finger of the right hand is on the key at the extreme right. Thus, every finger will be on an individual key with the thumbs on the keys nearest the centre. Always keep your fingers in these positions during the experiment.

Directly in front of you, you will see a small aperture. In this aperture you will see a geometrical pattern mounted on a particular coloured background. There are ten different patterns mounted on ten different backgrounds, each combination corresponding to one key on the keyboard. When you press the key corresponding to the particular combination showing in the aperture the slide will be released and a new one will appear. If you press a key and nothing happens it means that you are pressing the wrong key. The same slide will always be released when the key corresponding to it is pressed, regardless of the order in which it appears.

The importance of keeping the experimental situation constant cannot be over-emphasized. The results of an inconstancy, unwittingly introduced with Group IV, will become evident when we consider the data. The experiments with Group III were the most successful from this point of view. In this group it was possible to have the subjects come at the same hour of day, every two days for the original learnings, and exactly eight days later for the relearning. Although this was attempted with Groups II and IV there were wide variations which were unavoidable.

What can we say about the factors within the learner which may influence learning ? One thinks first of intelligence. In the present experiments, Groups II and III were given the Army Alpha Test by a skilled tester and the results correlated with the learning performance. In Group II the correlation was +.41 and with Group III +.42. Many other experimenters in the field of learning have found correlations of this order between learning performance and intelligence as measured by various tests.[1] Though the correlations are consistent and fairly high, they are far from perfect. It seems logical to suppose that other factors are also operative. What type of factors could these be ? Motivation has been the recent answer, especially since it was shown that mere repetition of a stimulus and a response does not in itself lead to

1. *Cf.* Lumley,F.H. 'An investigation of the responses made in learning a multiple choice maze.' *Psychol. Monog.*,1931,*42*, No.2, 1–61 ; and Schultz,R.S. 'The relation of maze adaptability, maze learning, and general intelligence.' *Amer. J. Psychol.*,1932,*44*, 249–262.

learning.[1] Muenzinger [2] has recently studied learning and motivation in human subjects. He divided them into two groups and motivated one group with an electric shock each time the wrong response was made. The other half of the group acted as controls. He found no significant differences and concluded that humans are so completely motivated in the usual laboratory situation that the addition of a shock cannot produce an accelerating effect upon the learning. This was taken for granted in our experiments.

Learning

In every learning experiment some arbitrary stage of mastery must be chosen in order that the performances of the subjects are comparable. Throughout the present experiments the state of mastery was set at correct responses to twenty successive slides beginning with the slide first presented. The same standard was set for the relearning sections of the experiments. In no instance did a subject learn beyond this point.

If we analyse the learning performance it becomes clear that there are at least three feasible measures: first, the *number of errors* made in reaching the stage of mastery; second, the *total time* taken; and third, the *number of repetitions* of the stimuli required. Almost all previous studies of learning have used but one of these three measures. But since correlations between these measures are frequently low, it seems better to include them all in a single composite score: the Learning Index. The Learning Index is found by extracting the cube root of the product of the three scores. It has been checked statistically and appears to be an adequate measure of learning performance. By using the Learning Index as a measure we are able to compare the performance of a subject who makes a great many mistakes but requires only a short time with the performance of a subject who requires much

1. Thorndike, E.L. 'A fundamental theorem in modifiability.' *Proc. Nat. Acad. Science*, 1927, *V.13*, 15–18.
2. Muenzinger, K.F. 'Motivation in learning, II, The function of electric shock for right and wrong responses in human subjects.' *J. Exper. Psychol.*, 1934, *17*, 439–448.

time but makes comparatively few errors, or with a subject who requires many repetitions in comparison with the number of errors or total time taken.[1] All learning and relearning performances throughout these experiments are measured in terms of the Learning Index.

In order to obtain an estimate of the subjects' learning ability all of his original learning performances were measured in terms of errors, total time and repetitions and combined by the Learning Index formula. The subjects were then ranked on each performance and a composite rank order made from these individual rank orders. It is taken as representing total learning ability in a task of this type and was correlated with all of the personality variables.

Certain consistent correlations were found. They are :

Variable	*Group II*	*Group III*	*Group IV*	*Av.*
n Achievement . .		—.26	—.43	—.35
n Deference	—.28	—.22	—.42	—.31
n Exhibition	—.22	—.52	—.39	—.38
Exocathection . . .		—.31	—.36	—.36
Impulsion	—.55	—.28	—.21	—.35
Intensity	—.50	—.27	—.49	—.42
n Play	—.26	—.23	—.24	—.24
n Sex	—.28	—.26	—.42	—.32

Of these eight consistent correlations four are intimately related : Sex, Exocathection, Play and Impulsion. These four variables have been found elsewhere to always show consistent, significant intercorrelations with one another. It has been termed the Sensation Syndrome. If we combine these four variables into a single composite rank order and correlate it with learning, we obtain a correlation of —.47, which would seem to indicate that the 'good' learners are those whose interests are not concerned with the outer world but rather with inner values. The remaining four correlating variables are also prevailingly occupied with immedi-

1. For a complete discussion of measures of learning see : Langer, W.C. 'An experimental critique of the measures of learning.' *J. Psychol.*, 1936, *3*, 195–221.

ate external adaptation. If, however, we regard all of these factors as indicating a certain attitude toward the external environment and combine them into a composite rank order and correlate it with the Learning Index the result is —.83.

These correlations indicate rather definitely that 'introverts' are more efficient learners than 'extraverts.' This may seem strange at first glance since it is generally believed that the closer one's contact with external reality the easier it will be to learn a manual task. Such a conclusion may be easily drawn from the older associationist or connectionist theory of learning which maintained that learning consisted of the establishment of neural bonds between a definite external stimulus and a given response. The results obtained by the gestalt psychologists, however, have shown that this is not usually the case. Learning depends on organization. In our own experiments, for example, subjects found it impossible to learn the tasks by simply relating each of the ten stimuli with the keys corresponding to them. Approximately five stimulus-response patterns could be mastered in this manner. When this number was reached each new response learnt meant a loss of one previously established, the number known remaining rather constantly in the neighbourhood of five. What was necessary to master the entire task was some sort of cognitive scheme whereby all ten stimulus-response patterns could be organized into a single related whole. It is characteristic of the introvert to think in such terms. It is also characteristic of the introvert to think before he acts, or, as one subject reported : 'I would have turned in a better performance if I used my head more and my fingers less.' In the present task, since a scheme of some sort was necessary, the introvert had the advantage ; since he came to it sooner and could immediately proceed with the learning whereas the extravert was forced to think conceptually only after much time and effort had been wasted.

Due to an oversight, the conditions under which Group IV learned were not identical with the conditions for Groups II and III. The two latter groups (II and III) participated in this experiment before they had taken part in any other Clinic experiments.

All of them were unsophisticated from a psychological point of view, unfamiliar with this type of experiment, and unacquainted with the Clinic staff. It seems reasonable to suppose that under these circumstances a certain amount of anxiety would be aroused during the first few experiments; and this proved to be the case. Furthermore, in these two groups, consistent negative correlations, in addition to those already cited, were found with n Succorance, n Infavoidance, Intraception, Projectivity, Emotionality, Superego Conflict and Narcism. These variables have always been found to intercorrelate with one another throughout all the groups and may be designated as the Inferiority Syndrome. A composite rank order correlates —.59 with the learning R.O. which indicates that in a strange situation Infavoidance and its accompanying Emotionality are detrimental factors to efficient learning. This fits in with the observations of many writers on the subject. The closest definite proof is an experiment performed by Higginson[1] on rats, in which he concludes that 'anger and fear of the varieties aroused in our white rats immediately preceding their introduction into a standard circular maze, appear to modify habit formation in the maze as witnessed by an increase: (1) in the time spent by the rat in running the maze as well as the total time required for learning it; (2) in the degree of variability of performance from trial to trial; (3) in the total distance travelled; (4) in the number of errors; and (5) in the number of trials necessary for mastery.' Our experiments seem to indicate that under these experimental conditions emotion arising out of feelings of inferiority and insecurity tends to have a disturbing effect upon human subjects.

Quite a contrary effect was found in the learning performances of Group IV. The subjects in this group took part in the learning experiments about five months after they had begun work at the Clinic, during which time they had participated in some thirty experimental sessions. They were, consequently, familiar with all of the members of the Clinic staff, and knew about what to

1. Higginson, G.D. 'The after effects of certain emotional situations upon maze learning among white rats.' *J. Comp. Psychol.*, 1930, *10*, 1–10.

expect in an experiment. There was, therefore, far less tension than in the foregoing groups. An examination of the correlations between the personality variables and the learning performance of Group IV reveals a positive correlation with the entire Inferiority Syndrome which correlated negatively with learning in the two previous groups. In other words, the personality factors which proved detrimental when the situation was strange and uncertain became advantageous when the situation was a familiar one. One may suppose that the learning test presented itself to those with social inferiorities as an opportunity for self-vindication (substitute achievement).

Motor Impulsion Index

In the general discussion on measures of learning it was indicated that some subjects made more errors in comparison with the amount of time or number of repetitions required, while others made less. It was pointed out at that time that an adequate measure of learning must take all three factors into account. The Learning Index was invented for this purpose. It seems reasonable to assume that the comparative number of errors made in relation to the other factors would be an indication of the tendency to act without thinking; that is, of the impulsiveness of the subject. This factor will be termed *motor impulsion.*

A subject's score on motor impulsion was determined by the ratio of number of errors made to his total score on learning as measured by the Learning Index. The larger the ratio the more impulsive the subject. Only Groups III and IV were calculated. When the rank order on motor impulsion was correlated with the rank orders on the personality variables, consistent correlations were found with the following:

Variable	*Group III*	*Group IV*	*Av.*
n Aggression	.50	.54	.52
n Dominance	.39	.47	.43
Exocathection	.53	.51	.52
n Exhibition	.24	.56	.40
Impulsion	.22	.54	.38

Variable	*Group III*	*Group IV*	*Av.*
Intensity	.24	.46	.35
Sameness	—.26	—.26	—.26
n Succorance	—.39	—.30	—.35

An examination of these correlations reveals that the first five of these variables : Aggression, Dominance, Exhibition, Intensity and Impulsion (general), form a syndrome ; that is, they consistently intercorrelate with one another in all the groups. We may call this the Ascendance Syndrome for purposes of identification. If we follow the method of compositing the variables of a syndrome as outlined in the previous section we find a correlation of +.65 between Ascendance and motor impulsion. Ascendance, of course, is antipolar to n Succorance and, as one might expect, there is an average correlation of —.35 between this personality variable and motor impulsion. The positive correlation between motor impulsion and Exocathection and the negative correlation with Sameness conform to the nature of the Ascendance Syndrome.

Impedance

Just as there are individuals who make a disproportionate number of errors in comparison with their total learning, so there are individuals who require a disproportionate amount of time. We have designated this as *impedance* to action. Impulsion would be the opposite of impedance if it were not for the third variable of Learning, namely, number of repetitions, which is also operating. Just as motor impulsion was calculated from the ratio between the error score and the cube root of the product of all three scores, so impedance is calculated from the ratio between time score and the same product. The Impedance Index may be said to represent the amount of learning per second of time ; the less learning the more impedance. When a rank order is made of the subjects in terms of impedance and this rank order correlated with the rank orders on personality variables, the following results are obtained :

Variable	*Group III*	*Group IV*	*Av.*
n Abasement		.36	.36
n Aggression	—.37	—.46	—.42
n Counteraction		—.36	—.36
n Defendance	—.36	—.62	—.49
n Dominance	—.41	—.68	—.55
Impulsion	—.28	—.40	—.34
n Infavoidance	.64	.37	.51
Superego Integration	—.21	—.23	—.22
n Succorance	.40	.31	.36

Here the personality make-up is rather definite. We see the impeded individual as one overcome by his own feelings of inferiority and insecurity, poorly integrated and self-abasing. Pride and Inviolacy are low, as well as Counteraction and most of the positive needs.

Impermeability

The third factor in the Learning Index is the *number of repetitions.* If this is divided by the Learning Index one obtains a quotient which represents its disproportionality (relative to the other factors) in the learning process. It was found that subjects differ widely in this respect. In other words, time and errors held constant, some individuals must repeat a performance more often than others do before it is completely mastered. Lacking a fitting term for this quotient we have called it *impermeability*, since it seems to indicate a lack of clear ready perceptiveness and retentiveness. A typical subject of this class would be one who learns *most* of the task rather quickly (and to do this he must be an habitual conceptualizer), and hence can proceed with relatively few mistakes and at a relatively even pace. But he experiences difficulty in remembering *all* the items perfectly. On each trial he makes one or two 'careless' mistakes. Thus, it is necessary for him to repeat the attempt over and over again. This is rather characteristic of the clever obsessional introvert who, though conceptually capable, usually disregards the stimuli that do not fit into his somewhat confused scheme of thought. This supposition is supported by the correlations :

Variable	*Group III*	*Group IV*	*Av.*
Superego Conflict	.52	.27	.39
Endocathection	.33	.51	.42
n Rejection	.44	.42	.43

Transfer

An examination of the successive learning performances reveals that for every subject the second learning performance was more economical than the first, and the third more economical than the second, but the amount of improvement (*transfer*) varied widely with individuals. The degree of *transfer* was computed by taking the ratio of the third learning (which seems to be the most economical) to the first learning. The smaller this ratio, the more improvement would be indicated, irrespective of the subject's absolute learning ability.

When *transfer* is correlated with the personality variables only three consistent correlations appear :

Variable	*Group III*	*Group IV*	*Av.*
Conjunctivity	—.47	—.56	—.52
n Counteraction	—.47	—.43	—.45
Sameness	—.30	—.40	—.35

The picture is that of a disjunctive, changeable and impersistent individual who, it may be assumed, did rather poorly in his first test because he was slow to discover the necessity of a conceptual scheme. Once having made this discovery, however, he could do relatively well on later tests.

Interference

Though improvement was shown by all subjects, there must have been some *interference* from earlier learnings, due to the fact that in each test the same stimuli had to be associated with different responses, or, in other words, the same responses had to be associated with different stimuli. Thus, the subject had to inhibit the previous responses before he could learn the new ones. Interference of this sort may be manifested in two ways: (1) by overt responses which would have been correct in an earlier learning, and (2) by an increased time of response resulting from the inhibition of the incorrect tendency. Efforts to treat these two factors independently were unavailing, due to the fact that all subjects employed both types at different stages in learning. Consequently, the two effects were computed and combined in one rank order of *interference*, which correlated with the following personality variables:

Variable	*Group III*	*Group IV*	*Av.*
Anxiety		.51	.51
Emotionality	.45	.42	.44
n Harmavoidance		.35	.35
Impulsion	.22	.35	.29
n Infavoidance	.37	.31	.34
Intraception	.30	.32	.31
Projectivity	.54	.21	.38
n Sentience	.39	.20	.30
n Succorance	.57	.22	.40
Superego Conflict		.28	.28

All of these variables fit into two closely related syndromes. The first is the Inferiority Syndrome which we have mentioned previously, and the second is the Subjectivity Syndrome which is composed of Intraception, Projectivity, Impulsion and Sentience. If we make two composite rank orders, one for the variables most closely allied with Inferiority and one for the variables most closely allied to Subjectivity, we find that *interference* correlates +.48 with the first and +.42 with the second. When the two syndromes are combined into one, the composite rank order thus obtained correlates +.57 with *interference*. Since *interference* is comparable to the effects of a neurotic complex, we are not surprised to find it marked in individuals that are relatively timid, shy, dependent, emotional, subjective and projective (irrational in judgements).

Retention

After having learned the successive key-slide systems the subjects were recalled and all systems were relearned. The Learning Index on the original learning of each system was then compared with the Index on the relearning, the ratio of the two being a measure of *retention* in accordance with the 'saving method' of Ebbinghaus. The subjects were ranked for retention on each of the key-slide systems and from these a composite rank order was computed. The correlations with this rank order, however, were all comparatively low and largely meaningless. Probably the 'saving method' is not an adequate measure of *retention* in experiments such as this, in which three or four conflicting tasks are learned successively before an attempt is made to measure retention.

Initial Retention

In scoring the subjects on *retention* it was noticed that most subjects remembered the first key-slide system better than they did the second or the third. The tendency to remember what is learned first better than what is learned later runs counter to the powerful factor of recency, which is emphasized in most studies in retention. We have called it *initial retention*, the index for which is obtained by dividing the relearning score (Learning Index) on the first system by the relearning score (Learning Index) on the third system. The following consistent correlations were found :

Variable	*Group III*	*Group IV*	*Av.*
n Abasement	—.40	—.36	—.38
n Affiliation	—.30	—.34	—.32
n Aggression	.28	.38	.33
n Defendance	.23	.42	.33
n Deference	—.69	—.30	—.50
Endurance	.22	.28	.25
Exocathection	—.28	—.25	—.27
n Play	—.24	—.36	—.30
n Rejection	.23	.23	.23

These correlations fall into two groups, the negative and the positive. Among the negative correlations we find Deference, Affiliation, Exocathection, and Play. At first glance the lack of these variables seems to have little relation to *initial retention*, though it indicates a certain attitude toward the external world, namely, one of withdrawal. These four variables almost always intercorrelate with one another and may be said to form the Social Syndrome. This correlates —.44 with *initial retention*. On the positive side we have the three variables : Defendance, Aggression, and Rejection, which also form a syndrome : the Defensive Syndrome. This correlates +.45 with *initial retention*. Linked as it is here with Endurance, it suggests 'tenacity of purpose.' Thus, *initial retention* seems to characterize the individual who is negative to the social environment. He does not adapt quickly to changing conditions. He sticks to what he first assimilates and rejects whatever comes later to disturb it.

Time of Response

Time of response refers to the subject's average time of reaction to the visual stimuli. In these experiments no instructions were given as to how the subject should react. He was free to respond as quickly or as slowly as he chose, and since hundreds of measures were averaged in obtaining the index, it may be supposed that we have an approximate measure of each subject's normal reaction time. The *time of response* was measured from the exposure of the stimulus to the beginning of the first response, regardless of the correctness of the response. The following correlations were found :

Variable	*Group II*	*Group III*	*Group IV*	*Av.*
n Abasement	—.49		—.53	—.51
n Aggression	.32	.17	.36	.34
n Counteraction . .		.38	.66	.52
n Defendance . . .		.38	.35	.37
n Dominance		.43	.57	.50
Impulsion			.22	.22
Intensity		.27	.20	.24

Five of these variables form a syndrome. They are Defendance, Counteraction, Dominance, Aggression, and Intensity. It is reasonable to suppose that a subject possessing these characteristics would undertake problems with assurance and speed. The negative correlation with Abasement (Passivity) fits in well with this hypothesis.

Perseveration on Keys

Perseveration on the keys refers to the average length of time a subject kept his finger on the key in responding to a stimulus. The following correlations were obtained with this factor:

Variable	*Group II*	*Group III*	*Group IV*	*Av.*
n Achievement		.37	.22	.30
n Aggression		.61	.23	.42
Creativity		.32	.20	.26
n Dominance		.47	.30	.39
Intensity	.23	.34	.38	.32
Intraception		.31	.36	.34
Narcism	.46	.46	.56	.48
Projectivity		.24	.51	.38
Sameness	.38	.30	.32	.33
Superego Integration		—.29	—.27	—.28
n Understanding ..		.37	.31	.34

These figures reveal a peculiar combination of traits. We have four positive variables, Aggression, Dominance, Achievement, and Intensity, combined with the subjective variables: Intraception, Projectivity, Understanding, Creativity, and Narcism. The latter five always intercorrelate with one another, and therefore form a syndrome. A composite rank order on the latter correlates +.46 with *perseveration*. The group of positive aggressive variables seems to indicate 'strength and emphasis' of response, coupled with the subject's conviction that he cannot be wrong. Such a person presses the key harder and longer in the hope of 'forcing' the instrument to obey him. The positive correlation with Sameness indicates the continuance of an activity once inaugurated.

Summary and Conclusions

We have studied ten different factors that influence the learning process and their relation to personality variables. The correlations to these ten factors include every variable in one connection or another. Consequently, it should be possible to put a group of subjects through the learning tests as here described, analyse their performances, and predict the personality of each subject. An attempt of this sort was made with Group IV, using the correlations previously found with Groups II and III. Though the attempt was not very successful (due to the change in the experimental conditions with Group IV) the predictive value of the measurements was far better than chance. The average correlation for all variables between the predicted rank orders and the Clinic rank orders for Group IV was +.48.

17. EMOTIONAL CONDITIONING TEST

a. Galvanic Skin Response

CARL E. SMITH and KENNETH DIVEN

Purpose. The purpose of this procedure was to investigate some determinants of emotional conditioning ; this being the process whereby an organism becomes emotionally responsive to a once ineffective stimulus. More specifically, the aim was to study the change in a subject's differential emotional reaction to a list of words, one of which (critical word) was recurrently followed by a painful electric shock. Accepting the galvanic skin response (gsr), which records a sudden lowering of the electrical resistance of the skin, as an index of autonomic (emotional) change, the attempt was made to measure : general and specific reactivity, the immediate perseveration of the response, the speed and degree of conditioning to the critical word (primary displacement), and the rate of extinction that occurs when the painful stimulus is no longer administered.

Preliminary experiments[1] showed that the degree of gsr is significantly correlated with affectivity, or more exactly, with the

1. Smith,C.E. ' A study of the autonomic excitation resulting from the interaction

intensity of an expressed sentiment. The technique used in these experiments was as follows : subjects were asked to put down the degree of their agreement or disagreement (Yes 5 to No 5) after each of a series of statements pertaining to provocative social questions read to them by an experimenter. Four weeks later, while connected with the psychogalvanometer, the same statements were re-rated verbally by each S, but this time after the experimenter had announced (before reading each statement) the opinion of the majority of the group. Thus, in many cases a condition of conflict was set up between individual and public conviction. The data showed that :

1. Responses of 'no' are accompanied by greater gsr than are responses of 'yes.'

2. Responses *against* the group opinion are accompanied by greater gsr than are responses *with* the group opinion.

3. The magnitude of the gsr varies proportionally with the degree of conviction asserted, excluding indifference and absolute conviction.

4. The gsr accompanying 'zero' responses are greater than the gsr accompanying responses of the degree of conviction 'one.'

5. The gsr accompanying absolute conviction are smaller than the gsr accompanying the degree of conviction immediately preceding the absolute.

6. The accompanying gsr are graded in the order of ascending magnitude : (a) 'yes' *with* group opinion, (b) 'no' *with* group opinion, (c) 'yes' *against* group opinion, (d) 'no' *against* group opinion.

In a subsequent series of experiments it was shown that if a particular word in a word-list (read to the S by the E) recurs at irregular intervals and four to twelve seconds after each presentation of this word an electric shock is administered, it will not be long before the gsr — which at first occurs *after* the shock — is exhibited immediately after the critical word (several seconds *before* the shock). This experiment was merely a demonstration of what others [1] had shown, namely, that it is possible to con-

---

of individual opinion and group opinion.' *J. Abn. & Soc. Psychol.*,1936,*31*, 138–164.

1. *Cf. Landis,C.* 'Electrical phenomena of the skin.' *Psychol. Bull.*,1933,*29*, 693–752.

dition the gsr (primary displacement), but it was a discovery to find that many of the subjects who showed conditioning, by thus responding differentially to the critical word, were entirely unaware that it was this word which had been followed by shock.

Apparatus. The apparatus consisted of a Wechsler psychogalvanograph, containing a D'Arsonval galvanometer and a Wheatstone bridge. The characteristics of the galvanometer were: resistance, 500 ohms; period, 3 seconds; sensitivity per mm deflection on scale, 0.15 microamperes. A 6.0-volt storage battery used to impress a potential of 4.0 volts at the bridge. The potential was held constant by means of a potentiometer. Recording apparatus containing a roll of white paper 22.9 cm wide, moving at a rate of 20 cm per minute. The fluctuations of the beam of light were magnified 3.5 times when reflected to the recording paper, and were traced by a pen. The apparatus was located in a separate room. The electrodes were of the two-fluid type: normal saline and saturated zinc sulphate, held at 37° C by a water bath. A constant volume, 3.6 cc, of the index and third fingers of the left hand was determined by displacement, and exposed to the electrode. Surgical tape was put snugly around each finger, the distal edge coinciding with the boundary of the part exposed. A large clock dial was constructed 44.5 cm in diameter, the hand activated by a telechron attachment. Brass disks 2.5 cm by 0.2 cm were used for giving electric shocks from an inductorium activated by dry cells.

Procedure. The S was seated with the clock dial 2 meters in front of him. The index and the third finger of the left hand (after immersion in a tube of water until 3.6 cc had been displaced) were then taped at the wet-dry boundary and placed in the fluid electrodes, the forearm being comfortably supported in a horizontal position. The index and little finger of the right hand were placed on the finger platforms of the tremograph (to be described later). Next, the brass disks used for shocking the S were attached to the bare calf of one leg.

The S's resistance was then balanced in the bridge and when

it became substantially constant the following instructions were read :

> Sit as comfortably relaxed as you can. Please do not move your hands, arms or legs. Watch the clock. I shall read you a list of words. Five seconds after you have heard each word, please respond with the word that is in your mind at that time. Are there any questions ?

The word-list consisted of the first 15 words of the O'Connor Work Sample No. 35[1] with the addition of the word 'Night' (critical word) which recurred five times, in serial positions 4, 7, 11, 16, 20. Four seconds after each repetition of the word 'Night' (hence one second before the S had been instructed to respond) he was given an electric shock.

With one half the Ss the twenty-word list was repeated immediately to test for conditioning on the critical word. With the other half of the Ss a 24-hour interval or delay intervened before the test of conditioning. No shock was administered in either the immediate or the delayed second session.

Results. To measure the extent of the galvanic deflection on the graph an arbitrary base line was established by drawing a horizontal line at the mean height of the curve between the point of shock and the point one second before the shock. The degree of response was measured as the vertical distance from this base line to the peak of the deflection. The measure of each deflection was finally given in terms of per cent ohms change of apparent resistance.

Under the above set forth conditions it was found that all the subjects became conditioned to the word 'Night' after three or four repetitions, that is, when the word-list was re-read in the second session (without shock) the galvanic deflections after this word were markedly greater than those after other words. In some subjects the heightened reaction was focally limited to the critical word, in others it was spread to some extent over the entire list (free-floating anxiety).

Comparing the immediate second session with the delayed

1. O'Connor, J. *Born That Way.* Baltimore, 1928, p. 43.

second session, it was discovered that the elapse of time (24 hours) had a tendency to increase the conditional response to the critical word. It was supposed that this phenomena was an illustration of 'incubation' (the unconscious 'growth' or intensification of an emotional complex). Leaving off the shocking electrodes during the second session and assuring the subjects that no shock would be given did not affect the extent of the gsr. In some subjects conditioning was an entirely unconscious occurrence.

It was decided to try a new set of conditions with Group IV ; to combine the gsr with the tremograph (to be described) and, in order to bring out all the phenomena measurable by the latter instrument, to ask each subject to respond to each item in the word-list by speaking aloud words that came to mind one after another (chained associations), until told to stop. The stop signal was given 12 seconds after the stimulus word (after the subject had given about seven or eight associations) ; and when the stimulus word was critical ('Night') a shock was administered immediately after the stop signal. But when it was found that these first subjects had not been conditioned (due in part to the long interval (12 sec.) between the critical word and the shock and in part to the interposed associations) the technique was modified by shortening the interval to 10 seconds and then to 8 seconds. Under these conditions a few of the subjects showed primary displacement of the affect to the critical word, but others did not. Only later [1] was it found that if many associations are given by the subject no conditioning will take place unless the critical word is specially accented, by speaking it in a deep voice, for example. Unfortunately, this was not discovered in time, and in the experiments with Group IV conditions were changed from subject to subject in the hope of finding the right procedure for combining the psychogalvanometer and the tremograph in a single session. For this reason the data for Group IV are not comparable and no generalizations can be made.

1. Diven,K. 'Certain determinants in the conditioning of anxiety reactions.' *J. Psychol.*,1936,*3*, 291–308.

b. Tremor Responses

In a very suggestive book Luria [1] reported a series of experiments in which it was conclusively shown that muscular disco-ordination (finger tremors) could be used as a sensitive index of emotional excitement, and so, with the intention of combining this measure with the gsr, a more convenient apparatus than Luria's was designed for accurately recording tremulous movements of a finger. The details of this so-called tremograph have been described elsewhere.[2] Suffice it to say that it consists of a box (overall dimensions 20″ x 20″ x 7″) within which is set a recording case containing a film of bromide paper for photographically recording the movements transmitted from the fingers by means of a set of light levers. Protruding through the top of the box are two very delicate levers each with a little platform upon which the index finger and the little finger, respectively, of the right hand are rested lightly.

The subject, seated in a comfortable chair, is instructed to flex his index finger (and thereby depress the lever) just as he utters each responsive word, but to let his little finger ('passive' finger) remain quiet throughout the experiment.

Though this technique was used only with Group IV, it can be said, at least, that our findings were in complete accord with Luria's. In some cases an emotional upset was transmitted through the active (responding) finger, in some cases through the passive finger, and in some cases through both fingers. The curves of the two fingers being simultaneously recorded on the moving film, together with the moment of the stimulus word and the moment of the subject's verbal response, it was possible to measure accurately 1, any departure from simultaneity of verbal response and index finger flexion ; and 2, any irregularity (tremor) of either the active or the passive finger. The records clearly showed disco-ordination, first in connection with the electric shock and later in connection with the critical word. That is to say, finger

1. Luria, A. *The Nature of Human Conflicts*, New York, 1932.
2. Langer, W.C. 'The tremograph.' *J. Gen. Psychol.*, 1936, *15*, 459–465.

tremors, as well as the gsr, can be conditioned by the above mentioned technique. It was not possible, because of the frequent changes of procedure, in these preliminary experiments to make precise correlations between muscular disco-ordinations and galvanic deflections, but it was seen that in many instances they ran parallel.

In testing Group IV the word-list was lengthened and several provocative words ('cheating,' 'homosexual,' 'coward') were added. In the majority of cases the tremor reactions accompanying the associations to these words were more marked than those that followed the other words.

18–22. EXPLORATION OF COVERT AND UNCONSCIOUS THEMAS: PROJECTION TESTS

H. A. Murray

In an attempt to discover the covert (inhibited) and unconscious (partially repressed) tendencies of normal persons, a number of procedures were devised. These procedures are simply different methods of stimulating imaginative processes and facilitating their expression in words or in action. Under the term 'imaginative processes' have been included: single words or phrases, verbal associations, single or compound images, thematic constructions (fantasies) and conceptualizations.

Facilitation was partially achieved, in all procedures, by having the S use his imagination in describing some object or constructing a dramatic presentation with objects or with words. His attention was thus diverted from his psychic processes, as such. He was, it seemed to him, talking about the material, not about himself. This is important because almost everyone is put on the defensive by a direct attempt to penetrate below his peripheral personality. This is true even for neurotics who have been assured that the cure of their suffering depends upon the uninhibited expression of their free associations. It takes months of analysis sometimes before the resistance of a subject is sufficiently dissolved to allow him to talk freely about certain matters which were perfectly conscious to him at the beginning of his treatment. If such defensive measures are found in patients who have confidence in their physicians, much more frequently are they encountered in everyday life and most particularly in clinical experimentation with subjects who have little to gain, and perhaps something to lose, by exposing themselves. Consequently, subjects must not have it in mind that they are talking about themselves. They must believe that they are demonstrating their ability to interpret or create something which is external to them.

The procedures which have been used in our exploration of personality are the following: 1, Thematic Apperception Test (Morgan and Murray); 2, Beta Ink Blot Test (Wheeler); 3, Similes Test (Wheeler); 4, Minister's Black Veil Test (Wheeler); 5, Musical Reverie Test (Kunze); 6, Rorschach Test (Beck); and 7, Dramatic Productions Test (Homburger). Each of these tests may be used as an index of the following variables: Intraception, Creativity (literary and artistic), and to some extent Projectivity and Narcism. They are chiefly useful, however, in revealing the latent images, needs and sentiments of individual subjects and, thus, providing data for a speculative reconstruction of unconscious thematic patterns. The Rorschach Test has, of course, additional advantages.

During the year following the completion of these studies several more 'projection' procedures were devised, all of which proved effective in provoking imaginative thought.[1]

18. THEMATIC APPERCEPTION TEST[2]

Christiana D. Morgan and H. A. Murray

Purpose. The purpose of this procedure is to stimulate literary creativity and thereby evoke fantasies that reveal covert and unconscious complexes.

1. Murray, H.A. 'Techniques for a systematic investigation of fantasy.' *J. Psychol.*, 1936, *3*, 115–143.
2. By permission of the editors, a good part of this report is quoted from: Morgan, C.D. and Murray, H.A. 'A method for investigating fantasies.' *Arch. Neur. & Psychiat.*, 1935, *34*, 289–306.

The test is based upon the well-recognized fact that when a person interprets an ambiguous social situation he is apt to expose his own personality as much as the phenomenon to which he is attending. Absorbed in his attempt to explain the objective occurrence, he becomes naïvely unconscious of himself and of the scrutiny of others and, therefore, defensively less vigilant. To one with double hearing, however, he is disclosing certain inner tendencies and cathexes : wishes, fears, and traces of past experiences. Another fact which was relied upon in devising the present method is this : that a great deal of written fiction is the conscious or unconscious expression of the author's experiences or fantasies.

The original plan was to present subjects with a series of pictures each of which depicted a dramatic event of some sort with instructions to interpret the action in each picture and make a plausible guess as to the preceding events and the final outcome. It was anticipated that in the performance of this task a subject would necessarily be forced to project some of his own fantasies into the material and thus reveal his more prevailing thematic tendencies. As the subjects who took this test were asked to interpret each picture — that is, to apperceive the plot or dramatic structure exhibited by each picture — we named it the 'Thematic Apperception Test.' Only by experience did we discover that much more of the personality is revealed if the S is asked to create a dramatic fiction rather than to guess the probable facts.

Since, for purposes of comparison, it is desirable to devise a procedure which is as uniform as possible, the attempt was made to arrive at a set of pictures which could be considered standard. Each picture should suggest some critical situation and be effective in evoking a fantasy relating to it. The set must be comprehensive. Ideally, there should be a picture which could act as a trellis to support the unfolding of every primal fantasy. It was considered, and the idea was later confirmed by experience, that in most pictures there should be at least one person (*evocative object*) with whom the subject could easily empathize and identify himself. Thus, there should be a separate set of pictures for males and females, and also for children, young adults and elders. Since in the present experiments the subjects were all young men between the ages of twenty and thirty, most of the pictures in our set included at least one figure of that sex and age. After a preliminary selection from several hundred pictures and an elimination of those which on repeated trials proved unproductive, we arrived at a set of twenty which gave good results.

Procedure. The subject was seated in a comfortable chair with his back to the experimenter and the following directions were read to him :

This is a test of your creative imagination. I shall show you a picture and I want you to make up a plot or story for which it might be used as an illustration. What is the relation of the individuals in the picture ? What has happened to them ? What are their present thoughts and feelings ? What will be the outcome ? Do your very best. Since I am asking you to indulge your literary imagination you may make your story as long and as detailed as you wish.

The subject was then handed Picture No. 1 and the experimenter wrote down everything he said. If, in giving his story, the subject omitted the antecedent circumstances or the outcome, he was prompted by such remarks as, 'What led up to this situation ?' 'How will it end ?' and so forth. When the subject finished his story he was handed Picture No. 2 and asked to proceed as before. There were twenty pictures in the series, but as the test was stopped after an hour, most of the subjects did not have time to make up stories for more than two-thirds of them.

After a few days had elapsed each subject was interviewed. This time the experimenter explained that he was studying the factors which operate in the imaginative construction of literary plots, and that he wished to know whether what eminent writers had written about their creative experiences was true for everyone. The subject was asked whether he would co-operate by saying what came to his mind when certain words or topics were mentioned. The S was then reminded one by one of the more important items or situations which he had recounted. The S was also asked whether his story had come from something which he had seen or read or whether it had come out of his personal experience.

Results. Examination of the stories concocted by our subjects in conjunction with material obtained from introspections, autobiographies, hours of free association, interviews and so forth, shows that there were four chief sources from which the plots and the items of the plots were drawn : 1, books and moving pictures ; 2, actual events in which a friend or member of the family participated ; 3, experiences (subjective or objective) in the subject's own life ; and 4, the subject's conscious and unconscious fantasies.

Although the material from the first two of these four sources may seem at first blush to be of little importance, it was discovered that even here much of significance was revealed. It would appear that the external events which excite sympathetic vibrations (empathy) within the psyche are generally those which make the deepest impression and are most enduringly remembered, and so when we hear the recounting of such events we may tentatively suppose that the theme of the objective occurrence is a clue to the subject's personality.

That every subject almost immediately projects his own circumstances, experiences or preoccupations into the evocative object was only too obvious. For instance, in one of the early experiments six of the eleven college men who took the test said that the youth in one picture was a student ; whereas none of the twelve non-college men who acted as subjects described him as such. To take another case, one of our subjects, whose father had been a ship's carpenter, wanted to go to sea himself, to travel and see the world. This was his dominant fantasy. In his stories three of the scenes were laid on board ship, two in the Orient. About a picture which illustrates a middle-aged man talking to a younger man, the subject said : 'The older man is educated and has traveled a lot. He convinces the other to travel ; to take a job that will take him to different places.' In a picture which illustrates a young man sitting in a chair brooding rather disconsolately, this subject said : 'This is a business man who runs quite a business in town. He is weighing the possibility of a European trip. He has been arguing with his wife on the subject. She got angry because he would not go, and finally took up her hat and left. He is thinking it over. He changes his opinion, goes out and buys tickets.' In another picture illustrating two labourers engaged in conversation, the same subject said : 'These two fellows are a pair of adventurers. They always manage to meet in out-of-the-way places. They are now in India. They have heard of a new revolution in South America, and they are planning how they can get there. . . In the end they work their way in a freighter.'

Many other examples of this sort of thing could be cited. No subject failed to exemplify it. Some of them, in fact, gave stories which were frank and unabashed autobiographies.

If the procedure had merely exposed conscious fantasies and remembered events it would have been useful enough, but it did more than this. It gave the experimenter excellent clues for the divination of unconscious thematic formations. The following mode of analysis and summary was used : each of the subject's stories was read and diagnosed separately and then the attempt was made to find a unifying thema. If such was evident, each story, if necessary, was re-interpreted and with some elimination and curtailment the series was re-arranged in such a way as to emphasize the important trends, and demonstrate their inter-relations. To illustrate the procedure we have chosen a few stories (given by one subject) that require the minimal amount of interpretation. Most of them are variations of a single underlying complex thema.

Case : Virt

Virt was a Russian Jew working for a Ph.D. in Science. He was born near the German frontier. Six months after his birth his father emigrated to America, and left him, an only child, with his mother. When he was two the Great War broke out and for four years mother and son experienced 'terrible suffering.' To keep alive the mother 'resorted to that dangerous but quite remunerative sport of smuggling.' Not until Virt was eleven years old did the father send for his wife to join him in Pennsylvania.

Before going to America Virt also experienced the horrors of religious persecution. 'Recollections of those persecutions,' he writes, 'still prey on my mind : dead bodies with torn limbs dragged in heaps to the cemetery ; my uncle forced to dig his own grave before my eyes ; my aunt shot in cold blood at my hand ; bombs thrown a few feet before me' (p Aggression). In his autobiography he reports two recollections of note, one in which he and his mother and a group of others were barricaded in a cellar without water (p Lack : Water, Food). 'Suddenly the door was blown open,' he writes, 'my mother and I stood quite near. I at once ran out to the next building, intent on procuring food and drink. . . I darted across through the bullets and shrapnel and forced open the door of the next building. Imagine the fright of the inmates. They refused to let me go back' (p Dominance : Restraint : Enforced Separation from Mother). Virt's other memory was of being left alone (p Insupport : Separation from Mother), a lad of eight, at a hotel in Warsaw while his mother went to procure passports. 'Tired of staying at home, I ventured out,' he writes. 'I determined in some way to go to her' (n Succorance for Mother). He happened to pick up a transfer, took the first car and eventually found his mother. 'Luckily for me, it was the right car. Otherwise I would have been lost in a strange large city. The surprise of my mother was great when she saw me.'

These memories are concerned with separation from the mother and anxiety about reunion. They seem to be repetitions of the numerous earlier experiences of being left by his mother. 'While fighting was going on in one village, she used to come there with products from a more peaceful town. She stood the danger of being killed, or if caught, of being hanged, or maltreated by the soldiers' (Fear of p Insupport : Death of Mother).

Soon after arriving in this country the faults of Virt's father became glaringly apparent to him and to his mother (p Insupport : Inferior Father). Quarrels, in which Virt always took his mother's part, commenced and persisted (Oedipus complex). Lately, the mother has become very nervous. Her son fears heart failure (Fear of p Loss : Death of Mother).

Virt worked his, way through school and college and is now planning to become a schoolteacher. 'I know that such a position would satisfy my mother, whom above all I want to please' (Positive cathection : Mother), he writes. A short time ago he formed a serious attachment for a girl his own age and for a time enjoyed intercourse with her (Fn Sex Aff). Now, he is trying to break away from her on the ground that he will not have the money to marry her for several years (n Rejection : Renunciation of Love for Achievement).

Virt reported that he had occasional nightmares reminiscent of the shocking experiences of his youth. Otherwise there were no unusual manifestations. He appeared to be a quiet, self-contained and self-reliant young man. Since he had a leaning towards pessimism the philosophy of Schopenhauer was especially congenial to him. He said that he feared a general failure. As he put it, he had a 'fear of coming to such a state in life that you have no economic means, no interests, no social standing, nothing seems to interest you and you can't seem to make your way in the world.'

Thematic Apperceptions

Picture No. 13. (On the floor against the couch is the huddled form of a boy with his head bowed on his right arm. Beside him on the floor is an object which resembles a revolver.)

S : Some great trouble has occurred. Someone he loved has shot herself. Probably it is his mother. She may have done it out of poverty. He, being fairly grown up, sees the misery of it all and would like to shoot himself. But he is young and braces up after a while. For some time he lives in misery — the first few months thinking of death. (p Loss : Death of Mother → Dejection (or Suicide with reunion after death))

Here, the possible death of the mother appears as one determinant of his present pessimism. The story is one variety of a large class of complex themas — the Tragic Love thema.

In his introspections the subject said : 'This comes out of my own experience. We have often been very poor and I have been very close to my mother and seen her struggles, known her discouragement (Identification with Mother) and thought of a

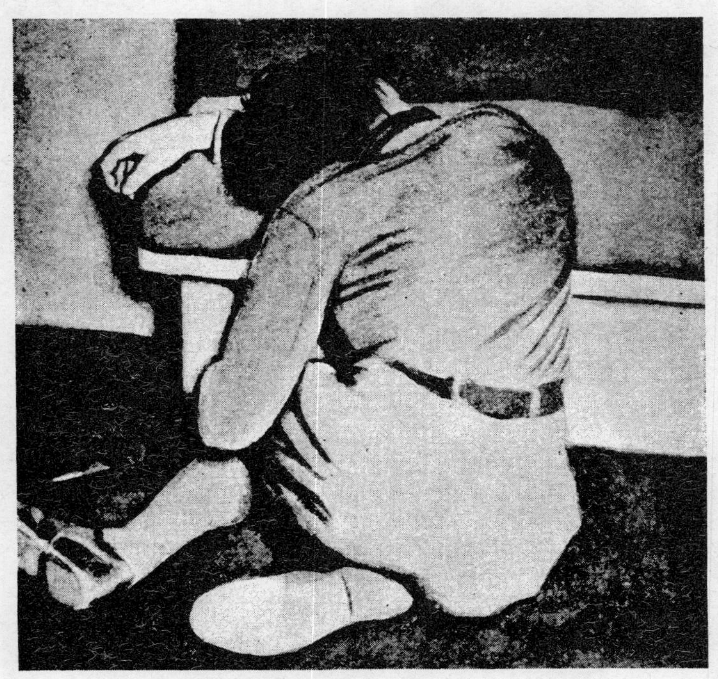

Picture No. 13

poverty so awful (p Insupport : Poverty) it could lead to suicide. As a child I used to think about poverty and death.'

Picture No. 11. (A short elderly woman stands with her back turned to a tall young man. The latter is looking downward with a perplexed expression, his hat in his hands.)

S : Mother and boy were living happily. She had no husband (Oedipus complex). Her son was her only support (n Nurturance for Mother). Then the boy got into bad company and participated in a gang robbery, playing a minor part. He was found out and sentenced to five years in prison. Picture represents him parting with his mother. Mother is sad,

Picture No. 11

feeling ashamed of him. Boy is very much ashamed. He cares more about the harm he did his mother than about going to prison. He gets out for good behaviour but the mother dies. He repents for what he has done but he finds that his reputation is lost in the city. No one will employ him. He again meets bad companions and in despair he joins them in crime. However, he meets a girl with whom he falls in love. She suggests that he quit the gang. He decides to quit after one more hold-up. He is caught and sent to prison. In the meantime, the girl has met someone else. When he comes out he is quite old and spends the rest of his life repenting in misery. (p Dominance : Bad Influence (externalization of blame) & n Acquisition : Robbery (Crime) → p Aggression : Imprisonment (Punishment) & p Loss : Death of Mother (also as a punishment) → n Abasement : Remorse & Dejection. The entire complex thema is then repeated with p Rejection : Preference for Rival instead of p Loss : Death of Mother)

The subject presents the Son-Lover thema followed by the death of the mother, and later the Love thema followed by desertion. In neither case is union between the lovers achieved. We also find a conflict between mother and son over the question of crime and gang robberies. Since the subject's desire for achievement and marriage are much restricted by poverty, and since his much-respected mother was a smuggler in Russia, we may suppose that temptations to rob and cheat have at times occurred to him. (N.B. He cheated repeatedly in the Ethical Standards Test.)

The conflict of the hero with the mother brings to mind some incidents mentioned by the subject when giving his childhood memories. He said that he had occasionally quarrelled with his mother because she nagged him. Once when he was thirteen he ran away and got a job in Pittsburgh. Another time he ran away to Newport News on account of a romantic longing he had for adventure. In regard to the repentance theme in the last story the subject said in his introspections : 'That's the way I would feel. If I took my car and stayed out all night I would be ashamed for having hurt my mother (n Nurturance for Mother), not for anything I might have done. We are really close to each other. She confides every thing to me (p Succorance). She doesn't get on well with my father.' The subject's conscience is a personal one. It prohibits him from hurting the woman he loves. He is not guided by an impersonal ethical standard.

Picture No. 16. (A dimly indicated figure of an man clinging to a rope. He is in the act of climbing up or down.)

S : It is a terrible fire in a place where there is no modern apparatus. While they wait, a rope is cast down and most of them escape by this rope. One man goes down and remembers that his wife is there too. What shall he do ? Engines come with a ladder. They are about to climb up,

Picture No. 16

but it is too dangerous. He decides to do so. As he is about to go up, he sees his wife at a window. She asks him not to go. Firemen keep him back. His wife dies in the flames. After the death of his wife, he is in great distress. He believes he should have gone up in spite of firemen. He blames the death of his wife on himself. Nothing more seems to interest him. He dies an early death. (object-p Danger : Fire → n Nurturance : Rescue → p Dominance : Restraint → p Loss : Death of Loved O → n Abasement : Self-blame & Dejection)

The accidental death of the beloved and the failure to rescue her calls to mind this subject's earliest experiences — the departure of his mother upon hazardous enterprises, his fear of losing her, and particularly the men restraining him when he wished to carry water to his mother. The subject says that after the hero loses his wife 'nothing more seems to interest him.' This sentence reminds us of his answer to the question, 'What are you most afraid of ?' The reply was this : 'Fear of coming to such a state in life that you have no economic means, no interests, no social standing ; nothing seems to interest you and you can't seem to make your way in the world.' One might guess that what he feared most was the death of his mother. She was living for him and he for her. This may have become imbedded at the time when his mother was his only means of support.

Picture A. (A heavily-built man naked to the waist gazing at the ground with his arms hanging limply at his side.)

S : Shipwrecked man. The boy had a girl in a boat. He tried to save her, but became exhausted. He brought her to shore — an island somewhere. She seems to be absolutely dead. He looks tired, exhausted. He tries to revive her but can't. Apparently she had died. He is very troubled. He doesn't know what to do. Should he commit suicide now that she is lost to him ? Or, should he go on living ? He decides to go back. He finds life unbearable for a while. He never marries. He gets old quick. (object-p Danger : Water → n Nurturance : Rescue Failure → p Loss : Death of Loved O → Dejection (or Suicide))

The fact that here the complex thema is the same as that in the preceding story indicates that it is the reverberation of a fixed unconscious fantasy.

Picture B. (A formal design of a young woman holding a baby in her arms. She seems to be running. Her long hair streams out behind.)

S : Two people about to be married were prevented by both father and mother on both sides. The boy is sent away. In the meantime an illegitimate child is born and the young girl is sent out of the city. She comes to

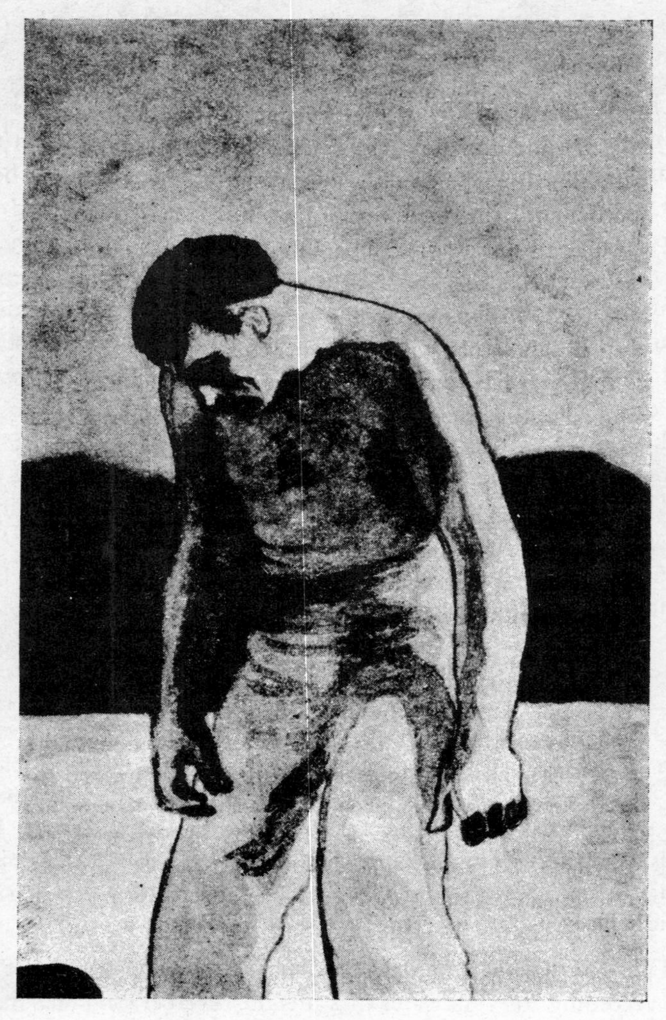

Picture A

some woods. She takes care of her child. In the meantime the father of the child comes back. He is not told about the child, but is told that the girl has killed herself. He rushes out of the house and goes to the woods. He doesn't know what has become of her. (N.B. At this point the subject said : 'I don't want them to come together.') The mother grows old

Picture B

and dies. The man and the child come together. (n Sex : Mutual Love → p Dominance : Restraint : Separation from Loved O → p Birth of Offspring → p Loss : Death of Beloved O)

The subject's interpolated remark — 'I don't want them to come together' — shows how deeply the Tragic Love thema is rooted. For Virt, mother, wife and the beloved object seem to be one and the same.

In these five pictures we find themas which are very similar or easily integrated. The Son-Lover thema, interrupted by an accident or stroke of fate which separates the boy from his mother, the Rescue Failure thema, the occurrence of p Loss : Death of Beloved O and, finally, the Suicide thema or the Dejection and Death thema. All this seems to be a reverberation of actual experiences and fantasies which occurred in childhood. They may be subsumed under the Tragic Love (or *Liebestod*) thema.

In three other stories the Renunciation of Love for Achievement thema appears. This describes his present predicament. He is in love, but he has nothing saved up in the bank and he must help support his mother. One wonders, however, whether his present erotic renunciation may not be the result of his mother fixation as well as an objectification of the Tragic Love thema — 'the lovers must not unite.'

The question arises : Is the prescribed tragic ending a result of his former constant fear that his mother would be killed or is it the recognition of the incest barrier ? As a boy he may have come to the tragic realization that, though his father was away and could not interfere, he would never reach (possess) his mother. This would account for his underlying pessimism.

Further Results. It was possible from the material obtained to assign marks to each subject on most of the latent variables : covert Aggression, covert Acquisition and covert Succorance being particularly evident. The experimenters also found that this test offered favourable conditions for measuring Intraception, literary Creativity, Projectivity, Intensity, Emotionality and verbal Conjunctivity.

'Optimism' was measured as the ratio : pleasant/unpleasant endings. The scale used for each story ran from —2 (very unpleasant : frustration, failure, death) to +2 (very pleasant : success and happiness). To obtain the final index the algebraic sum of these scores was divided by the number of stories. The degree of optimism or pessimism as measured in this way seemed to fit in with other findings.

Summary. The experimenters came to regard this test as the one which could be most certainly relied upon to supply the necessary clues for the divination of the unity thema. One of its chief virtues is that the subject reveals some of his innermost fantasies without being aware that he is doing so.

19. IMAGINAL PRODUCTIVITY TESTS

D. R. Wheeler

a. Beta Ink Blot Test

The Beta Ink Blot Test was suggested by one of a series of experiments conducted by Bartlett to shed light on the subjective nature of perceiving and imagining.[1] In addition to other materials, Bartlett employed a series of thirty-six ink blots of his own design. His subjects were requested to state everything that was suggested to them by the blots. While Bartlett was not primarily concerned with the question of individual differences among his subjects, he noted, as did the subjects themselves, that the interpretations of the blots were to a large extent conditioned by the individual's vocation, special interests, and past experiences. 'It has of course been noted before that this sort of test may throw a good deal of light on a person's interests and perhaps on his occupation. The subjects themselves often called attention to this. "You ought to be able to tell a lot about a man's interests and character from this sort of thing," they would say. . . The subject who was reminded by one of the blots of "Nebuchadnezzar's fiery furnace, with two men on either side at the top, and two in the middle" was a parson; while the same blot reminded a scientist interested in physiology of "an exposure of the basal lumbar region of the digestive system as far back as the vertebral columns up to the floating ribs."'[2]

1. Bartlett, F.C. 'An experimental study of some problems on perceiving and imaging.' *Brit. J. Psychol.*, 1916, VIII, Part 2, 222–266.
2. *Op. cit.*, p.255.

This suggested the obvious possibility that a careful analysis of the subject's responses to such a series of ink blots might yield information in regard not only to his interests but also to his dominant needs and themas. Hence thirteen of Bartlett's blots were mounted on cards and used with the thirteen Ss in Group III and ten of the Ss in Group IV; one of which is here reproduced.

In administering the test the E tried at the start to get into

good rapport with the S and to elicit his fullest co-operation. The S was invited to smoke and to make himself as comfortable as possible. The instructions, a modification of Bartlett's, were not read to him but were delivered from memory in a conversational tone of voice. They were as follows:

'I am going to ask you to look at some ink blots. These blots are not intended to represent anything in particular. They may, however, suggest something to you, as you sometimes see shapes in clouds or faces in a fire. So please look at each blot and tell me everything you see in it, everything it suggests or recalls, everything it might possibly be. You will probably find it easier if you adopt a relaxed and unself-critical attitude.'

The S was not allowed to spend more than two minutes on each blot. If his efforts seemed to be too superficial or if he was suspected of wool-gathering, he was occasionally prodded with some such query as, 'Anything else on that blot?' All of his responses and asides were noted by the E.

The interpretations obtained were also utilized as a basis for an estimate of the S's Intraception. These estimates were expressed in terms of an absolute scale of from 0 to 5. The S's mark depended on the quality as well as the quantity of his productions. Marks of 0 or 1 were given to those whose interpretations were obvious, stereotyped, or completely unelaborated, while a mark of 4 or 5 was awarded for a preponderance of detailed and ingenious interpretations, for highly improbable or fantastic elaborations, or for a marked tendency to interpret in terms of animate beings and to ascribe to them purposes, thoughts, emotions, traits, or talents.

Actually the Ss showed wide variations in both the quantity and quality of their associations. The number of productions that could be classed as 'intraceptive' ranged from 0 to 67. In quality they varied from such uninspired interpretations as 'This might possibly be some sort of jagged rock' to such a projection as 'This is somebody extending one arm to shake hands and raising the other up in the air as if saying "Hi there, old top!"' The latter interpretation was supplied by a S who had a strong need for Affiliation which he had not been very successful in satisfying. Considerable Intraception with less projection is illustrated by such a statement as 'I can see two faces, each of which is very grotesque. One face has a rather frowning look, and the other is very frightened. The frightened one is hairy and unkempt.'

b. Similes Test

The Similes Test was usually administered in the same interview with the Beta Ink Blot Test. The instructions were as follows:

'I am going to give you some adjectives. I wish that for each one you would give me several of the most apt or striking or effective similes that you can think of. They must be original with you.'

Usually it was also necessary to define a simile and give one or two examples. The S was then given the following ten adjectives at intervals of two or three minutes each : pathetic, incongruous, hot, artificial, conspicuous, meek, dangerous, delightful, exciting, deceptive. The similes given were noted. As in the case of the Ink Blot Test responses, they were analysed both for thematic content and Intraception.

It was found that in many cases this relatively simple test furnished a surprising amount of information about the S. Certain of the adjectives employed proved especially effective in shedding light on particular points. For example 'deceptive' and 'artificial' tended to reveal the S's favourite objects of manifest or latent Aggression, 'delightful,' his sources of satisfaction, his cathexes, and 'dangerous,' his fears and anxieties. In some cases one or more themas of an apparently all-absorbing nature to the S kept reappearing in varied forms in response to several different adjectives.

The mark assigned the S for Intraception on the 0 to 5 scale was chiefly determined by the number of similes produced. Here again, however, in order that sheer quantity should not outweigh quality, no credit was given for such unoriginal and stereotyped comparisons as 'As dangerous as dynamite' or 'As delightful as spring weather.' It was assumed that the Ss who gave only striking and novel similes could have given the commonplace comparisons also had they been content to do so. 'As pathetic as a tugboat beside an ocean liner' and 'As artificial as a prelate's smile' might be cited as random examples of similes which were taken as indicative of Intraception.

c. The Minister's Black Veil

Before beginning this test the S was asked if he had ever read Hawthorne's story *The Minister's Black Veil.* In almost all cases the reply was in the negative. The one or two Ss who had read it could remember very little concerning Hawthorne's treatment of the theme, and they were asked to disregard what they could member. The following paragraph was then read, and after-ards left with the S for reference :

'This story by Hawthorne is laid in the last century. The ntral idea is that a minister, after many years with his congre-ation, appears in the pulpit one Sunday morning wearing a lack veil over his face, and thereafter for a long time is never en without it. It would be interesting if you would take this idea the nucleus for a story of your own. You may develop it in ıy way you please and make any modifications you desire. As our story will be marked on the basis of its literary value you ust try to make it as good as possible. Plan to spend about forty forty-five minutes on it.'

The E then left the room and did not return for forty-five inutes. If the S had not finished by that time, he was requested spend the next five or ten minutes summarizing the remainder the story. In no case was he allowed to work longer than an our.

The results obtained from this test were highly illuminating several different respects. In point of literary skill displayed e stories ranged from crude, disjunctive efforts scarcely worthy the proverbial school-boy, to compositions which approached rofessional standards of deftness. In the latter cases the choice phrase and metaphor, for example, was frequently excellent. loreover, the variations in adequacy of character delineation ere fully as striking as those in verbal expression. In some ıstances the protagonist was merely named, while in others his haracter and consciousness were explored in considerable detail. he motives assigned for his adoption of the veil ranged from howmanship, a desire to fill the collection plate, to shame over e delinquencies of a scapegrace younger brother. Real or imag-ıary sex guilt was of course a common theme.

The o to 5 scale was again employed in assigning a mark for ntraception. The points here taken into consideration were ose just mentioned, particularly the amount of descriptive elabo-ation provided, the adequacy of the character analyses and the amount of insight revealed in them, and the nature of the motivation ascribed to the minister.

The theme of the minister and his black veil was chosen for the Ss to write about because it posed a dramatic and intricate problem in motivation and then left the issue squarely up to them, thus forcing them to reveal in some measure the depth of their psychological insight. Its chief disadvantage lay in the fact that some Ss were so unfamiliar with, or antagonistic toward, all things smacking of Calvinistic theology that having to write about the problems of a nineteenth-century New England minister was repugnant or out of character. That despite this, the test was so generally successful in pointing to latent needs and themas (particularly those concerned with guilt), is attributed in no small measure to the brief time limit imposed upon the S. He had to produce a story in short order and tended to use the first material which came to hand, in most instances his own problems and obsessions. Moreover, the source of his ideas was by no means apparent to the S. The fact that so many of the stories lent themselves profitably to analysis from a psychoanalytic point of view (*cf.* the Case Study) indicates that whatever disguising took place was the work of unconscious rather than conscious mental processes.

20. MUSICAL REVERIE TEST

KARL KUNZE

Purpose. As with other procedures for the evocation of imaginal processes, the Musical Reverie Test is instrumental in the exhibition of fantasies which reveal underlying unconscious themas.

Procedure. The subject is seated in a comfortable, upholstered chair. A phonograph, covered with a piece of heavy cloth, which is effective in filtering out noises that arise because of mechanical defects of the instrument, is placed close to his head. The subject is told that the experimenter is interested in music, and that he is trying to discover what imagery or dramatic occurrences are commonly suggested by certain musical compositions. He is instructed to listen to the music, and when the record has terminated, to tell the episodes or series of images which the music suggested to him. The records that were used are :

1. *Symphony No. 4 in F minor*, by Tschaikowsky. This record usually suggested fear, agitation, mental or physical struggle.

2. *Don Juan*, by Richard Strauss. The last part of the second movement brought to mind love scenes, sentimental or romantic settings. The phonograph needle was placed at about one and one-half inches from the outside of the record to avoid the introductory passages which differ in tone-colour from the remainder of the piece.

3. *Symphony No. 6 in B minor (Pathetique)* by Tschaikowsky. Last movement only. This record brought forth stories of tragedy, despair and sometimes death.

4. *Quintet in G minor*, by Mozart. Closing movement. This suggested happy, light-hearted, animated action.

5. *Death and Transfiguration* by Richard Strauss commonly brought to mind feelings of reverence and solemnity, or ideas of regeneration.

6. *Afternoon of a Faun* by Debussy, placid and slow moving, seemed to facilitate reminiscing and philosophizing.

Other records were occasionally used if one kind of music seemed to be definitely more productive than the others.

Results. The results of this procedure demonstrate that the structure of the music (whether slow-moving with gradual departures from the key note, or fast in tempo with abrupt and frequent departures from the key note) is influential in bringing about rather characteristic attitudes and images, the form of which is influenced by the subject's past experiences. The little narratives often included a significant amount of information about the subject's own life and it was ordinarily possible to identify him with one of the leading characters.

Two kinds of mental processes occurred : unorganized free associations and unified fantasies. Some subjects ignored the instructions and allowed their minds to drift along with the music. Kast was one of these. 'At first I thought of wide open spaces, but then — a city — no people stand up in my mind. A conflict of some sort — the whole scene changes — a conflict between two people — the scene is changing all the time — . . .' A few Ss paid no attention to the music.

The dramatic stories were more valuable. Veal gives us an example of this kind of response : 'An old violin master in his room practising. Somebody comes into his room — about thirteen years old — a street beggar — has a violin too — the little fellow, an orphan, begs him for instruction. The child explains that a heartless man is taking his earnings. The child has run away from him. Master asks him to show his skill — Master decides he has skill and teaches him — in time pupil becomes famous — the fame is also transferred to his teacher.'

21. DRAMATIC PRODUCTIONS TEST [1]

Erik Homburger

Play that is of concern to psychology ranges from the first playful movements of the baby to the various manifestations of the need for Play in adults. Taking the most fascinating extremes of 'play,' the child's play on the one hand and the productions of the artist on the other, we find that, in spite of the testimony of language, popular opinion tends to valuate them as antithetic phenomena, finding 'no sense' in children's play but looking at the artist's play as burdened — and in modern times, overburdened — with conscious problems and meanings.

When the present writer, a psycho-analyst for children, and therefore interested in the psychology of play, undertook to study with others at the Harvard Psychological Clinic the development and character-formation of a group of college men, it seemed of possible interest to place these subjects in a play situation and observe what their late adolescent imaginations would do with it.

1. This report appeared as part of a larger article : 'Configurations in play : clinical notes.' *Psychoanal. Quart.*, 1937, *6*, 139–214.

Description of the Procedure

Each subject was brought into a room where there was a table covered with small toys. He was told that the observer (who was unknown to him) was interested in ideas for moving picture plays and wished him to use the toys to construct on a second table a *dramatic scene*. After answering a few typical questions (e.g., 'Do I have to use all the toys ? '), the experimenter left the room for fifteen minutes, but watched the behaviour of the subject through a one-way screen. In the following pages these first observations, made while the subject believed that he was unobserved, are referred to as *Preparation Period*. After this the observer re-entered the room, wrote down the subject's explanations and sketched the scene (referred to as the *Dramatic Scene*).

Picture A shows the types of toys which were at the disposal of the subjects. Some types were provided in large numbers, for example : farmers, animals, furniture, automobiles, and blocks. The principal toys suggested to most of the subjects a family, consisting of father, mother, son, daughter, and a little girl. In addition, there were a maid and a policeman. Picture A also shows the symbols, used in the diagrams, for the different toys.

Picture A

Results

Five out of *twenty-two* subjects ignored the instructions and on the observer's return greeted him in a friendly way with some such remark as, 'Everything quiet! Just a nice, harmonious, country scene!' Of the remaining seventeen subjects only *four* constructed dramatic scenes which were not automobile accidents, while *thirteen* subjects put in the *centre an automobile accident* or an *arrangement which prevented one.* Nine times in these scenes the little girl was the object of danger or the victim of an accident, other females twice. In other parts of these same scenes seven females died, fainted, were kidnapped or were bitten by a dog. In all, *eighteen females (ten times the little girl) and no males, were in danger or perished,* a theme which can be called the typical fantasy of the average member of the group. On the other hand, a dog was the victim of an accident in the construction of the subject who could be classified as the most masculine and socially best adapted ; and the red racer (with its not specifically named driver) came to grief in the constructions of the two subjects who came nearest to manifest homosexuality and manifest psychosis, respectively.

Interpretation of Results

The examples to be given in this report will illustrate a few hypotheses which follow from the analysis of the results.

They suggest first that the five friendly subjects had not failed to understand the instructions ; they *could not construct a dramatic scene* because their first (most probably unconscious) response to the instruction was a configuration conforming to a *traumatic scene of their childhood.* This had to be suppressed.

It may be supposed on the other hand that, in most of the scenes that were dramatic, traumatic childhood memories were represented in a symbolic form, the typical theme being that *of an accident, in which the little girl was the victim.*

The constructed scenes will, of course, be the central object of our analytic efforts. As associative material we have what the subject said or did just before or just after the construction of his scene and what the subject did or said during other experiments or interviews.

I. Avoidance of Repetition by Separation

a.) Zeeno

1. *Preparation Period.* The first toy that Zeeno touched was one of the *twin beds.* He set it at the extreme edge of the table beyond the margin of the sheet of paper. He did the same with the other twin bed on the opposite edge so that they were *as far away as possible from each other* (Diagram 1). Next he placed a couch and *separated* it by a wall from the beds. Then the bathroom was constructed and *separated* ; the kitchen followed but was given no wall ; neither did the house as such have any surrounding walls.

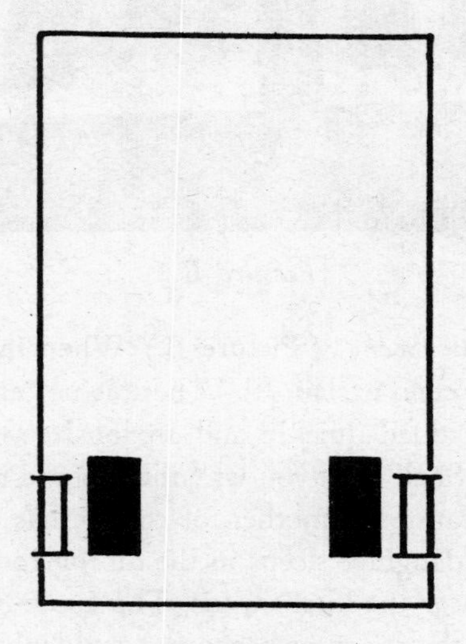

Diagram 1

Next he took, as the first toy person, the *maid.* Here, Zeeno was *doubtful* for a time — put the toy back and in a nervous manner touched the region of his penis. He looked around the room with a worried expression, then *shifted to a street scene.* First he placed the cars (the red racer and the green truck) and *then marked the street* (just as in the house scene he had first placed the objects and then built the walls of the rooms). Now he suddenly seemed able to continue more quickly, obviously lost in that concentration characteristic of undisturbed play. He placed other cars in more rapid succession, then put people quickly and decisively at certain places, *keeping males separate from females,* and the *daughter from the rest of the family.*

Picture B

2. *The Dramatic Scene.* (Picture B) When the observer entered the room, Zeeno exclaimed, 'There is not enough space in this house,' and added quickly and anxiously, as if he did not believe himself, 'Shall I tell you why the son and the father sleep in one bed? Because the mother, of course, has to be near the kitchen, and the daughter sleeps in the dining room because the maid has to be near the kitchen, too. The green truck drives on the highway and the red racer has to stop suddenly. Here (pointing to the extreme left of the scene) is a fisherman. He is disturbed by a man who is *looking for a lost lamb* with his four dogs.'

3. *Themas and Analytical Remarks.* Where is the dramatic scene

which was supposed to be constructed ? In the house *everybody is asleep*. Only the walls which separate people are built — not the outer walls which make the house a home. We saw the rhythm of *separation* : bed, wall, couch, wall ; later, men here, women there, their position only weakly rationalized. As for the *street* : a *collision is prevented*. Is this the dramatic event ? The scene at the left at best only implies a dramatic element : a *lamb has been lost* — an accident in the past, not a dramatic scene in the present. What has to be separated and why ? What do the subject's childhood memories suggest in regard to these themas ?

The report of another experimenter focuses our attention on the following event : '*Zeeno used to sleep in the same room with his sister who died* . . . She died about three o'clock in the morning before the doctor arrived.' He remembers 'lying in bed *not particularly concerned* about this.' The psychologist, however, to whom the subject tells this story makes the note that, 'He has a little *anxiety* about this. He was silent for some time afterwards.'

We know from our dream interpretations that the dream often disguises the dreamer's deep inner participation in a scene by having him see himself as a 'not particularly concerned' onlooker. The psycho-analyst of children can add to this well-confirmed interpretation the actual experience of having seen children accept a traumatic experience, especially the death of a relative, with complete calm, though every detail of a later neurosis indicated the pathogenic importance of this event. Can we assume that a feeling of guilt torments Zeeno in connection with this event about which he denies an entirely natural anxiety ? Children who mourn in the 'invisible' way described above are deeply concerned with the idea that some aggressive or sexual act or wish of theirs might have been the cause of the ambivalently loved person's death.

Several times during other sessions Zeeno voiced *thoughts of death*. When asked in the conference of what he was most afraid, Zeeno answered, 'That I am not going to live terribly long.' To one of the ink blots he said, 'I immediately think of a skeleton and ribs, and on each side above I see two faces looking at each other, guarding these ribs with an austere expression, like twins' — a detail which might be significant when one considers the fact that some years ago he fell in love with 'two sweet *twins*' who were *older* than he, as were his two sisters. He had shared the bedroom with his second sister after the first had died. At the very time of his sister's illness Zeeno remembers having had 'mimic intercourse' several times with an *older* girl. Could this have been one of his sisters? We do not know; probably it was one of her friends. Experiences with girls, however, and punishments connected with them, might easily have come into associative connection with his sister's death. It may be anxiety on this score which he is trying to overcome by the repeated self-assurance: 'I know a lot of people older than myself who have actually asked me to advise them on certain (sexual) subjects. This always made me think that my advice was pretty good.'

For his actual sexual experiences Zeeno uses a queer and detached language. 'I never mingle in intimate relations.' . . . 'I have never desired to indulge with a virgin.' . . . 'I decided I might indulge in sexual congress.' . . . 'Having found a very suitable person, I took part in coitus on various occasions.' In these carefully chosen expressions we may see an effort to *separate the experience from its affect.*

As for the *search for the lost lamb* — the part of the scene which, in spite of its inconspicuous placement at the edge of the table, more nearly approaches a dramatic content than any other part — I assume that it represents the unanswered question in the subject's mind, what happened to the 'lamb,' the little sister. One can only regret that other details of this scene which we could bring forward as confirming our interpretation, reveal so much about the actual family constellation of the subject's childhood, that we cannot use them here.

4. *Interpretative Hypothesis.* In selecting and comparing certain elements of the subject's memories and of his play, we point to the *probability* of the importance of a certain event in his life. As a psychic reality, so we assume, the thema of that traumatic event still imposes its content, as well as certain structural elements, on

the subject's autoplastic and alloplastic behaviour, i.e., it imposes certain configurations upon an arrangement of toys on the table.[1] In Zeeno's case we suggest the interpretation that in his life as well as in his play construction he has to separate certain elements because their connection arouses anxiety in him, and that these elements correspond to the details of his experiences with his sister. In this short account we are forced to neglect the fact that in the formulation of every psychic thema it is possible to interchange active and passive, subject and object, without having the thema lose either its importance or its inner truth ; that is to say, we may assume that Zeeno is afraid of dying young (like his sister) according to the primitive notion of 'an eye for an eye,' or that he, being younger, was or felt seduced by his sister, shared some kind of guilt with her and was afraid of having to die as she did.

Other interpretations would perhaps suggest themselves to persons familiar with the subject's life history. Our point, which can be substantiated here only vertically, through comparison with other constructions, not horizontally, through further search in this subject's history, is this : he is unable to construct a dramatic situation, but gives some evidence at the very edge of the construction of the *traumatic situation in his memories* which tried to impose itself on his mind when, at our authoritative suggestion 'to play,' a safety valve was opened—and quickly closed again.

b.) Berry

1. *Preparation Period.* Without any hesitation Berry builds the form shown in Diagram 2. Then he changes the form and constructs a scene (touching the maid first, as did more than half of the group) : Father and Mother *discover* the *son* with the *maid* in the kitchen (Diagram 3). But he doesn't like this scene. He builds another house, without doors, in which the kitchen is separated from the living room and the son and maid from the parents,

1. In Kurt Lewin's terms : A 'structuralization of the life-space' represented in toys — materials which are less 'refractory' than the objects encountered in real life.

who, in addition, are completely shut in by a ceiling — the only one to be found in these constructions.

2. *The Dramatic Scene.* (Picture C) He explains the scene more impersonally than the other subjects. 'The owner of the house and his wife, a visitor in the kitchen.' Behind the house in the garden sits 'a member of the family,' and on the street *the policeman stops traffic in order to let the little girl pass safely.*

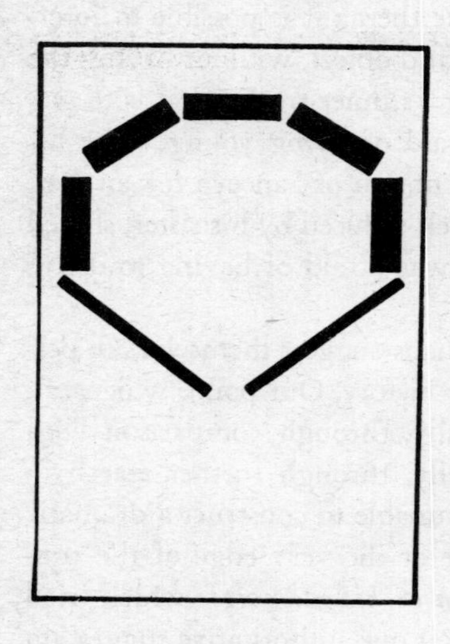

Diagram 2

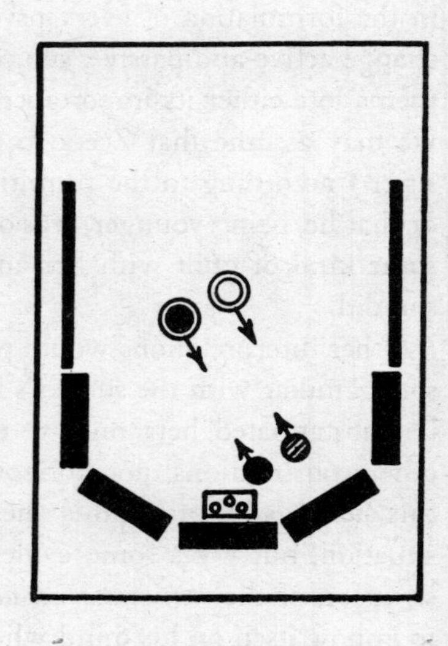

Diagram 3

3. *Themas and Analytical Remarks.* As in so many other cases we vainly expected a dramatic situation. Two are suggested by the effort to avoid them — *discovery and accident.*

Among the subject's memories we find the following event: At the age of 6, a *garden behind the house, and a little girl* with whom he eats onions. He kisses the girl. One day the girl doesn't come back. She is *not allowed to come* any more. 'Is this because of me?' he asks his mother. 'I doubt it,' is the answer. In this moment he says he *learned what it meant to doubt* — a statement which justifies our taking this scene seriously. A recurring event of his later childhood awoke this bitter feeling of doubt in him again and again: doubt of the justice of parents. If he had a *quar-*

rel with his sister, the parents most often *intervened* in her favor.

Discovery, intervention, punishment appear in the material of the Clinic in a rather decisive way : Hawthorne's vicar, for example, wears the black veil — so the subject concludes in completing the story — because he had *discovered his brother with a woman*. Thus the vicar in wearing the veil punishes himself *for*

Picture C

what he has seen. In the autobiography we find the statement : 'I had an *exceptionally curious* mind regarding sex matters and read a great variety of *medical books* from the age of ten to fifteen,' which throws a sudden light on his neurotic reading difficulty. But this inhibition had a history. First, Berry had developed an *inhibition to play with girls* or to touch them at all, which concerned especially his *sister*. Later on, this inhibition extended to reading, in which his curiosity obviously had found refuge. Visions of the past, so he says, came between him and the reading matter, and it tormented him that there should be so little personal feeling in these visions — a subjective account of that separation of experience and affect which we found in Zeeno.

We now may come back to his first house form (Diagram 2) :

does it not suggest a diagrammatic *cross section of a female body* ? He himself in another experiment (Beta Ink Blot Test) tells us what he perceives : 'Cross section through a female body, as one sees it in *medical books.*' Other blots remind him of *embryos* or portions of a *miscarriage* ; others of ulcers and decomposed animals. Thus the house seems first to represent the (female) *body*, which contains what one wants to know. It then takes the form of a real house which *contains the body* which one wants to know about (son, maid, and intervention). But if one tries to enter and discover the secret, so Berry remembers, one is oneself discovered and separated from the object of curiosity. Therefore, it seems better to *avoid discovery by separating* all dangerous elements from the beginning. Thus in his play construction *parents* are *closed in so that they are unable to discover* the son (nor can he, we may add, see what they are doing). This avoidance again (as in Zeeno's case) has its *parallel in a precaution on the street* : the *traffic is stopped in order to let the little girl pass safely.* In this way a traumatic outcome is avoided, but at the same time a *dramatic situation has become impossible.*

Separated and alone, 'a member of the family' sits behind the house in a special arrangement similar to Zeeno's 'sister.' Is she the *girl in the garden behind the house* of his childhood, the girl whose disappearance caused or was caused by guilt ? We can only guess. But wherever in these constructions we feel able to interpret lasting concern about a person who disappeared during childhood, we find the toy representation of that person *set outside of a closed house or room* (always to the right of the subject). In one case, the 'best boy' of the whole group, a dead rival-cousin was even placed on another table where he too, 'walked in safety.' One cannot help comparing this with the custom of some primitive peoples who make a hole in their houses through which they push the corpses of their dead, only to close it again so that the dead cannot come back into the house. We will find a *house without doors* (neither Zeeno's nor Berry's had doors) in the construction of the subjects in whose mind the idea of death and sex, the dark room whence we come (the womb, the inside of the female body) and the one where we go (the tomb, the beyond) — symbolically one idea in primitive thinking — have been permanently associated by a traumatic experience at that stage of childhood for which this association in its abortive form is typical (the phallic-sadistic and locomotor stage of libido-organization).

Here we might make another suggestion. In so far as the first house form represented a cross section through a female body, it contains the secret with which Berry was very much concerned, as his memories as well as his ink blot fantasies of embryos and miscarriages suggest. In his childhood he had heard that before he was born his mother had given birth to a *girl who died* — a fact which had strengthened his sexual curiosity (medical books) and influenced his mental development.

c.) Asper

Because of its clinical interest, I add here the most psychotic construction, an extreme example of separation (Diagram 4).

1. *Preparation Period and Dramatic Scene.* Asper puts six peasants near to one another like soldiers ; stares at them for several minutes, looking very unhappy, almost paralysed. Then he places some cars. In the green truck he puts a policeman, smaller cars and a man with a dog are approaching ; again a long paralysed hesitation, as if one single movement would bring about catastrophe. Then he suddenly arranges that the *red racer crashes* into a block and overturns. After this the subject seems immediately freer, as if a magic word had been spoken, and completes the scene quickly. He puts the little girl into a corner and *surrounds her with animals, surrounds the policeman's car with peasants,* and turns the peasant with the dog around so that he (to speak with Lewin) '*leaves the field.*'

2. *Thema and Analytical Remarks.* When the observer enters the room the subject says, 'The imagination does not have enough to work on. *Everything here is symbolical.*' He adds (about the little girl) : '*She does not understand* what it is all about. The animals are her pets.' About the green truck : 'An army truck. These men could easily be taken into the truck.' He puts them

in. About the peasant : '*He is immune to* all of us, he lives in the woods, *he is outside, he can't be touched.*'

The subject, in his nearness to mental disintegration (even the word '*incongruous* becomes meaningless after a while,' he says elsewhere), is the only one who feels that his construction is symbolic and at the same time (paradoxically enough) seems to

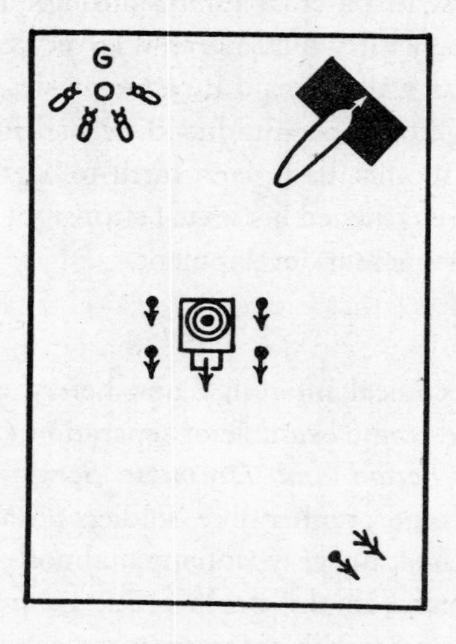

Diagram 4

feel the danger of play-omnipotence as real. Nearer to 'catastrophe' than all the other subjects, he scarcely dares move and go on. He keeps a strict organization of cars and soldiers, puts the soldiers closer and closer to the policeman and feels easier only after he has rendered the red racer no longer dangerous. The peasant with his dog goes silently away : 'He is outside, he can't be touched.'

Much could be said about the psychotic characteristics of this play construction : the danger of symbolic expression in infantile material is feared as a real danger, the plot shrinks to a mere spatial arrangement upholding the principles of order and constructiveness ('right in time, right in space, not too late, not too soon, just right,' as one of the inmates of the Worcester State Hospital remarked when he showed me his construction). It is in agreement with this need of upholding the last psychic barriers which keep the patients from infantile chaos, that the only person to protest against the 'childish' aspect of our task (which was given to 40 normal, neurotic and psychotic adults and children in all) was an inmate of the Worcester State Hospital.

He, too, had suggested he could build an accident but refrained from it. Instead, he just put toys (furniture, people, cars, animals) in curved rows. He, too, tried to put the little girl into a bed but smiled thoughtfully and gave it up to arrange another long row of toys. Reminded by the observer that he wanted to build an accident, he said : 'Well, well, well, a child might do that, if it cared to.' For a moment he threw the cars around furiously, as if illustrating what a child would do ; then, putting the blocks *two and two together*, he said, 'Some people forget their childhood, others go back to it.' Building then a solid square of blocks : 'This *could be the foundation for a house*—or wharf. And this (putting two blocks together) is a breakwater. It is supposed to turn waves backwards.' After a thoughtful moment he began to whirl the breakwater around as if it were helpless against the waves, and said slowly, '*Do you think—a wave—can flow—backwards?*'

II. Repetition and Self-punishment

'Nothing happens to the girls and nothing happens anyway' seems to be the slogan of the small group of cautious subjects represented by Zeeno and Berry. 'Something happens and it happens to the girl' is the slogan of the majority, whose spokesman we shall now hear.

a.) Oriol

1. *Preparation Period*. After receiving his instructions the subject jokes. He takes the *toy toilet* between his fingers and smiles broadly at the observer. Left to himself he grows serious : Let's see. Little girl ? No. Maid ? No. Baby carriage ? No. Highly dis-

satisfied, he suddenly, with sweeping movements, makes three piles — people, cars, blocks. He then finds excited satisfaction in taking *single objects out of the piles* and constructing his scene.

In the centre of his construction he first puts a *policeman standing on the block* and four cars pointing straight at him from four directions. If real, this scene could represent only a *suicidal demonstration against the authority of the state.* And, although in the

Picture D

final scene he had turned the cars so that they were not pointing at the policeman, his first remark when the observer entered the room continued the *thema of revolt.*

2. *The Dramatic Scene.* (Picture D) 'This is like the Place de la Concorde, where the riots were,' and about the policeman, 'He stands in his box higher than the other people' (suggesting probably something like the Napoleon column in the Place de la Vendôme). *The little girl is run over* — thus suffering the fate for which at first the policeman was destined — 'because the maid chats with an old friend of her mother and does not watch the girl.' The parents, *by coincidence*, arrive at this moment and are *witnesses to their daughter's death.*

On leaving, the subject *again takes the toilet*, laughs and says, 'I suppose some people use this to express their ideas. *I haven't come to that stage.*'

3. *Themas and Analytical Remarks*. Though the subject jokes twice about the *toy toilet*, he assures us, without being asked, that he does not use the medium through which he supposes 'some people' express their ideas. This, and his strange pleasure in piling the toys and in taking single pieces out of the piles, arouses a suspicion as to the psychic reality of an unusual element in the subject's memories : at the *age of eight* (a very advanced age for the breaking through of aggression in this direction) Oriol was found *smearing faeces*. This story is often repeated at home to family intimates, much to his discomfort, and is advanced by his family as a reason for wondering how he ever got into college.

In addition to the *riot thema* and the hints in regard to the *anal riot* of his childhood, there are spatial arrangements in his construction which possibly indicate the subject's main psychic (and maybe physiological) quandary in life : *to retain or to release*. First he builds one street, then a square with four entrances and, finally, points out explicitly that the square has many exits. We may add that no one who has heard the subject talk would fail to notice his speech which often approaches an *oral riot* — the flow of intellectually defiant words which he continuously releases. In his childhood, he is said to have learned to talk very late.

Oriol likes to play with the idea of *running away from home* ; but has decided to run away, so to speak, intellectually ; he keeps his mouth shut when with his father, but remains intellectually his own boss, and says so to whoever wants (or does not want) to hear it. While his memories are full of humiliating experiences, his confessions express the wish to overcome humiliation through greatness, and to overcome unclean tendencies by producing beauty. 'If I could remodel the world I would like to be the greatest writer.' But, 'I am afraid of life and afraid of death.' Certain of humiliation whenever he expresses his immature and unconsolidated impulses, he must choose masochistic wish-fulfilment in order to gain satisfaction. He wants to be a poet—but he wants to be a martyr poet : '*I want to expose myself and suffer.*' (Here, even were it not suggested by other constructions, one would suspect that the girl in the accident somehow symbolizes the subject himself : the parents witness his suffering.)

As to his construction, Oriol is right in saying, 'I haven't come to the stage where I would use the toilet to express my ideas'; for he obviously prefers a suicidal accident to riot, after a riot in his past (playing with faeces) has been suggested to him by the stimulus situation of being confronted with toys. But in spite of his objection, he repeats the event he wants to avoid in the formal elements of his construction (piling : playing).

4. *Second Construction.* Oriol was asked to construct another dramatic scene a year later. In the evaluation of such a repetition we must remember that the first construction a year earlier took 20 minutes, was not understood by the subject as 'meaning' anything, and was not mentioned to him by anybody afterwards. Now Oriol again *piles* the blocks before he starts. His *square* this time is first *round, with one exit leading to the water.* A truck (coming from the direction of the water) is headed straight for the policeman. There is a *dog* in front of the truck : '*It will not be run over,*' the rebellious subject says (a fact which we shall remember later when, in reviewing the construction of well-educated, pious Mauve, we do find a dog run over). In changing the square all form is abandoned, the blocks and furniture appear in *piles* ; again the *memorial for a revolutionist* takes the centre. This time it is a communist worker. Quite independent of this scene, another part of the table is supposed to be the inside of a house. The little girl stands in front of a mirror '*admiring herself and stubborn.* She is defiant. She does not like people. Later, she will go to the maid *who cannot tell her to "Shut up"*!' This parallel to the communistic orator on the memorial characterizes well the state of continuous narcissistic and oral revolt in which our subject lives.

When the observer re-enters the room, Oriol has the *red racer in his hand.* After having given his other explanations, he adds it to the scene, remarking as if excusing himself, '*This one does not mean anything.*' Then, in going out, he says : 'I left the bathroom empty. I would be embarrassed —' Thus, he seems to follow the pattern of his first construction which he had left with the words, 'I suppose some people use this (toilet) to express their ideas. I haven't come to that stage.' We have supposed that this last *negation really was a double affirmation.* Can we assume the same about the claimed unimportance of the red racer ? Does the subject's remark dispense with a possible *phallic revolt* ?

5. *Interpretative Hypotheses.* Oriol's construction shows the confusion which can extend to the adolescent mind from childhood experiences in an almost tragi-comical way. Only with weak negations does he separate himself from the most embarrassing childhood situations. Here we must suspect that the wish 'to expose himself' was decisive.

Oriol did not talk when he was expected to. He still soiled when he was no longer expected to—and this 'stubbornness' (which might well be based on a constitutional or early traumatic factor) still pervades everything he says and does, with typical pregenital ambivalence. Not independent enough to do without love and protection, he still is not able to return love, because this would have meant in childhood the unconditional surrender of jurisdiction over parts of his body, and would mean now the final socialization of modes of behaviour which are derived from those organic functions. Oriol does not soil, because he is neither child nor psychotic. Still, elimination and retention in their characterological and mental aspects are his problem. What is presented here by Oriol, in his chaotic way, that pertains to anal sadistic characteristics, differs only quantitatively, not qualitatively, from the general problems facing our whole group of late adolescents. Did their genitality make itself independent of regressive association with the psycho-biologically significant drives of childhood ? We know that lack of genital consolidation necessitates a continuous state of defence against the guerilla warfare of infantile impulses which still resist 'don't's' long since senseless, promise paradises which do not exist, and urge the individual to subdue love objects or to surrender to them — in an oscillation between love and hate.

But since we may expect to be called to order for the 'clinical predilections' in our observation of a group of individuals who, after all, did not come as patients and are not patients, it might be of special interest to see, after the illustration of Oriol's fixation on oral and anal sadistic autoerotism, the construction of Mauve, who is perhaps the best organized personality in the group. His construction shows a typical attempt to overcome the pre-genital ambivalence menacing our best organized young men in their relationships with the other sex. Between Oriol and Mauve lies the problem of the whole group : how (in a society which with moral and economic means discourages unbroken psycho-sexual progress) can one adapt without sacrificing one's genital masculinity ; how develop without rebellion ; how wait without regression ; how love without suspicion, fear, and hate ; in a word, how *overcome ambivalence*, the counterpart of obedience ? This is the moral problem of adolescence ; various cultures find various ways of dealing with it.

b.) Mauve

1. *Preparation Period*. Mauve took off his coat and, obviously pleased with himself and ready to serve scientific purposes, began his construction like a good organizer, quickly and without interruption. A growing excitement was evident — he became engaged by his ideas.

2. *The Dramatic Scene*. (Picture E) Mauve explains : '*The green truck is running over a dog* — it is the little girl's dog. A car coming after it *bumps into the truck*, a second one is *just turning over*, a third one tries to avoid the crash.' In the kitchen '*the maid is fainting* ; she has a little dog herself and this is the reason why she feels like that.' In the living room we see '*a young lady on the couch in the first stage of pneumonia*. Something very emotional in this scene. Her fiancé and her doctor are looking down on her. *The mother does not feel well* and has gone to bed.'

3. *Themas and Analytical Remarks*. This is the only time a

dog is run over instead of a woman ; we are therefore interested to hear Mauve, in another interview, say : 'Women are faithful, *they are dogs. They have been dogs for so many centuries.'* In his outlook on life, as well as in his conception of himself, we see him separate himself from the '*animal in us.*' 'My standards are high and I intend to keep them.' Woman and drives belong to

Picture E

another, an animalistic world which is separated from the young man's world of clear standards.

On the other hand his standards are derived from his education by his mother and his aunt. Younger than the father, the mother is deeply attached to the son and he accounts for their emotional relationship in the most explicit Oedipus fantasy offered by any of the group. Overobedient to her wishes, he says he 'almost *dedicated his life* to the avoidance of drinking, smoking and swearing.' And yet certain circumstances in his relationship to his mother seem to draw him deeply into ambivalence towards the weaker sex.

His mother is 'handicapped by lung trouble which periodically disables her completely' and she always tried to keep the healthy active boy close to home — as he complains, though he has been taking care of his mother in a most touching manner. If, in the 'dog running on the street' we want to see a symbolic rebellion of the son against all the careful obedience which a physically weakened authority is imposing on him, we may understand that it is his drive, the 'animal in us,' which is punished by being run over. (On the other hand, the dog, as we saw, joins the group of all the human beings in this construction to whom something happens : they are all female.)

If we confront this subject's outbreak with his remarks about women on the one side and his educational indebtedness to his mother and other women on the other, a conscious or unconscious duality of attitude towards women quite common in our civilization is represented : men easily identify women with the wishes which they stimulate. If they learned to have contempt for 'lower' drives (and their pregenital components) they may also have contempt for women in so far as they are the objects of their wishes. As beings, however, held in high esteem ('like your mother and aunt or teacher') from a very early time, women are also identified with the strictest and most idealistic concepts of conscience. 'Angels' or 'dogs' — women awake uncomfortable ambivalent feelings, feelings which spoil the perspective of sex life. A not unusual type of rather well adapted young man (whom Mauve seems to represent) learns to live and to care for a world of achievements which have 'nothing to do with women'; it is characteristic of this type that in order to satisfy his conscious and potent genital wishes he goes 'to Paris' — as Mauve says he plans to do. There, then, women are neither angels nor dogs ; they are French. The girl who does not belong to one's own culture or class (in other constructions often the girl who does not belong to the family, namely, the maid) is the object of more conscious fantasies.

4. *Interpretative Hypotheses.* Returning from the exception (the running over of a dog) we may ask ourselves what the little girl, to whom the subjects pay so much damaging attention, might represent. It is hard to give the reader an impression of the

uncanny regularity with which these (normal, neurotic, psychotic) young men took and examined the little girl and — as if they were following a ritualistic duty — seriously put her under the green or the red car, or placed a policeman in the centre of the scene to protect her. The majority of the subjects who failed to have this thema in their final scene at least considered and rehearsed it during the preparation time. A great number of problems must be evoked by this little girl and the crux of the matter must be symbolized by the accident which happens to her.

Some of the possible explanations, all suggested by material which cannot be fully quoted here, are :

a.) The little girl may represent *a little girl of importance* (i.e., the sister) in the subject's childhood. The uniform and typical handling of this toy, however, suggests that she represents rather a symbol than an historical individual.

b.) The little girl, as the *youngest among* the toys, might appear to be the representative of 'the child,' the most endangered and therefore the most protected human being in traffic. Can we assume that in spite of the abundance of dramatic moments in life and literature, movies and newspapers, accidents resulting in the death of children are emotionally important enough to be the dramatic scene par excellence for the majority of twenty Harvard students ? In that case, our psycho-analytic explanations are less valuable, though not entirely worthless since they show the unconscious meaning of this accident in its relationship to other unconscious concepts of 'what happens to children.'

c.) The emphasis may lie on *girl*. Since, according to common infantile theories, girls are made girls, not born girls,[1] violence may become associated with the idea of sex. The accident, then, which belongs to the 'complex' of related symbols dominating our construction, may represent the act of violence of which girls are the victims.

1. Everyday example : Marlborough Street, Boston, Mass. A little boy tries to climb a small tree ; he scratches his legs and hurts his penis. 'Be careful,' his mother says, 'or else we shall have to cut it off.' For a moment he stands with his mouth open. 'Is that what happened to Marion ?'

d.) Since, beside the little girl, other female toys, and only female toys, are the victims in these accidents, the little girl may represent a *pars pro toto*, namely, the female world, in which case it might have been selected because it provokes the least conscious aggressive fantasies and allows the subject to feel himself consciously free of any participation in the committed violence. We shall presently come back to this point.

e.) The little girl may represent a *totum pro parte*. Freud remarks that in dreams 'children often signify the genitals since men and women are in the habit of referring to their genital organs as "little man," "little woman," "little thing." To play with or to beat a little child is often the dream's representation of masturbation.'[1] It is a big step from our first tentative explanation to this interpretation; but I am afraid the reader will have to decide to make this step tentatively with us—or decide to leave the question open. Psycho-analytic method, waiting for the most part for associative material in order to interpret any product of the mind, uses only a few 'established' symbols, the uniform 'translation' of which has been amply justified in long and exhaustive studies. Two of these symbols with which we are concerned here are put together by Freud in a title to the interpretation of a woman's dream which states bluntly: *The 'little one' as the genital organ. Being run over as a symbol of sexual intercourse.* Dream interpretation thus suggests that what the subjects do with the little girl corresponds in their unconscious with ideas of autoerotic and alloerotic sexual acts, in which something happens to the partner's or the subject's own sexual organs. There is nothing in their strange behaviour which could refute a priori such a strange notion.

f.) We cannot avoid pointing to a sociological factor, namely, the sexual life typical for a group of biologically mature individuals like our subjects. As everybody knows, their sexual activities are autoerotic or consist of a kind of mutual heterosexual autoerotism more or less sanctioned by society. The danger of this form of gratification is the conditioning of masculine impulses by the

1. Freud, S., *The Interpretation of Dreams*, Revised Edition, New York, 1933, p. 338.

repetition of a situation with infantile characteristics. Mobilized with other impulses participating in the pattern of complete sexual satisfaction whenever a suitable object presents itself, biologically and psychologically most important impulses — namely, masculine intrusion and certain related sadistic tendencies — fail to be disarmed in this mere play. It is, I think, this continuously frustrated intrusive component of masculinity which in our subjects has not yet found its wholesome amalgamation with the other factors of heterosexual partnership, and therefore in their secret fantasies appears in a certain homicidal and suicidal rudeness — which we may add here, has an important sociological counterpart in certain adolescent and cruel forms of public sensationalism not dissimilar to our constructions.

g.) The few female subjects who constructed scenes with the same toys showed as a common factor the *criminal man* (father). The five college girls among them (the same age as our subjects) constructed the following scenes :

1. A father who as a deserter in war, lives in shameful exile, picks up a little girl on the street who has been run over by a truck. She is his daughter.

2. A selfish father, who had neglected wife and children for years, comes home and finds everything destroyed and everybody killed by flood.

3. A father, now away in an insane asylum, comes home to murder his family.

4. A land-owner strangles his wife. His servant's daughter, to whom he had made advances, testifies against him at the trial.

5. Robbers steal a table out of a house in the middle of the night.

It would be interesting if further studies would substantiate the possibility that to the main theme of our male subjects ('Something happens or is prevented from happening to the girl'), there corresponds a female one : 'A man is (or is prevented from being) criminally aggressive.' The fact that — with few exceptions — by both sexes a member of the *opposite sex* is put in the centre of the construction, clearly points to an at least partially sexual meaning of the scenes we are witnessing. We can only regret that a historical handicap (the fact that Freud first studied psycho-neurotics) hinders us from reaching the all-important problem of aggression beneath its sadistic (which means *also* sexual) surface.

c.) Krumb

1. *Preparation Period and Dramatic Scene.* Krumb considers for a while the problem of whether to use *one* or *two* tables. He decides on one. With two blocks he builds a wall, puts the *red racer* at an angle of 45° toward it and then makes a *small opening* in it. Then he puts the father into the house so that the red racer,

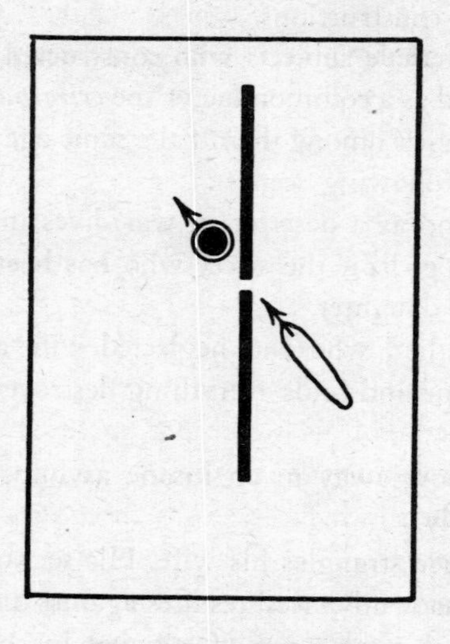

Diagram 5

if driving, would run *through the hole* in the house and *hit the father in the back*. (Diagram 5) After this his doubts disappear. He obviously gets a funny idea and, laughing, puts the *son and the maid together into a bed*. The scene is completed quickly as seen in Picture F. The father finds the son in bed with the maid and forbids intercourse. 'Nothing homosexual is going on in the other room,' adds the subject. The *little girl is caught between two cars* and that the red racer is *dangerously speeding* around the corner means one more danger for her. He seems not quite sure about which is the front and which the back of the racer, so that in reality it would, if 'dangerously speeding' hit door and father.

2. *Themas and Analytical Remarks.* This subject, the only one to put a boy and girl in a bed together, is a manifest homosexual—a fact which without any help from the rich but disorganized and

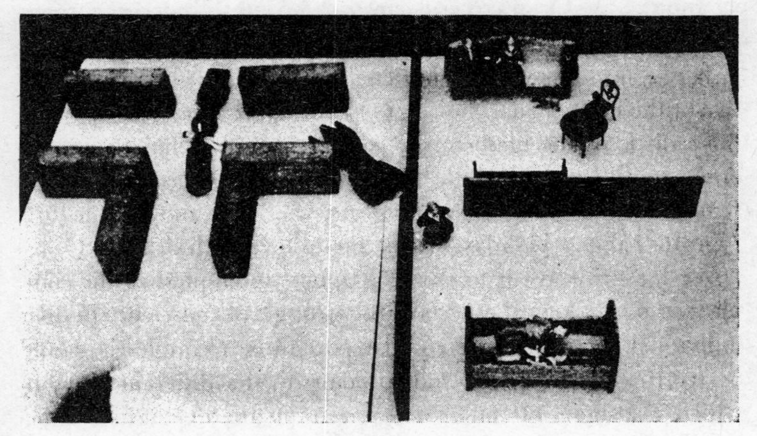

Picture F

complicated material of his life history, makes it possible for us to understand the meaning of the almost 'topological' description of his inner conflicts in his scene ; *the living between two alternatives, both dangerous.*

'Last year I had affairs with about three women and some fifteen men. Now it is only with men that I can find happiness. Being homosexual makes it possible for me to repress sexual impulses. I wish I could repress my feelings of guilt also.'

It seems that Krumb tries to appease his growing feeling of guilt by the following arrangement : the *father, between two rooms* with a couple of the same sex in one and a couple of heterosexual lovers in the other, turns to the latter and forbids what they are doing. Thus the father himself decides against heterosexuality. The subject assures us that 'nothing homosexual' happens in the other room. But then, we did not ask ; the subject did not even know whether or not we were informed of his sexual predilections. Neither did he know that he had given himself away in his very first move : the arrangement of the racer, the door and the father. Knowing how often a house symbolizes a body and a car the genitals, we assume that this first construction represented the form and mode of a homosexual act : intercourse per anum. (See Oriol's second construction.) His indecision, then, as to which direction the car is going (whether crashing into the father or into the already mutilated girl) represents the alternative of the homosexual choice : to be the aggressive or the passive, the sadistic or the masochistic, partner. Again a choice ; and no doubt guilt drives him into the masochistic part, as many of his remarks in other interviews indicate, i.e., 'The moving picture, "Death Takes a Holiday," made me in love with death.'

We have to leave it to the biographers to emphasize the complicated psychological aspects of the struggle of conscience in their individual subjects. If we could report more examples it would be worthwhile to define and to compare the different ways in which a struggle of conscience appears in the preparation time, with the outcome as represented in the final scene. In the succession of toys which the subjects take and refuse at the beginning, one notices a peculiar alternation of symbols of repressed forces (maid, bed) to symbols of repressing forces (father, policeman) or vice versa ; the street seems always to offer a welcome opportunity for shifting the problem to the impersonal. The subjects show all variations of guilt feeling from the anxiety of losing love and protection (i.e., in building harmonious scenes with the mother at the table and the maid at the stove — entirely forgetful of the instructions) to the fear of catastrophe (i.e., policeman regulating traffic and preventing accidents as the only 'dramatic' element), to various forms of self-punishment. It is as if these subjects, in the painfully slow process of civilized maturation, had to find a painfully individual substitute for that sacrifice of a tooth, or other symbol, which 'cruel' primitives in their puberty rites inflict uniformly and once for all on the boys of their community.

Second Construction. One year after this construction and interpretation (it might be well to state here again that not one word of interpretation was given to the subjects) Krumb was again asked to construct a scene. He immediately asked : '*May two things happen?,*' thus taking up again the dualism of the first construction. He builds first *two houses*, then one house with *two*

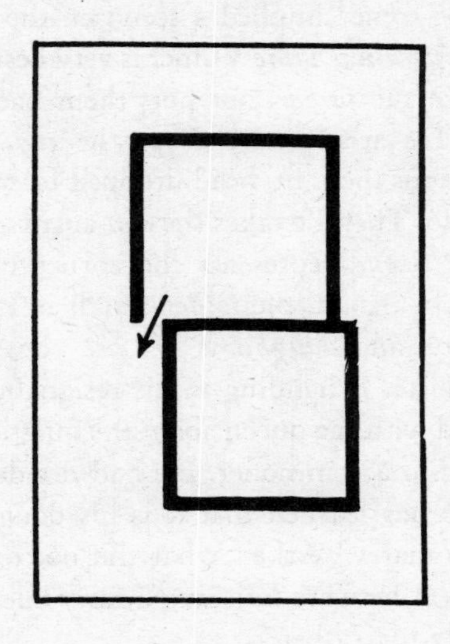

Diagram 6

parts, two rooms in each part. Again males and females are separated. The *father*, he says, *has a homosexual crush on a severely wounded soldier*, and is in the bathroom — while in the street the *red racer is wrecked* by the green truck. 'I have a feeling,' the subject remarks, 'that I have repeated my last construction. I struggled for three minutes to overcome the feeling that I did the same thing. Then I did — and found that *I had expressed homosexuality* this time, which it seems I could *avoid last time*.' Finally, Krumb gives a confirmation of our first assumption, which no doubt to many readers seemed hazardous, if not disgusting, namely, that the small hole in the house of the first construction symbolized the homosexually attacked rectum : the house of the second construction, again, and at the same place, has a small hole. (Diagram 6) Krumb remarks about it : 'The house is badly built, bad odours come out of here.'

III. Drama

Vulner

This is the construction of the only subject to whom the suggestion 'dramatic scene' implied a scene on the stage.

During the *Preparation Time* Vulner is very hesitating. He takes the *son* first, then the *father*, but puts them back and seems to think seriously. He accidentally *drops* the *son*, plays with the policeman, in serious thought, head dropped forward : Should he take the *cow* ? No. Then he takes the *son* again and acts quickly.

The *Dramatic Scene* represents the corner of a room. The *mother* is sitting in a chair, the *father* stands in front of her. In a doorway stand *son* and *daughter*.

'The head minister is handing in his resignation. The day before he had talked with the queen about the question of the crown prince's marriage to a commoner. He had decided against it. In the meantime he has learned that it is his daughter whom the prince wishes to marry.' Asked what the outcome will be, the subject replies, as if he were finishing a fairy tale told to a child, 'He will probably marry her.'

Remarks. The most interesting aspect of this 'really dramatic' construction is, that there is very little to say about it. The scene possibly contains some hints in regard to the subject's family situation ; he has one sister. But essentially the scene is a dramatic cliché and does not suggest any detail of the subject's biography, except that his mother is a writer and that, as a boy, he has often participated in dramatic plays.

IV. Final Remarks

Having asked our subjects for a *dramatic* scene, we find a product of *traumatic* tension ; instead of tragedy we find accident.

Dramatic and traumatic moments have one psychological element in common. Both are events which transgress the boundaries of the human Ego, the first in widening it beyond individuation, he second in nearly extinguishing it. In other words, in a truly *lramatic moment* the individual is confronted with a choice which nay make him the heroic or tragic master of human fate in its :ternal aspects ; he is allowed one chance of overcoming the bondige of gravity and repetition. The *traumatic moment* destroys ndividuation, chance and choice, and makes the individual the ielpless victim of repetition compulsion.

To be sure, in offering the little toys for a dramatic task we probably asked our subjects to take a too-difficult step from the idiculous to the sublime. In offering play material we ourselves iave provoked the spirit of infantile conflict, since play 'presupposes a psychic substance which is not quite structuralized yet.' (Robert Wälder) The specific conflicts appearing in the constructions indicate that the subjects when confronted with toys, continued where they had left off in their childhood play with the attempt to overcome passive traumatic experience by active repetition in play.

In describing these results we naturally do not describe or characterize individuals in their conscious and rational individuation ; as little as a war correspondent in the trenches can describe the state of the country behind. The psycho-analytic microscope first focuses on *neurotic material in its specific psycho-sexual characteristics*. It shows us the inner frontier where the rational human mind — whether in the state of infancy, savagery or civilization — is constantly faced by the wilderness of the irrational.

The set-up of this particular study is not of any general value and will not be recommended as a psychological experiment. But the results of this accidental undertaking may be of some interest in regard to the psychology and the psychopathology of play (important for the treatment of patients who cannot or do not want to speak, i.e., children and psychotics). We can observe directly the structuration of a given space in accordance with the qualities of a traumatic configuration, which imposes on the subjects' autoplastic and alloplastic behaviour spatial elements of a past event or of the way in which the subject has armed himself against the (irrational) danger of its recurrence.

Further deciphering of play hieroglyphs — especially in the legitimate sphere of childhood — may offer valuable keys for the understanding of the prelinguistic and alinguistic strata of the human mind.

22. RORSCHACH TEST

S. J. Beck

The Rorschach Test was given to ten of the Ss of Group IV by Dr. S. J. Beck of the Boston Psychopathic Hospital. The nature and technique of this test is too familiar to need discussion here. Rorschach findings on one subject, interpreted independently, without reference to the results of other sessions, but in many respects remarkably consistent with these, constitute part of the Case Study.

23. MISCELLANEOUS PROCEDURES

H. A. Murray

Under this heading may be mentioned some of the tests and experiments which were used in examining one or more of the first three groups of subjects, but which were not included, for one reason or another, in the final program of sessions.

Mrs. Whitman administered Form 5 of the Revised Army Alpha [1] to the first three groups of subjects. Dr. Sanford employed a battery of eight speed tests which measured reaction time with the highest precision. Dr. Shevach devised a set of nine tests of sensory perseveration, each of which showed high reliability ; but the intercorrelations were low and inconsistent and none of the tests correlated repeatedly with any of the personality variables.[2] Mrs. Morgan used a number of procedures based on techniques devised by Kendig,[3] for the induction of enduring, compulsive mental activity. The aim of these tests was to study the post-experimental recurrence of monotonously repeated sense impressions (visual

1. Revised under the supervision of Dr.F.L.Wells at the Boston Psychopathic Hospital, 1932.
2. Shevach,B.J. 'Studies in perseveration,' VI, VII. *J. Psychol.*,1936,*3*, 381–427.
3. Kendig,I. 'Studies in perseveration,' II, III, IV, V. *J. Psychol.*,1936,*3*, 231–264.

and auditory). The results were difficult to interpret. Mrs. Frank administered a number of tests of cognitive perseveration, but, again, the intercorrelations were low. Two tests of associative memory (faces and sayings; faces and names) were investigated by Miss Leventhal. The results did not correlate consistently with any other variables. Mrs. Jones devised a method for judging the accuracy of casual observation and aesthetic appreciation, but the attempt to establish objective criteria for estimating the results proved unsuccessful. Several tests of persistence, each of which seemed to be loaded with specificity, were devised, tried and abandoned by Dr. Rosenzweig. Dr. Wheeler used Watson's 'Survey of Public Opinion on Some Religious and Economic Issues'[1] as a measure of prejudice. A high correlation with Intraception (subjectivity) was expected, but the opposite was found. Prejudice, by this measure, correlated with: Extraception +.48, Exocathection +.56, Ascendance (A–S Reaction Study) +.54, Extraversion (Guilford) +.54, Extrapunitiveness (Rosenzweig) +.47, Aspiration level/performance level (Frank) +.60, Moore-Gilliland Test +.41. Clearly, the prejudiced individual, as revealed here, is not the subjective introvert but the projective, aggressive extravert. Besides a host of questionnaires, several other techniques were tried and abandoned: tests for suggestibility, tempo of activity and so forth.

Dr. Sears devised a number of experiments and tests pertaining to humour.[2] He came to the conclusion that a joke can be analysed into two sets of factors: schematic and thematic. Schematic factors are those which characterize the general structure of a joke. They are three in number: (1) an original tendency to closure, and (2) the *sudden* dislocation of this tendency, by (3) the substitution of another closure which is incongruously related to the first. Without this schema existing in a *novel* form there is no joke; the 'essence' of which is *playful* departure from

1. *Cf.* Watson,G.B. 'The Measurement of Fair-Mindedness.' Teachers College Contribution to Education, No.176, 1925.
2. Sears,R.N. 'Dynamic Factors in the Psychology of Humor.' Doctoral thesis, 1934, Harvard University Library.

an expected and conventional form. Thematic elements, though usually present, are variable and not essential. When present they constitute the meaningful human content, or plot, of a joke, and it is this which evokes the asocial or repressed needs : principally Aggression, Superiority and Sex. Such a joke is the imaginal presentation of a thema which provides — suddenly and gratuitously — the end situation of one of the subject's needs, fused with n Play. The mirth-thema, then, brings added delight by satisfying in fantasy some purely egocentric and usually hostile wish. The delight is not inhibited, for it can escape disguised by the playful social feelings engendered by the mirth-schema in which the mirth-thema is embedded. Some of the thematic factors are general, determining what need is gratified ; and some are specific, having to do with negatively cathected people, institutions or events. For one of his experiments Dr. Sears collected jokes and humorous cartoons which represented mirth-themas that released a variety of commonly suppressed tendencies. They were classified as follows : self-enhancement, self-degradation, degradation (of others), violence, overt anal, covert anal, sex, sexual curiosity and nurturance. Subjects were asked to mark the humorousness of each item on a seven point scale. The score for each category of joke was then computed by taking the ratio of the average mark for jokes in this category to the average mark of all jokes. The intercorrelations (by the rank order method) between the different categories were suggestive though of negligible statistical significance (since only thirteen subjects were used). The results showed that degradation of others, overt anal and covert anal were consistently correlated (aver. $r = +.36$), and that a composite rank order of the three was highly correlated with repressed Aggression, as estimated by the Clinic staff. The rank order on nurturance (entirely kindly) jokes was negatively correlated with this anal Aggression syndrome (—.54). Violence correlated positively (+.69) with self-degradation (sado-masochistic complex) and both correlated negatively with self-enhancement (—.26, —.41). This syndrome showed a negative correlation with anal Aggression, with sex and with sexual curiosity.

These tests for mirth complexes, as well as the two procedures next to be described by Dr. Rosenzweig and Dr. Rickers-Ovsiankina, were considered thoroughly worth-while and, if it had been possible, they would have been included in the program for Group IV.

24. THE EXPERIMENTAL MEASUREMENT OF TYPES OF REACTION TO FRUSTRATION

SAUL ROSENZWEIG

In the course of certain experiments devised as part of a program for studying under laboratory conditions some of the general concepts of psycho-analysis, such as repression, it was found incidentally, and only as an impression of the experimenter, that there were marked personality differences between subjects tending to recall successes better than failures and those tending to recall failures better than successes. It was from these casual observations that the present schema of types of reaction to frustration arose, for it appeared that individuals who favoured successes in recall tended to gloss over their failures when these were first experienced whereas individuals who favoured failures in recall tended to concentrate upon blame, either of themselves or of the outer world, in experiencing frustration. The test for types of reaction to frustration that will be here described has been devised with the primary objective of employing it later in studying the problem of memory for successes and failures, though it is not difficult to see that if the instrument is successful it should have numerous other applications.[1]

The schema upon which the test is based must first be described.[2] Its purpose is to classify subjective types of immediate and pri-

1. *Cf.* the more detailed description on p. 472. As stated there it is regrettable that there was no opportunity in the present series of studies to attempt with the same group of subjects both the test for types of reaction to frustration and the experiments on the recall of successes and failures.

2. *Cf.* my brief paper, 'Types of reaction to frustration,' *J. of Ab. & Soc. Psychol.*, 1934,29, 298–300 ; also 'A test for types of reaction to frustration,' *Amer. J. Orthopsychiat.*,1935,5, 395–403. The latter is a version of the present account.

marily conscious reaction to frustration. The accompanying chart presents its salient points.

TYPES OF SUBJECTIVE REACTION TO FRUSTRATION

Name of Type	'EXTRAPUNITIVE'	'INTROPUNITIVE'	'IMPUNITIVE'
Pathognomonic Features (upon frustration)			
Emotions:	Anger (with hostility)	Guilt (with remorse)	Embarrassment (with shame)
Judgements:	Condemnation of outer world	Condemnation of self	Condonement of others and self
Hypothetically Associated Psycho-analytic Concepts			
Dynamic and Genetic Basis			
Instincts:	Aggressive needs outwardly directed ('Hate-guilt')	Aggressive needs inwardly directed ('Hate-guilt')	Erotic needs ('Love-guilt')
Attitudes of identification:	Fear of punishment. Need for punishment	Fear of punishment. Need for punishment	Fear of loss of love
Psychopathological Aspects			
Modes of defence:	Projection	Displacement and isolation	Repression (with self-deception)
Mental disorders:	Paranoid (Paranoid type of schizophrenia)	Compulsive and obsessional (Catatonic type of schizophrenia)	Hysterical (Hebephrenic type of schizophrenia)
Libidinal types (Freud):	'Narcissistic'	'Compulsive'	'Erotic'

When an individual experiences frustration, in so far as he does not allocate responsibility for the unhappy occurrence in an objective way, he may respond in one of the three following typical subjective ways or some combination of them: (1) He may manifest the emotion of anger and condemn the outer world (other persons, objects and circumstances) for his frustration, adopting an attitude of hostility toward his environment. This type of reaction may be termed 'extrapunitive.' (2) He may react with emotions of guilt and remorse and tend to condemn himself as the blameworthy object. This type of reaction may be termed 'intropunitive.' (3) He may experience emotions of embarrassment and shame, making little of blame and emphasizing instead the conciliation of others and himself to the disagreeable situation. In this case he will be more interested in condoning than in condemning and will pass off the frustration as lightly as possible by making references, even at the price of self-deception, to unavoidable circumstances. This type of reaction may be termed 'impunitive.' To take an extreme example of each of the three types, disappointment in love may be reacted to by murder of the loved object — which might be extrapunitive — or by suicide — which might be intropunitive — or by an over-compensating merriment, accompanied perhaps by drunkenness, into which protestations of one's own unconcern would enter — which might be impunitive.

Before proceeding, it should be made clear that this schema refers primarily to types of reaction and not to types of personality. Any given individual may exemplify all of these sorts of reaction on different occasions and may even combine two or all three of them at some one time. Whether persons have a characteristic way of subjective reaction to frustration which they consistently display, at least in a given kind of situation, is one of the problems to be investigated.

Another point that should be borne in mind is that these types are inapplicable in so far as the reaction to frustration is determined by the objective facts of the matter. They have to do only with distortions of the facts, either by overemphasis of some element actually present or by complete misinterpretation according to the subject's own traits and needs. They are, in other words, types of *subjective* reaction.

The supposed relevance of this schema to the problems of clinical psychopathology may be shown by a brief mention of some hypothetically associated psycho-analytic concepts (*cf.*

chart). Speculative comments included there are not, however, intended to have more than a suggestive value.

The dynamic basis of the extrapunitive reaction may conceivably be the outwardly directed aggressive needs. The corresponding basis of the intropunitive reaction may be conceived as likewise aggressive, but with the aggression turned in upon the self.[1] The common aggressive aspect of both these types of reaction indicates that it may be necessary to regard them as two periods of one inclusive cycle. The name 'hate-guilt' is suggested to describe the dynamism of this hypothetical cycle. In contrast to the extrapunitive and intropunitive reactions as thus conceived, and not intermediate to them as might at first glance be supposed, stands the impunitive type of reaction with the erotic needs as its dynamic basis. The term 'love-guilt' is suggested for the dynamism involved in this case.

On the genetic side, fear of punishment as an attitude toward the parents and other educators may be thought to underlie the extrapunitive type of reaction, while the need for punishment from the same authorities may be related to the intropunitive mode of response. Finally, fear of loss of love would be the corresponding genetic factor for the impunitive type of reaction.

To touch briefly upon the psychopathological aspects of the present schema, the characteristic mode of defence for the extrapunitive type of reaction would be projection; corresponding to this for the intropunitive type would be displacement and isolation, and for the impunitive type, repression in its most complete form. The mental disorders best illustrating each type of reaction would then naturally be as follows: for the extrapunitive, paranoid complaints; for the intropunitive, compulsive and obsessional ones; and for the impunitive, hysterical ones. With special

1. The psycho-analyst might appropriately call the turning of aggression upon the individual's own self 'nemesism' from the name of the Greek goddess of vengeance. Nemesism could then be thought of as the counterpart of narcism, the investment of the self with libido (erotic). The phenomena of narcism and nemesism are by no means mutually exclusive but are instead often found together. The ways in which they are related to each other would well repay experimental study.

reference to the potpourri included under the heading of schizophrenia, it may be worth pointing out that the paranoid reactions appear to be predominantly extrapunitive, the catatonic ones intropunitive, and the hebephrenic ones impunitive. Finally, though in this it is practically assumed that these types are found characteristically and consistently in given individuals — a conclusion which, as has been said, must await further investigation — Freud's libidinal types, as recently outlined,[1] come very close to the present schema. The extrapunitive reaction may be thought of as related to Freud's Narcissistic type, the intropunitive reaction to his Compulsive type, and the impunitive reaction to his Erotic type.

Needless to say, this schema — which, like others, is a convenient condensation — is not intended to be taken with too strict literalness. The arbitrary divisions that a brief presentation such as this necessitates should be allowed for fully or misconceptions are inevitable.

The behavioural test that has been devised on the basis of the present schema may now be described. In so doing, much greater emphasis will be placed upon the technique employed than upon the results it has yielded. The reason for this procedure is that the test is still in the formative stage. Work on it has up to the present been done with three small groups of subjects. With each group the test has been changed on the basis of the experience obtained previously. It has been thought unwise to attempt anything like standardization on a large group of subjects until these preliminary experiments have, by the method of successive approximation, given rise to an instrument that is, in essentials at least, theoretically comprehensible. Special attention will be paid to the work done with the third group of subjects, references to the other two being made only when this is necessary for purposes of comparison and confirmation.

The ultimate purpose of the test is to determine whether individuals characteristically follow some one or some combination of the three types of reaction to frustration just outlined. In the

1. S. Freud, 'Libidinal types.' *Psychoanal. Quart.*, 1932, *1*, 3–6.

preliminary work the main object was to find the best means of readily eliciting reactions to frustration such as could eventually be used in an instrument for classifying individuals, if they can be so classified, in accordance with the present schema or any other that the experiments revealed.

In order to avoid the pitfalls of the usual personality questionnaire — the answers to which generally embody the 'opinion-error,' i.e., tell more about the subject's opinions of himself than about the facts which the questionnaire is intended to reveal — the method was adopted of presenting subjects with problems of different kinds under such conditions as would make it possible to study their behavioural reactions in solving them. The behaviour of importance for the present purpose is, of course, that attendant upon failure. Despite its theoretical advantages over personality tests of the questionnaire variety, this technique is also obviously imperfect because, in the first place, it measures reactions not to all types of frustration, but only to failure in satisfying certain needs of the ego (assuming that the instructions of the test arouse these needs, which is also a matter of doubt in some cases); and it does not even involve all kinds of failure of ego striving but only failure on such intellectual problems as are feasible in the test situation. Moreover, only a sample of the sort of problems that can be called intellectual is adapted to the present purpose. One of the chief objects of the successive revisions of the test is to broaden its scope to the greatest possible extent in spite of these limitations.

The test was given to three groups of about fifteen subjects each, mostly men, between the ages of 18 and 30, the majority of them being university students.

The technique now to be described in detail is the one used with Group C (Clinic Group III). With Group A (Clinic Group II) the test was administered in one session, only one kind of problem (linguistic) was utilized, and the subjects were tested individually. Group B (none of whom took part in the other Clinic experiments) was given the test in two sessions, with a different variety of problems in each (linguistic, arithmetical).

In this case the subjects were tested in a group. Group C, with which this account is mainly concerned, also had two sessions of testing and two sorts of problems. Here, however, problems of both kinds were included in each session. Like Group A, the subjects in Group C were tested individually.

After a few minutes of rapport-making conversation in the experimental room, the subject was read the following instructions :

The problems you are to solve in this test are of two types. One involves putting together geometrical forms to make a rectangle of given size — a sort of paper-and-pencil jig-saw puzzle. Here is a sample to examine. (Hand sample.) Is that clear ?

The other sort deals with letters which are to be arranged to form a word. All the letters given in each case must, of course, be used in the solution. Here is a sample. (Hand sample.) Is that clear ?

Now, before beginning the test, I wish to explain several things.

Three minutes will be allowed for the solution of each of the problems. At the end of each three-minute interval, I shall ring a bell. You will then put down on the problem sheet one of the three following :

1. The solution of the problem, in the space provided. You may, of course, write in this space while working the problem. If you get the answer before the end of the allotted time, notify me so that we may go on to the next problem without delay.

2. A check mark on the line beside the cross — which will indicate that you have not been able to solve the problem in the time allowed but believe it can be solved.

3. A check mark on the line beside the zero — which will indicate that you believe the problem has no solution. (If asked whether some are actually unsolvable, reply : That is for you to decide.)

Be sure to answer every problem, but remember that only these three types of reply will be accepted.

Are there any questions ?

Then we may begin.

(The subject is now handed the test leaflet.)

On the day following the first session, the subjects returned for the second part of the test. The instructions for this session were as follows :

Today we are to do the second part of the test of which you did the first part yesterday.

The problems are of the same types as those you have already done. The procedure is also identical. I will simply remind you of the three-minute limit for each problem and of the three alternative modes of response :

1. The solution.

2. A check beside the cross — to indicate that you have not been able to solve the problem in the time allowed but believe it can be solved.

3. A check beside the zero — to indicate that you believe the problem has no solution.

Be sure to answer every problem but remember that only these three types of reply will be accepted.

Are there any questions ?

Then we may begin ?

(Subject is handed leaflet.)

In each session twelve problems were given, six of each of the two kinds.[1] The two kinds of problems did not alternate with each other but came in a haphazard order. This order was, however, constant for all subjects. The test leaflets contained only one problem on a page so that, since each sheet was turned over when the problem on it was finished, any tendency the subject might have to keep a score of his successes and of his failure reactions would be hindered.

Since the problems were so chosen that the majority of them should not be solvable in three minutes, every subject experienced a number of failures and his reactions to these could be scored on the basis of his own check marks as extrapunitive (if the subject stated that the problem could not be solved) or as non-extrapunitive (if he stated that the problem could be solved). An extrapunitive percentage score, based naturally upon the failures only, could then be calculated for each subject. Since many subjects presented as correct solutions those which they were only guessing at and which could therefore not be scored either as

1. The kinds of problems given the subjects for solution seem to be sufficiently described in the instructions, which are quoted in full. It may, however, be added that one kind consisted in rearranging a group of mixed up letters to form a word, the other consisted in drawing given geometrical forms into a larger rectangle which the smaller figures all together were required to fit perfectly.

right, as extrapunitive or as non-extrapunitive, a score on guessed solutions could be obtained. This result may help to analyse out the impunitive factor, with its component of self-deception, in the non-extrapunitive responses which, in the present form of the test, include both the intropunitive and the impunitive types of reaction.

It should be noted that half of the problems of each kind actually had no solutions, though this fact could by no means be easily detected in any case. The reason for this device was to offer an opportunity for non-extrapunitive replies to be as often invalid objectively as the solvable problems made possible the objective invalidity of extrapunitive replies. In this way, it was thought, there could be somewhat greater certainty about the subjectivity of the reactions.

It may be questioned why such a short time as three minutes was allowed for the solution of each problem. The object of this procedure was to give the individual so little time for objectively evaluating the task in hand that his reaction to the failures would reflect, as far as possible, his habitual behaviour upon frustration in the past. Thus, once more, the subjectivity of the responses and their dependence upon the possible personality traits the test was studying would be favoured.

It is theoretically likely that the amount of ability an individual possesses for a given sort of task will to some extent influence his reactions to failure on such tasks. This was why two kinds of problems of widely differing intellectual character were utilized. An attempt was also made to find out by direct questioning which of the two sorts of problems the subjects generally preferred and in which they usually did the better work. It was hoped that the answers to these questions would shed light upon the frustration reactions in the present test. Another closely associated problem concerns the relationship between the degree of success achieved in this test itself and the type of reaction to the failures in it. A complete analysis of the results of the test would have to take this matter seriously into consideration.

A final and important feature of the technique was the division of the test into two sessions to allow for the manifestation of any cyclic or pendulum effects in reaction to frustration.

A brief account of the results of the test may now be given. Though the main purpose of the present account is to point out the implications of the problem under investigation and to describe the experimental technique adopted, a sample of the data that have accumulated may profitably be reported. These results must not, however, be regarded as final in any sense but rather as illustrative of the kind of material that the test yields and the sort of interpretation of this material that may be made. In this discussion Group C will again be mainly considered but even in the case of this group, no attempt at a complete presentation of the results will be made.

The range of scores on extrapunitiveness for session I was from 13 to 86%, with a median of 44%; for session II the range was from 20 to 100%, with a median of 45%. The indication is that individuals certainly do react differently to the frustration experiences in the test.

A study of the results of Group C to determine the relationship between success on the test and type of reaction to frustration reveals one or two noteworthy points. The highest number of successes achieved by any subject in the two sessions combined was 7, the lowest number, 2. At least one problem was solved by every subject in each session and some individuals succeeded in as many as five in one session. The study of the results thus far completed does not, however, reveal any consistent relationship between degree of success and type of reaction to frustration when the individual is taken as the basis of analysis. If, on the other hand, the group is made the unit of study and the results on the two kinds of problems are totaled up separately, it is found that in the first session the median extrapunitive percentage for form problems was 25, for linguistic problems, 60; and in the second session the corresponding averages were 33 and 67. This indicates that the group as a whole tended to be markedly more extrapunitive on linguistic than on form problems, and when this fact is coupled with the further one that 11 of the 13 subjects stated that they preferred and that they did better in literary than in mechanical work,[1] the conclusion is suggested that there is a tendency for greater extrapunitiveness in fields where the subject has or feels that he has greater competence. The result just reported is borne out by evidence from Group B, in the case of whom the median extrapunitive score on the linguistic material was 67%, while that on the arithmetical material was 45%. In that group, too, 11 of the 17 subjects participating in the test stated a preference for and alleged greater success in the kind of work (literary) in which more extrapunitiveness was manifested. Further evidence in the same direction is presented further on.

In view of the facts just mentioned, it is not surprising that the coefficient of correlation between extrapunitive scores on the linguistic and on the form material, each taken separately, is only .18. One implication of this low correlation is perhaps that the type of reaction to frustration is specific to the type of situation involved. It is, however, too early to draw this conclusion.

As for split-half reliability, taking each session separately, simple inspection of that data reveals that this is extremely low. This result is not to be wondered at, however, since the number of problems in each session on which the extrapunitive scores were based was about nine, and no one would seriously consider taking the results on half of such a number of items as a basis for prediction about the other half. The folly of such an attempt is even greater when the apparent specificity of reaction to frustration, as indicated in the last paragraph, is called to mind. In the future, an attempt must be made to increase the length of the test as much as possible without interfering with other desiderata, but this objective will be difficult to achieve in view of the importance of such factors as fatigue in a test of this sort.

It might be thought that the retest reliability could be more profitably weighed. There were, after all, two sessions of the test, and it is therefore possible to correlate the scores obtained on the

1. The identification of the form and arithmetical problems with things mechanical and of the linguistic or verbal problems with things literary may well be questioned. No major conclusions are, however, based upon this interpretation.

separate occasions. If, with this consideration in mind, the correlation between the scores obtained in the separate sessions is calculated, the coefficient (rank order method) is found to be very low — only .26. From another point of view, however, this low correlation may be regarded as a positive result, for it tends to bear out the original reason for dividing the test into two sessions. It will be recalled that this division was introduced to make possible the study of any shifts in the type of reaction of frustration that might occur from session to session. The significance of the low correlation between sessions may, therefore, have a very different meaning from the one that would be attributed to it from the standpoint of reliability. It is impossible to define this significance with any finality on the basis of the present meagre data, but close scrutiny of the results of the individual subjects indicates a tendency towards compensation in the second session for the type of reaction exhibited in the first.

While no effort has yet been put forth systematically to validate the present test, some attempt in this direction was made possible by the fact that the subjects in Groups A and C were among those studied at the Clinic. Though a correlation coefficient derived from as small a number of measures as 13 must be about .52 before it is equal to four times its probable error, when it may *perhaps* be regarded as significant, such comparisons do have at least a suggestive value. They can certainly not be regarded as having any higher value. If this estimate of their importance is kept in mind, one or two of the results obtained from the correlation of the rank orders of the present test with the rank orders just referred to may be mentioned with equanimity.[1]

It has previously been pointed out that certain of the subjects presented as correct solutions some that were not correct and were apparently only guessed at or at any rate not very critically considered. One individual made six such responses — 25% of the

1. The rather striking relationship between the present test and that dealing with changes in the level of aspiration deserves a word of comment. The result signifies that high extrapunitiveness is negatively related to the tendency to reduce the level of aspiration after failure. The common note is apparently one of defiance.

total number. At the other extreme of the scale are those individuals who gave no replies of this sort. The meaning of the behaviour seems more intelligible if the rank order of subjects in respect to 'guessed' solutions is correlated with the rank orders on the variables estimated by the Clinic staff. The following coefficients are worthy of note : with Aggression +.67 ; with Dominance +.51 ; with Exocathection +.60 ; with Superego Conflict —.53. The interpretation suggested by these results is that the offering of incorrect solutions as correct is more characteristic of individuals who have a high degree of Aggression and a strong need for Dominance — thus being ready to assert themselves without hesitation — and who are rather markedly extraverted and lacking in Superego determination — thus not being easily inhibited by conscientious scruples and critical doubts.

This view is somewhat substantiated by the consideration of another sort of behaviour that occurred in the case of four of the subjects in Group C. This consisted in a marked fluctuation of the hand from one side of the problem sheet to the other at the moment when it became necessary to check off a problem as solvable or not. Since the symbols between which a choice was to be made were printed at opposite sides of the page, there was an opportunity in the instances mentioned to observe the conflict attending choice. Interestingly enough the subject who manifested this behaviour to the greatest extent — practically every time the need for making a choice arose — in no case presented an incorrect solution as correct. Two of the other three subjects with overtly manifested conflict of this kind are likewise found in the lower half of the rank order on 'guessed' solutions. On the other hand, the first three subjects in this rank order failed to give any indications of such conduct.[1] It then appears that guessing and doubting as occasionally manifested objectively in the present experiment probably represent opposed ways of behaving, related to different patterns of frustration reaction.

1. Since only four of the thirteen subjects showed fluctuations of the hand at the time of choice, a rank order could not very well be drawn up. A statistical correlation with the rank order on 'guesses' was therefore not possible.

Another result worth noting is a rank order correlation of .40 between extrapunitive score (average for the two sessions) and the variable of Narcism as estimated by the Clinic investigators. This finding is, moreover, somewhat confirmed by a coefficient of correlation of +.35 between extrapunitiveness and Narcism for the subjects in Group A.[1] The interpretation of this result, assuming that it has any statistical significance, seems to be the rather obvious one that, if it is legitimate to regard a given type or combination of types of reaction to frustration as belonging to a relatively congruent and consistent constellation of personality traits, then the constellation containing extrapunitiveness will also contain Narcism. The previously described results on the relation of subjective competence to extrapunitiveness afford corroborative evidence of the present association of Narcism with extrapunitiveness.

Only one other correlation will be discussed : —.51 between the subjects' extrapunitive scores in session I and their need for Affiliation as estimated by the Clinic. Non-extrapunitiveness and the need for Affiliation seem, on this evidence, to belong to the same personality syndrome. The correlation between extrapunitiveness in session II and the same need for Affiliation is, moreover, +.11, a difference from the previous result which tends to confirm its significance. For it seems plausible that a strong need for a good rapport with the experimenter would inhibit the extrapunitive type of response in the first session, when this social relationship would naturally be more of a problem for the subject, whereas by the second session this dependence upon the experimenter's good opinion would have given way somewhat to the other aspects of the situation.

Now, if Affiliation be regarded as a representative of object-love, the *negative* correlation of this variable with extrapunitiveness and the previously mentioned positive correlation of Narcism with extrapunitiveness may be interestingly coupled. The implication is that self-love is associated with high extrapunitiveness, object-love with low extrapunitiveness. This sort of interpretation,

1. No ratings on Narcism were available for the subjects in Group B.

however, obviously implies that type of reaction to frustration is to be given the status of a rather consistent personality trait and it must be again stated that the evidence on this point thus far gathered is far from conclusive. Until a great deal more research has therefore been done, such an interpretation, or any similar one, must be regarded as tentative to a very high degree.

In conclusion it may be mentioned that the test under discussion is now being revised and improved on the basis of the previous results. A complete description of the revision would be out of place here but it may be noted, to round out the account already given, that this new version will have at least three kinds of problems and a larger total number of tasks, and that provision will be made in it for two possible non-extrapunitive replies, one of which, it is hoped, will approximate the intropunitive and the other the impunitive type of reaction.

25. SOCIAL INTERACTION

MARIA RICKERS-OVSIANKINA

Purpose. It is obvious that in an investigation aiming to study the personality from as many angles as possible a consideration of its social aspects is essential. The majority of the contributions presented in this book naturally have social implications of one kind or another. In the one to be discussed now, however, the sociality of a person is the centre of attention.

For the choice of the method of attack a common observation of everyday life was determining. If two strangers find themselves confined for a period of time in a relatively closed space, such as a train compartment, and if there is no particular activity occupying one or both of them individually, then it is very likely that they will become engaged in some form of social behaviour. Spatial proximity combined with absence of any definite occupation thus seem to facilitate social interaction. With this principle in mind the following experimental setting was devised.

Procedure. The S, who had already taken part in a number of the studies described in this book, was informed upon entering that he would have to wait a short while for the E. He was then conducted into a room in which he could be observed through a one-way screen. In this room he found another student, presumably also waiting. In reality the latter was an assistant of the E and was acting according to definite instructions.

The room was furnished simply with a few chairs, two tables, a mirror, and several pictures on the walls. There were, further, a number of objects scattered around the room : 1, an open box with cigarettes, 2, several puzzles of medium difficulty, 3, a mechanical toy constructed in such a fashion that a person manipulating it would easily get the impression of having broken it, 4, a box full of nails and other small objects, which in the course of the experiment was dropped on the floor by the assistant as if by accident. No reading material was left in the room or in the hall through which the S entered. If he had something with him to read, however, this activity could not be prevented.

The objects which have been described had a dual purpose in the experiment. In the first place, it was hoped that they would provide the medium for actions or events of a social nature. It was interesting to observe whether or not the Ss would use the objects without permission from some member of the Clinic staff. Furthermore, the puzzles presented good material for the development of either co-operation or competition ; the dropping of the nail box gave an opportunity to be helpful in repairing the damage ; while the 'breaking' of the mechanical toy might create embarrassment or guilt feelings. In the second place, the presence of the objects in the room furnished the possibility of differentiating between those persons who were more interested in the opportunity for social contact and those who preferred to concentrate on the objects.

Upon the S's arrival the experimental assistant asked the newcomer whether he had been in the Clinic before and intimated that this was his own first visit. This was done to encourage the S to take the initiative in establishing some kind of social relationship. For the first fifteen minutes of the total thirty-minute observation period the assistant remained rather passive with respect to the S, confining his activities to the objects. If the S let this time pass without paying much attention either to his partner or to the objects in the room, then the assistant took the lead in the second part of the observation period by asking questions about the S or about the Clinic and by suggesting that they investigate the different objects in the room. Between the two sections of the experiment the assistant left the room upon some pretext for two or three minutes to provide the possibility of observing any change in the behaviour of the S when left alone.

Two people were thus thrown together in spatial proximity; the situation of waiting precluded any intensive occupation; and the fact that they were both experimental subjects put them on an equal footing. In this way was created a situation favourable to social interaction; consequently the extent to which the S was influenced by the facilitating circumstances may be considered an indication of the degree of his social responsiveness.

Results. The procedure proved fruitful in procuring typical differences in the S's reactions. The social attitudes displayed ranged from a companion-like 'we'-relation to a situation of separate existence in which the other person either did not exist psychologically or belonged to an 'out-group.' The former was characterized by friendly chatting about personal matters, a confidential communication of opinion in regard to the Clinic, taking and giving suggestions, an absence of suspicion towards the assistant, and common occupation with the objects. The opposite attitude expressed itself in great reserve and reluctance to take part in common occupation. The conversation, if any, was not a social act directed towards the other person, but rather a manifestation of the S's own restlessness. An apprehensive attitude towards the assistant was typical. The S offered no spontaneous statements about the Clinic, and if asked for an opinion gave very non-committal replies.

The analysis of these various behaviour patterns may be pursued in two directions. On the one hand, the data lend themselves to speculation concerning the topology of social situations such as the one created. On the other hand, they can be utilized for studies of individual differences, since they yield information pertaining to the degree of social responsiveness.

This twofold analysis of the material is given in another place. At this point the observed forms of social interaction will merely be illustrated by examples taken from their extreme poles.

A good instance of the 'we'-relation is found in the case of Oriol and a contrast to this is offered by Zill.

Example 1. Oriol inspects the room briefly, answers the assistant's usual question, combs his hair before the mirror, complains about the heat — all in the first minute. Then he stops before the table, examines the toy tower and winds up its mechanism. He invites the assistant to join him in trying to find out how the object functions. Oriol is very active but not persistent. Soon he takes a sandwich out of his pocket and eats it, explaining that he has had no breakfast. He engages in a conversation with his partner, asking rather inquisitively what the latter knows about the tests, and what he expects to gain from them. Then, in his turn, he starts describing the different procedures he has been through but soon interrupts himself and, with an apology, takes another sandwich out of his pocket. The assistant now asks where he can get a drink of water. Oriol offers to show the way. They return together and Oriol begins to discuss the reasons for their being kept waiting. He advances the theory of a test of patience and starts to make some other interpretations but drops them half-formulated. With an energetic movement he tilts the mechanical tower over and examines it with zest, displaying frank enjoyment at every new discovery. After three minutes, however, this activity is dropped for the sake of a puzzle. About the latter he expresses the opinion that it might have no solution and he is distinctly disappointed when the assistant disproves this by mentioning his own success with the puzzle. For the rest of the observation time (about five minutes) Oriol goes once more over the different puzzles, showing interest but no persistence. He responds goodnaturedly when the assistant laughs at his failures. Shortly before the end he states again his suspicion with regard to the purpose of their being kept waiting. The situation throughout is one of being together as companions.

Example 2. Zill relaxes without hesitation in an armchair and at once takes a cigarette from the box on the table. In answer to the question of the assistant whether he has been in the Clinic for a long time, he mutters something indistinct and takes out of his pocket a college journal which he begins to read. After three minutes the assistant attempts to encourage a conversation by asking whether the tests at the Clinic were interesting. The S answers curtly: 'Most are rather interesting,' and then asks, 'Are you a patient here?' Soon silence prevails again. Zill continues to read and smoke placidly, leaning back in the armchair self-indulgently. He pays no attention to the other one, who keeps in the background.

After nearly a quarter of an hour Zill puts the paper aside, walks about a little, looks casually at a few of the objects on the table, glances at the mirror on the wall and tries out one of the puzzles for a few seconds. When the assistant asks where he can find the toilet the S directs him briefly. The assistant leaves and immediately Zill turns towards the mirror. He spends a good deal of time in front of it, 'primping' with great absorption. Then he starts to pace the room, and as he passes the mirror, he stops, as if enthralled, to take another look. The assistant returns and tries to interest the S in the solution of one of the puzzles, but the latter declines the suggestion, remarking, 'I don't think you should touch it, they might object.' He leaves the room to get himself a newspaper and sits down to read it, not without having first surreptitiously caught a glance of his image in the mirror. The assistant, who has been occupied since his return with the puzzles, offers Zill a ring puzzle and asks whether he knows the solution. Zill takes the rings and begins to manipulate them rather indifferently for a couple of minutes. The assistant drops the box containing the nails, clippings, etc., whereupon the S smiles condescendingly, without making any attempt to help in the replacement of the objects, and continues to fumble with the puzzle. He remains aloof when the box falls a second time and some of the contents roll right to his feet. Soon after this occurrence he returns the puzzle, which he has kept in his hand, and also takes special care to put the box of nails exactly in the same position in which it had been before falling down. A new attempt of the assistant to interest him in a mutual occupation with the mechanical toy is unsuccessful. A few moments later the S is called out of the room.

Chapter VII
THE CASE OF EARNST

R. W. WHITE

INTRODUCTION

H. A. MURRAY

As soon as all the examinations (as outlined in the previous chapter) were completed a biographer was selected for each of the subjects. The function of the biographer, who in every case was a member of the Diagnostic Council, was to collect all the observations and interpretations that had been made on the individual assigned to him, and then to fit them together as best he could into an understandable and convincing portrait. A 'portrait' meant a 'biography,' since the notion was accepted generally that the history of a personality *is* the personality. Consequently, it was necessary to pay particular attention to the events of childhood and their genetical relations, in order to discover some of the factors that had led to the particular pattern of traits which the subject exhibited during his three months' period at the Clinic.

Experience was to teach us that, though the reasons for many of the subject's responses were mysterious and much of his past entirely out of reach, it was possible to find in most individuals an underlying reaction system, termed by us *unity-thema*, which was the key to his unique nature. I say 'key' because if one assumed the activity of this unity-thema many superficially unintelligible actions and expressions became, as it were, psychologically inevitable. A *unity-thema* is a compound of interrelated — collaborating or conflicting — dominant needs that are linked to press to which the individual was exposed on one or more particular occasions, gratifying or traumatic, in early childhood. The thema may stand for a primary infantile experience or a subsequent reaction formation to that experience. But, whatever its nature and genesis, it repeats itself in many forms during later life.

As soon as we realized the force of the unity-thema its importance in the interpretation of each session began to dawn upon us. For if every response is the objectification of an aspect of a particular personality and the most fundamental and characteristic determinant of a personality is its unity-thema, then many responses cannot be fully understood except in terms of their relation to the unity-thema.

A single, significant response may be likened to one piece of a picture puzzle. The latter has a certain shape and exhibits certain colours, but these items *per se* are of little interest or importance. They only become meaningful when it is known how they are related to the attributes of other pieces and how together they contribute to the total unity. No doubt other more dynamic analogies for a single episode could be cited — one chord in a long musical composition, for example — but I think the general principle is clear : that, *by the observation of many parts one finally arrives at a conception of the whole and, then, having grasped the latter, one can re-interpret and understand the former.* This was the conception which guided every biographer in his analysis and reconstruction of the data that was accumulated about each individual.

As soon as the biographer finished his work, a meeting of all the experimenters was called to review the entire case. The biographer opened the meeting with a very brief account of his theoretical formulation : the hypothesis that he believed would be sustained by the facts to be related. Following this introduction each E in turn read a short report (3 to 20 minutes) of his session with the subject ; after each of which the biographer made a few interpretative comments to show how the observations fitted his formula. About four hours were spent in reading and discussing these reports ; at the end of which the biographer read his 'psychograph' of the case. The term 'psychograph has been used by

G. W. Allport,[1] A. A. Roback [2] and others to stand for a list of rated traits (comparable to our list of scored variables), but it was employed by us to mean 'abstract biography,' a matter that will be discussed in a little while.

After the psychograph there was general discussion ; and at the end the marks of the subject on each variable — those assigned by the Diagnostic Council and by other experimenters and those obtained from questionnaire scores — were put up for inspection and after brief consideration final ratings were given, disagreements being settled by majority vote. Except for the omission of the general discussion the Case Study presented in this chapter is an almost exact report of one of these final meetings.

It is regrettable that the necessity of putting our results between the covers of a single volume does not permit the inclusion of more than one case history,[3] for case histories are the proof of the pudding. That is to say, a personological theory can be tested best by utilizing it in the writing of biographies, and its worth judged positively by its general success in ordering the facts as well as by what it reveals beyond the facts ; and negatively by what it leaves uninterpreted. It should be an instrument that can suitably portray in their relations the subject's main directions and modes of effort and growth, and bring into sharp relief the pertinent variables which operated in the episodes that chiefly determined these strivings and developments.

No scheme of technical symbols has been evolved to date that can stand alone. All proposed formulations must be supplemented by the language of common speech. Perhaps some day concise symbols for the variables (or themas) will be devised ; in which event the psychologist will be able to set down in the briefest possible fashion the known episodes of a man's life in their proper sequence, just as now a competent musician with his system of notation can clearly represent a complicated temporal arrange-

1. Allport,G.W. *J. Abn. & Soc. Psychol.*,1921,*16*, 6–40.
2. Roback,A.A. *The Psychology of Character*, New York,1927.
3. A very interesting case study by Dr.Barrett had to be eliminated at the eleventh hour. We trust that it can be published in a later volume.

ment of musical sounds. Though it seems inadvisable to attempt such a thing before there is reasonable conviction as to what variables are most essential, one can imagine by picturing a musical score how it could be done. Along the top line, let us say, there might be represented the succession of alpha press : the significant environmental forces (in so far as they were objectively discernible). The second line could be used to depict the beta press : the environment with its objects as the S apperceived it (the so-called 'psychological environment'). The third could be devoted to the subject's behavioural reactions (needs and modes) ; the fourth to his emotions and hedonic affections ; and, finally, the fifth line to his thought processes : fantasies or intellections. A simpler plan would be to eliminate everything but the second and third lines ; or even, by adopting a symbol for every press-need combination (thema), to represent the succession of episodes on a single line. But this is not for the present.

Nowadays the psychologist is forced to employ non-technical language and consequently the writing of case histories (which should provide the factual substance for a true science of psychology) must lie somewhere on the continuum between biology (science) and literature (art). It seems reasonable to speak of such a continuum, for there are scientists who in the presentation of their material employ with telling effect the resources of imaginative writers (imagery, simile, metaphor, style), and there are novelists who record their observations of man and nature with the detachment and detailed precision of trained scientists. Those who are acquainted with the writings of William Morton Wheeler, for example, know that an eminent and scientifically scrupulous biologist can, without compromising truth, work his data into enduring literature. And one must acknowledge the modicum of truth that resides in the remark that Henry James wrote novels like a psychologist and William James wrote psychology like a novelist ; something which might be said with equal fitness of Aldous Huxley, the novelist, and Julian Huxley, the naturalist.

I should favour as a hovering ideal a system of symbols which could be used to record what was psychologically pertinent in any occurrence. At least the attempt to develop such a system [1] would serve to bring clearly to consciousness the essential variables, many of which find their way into literary accounts without clearly announcing their presence. With adequate notation the psychologist could function at the scientific end of the continuum ; without it he must write, to some extent, as a historian.

The next thing to a system of notation is a conceptual scheme which is complete enough to represent everything important in technical language. This would naturally have to precede any meaningful system of notation. In our work we attempted to make our theory as elastic as possible, but when it came to the test of writing biographies it fell far short of the requirements. Much was observed which could not be held in the net. We had to decide whether to squeeze the life out of our subjects by lacing them up in the rigid vestments of our constructs, or loosen the scheme and use what literary ability we possessed to catch some of the conceptually unmanageable life. The final result was a compromise. I cannot recall reading any case histories that are more scientific than ours, if by scientific one means systematic observation, the organization of observed facts in terms of a scheme of defined categories, the measurement of variables and the determination of causal factors. But compared to other varieties of scientific writing they appear extremely uncritical. And we must also acknowledge that they fall short of the portrayal of personality in good literature ; though, in some instances, the concepts have made matters which novelists only suggestively touch upon, explicitly intelligible.

Until theory has been much further developed we would be inclined to favour the use of clear literary language, despite the current tendency among American psychologists to become suspicious whenever there appears in the writings or speech of a fellow-scientist the slightest trace of aesthetic feeling. A psycholo-

1. Lewin has attempted to do this, but I do not find that his system can be applied to complex situations. (*Cf.* Lewin,K. *Principles of Topological Psychology,* New York,1936.)

gist who believes that he can tell the truth without being 'literary' has only to try writing a case history or biography, and then compare what he has done to a character sketch by any novelist of the first order. We academic psychologists have yet to discover how much can be learnt from the realists of literature. A little humility here would add to our stature.

What are the necessary components and what is the best form for an abstract biography? Over and over again we have asked ourselves this question. In our minds it is not very different from the primary question, What is personality? since the proper conceptualization of a human life (abstract biography) *is* the personality in so far as it can be scientifically formulated. We can think of no problem more important than this. Its adequate solution would provide a framework within which all more specific problems could be set. As Dollard[1] has so pregnantly observed, it is the logical meeting ground of psychology and sociology. For the individual is always imbedded in his culture. He assimilates it, is changed by it, conserves it, represents it, conveys it, modifies it, creates it. The culture is expressed through personalities, and personalities are expressed in the culture. Furthermore, if one takes the general drift of passionate preoccupation as a criterion, it becomes apparent that personality—the concrete, individual, human soul—is attracting the attention of creative genius as it never has before. Witness the rapid rise of biography, the prodigious increase of autobiographical literature and of autobiographical art in general. Witness also the attention that is being paid to-day to the individual child in the family and in the school; and the recently emerging conception of what Plant[2] calls an 'individual-centered culture.' It does not require unusual perceptiveness to see that this new direction and focussing of profound concern is closely related to the setting of the sun of orthodox theology. It parallels the growing conviction that the religious vision is the ecstatic creation of the suffering, frustrated, longing, human soul; that Deity is not something 'up there,' but some-

1. Dollard, J. *Criteria for the Life History*, New Haven, 1935.
2. Plant, J.S. *Personality and the Culture Pattern*, New York, 1937.

thing in personality — in the mostly unconscious depths of personality. This conviction does not quell the forces that in the past have given rise to religions, but it gives them an entirely different significance and aim. The point I wish to make is this : many able people in different places from different standpoints and with different methods are attempting to discover and portray the workings of the human mind. All roads are leading to personality ; and psychologists should see to it that in the coming developments their science plays a decisive part, as it should by definition. Above all, it is necessary to find abstractions that do not imprison life in hollow categories but — like 'all the pens that poets ever held' — portray its richness and its depths.

For those who feel that this conception is nothing but an idle, sentimental dream, I can only cite again, as an analogy, the score of a musical composition. Though abstract, it conveys *all* the music to anyone who can read. I admit that this is a counteractive 'far cry' provoked by the realization that our own conceptual scheme was not equal to the life that we observed.

Because we were led to attribute (rightly or wrongly) great importance to the earliest experiences of life, we would have liked to discover as many facts as possible about each subject's babyhood : the special circumstances attending his birth, his earliest reactions, the dispositions he displayed in the cradle, the manner of weaning, his initial ambulatory and predatory efforts. But since all our information about the past was gained from the subjects themselves and they rarely remembered anything that occurred before the third year, the drama of infancy has been left unchronicled. In a few instances subjects reported events which their parents had related to them — difficulty of labour, being fed by a spoon from birth, falling into a tub of water at an early age and so forth — but these were exceptional.

In general, then, our consecutively arranged records based upon the subjects' memories of the past begin with a few rather dubious reports pertaining to the third or fourth year of life ; but, from then on, consist of an increasing number of less questionable facts. The memories bring the history up to the period of our three months' intensive examination. With this series of successive items as a basis, we have attempted in each case to extrapolate backwards to birth. Thus, our psychographs commence with a four-year segment of hypothetical occurrences that have been inferred in accordance with certain tentatively accepted principles of conditioning. This is followed by a sixteen-year segment of the personality that is mostly based on memories ; and at the end there is a short but fuller segment covering the period of testing and interviewing. This is the nearest that we have been able to come to the natural history of each personality.

We wanted to make a record of such successions in order to discover what developmental processes — progressions, inhibitions, repressions, dissociations, sublimations, regressions, socializations, contrafactions, integrations, differentiations, unifications, substitutions, counteractions — had most influentially occurred. Knowing these, it is possible to make certain inferences in regard to the structural dynamics and relative stability of the contemporary personality.

We expect most readers to be skeptical of our reconstructions of infancy, and we take it for granted that those who have been trained in psycho-analysis will consider the evidence insufficient. This is precisely our own opinion. Our reconstructions are speculative and entirely hypothetical. We are taking them with more than one grain of salt. But we consider that they may be important as leads to further research. For we are not cured of the prejudice that *some* experiences of infancy are determining. Probably most impressions become entirely obliterated — though of this one can never be certain — and many habits are outgrown and never re-instituted. But there are critical occurrences in every life — and one is usually taxed to state just why they are critical — which register in the brain and thenceforth are ever ready to be revived by an appropriate press.

As an example of this, we may cite an experiment performed by Diven.[1] This investigator found that when a group of sub-

1. Diven, K. 'Certain determinants in the conditioning of anxiety reactions.' *J. Psychol.*, 1936, *3*, 291–308.

jects were read a word-list containing 'urban' words ('taxi,' 'subway,' etc.) and 'rural' words ('hay,' 'plough,' etc.), some subjects gave marked galvanic skin responses to the 'urban' words whereas others responded to the 'rural' words. Here was a clear-cut difference. How is it to be explained? The reader could hardly be expected to answer this question without further information. The solution is provided by the knowledge that on the previous day the subjects who gave gsr's to the urban words had regularly received an electric shock after the word *taxi*, whereas those who gave gsr's to the rural words had regularly received an electric shock after the word *barn*. The potency of the critical word had spread to other words having a similar locational reference. Here, we suppose that a trace of the electric shock persisted and this 'persistent' must be included as a determinant of the present event.

As a clinical analogy we may take the case of Frost who, when shown a picture of a mill in the Aesthetic Appreciation Test, was the only subject to note and comment upon a barely perceptible brook in the corner of the picture. To a picture of a train passing along the bank of a river the subject said that it looked as if the train were about 'to topple in the water.' Since it did not appear in this way to the experimenter or to any of the other subjects, one is left to wonder why Frost gave this unique response. The solution seems to be partially indicated by the following facts:

1. In childhood Frost had a nightmare of a train falling from a bridge into a river. (Evidently this is the fantasy that was projected into the picture.)

2. Frost used to enjoy building bridges with blocks. (Possibly as a counteraction to falling into water.)

3. He was afraid of water and did not learn to swim until he was 11 years of age. (This suggests that Frost identified himself with the train.)

4. The fear of water can be attributed partly to the dramatic stories told him in infancy of a dreadful flood that had inundated the Ohio countryside before his birth, and partly to the fact that Frost was a chronic bed-wetter.

5. At the present day Frost's nocturnal emissions occur in conjunction with dreams of prodigious urination (urethral erotism).

6. Frost has been occasionally bothered by a compulsion to turn off faucets. He is made uncomfortable by hearing water running and on certain occasions has been forced by inner promptings to make sure, by a twist of the wrist, that every faucet in the house was securely shut off. [This compulsion might be interpreted as a symbolic prohibition of urethral erotism.]

Thus, there are reasons to suppose that an association had occurred between ejaculation (or infantile masturbation), bed-wetting (flooding the room), and the fear of falling into water and drowning. The dream of the train toppling into the river symbolized the anxiety associated with this complex, and his attempts in play to build strong bridges probably represented an effort to protect himself against such an accident, as well as an externalization of his attempt to overcome bed-wetting (urethral erotism). Whether or not this formulation is entirely correct the autobiographical data certainly have some bearing upon the peculiar response which Frost gave to the picture of the train skirting the river, for without this data his remark is merely freakish.

Such genetical interpretations are commonplaces to psychoanalysts. But usually what appears to them most probable is what psychologists of other denominations are least inclined to accept, and so it is important at the present time to collect as much evidence as possible that bears upon the various theories of development proposed by Freud and other analysts.

The case history interpreted by Dr. White that constitutes the bulk of this chapter is that of a representative subject. In respect to quantity and richness of subjective or personal data it ranks clearly in the upper half of our biographies. It is not as unusual, as complex or as deeply revealing as a few of our cases, but there is plenty of grist in it for a psychologist's mill.

In publishing this analysis of a young scientist who all his life has fought with great determination against almost overwhelming odds, we are sensible that a record of this kind which purposely leaves out all valuations cannot possibly do justice to a human being. For the man's personal appeal, ability, status and moral fibre are almost entirely neglected, while his actions and words are disinterestedly dissected to their elementary, infantile roots. The subject is stripped bare, and shown — at least to those who are unaccustomed to such analyses — in the very worst light. Of course, this procedure did not depreciate the subjects in the eyes of the experimenters. For most of us knew full well that in our own personalities there was enough to match almost every complex that we discovered in our subjects. And we had come to accept and live on reasonably friendly terms with these goblins. We may even have been a little proud of them when we recalled how many mediocre men and how few great men are without them. This, however, is an attitude which comes to a practising psychologist through bitter-thick experience ; it is not one which is typical of the average human being. In everyday life it takes a rare sort of rectitude to see without a wince the crude formula of one's personality written plain. Appreciating this, we were full of respect when every subject, to a man, sent us his permission to publish the findings.[1] The following are chosen at random.

It is a pleasure to give my complete consent to the use of any results. It really was more of a pleasure than a task to work at the Clinic.

I am entirely in sympathy with your aims and am perfectly willing that you use any and all the facts about me in any way that you wish.

What you ask me is so very little. I would that I were able to do something of worth.

I am very much interested to learn that you intend to publish some of the results of your experiments. Of course, I shall be very happy to have you dissect me in any way which you see fit. Indeed, I am quite pleased.

You know that you need not have asked my consent to using my case in your book. I am perfectly willing for you to do anything which you

1. In publishing the biographical data a few items have been omitted and slight changes in irrelevant details have been made here and there in order to conceal the identity of the subject.

consider proper with any information you may have gained from studying me during this year. In fact, since you are going to use me, I shall be glad to furnish you any more information about me that you may want, gladly and frankly (that is, subject to my own little personal simplexes and complexes).

Naturally, it was a privilege to work with men of this stamp.

THE CASE OF EARNST

R. W. White

Summary

Earnst is a tall, slender young man of twenty-four. His asthenic features, narrow shoulders, and thin nasal speech convey an impression of extreme physical frailness which subsequent acquaintance proves to be but partly correct. He was born on a farm in Wisconsin, the youngest of a large family, and received most of his education at country schools until he entered an engineering college. Almost from birth he was exposed to the press of Frequent Illness; the press of Family Poverty rarely abated; while the press of Family Discord had an effect of special significance, as the subsequent reports will show.

The following events of his life are relevant to the present study:

Age	Event
6 weeks	Measles
1–5 years	Succession of illnesses
6	Mother began long absences
7	Began school; badly bullied
10	Changed school; began to excel in studies
14	Death of mother
15	Father became an invalid
18	Left farm and entered engineering college
22	Engaged to be married
23	Death of father
	Engagement broken
	Left graduate school; began work for engineering firm

When Earnst first came to the Clinic, he was a student in engineering. Before long he was forced to abandon this pursuit because he reached the end of his funds. Then followed several months of hand-to-mouth existence, during which, though much depressed, he sought unremittingly for employment in the profession for which he was trained. Many of the session reports reflect the exhaustion and despair engendered by long late hours of grubbing work on which was imposed the heartache of continual rebuffs in his search. At the same time the affections of the girl to whom he was engaged were gradually transferred to a luckily situated rival, and the engagement was broken. Not until a few days after the Final Interview did the quest for employment succeed. He left in high spirits for Cleveland to begin work in the laboratory of an engineering concern.

Manifest Personality. Earnst is outstandingly low in all the affiliative variables : n Affiliation, 1 ; n Nurturance, 1 ; n Deference, 1 ; n Sex, 1 ; and he is low in the socially directed needs for Dominance and Exhibition. Thus it is clear at the start that Earnst is not an out-going person confident of his ability to manage, amuse or win the affections of others. Among the high manifest variables we find a syndrome oriented about Anxiety : n Harmavoidance, 4 ; n Infavoidance, 4 ; Emotionality, 4 ; a combination which is typical of the sensitive, avoidant introvert (*vide* p. 240). But that this does not portray the entire personality is indicated by high marks on the variables associated with proud Inviolacy : Narcism, 4 ; Ego Ideal, 4 ; n Autonomy, 4 ; n Defendance, 4 ; Radical Sentiments, 4. Finally, the high score on Projectivity suggests that we are dealing with a hypersensitive subject who shows a marked tendency to ascribe some constituents (needs and press) of his own thematic tendencies (complexes) to others.

Anxiety, n Infavoidance and n Defendance suggest strong feelings of inferiority which cannot be dispelled by the bolder course of Counteraction. The n Abasement, which is above average, prevents the n Defendance and n Infavoidance from being maximal.

A collapse of defences and a complete admission of weakness occurs if the press is too severe. Slender indication of n Deference, n Nurturance, and n Affiliation suggests a difficulty on the part of the subject in establishing a warm feeling for others, and is consonant with the more-than-average strength of a n Aggression at both manifest and latent levels. He has few friends, older,

PERSONALITY SCORES

MANIFEST VARIABLES: SCALES 0 TO 5

Int	2	n Dom	1	N	4	n Harm	4	EI	4
End	1	n Agg	3	n Aff	1	Anx	4	n Ach	3
Imp	3	Rd St	4	n Rej	2	n Inf	4	n Play	2
Emo	4	n Auto	4	n Nur	1	n Dfd	4	Exo	3
Sa	2	n Def	1	n Sex	1	n Cnt	2	Intra	2
Conj	2	n Aba	3	n Sen	2	Se C	2	Proj	4
n Ord	1	n Suc	3	n Exh	1	Se I	3	n Und	2
LATENT VARIABLES: SCALE 0 TO 3								Cr	2
n Suc	3	n Agg	2	n Exh	0	n Acq	2		
n Dom	1	n Aba	1	n Cog	1	n Sex	1	n Homo-Sex	1

younger, or contemporary, and there is little to suggest that he regrets it. The n Autonomy, shown in his strenuous efforts to be beholden to no one, despite extreme poverty, is in obvious conflict with the very strong, though largely latent, as if repressed, n Succorance. It is natural to infer that the latter has been severely frustrated, and Autonomy adopted *faut de mieux* in a barren environment. Why this heroic stratagem was necessary will be discovered in the ensuing reports.

Present Status. At the present time Earnst, though only twenty-four, is completely severed from his early life and from his family.

He looks back upon his years on the farm with bitter loathing. Both parents are dead, and he makes no effort to see his numerous brothers and sisters. Nor does he attempt to establish himself in a new social *milieu*. He is content to be on the whole solitary, hard-working, driving on to some brighter future, demanding little diversion in the present. He is almost completely preoccupied with his work, as if a vast compulsive concentration of his energies had occurred which permitted no deviation from the urgent march. No other member of the family was trained for a profession. Earnst has considerable aptitude for his work, but by no means the exceptional endowment which would itself explain his advancement. A long way from equilibrium with his environment, he suggests a system under great tension which cannot yet be discharged. For his whole life up to the present he makes little claim ; it is by future accomplishments that he would be weighed.

Unconscious Themas. The attempt to understand this manifest personality carries us inevitably into the past, and leads to the speculative construction of four themas. A summary statement of these at the outset no doubt invites skepticism, but this risk must be run for the sake of directing the reader's attention, in the session reports, to the evidence from which the inductions were made.

1. *Oral Succorance Thema*. It is supposed that the S, due in part to his own and his mother's illness, was for an appreciable time, unable to secure sufficient nourishment (oral pleasure, maternal love) to satisfy him. This circumstance generated a thema of oral Succorance, the signs of which are preoccupation with thirst and starvation, an interest in food and drink out of all proportion to his present deprivations, and an underlying craving for sympathy.

2. *Provision Quest Thema*. In consequence of this frustration the S, it is believed, was filled with an intense desire to extract more nourishment (love) from his mother's body. This aggressive demand, which may have been carried into such ineffectual actions as his slender strength permitted, created an emotional ambivalence — for the mother was still the chief source of whatever nurture he received — and at length was embodied in the un-

conscious fantasy of robbing his mother of the withheld nourishment.

3. *Predator Thema.* The next thema is a peculiar one, and it is here that the press of Family Discord is fancied to have worked its distinctive effect. In the S's mind, it is supposed, there was formed the idea that his father had robbed his mother of nourishment, and thus indirectly robbed the child. As a result his mother, herself a victim, was restored to affection, and his father became the object of fantasied aggression.

4. *Forced-Robbery Thema.* As a direct derivative of the Predator Thema, it is supposed that the S projected the aggressive fantasy which he had entertained against the mother, attributing his own wish to the father, and his own fantasied robberies to the latter's power over him. In this manner he freed himself from guilt.

The evidence for these unconscious themas will be collected and weighed in the psychograph. At this point, however, when the reader must feel disposed to doubt our constructions and to cry out against the projection of elaborate fantasies into the innocent head of a tiny baby, it will be well to indicate the sources from which our hypotheses are drawn and to explain in what sense we attribute a fantasy to the earliest years of life. The sources of evidence are threefold. In the first place, we rely on facts related by the S himself; that both he and his mother were sickly, for instance, and that he feared and hated his father. Secondly, there is the current fantasy material offered by the S, wherein it is possible to observe the type of thema to which he seems predisposed, and to detect repeated peculiarities, such as the questing for treasure in a barren world, or incongruent items, like the compelling of robberies by a person with superior power. Finally, there are those peculiarities in the S's present attitudes, sentiments, even choice of words and metaphors, which strike us as disproportionate to any probable contemporary circumstances. It is from a pooling of these resources that we derive the unconscious themas. We do not wish to be understood as attributing fantasies in full imaginal form to the early years of life to which they bear reference. Our hypothetical themas are not precisely dated. We believe that they represent a reverberation of the more simply *felt* experiences of infancy, which became associated with an imagery and indeed a knowledge of life derived from later events. Thus it is by no means our notion that the Predator Thema was conceived by a few-months-old baby in such terms as we must now use to express it ; on the contrary, we are inclined to suppose that somewhat later experiences, involving guilt on account of aggression toward the mother, and hatred for the terrifying father, have been cast back as an interpretation of an uneffaced sequence of primitive feelings : hunger, helplessness, frustration and resentment.

The four unconscious themas just described may be subsumed under a single unity-thema which is highly characteristic of Earnst at the present day. In the accompanying diagram this is given in formula, followed by the concrete forms it has assumed with reference to successive periods of his life.

UNITY THEMA

Deprivation (Barrenness) ⟶	Anxiety ⟶	Aggressive Quest for Provision
1. Oral, by Mother	Thirst, starvation	Fantasy of robbing M
2. Oral, by Father	Thirst, starvation	Fantasy of killing F
3. Social	Neglect, mutilation	Fantasy of provision (story-books); substitute achievement (school work)
4. Economic, by Father	Barren life	College education
5. Economic, by world	Barren life	Professional employment

1. CONFERENCE

H. A. Murray

Earnst was very ill at ease. He appeared frightened and cast suspicious glances from one E to another. He said that Engineering (Extra) [1] was his field of concentration.

E : Were your parents in sympathy with your choice ?

S : Well, my parents really didn't have anything to do with the

1. The diagnoses that are thus inserted in the text are merely suggestive and, of course, tentative.

matter. My mother died when I was 14 and my father was never especially interested in education (p Insupport : Death of M, Inferior F).

E : What vocation are you intending to follow ?

S : Research.

E : Do you like to speculate and discuss theories ?

S : At times. I never go to extremes (low Int). At Harvard I got plenty of theories to *grasp*. I don't have time to *dig up* more (low Cr).

E : How did you get on with the other boys at school ?

S : I never saw a great deal of them (p Rejection (Social)). I got along with most of them in a casual way, but I didn't go out for activities (n Inf).

E : How did you get along with girls ?

S : In high school, I had no contacts to speak of (n Sec). I didn't dance very well and made a poor impression (Inferiority (Social)) and that kept me out of that (n Inf). I worked in a dance hall nights after that. I started checking. The last year I was there I worked at the soda fountain. The girls were used to dancing and I picked it up quite easily (n Cnt, Inferiority Restriving).

E : What was the general opinion about you at school ?

S : I really don't know. I don't believe they knew I was there for the most part (n Sec, p Rejection (Social)). The teachers and faculty were usually helpful as far as they could be (n Suc).

E : Were you ever a leader, or if not, did you want to be a leader ?

S : I had such ambitions, and I still have (ln Dom).

E : What is the worst blunder that you ever made ?

S : I don't know. I have made a bunch of them (n Aba). One incident I recall vividly is taking a girl to a dance and then not being able to dance after I got there (Inferiority (Social)).

E : What are your chief faults from a social standpoint ?

S : Well, of course, one of the first things would be that I don't make friends readily (Inferiority (Social)). Another one is that sometimes I am self-conscious (n Inf, N). If I am studying during the day, it is awfully hard for me to adjust myself to things that are external (N, Proj, delusions of self-reference). I feel awfully sensitive and self-conscious (n Inv, n Inf).

E : Do you feel people are looking at you ?

S : Yes, that you are an eyesore, or something of that sort (Proj, N, Inferiority feelings).

E : Do you like animals ?

S : Not particularly. I don't mind them (low n Nur).

Sentiments Questionnaire : Radical Sentiments, 35 (R.O. 2 out of 15) ; Intensity, 3.9 (R.O. 5) ; Total time, 5 min. 30 sec. (R.O. 14). In his answers Earnst was unusually negative and aggressive. For instance :

4. Communistic propaganda should be prohibited in America.

S : No — 5. Communistic propaganda represents new ideas and new ideas must be introduced before the old ones will be changed, and there is a necessity for new ideas (ln Agg, Ch).

5. Harvard is easily the best college in this country.

S : No — 5. Because of the fact that when you say 'best' you don't define what you mean by 'best,' and therefore the statement doesn't mean anything (n Agg).

Picture A : (A heavily-built man standing in his undershirt gazing at the ground with his arms hanging limply at his sides).

S : That looks like a chap who is suffering from intense thirst (p Lack : Water, Oral complex), or fatigue (Passivity), perhaps in a desert without water or food (p Lack : Water, Food). He looks as though he was in a poor condition (p Illness). I think he stands a chance of dying before long (Death from lack of water and food).

Picture C : (A young man lying prostrate on a bed and a young woman standing outside the door with her head buried in her hand).

E : This is a married couple — old friends of yours. The husband has been taught by another man to take morphine. If you came upon this scene, what would you do?

S: I would get medical attention for the man. That would be the only sensible thing to do because I wouldn't know what to do for an addict. The surroundings seem to indicate poverty (p Lack: Economic), I should say. Therefore, it might be a good idea to call on the state authorities (n Suc). If the wife has to be taken care of, that would be up to the state authorities; I am darned sure I couldn't do anything (low n Nur, low n Dom). Take me just as I am, I couldn't help her very much (Inferiority feelings, p Lack). It would be hard to find out who taught him. That would again be up to the authorities (n Suc). I might have some desire for vengeance (n Agg), but I couldn't very well take it myself (n Harm, n Inf).

Blank Card.

S: Yes, I can imagine a picture. It is a sandy plain (*cf.* the desert in Picture A, p Lack: Water, Food), possibly a poor road on it, travelled by a few solitary people (p Rejection, n Sec), perhaps oil derricks dotted here and there. The only person I can think of would be one of these people who go around looking for new mines—a prospector (Quest for Provision, or Quest for the Cathected Object thema). A very easy story might be that of two prospectors going along in an old flivver looking for gold fields. There would always have to be trouble, and a villainous person (p Aggression: Malicious Hostility) to throw a monkey wrench into the machinery. To make the story amusing, it would be necessary to have them succeed in getting the gold (Digging for Provision or Digging for the Cathected Object thema). (As an interpretation of this story it might be suggested that searching for new oil wells or digging for gold is somehow connected with an infantile conception of getting liquid and food from the body of the mother.)

Names of persons admired: Abraham Lincoln, Mary Baker Eddy, George Washington, Thomas Edison. (Hypothesis:

Mary Baker Eddy is a mother surrogate who gives spiritual nourishment.)

The S failed to do the puzzle.

E : Would you like to take another puzzle or would you like to continue trying to solve this one?

S : No difference. I never do any puzzles because it hurts my eyes (n Inf, n Dfd).

E : Were you nervous doing the puzzle before all of us?

S : There was no tension (n Dfd). I didn't mind people in this case; sometimes I do. They make me nervous (n Inf).

Eye Test : (R.O. 5 out of 15); Time, 27.7 sec., very slow (inverse R.O. 2); Increase of time with staring, —7.9 sec. (R.O. 15). The S was rattled, but he did better when he looked the E in the eye (i.e., an aggressive attitude helped him).

E : What things or situations are you most afraid of?

S : Well, the situation I am really most afraid of is that of being about to do something that I am supposed to be able to do, and being a complete failure (n Inv, n Inf, Inferiority feelings).

E : What do you do in those conditions? Do you avoid the situation?

S : Yes, unless I have something definite to gain by going through with them (n Inf).

Summary. Earnst is a physically feeble, extremely nervous young man who seems to be engaged in a struggle against inferiority feelings. In the conference he looked as if he wished to take flight and yet he denied that he found any of it disagreeable (n Dfd). The conflict seems to be one between the n Infavoidance and the n Counteraction. The former is stronger at present. The marked degree of Radicalism, his apparent negativism (n Auto) and his latent, though impotent, Aggression point to a high degree of Narcism. He says that he is sensitive and self-conscious (N, n Inv, n Inf). His libido is still intraNurturant. His stories (p Lack : Water, Food, and the recurrence of p Rejection), his low need for Nurturance, and his scarcely concealed n Succorance suggest an early oral frustration (Oral Succorance thema). The story of the prospectors (Quest and Digging for Provision, or for Cathected Object thema) also points to a thema of p Lack : Food or to a thema of p Acquisition : Robbery. This sometimes arises when a child is given an enema by a parent ; in which case the fantasy would be connected with anal erotism. That his complex is oral is suggested by words used in the early part of the conference : 'At Harvard I got plenty of theories to *grasp* (oral Acquisition). I don't have time to *dig up* more.' Perhaps this fantasy partly determined his decision to become a research engineer.

Prediction of Underlying Factors : p Insupport, p Lack : Water, Food, Oral Succorance thema, p Rejection, Quest for Provision or for Cathected Object thema, p Acquisition : Robbery, n Acquisition : Robbery, n Autonomy : Rebel, n Aggression : Revenge, Passivity : Exhaustion, themas of Death and Inferiority.

Biographer's Note : At the final interview the S said that he had lately become a Christian Scientist 'by choice,' though in accordance with his fiancée's wishes. He described Christian Science as a 'very practical religion,' that is, in its 'feeling aspect,' despite the failure of a practitioner to relieve his eye trouble.

1a. MEMORY FOR THE CONFERENCE
(Six Months Later)

R. W. White

Earnst settled himself to recount the events of the conference item by item, beginning with his own feelings before he entered the library. 'I was rather excited ; it was something new, and I'm always anticipating. — Yes, it was apprehension to a certain extent. I had every faculty with me ; I usually do in a new situation of which I'm aware' (Anxiety, Inferiority feelings).

He recalled being met in the hall by Dr. Murray ; he entered the library and saw the group around the table. 'Each one had a glass of water in front of him' (Cathexis of water, Oral Succorance complex). 'They all looked me over very carefully (N, projections of self-reference). Each man put me through a test of some kind. They asked me whether I ever made great blunders, and I said, "I have, lots of them."' Earnst remembered that he was questioned on incidents of childhood and adolescence, and asked to recall 'social situations which were outstanding' in his mind. He was undecided as to his greatest blunder, and so mentioned the humiliating incident when he was unable to dance. He came to the blank card, and now, warming to his narrative, he described the rest of the Conference with quiet, dry satire, taking off the voices of the different experimenters. '"On these cards,"' Earnst quoted, '"you will see scenes representing various episodes of something or other." So I immediately proceeded to project a scene of the desert. There had to be something moving, apparently, so I found a desert road and an old flivver, with two boys in it. I may have been wrong, but I had the feeling they would have preferred a young lady (ln Homo-Sex). They asked me who these boys were, what they were doing, and what they were going to do — so I filled in a Horatio Alger plot — they were boys who had come west to search for a fortune in order to lift the mortgage off the old farm. They asked for the outcome, and I said, "They lifted the mortgage."' Laughing, Earnst said to the interviewer, 'If I break down you'll have to carry me out' (Passivity, ln Suc). Then he continued, 'They all seemed to be the most intent on one scene, a bedroom scene. A young woman found her husband unconscious from some malady. She was afflicted with great shame, distress, and horror. That was probably to stimulate my imagination, and I was asked to fill in the horrible details. So I took the least obvious explanation, and revealed the young man as a dope addict. Circumstances strongly pointed to something else, I mean to some sexual disorder. I was strongly aroused that evening.' The interviewer said. 'Why?' and the subject continued, 'I had a nasty feeling this chap was a Freudian psychologist. I rather dislike them — too narrow in their belief. I've read enough so I dislike the idea of relating everything to sex. No doubt the Freudian school has its very decent place in psychology, just the same as the gold standard has its significant place in economics. Yeah, money and sex.' After this digression Earnst returned to the picture, and from it continued to a question put him by one of the experimenters whose name he remembered incorrectly, a question 'in regard to my preference for the female sex, whether I enjoyed the companionship of the other sex.' 'Then,' said Earnst, 'Dr. Murray announced that the session was concluded. Before I could say a word, all the men at the table rapped out "Good-night" like so many machine guns going off (projection of p Aggression). I went outside with the uncomfortable feeling of being at a loss. I wondered if they said it that way to create a psychological situation.' Earnst laughed at this, and the interviewer asked whether the men seemed unfriendly. 'Well, it was most unusual, as I was sitting there answering questions in a very friendly way, they went right around the table like pop-guns. I couldn't have been more surprised if they'd shoved revolvers into my face (suggestion of paranoid delusion and passive homosexuality). Possibly they were very busy. Incidentally, this is my only way of getting back at them' (ln Aggression : Revenge).

From this interview it is apparent that Earnst perceived the Conference as a humiliation, the experimenters as men who, secure and comfortable with their glasses of water, ridiculed him and exposed his inferiorities, finally to blow him abruptly out of the room, a dissected specimen thrown to one side. The interview six months later afforded a welcome opportunity for a catharsis of the long-stored aggression, and memory furnished a multitude of painful but by now depersonalized details. Earnst is a worm who turns, circumspectly, in his own good time. It is evident that he watched his questioners closely, reading their motives and projecting some feelings of his own. Curiously, he attributed to himself the interpretation of the man in Picture C as a morphine addict, and represented that in this way he dodged the sexual interpretation which he believed the examiners preferred.

2. AUTOBIOGRAPHY

H. A. Murray

Family Situation. Earnst summarizes the family situation in a few words.

I was born in January, 1911, of elderly parents (mother 44, father 54), the youngest of nine children. My next youngest brother was five at the time of my birth. Mother and father are both American. My father was a combination farmer and cooper, and had been during his lifetime a woodsman, trapper, engineman and various other things. Mother was an intelligent, gentle, loving woman, and was much thought of by friends and neighbours.

Childhood. The subject's early years were unhappy :

My earliest impressions of life that I can remember now, were to a large extent miserable. As a baby I was constantly ailing (p Illness), apparently having one childhood disease after another, starting off with measles at the age of six weeks. During the first few years of my life there were more or less frequent occasions when all hope of my living was given up (Death thema). One thing which impressed me greatly as a baby was a large china mug or cup inlaid with gold (cathected object) which was used only when company was present. I remember drinking water from a tin dipper for days, a sip at a time, to ease the feverish burning of my throat (p Lack : Water, oral complex). This was during the war. Also, I can remember the talk of big guns and had frightened visions of Germans setting off cannons in the field across from our house and shooting at us (n Harm, projection of p Aggression).

My father was at times a brutal man and inclined, when drinking, to be vindictive toward me (p Aggression, p Insupport : Inferior Father). At such times he would make fun of me, call me all sorts of unpleasant names and say that I probably wouldn't live the year out, and that it would be better if I didn't (p Aggression : Belittlement). I was extremely sensitive and cried rather easily at such things (N, n Suc, n Inf, n Harm). Somehow during those years, I acquired a feeling of inadequacy (Inferiority feelings) which stayed with me and crops up even now on occasions. I get the feeling that there is something wrong with me, and can hardly look another person in the eyes (n Inf). Sometimes, also, I see a person laughing on the street and looking in my direction and I have the instant impression that the said person is laughing at me (paranoid projection of self-reference). Reasoning, checking this up, I always find this impression wrong, yet it comes back again and again.

As a small child I played with two little girls, daughters of one of our neighbours. I cannot recall many playtime incidents except that once I saw some spikes, new shining ones, in the neighbour's woodshed and carried them home with me, not realizing their use (n Acq, cathexis of shining object (phallic)). Mother punished me for this and said it was stealing. I was greatly impressed with the fact I had done wrong (SeC), although it wasn't until somewhat later that I realized what stealing actually was and why I had done wrong. The punishment consisted in talking to me. I had such an acute terror of the whip, however, that I usually went into hysterics at the mere sight of one, hence it was seldom used on me (n Harm).

I entered school at the age of seven, a school where the large percentage of the pupils were Swedish. The only Americans besides myself were the two neighbour girls I spoke of. I immediately received more than my share of the brutal treatment (p Aggression : Maltreatment) which was forthcoming to the smaller children (Inferiority (Physical)) in schools of that type, and developed at once into a 'cry-baby,' coward and so forth (n Aba, n Suc, n Harm, n Inf). I was too puny to get anywhere fighting for myself even with children my size, hence I acquired a fear of other people menacing me with physical punishment, which again is something I have never entirely overcome (n Harm). I soon became ashamed of being a coward, yet could do nothing about it, so life became intolerable to me as it was. I began to avoid as much as possible the company of other children (n Inf, n Sec), and as soon as I learned to read, found great satisfaction in following the adventures of various heroes. I lived the stories I read (Intra, Endo) — a kind of recreation and enjoyment which was not forthcoming of some kind of physical pain (n Harm).

Development

I was at first a rather dull pupil in school, but as I became interested in my studies and found that I could do better than the other children in some studies (Superiority (Intellectual)), I immediately concentrated all my attention on school, and this became the medium through which I was able to show my superiority and in a measure, to justify my existence (Substitute Achievement thema).

My mother encouraged me in school work and praised me highly when I did well (p Deference : Acclaimance). It was at this time that I began to enjoy life and to look around me a bit, instead of living a more or less painful and secluded existence (n Sec). My parents moved to a new farm when I was ten and I started in school with a new group of children. It was a much smaller group and I acquired the scholastic leadership immediately (Superiority (Intellectual)). While at this school I fought in my own cause one day (n Agg, n Inv) and was so braced up by my success that I never allowed myself to be picked on thenceforth (n Cnt), unless my tormentors were comparatively large. However, I still experience that thrill of fear of others at times (n Harm, n Inf), even though my temper (n Agg, Imp, Emo), occasionally leads me to have fear of nothing under the sun.

I entered high school at the age of thirteen and graduated on my seventeenth birthday. During this time my mother died (p Insupport : Death of Mother), and the farm, mortgaged to the hilt, was lost (p Loss : Economic). My father went to live with a brother in Racine, Wisconsin, and I finished school, living with a brother and his wife. I couldn't get along with my sister-in-law (n Agg) and left them immediately after finishing high school (n Rej, n Auto). My father had become an invalid, I forgot to mention, shortly after mother died.

The brother in Racine got me a job at the place where he worked as an apprentice machinist (Extra). Six months of this taught me that I wasn't going to get anywhere as a mechanic, and since I had been saving money very carefully (n Ret), I planned on saving enough to start college the following fall — this I was able to do and, through one break and another, was able to complete my work for a degree, without receiving aid from anyone (n Inv, n Auto), and without running into debt (n Cnt).

I am, in general, retiring (n Sec, n Inf) when with a group or at least I never assume leadership (low n Dom) — am never the 'life of the party' (low n Exh).

Sex History

The only sex experience I remember at this early age was an incident which was greatly interesting to me although subsequent fright prevented any more of them from happening. A Swedish boy and his sister came over to play with me, and during the course of the afternoon he made his sister take her clothes off, and played with her sexual organs (n Cog : Voyeurism). This interested me and I played with them too, finding great delight in doing so (p Sex : Exposure). The next evening while playing around the kitchen table I noticed my older sister's legs and touched one of them considerably above the knee. I was immediately treated to a shower of slaps and blows (p Aggression : Punishment), which quite took away my *appetite* (oral complex) for any further adventures under tables.

My sexual experiences have been very limited (low n Sex). I remember other boys indulging in masturbation, and inviting me to indulge in such activities with them. The practice always seemed indecent to me and I never engaged in it (Se I). I was never out on a date with a girl until my third year in college (n Sec, n Inf), and found at that time that I had been missing girls a bit in the way of feminine companionship. Since then I have had a great deal of pleasure in finding out what one has to do to arouse the interest of a girl, and have found that the best thing to do is to trust to luck (low n Dom, Passivity). I eventually fell in love with a girl (n Sex) who happened to have some regard for me, and I am engaged to her at the present time. I have never had sexual intercourse, and certainly wouldn't want to have with anyone for whom I had any deep feeling — unless, of course, we were married (Se I).

Opinion of the Self and of the World

I most resemble my mother in temperament (Mother Identification), and so forth, although I have some of my father's traits (bad temper (n Agg, Emo) if aroused), but not so extreme (negative cathexis of Father, Oedipus complex).

My general estimate of myself can best be expressed in terms of what I think I shall eventually become, and that is a great success (E I) or a dismal failure (n Aba, Passivity, Inferiority feelings). I couldn't be in between, I am quite sure. I want to be a research engineer, although sometimes I doubt if I have the ability to be a good one (Inferiority feelings).

The subject's paper was extremely untidy and his handwriting was rather poor (n Order : R.O. 14 out of 15).

Summary. This is the story of the youngest of nine children whose childhood was a long series of fears and terrors : fear of death, of illness, of physical injury, and of his father's punishments, of his older brother's aggression. No doubt the Oedipus thema developed, for his father was a monster to him and his mother gentle and loving. He was so thoroughly frightened that he has not yet recovered. His early school years were no better. He was naturally a timid boy, the prey of bullies (n Harm, n Inf, n Aba). When he discovered that he was bright at studies he turned to them with zest. They proved an opportunity for substitute Achievement. Gradually, against great odds, he has been winning self-respect (n Cnt). He has high ambition (E I) and works hard (n Ach). The n Succorance was certainly frustrated at an early age. There are some suggestions of oral deprivation (thirst) and subsequent acquisitive tendencies : memory of gold cup, stealing spikes, saving money, economy and so forth.

All his energy has gone into an attempt to overcome inferiority but the n Counteraction has not yet become dominant. His Sex need is rather low. His selection of research may be related to the sudden frustration of his early voyeurism.

Hypothetical Diagnosis, Underlying Factors. Inferiority (Physical), p Aggression : Maltreatment, Quest for Provision or for Cathected Object thema, n Retention, p Lack : Water, p Illness, Substitute Achievement and Achievement Failure themas, Death thema.

3. CHILDHOOD MEMORIES

H. S. Mekeel

In his questionnaire Earnst did not fill out the section relating to siblings. When interviewed, he had some difficulty in recalling the names, ages and even the number of his brothers and sisters. He said that early in his childhood most of them had married and gone away. It was only after several rehearsals of the list that he could give the ages even approximately, and then at the last he remembered a brother 17 years older whom he had forgotten until this point.

Answers to Questions

Group I. *Family Relations*

'Was very much attached to Mother, who died when I was 14. As a youngster I was afraid of my father, and at times hated him. However, since he has become an invalid, and in a more or less pitiful condition I have lost the old feeling of fear and hate and now feel only kindliness and sympathy for him.'

Group II. *School Activities*

Leisure Time. 'I never seem to reach the point where I have nothing to do. I imagine I could *dig up* something to do at almost any time. When I do want recreation I usually go to a dance, see a play, or, formerly, read a book. In the last two or three years I have gotten away from reading because of trouble with my eyes.'

Group III. *Authority and Punishment*

Earnst says, 'The setting of standards was on a co-operative basis in our family; that is, between Dad and Mother. Dad furnished the limitations and mother supplied the ideals.'

'I was seldom punished as a child, and what discipline I was subjected to was probably taken for granted, for I remember little about it. I hadn't the spirit to be a precocious child. I much feared punishment by my father (n Harm) although I was seldom punished by either parent. Dad was a rather harsh sort of man (p Aggression : Maltreatment), and it was quite natural that I should be afraid of him.'

In regard to prohibitions Earnst says, 'Smoking, running away were prohibited. I have not cared for smoking since the ban was removed, and there is nothing to run away for or from, now.'

An older sister took charge of his early care.

Childhood Memories

'One of my earliest memories was that of being sick. I was quite sickly as a child. It just happened to be a particularly embarrassing situation. I was sitting at the breakfast table in a high chair. I was afflicted with some sort of diarrhoea (Ejection vector) and an accident took place which of course was very revolting to the other people at the table, and made me feel very embarrassed. That is about all there is to it. I was about five. I can remember an incident particularly trying to learn the alphabet. I did learn it before I was 7, before I started school. I should say that was something around 6.

'When I first started in school I had to learn the multiplication tables — all of them up to 12 at once, and that looked to me to be an impossible task. I thought I couldn't do it. I was completely discouraged. Mother talked to me and said of course I could do it, and she helped me (p Nurturance). She was very good at teaching things of that sort.

'I remember the fascination that I used to hold for a large china cup we had in the china-closet. It was extremely colourful. It was more or less trotted out when company came. I remember I formulated the word "company" for that cup, and it took some training to break me of that association. I persisted in calling it "company." Things don't come back without effort. I *try to drag them out.*

'I was brought up on a farm, and I used to accompany the folks to the fields. Oh yes, there was a devilish hail storm one time (p Danger : Inclement weather) and we had a horse and wagon to carry implements. The storm came up rather suddenly and I caught a bad cold from it. It nearly finished me (Death thema). I remember riding home in it and the hail hitting me on the face and head (p Aggression) and the horse tearing along the road. I was not quite seven.

'There are many more incidents occurring between seven and twelve I suppose than before seven. I had a pernicious hip disease that put me out of running for about a year or so. I remember all sorts of things in connection with that. The knee used to get me at first if I got my feet wet, and a day or two later I would have a pain in my hip. It got to be the worst on the 4th of July and we were to go to a reunion at my sister's place, an older sister who was married, and my brother-in-law had to carry me out to the car and I particularly disliked this brother-in-law and I didn't like being carried out by him. Another incident connected with this disease took place in one of the hospitals in a nearby town. I had to have an X-ray taken of the hip, and I went in to the X-ray room and took my clothes off and was duly placed on a table and then I stood there and a nurse came in and I remember being distinctly embarrassed because I didn't have any clothes on. I was extremely sensitive about things of that sort as a child. I was about nine or ten. I had a sort of tuberculosis of the hip.

'I remember being away from school for various reasons. My brother and I skipped one day. We ran off with a chap who was taking cattle and had a very enjoyable day (Egression vector, n Auto). When the folks found we were not in school we were punished. I remember my older brother was whipped slightly, and I was supposed to be and wasn't. At the supper table my father told us what he was going to do and we had the time until supper was over to think about it. Another time three or four kids, three of us, a girl and her brother and I, went out chasing after butterflies and the school bell rang and we were half a mile away and we hurried back and we were fifteen minutes late or something like that and our punishment was to copy out of a book, a text book, a page of it on paper. I think I got a stubborn streak and I decided I wouldn't do it (n Auto), and the teacher said I would have to stay after school, and I stayed until after 6:30 and the teacher got tired and let me go home. The teacher wasn't just tired, the boy friend came around. The two of them tried to coax me into writing the thing, but I wouldn't do it and didn't (n Auto : Resistance).

'A horse kicked me one time. A pet horse. He was bad-tempered at times. I was very incautious one night in the dark I walked into the stable and through the other part of the barn, and I was going through the manger and I walked up in the stall and slapped him and about that time he let me have it with both feet. It began to ache after a while and it ached like the deuce. He used to bite women because women were afraid of him, and he used to bite me a lot when I was a little chap (p oral Aggression). On the arm. He never bit anyone very hard. Just pinch a little. No one could come very close to him because he would make this awful face, his lips back from his teeth, sort of fierce looking. He was an old horse and his teeth were yellow.

(The E asked the S whether he got along pretty well with his brother.) 'There were times when we were very amicable, but there were times when I was putting something over on him, or he was putting something over on me. He was five years older than I. I was telling Dr. Barrett about throwing stones at each other (n Aggression : Quarrel). Dad and Mother were going away visiting somewhere and we were throwing stones and I scored the last hit. I tried to retreat while the time was good so I went into the house. My brother didn't care. He knew that just as soon as Dad and Mother cleared out, his time would come. I couldn't tell them I had hit him with a stone. I couldn't say anything, and they went, and then the chase began. We were running around the house and at every corner he would throw a stone. Then he got the idea of yelling at me. He threw a stone and yelled " Look out " and I turned and ran to the left and ran right into the stone. It nailed me in the back of the head and put me out. I woke up being carried into the house, and he fixed me up with all sorts of quilts and pillows. He was very good to me that evening.'

Favourite fairy or animal story—Earnst remembers only 'Black Beauty' and a story about city children on a farm.

Night dreams—Earnst says, 'The only thing I can remember dreaming was that of being chased by a bear (p oral Aggression) and not being able to run, and not being able to move (Passivity). That sort of thing occurred in more than one dream. The circumstances might not have been the same. A man might be chasing me, and the next minute it would turn into a dog (p oral Aggression). Things of that sort. Never any continuity to them.'

Day dreams—'When I was in school I used to have day dreams at the time I was supposed to be studying. I would often wander away so that I wouldn't hear if anybody spoke to me, visualizing myself in various adventures (Intra). When I was 8 or 9 I began to read dime novels, " Young Wild West " and that sort of thing. I used to picture myself having the adventures this fellow had. A person would have to speak to me three or four times before I would hear (Endo). I used to have the same thing in reading. I would concentrate so completely on a book that I would not hear the first time a person spoke to me.'

Adolescent Memories

Usually Earnst walked the four miles from his house to the high school, although sometimes he would take a trolley. Frequently in winter he was snow-bound. He used to get up about six or six-thirty in the morning. Now he gets up quite late because he is working at night. For instance, the night previous to the interview he was up until three o'clock working on a report. In the latter half of his freshman year he shifted to a high school in a neighbouring town. This was after the death of his mother at Christmas.

He was not particularly ambitious then. The last two years of high school he kept house for his father. He was not remarkable at housekeeping, but what he did served the purpose. He hated dish washing particularly, and would let the dishes pile up for two or three days. He remembered with a good deal of resentment the time that his father invited the thrashers to supper. It was, of course, the custom for his father to invite them to eat, yet his father didn't really have to have the thrashers because they knew there was no woman in the house. The subject did his best for the meal, but since he was tired both mentally and physically he himself did not eat and went on upstairs after he had prepared the meal. He said he was quite angry with his Dad for having asked them to supper. The first summer the subject was able to take care of the place fairly easily because he had extra help. Then his father had a stroke which prohibited him from working on the farm. The second summer Earnst did the larger part of the work. It was a farm of about 100 acres. The subject did all the ploughing and he had a good team of horses to work with. This reminded him of the first time he ploughed which was at the age of 14. He experienced great difficulty in driving the horses. It was hard to follow them and hard to keep them going straight. He mentioned with some guilt that he developed a good vocabulary of oaths at this time, and then mentioned that he discovered that one had to have patience.

Earnst prefers to work for a large organization because it is impersonal, and there is more chance for advancement. In such an organization it is easier to get along with people.

Biographer's Note : At the Final Interview the S added to his early memories the following items. (1) At 4 or 5, he was given on Christmas morning a small red wagon ; his sister showed it to him (n Acq, cathexis of object). (2) There was a chain pump on the farm ; his brother would 'crank furiously and drink the water in large quantities' (Cathexis of water, Oral Succorance complex). He repeated the report about his childhood dreams, using the phrases 'ferocious beasts' and 'hungry animals' (p oral Aggression).

The references to food and drink are noticeably frequent in this report. The image of the extortionate father also emerges with striking clarity, especially in the incident when the thrashers were invited to supper.

4. SEXUAL DEVELOPMENT

W. G. Barrett

Earnst blushed freely as he lay down on the couch and seemed more embarrassed and uncomfortable than had any other member of the group. He twisted uncomfortably in order to be able to see the E while the instructions were being given, and also kept one foot on the floor. The S attempted to cover his anxiety by a defiant attitude, but the fundamental insecurity became more apparent as the interview progressed.

He began his associations by telling about an examination of that morning. It was 'rather easy,' but the S 'wasn't feeling particularly brilliant (and does not) know whether (he) made any mistakes or not.' He does not dare be outright about it, apparently. This examination was important for a scholarship, and the S went on to tell at length why it is not advisable to borrow money even if one is able to : there is little likelihood of being able to pay it back, he thinks.

When the E suggested he avoid telling stories and try to report just whatever came into his mind, he went on : 'I wonder how my Dad is getting along. He is on his last legs, so to speak. Dad and I never got along very well.' He then related an incident wherein his father 'was angry as the devil. He . . . made a beeline for me and . . . took a healthy swing at me with his foot as I went by, and he slipped and nearly broke his arm on the wet grass.' At this point the S turned way around to look at the E. When asked why, he said, 'to look directly at you.' With exaggerated casualness he repeated the look, and when asked why he wished to look directly at the E, explained, 'I usually do when talking with anyone. If you are trying to put over a point and look directly at the person it is generally better.' Asked what point he was trying to put over, he said, 'That was the point I thought I had told you about : In making a point to look directly at the person.' By this time he was almost completely turned around the better to look at the E. He went on to tell of the importance of this in connection with salesmanship.

It is obvious that the S is attempting to rationalize his feelings of anxiety. These probably arose on the basis of an identification of the E with the F, and he wished to be sure that there would be no kick this time. If one considers the 'couch reaction' along with this material, one may infer that the S is compensating for passive homosexuality. The aggressive trend which follows adds weight to this inference.

The E repeated the instructions, pointing out that they were quite different than the S's attempt to sell himself would indicate. A long pause followed. Then, 'I am to report what comes into my mind and nothing seems to come in. I don't care much for your paintings that you have, or whatever they are.' Asked what he disliked about the simple steel engraving, he said, 'I have disagreeable memories of paintings of that type. . . The framed diploma is a plain looking thing to have on the wall. Is that yours, by the way ?' This comment referred to a steel engraving of Franklin at the foot of the couch, which may have been partially obscured by a bright light on its glass. The S was asked to tell his thoughts about it. 'I thought it might be yours, but when I look at the inscription it says "M.D.," so I guess that can't be yours.'

After this sally the S asked two questions. When the E explained that it would be best to look upon these as associations rather than questions for the time being, he said, imperiously, 'When I ask questions I will answer them myself.' His effort to prove himself autonomous is apparent. It was noted that he was more tense, however, and soon complained of being 'under a tension,' but attributed it to the examination of the morning.

Associations then went on as follows : the exam was simple but he had studied the wrong thing ; he lost his door-key last night ; his appearance is not what it should be because he has to earn money ; he is uneasy about the exam ; he had actually failed a problem in the exam, one he 'had done hundreds of times without thinking of it.' Here we see how the S attempts to avoid recognition of his failure : the 'door key' means the intellectual key to the examination, and the 'appearance' is actually that of his exam paper. He would like to believe that his having to work is an adequate excuse for the failure which only with great reluctance does he admit directly. He then related previous experiences when being in a particular room had, for some unknown reason, prevented his doing the good work of which he was capable, and caused him to fail examinations in spite of the fact that he had coached others who passed them. He justified his needs to 'blame his tools' by telling how, in a particular room where there was 'hardly ever any one around,' he wrote an excellent examination.

We see in this material an extreme attempt to avoid inferiority feelings. This goes so far that we are led to fear a fundamental lack of integrity and to suspect what transpires under the conditions of isolation he mentions, as necessary to good performance. His attitude suggests that he constantly finds himself in a world of enemies and that he is prepared to 'fight fire with fire,' and take advantage of fair means or foul to gain his ends. There is a mild paranoid tendency evidenced in his continued finding fault with the conditions under which he must work.

The early memories deal with a successful attack upon an older brother, gang fights at school, extreme dislike for a brother-in-law, throwing stones at people and an early attack of diarrhoea while dining with the family. He reported this in a 'served-them-right' tone of voice.

The S was the youngest of a large family : one brother was more than 25 years older. He was 'rather a puny brat' and very dependent upon his mother. He lived in fear of losing her as she was frequently sick and away from home months at a time. His father, whom he feared, showed no affection for him and treated him roughly. Earnst was sickly for a while and retreated into the world of books. There was conflict with his brothers and he remembers 'always getting the short end of it.' He says, 'I wonder if (this) was not the cause of the inferiority complex I had as a child, and still have to a certain extent.' Such an admission of inferiority feelings would hardly have been expected from the S's previous attitude, and can be looked upon as a hopeful prognostic sign.

The S 'supposes' his mother instructed him as to sexual differences. At about 7 years an older boy undressed his sister and played with her sexually for the S's benefit. He was not surprised and believes that living on a farm acquainted him with these facts sooner than if he had lived in a city. His mother saw to it that he was not of the party that took the cow to the bull, but his brother later reported what happened. He cannot recall when he learned of birth, nor any theories he may have had.

Of masturbation, Earnst says, 'I never indulged in (it), for some reason or other.' He knows this is contrary to the general rule and believes that what he saw of a brother's practices, alone and with a group, disgusted him so intensely as to prevent it. Another reason : 'I used to spend all my . . . spare time reading. Of course, I didn't do anything that would lead me in that direction.' When the E remarked that copious reading and masturbation frequently went together, the S suggested that he might 'have possibly done it when (a) very small child, 4 or 5 years.' He then promptly asked what time it was, saying that he had an appointment on the hour. One is inclined to suspect that the S's denial of masturbation is in the service of inferiority inviolacy and that his inquiry regarding the time represents a wish a escape from the interview.

The S has 'never looked around for some one who would provide intercourse,' and when rare opportunities have arisen he has been unprepared with contraceptives. 'I always intended to (buy them), but I didn't.' He does not have strong sex urges because his energy is 'bound up in trying to get ahead.' He has had nocturnal emissions, also occasional necking parties. He is not afraid of venereal disease.

If approached by a homosexual, he would 'attempt to use violence.' He would feel insulted, and says, 'It is a vile thing, I think. The idea of any one associating me with doing that sort of thing would make me very angry.' The violence of this reaction suggests that there is a struggle against homosexual urges quite near the surface. Note the above-mentioned hypothesis of passive homosexuality and the emphasis throughout upon conflict with men rather than affiliation.

When given opportunity to question the E, Earnst wished to know what brought about homosexuality. After the E had discussed this briefly, the S asked if it could be cured. He also wished to know whether the E knew of other instances where adolescent masturbation had not occurred. The E stated that this finding was rare and due to especially strong repression. The S thought that his having observed several boys masturbating together might have made it particularly revolting to him. This, of course, emphasizes the homosexual element in which we have been interested in this case.

Biographer's Note : At the final interview the S was questioned about his mother's absence. He said, 'My mother became very frail. She went away for months at a time to escape farm routine.' Asked how this affected him, he replied, 'When she would go, I was dismayed as to what my future would be.' She was away an entire year shortly before her death. The latter event was for the S 'a great shock ; it seemed like the beginning of a new world for me.'

5. PRESENT DILEMMAS

M. Moore

The subject's main problem is one that occupies most of his consciousness : he is in acute need of a job. He has no money and lives on what he can borrow from his brother ; his meals are earned by working in a restaurant. He has some training in engineering and refuses to give up the idea of working in that line.

Though he is an odd looking boy, he has a pleasant expression and appears to be in a good frame of mind though naturally he is not elated at his present circumstances. His mood seems dependable and on the whole quite stable. He has no acute emotional problems at present, or if he has they are submerged by the economic problem he is facing. I believe he is a simple, plain, straightforward fellow with considerable character and many original ideas.

He states that he was brought up on a farm and lived there until he was seventeen. Both parents are dead and he is for all intents and purposes alone in the world, since his brothers have their own families and interests and none are well off. In simplest terms, here is a solitary organism trying to keep its balance and find sustenance in a difficult world. I feel that his general psychological reaction to the whole situation is admirable and that he is a superior fellow well worth advising and helping, if possible. I would not regard him as a weak or unstable character.

He will probably go through life in a very even tempo and probably will never strike the nadir or the zenith in mood. He is deeply appreciative of any help and indicated this when the E offered to introduce him to a man who might help him find work. A friend is helping him by allowing him to earn his meals and permitting him to take time off as necessary in order to look for a job.

The material revealed in the interview was largely factual and was surprisingly lacking in affect. I do not mean that the boy's personality was lacking in colour but it seemed that he was purposely refraining from telling how he felt about his troubles for fear that it would seem that he was complaining. Probably the privations he has suffered are not different from those of many men his age in the present depressed economic era, but I doubt whether many others present such a realistic response as does this subject.

Biographer's Note : Observe that Earnst, in an unexacting situation, may appear composed and self-possessed.

6. CONVERSATIONS

ELEANOR C. JONES

The air of dogged patience, of tolerant resignation to an economic and emotional incubus, the overwhelming periodic fatigues, and the detached impersonality which at first appear to characterize the general behaviour of Earnst are more than a little deceptive. Contrasting with these signs of an overburdened debility, one comes to discover a firmness — qualified mainly, perhaps, by commercial failure — and an understated, intermittent, but accurate satire, delivered in a subtle mimicry, a few sufficient words or tones — his head resting, in this releasing interim of assertion, back against a chair, and just a flicker in his face, as if peace were coming at last in this belated aggression. And in spite of his desperate poverty he exhibits signs of elegance — in two rings, a striped silk muffler folded about his shoulders, the handkerchief arranged with careful negligence, and in his grey spats which, one feels, may serve a triple purpose of adornment, warmth, and a conceivable lack of socks. Also, to offset his weariness, he shows a surprising power of recuperation ; and, as an extension of his usually non-censorious detachment, a nurture which, experienced and disillusioned, is all the kinder and more constant. As he sits with hunched-up shoulders, elevating himself on the toes of his sideways-twisted feet, making scrupulous, tired marks (also making mistakes in scoring), one is further struck by the sudden passionate gesture of his hand to his head, a gesture which starts to be extravagantly expressive but is abruptly checked perhaps through definite control, perhaps through a compulsive regard for the arrangement of his hair. For in his use of the phrase : 'I can be quite *top*, if I have to,' one feels an evidence of compensation in his luxuriant, deeply wavy, always carefully washed and brushed black hair. He never wears a hat. 'I haven't a hat,' he says and diagnoses the difficulty : 'I'm going to get one, but I can never find one that's becoming.' Thus he walks the street exhibiting his hair, which plays the major part, perhaps, in 'relieving the monotony,' a phrase he uses more than once in describing his momentary evasions of a reality which he recognizes as only too real.

In Earnst's frustrated and unhappy love affair — for which he considers his assiduous devotion to be partly responsible (he used, after a day's work, to hitch a ride, take a bus part way, and walk the rest in order to spend an hour or at longest two with his girl in Connecticut, leave there at midnight, debark in Boston at four in the morning, and walk out to Cambridge) — from this eventually fruitless labour of love one may draw several analogies to his insolvent position with society. Yet he is realistically fair to the qualities of his rival, according to him both brains and the money, which he himself so patently lacks, to amuse his sweetheart as a young girl ought to be amused. 'I got her up here in spite of her parents' opposition, and now I want her to have the good time I am not at present in a position to give her.' But when the rival remarks that he finds it impossible to 'talk to' Earnst, Earnst exclaims : 'Of course he couldn't talk to me — the big stiff ! ' Of his girl he says : 'I never thought when I first saw her ' (at something like a church supper) 'that there was anything to fall in love with, but as time went on I found that there was something which made her the only one for me.' . . 'Yes, she is very blond,' he answers, 'and I am dark,' — here one again detects a pride in his hair — yet later, in an extenuation of her infidelity, he says with a self-satiric smile, 'I'm not exactly a romantic figure.' When his cumulative suffering and confusion grew too great, 'I wanted to keep my head,' he says, 'so I sat down at the typewriter and put the whole thing down on paper ' — but at a later session he admits : 'No, I don't do that any more — I've given up trying to understand or to direct it, or else I might go crazy.'

Concerning a statement about a wife, he asks defendingly : 'Does anyone like to stay at home and keep house ? — sounds pretty prosy to me,' perhaps an extenuation of his mother's absence when he was a child and a momentary rationalization of his girl's evening adventures.

To circumvent the daily waking to frustration and dog-labour, Earnst has originated his own self-inflationary devices. When, for instance, the practical methods of getting a government job are reported by the E ('You must swagger, bluster, bawl them out before they bully you'), he shows no concern at all, only a seasoned sense of adequacy and a conviction that 'it is always just as well to know somebody.' 'Oh,' he says, 'I can be quite *top*, if I have to, but I don't like to do it'—speaking as one who is accustomed to dealing airy yet crushing reprimand when pushed too far. Yet he confesses that his capabilities—in which he has a thorough verbal confidence ('If you know anyone who wants a good engineer')—are 'paralysed' before an interview: 'I'm not good at pep-talks to the Big Executive. . . I can't come back and describe at length how I said so-and-so to the Big Shot.' . . 'At least I don't have to look for my *first* job—that's *horrible*—I've done it many times since then.' Yet also he is at pains, in speaking of his girl, to imply that though he would never marry a woman who smoked, he himself has been about, somewhat dashingly, in company; is not unversed either in drink or in flirtation; has had in general a quite successful social time—and his small tyrannies are to be mainly exercised in the protection of the girl who has already eluded his alternately indulgent and restrictive grasp.

Despite his deprivations, Earnst can on occasion be surprisingly free from bitterness. Even in a discussion tinged with socialistic sympathies, he is not to be led away to radical assertions, his pragmatic attitude toward the muddled human lot causing him to be humanely fair even toward the stereotyped external image of an all-fortunate oppressor. Although he speaks of mediaeval, anonymous groups of workers and craftsmen commissioned by royal patronage, his sympathies are socialistic rather than communistic, and his native tolerance would modify any really 'radical' theory by a projected fantasy of 'hard times for all.' This is the human lot, he would imply; money is not everything (though the fulfillment of his desperate and abiding desire appears to depend upon it, however meagre the half-satisfaction) : this is the human lot, compromised from the day of birth, and everyone is miserable.

And in the meantime, while trying to hope for happier consummations in which nothing so far has made him really able to believe, he suffers a great deal, smiles a little with that mimicry which reveals a close and hidden observation of the enemy, recovers briefly, and so shoves himself from day to day, subsisting on the short-time plans and sops which suffice to get him up in the morning, after the hours — broken by work and pain — of the night before.

7. PREDICTIONS AND SENTIMENTS TEST

K. Kunze

I. *Interest Distribution and Outstanding or Typical Sentiments*

1. Interest Distribution : Science 37%, Politics and Government 20%, Religion 19%, all others under 10%.

2. Outstanding or Typical Interests :

a. Because of a persistent negative reaction to the test statements, the experimenter experienced difficulty in his attempt to determine the fields of activity that appeal to Earnst in a positive way. Science attracts his attention, especially a flexible type of science that does not depend too much upon physical elements and mathematics.

b. He has religious inclinations and maintains that moral decadence would follow a society's renunciation of religion : 'Religion will never be a thing of the past, I hope. If it ever does become submerged in the modern whirl of civilization, the quality of civilization will tend to degenerate.

II. *Interpretation of Test Data*

1. Correspondence of the tests : Rank Order 9 out of 15.

2. Sentimentive Intensity : Rank Order, Predictions 11.5 ; Sentiments 11.

3. Intraception-Extraception Index : Rank Order 12.
4. Radical-Conservative Index : Rank Order 11.
5. Need Variables :

a. n Autonomy. Earnst furnishes us with a unique picture of an individual who is undoubtedly high in Radical Sentiments yet who ranks low in the Radical-Conservative Index. We may look to the phrasing of the statements for a clue to the solution of this apparent paradox. Most of the statements take a positive form, such as : 'Church properties should be taxed by the government,' and because Earnst is compelled to be negativistic, his reactions reveal an antagonism toward change. Perhaps if the statements had reflected negative aspects, Earnst would have answered with his usual 'No,' which would have resulted in a high Radical Index. This explanation does not seem so far removed from the truth when we note that he disagreed with himself in order to maintain this attitude. As one instance, Earnst contended that society should not impose fewer restrictions on the amount of wealth an individual may accumulate, and in the same breath reacted negatively to the suggestion that rugged individualism should be encouraged. In the Sentiments Test, Earnst reacted to only four of the seventy statements with a 'Yes 3' response, and in the two tests, two-thirds of the reactions were negative ones. The average response with other individuals has been about two to one in favour of 'Yes' reactions.

b. n Order. The layout of the paper with his written reactions and his handwriting indicate a lack of the need for Order.

c. n Aggression. His apparent negativism might be considered as a form of covert Aggression. This is substantiated by the fact that his written reactions were in the main terse, derogatory, and more destructive than constructive.

Biographer's Note : There is a striking difference between the aggressive, negativistic Earnst of this report and the tempered, tolerant young man described in the previous one. While partly a function of the time — for Earnst developed a guarded friendly feeling for the Clinic only in the last weeks of his visits — this is mainly determined by the character of the session and sex of the interviewer. He was usually anxious and hostile, but when the atmosphere was unquestionably sympathetic he could be induced to lay down his weapons and display the maturer attitude described in Mrs. Jones's report.

8. QUESTIONNAIRES

H. A. Murray

Earnst displayed more than the average amount of sentimentive intensity in the marking of his questionnaires. He differed by more than one point from the marks assigned by the Clinic on eight variables :

Two points higher : n Dominance (3 instead of 1) ; n Affiliation (3 instead of 1), n Nurturance (3 instead of 1) ; n Rejection (3 instead of 1), n Play (3 instead of 1), Ego Ideal (4 instead of 2).

Two points lower : n Harmavoidance (3 instead of 5) ; Narcism (2 instead of 4).

It will be noticed that Earnst marks himself *up* on 'desirable' variables. We may suppose from this that he is high on Projectivity. An examination of the questionnaire reveals nothing unusual. The S evidently regards himself as a very normal sort of fellow, slightly more sociable and assertive than the average. This is clearly a wish-fulfillment. Perhaps the Clinic should raise their marks on Rejection and Ego Ideal. The S marks all the Ego Ideal questions high. The S made one note on his questionnaire. To the statement : I am drawn to women who are sympathetic and understanding, he adds : 'Who isn't ? ' Nevertheless his mark is only 3. In the Aphorisms test he gave highest ratings to the following statements :

Men are just what they seem to be, and that is the worst that can be said of them.

Few men are raised in our estimate by being too closely examined.

Familiarity breeds contempt.

No bird soars too high if he soars with his own wings.

The S seems to be high on n Defendance : Concealment. He says that he hates to discuss his inner problems with anyone.

On the A–S Reaction Study Earnst scored —12 (R.O. 5 out of 15).

On the Study of Values test he showed an unusually even distribution. Theoretical and Political Interests were slightly higher than the others. The Endopsychic/Exopsychic ratio was .9 (R.O. 13 out of 15) indicating a definite predominance of Exocathection.

9. ABILITIES TEST

E. Inglis

The S was nervous and it was extremely difficult to get him talking. He did not co-operate as did most of the others. He was rather dull, somewhat shy, and did not seem to be possessed of much insight.

Physical. 3 — 3[1]

'I'm not an athlete at all. I never had much time to go in for games in a big way. I do pick up games rather easily. I went out for baseball and basketball at college, but didn't make either team. I had the same experience when I was in high school. I haven't done anything much in the way of athletics for the last three years.'

Although he says he picks up games quickly, he gave no specific examples of this ability, and dodged the question when it was asked.

Mechanical. 5 — 5

The S is the only one who has rated himself 5 on this ability, but he seems to deserve it.

'I have a definite knack for doing mechanical things. I've been interested in mechanical things for many years, and I've always been interested in things along that line. I've designed an electrical measuring instrument, and I usually manage to make im-

1. These figures refer to the ratings the S gave himself : 1, when filling out the questionnaire and 2, later when face to face with the E.

provements on the apparatus in the shop. I work in the laboratory and in the shop a great deal. I've done a lot in the machine shop, and turned out pretty good work.'

The kind of work S is doing requires high mechanical ability, and he is making good at his job.

Social. 3 — 3

'There isn't a great deal to be said about this. I make some friends and lose others. I find myself just about average.'

Attracting and Entertaining. 1 — 1

'I'm no wonder at this; I never was able to talk fluently. I'm no good at entertaining when the situation demands that I do something. I'm reluctant to try to amuse people on my own initiative.' . . 'I had some little dramatic experience at college — I was a young lady in a play.' This last statement was followed by swallowing and a slight blush.

S is apparently quite self-conscious, and never at ease when he has to entertain or say something before a group.

General Intellectual. 4 — 3

'I was on the honour list at college. I'm in an engineering honour society now. So far I've won a scholarship every year to cover my tuition expenses.'

S has always stood well in his classes, and has done better work in engineering and mechanical fields than in any of the liberal arts.

Scientific Understanding. 4 — 4

'In engineering we have to think in terms of mathematical analysis. This is true of my own field in particular. I studied biology and psychology and did better with biology. I did fairly well in economics, and sociology — I got mostly A's in these subjects.'

It is plain that S's real interest is in engineering, and his ability to think in terms of mathematical analysis is well above the average. His standing at the engineering school would indicate the validity of his self-rating. He might even have given himself a 5 without over-rating.

Psychological Understanding. 4—2

'I consider myself good at that (understanding others). But my confidence in this particular ability has been rather shaken. I don't, however, seek to understand people who have no direct relation to me.'

Further discussion led S to state that he guessed his ability to understand the attitudes and motives of others was not quite average, and in re-rating, he gave himself a 2.

Artistic Contemplation and Judgement. 1—2

'I enjoy music and certain types of painting. However, I'm not enthusiastic over any of the Arts. This may be due to my early environment—I was brought up in a rural community and there was little opportunity to hear any good music, or see any fine painting. I didn't get a glimpse of any real art or music until I was eighteen.' . . 'I enjoy scenery, especially the green of the countryside. I remember seeing some marble buildings reflected in the water, and I remember the pleasure I got from seeing mist lifting from a field of daisies. I've seen a lot of beautiful sunsets, and I enjoyed them.'

S has no highly cultivated taste for any of the Arts, but his enjoyment of beauty warrants a rating higher than 1. He changed this to 2 after the interview.

Art-Creative. 1—2

'To tell the truth I play the violin very poorly. I've tried writing short stories, but never sold any. I'm sadly wanting in this ability.' . . 'I think the factor of early training comes into this—I had hardly any chance, as a youngster, to learn to do this sort of stuff.'

Extreme Ratings. One 5, three 4's, one 1, and no 0.

The S has apparently over-rated himself on Physical Ability. His build is definitely not of the athletic type, and he admits that he is 'not an athlete at all.' He gives no examples of proficiency in any sport. A 1 or a 2 would be a more accurate rating.

He has under-rated himself on Artistic Contemplation and Judgement. Although he has had no extensive training in any one of the Arts, he is sensitive to beauty, as evidenced by his memory of sensuous scenes, and he enjoys music and painting. A 3 would be more accurate.

Biographer's Note : It is a quite characteristic sequence with this S for Abasement to be followed by Defendance ; when obliged to confess a weakness, he gives an extrapunitive excuse. His country origin serves most frequently in this capacity.

10. AESTHETIC APPRECIATION TEST

KENNETH DIVEN

Earnst shook hands and then stood impassively in the middle of the floor until told where to sit. When told about the requirements of the procedure he expressed a long sigh saying, 'I'll do what I can but don't really know anything about such matters.' Earnst sighed a great deal, seldom stirring out of a dogged pace and expression.

In the correlation of his rank orders with the standards he ranked ninth place out of ten on the poems, and seventh place on the pictures. He ranked seventh on Projectivity.

POEM 1. *Shelley* : POLITICAL GREATNESS

. . . Man who man would be,
Must rule the empire of himself . . .

'I like the idea of ambition and domination of oneself first.'

POEM 2. *Thomas Hardy* : TO LIFE

O Life with the sad seared face,
I weary of seeing thee,

. . . . . .

And thy too forced pleasantry !

(The S drew a long sigh) 'Yes, I like it, it fits in with some of my moods. It is a mood, and while in it the poet could be very sincere. Good. I liked it better than the first one.'

POEM 4. *Byron* : 'AND DOST THOU ASK THE REASON OF MY SADNESS ?'

My wounds are for too deep for simple grief ;

. . . .

Revenge is left, and is not left in vain.

'Don't care especially for that. The spirit of revenge always seems futile to me. I'd like it fairly well if the last stanza wasn't there. I like especially the second stanza.'

POEM 6. *John Donne* : No. 5 from HOLY SONNETS

I am a little world made cunningly
Of elements, and an angelic sprite ;
But black sin hath betray'd to endless night

. . . .

. . . And burn me, O Lord, with a fiery zeal
. . . which doth in eating heal.

'I like the first two lines and that's about all. It seems rather trite or something. Religious ecstasy does happen like this, but carried too far it's a form of madness.'

POEM 7. *Keats* : SONNET (To Fanny Brawne)

I cry your mercy — pity — aye, love !
. . . give me all,
Withhold no atom's atom or I die.

'I like this more than the others, it happens to express something I have felt. . . (The S made a pause) . . . by the way . . . do . . . do you know where I can get hold of this ? This . . . this is very real.' After the session was over, Earnst was given the reference which he copied and put in his wallet.

POEM 8. *Untermeyer* : INFIDELITY

You have not conquered me — it is the surge
Of love itself . . .
It is not you I love . . .

'If this is written by a true lover it's not sincere because he, if he was really in love, couldn't have analysed himself this way . . . this was written by a cynic, not a true lover. We all *do* this, but when in love we couldn't possibly analyse it.'

POEM 9. *Stephen Spender* : MY PARENTS QUARREL IN THE NEIGHBOUR ROOM

How can they sleep, who eat upon their fear
And watch their dreadful love fade . . .

'Uh — this is an unpleasant one. I never did go in for nightmares. . . (The S laughed self-consciously and got very restless.) A shell-shocked post-war poet must have done this. . . It indicates younger thoughts — sounds plain miserable as an idea . . . the spirit of the thing is depressing if one reads very much . . . nothing here . . . it seems just miserable to me . . . all blurred and jumbled up.' This poem was put last in the R.O., as Earnst said, 'Certainly wouldn't ever want to see this again.'

Pictures

Picture 6 (Cain slaying Abel) : 'I can't make out whether this is a man or a woman. The artist attempts to show life in the raw, he probably has evil intentions. She seems to have her legs crossed as though she suspected him. The man's tactics seem to be a bit odd.' (The S laughed.) Earnst gave this picture fifth place in his R.O., saying, 'Don't care about it.'

Picture 7 (Two men in a Victorian drawing-room) : 'Just a couple of stuffed shirts so far as I can see. Can't like this stuff. We always had things like this hanging around our house. (The S kept looking continuously at the picture, taking a much longer time than over any picture so far.) No appeal. It bores me, to tell the truth.' This picture was put in ninth place in the R.O., as the S said, 'Never want to see again.'

Biographer's Note : The S's preoccupation with his fading love affair appears in his comments on Poems 7 and 8. The second and fourth poems, with their emphasis on sadness, appeal to him, but when the note of revenge is struck he backs away. This probably denotes anxiety ; the futility of revenge must have been driven home to him in many a bitter incident of early years. Poems 1 and 6 appeal to his n Autonomy, but the introduction of black sin in the latter draws from him the curious adjective 'trite.' It may be assumed that the extrapunitive tendency, so clearly marked in this S, makes the idea of sin in himself entirely unreal ; for the most threadbare truism scarcely seems trite if it fits neatly with one's own experience. The marked emotional response to Poem 9 is significant.

The misinterpretation of Picture 6 gives striking indication of a close linkage in the S's mind between Sex and Aggression. The response to Picture 7 suggests an indirect outburst against the father.

11. HYPNOTIC TEST

R. W. White

(Hypnotic Index, 3.75. R.O. 4)

(R.O. predicted by Diagnostic Council, 15)

The story which Earnst gave for the hypnosis picture (Thematic Apperception Test) led to an expectation of extreme resistance to hypnosis. He began with the comment, 'The hypnotist has no chin, doesn't look very powerful,' and ended by saying, 'the hypnotist is not a man of power, but the young man is, and when that happens, you don't get hypnotism.' Between these deprecatory remarks he told a story representing the hypnotist as a barroom acquaintance of the subject's, who performs his experiment with a view to robbery. The subject and his parents are wealthy :

in the family safe is to be found 'a large amount of money and the family jewels.' The hypnotist, supplementing his own efforts with a 'strange drug,' secures from his semi-conscious victim the combination of the safe, but in the end is arrested while breaking into the house.

When Earnst came to the experiment, the cautious defensiveness of his attitude again conveyed an impression of resistance. The hypnotist was therefore astonished to find him responding to all the suggestions after the first, and giving outward evidence of deep drowsiness. After being awakened, he still appeared sleepy, and said, 'I think I'll go back to sleep again.' He was unable to recall anything that had happened ; in the attempt he was uneasy and hesitant, shifted his gaze continually and closed his eyes several times. 'I don't think I got up and walked around,' he murmured. 'You were sitting there beside me, weren't you ?'

In the course of his vain effort to remember, Earnst said, 'It was like gas,' and went on to recount the extraction of his upper teeth, several years ago. He was, in his own phrase, 'a green farm boy, right from the sticks,' not prepared for the quick clapping of the ether cone over his face, still less for the sight of a 'terrible looking instrument' which came into view, or the doctors' discussion of their 'plan of attack' before he lost consciousness—'it would be best to start at the left and sweep across.' Naturally, he struggled, became panicky, but found himself 'too far gone.' Then he had an impression of things happening rather remote from him : it was this remoteness which formed the association with hypnosis. He saw doctors hammering and pounding the teeth out of a fellow with big hammers, while he himself watched, laughed, and thought how terribly funny it was. Then the fellow and the pounding began to get nearer, until at last he realized that he was being pounded : 'Then the joke was on me.' This recollection of Earnst's shows an interesting projection of the trauma and its mastery by derogatory laughter, a mechanism which he may employ at other times without the aid of an anaesthetic.

When he returned for the second test, Earnst began at once,

'I was deceiving you a little last time. I was curious and wanted to watch the technique. When you knock around the world you learn to keep your eyes open. I wouldn't really let myself in for a thing like hypnotism.' In words taken down later by the second interviewer, he said, 'I felt slight apprehension in allowing myself to become subjected to someone else's will. Almost anyone would have a disinclination to let go the great "I am." I particularly wondered what he was going to ask me or make me do. I pretended to be hypnotized the first time in order to satisfy my curiosity as to what the entire experiment would be like.' Asked if he suspected an ulterior purpose, he replied, 'If there was such a purpose I wanted to find out what it was before losing control of myself.' At still another time he said, 'I knew if I didn't help him along I'd never get away.'

The second hypnotic test followed a course very much like the first. Two of the five suggested catalepsies were successful, and there was partial amnesia. This time Earnst thought, 'it was more genuine. I felt as though I were myself, and yet it seems as if I felt a strong sense of duty to do what you told me to. I had no clear thoughts at all. I sort of felt I was there, and yet I went ahead and did the things just the same.'

Incidents too numerous to mention leave no doubt of the fact that Earnst, in the first test, was genuinely hypnotized. His introspection on the second trial furnishes an explanation for his own contrary belief. It may be assumed that at the outset he experienced that division of self, that feeling of the self as still present in the capacity of a passive onlooker, so characteristic of light hypnotic sleep. Perhaps this consciousness remained throughout, sufficiently to satisfy him that he was watching the whole procedure and preserving his autonomy. Since Earnst was so determined not to be hypnotized, his actual yielding must have been due to a motive of impressive strength awakened in him by the experiment. It is probable that he exemplifies Freud's description (*Group Psychology and the Analysis of the Ego*, p. 99): 'What is thus awakened is the idea of a paramount and dangerous personality, towards whom only a passive-masochistic attitude is possible, to whom one's will has to be surrendered.' Earnst's use of the phrase, 'a strong sense of duty,' supports the belief that in hypnosis the father-image overwhelmed him (n Aba). In retrospect, this became unbearable, and had to be denied (n Dfd).

12. LEVEL OF ASPIRATION TEST

ELIZABETH A. COBB

Earnst was the only one of the ten who had the Ethical Standards Test *before* he did the test for the Level of Aspiration, in fact he went to Mr. Christenson on the morning of the same day. About half way through the session, he said, 'Funny this test is O.K. till you get nervous, then you can't do a thing. . . I consider myself nervous today — many things have been happening lately and I had to do some puzzles this morning that got me all nerved up' (n Suc). He certainly appeared much upset, working inaccurately, jiggling his foot and knee most of the time, perspiring freely, sighing, yawning, stretching, head sunk in hands from time to time (n Suc), altogether the picture of one who had quite lost his grip (n Suc). Almost at once, after printing the third card and hearing that he had not reached his goal he said, 'I resign — I knew I fiddled around there and was slow' (n Aba). He then started talking about the apparatus in the street and when it was suggested that he go on with the next card, he said, 'I was just looking out the window trying to relax my nerves or something.' He was obviously very tense and began the next card without waiting for the signal.

Later when he did better he would draw attention to the fact. 'Hurray' 'Remarkable' (n Exh). After more improvement the n Ach seemed to gain hold and he suddenly said, 'Do you mind if I take my coat off, my sleeve catches and hampers my style.' Whereupon he stripped his coat and rolled up both sleeves.

During the rest period he asked how he compared with others on this test and then said that he had never been very good at manual things (n Dfd Sn Inv), that back home on the farm his sister could always pick twice as many cherries in a day as he without getting nearly so tired. He thought this test was like learning the Morse Code, you stay on the same level for a month, then suddenly improve (low End).

At the close of the experiment when asked about his attitude, he said, 'At first I was interested but soon I had to force myself (low End). My mental discipline is not as good as it might be. I can't always control myself in focussing my attention. I felt nervous and wished the test was over. When I did better than I said, I felt momentary elation and when I took longer I was resigned. You have to take what you get, like in an examination and I rationalized in regard to my fumbling. . . I found I increased my speed by not pressing myself. I figured the decrease of time I should be able to bring about by eliminating errors made in previous attempts ; and so set the time I thought I could make, but other unlooked for errors would come up.'

In respect to average difference between level of aspiration and level of performance Earnst ranked second, with the very large score of +2.5. The difference decreased relatively little (rank order 9) during the course of the session. However, the S ranked eleventh in rigidity of the level of aspiration. In other words, his level of aspiration fluctuated considerably, but tended to remain, as it started, well ahead of his level of performance.

Biographer's Note : Again in this session the sex of the E influenced the variables shown by the S. The characteristic sequence, Abasement — Defendance, is but slightly apparent and the n Succorance and n Exhibition emerge to prominence. The S's mother used to encourage and praise him, when everyone else disheartened and ridiculed.

13. MEMORY FOR FAILURES TEST

E. H. Trowbridge

In the Memory for Failures Test, Earnst remembered more successes than failures, ranking 6.5 (out of 15) whereas his predicted rank order was 3. In another session, for which there were too few designs remembered to make it significant Earnst ranked 10.5.

Before the test began, Earnst started to make excuses. He said he had never done puzzles and would probably be poor at them (n Dfd). Two among many of his excuses are contained in the following remarks quoted *verbatim* : 'Had too damned much sleep last night and am now in a sort of lethargy!' and, 'My eyes are going to prevent me from achieving my greatest degree of efficiency.'

Earnst had a nervous twitch about his mouth and frequently bounced his fingers nervously on the table. The experimenter interpreted them as symptoms of a repressed need for Aggression. 'Occasionally this Aggression would manifest itself, and at one time he emphatically criticized the design on the box as being a misrepresentation of the finished puzzle (extrapunitive reaction).

It was found that a series of successes tended to increase Earnst's efficiency. This is interesting in view of his rank order which showed that Earnst's preponderance of success recall was greater than the majority.

14. ETHICAL STANDARDS TEST

J. A. CHRISTENSON, JR.

Session I

Part A. Earnst was quiet, unassuming, and quick. He was deliberate, and never did anything excitingly original.

Part B. He failed three puzzles in complete honesty, then after touching his tie, began again ahead of time, as he did with all other puzzles, but with no better success. On one puzzle he stopped ahead of time displaying Infavoidance and Abasement. After the fifth puzzle was in the box he looked at the solution. His pace remained steady and rather fast except that three times in the last ten minutes he remained motionless for a minute at a time, as if he was exhausted or in a trance.

Session II

Part A. Uneventful except for his remarks after his two successes : (1) 'that sure went together,' (2) 'I seem to have mixed up my material here somewhere. Oh, a piece was bottom side up.'

Part B. Earnst started ahead of the bell. He completed five puzzles, stopped on the bell for 3 of his failures, and stopped early on the remaining two (Low Endurance, Abasement and Infavoidance). After one success, and after a failure, he looked at the solution.

Earnst was paid before the second session. His striving seems to have been rather low at first, but increased as he became more involved. In ability he ranked 4th out of 15. In honesty he ranked 10th, as against a prediction of 8th.

Biographer's Note : Strict honesty in this session was evidently not demanded by the S's conscience. As will be shown later (# 18), his father's influence was excluded as far as possible from the formation of his Superego. Gaps in his conscience during a competition of this type are accordingly not surprising.

15. OBSERVATIONS OF EXPERIMENTS AND POST-EXPERIMENTAL INTERVIEWS

R. N. SANFORD

Observation of the Memory for Failures Test (Second Session)

The S seemed serious and somewhat unfriendly. He complied with the E's requests readily but with no enthusiasm. He seemed indifferent or perhaps a little annoyed with the procedure. When criticized for his earlier performance he remained silent and his countenance revealed nothing. His manner in attacking the puzzles was perfunctory and his effort was only moderate. He seemed to show some orderliness, precision, conjunctivity, and an unwillingness to be hurried. He took little notice of the E, rarely glancing in his direction, and when he spoke it was usually to make some objective comment upon the puzzles. When at the close of the session he was asked to comment on the puzzles S offered excuses for his not doing well — the bases of these were his eye strain and his worries over other matters — and expressed some doubt that the test really revealed mechanical aptitude. There was a somewhat plaintive note in his voice as he gave his excuses, but this was the only time that his manner was not detached and impersonal.

For this performance S should be marked high on Conjunctivity, low on Intensity, Endurance and Impulsion. n Rejection, n Autonomy, and n Defendance seemed to be the most important needs, and there was some evidence of n Succorance. His failure to affiliate was marked. His abasive behaviour was indifferent, as if it gave him less bother to behave in this way.

Interview I

S smiled faintly when greeted by the interviewer, and his manner seemed dignified and restrained. He described his experiences in a serious and orderly manner, giving the impression of detachment or aloofness and revealing at times a somewhat scornful humour. He stated that because of eye strain he had not done very well with the puzzles just completed and that because he was distracted by worries he had not done well in the earlier session. He said he liked to do well and that he had tried quite hard. 'He told me I hadn't done well before and I felt I ought to show him. So (with detached amusement) I grimly went at it.' Asked whether or not he had expected to do well, he said, 'You can't expect anything,' thus revealing that he had probably prepared excuses in advance. 'To tell the truth,' he said with feeling, 'I detest jig-saw puzzles,' but on a later occasion he admitted, 'They are fascinating when you get started.'

Concerning the E's attitude the S said, 'As a matter of fact I didn't have much of an impression of him. I was preoccupied with the puzzles. He was courteous enough, but he certainly had nothing remarkable in the way of a friendly personality. He appears critical, and seems to take the attitude that you're an experimental subject and nothing else. I wasn't responsive. In fact, I felt some slight antagonism. I do this often for no particular reason. I told him about my eyes and other troubles and he was nice. I thought he was nice, really. I had a notion he was being disappointed at my not doing better. He was quite young and hasn't the professional manner. I haven't anything against him, but to tell you the truth, I felt those tests didn't amount to a damn.'

When the interviewer thanked the S for the co-operation he said, 'Well, I'm glad to have been of help to you. I can imagine your difficulties.' He seemed genuine in this, though his manner was somewhat formal. As he left the room he was thanked again and he said, 'You're welcome I'm sure,' and his handclasp was firm and his gaze steady.

In his relations with the interviewer S showed n Succorance and a small degree of n Nurturance and n Affiliation. To an extent, good fellowship was obtained because the interviewer was a kind of silent partner to S's criticism of other people, but formality, reserve, detachment seemed to be the most important aspects of his demeanour. In his conversation S revealed relatively high n Rejection, n Aggression, n Defendance, n Counteraction, n Autonomy and n Succorance.

Observation of the Ethical Standards Test (Second Session)

S seemed frankly bored in this situation. His manner seemed to reveal resignation and a degree of self-pity. He accepted the E's instructions readily but indifferently and mechanically, and showed only moderate effort when working on the puzzles. He was slow and deliberate in his performance, pausing frequently to gaze at the work before him, and it was impossible to know whether he was studying it or thinking about something else. From time to time he sighed deeply and his facial expression was usually gloomy. This picture was altered for a moment after his first success when he leaned back in his chair and said, laughingly, 'That sure had me puzzled.' He seemed slightly annoyed by his failures, after which such activity as drumming on the table, sighing, pursing the lips and stroking the nose became more pronounced.

The S's extremely low Intensity and Endurance were in part due to physical fatigue, for his features were haggard and bodily movements seemed to cost him much effort, but they might have been closely related to his lack of concern for this situation. Low Emotionality and Impulsion were shown and n Abasement seemed to be the outstanding manifest need. There were a few feeble attempts at affiliation but he remained for the most part detached and self-sufficient.

Interview II

The S seemed physically worn out. He rubbed his face with both hands, sighed deeply, and slumped in his chair. His responses to questions were parsimonious, vague, and superficial, as if speaking or even controlling his mental processes were almost beyond his strength. He was not unfriendly, but he showed no effort to please the interviewer and gave the impression that more than anything else he desired physical and mental rest. 'I haven't done anything very remarkable with these puzzles,' he said with grim humour. But he added that he had come up to his expectations, and that he thought he had done better work this time than on the previous occasion. He confessed an attitude of boredom towards the puzzles. 'I honestly tried, but I can't concentrate on them. My mind begins to wander. I think about other things. I think I haven't much power to concentrate anyway. Most of my concentration is involuntary, I suppose.' In explaining his motive for trying 'fairly hard,' he said, 'It's a test for mechanical ability, and of course if one doesn't enter in it's not a good test. Inasmuch as I'm being paid I thought I should co-operate. But frankly I'm tired of puzzles. There must have been 70 or 80 all together.' He denied that the incentive of double pay had been effective. 'I doubted if I would be in the upper three, and there was motive enough anyway.' He considered the E 'just naturally nice.'

Of the other experiments he enjoyed writing the short story most. He spoke indifferently of the Ink Blot Test which he considered 'very interesting,' and of the Musical Reverie Test which he found 'amusing.' He said he had gained something from the experiments as a whole in that 'I was compelled to use my intellect more in analysing my motives and reactions than I otherwise would have done. Of course I have a tendency to wander a bit to the introspective side.'

When the interviewer offered to close the interview at this point S was apologetic : 'I fear I'm not very helpful to-day,' and then he excused himself on the basis of 'energy phases' which characterize his waking hours. This was a period of low energy. Though he sometimes works all night he never becomes really 'waked up' until noon on any day.

Although the subject's responses in this interview seemed profoundly influenced by his weariness, he nevertheless showed the defensive, somewhat critical attitude, the striving for detachment and self-sufficiency, the low n Affiliation, the indifferent compliance (n Abasement), the preoccupation with his own troubles, and the suppressed n Succorance which had characterized his behaviour in the experimental sessions and in the previous interview. There is thus evidence of a rather high degree of Narcism. Subject's immediate response to a humiliating situation seems to be extreme n Defendance fused with a suppressed n Succorance, while n Defendance, n Aggression, n Rejection and n Autonomy seem to constitute a more or less permanent armour for his sensitive Ego against a hostile world. There is a fair amount of n Counteraction, but n Defendance and then n Infavoidance seem to be more characteristic. The S seems to avoid, as far as he can, becoming involved in personal relationships, and he has given evidence that in any close relationship of this kind, his would be the role of the dependent or pitied one.

16. SENSORIMOTOR LEARNING TEST

WALTER C. LANGER

Earnst was not very co-operative in these experiments. He was fifteen minutes late for the first appointment, twenty minutes late for the second and cut the third one entirely without making any effort to get in touch with the experimenter. He could not be reached by telephone and consequently a postcard was sent him with the time of the new appointment. Again he failed to appear and again he failed to notify the E of his inability to keep the appointment. After numerous efforts he was finally reached by telephone. He was full of apologies and described to the experimenter how he had tried hour after hour to reach the Clinic and cancel his appointment, but the telephone was always busy or nobody answered. The explanations did not ring true and the experimenter interpreted his behaviour as evidence of n Autonomy and lack of Deference. Unfortunately the delay between sessions was most unequal and has undoubtedly discoloured the picture of the learning process in its various phases.

Early in the learning of the first key-slide system the subject was very impulsive, disorderly and unmethodical. He frequently pressed the same key two or three times in succession as though he were sure it was the right key when there was little possibility of his knowing which key it really was. After about fifteen minutes he became more deliberative in his responses and learned rapidly. His rank for the learning of the three key-slide systems was 3. His rank on motor impulsion in the learning of the first system was 4, although in the succeeding systems he became more and more deliberative.

The interference between the key-slide systems was slightly more than the average. The greater part of the interference effect was in terms of overt responses which would have been correct in previously learned systems (Imp), while the inhibitory effects were slight. In all other respects his learning was just about average, the ranks varying from six to nine.

His introspective reports were poorly written and were not neat. One line he would write and the next line he would letter (low n Order). He named only one of ten slides for purposes of identification. At the end of the first session he wrote in answer to the question 'How would you improve your performance if you had it to do over,' 'I don't know.' At the end of the second session he wrote that since the first session he had thought it over and 'decided that it would be more efficient to concentrate on each figure as it arose the first time and then think about it longer when it came up again—instead of stabbing indiscriminately when puzzled.'

Since all of the ranks on the ten measured relating to learning are fairly close to the middle of the rank order, we do not get sufficient weighting to make definite predictions.

17. EMOTIONAL CONDITIONING TEST

a. Galvanic Skin Response

C. E. Smith

While waiting for the experiment to begin, Earnst asked whether there was any objection to talking, and on being told that there was, continued to comment on a faint stinging in his fingers, which he thought might be due to voltage or to an abrasion in the skin. In general reactivity, Earnst was 3rd. In the rank orders of reactivity to the three provocative words, he was 3rd on 'cheating,' 6th on 'coward,' and 3rd on 'homosexual.' In the interview, the S immediately recalled 'homosexual,' and at three different times referred to questioning by one of the E's about the S's homosexual inclinations. Earnst still resented this session.

In the conditioning experiment, Earnst was much affected by the shock. On the first application he jumped up and cried, 'My God!' and then after a pause, 'I'm sorry.' He spent most of the time thinking of the next shock. He explained that in his work in engineering he had received many shocks, but 'You don't get used to shocks, you dread them.' Earnst was very angry at being shocked. 'I can't get mad all at once. I think after a few more shocks I would have expressed myself quite clearly. I dislike them very much. They aren't so bad when you aren't expecting them. When you know you are going to get one it is a very different matter. I would like to work on you fellows a little bit. I have a few ideas.' This S made no association between the critical word 'night' and the shock.

In the extinction experiment, Earnst was waiting for the shock.

The previous evening he had told three persons about his punishment; just before coming to this session he told another E that he might tear up the apparatus if too many shocks were given. When no shocks were forthcoming, the S thought that the E was trying to get him in an unsuspecting attitude, and then 'deliver the goods.' During the interview the E had forgotten to remove the electrodes (not functioning in this experiment) from the S's leg, and the E apologized for this neglect. 'I was wondering if you were going to see what I would say.' The S had been apprehensive of a sudden shock during the interview.

There was no evidence of conditioning to the critical word 'night.' The average gsr to the neutral stimulus words in the extinction series was 1.58 times as great as that in the conditioning series, which is suggestive of diffuse anxiety.

b. Tremor Responses

WALTER C. LANGER

During the first session Earnst manifested more anxiety than any of the other subjects. From the very beginning of the experiment, before any shocks were given, there were tremors in both the active and the passive fingers, and all the finger responses were characterized by disco-ordination. The condition persisted throughout the first session which makes it extremely difficult to select the emotionally toned words. This condition is probably due to two factors: (1) the subject having trained in engineering must have had a good idea when the electrodes were put on his leg that he was going to get a shock, although he reported that he hadn't thought about it. He reported, however, that shocks were extremely unpleasant to him due to his wide and varied experience with them. It seems logical to suppose that an unconscious recognition that he would be given a shock of unknown severity brought on the first diffuse anxiety, while the fact that he did not become conditioned to the word 'night' kept the anxiety in this diffuse condition. (2) Considerable anger was aroused by the shocks, which undoubtedly contributed to his disco-ordination.

In the second session, despite the fact that he anticipated more shocks, the subject had himself well in hand. There were few tremors and rather few broken responses. The whole performance seemed to be of a studied and restrained type. It is likely that between the responses the subject lifted his fingers from the platform.

In the subject's associations several definite trends are to be found. The associations to the word 'day' provide an example. 'Day' was given twelve times in the two sessions. The first association on eleven of these occasions was 'night.' The general trend in the train of associations to this word was to something in the country : trees, rivers, canoes, poles, music, house and barn. Most of these responses were badly broken and it is possible that they are connected with memories of playing 'hookey' and going to the river to fish, then the scene in the house upon return and the infliction of punishment in the barn, although we have no concrete evidence to substantiate such an hypothesis except the frequent occurrence of the trend. In three of the chains 'baby' and 'girls' occur, while on the last presentation of the word 'day' in the experiment he gave 'night,' the motor response being long and broken, then 'star' (motor response broken), then a long pause followed by 'pall' (motor response very long and tremored), followed by 'vinegar' which was long and tremored.

To ten presentations of 'night' the first association in seven instances was 'day' (Sameness). Again the general tendency was to go back to the farm, but here we find more 'roads,' 'bushes,' 'walls,' and means of locomotion such as 'horses,' 'automobiles,' 'bicycles,' and the like. 'Girl' occurred only once but there were a number of repressed verbal responses in connection with this stimulus word, both in the first and second sessions. On the last presentation of 'night' the S gave 'darkness' (pause), 'stealth' (pause), 'gun' (pause), 'tree.' The same thema occurs in connection with a number of other words and it is possible that behind it are fantasies or experiences with which guilt is connected.

Other words which seem to be emotionally toned are :

Sickness — First session : 'disease, death, life, angel, church, organ, wire, seats, people,' all accompanied by disco-ordination. Second session : (repressed verbal response), 'health,' (tremored), (repressed verbal response), 'disease' (very disorganized), (repressed response), 'cold' (very disorganized and followed by a long tremor).

Eating — First session : 'drinking, sleeping,' (repressed verbal response), 'work,' (repressed verbal response), 'farm, hay, corn, fight.' Second session : 'sleeping, drinking, wine, glass, lights, bread.'

Soft — First session : (heavy tremor), 'hard, egg, shell, cook, table, counter, coffee,' (very disorganized), 'cup, glass, urn.' Second session : 'hard, road, mud, onion,' (repressed verbal response), 'air.'

Fruit — First session : 'United Fruit, ship, South America, jests, School, Halloway.' Second session : 'orange, apple, banana, pineapple, prune, peach.'

Clinic — First session : 'Psychology, Ingalls, desk, phone, stairway, room.' Second session : (the greatest amount of disco-ordination), 'psychology, house, stairs, telephone, tea.'

Sweet — First session : 'sour, bitter, coffee, tea, vinegar, pickles,' (repressed verbal response and heavy tremor). Second session : 'sour, bitter, strong, weak, house, barn.'

River — First session : 'bridge, smoke, tide, ferry, people, road.' Second session : 'boat, smoke, paddle,' (repressed response), 'canoe.'

Cheating — First session : 'lying, cheating, politics, Washington, Capitol, Alexandria,' (heavy tremors). Second session : 'lying, stealing,' (long pause), 'thievery, politics.'

Homosexual — First session : 'table, room, question, couch, rug, door.' Second session : 'room, couch, man, red, pencil.'

The co-ordination throughout the experiment was poor. The motor response always preceded the verbal response, sometimes by as much as two seconds. Motor responses without a verbal accompaniment were frequent. This would seem to indicate an alternation of impulsion and inhibition combined with manifest anxiety.

Biographer's Note : The passage of six months, it can be seen in these two reports, had done little to abate Earnst's anger connected with the hour on Sexual Development (# 5), especially the questioning in regard to homosexual feelings. Food and drink appear in the associations with marked emotional accompaniments. After one of the sessions the S remarked, ' Some words brought up vivid pictures of my life, a quick history of it.' One sequence seems to fit this description particularly well : ' House —barn, farm, road, town, safe, travel, college.'

18. THEMATIC APPERCEPTION TEST

CHRISTIANA D. MORGAN

The subject did 13 pictures for which he offered 14 themas.

The score for latent Aggression was 12/13 = 0.92 (R.O. 3 out of 10). The score for Optimism (Pleasant/Unpleasant) P/U = 1.33 (R.O. 3 out of 15). Suggested ratings : Projectivity, 4 ; Intraception, 3 ; Creativity, 2.

Dominant Themas : p Monotony : Barren Environment occurs four times, Achievement thema four times, and Crime-Punishment thema four times. Achievement Failure thema is given three times and Dejection three times. The thema of p Dominance : Coercion (by an older man) occurs four times. In each instance the older man is a criminal who is exerting his power over a younger one with the aim of using him as an accomplice.

Earnst's introspections are meagre. He showed strong Inviolacy reactions to all questions and was aggressively defensive until near the end of the second hour.

Before one can understand the stories one must look at Earnst's introspections in order to realize how intensely he feared and hated his father. He says : ' My father was always trying to oppose my ambition. He wanted to keep me on the farm. . . Sometimes I got very hopeless . . . I once thought of suicide. It was when I was in the last year of High School and it looked as though I wouldn't be able to finish. My father was trying to make me stop and to help him on the farm. We had awful arguments and rows all the time. I used to feel that if I couldn't get on with my education I would kill myself. . . I used to think of suicide quite often . . . I hated the farm so dreadfully and the farm work — and I had such rows with my father.'

The S's physical fear of his father is indicated in the following statement : 'My father sometimes got drunk. He was a great big powerful man and we were always afraid of what he might do as we none of us could have defended ourselves against him if he became violent.'

In one story (Picture No. 16) the man is a robber who has committed several murders and who has 'great brute strength.'

Picture G (A middle-aged man leaning forward with his jaw thrust out and his fists clenched).

S : . . . This is an angry parent. His son had joined a gang to let the air out of automobile tires on Hallowe'en. . . The father is thinking how to punish the boy for he has discovered the air is out of his own automobile tires. . . He will give him an angry talking to, and a beating, but will not injure him badly. (n Aggression : Destruction (Crime) → p Aggression : Beating (Punishment))

It is of interest to note here the signs of repressed Anxiety. The S is careful to inform us that the boy is not injured badly. The Aggression against the father is disguised as an innocent prank (Injection vector). The boy has the protection of numbers ; he is one of the gang.

The same thema is apparent in the following story.

Picture D (A small boy is standing leaning against a fence looking at a factory dimly outlined in the distance).

S : This little boy is the son of a smelter worker in the coal regions. . . The child is cold and miserable. . . He is looking at the plant where his father works. . . He dreads the appearance of the big plant which seems like a monster. . . The boy feels there is something wrong with this place. He feels he doesn't want to work there. That feeling stirs up a spark of ambition which leads him to get an education through his own efforts. Eventually he becomes an educator. He tries to teach the iron workers that they are downtrodden, and that big powerful finance should be broken. He turns Socialist and leads a successful life. (p Insupport : Poverty & p Dominance : Coercion → n Autonomy & n Achievement (Intellectual) → n Dominance : Agitation of Aggression)

In his introspections the S said : 'Mellon who owns those factories had great power and just exploited the workers and made them do anything he wanted them to do. He was very powerful and they couldn't fight him.'

In this story the powerful father and the hateful factory (farm) seem to be combined to form the image of a monster, or dragon. The S does not, apparently, feel himself to be sufficient of a hero to meet the beast in single-handed combat, but as an agitator he will stir up others to fight. We may note that in the introspections the S speaks of Mellon as exploiting the workers to make them 'do anything he wanted them to do.' This press of Dominance : Coercion is important as we shall see later.

Earnst has told us in his introspections how much he hated the farm and the farm work. He says, 'I was wild to get away. I couldn't stand the thought of the farm.' This bitter loathing is reflected in the press of Monotony : Barren Environment which occurs in four stories.

Picture No. 13 (On the floor against the couch is the huddled form of a boy with his head bowed on his right arm. Beside him on the floor is an object which resembles a revolver).

S : This youngster is discontented about something. He is trying to find something which he can do to amuse himself. His store of resources has given out. He is bored to tears. At present he is weary of himself. He is thinking of stories which he has read of people who have done things. He is wishing he were a hero, or he might have a hero with whom to identify himself. He wishes he were doing something else than just hanging around. If he is like the usual boy of 14 he feels he isn't understood at home and should be out in the big world. (p Monotony & p Rejection : Parental Indifference → Ego Idealism & n Achievement)

The S says in his introspections, 'At first when I had these hopeless feelings I didn't know what to do about them. Now, when they come on I just go to the movies to get over them as quickly as possible. I think it is abnormal to have such feelings. I attribute them to the hard time I had as a child.'

Picture No. 4 (The silhouette of a man's figure against a bright window. The rest of the picture is totally dark).

S : This picture is a sequel to the other one. This young man is probably a farm hand. . . He tells himself that he doesn't belong where he is. He wants to get away and lead the life that he feels he ought to lead. . . He finds a way of getting ahead. (p Monotony → n Rejection : Egression → n Achievement)

Picture No. 12 (A man helplessly clutched from behind by two hands, one on each of his shoulders. The figure of his antagonist is invisible).

S : . . . This chap is unconscious. He is drunk. . . He gets very little personal glory. He feels that he must do something to enjoy life. . . He drinks more and passes out completely. (p Rejection : Social Indifference → Dissipation → Death)

Here we have suicide by regression to an oral mode of activity. In the story given for Picture E, a young man has failed in his examinations and feels that there is nothing left to live for.

Earnst says in his introspections : 'I used to feel that if I couldn't go on with my education I would kill myself (intrAgg). The idea of living and knowing that people knew more than I did was intolerable to me (E I, n Inviolacy). I used to think of suicide quite often (n Abasement : Surrender). Luckily, I was able to finish High School (in spite of my father). Afterwards, I saved up $500 to enable me to get to college which was pretty good.'

For Earnst, money meant education and education meant freedom from the farm. It was his only weapon against the intolerable domination of his father. On money, which would enable him to get an education, depended his manhood and his salvation.

The press of Dominance : Coercion (on the part of an older man) deserves special attention for the S repeated this four times, in three stories and in one introspection which has already been mentioned.

Picture No. 14 (A young man lying on a couch with his eyes closed. Sitting beside the couch is an elderly man leaning forward with one hand raised above the forehead of the reclining figure).

S : . . . The hypnotist wants the money of this young man. He is unscrupulous and he has acquired the knowledge that the young man's parents keep in the safe of their house a large amount of money and the family jewels. The young man knows the combination of the safe. . . The hypnotist drugs the young man by some strange drug. While he is semi-conscious the hypnotist got him in his power . . . he is trying to get the combination of the safe from the young man. The hypnotist is trapped and arrested for robbery. The young man . . . gets out from under the hypnotist's spell and leads a normal life. . . In the picture the hypnotist is not a man of power but the young man is, and when that happens you don't get hypnotism. (p Dominance : Coercion & p Cognizance : Cross Questioning & p Acquisition : Robbery → n Harmavoidance : Escape & n Aggression : Imprisonment (Punishment))

The hypnotist is clearly the father from whose spell the subject tried for so many years to escape. In the interpolated remark at the end of the story the S again betrays his anxiety.

Picture F (A young man sitting opposite to an older man. The latter has his hand out as though emphasizing some point in an argument).

S : The younger man is a clerk in a bank who has been gambling — and he is in debt to the older man. The older man is trying to get him to engage in shady business with the bank. The younger man is objecting, not from conscience, but because he is running his neck into a noose. The young man is intelligent and will find a way . . . to get out of the man's power. It will be some drastic method. He might take the older man out in the dark and quietly throttle him and throw him over the brink. (p Dominance : Coercion for Acquisition : Robbery (Crime) → n Aggression : Murder)

The subject's parricidal fantasy is evident in this story.

Picture No. 15 (A grey-haired man is looking at a young man who is sullenly staring into space).

S : The older man is a miser who is out for money. He employs this young man to help him. . . These two are now in conference about the most likely way to get money controlled by an old lady. . . Years ago the old lady had a son. He disappeared completely and she never found him. This old man knows about it and is going to foist this disreputable young man on the old lady as her son. (In the cause of justice this mustn't succeed.) . . . One day the old lady sees that there is no such birth mark on this man as there was on her son — and so she calls the police. (p Dominance : Coercion → n Deference : Compliance (n Acquisition : Robbery) → p Aggression (Punishment))

All these stories haye this in common : an older man uses a younger man as his tool in order to steal something : jewels from his mother's safe, money from the bank, money from his supposed mother. Superficially this seems to be related to the S's feeling that his father was exploiting him by making him do the hateful work on the farm (to make money for him by digging into the earth). More deeply, perhaps, it suggests the fantasy of an enforced robbery of the mother (safe = bank = woman's body).

The subject has told us in his introspections that he thought of suicide when his father was trying to make him stop his education in order to help on the farm. The reason that his father gave for this demand was the lack of funds. The boy probably felt that this labour was being forced upon him by his father because the latter wanted to save and make money for himself. His father would have appeared as a greedy miser who was attempting to thwart his son's thirst for knowledge. It has already been suggested what an education meant for the subject. The fact that the plot of enforced robbery is repeated with little variation justifies us in looking for a deeper interpretation ; and the hypothesis which suggests itself is that the subject had a fantasy that his father wanted to compel him to rob his mother.

It is evident that the son was unable to admire his father. In Picture No. 13, the boy 'wishes that he had some hero with whom he could identify himself.' He could not use the father as an exemplar for Superego formation because he hated him as a monster, the personification of all evil. The father, however, served very well as a figure into whom the boy could project his own Id tendencies. In this way he could shift the blame and dismiss guilt feelings. This is the mechanism that occurs in paranoia.

We have yet to understand why the subject interpreted the father's relation to the mother in the way that he did. The father was the robber who exploited the mother or robbed her for his own greed.

Picture No. 11 (A young man with his head buried in the lap of a young woman who bends over him with a tender expression).

S : . . . Husband and wife. . . He is fired and feels that he is a failure. . . He tries to tell his wife courageously, but his sense of personal failure overcomes him. . . She comforts him. . . This happens late in the evening. She makes him some coffee and gets him lunch knowing that this cheers a discouraged person. . . The following day he gets up with courage. . . He gets something later in his own line and leads a happy life. (n Achievement Failure → Dejection → p Nurturance : Nourishment → n Achievement (Counteraction) Success)

Since this is the only time that a subject has specifically mentioned food and drink in connection with womanly sympathy the association probably has significance. When the subject was asked to give the first thought that came to his mind in relation to thirst, he said, 'The only thing that comes to my mind is the awful thirst you get on the farm working in summer. You are so bound to the soil that you can't leave it and walk for half a mile for a drink. I remember when I was eleven that I had to hoe a great corn field. I was very young and those rows seemed to stretch as far as I could see like a great desert. I have never forgotten the heat and the intolerable thirst.'

It seems reasonable to suppose that the subject's memory of his father forcing him to work in the fields and suffer thirst is a modified reverberation of an underlying fantasy of the father as the frustrator of his earliest oral wishes. From Picture D and other evidence it seems that the subject dreamed of his father as a monstrous plunderer. Thus the content of the primal fantasy might have been this : 'My greedy father takes all the nourishment from my mother. Because of him I thirst.' And later : 'My coercive father forces me to carry out his predatory designs against my mother' ; the unproviding mother being later equated with the parched earth (desert). It is possible that the Oedipus fantasy was built up on this thema.

It is probable that education offered this subject his only opportunity to escape from and then overcome his father. He says, 'My hatred of the farm made me more ambitious than I should otherwise have been if I hadn't hated it so much.'

Summary. The data which Earnst gives us in this test suggests that oral frustration gave rise to a fantasy of robbing the mother and that the earliest Oedipus wishes followed an acquisitive oral receptive pattern. These tendencies were frustrated by his father — the robber baron — who thus became responsible for his deprivation. By projection his own acquisitive tendencies were attributed to the father : 'he forces me to steal.' The subject may have identified himself with his mother in a castration fantasy, 'My father wants to rob me as he robbed my mother.'

The predominant variables are n Infavoidance, n Aggression, n Dominance, n Autonomy, n Achievement. The conspicuous latent variables are Anxiety and n Harmavoidance (physical fears).

19. IMAGINAL PRODUCTIVITY TESTS

D. R. Wheeler

a. Beta Ink Blot Test

Earnst's ink blot interpretations were copious but entirely lacking in thematic significance. One of his most fantastic associations was that for blot 9 : 'Looks something like a bear in a cowboy suit just after having jumped out of an airplane in a parachute.'

b. Similes Test

On the Similes Test two factors recurred : p Loss of Loved Object and n Aggression (mostly against politicians).

p Loss of Loved Object (p Family Insupport, p Rejection) :

As pathetic as a cat that has just lost its brood of kittens.

As pathetic as an orphan who is being returned to an asylum.

As pathetic as a cub trying to awaken its mother that has been shot.

As deceptive as the young lady who announced her engagement to someone you hadn't even heard about — that was my unpleasant experience at one time.

n Aggression :

As incongruous as a Bronx statesman's platform — they promise everything to everybody.

As artificial as a politician's sentimentality.

As dangerous as a dictator who is merely seeking his own ends.

As dangerous as the ideal of communism.

As deceptive as 50% of our congressmen — you can see I'm quite a ranter on politics.

As artificial as the culture of a department store clerk — I don't intend to condemn department store clerks, I just . . .

As conspicuous as a person picking a fight with a policeman.

On the adjective 'delightful' he remarked, 'I'm stuck on this one because I'm not a person who has many delights — I'm not given much to ecstasies.' At the conclusion of the hour the S said, 'I should think it would be quite a job to classify all these. You'll have to go by your own standards and you can't be sure that they are right' (ln Agg).

Combining the two factors that appear in these tests, one gets the formula : p Rejection (or p Loss of Loved O) → (ln Succorance) → n suprAggression. The universe is first a void and then a tyrant (politician, communism).

c. The Minister's Black Veil

by Earnst

The brazen clamor of a poorly wrought bell cut the stillness of the frosty air as Hepzibah Winters profoundly discharged his passengers in front of the low but aspiring brick church. Mrs. Winters, in charge of her family group, herded them to the walk, turning grimly to admonish Hepzibah with a meaning glance.

He, shrinking under the barbed look, instantly curtailed all thoughts of dallying in the sheds where the horses were stabled. Like all good husbandmen he enjoyed a brief talk on affairs with a few cronies to spice the occasion and make up for the dullness of the sermon (n Aggression con p Dominance (moralizing)).

Not that Parson Snow was a dull man. No, indeed! With snapping black eyes set on either side of an acquiline nose, the ensemble flanked by bushy eyebrows, mustache, and beard; a huge, formidable person was he in the pulpit. Let him fasten an accusing glance on a small boy scoffer in the congregation and Lo and Behold! the youngster stiffens in his seat, turns pale, and is as still as a wooden post during the rest of the sermon (n Harm). Parson Snow was called a good man by the respectful, tea-drinking biddies of his brood, but manifestly his ideas about the 'good' in the world were narrow and cynical; his sermons were wrathful invectives against straying from the straight and narrow (p Agg). Obviously, he thought that talking wouldn't help much but he would at least do his duty. He did it fifty-two Sundays a year, admonishing with shaking locks and bellowing voice against the whole category of crimes; his face revealing conclusively his suspicions of the whole of the congregation.

Parson Snow had now delivered forty-three of his fear-producing, devil-chasing sermons whence arose the reluctance of sundry male members of the congregation to enter the church until the last moment; those innocent souls who playfully indulged in a little horse trading, betting, and fighting cocks, just couldn't relish the idea of having so many of their sins paraded before them and dreading the possibilities of being exposed.

'There's no gettin' away from that danged hell-roarer — he sure makes a man think dang little of himself,' impolitely criticized one slightly uncultured gentleman.

As Hepzibah bravely dared the forbidding portals (the organ was just beginning to wheeze its message of blessedness) he felt a tenseness in the air. He looked — the Parson was wearing a black veil! Rubbing his eyes did no good, the veil was there all right. A solemn swath of black around the man's head and face which darkened his features so that only his flashing eyes were distinguishable.

The Parson was otherwise the same as usual. His denunciations of evil did not flag, his style of conveying reproach had not altered a whit. It is to be suspected that the brimstone and thunder lost some of their effects this particular morning because of the veil. The good people of Vangel were wondering about that veil and they could only wonder about one thing at a time.

The sermon went its way, so did the Sabbath, likewise the minister, but rumor arose and flew furiously about the little township. What ? Who ? Where ? — Small-pox ? Burn his face ? Augmented by further appearances of its parson in his new regalia (he didn't appear without it, in fact) the gossip resulting therefor kept the eager villagers entertained for some time. Time advanced — the interest in the veil waned — new gossip arose. The parson visited, preached, walked, his features secluded like those of a harem beauty.

Exactly twenty-three sermons after the appearance of the black veil a bomb of excitement burst forth in Vangel. The congregation was gathered and ready for the twenty-fourth sermon. Usually punctual to the hour, Parson Snow was late. The people waited, no parson came. A group of townsmen went to the parsonage presided over by Martha Peabody, who was old, deaf, failing in mental activity. The Parson had left at his usual time, said she. Funny thing though, he took his grip sack. Maybe — 'Maybe what ? ' chorused the inquirers. 'Maybe it had something to do with those trunks and boxes he shipped away last week,' said she. Trunks ! Boxes ! ? ? ?

At ten o'clock Monday morning Jacob Hirch, the hotel man, was surprised by an inquiry for the town parson.

'I thought everybody knew he'd disappeared,' quoth he.

'Disappeared ! Damnation,' swore the inquiring individual. 'I've tracked that scoundrel for two years. He's "Preacher Dan" Morgan, and is wanted by the Federal Government as well as a dozen or so State Governments. I'll get him yet,' he grimly concluded. 'I've been after that bird a long time and I was already to gather him under my wing. My wing will reach out and gather him in, you'll see!'

Biographer's Note: This story fits well with the hypotheses developed in Report No. 18. The alarming preacher strongly suggests the S's father, and at the end of the story he is discovered to be a robber.

20. MUSICAL REVERIE TEST

K. KUNZE

To record No. 1 Earnst said: 'At the beginning I visualized a boredom, then a friction, and lastly a quarrel. It was a time of distress, the angry lover is leaving. It is a crisis. The girl is thinking things over. She realizes something she has done for which she is repentant. She has written to her lover and told him about it. She waits in high expectancy. He has come back, and there is great feasting and celebration. A wedding.'

The story starts with a state of boredom (p Monotony), which is followed by an argument (n Agg: Quarrel) and the departure of the lover (n Rej). The woman, finding herself in the wrong, repents and to complete the wish-fulfillment the situation terminates with a reunion and wedding which is celebrated with *feasting*.

To the first part of record No. 2 Earnst said, 'The soft music suggested a silent sadness. The music brought to mind a funeral. The funeral of a great poet. A long procession moves down the street. Spectators weep bitterly while the sombre procession moves on.'

This suggests a fantasy of his own death for which others are probably responsible (Imposed Guilt thema). The story also involves n Achievement (oral mode).

To the last half of record No. 2 Earnst said, 'A peasant girl is tiring of her dull life. She dreams but does not derive happiness from them. She is disconsolate — sometimes almost passionate in hating her life. (The conductor isn't following my thoughts at all.) She tends her daily routine and goes through her chores. (I thought the music would change.)' The record ends at this point. Earnst continues, 'Relatives in the city send for her and at the city she has an unhappy time—pitfall, etc.—and eventually goes into disillusionment. There is a sorrowful and unhappy ending.'

Earnst identifies himself with the girl, and again begins his reverie with barrenness and monotony. This girl was a peasant girl and we suspect that her dejection was due, in part at least, to her status in society. This is the first indication of an 'unjust society,' a conception that recurs later. The ending is tragic.

To record No. 5 Earnst said, 'This is the launching of a great ship. It has been christened and is now going down the ways. It hits the water with a great splash. Cheering increases to a great pitch and the crowd is frantic. The launcher feels happy after accomplishing so much. The great ship starts across the ocean and is not heard from. There are no radio messages. There is fear and anxiety and depression of the people whose relatives are on the ship. Then rumors flash across the ocean. Perhaps the ship has been torpedoed—perhaps it has merely lost its course. Speculation continues. No one ever knows what happened.'

Here we find the thema of Death (Sinking) from p Physical Insupport. The launching suggests birth. The statement 'The launcher feels happy after accomplishing so much' suggests the operation of the n Achievement.

The story given to record No. 6 is as follows: 'A happy life of a young couple in a rustic community. They are deeply in love and follow life peacefully with small woes and small joys. They are to be married—when, they don't know. It has been a hard struggle for them to live. Times are hard and it seems as though their marriage were getting farther away. A note of hope springs up. There may be a great national revolution which will give poor people a chance to earn their living and give them a possible life. Their love continues on. Sometimes they are happy, sometimes they are afraid. The young man has his family to take care of and she cannot leave her motherless brothers and sisters. They are caught in a trap of fate and go on and on. The end is merely dull disappointment.'

In this story we find p Lack : Economic and the hope of revolution (n suprAggression). Once more the notion of an 'unjust society' is expressed when Earnst says, 'There may be a great national revolution which will give poor people a chance to earn their living and give them a possible life.' The fantasy closes with a tone of failure and resigned exhaustion.

Summary. Without being distinguished for Creativity, Earnst entertains all kinds of fantasies, of Aggression and of Achievement. Fears and anxieties are also indicated. Social injustice leading to failure and exhaustion suggest a covert need for Succorance. The S has a high degree of Emotionality.

Biographer's Note : The first story, reflecting even in detail the momentary status of the S's love affair, has a happy ending. All the rest finish with gloom, doubt, despair, frustration ; symbolic, it is easy to imagine, of his own dubious future, with its alternatives of 'great success' and 'dismal failure' (see Report # 3). The Musical Reverie Test was given at one of his darkest moments, when the pilgrimage away from the farm must have seemed doomed to a barren ending.

Identification with the mother (Bi-sexuality) is indicated in these stories. The funeral of the great poet suggests not only death of the self but death of the mother, who had poetical and musical pretensions ; in the next story it is a 'peasant girl' who lives what is obviously the S's own history ; and the sinking of a ship recalls the manner of death he ascribed to his mother in a story written a few years ago, collapse of a trestle under her train. The mother left the farm to escape its routine (Report # 5, Note) and Earnst, too, wished to escape. The mother taught herself to play the violin, which instrument Earnst in turn attempted to master. The S's suicidal fantasies came in the years immediately following his mother's death. All these parallels support the hypothesis of identification.

21. DRAMATIC PRODUCTIONS TEST

ERIK HOMBURGER

The S explained his play construction as follows : A sick girl is lying on a couch. Her mother, standing at the window, sees the man to whom the sick girl is formally engaged, across the street, kissing the little girl. The dramatic question : shall she tell the sick girl what she has seen ?

Biographer's Note : If the sexes are reversed, this story becomes Earnst's own ; he sees himself as losing his girl to a rival on account of poverty. It is perhaps legitimate to assume this reversal since the S made it so unmistakably in the Musical Reveries Test, and it harmonizes readily with the hypothesis of mother identification. The dramatic question may reflect in disguised form, like a dream, his unwillingness to admit that the girl's affections are lost.

22. RORSCHACH TEST

S. J. BECK

Most of the marks indicative of very rich mentality stand out in Earnst's response record. With them there appear, however, unquestioned signs of an illogical procedure and peculiarity of thinking. These reactions are more characteristic of clinical groups, and raise the question of certain special processes coursing through this otherwise well-endowed personality.

Psychic structure : Ability to grasp relationships, creative capacity, breadth of interest, percentage of the most obvious (stereotyped) reactions, are all well within the range of the very superior adult. A discrepancy is first noted in respect to form accuracy. This is not at the level maintained by the healthiest members of his group. Secondly, we note an occasional tendency for logical procedure to break down, although, to be sure, it remains orderly more often than not ; it is a trend away from control, but still on a background of control, which the S manifests. Thirdly, is the

S's intellectual method : an over-emphasis on the generalized-abstract, with a less than normal distribution of attention to the practical-concrete, and to the finer points ; in other words, the S may react to global situations with relatively inadequate analysis of them into the essential component elements.

Turning to the affective life, the findings indicate that emotional experiences such as come to outward expression will be relatively few. Such as are indicated show the S to be of the more unstable, sensitive variety, tending towards the egocentric. Some capacity for more mature emotional control, that in which regard for the environment plays a role, also appears.

It is in respect to the S's inner, fantasy life that the findings are most telling. They show that (a) the S is capable of very much of this kind of experience ; (b) he may hold it in abeyance for a long time, bringing it out only under special stimulation ; (c) in some of it he expresses special fantasies peculiar to his own needs. The great amount of fantasy activity has to be considered also in the light of the already noted lowered accuracy of perception (form). Were this much lower than it is, the pattern would be that of personalities noted for autistic thinking. As the findings now stand, they are interpretable as no worse than an inventiveness which expresses values useful to the S personally, rather than some of more universal application. Individually studied, the fantasy responses are seen as more consistent with indications of a struggling activity than the resigned sort. These, in Rorschach experiments, have been found a good sign. They are characteristic of individuals fighting against, rather than surrendering to, their inner difficulties.

Confirmation of this struggle is found in another factor, namely, the large amount of self-will, of resistiveness, indicated in the test findings. In this respect the S shows himself notably above the average of his (the superior adult) group. Considered on the background of the great amount of inner living and of its overbalancing the affective trends (introversive personality), this self-will points to a resistance by the S to his own, innermost, unconscious trends. This self-will needs to be considered also in the light of evidence yielded in the test findings of a great amount of inferiority feeling. To what extent the resistance is compensatory for the inferiority consciousness is a question that can only be raised.

All the foregoing assumes special significance in view of several responses which are unique and unusual to the point of being wide deviations from those found in the healthy. They resemble rather the odd twistings of meaning produced in schizophrenia. Considering now the several findings in one *Gestalt* : much building of relationships, persistence, odd constructions—they form the paranoid picture. However, with percentage of form accuracy definitely within the range of the healthy average (even if below that of the S's group, the superiors), with logical orderliness in general maintained, and with no oversensitivity to the inconsequential values, one cannot speak here of any actual break-down of mental functioning. The pattern is, in fact, found in many of the superior group : schizoid (not schizophrenic) personalities. The paranoid trend can be detected, but control such as is reflected in perceptual accuracy (regard for the real world) and intellectual orderliness (obedience to logical canons) are maintained. Whether these individuals reap the full benefit of their rich potentialities is another question.

Recurring themes which may, on investigation, prove to have personal value for the S include : romantically coloured landscapes ; winter scenes ; scientific topics, more especially biological ; mine shafts, or allied material, in cross section.

Biographer's Note : Since the Rorschach findings were not in the biographer's hands when the Psychograph was written, they offer an entirely independent confirmation of some of the characteristics there described. Attention is particularly called to the following observations : the S's sensitiveness and egocentricity, together with some capacity for more mature emotional control ; his power to hold the expression of fantasy in abeyance ; his struggling activity ; his self-will and resistiveness ; the evidences of inferiority feelings ; and the paranoid pattern in some of this thinking.

23. PSYCHOGRAPH

R. W. White

1. *Press : Frequent Illness, Lack of Nourishment*

Oral Succorance Thema. Beginning at six weeks with measles, Earnst went through a series of illnesses so grave that his life was more than once in danger. The hypothesis that the problem of his nourishment was acute, that he suffered an early, severe, and long-continued oral frustration, seems from these circumstances alone highly probable, and is encouraged by the following indications.

a. Negative Cathexes : Aridity (p Lack : Water, Food). Among all the subjects, none made such frequent references to thirst and starvation as Earnst. His memories of childhood begin with a large china cup and a painful drinking 'for days, a sip at a time, to ease the feverish burning of my throat' (# 2). In the session devoted to Childhood Memories (# 3) the first item mentioned was a diarrhoea at the breakfast table, an image, perhaps, of the fugitive character of nourishment, no sooner gained than lost. When asked for a free association on thirst, he described the hot summer fields, likened them to 'a great desert,' and added, 'I have never forgotten . . . the intolerable thirst' (# 18). At the Conference (# 1) he saw in Picture A a man 'suffering from intense thirst,' who 'stands a chance of dying before long,' and on the Blank Card he projected a scene of the *desert.*

b. Positive Cathexes : Water, Food. Equally prominent are the references to food and drink. It did not escape his notice that the Es at the Conference had glasses of water (# 1a) ; and among his childhood memories was one of his brother cranking furiously at the chain pump and drinking the water 'in large quantities' (# 3, note). When at the age of nineteen he began a diary, the event was signalized by drinking to its health a glass of water drawn from the bathroom tap. There are few direct references to the S's own oral gratification, but in his fantasies provision is often obtained in generous measure. Thus, in the Thematic Apperception Test (# 18, Picture No. 11) he represents comfort as being administered chiefly through the agency of coffee and lunch, he does not omit feasting when mentioning a wedding (# 20), and in his story called 'Life Is Like That,' so clearly a fantasy of what life ought to be like, he introduces, quite without relevance, the preparation and eating of two lunches. The preoccupation emerges once more in the frequency and affective tone of words signifying food and drink in the Emotional Conditioning Test (# 17).

As the S gained in strength, grew more active, and found himself less utterly the helpless recipient of such slender favour as a hostile world seemed inclined to bestow, the unity thema evolved into a form which will be called the Provision Quest thema.

2. *Press : Oral Frustration, p Loss of Nourishment, Weaning*

Provision Quest Thema. The infant Earnst will not remain helpless. He will search for the stubborn nourishment, find where it is hidden, pull it forth, drag it up, and somehow still his thirsty craving — the mother's body shall yield up its treasure. Evidence as follows may be cited in support of this development. When shown the Blank Card at the Conference (# 1), Earnst, as already mentioned, projected a scene of the desert. On it he placed oil derricks, then saw two prospectors looking for gold fields, and concluded, 'To make the story amusing, it would be necessary to have them succeed in getting the gold.' At the Final Interview, he told, with mild amusement, of his attempt about three years ago to write a novel : 'A great scientist, a brave man, went to another continent in search of something or other. I'll be darned if I can remember what the object of it was. Can't remember what the great quest was for. Something very great.' Among the Memories was the stealing of some new, shiny spikes from a neighbour's woodshed (# 2), and a pursuit of butterflies so engrossing that he was very late to school (# 3). In both instances, the S had great difficulty in seeing that what he had done was wrong — in the latter case he stubbornly resisted the punishment — from which an extreme cathexis of the objects may be inferred.

But the most telling evidence came to light in the Thematic Apperception Test (# 18), where the Robbery thema was given three times, in a special form which will be discussed later.

In Earnst's conversation there occur rather frequently figures of speech derived from the Provision Quest thema. He speaks of '*grasping*' theories, of having no time to '*dig up*' more (# 1), refers to his '*appetite*' for adventures under tables (# 2), fancies he could '*dig up* something to do almost any time' (# 3), and represents himself as trying to '*drag out*' his memories (# 3).

The unity thema which has been proposed for this subject, namely :

p Deprivation (Barrenness) → Anxiety → Provision Quest was thus strenuously activated during the oral period. In the chart on p. 620 this thema was represented to have repeated itself with appropriate modifications at all stages of the S's development down to the present, the terms 'barrenness' and 'provision,' as his experience widened, assuming correspondingly broader meanings. But in the second line of the chart, and at the point we have now reached in reconstructing the S's history, a curious turn of the thema was introduced, unique to Earnst : the hypothesis was made that blame for oral deprivation was transferred from the mother to the father, who appeared as robbing and exploiting the mother for his own good, at the child's expense.

3. *Press : p Aggression (Predatory and Coercive Father), p Family Insupport : Ailing Mother, Family Discord*

Predator Thema. It is assumed that in some way the S came to imagine that his father had robbed his mother of the nourishment intended for himself. His mother, he says, 'became very frail' at the time of his birth or shortly thereafter. His father appears on the scene from the very start as a storming, dangerous man, of whose ungovernable temper the mother herself is afraid. At some point there took place in the child's mind a linking of thirst, the mother's frailness, and the father's aggression. That he witnessed parental intercourse and interpreted it as robbery for the sake of nourishment is suggested by some of the material. His own Aggression was now directed toward the exploiting father, but was rendered impotent by the latter's enormous strength : ' He was a great big man . . . none of us could have defended ourselves against him if he became violent ' (# 18).

In weighing the evidence for this thema, we shall first point out that some hypothesis is necessary to explain the transfer of the S's resentment from his mother to his father. It is difficult to believe that the present focalization of hostility upon father-figures prevailed also during early infancy. An extreme deprivation in the oral period, leading to an active quest for provision, may be expected to result in no little aggressive feeling toward the person responsible for the loss. The subsequent history of this feeling may lie along two paths. It may continue in the form of a marked, even when latent, Aggression toward mother-figures, sometimes even toward women in general, to whom will be attributed a selfish, withholding, faithless nature ; or, if affection for the mother cannot be foregone, the aggressive fantasies may be repressed with guilt feelings (intraAggression). A subject with a history of oral frustration such as Earnst's might be expected to show Aggression toward mother-figures, or guilt feelings, if not both.

In point of fact, traces of deeply latent Aggression against the mother have appeared in Earnst. In his story, ' Life Is Like That,' written with a view to publication some three years ago, he begins quite irrelevantly with an account of the death of his mother — the story being told in the first person — somewhat freely altered. ' She had been an invalid since my birth, and was on her way to Colorado for her health when a trestle collapsed under the train upon which she was riding. . . We couldn't see her because she was so mangled.' In two themes and a poem written at about the same time, the greed of women and their joy in possessions furnish Earnst with his topic. But on the whole the absence of Aggression against women was more remarkable than these small evidences, none of which are contemporary. Though his mother by her long absences deserted him more than once, though now his love affair is threatened with an unhappy ending, his predominant attitude toward women is one of Succorance (# 6,

12), and in none of the tests dealing with fantasy (# 10, 18, 19, 20, 21), did he avail himself of his numerous opportunities to express Aggression.

This apparently easy transcendance of Aggression against the mother would be less surprising if Earnst showed guilt feelings. But there is practically no evidence of these. Earnst is markedly extrapunitive ; he blames his country childhood (# 9), his father (# 18), his poverty (# 6, 17b), big business (# 5, 6), but seldom himself. Outspoken as well as latent Aggression against father-figures has been noted in practically every report. Something must have happened in the course of Earnst's career which absolved the mother from blame for his deprivations and restored her to his affection, while implicating as the true villain his already dreaded father.

It will be observed that the evidence so far examined does not constrain us to attribute the Predator Thema to the first few years of life. As a first approximation we may suggest that the events of late childhood and early adolescence sufficiently explain the S's current attitudes. His mother was gentle and nurturant, inspiring him to higher accomplishment ; his father, on the contrary, ill-tempered and violent, steadily sought to block the avenue to achievement and reduce him to hateful servitude as an exploited farm labourer. Earnst vividly describes his adolescent clashes with his father, and the bitterness and despair which they evoked. His present attitudes toward men and women faithfully reflect this epoch of his history.

Nevertheless, despite the attractive parsimony of this supposition, there is reason to assume that the Predator thema was engendered much earlier in the S's life. It is not likely that his parents changed their roles ; brutalities on the father's part and displays of affectionate care by the mother are reported well back into the earliest years. Furthermore, in spite of her nurturant attitude when at home, Earnst's mother by her protracted absences, beginning when he was six and continuing until her death, gave ample cause for resentment ; yet almost none of the usual precipitates of this feeling are discernible in the S's sentiments or fantasies.

The Predator thema, we believe, began as soon as the child experienced guilt feelings on account of his succorant desires and fantasied aggressions against his mother ; it served to project both his resentment and his self-blame on to a worse criminal, and forthwith functioned to exculpate the mother even in her desertions.

In the evidence which supports the Predator thema there is much to suggest a relatively early formation. We shall examine this evidence under two captions, the confusion of sexuality with aggression, and the thema of robbery. Our hypothesis is that the child witnessed or inferred parental intercourse and interpreted it in terms of his own fantasies as a robbery for the sake of nourishment ; this remembered experience served as a kind of basic image for the thema.

a. Sexuality as Aggression. The S was aroused to considerable emotion by the Spender poem (# 10). He called it 'plain miserable' and said, 'It indicates younger thoughts' ; later he declared, 'Certainly wouldn't ever want to see this again.' The affective reaction and the phrases used suggest that this poem, hinting the scene of parental intercourse, found its mark in the unconscious. Earnst was also displeased, in the Aesthetic Appreciation Test (# 10), by the picture of Cain murdering Abel, the dim outlines of which allowed him to perceive a violent sexual assault on a woman. The same confusion of sexuality and aggression reappeared in his story, 'Life Is Like That' : after the hero and heroine had been 'the victims of an age old urge,' the girl fainted and the hero thought she was dead. In the interviews, Earnst was apt to become defensive and indirectly aggressive (# 1a, 4) when questioned concerning his sexual life.

b. Robbery Thema. In the Thematic Apperception Test (# 18) the Robbery thema occurs three times (Pictures No. 14, F, 15). In two cases, the circumstances given for the crime suggest robbery from the mother's body : a family safe is to be robbed of money and jewels, and some money 'controlled by an old lady' is to be stolen. The thief is in all three instances an older man, variously described as 'unscrupulous,' 'shady,' and 'a miser.' The thema of robbery and exploitation appears repeatedly in Earnst's references to politicians, business barons, and persons in authority, father-figures against whom he feels a bitter resentment (# 1, 6, 7, 10, 19). The most striking evidence is furnished by his completion of 'The Minister's Black Veil' (# 19), wherein the huge, formidable, hell-roaring preacher is discovered in the course of the story to have been all along, despite his professions of goodness, a scoundrel. From the trunks and boxes which 'Preacher Dan' shipped away, it may be inferred that his crimes were robberies. This story, the writing of which the S enjoyed more than any other session (# 15), describes the very process which according to our hypothesis occurred in the child's mind, with the addition of a happy ending.

It was noticed in the Thematic Apperception Test (# 18) that another very unusual plot presented itself in connection with the Robbery thema. This was referred to as the thema of p Dominance : Coercion ; it will here be abbreviated as the Forced-Robbery thema. It may now be explained as a derivative of the Predator thema in the following manner.

4. *Forced-Robbery Thema*

The hypothesis is made that the S's fantasy of aggressive search into the mother's body was not free from guilt, his attitude toward her being quite naturally ambivalent. When he developed the Predator fantasy, he absolved himself from such of this guilt as remained by a further projection. It was his father who forced him to rob his mother, who put the guilt-burdened thoughts into his mind. This seems indeed a fantastic hypothesis, but not more peculiar than the plots of the S's stories to explain which it has been formulated. For in each story of robbery, the crime is planned by an older man for his own benefit, but executed, unwillingly, by a young man (the 'evocative object' in the picture), because of hypnotic influence or financial control by means of which the villainous elder forces him to serve as a tool. The same thema is given in the S's introspection on Picture D, where the factory owner is described as exploiting the workers and making them do anything he wants.

By a fortunate chance an original of one of Earnst's stories of robbery was discovered. In the session devoted to Present Dilemmas (# 5), he told how his former dance hall employer secured land for a golf course and dance place outside of Boston. This man obtained as his agent a poor fellow who was 'on the town,' and who bought the land at a ridiculous price by means of a pathetic plea addressed to the elderly widow who owned it. The agent then turned over the property to the true buyer at a handsome commission. If this story is compared with the S's plot for Picture No. 15, the similarity will be at once clear ; but there are two important changes. In the first place, the agent is turned into a false son — a motif already interpreted (# 18). Secondly, the fact that the agent benefits from the transaction is entirely suppressed. This significant alteration our hypothesis explains with special aptness : the Forced-Robbery thema, here reactivated, demands the *complete projection* of the S's fantasied attack on the mother ; it is *the father alone* who benefits. The S's departure from the plot of a story already known to him suggests unconscious steering toward a thema fundamentally more congenial.

The projection process which we assume to have produced the Forced-Robbery thema is, as already observed (# 18), not unlike the paranoid mechanism. The child Earnst interprets his father's behaviour toward his mother in the only terms known to his limited experience, those of his own guilt-laden thirsty desires. The further step is irresistibly easy. The father, whose power seems endless, is the sole source of those desires. Mother and son alike are the victims of his greed. A considerable identification with his mother now takes place ; it is she who starts the fashion of leaving the farm to escape the burden of its routine and the demands of the father, a move which is later to become Earnst's own burning preoccupation.

It is not probable that the four related themas so far discussed were ever clearly focussed in consciousness. As the child grew up they functioned as unconscious determining factors which influenced the outlines of new experience and gave to his personality certain salient features. Earnst was prepared to find the world hostile, extortionate, irrationally aggressive, too strong to invite counteraction ; he could hope at most for an occasional chance to draw on its slender fund of nourishment and sympathy by dint of exhausting effort. He was acquainted with constant anxiety. All of this may well have taken place by the time when the Oedipus thema is usually regarded as becoming acute, and it cannot be thought that the menace of castration or mutilation, if it occurred at all, would have added much to the threats already received from the father. We are inclined to believe that the Oedipus situation was conceived in terms of oral wishes. Earnst's childhood dreams were filled with figures of hungry animals about to bite him (# 3) ; his memories contain one of a hideous horse which he said 'used to bite women because women were afraid of him, and he used to bite me a lot' (# 3). These so-called 'castration symbols,' however, find their explanation in terms of the Predator thema as projections of oral desires rather than as fears of genital mutilation.

The formation of the Superego was conditioned accordingly. There was no identification with the monster-father (# 18, Picture No. 13), whose punishments, Earnst said in the final interview, were administered 'just after he lost his temper, otherwise he would have been chicken-hearted about it.' Misbehaviour which provoked the father's wrath, in other words, easily lost its guilty character (# 18, Picture G). Superego formation was accomplished entirely by identification with the mother and introjection of her precepts ; of her punishments he said, 'You knew if you did a thing that was bad enough you would get what was coming to you.' It is quite in accordance with this that Earnst started ahead of the bell in the Ethical Standards Test (# 14), a competition with other men, and condoned the sharp practices of a former employer with the words, 'In a business way it is perfectly all right.' His espousal of Christian Science (# 1 and note), despite its failure to cure his eye trouble, may be helped by his finding therein the counterpart of his own Superego structure — the Father-figure too abstract to evoke anxiety, the figure of 'Mother Eddy' warmly and humanly in the foreground.

When Earnst was old enough to go to school he was bullied and humiliated, a new form of deprivation. This evoked the n Infavoidance and the n Abasement, already well practised by his father and next older brother. The n Aggression and the n Counteraction had to be smothered until the intolerable world could be forgotten in story books. It was a critical moment in the S's life when he found the path of substitute achievement in school work. So stimulating was this to his self-respect that a few direct counteractions took place (# 2). The aggressive quest for provision now began to be crowned with success. But there was no possibility of expanding this success, no warming of the old embittered relations, no collapse of the hostile forces around him. Intellectual superiority was far from provoking affiliative tendencies in others. The S's mother, sole source of p Nurturance, died. He could not get along with his sister-in-law (# 2) ; he refused to be subordinate to his brother-in-law (# 3). His father claimed him for the farm and tried to block the pathway to achievement, the escape from a barren life. If the only solid satisfaction hitherto granted him was not to be lost, and he would have preferred suicide to losing it (# 18), he must escape from the whole scene and make his way in the world alone. To do this, Succorance, Anxiety and Abasement must all be forsworn, rigorously repressed ; the n Autonomy was forced to the front in a subject who really wanted to be loved and nurtured. Earnst now became, as he has since remained, 'a solitary organism trying to keep its balance and find sustenance in a difficult world' (# 5). He saved money, escaped from the farm, and put himself through college, as he said in his Autobiography (# 2), 'without receiving aid from anyone.'

In this drive for achievement, the S's sexuality has been comparatively neglected. There is considerable evidence for latent passive homosexuality. The S's behaviour in the session on Sexual Development (# 4), his enduring resentment at being questioned on homosexual feelings (# 17), and his unexpected susceptibility to hypnosis together with his subsequent denial of its success (# 11), contribute to the impression of a passive sexual fantasy under considerable repression. The discovery of such a fantasy in a S who shows definite evidences of paranoid projection accords well with Freud's theory concerning the nature of the paranoid reaction. It must be remembered, however, that Earnst's relations with men — his father, older brothers, and school friends — have always been dominated by a struggle for power with little hope of success. The Anxiety, Abasement, and Defendance which he showed in many of the sessions conducted by men, and indeed his paranoid tendency itself, may be derived from omnipotence fantasies rather than erotic ones, may in fact be stirred by the danger of abasive collapse, the compulsive quality of which arises out of the reactivated Predator thema with its figure of the terrible monster whose power is boundless. The S evidently experienced the greatest difficulty in leaving the farm contrary to his father's wishes. Our evidence does not permit us to decide whether a subtle erotic tie or an unconscious abasement to an omnipotent being determined this hesitation.

It is assumed that sexual development in this S was bound up with the fate of his chief latent need, the n Succorance. The virtual starvation of this need during adolescence served to restrict sexuality, which could express itself only through intraNurturance. To a large extent it is still so directed. External object-choice was guided by the possibility of a relation either succorant or nurturant. In his awkward sentence, 'I found that I had been missing girls a bit in the way of feminine companionship' (# 2), the S perhaps tried to convey his pleasure at discovering such a possibility, at learning that not all human relationships awakened the relentless fear of inferiority and abasement. The way seems clear to heterosexual adjustment.

The present and future problems which beset Earnst have less to do with sexuality than with his ego. The world may perhaps be kinder to his ln Succorance than to his self-respect. In marriage he may bring the former to a relative equilibrium, but it is not easy to imagine the conditions releasing him from the fear of inferiority. A modicum of success will tempt him to vast overcompensation ; failure, to unresigned bitterness, perhaps rebellion. His assets and liabilities in the presence of such temptations deserve scrutiny.

Assets. To survive without physical or mental mishap the press which bore on Earnst—early and continued illness, danger of death, extreme oral frustration, family discord, violence from father, brother and schoolmates, absences and death of mother, poverty and lack of support in his enterprises—one cannot be a weakling. Despite a slender physique and frequent exhaustion, he has always worked hard and incredibly long, his school work but a fraction of his total employment. Against odds overwhelming both physically and emotionally, a driving force has pushed him toward the goals of self-respect and successful achievement. As early as two years, he had learned how little the world cares for its children, had faced the disillusionment which sometimes wrecks a career at two-and-twenty. Not much later he sensed and started to pursue the virtue of self-reliance. At twenty-four he is well able to take care of himself, coolly realistic, his hopes and expectations tempered as if by a long seasoned wisdom. Further, least to be expected as the issue of his battered career, he shows a dispassionate detachment in regard to even the most irksome human press : condones the exploiting business baron, is fair to his successful rival in love, even excuses by reference to an unfortunate life the violent aggressions of his father. He knows well enough now what the paranoid patient never learns, that the world is not a designing one, it is simply impersonal.

Liabilities. These impressive assets would leave little room for liabilities, were they all securely won. But the unconscious yields stubbornly. A press which too strongly reactivates the father-image opens up the latent fund of resentment, bitterness and anxiety. A danger of exposed weakness thrusts the S quickly from humorous self-depreciation to strenuous Defendance and extrAggression. And surely the statement in his Autobiography (# 2), 'I think I shall eventually become . . . a great success or a dismal failure ; I couldn't be in between,' is no less candid than the tempered expectations which he revealed in later interviews. It will be hard for Earnst to accept the relative insignificance which is the lot of nearly everyone. These liabilities — a deeply-placed, over-compensating ambition, an undercurrent anxious feeling of inferiority, a latent aggression toward rivals in a competitive world — must be counted in weighing the S's equipment for the life ahead of him. He is working all the time to bring them under control of the Ego, to achieve conscious mastery. He succeeds when the atmosphere is friendly : in the Clinic when he is talking with an E who is sympathetic. He fails when the press touches off the old themas ; when strange Es around a table attack him with too personal questions and threaten to expose his faults. Which situation will the world of his immediate future resemble ? With what success will the Quest for Provision meet ? How fast and how far will Ego-mastery proceed ? Here is a complicated field of forces whose ultimate distribution it would be rash to foretell.

Chapter VIII
CONCLUSIONS

H. A. MURRAY

In writing up the biographical material we ventured further than our scientific consciences advised. We did not always hug the solid shore of fact, but sometimes let reflection take us out to sea — 'very much at sea,' will be our critics' comment. For us this loosening of constraints was a desirable refreshment which allowed the inclusion of impressions that were beyond the subtlety and flexibility of our abstractions. It did not delude us into thinking that we were voyaging on *terra firma*. But now we have come to the end of our explorations and must somehow make a landing, as far up the beach as possible ; there to write our findings in the sand, since we have nothing to carve in stone, our work being merely a prelude to more substantial studies.

As stated in the Preface, several of the sessions were controlled and conducted as true experiments pertinent to specific problems. These led to more or less definitive conclusions that constituted our least equivocal, though not necessarily our most fruitful, findings. But they have been reported in sundry journals and will not be included in the present volume. With these omitted, we now must ask ourselves : what remains that is worth recording ? Or, first : what kind of fruits can be reasonably expected from such an enterprise as ours ? The general procedure that we employed was comparable to that which for some time has been pursued with profit in clinical medicine. Patients admitted to a hospital are observed and tested by different specialists using a variety of methods, the findings are discussed and interpreted, and the final conclusions tabulated. When a sufficient number of cases of a certain nosological group have been so studied the data are assembled and submitted to the simplest statistical procedure ; the final results being of this nature : in 70 per cent of the cases symptom x was present ; in 83 per cent of the cases the concentration of z in the blood was below normal ; the majority of the patients were between 30 and 40 years of age ; 75 per cent showed definite improvement when drug y was regularly administered, and so forth. It is results of this general sort which have constituted the factual foundations of medicine ; and which will eventually constitute, according to my way of thinking, the foundations of personology. Our own program was inaugurated with the hope of obtaining such facts, but because of the small number of subjects, the marked diversities among them, and the continuous changes in procedure, our comparable data are not sufficient to form a basis for inductions that are valid. As has been stated, we were forced in the beginning of the research to choose between two courses : 1, to maintain our original concepts and procedures unchanged throughout ; or 2, to profit by our mistakes and better intuitions and improve our scheme before each new series of examinations. The latter plan was chosen because it was thought that the chief necessity for the present was a workable frame of reference and the attempt to construct such a frame should take precedence over other aims. We are satisfied with our decision because the original theory as well as the original schedule of procedure proved to be utterly inadequate ; and even though by adhering to them we should now be able to conclude with an imposing array of facts, the facts would be of little interest to a discerner. If, at the outset, we had had the wit to conceive of our final scheme, and had persisted with it until a hundred subjects had been studied, doubtless we should have obtained results that were relatively definite.

In medicine the facts are oriented, for the most part, about each disease entity, but in psychology there are numberless foci for correlation ; foci of different sorts but of almost equal interest. For example, one could investigate with benefit the correlations of poverty, of high social status, of the birth of a sibling during infancy, of press Insupport, of fantasies of carnivorous pursuit, of each variety of the Oedipus complex, of press Rejection, of inhibited Aggression, of physical ability, of early puberty, of prolonged masturbation, of artistic leanings, of philosophical interest, and so forth. It would be of some significance if certain common tendencies could be demonstrated statistically : that most subjects with this or that infantile complex later developed this or that cathexis or syndrome of needs. At present there are no conclusive data pertaining to such relations. There are only individual case records, theoretical conjectures and the unproved knowledge of intuitive observers.

Though, for the reasons given, we lack the facts necessary for statistical computations, we shall attempt to extract what sap we can out of the living trunk of our experience. As topics for discussion there are : the general plan, the conceptual scheme, the special procedures and, finally, the reflections provoked by a review of the case histories.

A. *General Procedure*. If we have made any contribution to personology it is probably to be found in our general plan of action : numerous sessions, of which as many as possible are controlled experiments, conducted by different examiners who work independently until at a final session they meet to exchange their findings and interpretations. By following this program a great deal of information is assembled which can be used to interpret the reactions of each subject in each experiment. In this way an experimenter is able to discover many of the operating variables, rather than having to content himself with crude, merely statistical results, such as are obtained in most experiments (which are performed on a large number of subjects about whose personalities nothing is known). What laws could have been discovered in chemistry if investigators had not ascertained what elements or compounds they were dealing with ? I venture the opinion that our program will eventually be most useful to the experimentalist, the very man who at first glance may find it least appealing. I say this because the ultimate goal of the experimentalist is to find for a psychological event its complete formulation, employing only those variables that are operating at the moment ; some of which are in the environment and some in the subject. Among the latter the pertinent traces of past events (conditionings) are to be numbered. These can only be discovered by biographical investigations. The traces are factors which must be included in the formulation since it is they that are chiefly responsible for the individual differences among responses to a given situation. To determine the role of the external factors the E changes them one by one (using, if possible, the same subjects); to determine the role of the internal factors the E changes these (by using a group of subjects that have and a group that have not a certain internal factor, or by previously evoking a certain internal factor in one group of subjects and not in another), maintaining the external situation constant. Ideally, these two modes of experimentation should be combined. But since it is not possible to do everything at once one must exercise a prejudice and push it to the limit, or adopt one approach after the other. Instead of attempting a detailed statement of the environmental factors, as Lewin has been doing so effectively, we concentrated on the inner variables. Actually, we attempted to determine a little of everything, which was much too much: the principal traces, the habitual reaction systems (need integrates), the common responses to a few specified situations, and, in two or three controlled experiments, the effect of certain situational changes (change of outcome, change of press). Though the result of spreading in this way was that we obtained nothing conclusive, we hit upon what seems to us to be the ideal method of experimenting with human subjects.

Another advantage of the method of multifarious sessions is that different aspects of the personality are brought to light by the different press that are presented. As a rule the analyst's patient or the experimenter's subject is confronted by a single situation only, one man and one routine. How he would have acted under different conditions or with an analyst or experimenter of another sex, age or temperament, is never known.

A third advantage of our plan is that it minimizes the errors which arise from the experimenter's personal viewpoint. The psycho-analyst is quick to note the projections and egocentric rationalizations of his patient, but it is difficult for him to be equally aware of his own. As few, if any, other analysts have seen his patient on equally familiar terms, there is rarely anyone who can confront his conclusions with a different set of facts.

In our experience, a well-managed discussion of a particular case by a number of trained examiners, each of whom has personally observed the subject, is as profitable as any other part of the program. Discussions of individual personalities, however, do not come to anything if there is insufficient agreement about the frame of reference, which is usually the case in the beginning. Hence, the early discussions almost invariably turn into arguments about terminology. At such times it is most important that each participant adhere to the principle that a concept (word) signifies either (a) a certain observed uniformity among events, or (b) an imagined process, the occurrence of which may be inferred when certain designated facts are found. The first question, then, should always be this : what are the facts ? and, in psychological discussions, the second may properly be : what conceptualized process do these facts suggest ?

Our plan provides the conditions that enhance the evolution of an effective policy of experimental action. Indeed, it so forces the growth of theory that one is apt to get an over-production of mere stop-gaps. The theory, however, is bound to be one which is intelligible to more than one mind and does not wildly overreach the observations ; since at the centre of collective attention there is always the individual case, the specific phenomenon to be interpreted ; and ideas that merely float aesthetically over life are brought soon enough to earth and torn to pieces by the rub of substantial facts.

Our system is not composed of highly abstract conceptions that spring from ideal notions at a distance from everyday experience, such as those based on physical models. Every technical term has been defined so as to call to mind a number of similar facts, subjective or objective ; each of which, on the other hand, is considered to be a manifestation of the process designated by the term. Thus, our scheme bound us to the data, and when we departed from them — which, let us confess, happened only too frequently

— we were thoughtless and not ignorant of accepted principles. Such was the method followed in constructing our framework; a method which seems less objectionable to us than its product, the theory, which now requires our attention.

B. *Conceptual Scheme.* We are prepared to heap criticisms upon our system but not in most instances to offer adequate substitute conceptions. However, others may succeed where we have failed, and with this expectation I shall list a few of the objections that have occurred to us. Let us start with 'need.'

i. *Need.* Needs are too abstract; and in the present study have been over-emphasized. Perhaps these are two ways of saying one thing, since a need can be made less abstract by adding certain limiting variables (which define more precisely its mode of expression and focus of application), and with each addition the emphasis on the need itself diminishes relatively.

Certainly the quantitative analysis of an epoch of personality into needs of various strength is an abstraction which disrupts the dynamic patterns that are characteristic of the individual. We believe now that this need analysis is necessary and that the method of scoring needs on a zero to five scale is satisfactory, but we do not believe that matters should be allowed to end here. In organic chemistry the first step in the identification of a compound is often an analysis which shows what elements are present and in what proportion. (This is analogous to need analysis.) The second step, however, consists of the determination, by appropriate methods, of the probable structure of the substance. This displays how the molecules are bound together. Later, the chemist may test the reactions of the compound to a variety of other compounds. (This is analogous to thema analysis.) At the end of our studies 'thema' was the concept that drew all things to it, but in the beginning it was 'need' which, being installed earlier, was in a more developed state and readier for use when it came to writing the biographies. Consequently, it was over-worked. The concept of need is dynamic, but the practice of listing and scoring needs gives them a somewhat static form, since it obliterates their relatedness to the environment (which is represented in thema analysis) and their relatedness to each other. The score on a need, as we assigned it, was a composite figure which served as an index of both intensity and frequency. If these attributes were separately marked to characterize distinctive epochs of the life history a more revealing longitudinal portrait would result.

We agree that the need categories are large, that they include a great variety of action patterns ; but this defect could have been remedied only by employing a much greater number of variables — more than unpractised experimenters could well begin with. It seems to me that most of the supplementary notions which the concept of need requires to prevent the psychologist from slipping into soft mud have been outlined (*vide* Chapter II), but since these elaborations were not firmly imbedded in thought during the entire season of our experiments they were not utilized very much in writing the biographies. To illustrate the utility of these supplementary notions I shall select the Aggression drive, which by itself conveys a vague impression of an irritable or angry force directed injuriously towards one or more objects in the external world. The notion of *overt* and *covert* needs distinguishes aggressive tendencies that are openly displayed from those that smoulder sullenly behind a barrier of restraint. The principal *actones* are divided into those that are physical (striking, pushing, kicking) and those that are verbal (cursing, insulting, blaming). If it is a matter of physical aggression, certain *zones* or organs of the body may be typically utilized (mouth for biting, nails for scratching, feet for kicking) or certain agency objects may be specially cathected (knife, gun, poison). The score on the variables Intensity, Endurance, Impulsion and Emotionality tells us whether Aggression comes as a sudden violent storm, or as a coolly calculated piece of malice. The conceptions of *fusion* and *subsidiation* call attention to the relation of this need to other needs. When compounded with Autonomy, for example, we have rebellious attacks on authority or violent freedom-seeking struggles. When compounded with Dominance we have ruthless self-assertion or the use of threats to control others. In the service of Acquisition,

Aggression takes the form of forceful seizures and hold-ups. *Sociocentric* Aggression describes behaviour which operates legally in the service of one's culture (the Nation or a recognized institution of the Nation). Here, the individual is usually supported by others and his activity is directed against public enemies (foreign soldiers, revolutionists, criminals and misbehaving children). Aggression based upon conscience — ideals that are more elevated than those which govern social practice — may be called *Superego* Aggression (ex : Zola's *J'Accuse*). *Asocial* or culpable Aggression includes all acts which do not conform to the tpmo scheme (*vide* p. 136) of the social environment. These are punishable. Aggressive behaviour may be *initiatory* or *retaliatory* — unprovoked or provoked by press Aggression. Finally, the *nature of the negatively cathected objects* towards which Aggression is typically directed is usually a matter of importance. We may, first of all, distinguish : things, animals, humans, institutions and ideas ; the principal human classes being superiors and inferiors, males and females. Further particularization of the environment may be had by utilizing the concept of thema (need integrate, complex), since this defines the press of the stimulating object. There is a great variety of press for Aggression : assault, coercion, restraint, belittlement, accusation, pretentiousness, acquisitiveness, any sort of asocial behaviour, and so forth. Among cultivated people a common form of verbal activity is *ideological* Aggression (criticism or censure directed against sentiments, political principles, literary judgements, scientific theories or religious beliefs). As soon as we learn to analyse ideologies into variables of psychological significance, we shall be better prepared to understand in individual cases the significance of ideological cathexes. In our studies only one distinction was made : that between sentiments and ideas which are conservative (long established, accredited, in harmony with the status quo, commonly expressed, held by the subject's parents etc.) and sentiments which are radical (new, revolutionary, supported by a small minority, unaccredited, contrary to parental teaching etc.). Lacking the necessary variables into which an ideology can be resolved we were forced to employ common terms : Republican Party,

Catholic Church, Communism, Cubism, Pragmatism, and so forth.

A need becomes less vague and abstract as soon as some of the above-mentioned defining attributes have been distinguished, and it should be possible for a seasoned psychologist to do so. We would recommend, for example, that the common modes, fusions and subsidiations of each need be recorded (as an almost necessary concretization). At first hearing, this suggestion may appear as the prescription of another inexpedient elaboration to confuse the concept-crammed head of the psychologist, but, in my opinion, this is not so. For, once the principal forms of need integration (compounds) have been properly distinguished and memorized, it is easier when witnessing behaviour to perceive examples of them than it is to analyse a reaction into separable elements (needs) at the moment of its appearance.

ii. *Trait.* Before dismissing the topic of motivational forces I am persuaded by the arrival of G. W. Allport's just published volume [1] to say a few words about the theory of traits as an alternative to the theory of needs. I can do no more than record first impressions, since I have not kept abreast of the trait theory's recent developments and time prohibits a sufficient study of Allport's detailed and carefully reasoned argument.

Glancing over our list of variables it will be seen that a fair proportion (Intensity, Impulsion, Conjunctivity, Emotionality and so forth) are qualities which, if repeatedly exemplified by a subject, would undoubtedly be assimilated to the category of traits. Also, by slight modifications in definition, the remaining variables — which we have termed needs — could be subsumed under the same heading. They would fall into a special class : 'motivational traits.' Thus, our work could be represented, by a little terminological juggling, as a study of personality traits.

Can it be true that the differences between the trait theory and

1. Allport, G.W. *Personality*, New York, 1937. I regret that limitation of time makes it impossible for me to read and mull over Professor Allport's theories before getting the present volume to the publishers, for I would enjoy nothing better than the opportunity to comment on the many points of agreement as well as on the few points of disagreement.

the need theory is merely verbal? Are similar phenomena designated by the terms 'trait of orderliness' and 'need for Order,' 'trait of sociability' and 'need for Affiliation,' 'trait of reclusion' and 'need for Seclusion' and so forth? It would seem so, since, according to theory, both trait and need are hypothetical 'somethings' in the organism which direct behaviour. Let us see whether any valid differences between trait and need can be discovered.

I am struck, first of all, by a difference in approach. Allport starts with the word 'trait' (as he does with the words 'personality,' 'attitude,' 'sentiment,' 'interest'), attempts to discover, by examining the history of its usage, what it has meant in the past and then comes to his own definition. In contrast to this, my method has been to start with concrete phenomena (objective and subjective), attempt to distinguish separable variables and then give each defined uniformity a suitable name. Allport has had his eye set for recurrences and consistencies; whereas my primary aim has been to formulate a single man-environment event. To do this the event had to be analysed into phases or processes. Of the latter the general directedness (aim, goal) of the subject's activity seemed especially significant. This led to the concept of need, which was considered to be but one of many operating variables. The difference in our points of departure, however, turns out to be unimportant since we end in approximately the same place.

According to Allport a trait is an internal state (readiness), the existence of which is inferred because of the repeated recurrence during an individual's life of actions having the same general significance. The concept calls attention to consistencies of conduct which are supposed, with reason, to depend on something stable in the organism. One cannot properly speak of a trait until one has observed a number of similar or equivalent bits of behaviour. Almost every conceivable consistent attribute of a personality is a trait. There are *individual* traits which but few people possess and there are *common* traits which are shared to some extent by almost everyone. Some traits are *motivational* (comparable to 'needs') and some *instrumental* (comparable to 'modes'). To include our studies within this frame it is only necessary to state that we limited ourselves to *common* traits, and of these emphasized particularly those that were *motivational*. We do not deny the existence or importance of *individual* and *instrumental* traits, but since one cannot study everything at once, one might just as well start by studying the more common tendencies. It would take years to study the varieties of dispositions (individualities) that result from different compoundings (fusions and subsidiations) of common needs. Chemistry, for example, has already discovered over seven hundred thousand distinguishable substances; perhaps a fourth of which are compounds of a very few elements: mostly hydrogen, oxygen, carbon and nitrogen.

There appear to be but two points of difference between a need and a common motivational trait: 1, the former is a momentary process which may operate *but once* in a man's life, whereas the latter is a *recurrent* reaction pattern; and 2, the former is an internal process with a *subjective correlate* which may or *may not* manifest itself directly or overtly, whereas the latter is a demonstrable attribute from which an internal condition *with no subjective correlate* is inferred. The first point of difference is important to us in so far as it permits the designation of a trend regardless of whether it has ever occurred before or ever will again. A baby has a personality according to the need theory, but none according to the trait theory (for it has no consistent habits). Since our conception of personality is that of a long succession of events, each of which may be partly characterized by naming the subject's trend (need), we should hold that one can only arrive at the abstract notion of a consistent motivational readiness (trait) by observing the frequent repetition of similar or equivalent trends. The more often a given need recurs the more of a trait it becomes; and, contrariwise, a need that is evoked seldom cannot be a trait. Since in studying a personality one always does look for consistencies, it is to be expected that the list of recurrent needs will correspond to the list of motivational traits. Thus, the first point of difference may in practice disappear. The second point of difference, however, is more radical.

'Trait' was originally used to refer to an objective attribute of conduct, and only lately has it been made to stand for an inner disposition. 'Need,' on the other hand, has been commonly employed in the past to designate a subjective experience (a desire, or feeling of want), and not until recently has it been defined on the basis of objective findings. For this reason, the words 'trait' and 'need' start the mind running in different directions. To a detached observer, the term 'trait of sexuality' may seem appropriate to describe an ardent and lustful lover, but the man himself, driven from his social duties by erotic desire, would hardly think that this was an adequate expression for his experience. (And, of course, it could not be used to describe a boy's first excursion into the realm of sex, since at that time no pattern would have become established.) A preference for one term or the other is an illustration of word-magic, since it has a realistic behavioural consequence : the psychologists who think of personality as a congruence of inter-dependent traits and those who think of it as a temporal pattern of inter-dependent 'drives' focus attention on different phenomena, use different methods and end with different accounts. Thus, people being what they are, it *does* make a difference what word is selected. Though the conscious definitions are similar, the unconscious and overtly pragmatic definitions are dissimilar. Dynamic ('drive') psychologists pay attention to the observable traits — even those that are most eccentric — but they are not content with bare facts. They are impelled by an insistent compulsion to analyse each trait and to discover its derivations. To do this they explore consciousness ; and, not being satisfied with this, devise methods that will change the state of consciousness in such a way that factors habitually eliminated (unconscious) will emerge. It must be admitted that trait psychologists, concentrating as they do upon what is manifest, remain on firmer ground ; but this ground is obvious to all (the subject included). The dynamicist starts there and, let us hope, can always return there ; but if an understanding is to be had of why and how an observed response 'wins the moment,' it is necessary to study consciousness (with its clues to unconsciousness) in order to discover the numberless interactions, conflicts, and integrations of which the given response is a resultant. Depth psychology flowered because trait psychology failed to 'explain' phenomena, failed to get at the root of things. Nineteenth-century psychiatry is an example of trait psychology. It has proved insufficient.

According to my prejudice, trait psychology is over-concerned with recurrences, with consistency, with what is clearly manifested (the surface of personality), with what is conscious, ordered and rational. It minimizes the importance of physiological occurrences, irrational impulses and beliefs, infantile experiences, unconscious and inhibited drives as well as environmental (sociological) factors. Hence, it does not seem fitted to cope with such phenomena as: dreams and fantasies, the behaviour and thought of children or savages, neurotic symptoms (morbid anxiety, phobias, compulsions, delusions), insanity and creative activity (artistic or religious). It stops short precisely at the point where a psychology is needed, the point at which it begins to be difficult to understand what is going on.

Allport insists very properly upon the concrete individuality of every human being, but the dynamicists go further. They insist upon the concrete individuality of every episode of a human being. Thus, they provide a place for inconsistencies: random impulses, sudden regressions and sudden creative advances. Let us grant that there are no identities. But if one can find similarities between two events of a single personality (as the word 'trait' affirms), one can find similarities between two events of different personalities. If this were not so, comparison—and hence science—would be impossible. Experimentation would be futile. No laws could be discovered or demonstrated. Every sparrow would have to be separately identified, named and intuitively understood. To be recognized and loved uniquely, this is what everybody longs for in his soul. And the almost inevitable partial frustration of this craving has produced, for the soul's assuagement, the conception of a personal God who knows the fate even of every sparrow. ('Nobody knows the trouble I seen, Nobody knows but Jesus'). Someday Science may create this God—if, as Claude Bernard predicted, it weds with Poetry. But now Science is ruthless of particularities; which explains why it can be no more than an accessory to wisdom.

iii. *Classification of Needs.* To return once more to the concept of need, a word should be said about the problem that gave us as much concern as any other. I refer to the classification of needs. Some sort of classification seemed necessary, as necessary as the classification of elements in chemistry, even though we did not propose to regard all the separable drives as basic instinctual units. We merely wanted to distinguish and name commonly observed general trends (needs, desires, goals), irrespective of what specific modes were employed or what specific objects were cathected. The fact that we were not able to find unequivocal criteria for setting up the categories is one of the weak points in our system. We used very much the same indices as McDougall has enumerated, but without satisfaction: differentiation according to distinguishable press, distinguishable emotions, distinguishable vectors and distinguishable effects (in terms of survival or inner satisfaction). The last index was considered crucial, the others merely helpful. Furthermore, we considered the most distinctive forms of animal behaviour as well as the exaggerated 'pure' tendencies exhibited by the insane. The kind of difficulty that is encountered may be illustrated by starting with any one of the above-mentioned criteria. Take fear, for example. At first blush, physical danger (press), fear (emotion), abience (vector) and security (effect) comprise a more or less unitary thema or reaction equation. But fear (anxiety, apprehension, worry) is found in many other combinations. It is set off by other press: the possibility of starving, of catching an infectious disease, of becoming bankrupt, of being ostracized, of being imprisoned, of failing in an examination, of losing a beloved object. And it leads to a variety of actions: self-concealment, walking very cautiously on the edge of a precipice, begging for food, going to the doctor, wearing rubbers, getting to the office early, observing the proprieties and inhibiting criticizable tendencies, seclusion, reticence, studying late at night, nursing a sick child. The goal in all instances may be termed 'security,' but it takes different forms : physical security, economic security, social or prestige security, security from guilt and inferiority feelings, the security of beloved objects and so forth. When man is faced by a sudden critical situation he is apt to act, as an animal acts, instinctively ; in which case a common rather clear-cut action pattern may be displayed. But in much of his everyday behaviour there is a most confusing mixture of emotion, actone, sub-need, need and effect. Most of the difficulties can be cleared up by a thorough analysis of the subsidiations, but, in our experience at least, problems may remain which defy intuition and logic. However, this is a complicated matter and until we are prepared to offer a classification that is clearly better than the one we have expounded we have deemed it advisable to let things stand as they are.

iv. *Cathexis*.. A necessary complement of the need concept that was not given its full weight in this study is the concept of cathexis. This refers to the evoking power of an object. Though 'cathexis' may be applied to an object on a single occasion, it is often used to indicate a recurrent phenomenon. Hence, the question may be asked : what objects are consistently cathected by each need ? By enumerating them the specificities of the drives are made apparent. Our practice has been, when scoring needs, to view them as diffuse general traits, and to give a high rating if the need in question was evoked frequently by many and varied objects. Here the cathexes were of minor significance. When, however, it was found that a certain need in a subject was *diffusely low* but *focally high* — that is, the need was intensely excited by one or two objects but not at all by others — then it became important to record the cathexis (something rather special that had evoked a commonly dormant need). It appears that some people are characterized by well-defined specificities — like Kuno Kursbold who slew the lion but fled from women and apples —, and some by marked generalities of attitude ; but most are in the middle — they have a moderate amount of diffuseness and a moderate amount of focality. In distinguishing these average people, focalities (enduring cathexes) are as important as generalities (needs). This fact immediately suggests a type of questionnaire which would be better than or supplementary to the one we used. Instead of asking questions about emotions and needs (ex : Are you easily irritated ? Are you apt to comply readily to rules and regulations ? Do you accept invitations to social gatherings ? etc.), one might ask questions about objects. Such a questionnaire could be modelled on some of the already devised attitude or annoyance questionnaires. It would consist, let us say, of a long list of commonly liked and disliked objects or situations which the subject would be asked to score on an affective basis. For example, the subject might be asked : Which of the following objects or conditions arouse anxiety (or irritation, good-feeling, compassion, disgust, etc.) and to what extent ? In this way the number and intensity as well as the nature of the cathexes could be roughly determined ; and this would provide a measure of the generality as well as of the specificity of each need.

According to our view, however, the naming of the specifically cathected object is insufficient. It gives psychological information only to the man who is acquainted with it and can discern intuitively its dynamic attributes (press). It is the psychologist's function rather than the reader's to make this analysis. It is not important to know that a certain subject likes an object named John Doe, but it is important to know that he likes a person of lower status who praises him, complies with his wishes and adopts his sentiments (press Deference).

For conveniences all the press cathected by adient needs may be put into one class, and all those cathected by abient and contrient needs into another. The ideological objects, however, should be treated separately, since it is desirable to be able to consider together the moral principles, aesthetical standards, scientific theories and religious conceptions which the S likes, praises, accepts, practices, attempts to develop further, and those which he dislikes, belittles, ridicules, censures or scornfully discards. In this way most of the subject's sentiments will be recorded.

v. *Social Memberships.* There is a widespread tendency among human beings to aggregate and form a group about a common focus (interest) : a locality (hamlet, village, town, city), an elementary need (food, security, conquest), an avocation (agriculture, commerce, construction, government, exploration, warfare, education, therapy, art, science), an ideology (political creed, aesthetical principle, scientific theory, religious or philosophical ideal). Each constellating process is initiated or furthered by a leader who functions as the focus or as the personalization of the focus. A given grouping may be due chiefly to the magnetism, assurance and will-to-power (Dominance) of the leader, complemented by the insecurity, perplexity, suggestibility and need for guidance (Deference) of the crowd ; or it may be due chiefly to the goal and the mode of attaining it seductively advocated by the leader, complemented by the herd's conscious or unconscious need for just that activity and just that end. Every social constellation, then, involves an aggregation of conforming people with admiration for and compliance to a leader (n Deference), and a distinguishable complex of aims (the goals of other needs) which are promoted by group action. For the good of the group, a member must inhibit the impulses of his Autonomy drive, and direct his Rejection and Aggression towards outsiders. Affiliation and Nurturance are strongly encouraged and Succorance is accepted. Evidently the group is an object which absorbs some of the subject's Narcism. Whether it is the members, the leader or the activity (interest or ideology) of the organization that attracts and binds cathexis, the object, taken as a unit, is for the 'good member' something 'higher' than himself (if only because it involves more people). Furthermore, it provides a channel for his energies. He works for the advancement of the group, acts as its advocate, is elated and feels enlarged when it succeeds, is depressed and feels diminished when it fails ; he is hurt or annoyed when it is criticized, does not enjoy jokes at its expense and is ready to attack other groups that oppose it. Sometimes his very life is in the Cause. In extreme cases he may die for it. If this transfer of Narcism involves the acceptance of an already current interest or ideology as well as co-operation with other members and deference to its leaders, the phenomenon may be termed *sociocentrism*, and the group with which the subject has identified himself may be termed an *affiliate*. (To complete the scheme we might call a group that is attacked by the subject a *rejectate*.) It is clear in such cases that the group belongs among the subject's cathexes of Affiliation, but it may be distinguished from other objects — a single friend, let us say — by the fact that it represents a goal (or a complex of goals), which usually involves the n Achievement in a sociocentric form.

This aspect of the personality is particularly significant to the sociologist who concerns himself with groups and institutions ; since he can get a quicker understanding of a personality by ascertaining his affiliates and rejectates than by inquiring into other matters. This is due to the fact that his thorough study of the nature of the different groups has provided him with 'knowns' by which to judge the 'unknown.' The psychologist, on the other hand, being less interested in social institutions, understands the individual better than any group with which he is affiliated. Hence, he can learn more about the group from the subject than he can learn about the subject from the group.

We must agree that among the positive and negative cathexes of a subject the psychologist should take special note of the affiliates and rejectates. A list of affiliates for one subject might be something of this nature : Hillbilly High School, Eutopia College, Epselon Society, Beansboro Boating Club, Pacific Association of Druggists, Republican Party, All Souls Church. The question is : what is the scientific value of such a list ? Unless I am mistaken, it has some value to a sociologist. To a psychologist, however, it has value only after each group has been analysed into meaningful factors. The question is : why did the S join this group rather than another, and after joining it, what did it mean to him and what did it do to him ? Naturally, the groups are important in the sense that if one wanted to find this particular subject on a summer Saturday afternoon one might guess that he was at the Boating Club. The subject's affiliates, as listed above, are concrete items — like the number of his house, size of his collar, name of his tailor. But as such, they are irrelevant to science. What the psychologist expects from the sociologist is a pertinent analysis of each important institution into significant variables. There is, first of all, the purpose or aim of the group, which should be analysable into needs (assuming that needs have been properly distinguished), and second the nature of the scheme (ideology) which is being advocated to satisfy these needs. Then there is the structure of the group, the degree and type of organization. And, finally, there is the group as a compound of press and object-abilities impinging upon each individual member. Are the other members sociable (p Aff) or protective (p Nur) ? Are the dues high (p Acq) ? Is there much coercion or restraint (p Dom) ? Is one entertained (p Exh) or instructed (p Exp) ? Does the building serve as a quiet retreat (p Claustrum) ? and so forth. Until such an analysis is achieved, the psychologist must discover from each S the significance to him of each affiliate and each rejectate.

We cannot, of course, agree with the sociologist who maintains that a personality is the sum of its social memberships. ('There are more things in heaven and earth, Horatio . . .') The greater part of a person's life is private and subjective ; much of it is related directly to Nature and much is either casually or informally social or involves only one other person. And this includes the 'joiners.' Also there are many people, particularly women, who have no or very few institutional attachments. Has the anchorite no personality ? Moreover, many social memberships are half-hearted, perfunctory or insincere and others merely inherited affiliations (ex : Church membership). Even in the case of loyal and representative members of an organization one does not know whether they were like the others before they joined or became so afterward. An institution may strengthen some personal tendencies and weaken others. Moreover, to be told that a man belongs to a certain society gives us no information as to whether he is taking a leading role in shaping its policies (ex : Hitler) or is deferentially following the others. How are revolutions within a group to be explained if not by reference to the psychology of the anti-group leaders ? Finally, membership does not characterize the personality if the group has not already been formulated in psychological terms and as yet no group has been so formulated ; and even were such a formulation to be made it would be found that it did not apply to all the members. An institution 'means' one thing to one man and something else to another.

vi. *Psycho-analysis*. No doubt there will be many to tell us that our hypothetical reconstructions of infancy, as illustrated by the psychograph, were not supported by sufficient facts, that they were too speculative to be of significance ; and, no doubt some critics will add, there was too much Freudian theory. To this we can only say that we obtained what facts we could within the limitations imposed by time and our ability to devise appropriate techniques. The data were meagre compared to what a psycho-analyst obtains as a basis for his conclusions, but we thought that it would be an unprofitable expenditure of time merely to portray the skin of our material without attempting to get at the heart and bowels of it. We regarded our reconstructions as questionable hypotheses which might nevertheless be useful as guides for future searches. Since we were of the opinion that to-day psycho-analysis, in conjunction with its several derivatives, provides the best orientation for the study of human personality, it was natural for us to adopt this point of view. Furthermore, since four of us had been practising Freudian psycho-analysis, the group as a whole were partial to and better acquainted with the theories of this school. But perhaps the most potent reason for selecting the Freudian approach was that we wanted, first of all, to investigate personality as a series of genetical experiences, and Freud's theories seemed to provide, if not the open sesame, the only comprehensive and coherent scheme for dealing with the events and fantasies of infancy.

I have explained elsewhere (*vide* p. 282f) why the genetical approach seemed particularly important at the time. If we had adopted the point of view that everything really significant can be found in the existing circumstances — and here one should include the subject's aims and expectations — then we should have had to depend more on Jung, Rank and Lewin for guidance. But to apperceive the chief variables in a person's present situation, to understand his perplexities and conflicts, and to surmise correctly the direction in which he is heading is a task for only the most experienced and intuitively expert psychologists. It did not seem wise for us to put all our eggs in this basket. It seemed better to distribute them and devote a fair proportion of time to a study of personal and social background with the expectation of discovering consistent patterns that would aid us in understanding present tendencies and states. Here our experience confirmed our original opinion : that the Freudian system has more resolving power than any other with which we are acquainted. Among Freud's numerous contributions the following proved most useful to us :

a. The theory that there are unconscious processes influencing consciousness and behaviour which resemble conscious processes.

b. The hypothesis that among active unconscious processes are to be found the traces of infantile themas or similes of these themas.

c. The observation that there are certain classical infantile themas that are especially influential in determining development ; the prevalence of these themas being due to the universality of certain conditions and activities : birth, sucking, weaning, bowel training, the presence of a maternal and a paternal figure, the birth of another sibling, the lack of sexual information, the necessity of being parted from the parents, and so forth.

d. Facts pertaining to the sexual instinct, its combinations, permutations, sublimations ; and the barriers that are set up against it. Here we must include the erotization of non-sexual tendencies. If Freud's theories — and terminology ! — had not shockingly arrested the world's interest, generations might have passed before an academic psychologist was true and bold enough to give sex more than aloof and perfunctory consideration.

e. A theory which draws attention to the eternal conflict between an individual and his culture; which shows how the culture becomes internalized (Superego) and thus engenders battles 'within the cave' which split (Hamletize) the personality and, in many instances, produce neurotic illness.

f. The theory of repression and the enumeration of various modes by which repressed tendencies commonly find disguised expression.

g. The concepts of projection and rationalization.

When it comes to a criticism of the Freudian system, I must speak for myself as, at this point, the opinion of the staff was by no means unanimous. In my judgement a critique should include the following points:

a. The confusion of fact and theory (ex: meaningless statements such as: 'the amount of libido is always constant').

b. The distorting effect of pan-sexualism (ex: referring all anxiety to castration anxiety).

c. The neglect of the muscles, arms and legs and the necessities and pleasures of locomotion (the conquest of gravity) and the manipulation of objects (power over substance). Freudian psychology is limited to the torso.

d. The absence of concepts to account for Ego structuration and the pleasures of will and self-mastery; the neglect of the needs for Achievement (power in general), Dominance (power over men) and Recognition (high status, honours, fame); the confusion of the Ego Ideal (standard of success — mostly excitatory) with the Superego (standard of morality — mostly inhibitory). Freudian theories do not recognize the fact that fear (cowardice, 'sissy') is more shameful than lust or aggression, and, therefore, must above all processes be inhibited.

e. The conceptualization of fear and its behavioural modes (riddance, flight, avoidance and inhibition) as an affect merely, rather than as an instinctual tendency on a par with sex and aggression.

f. The misinterpretation or neglect of the feelings and reactions which we have subsumed under the n Inviolacy: pride, self-respect, reticence ('shell'), independence, individuation, defence of status, self-vindication, fighting for honour's sake, scorn of weakness, counteractive attempts to regain status after traumas and defeats. These reactions are only partially accounted for by the concept of Narcism and the concept of Ego defence.

g. The notion that normal development can be explained entirely on the basis of a series of enforced frustrations which necessitate the selection of 'higher' substitutes. All individuals do not go through life 'tied to their mother's apron strings' with backward glances at the joys that have been denied them. Children clearly exhibit a tendency to seek change, to wander, explore, test their powers of mastery, act like 'grown-ups,' gain self-reliance and creatively conceive of things that are 'higher' than anything that their parents ever taught them.

h. The derivation of the general from the particular (ex : all attraction from sexual attraction, the emotion of love from localized tactile sensations, character traits from the hypersensitivity of one or another zone, hatred of authority from the Oedipus complex, and so forth).

i. The disposition to over-simplify, which leads analysts to overlook many reaction systems (Acquisition, Rejection, Deference, Nurturance, Succorance etc.) that require attention.

j. The neglect of what the ordinary man thinks of as the major factors in his psychology : abilities and disabilities, tastes, sentiments and social attitudes, friendships and affiliations, conscious interests and religious aims.

k. The minimization of sociological factors : local mores, cultural patterns, group interests, and the accepted social status of the individual.

vii. *Neglected Variables*. There will be many psychologists, no doubt, who will fail to find among our variables some favourite traits of their adoption, but it can hardly be said that our supply was limited in number or variety. We were not contained by any one system. We did not, like the catbird, lay our eggs in another's nest. Rather did we rob others to fill our own nest ; and if there had been any more eggs to sit on some of them would not have been given heat enough to hatch. We found that we had to become very familiar with a set of variables before we could, without embarrassing our minds, add more. For instance, there were but ten traits on our list when we studied the first group of subjects and over forty when we studied the fourth. In further studies it should be possible to hold in mind a greater number. It might be well to add certain attributes of mental activity : fine (subtle, sensitive, delicate, precise) as opposed to coarse (obvious, crude, rough, gross), and rich (abundant, expansive, inclusive) as opposed to meagre (scanty, thin, condensed). Taken together with Creativity, Conjunctivity, Intensity, and Sameness, these variables might serve reasonably well to define the formal qualities of intellection. Speed of reaction and tempo might well be included, as well as a variable which takes account of will power (strength of character, self-control, ability to inhibit, solidity, dependability).

We failed in several notable instances to bring our variables into accord with some useful concepts proposed by other psychologists. For example, Jung's formulation of four functions [1] — thinking, feeling, sensation and intuition — is very useful at times in distinguishing certain types of individuals, as well as in formulating some common internal conflicts, but we have not been able to assimilate it to our own scheme. First, because it is not clear enough to us ; second, because, by itself, it seems insufficient ; and third, because it overlaps, though it cannot be made to fit, our own conceptions. But because it seems to say something important it cannot be dismissed altogether. Our own modified version of the classification may be briefly summarized. The function of Thinking has a fairly definite aim : to make explicit discriminations, to name, define, classify and relate, in order to construct logical formulations that will truly represent and make intelligible selected aspects of the order of nature, subjective or objective (Spranger's Theoretical Attitude' [2]). This is covered by our need for Understanding (a not too happy term). The function of Feeling may be roughly described by such words as goodwill,

1. Jung,C.G. *Psychological Types*, New York,1924.
2. Spranger,E. *Types of Men*, Halle,1928.

sociability, friendliness, affection, sympathy, tenderness, love (Spranger's 'Social Attitude'). Its effect is to establish harmonious social relations (solid family life, enduring friendships) and to bring together those who 'belong' together, as well as to reject those who do not 'belong.' This is covered by the three positive social needs : Affiliation, Deference, Nurturance. The function of Sensation, in our opinion, is concerned with the enjoyment of sensuous impressions, bodily and emotional excitement, novelty, thrills, dramatic events, and aesthetic delights (some of which may be classed under Spranger's 'Aesthetic Attitude'). These activities are covered rather inadequately by the needs for Sex, Sentience, Play, Exhibition and Change. Intuition we do not recognize as a separate function. Any function may operate intuitively ; that is to say, by unconscious inferences. In its place we should substitute Action, the importance of which is minimized in all of Jung's writings. By Action we mean the practical and effective manipulation of the physical or social environment, its aim being tangible achievement, power and possession (Spranger's 'Economic and Political Attitudes'). These tendencies could be subsumed under Achievement, Acquisition, Dominance and Aggression. Thus, we have four common types : the theorist (scientist, generalizer, systematizer, obsessional thinker, rationalist, logician, philosopher, writer of programs and principles), the humanitarian (kind parent, considerate friend, co-operative associate, dependable party man, tactful host, devoted physician, priest, as well as faithful lover), the sensationist (pleasure-seeker, enjoyer, sensualist, playboy, romantic adventurer, performer, actor, lover of form and elegance, sensitive appreciator, as well as artist) and the practical man of action (farmer, labourer, technician, soldier, business man, efficiency expert, political executive, surgeon, explorer, bishop). Jung has emphasized Thinking and the various conceptual attitudes towards life ; Freud has maximized Sensation and the craving for primitive erotic expression ; and Adler has stressed Action and the will to power. It has been left for American sociologists to concentrate on the external aspects of Feeling : imitation, conformity, co-operation, group membership, social status. This formulation of the functions does not exactly correspond or do justice to Jung's vivid though elusive exposition, but there are reasons for departing from his scheme, — reasons which cannot be properly discussed in the space at my disposal.

C. *Methods.* Of our technical procedures the series that were termed Projection Tests (*vide* p. 529), which were designed to evoke imagery and fantasy, brought to light the most significant data. It was the data which most often revealed emotionally logical connections between past events and present behaviour, and thereby enabled the experimenter to find a formulation which would give meaning to otherwise disparate facts. In all projection procedures the subject is asked to give shape to ambiguous material. The Thematic Apperception Test, for example, calls for stories suggested by a series of dramatic pictures. To do this the subject cannot avoid drawing on his past experiences, his fantasies, his anticipations of the future, or, at the least, his memories of books and plays that especially appealed to him. Under the stress of the test what comes most readily to mind are his own feelings, emotions and attitudes when confronted by this or that situation, and so, though attending to the material, the subject talks mostly about himself. Indeed, the content of the stories, as well as their style and manner of composition, exposes so much to a discerning experimenter that the latter can hardly escape the feeling that he is prying. The subject is, or should be, intent upon following the instructions : to demonstrate his imaginative ability. Hence, he is 'set' for the fullest expression, not for reticence. Furthermore, the test requires a dramatic narrative, and what is most dramatic to the subject are the themas which have shaped his life. As someone has said of races : 'The soul of a people is mirrored in their legends.' Thus, unless the subject is inhibited by the experimenter's attitude he is certain to expose more than he would ordinarily confess, and what's more, more than he knows — because he is unconscious of it.

To be significant, of course, the data must be interpretable in the light of what is known about how the child's mind commonly reconstructs or poetically elaborates its experiences. In our studies the data appeared to lend themselves to such genetical interpretations and no doubt, at first, we were too fascinated by the mere ingenuity of the hypotheses to be critical of their factual foundations. But later, our dissatisfaction with plausible guesses led us to adopt several techniques of verification [1] which after the termination of these explorations were tried out and found useful.

We believe that we have had a glimpse of a most wondrous terrain for rewarding exploration. The paths made by the pioneers of psycho-analysis lie before us. It is a land of mysterious formations, so many of which are unfamiliar that much preliminary reconnoitring will have to be done before experimenters can get their bearings. Nevertheless, with some confidence, we put forward our set of projection methods as a step towards the development of roughly standardizable procedures for the systematic investigation of covert mental processes. Suitable techniques of verification should be practised as a rite, otherwise there will be no limit to what the imagination can do with the material.

Among our other techniques, those in which the subject was presented with similes of everyday situations gave the greatest promise of further development. I refer particularly to the sessions which tested emotional conditioning, level of aspiration, reactions to ethical prohibitions and reactions to frustration, many of which were suggested by the work of Lewin and his associates.[2] None of these procedures (except the Level of Aspiration Test) were carried out with maximum efficiency during the present series of examinations. But when used at other times they have proved effective. Methods of this sort allow the experimenter to observe the progression of critically important dynamic processes during a short segment of time. They provide opportunity for the investigation of one external factor after another, and if the sessions are

1. Murray,H.A. 'Techniques for a systematic investigation of fantasy.' *Jour. of Psychol.*,1936,*3*, 115–143.
2. Lewin,K. *A Dynamic Theory of Personality*, New York,1935.

placed near the end of the program, the experimenter will have enough data from the previous sessions for predicting the responses of each personality. In this way the internal factors may be identified.

D. *Case Histories*. What unsystematic conclusions we have here to offer must be limited, of course, to the particular group of young men studied. I might say that we had no reason to suppose that our subjects — though none belonged to the over-privileged minority of college students — were not representative of present day Harvard men, but this statement is almost meaningless, since there are so many varieties of human nature that there is little probability that fifty subjects chosen at random will constitute a fair sample of any much larger group. Though I have been advised often enough by those from other colleges that Harvard men are not entirely typical, it is perhaps over-cautious to say 'Harvard men' instead of 'American college men,' since our analyses always cut through the derm of recently adopted social attitudes and memberships to expose the more basic thematic tendencies. But it is perhaps more accurate to speak of our subjects simply as fifty *individuals* of college age, a heterogeneous group unrepresentative of any category. In the remarks that follow I shall limit myself to the twenty-eight subjects who constituted the last two groups examined, since our first groups were not studied with sufficient thoroughness or competence to yield data that are reliable enough even for the most tentative generalizations.

1. Most of our subjects were carrying what seemed to us a heavy load of crippling anxiety, inferiority feelings, guilt feelings or dejection. Many of them, of course, were troubled by thoughts of financial insecurity, but the majority were more concerned about their general social status. They doubted that they could live up to their own standards or to the expectations of their parents. Frequently, they suffered from memories of stinging humiliations, and when they went to their books in the evening, over-riding apprehensive thoughts of future failure or depressing feelings of separateness and forsakenness prevented concentration. A basic sense of insupport aggravated by dissensions with one or

both parents was a frequent finding. This was commonly accompanied by moral conflict.

2. We found a sexual factor at the root of every clear-cut neurotic symptom. However, there were numerous traits (which could be called neurotic) that were more closely connected with physical fear, inferiority feelings, traumas of Insupport, the press of Rejection, Ego disorganization, stifled rebellion and complexes involving pride or vanity.

3. p Physical Insupport was marked in two cases (7 per cent). One subject had fallen into a boiler filled with water when he was a baby, but later enjoyed nothing so much as shinnying up flagpoles, jumping from high places and going far from home (Counteraction). He became a track man, and had a strong tendency to 'soar' in his thinking. The other subject had suffered from fears of falling. Once, after rising from bed at night, he dropped to the floor with the conviction that he was a victim of infantile paralysis. Later, he cultivated a springy step, went for long walks in the country by himself, abominated all restraints and had fantasies of travel and aviation. Thus, in both cases, there were traumas and fears involving physical Insupport, followed by counteractive attempts to conquer gravity, to move far and high in space. This combination may be termed an *Icarus* complex. As an example of its sublimation we may cite Nietzsche who with such passion, especially in *Zarathustra*, eulogized seamen, voyagers, mountain climbers, dancers, tight-rope walkers and eagles. It seems important to us because 1, it involves the elementary function of sitting, standing and walking (balancing and propelling the body against the forces of gravity), something which the child spends its first two years or more in learning ; 2, locomotive endeavours are frequently attended by falls, fears of Insupport, cautious avoidances and adherences to solid bodies (physical objects, parents and so forth) ; 3, the fear of Insupport resembles in many particulars a very common neurotic symptom, *agoraphobia* ; 4, bodily co-ordination (physical balance) and emotional co-ordination (mental balance) are probably related to some degree (*cf.* Yoga exercises, as well as certain theories pro-

posed by behaviourists) ; 5, in our group the two subjects who exhibited this complex were clearly the most unstable individuals that we studied ; one suffered from affective schizoid states with paranoid trends, the other had experienced a series of manic-depressive cycles which were almost severe enough to require treatment.

4. The press of Cultural Discord (*vide* p. 294) had been an unstabilizing factor in five (18 per cent) of the subjects, of whom three were Jews. It had engendered inner conflict between two ideologies. Three of the individuals adhered to their family's tradition, and two went over to the culture. Both of the latter suffered markedly from inferiority feelings.

5. At least 32 per cent of the subjects exhibited symptoms of oral Succorance. That this was among the most common diagnoses may have been due to the fact 1, that a majority of our subjects were concentrating in literature and that literature (an interest in words) is highly correlated with oral fixations, and/or 2, that we erred in ascribing importance to speech phenomena, food memories, and persistent thumb-sucking as indices of this complex. Whenever we discovered a covert, infantile, passive and receptively dependent attitude we were prone to think of the nursing period and oral frustration, and if we found in conjunction with this disposition symptoms that were specifically oral we did not hesitate to propose the hypothesis of oral Succorance.

6. Over a third of the men gave evidence of p Rejection in childhood. They were misunderstood or another sibling was preferred or their parents were considered heartless. Usually, this was accompanied by latent Succorance : the desire for a supporting, sympathetic parent substitute. But in some subjects it led to counteractive strivings to be independent and self-reliant.

7. p Birth of Sibling was an important factor in the early life of five subjects (18 per cent). It led to destructively investigative tendencies in two subjects and to aggressive fantasies against the newborn child in two. There was usually some aggression directed against the mother because of what was felt by the subject to be infidelity.

8. About 68 per cent of the subjects had suffered in the past or were suffering in the present from persistent inferiority feelings. Social inferiority was the commonest source of discomfort. Though sometimes this was based on a realization of class discriminations (only too prevalent at Harvard), in most cases it arose from the subject's suspicion that he was generally unattractive to others, unpopular, a 'fish out of water,' unable to make friends. Physical inferiority, dating from childhood, was found in 41 per cent of the cases. Most of these gave a history of shunning fights, of being worsted in physical tussles, of being bullied, or of being afraid to join in the rough and tumble of boyhood games. The proportion of Jews was low in this latter group, not because they had escaped the brutality of their fellows, but because the thought of being a 'sissy' did not overwhelm them with humiliation. They were more distressed by disapproval and rejection (lack of love) than they were by the inner conviction that they had acted in a cowardly manner. Among the Protestants there were half a dozen instances of deep-seated self-contempt engendered by a recognition of their own physical fears. Though several of our subjects were disheartened by failures in scholarship, and some of these were willing to admit that they were 'not very bright,' this form of inadequacy did not burn into their hearts. None of the three Catholic subjects suffered from any sort of discernible inferiority.

9. A classical Oedipus complex (loving attachment to mother, hatred of father) was found persisting in 28 per cent of cases. In 18 per cent there was evidence of subterranean hostility to the mother, and in 14 per cent the father was clearly the preferred parent.

10. Very marked guilt reactions occurred during the boyhood development of 32 per cent of the cases, and experiences of a similar though milder sort in most of the others. In fact, we found no cases in which guilt (pangs of conscience, irrational fears of punishment, remorse, reform) had been entirely absent. This phenomenon seems to be a prerequisite of socialization.

11. A slight degree of fetishism was found in two cases. Both of

these had been perplexed at the onset of puberty about the genital structure of woman and the role of the penis in man. The evidence pointed to a fantasy of a penis-endowed mother, the occurrence of which would serve to explain the subjects' confusion of the sexes. Both men exhibited signs of urethral erotism.

12. In a number of cases it appeared that choice of vocation had been guided by infantile or adolescent complexes. One subject who had fantasied the death of his parents in an automobile accident (a symbol of intercourse in his case) became a salesman of automobile insurance, which necessitated his hurrying to the scenes of accidents. The same subject had had, as a child, destructive fantasies against his dog and, as an adolescent, an obsession concerning the prevalence of bacteria in dust. Before becoming an insurance agent he sought a position in the Society for Prevention of Cruelty to Animals and later acted as a salesman of vacuum cleaners. He enjoyed nothing so much as giving personal demonstrations of how thoroughly his cleaner could rid a room of dust. A subject who had been seriously injured by striking a keg of dynamite became a chemist, and another, who had developed an exploratory compulsion after his mother had lied to him (at the birth of a sibling) about the origin of children, chose research (in chemistry) as a profession. One man who as a lad had fantasied adopting a poor boy (as an atonement for destructive fantasies against a cousin who died) went into business with the idea of making money and giving it philanthropically to needy young men. Several subjects who had had oral fixations or inhibitions went in, later, for public speaking. Two of these wanted to be poets. One subject who, at the tender age of four or five, had witnessed fearful cruelties committed against his Jewish relatives, upon graduation found employment with a Hebrew social service agency. A stutterer selected philology for his life-work, and a chronic bed-wetter, bridge-building. Finally, one subject who had imagined himself delivering and caring for a child of his mother's (as an atonement for aggressive fantasies against a sibling) chose pediatrics as a profession and later psychiatry. Only three men (12 per cent) followed in their fathers' footsteps. In several cases

it was also found that the topic for a dissertation or for graduate study was clearly related to infantile preoccupations. It was supposed that the unconscious thematic tendency was but one of several factors influencing such selections.

13. Three of our subjects with literary talent showed many of the traits of the Romantic artist (genius type) as depicted by Rank.[1] Two of them particularly were highly narcistic, subjective (intraceptive) and projective. They were extremely conscious of themselves as separate individuals and felt hopelessly or gloriously different, misunderstood and alienated from society. They were as much concerned about the growth and portrayal of their personalities as they were about literature and the technique of writing. Sex was recognized as a contributing though often conflicting instinct. Succorance and Passivity were strong though inhibited most of the time by Autonomy, the desire to ignore society (n Rej) and pursue an independent course. They were searching for a way that was appropriate to creative work and creative living.

14. Among the important common processes of development Counteraction stood out conspicuously. The reactions of this class were originally distinguished as a separate need, but later it was apperceived that Counteraction was the working of an egocentric need (Aggression, Achievement, Rejection, Autonomy) in the service of Inviolacy. It was, in short, either a sequent-action (*vide* p. 122) to failure or trauma, or a reaction to the press of injury or depreciation (experienced or anticipated), with the aim of maintaining or rehabilitating status (prestige, honour). We should not have made such an error of conceptualization if we had had the concept of thema clearly in mind. For Counteraction is not merely a particular kind of behaviour. It is a thema : a particular kind of behaviour following a specified outcome or press, one that lowers the status (social esteem or self-esteem) of the individual. Counteraction includes what some (Adlerians) have termed over-compensation (or simply compensation), 'repetition for mastery' (Freud) as well as other types of redressing sequent-action.

1. Rank,O. *Art and Artist*, New York,1932.

We found Counteraction occurring most often in a subjectified or semi-objectified form. For example, one subject (Zill) had fantasies and dreams of winning fist fights after being humiliated in a physical encounter. Another (Gay) played gladiator for a time after being bitten by a dog. Roll's grandfather was fond of pretending that he was a wolf. When he crept up, scratched on the bedclothes and said, 'I am going to eat you,' baby Roll was terrified. For a time the child was afraid of all animals, but the tide turned eventually, and he became passionately fond of them, and read every book of natural history that he could lay his hands on and ultimately became an authority in lycanthropy. Many of our subjects (Oriol, Asper, Zeeno and Given, particularly) had been quick to reject with high contempt those who had rejected them (Timon thema). Two men had flunked their entrance examinations, an outcome which had spurred them to more serious efforts, and eventually they passed and did very creditably from then on.

15. Most of the subjects' memories seemed to support surprisingly well the genetical hypotheses suggested by the intuitive observation of their behaviour. Among the facts revealed in the all-too-brief autobiographies we often found just what was indispensable as evidence. And this has caused us to wonder how it is that among the countless traces of past events the few that can be recovered are (or seem to be) so typical, so pertinent to an understanding of conditioning processes? To this question one might answer that, in general, the most pressive and arresting events are best conserved and hence 1, are most lastingly influential in behaviour and 2, most easily recoverable by consciousness. But if this is a general principle it is one which does not always hold; for there are other processes, such as repression, which oppose it. What is repressed is often well conserved and lastingly deterministic, though not readily available to consciousness. Consequently, it may be stated that the effects of events recalled are usually exhibited in behaviour, though much of the past that finds expression in behaviour is not recalled. With this in mind we have often been led to infer from a sample of behaviour the operation of conserved, though unremembered, traces — the exist-

ence of which could only be demonstrated by prolonged psychoanalysis.

We find it helpful to conceive of the brain as an extremely complex, differentiated resonator, composed of variously integrated traces (much modified residues of racial and personal experience). Anything in perception or thought which resembles or corresponds to a trace or cluster of traces sets the latter in motion. It is possible that a great many traces are made to vibrate by a pressive situation, but only a minority are strong enough to influence the regnancy (and thereby affect behaviour or thought); and of these only a small number become conscious. Since it seems that traces are commonly integrated along thematic (molar) lines, we suppose that every episode activates innumerable traces of events with similar themas. For example, when a man fails miserably to achieve his goal, traces of all past failures and reactions to such failures are enlivened, and what comes to mind are fragments (isolated words, images or themas) from the vibrating ensemble. One might say that the traces of the past which pertain to the present are activated, though what enters consciousness may seem—because it comes as a bit of unbodied thought—irrelevant, to an outsider as well as to the subject. With this conception in mind the conscientious pursuit of free associations with the intent of giving body to the erupted fragments becomes more intelligible.

It is possible that some of the autobiographically recited events would not have been recalled during some other epoch of the subject's life, and that they arose when they did because of their being related by similarity or contrast to the then active dispositions. This hypothesis would help to explain the emotional coherence of past history and observed conduct.

16. The biographical facts did not convince us that external occurrences (press) were the major determinants of infantile complexes. We did not find, for example, that any habitually maintained attitude on the part of one or both parents was correlated with any particular type of family (Oedipus) complex. Though it was common to find a remembered event or even a cluster of

memories that appeared to be functionally connected with an unconscious complex, these events were not always typical of the subject's childhood.

To illustrate, a subject may recall an occasion in his infancy when his mother (momentarily distracted) rebuffed (p Rejection) an affectionate advance; and it may be discovered that this event was followed in the boy's life by the development of inferiority feelings or misogynic sentiments. From this one may be tempted to infer that the complex was engendered primarily by the mother's attitude. However, if one finds — as we often did — that as a rule this subject's mother was exceptionally tender and affectionate, and, furthermore, that numerous other subjects with mothers that were habitually cold and rejective did not develop inferiority feelings or negative complexes towards women, then one becomes doubtful of the signal importance of p Rejection in the life history of the subject in question. It seems certain that a press, by itself, unless it be extremely strong and sudden, cannot generate an enduring complex. The fact that it is difficult to produce experimentally a lasting neurotic symptom in animals is favourable to this opinion. The unpredictable and objectively irrational manner in which complexes originate and expand during infancy invites us to the view that the state of the organism is more important than the external happening in establishing a focal tendency. And among the factors which determine the child's state of mind the most pregnant is the nature of the prevailing fantasies. The latter are influenced to some extent by previous experiences, but it does not seem that they can be explained on this basis entirely. We are finally driven, I think, to Jung's conception of racially determined sequences of fantasy (progressing with the stages of maturation) that successively occupy the infant's mind provided the external world offers correspondences to feed them. This may be called racial or archetypal determination. According to this view an infantile complex which endures is the result of the concatenation of an elemental fantasy and a sudden external press that appears as a confirmation of it (*cf.* 'Chance and the prepared mind'). Thus the pith of a complex is always a product of subjective (imagined and irreal) and objective (perceived and real) conditions.

17. The Catholic subjects were conspicuously more solid and secure and most of the Jewish subjects conspicuously less so than the average. There was relatively little anxiety-linked material bubbling up in the minds of the Catholics. Their repressions were firmer and what occurred in their depths could only be inferred indirectly by interpreting their projections. It was as if their faith in an ultimate authority relieved them of the necessity of independently resolving fundamental issues. Their unconscious fears, one might say, were quieted by the hovering presence of the maternal Church. And if they were unable sometimes to live up to the precepts of their religion, they knew that forgiveness was always at hand. A secret, remorseful confession and once more they would be beneficently accepted members of the flock. It might be supposed that the irrational unconscious tendencies of these Catholics were so satisfactorily interpreted by a wise, human and altogether forgiving Church that they never knew what it was to feel themselves alone and forsaken in a maelstrom of incommunicable feelings and ideas. In the rationalized fantasy system of an effective Church there is a place for everything, and the faithful communicants do not have to face—and thus become conscious of and wrestle with—the naked impulses of their own souls. The problem of good and evil is settled and only the problem of moral will remains. Our Catholic subjects were relatively happy, free from neurotic symptoms, blissfully self-deceived, superficial in their psychological discernments, and always competent to clothe raw facts in the rational vestments of their faith. In these respects the Jewish subjects were outstandingly different. Most of them were highly self-conscious, relatively insecure, burdened by neurotic complexes, painfully aware of disturbing impulses and feelings, psychologically penetrating, and unusually quick to comprehend (and often to accept) even the least flattering interpretations of their behaviour. They were not contained by their religion and they never made use of its symbolism in depicting their difficulties.

18. Our findings indicated that the sex of the experimenter was a factor that modified the subjects' responses. This supposition was confirmed later by results obtained under more controlled conditions.

Because the topic falls outside the range of our endeavour I shall refrain from commenting upon the possible contribution of studies such as these to education. It seems obvious enough. For the essential function of a university is to promote intellectual activity, and since it is now evident that thinking is a function of the entire personality, rather than an isolated faculty, it is important to discover how and to what extent its advancement can be enhanced or blocked by other functions — feeling, sensuous perception, action. In every one of our subjects we found complexes that embarrassed learning and the zest of intellect. Is it not reasonable to suppose that teachers would be more realistically effective if they took account of such existences, if they had a better understanding of the young minds that they must interest and train ? Though it is doubtful whether members of a college faculty can be expected to have the wisdom that many a student longs to find in them, and by imparting it nourish the whole being of man, it is only too clear that high intellectual capacity without feeling and sensibility can choke young life most grievously.

Our explorations draw attention to two mutually dependent major problems for psychology : the formulation of small units (single episodes of personality) and the formulation of large units (individual lives). The two problems are mutually dependent because to understand a single episode one must know the settled past as well as the anticipated future, and to understand a life history one must be able to formulate the episodes that constitute it. The first problem calls for the experimental investigation of different reactions (immediate and delayed) to common press ; the method being to control one determinant (external or internal) after another. Among common press the following may be cited : (a) *mostly unpleasant and frustrating* : a physical barrier, prohibition, coercion, opposition, interruption, threat, accusation, censure, belittlement, ridicule, lack of appreciation, injustice, neglect, exclusion, rejection, expulsion, an unpleasant task, the superior achievement of rivals, failure, physical pain, noxious or disturbing sensations, the repellent behaviour of others, monotony, inquisitive questioning, unreasonable request, refusal to give or lend, sharp disagreement, protracted isolation ; and (b) *mostly pleasant and gratifying* : freedom, tolerance, rapt attention, appreciation, praise, respect, compliance, sympathy, friendliness, helpfulness, enthusiastic agreement, an appealing task, the inferior achievement of rivals, success, gifts, loans, pleasant sights and sounds, the presence of congenial people, variety, entertainment, wit, interesting information and opinion. In order to gain the knowledge that is necessary to understand the internal determinants of each response to any one of such press and in order to learn about certain situations and conditions, which cannot or should not be reproduced in the laboratory (situations involving parental action, sex, excretion, severe shock, great pain, illness), the psychologist must attempt to discover as much as he can about the life histories of his subjects. This brings him to the second major problem : the formulation of long units ; to achieve which he requires, first of all, a great many facts that must be obtained by observation, questioning and special methods. Here the therapist (physician, psycho-analyst) is in a peculiarly advantageous position, since people (subjects, patients) are more inclined to reveal their past humiliations and present secret life to one who is accustomed to receive such confessions with moral disinterestedness and who can be expected to understand what is involved and perhaps offer relief or guidance. For this and other reasons it may be confidently predicted that the happiest results for psychology will come from the closest working relations between research and practice.

The general procedure that has been outlined — modified to suit conditions — may be feasibly carried out by any department of psychology or by any clinic that can bring together six or more competent examiners and gain the co-operation of a sufficient number of subjects or patients. If this were done systematically for a few years at several different centres, psychology would soon have at its disposal a large assemblage of facts to build a foundation for personology and to direct attention to the most profitable problems for research.

GLOSSARY

A = Ambitendency : a complex composed of two opposing (anti-polar) needs. Ex : n Def — A — n Dom (Extreme compliance followed by extreme Dominance. The latter represents a Contrafaction).

n Aba = n Abasement (Abasive attitude). To surrender. To comply and accept punishment. To apologize, confess, atone. Self-depreciation. Masochism.

n Ach = n Achievement (Achievant attitude). To overcome obstacles, to exercise power, to strive to do something difficult as well and as quickly as possible. (This is an elementary Ego need which may alone prompt any action or be fused with any other need.)

n Acq = n Acquisition (Acquisitive attitude). To gain possessions and property. To grasp, snatch or steal things. To bargain or gamble. To work for money or goods.

actone = an action pattern *qua* action pattern. It is either a physical movement (motone) or a run of coherent words (verbone), considered apart from their external effects.

n Aff = n Affiliation (Affiliative attitude). To form friendships and associations. To greet, join, and live with others. To co-operate and converse sociably with others. To love. To join groups.

affection = a construct which stands for some process in the brain which manifests itself subjectively as feelings of pleasure or unpleasure and objectively as a compound of affective actones.

n Agg = n Aggression (Aggressive attitude). To assault or injure an O. To murder. To belittle, harm, blame, accuse or maliciously ridicule a person. To punish severely. Sadism.

Anx = Anxiety : startledness, apprehension, timidity, worry.

n Auto = n Autonomy (Autonomous attitude). To resist influence or coercion. To defy an authority or seek freedom in a new place. To strive for independence.

n Blam = n Blamavoidance (Blamavoidant attitude). To avoid blame, ostracism or punishment by inhibiting asocial or unconventional impulses. To be well-behaved and obey the law.

c = Cathexis, the power of an object to arouse a response of a certain kind in the subject (or the power of the subject to arouse such a response in other people).

C = Conflict of needs. Ex : n Exh — C — n Blam (The desire to show off in conflict with the fear of censure).

Ch = Change : a tendency to move and wander, to have no fixed habituation, to seek new friends, to adopt new fashions, to change one's interests and vocation. Inconsistency and instability.

n Cnt = n Counteraction (Counteractive attitude). Proudly to refuse admission of defeat by restriving and retaliating. To select the hardest tasks. To defend one's honour in action.

n Cog = n Cognizance (Inquiring attitude). To explore (moving and touching). To ask questions. To satisfy curiosity. To look, listen, inspect. To read and seek knowledge.

Conj = Conjunctivity : co-ordination of action and thought ; organization of behavioural trends and purposes. The *ability* to make a coherent pattern of one's life.

n Cons = n Construction (Constructive attitude). To organize and build.

Con St = Conservative sentiments : the maintenance of well-accredited conventional social sentiments. A dislike of innovations.

contrafaction = the activation of a need which is the antipole of a previously objectified need. The former serves to balance or rectify the latter.

Cr = Creativity : manifest ability to produce and develop original ideas ; to devise new methods, construct hypotheses, offer novel explanations, create a work of beauty.

n Def = n Deference (Deferent attitude). To admire and willingly follow a superior allied O. To co-operate with a leader, To serve gladly.

Del = Deliberation : inhibition, hesitation and reflection before action. Slow reaction time, spastic contraction, compulsive thinking. It is the opposite of Impulsion.

n Dfd = n Defendance (Defensive attitude). To defend oneself against blame or belittlement. To justify one's actions. To offer extenuations, explanations and excuses. To resist 'probing.'

Disj = Disjunctivity : disco-ordination of action and thought ; disordered and conflicting behaviour.

n Dom = n Dominance (Dominative attitude). To influence or control others. To persuade, prohibit, dictate. To lead and direct. To restrain. To organize the behaviour of a group.

E = Experimenter.

E I = Ego Ideal : the operation of images portraying the subject (or an accepted exemplar) achieving noteworthy successes. A high level of aspiration. This is the Achievement drive in a subjectified form.

emn = emotional need : a need evoked by sudden, close press, impulsively and emotionally objectified without forethought.

Emo = Emotionality : the amount of emotion, affection and autonomic excitement that a subject manifests : zest, elation, anger, fear, dejection, shame, etc. The opposite of Emotionality is Placidity.

empathy = an involuntary process whereby an observer experiences the feelings or emotions which in his personality are associated 1, with the situation in which the subject is placed or, 2, with the forms of behaviour that the subject exhibits.

End = Endurance : the protensity of a behavioural trend. 'Power of endurance,' persistence and conative perseveration.

Endo = Endocathection : the cathexis of thought or emotion for its own sake. A preoccupation with inner activities : feelings, fantasies, generalizations, theoretical reflections, artistic conceptions, religious ideas. Withdrawal from practical life.

Energy = need for Activity, zest, motility. Intensity combined with Endurance.

n Exh = n Exhibition (Exhibitionistic attitude). To attract attention to one's person. To excite, amuse, stir, shock, thrill others. Self-dramatization.

Exo = Exocathection : the positive cathexis of practical action and co-operative undertakings. Occupation with outer events : economic, political, or social occurrences. A strong inclination to participate in the contemporary world of affairs.

n Exp = n Exposition (Expositive attitude). To point and demonstrate. To relate facts. To give information, explain, interpret, lecture.

Extra = Extraception : the disposition to adhere to the obviously substantial facts. A practical 'down-to-earth' skeptical attitude. Enjoyment of clearly observable results. A tangible mechanical outlook.

Fn = Fusion of two or more needs. Ex : Fn Agg Auto (A violent attack against a coercing authority).

gratuity, or gratuitous end situation = something that satisfies a need without effort on the part of the S. Ex : The S inherits a fortune.

n Harm = n Harmavoidance (Harmavoidant attitude). To avoid pain, physical injury, illness and death. To escape from a dangerous situation. To take precautionary measures.

ideo n = ideological need : a need that manifests itself towards an ideology, a principle, an idea, a theory, a law.

idn = Id need : a need that is unacceptable or opposed to the 'best intentions' of the Ego. It usually refers to a need in its impulsive instinctual form.

Imp = Impulsion : the tendency to act quickly without reflection. Short reaction time, intuitive or emotional decisions. The inability to inhibit an impulse.

n Inf = n Infavoidance (Infavoidant attitude). To avoid failure, shame, humiliation, ridicule. To refrain from attempting to do something that is beyond one's powers. To conceal a disfigurement.

infra n = infravertive need : a need directed towards an inferior O.

Int = Intensity : strength of effort ; quick and forceful movements ; emphasis and zest during activity ; ardently expressed opinions ; power in expression.

intra n = intravertive need : a need that is turned in upon the subject.

Intra = Intraception : the dominance of feelings, fantasies, speculations, aspirations. An imaginative, subjective, human outlook. Romantic action.

n Inv = n Inviolacy (Inviolate attitude). This includes desires and attempts to prevent a depreciation of self-respect, to preserve one's 'good name,' to be immune from criticism, to maintain psychological 'distance.' It is based on pride and personal sensitiveness. It takes in the n Seclusion (isolation, reticence, self-concealment) which in our study was considered to be the opposite of n Exhibition and, for this reason, was not separately considered. The n Inviolacy has been broken up into three needs : n Infavoidance (the fear of and retraction from possible sources of humiliation), n Defendance (the verbal defence of errors and misdemeanours) and n Counteraction (the attempt to redeem failures, to prove one's worth after frustration, to revenge an insult). Counteraction is not truly a separate need. It is n Achievement or n Aggression acting in the service of n Inviolacy.

ln = latent need : covert or inhibited need. A semi-objectified or subjectified form of need expression.

motone = a muscular-motor action pattern (actone).

N = Narcism : self-love and egocentricity in any of its various forms.

need integrate = a complex of one or more needs with the images that depict the common objects and actones associated with these tendencies.

n Nur = n Nurturance (Nurturant attitude). To nourish, aid or protect a helpless O. To express sympathy. To 'mother' a child.

O = Object : any external entity (thing, animal, person) other than the subject.

Obj = objectivity : the disposition to judge oneself and others in a detached and disinterested manner ; psychological realism.

n Ord = n Order (Orderly attitude). To arrange, organize, put away objects. To be tidy and clean. To be scrupulously precise.

perseveration = the endurance of a process after its stimulus has ceased.

n Play = n Play (Playful attitude). To relax, amuse oneself, seek diversion and entertainment. To 'have fun,' to play games. To laugh, joke and be merry. To avoid serious tension.

p = press : kind of effect an object or situation is exerting or could exert upon the S. It is a temporal gestalt of stimuli which usually appears in the guise of a *threat of harm* or *promise of benefit* to the organism.

Proj = projectivity : the disposition to project unconsciously one's wish-engendered or anxiety-evoked beliefs. Mild forms of the delusions of self-reference, persecution, omnipotence, etc.

Rad St = Radical sentiments : the origination, promulgation or defence of novel or questionable sentiments, theories or ideologies that are opposed to traditionally established opinions.

n Rec = n Recognition (self-forwarding attitude). To excite praise and commendation. To demand respect. To boast and exhibit one's accomplishments. To seek distinction, social prestige, honours or high office.

recipathy = reciprocal feeling, the feeling or need in one person that is commonly evoked as a complement to a feeling or need in another person.

regnancy = a dynamically organized temporal segment of brain processes.

n Rej = n Rejection (Rejective attitude). To snub, ignore or exclude an O. To remain aloof and indifferent. To be discriminating.

n Ret = n Retention (Retentive attitude). To retain possession of things. To refuse to give or lend. To hoard. To be frugal, economical and miserly.

S = Subject : the focus of the psychologist's concern at a particular moment.

Sa = Sameness : adherence to certain places, people and modes of conduct. Fixation and limitation. Enduring sentiments and loyalties ; persistence of purpose ; consistency of conduct ; rigidity of habits.

Se = Superego : 'conscience' : inhibiting and punishing images representative of parental, social and religious authority. The operation of this factor may be 'quiet' (*cf.* unconscious inhibition without conflict) or it may be 'disturbing' (*cf.* conflict).

Se C = Superego Conflict : a condition of conflict in which asocial impulses are 'at war with conscience.' There may be some asocial conduct or there may be merely asocial desires (conscious or unconscious). These are opposed by domineering and prohibiting forces.

Se I = Superego Integration : a condition in which the dictates of 'conscience' have been so far accepted by the Ego that the subject *wills* the obligatory (the socially demanded action).

n Sec = n Seclusion (Seclusive attitude). This need has been taken as the opposite of Exhibition, not as a separate variable.

semi-objns = semi-objectifications, make-believe actions.

n Sen = n Sentience (Sentient attitude). To seek and enjoy sensuous impressions.

sentimentive intensity = the strength of expressed sentiments.

n Sex = n Sex (erotic attitude). To form and further an erotic relationship. To have sexual intercourse.

S.S. = stimulus situation. That part of the total environment to which the creature attends and reacts.

subjns = subjectifications : imaginal processes motivated by a need.

n Suc = n Succorance (Succorant attitude). To seek aid, protection or sympathy. To cry for help. To plead for mercy. To adhere to an affectionate, nurturant parent. To be dependent.

n Sup = n Superiority (Ambitious attitude). This need is considered to be a composite of Achievement and Recognition.

supra n = supravertive need : a need directed towards a superior object.

th = thema : a press-need combination. The dynamical structure of a single *episode* : a single creature-environment interaction. A dynamical structure of an event on a molar level. Simple th : combination of a particular press and a particular need. Complex th : a succession of related simple themas.

tpmo = time-place-mode-object formula acceptable to a particular culture.

n Und = n Understanding (Intellectual attitude). To analyse experience, to abstract, to discriminate among concepts, to define relations, to synthesize ideas.

v = vector, a general trend with spatial characteristics, which may serve one of several needs.

verbone = a verbal action pattern (actone).

INDEX

Definition of terms may be found in the Glossary.

For the convenience of the reader the more essential references in the Index that follows are printed in bold type.